Vital Statistics on the Presidency

George Washington to George W. Bush

Vital Statistics on the Presidency

George Washington to George W. Bush

Third Edition

Lyn Ragsdale
Rice University

A Division of SAGE
Washington, D.C.

CQ Press
2300 N Street, NW, Suite 800
Washington, DC 20037

Phone: 202-729-1900; toll-free, 1-866-4CQ-PRESS (1-866-427-7737)

Web: www.cqpress.com

Cover design: Mike Grove, MG Design
Cover photos: Photodisc
Composition: Judy Myers, Graphic Design, Alpine, California
Indexer: Julia Petrakis

∞ The paper used in this publication exceeds the requirements of the American National Standard for Information Sciences—Permanence of Paper for Printed Library Materials, ANSI Z39.48-1992.

Printed and bound in the United States of America

12 11 10 09 08 1 2 3 4 5

Library of Congress Cataloging-in-Publication Data

ISBN: 978-0-87289-529-4

In Memory of My Parents,
Carolyn and H. E. Ragsdale

Contents

Tables and Figures

Chapter 3 Presidential Elections

Chapter 4 Public Appearances

Chapter 5 Public Opinions

Chapter 7 Presidents in War and Diplomacy

Chapter 8 Presidential Policymaking

Chapter 9 Congressional Relations

Preface

Vital Statistics on the Presidency updates and expands material on the executive office from the time of George Washington through George W. Bush's second term. It has been twenty years since the first edition of this book was written; Ronald Reagan was then stepping down after two terms as president. This current edition ends with George W. Bush preparing to leave office. During the past two decades, the world and the challenges the president faces have changed dramatically: The Cold War ended, the Soviet Union collapsed. Summit meetings and nuclear arms control agreements have been replaced by American unilateralism, China's emergence as an economic superpower, and seemingly random terrorist attacks that are carefully planned, purposeful, and strategic. Deficit has been replaced by surplus, only to be replaced by deficit. We have moved from an era of limited military encounters to one of a protracted war with consequences well beyond the theatre of conflict. Yet amidst these historic changes, there are constants: a president's popularity grows when the economy improves, rises sharply when a president puts the nation at war, and falls dramatically if the war effort drags on or the economy turns soft. Over the same period, the size of the Executive Office of the President increased modestly, from 1,645 employees in 1988 to 1,719 employees in 2007. In 1988 President Reagan issued forty-five executive orders, covering such topics as military bases, agricultural subsidies, and abortion. In 2007 President Bush issued forty-five executive orders addressing these same topics. President Bush, like Reagan, made hundreds of ceremonial appearances in Washington, D.C., and across the country throughout his two terms in office. Both presidents made major addresses to the nation that boosted their approval ratings and rallied the country to their policies. These patterns of historic change and constancy in the institution of the presidency are examined throughout *Vital Statistics on the Presidency*.

The research for this book could not have been completed without the help of Shanon Nelson, Andrew Spiegelman, Ngoc Phan, and Jie Wu, who assisted on data collection efforts. Randall M. Smith graciously provided the data on treaties and executive agreements, which is the single most exhaustive and accurate data set now available on international agreements. My special thanks go to Richard Niemi and Harold Stanley for kindly sharing data that they have collected and to John Woolley and Gerhard Peters for their indispensable Web site, The American Presidency Project, at www.presidency.ucsb.edu.

I am also grateful to the fine professional team at CQ Press for facilitating a smooth and uncomplicated revision process. My thanks to Anna Baker, Andrea Pedolsky, and Anastazia Skolnitsky for their guidance and expertise on the many details of the book and for prodding me, the harried dean, to "get the book done." Kerry Kern again served as the copy and production editor, as she has on the book's previous editions, lending her considerable talents and creativity to the project.

Finally, I would like to thank my husband, Jerry Rusk, and my son, Matthew Ragsdale Rusk, my two best friends, for their unflagging encouragement and support and for making my life whole.

Introduction

This book presents a comprehensive statistical description of the American presidency. It offers a perspective on the presidency that deemphasizes the uniqueness of individual presidents and focuses instead on the presidency as an institution. This perspective suggests that institutions are "political actors in their own right" (March and Olsen, 1984, 738). Institutions are not simply the sum total of the behavior of individual participants. Rather, they have lives of their own that illuminate individual actions. Institutions are collections of regularly occurring patterns of behavior that help explain and predict the conduct of individual actors. Theoretically, the study of the presidency as an institution highlights continuities and patterns that can be observed from one president to the next. These patterns characterize the presidency as an elected office and offer an explanation of the organization of the Executive Office of the President, its relations with the public, its policy decisions, and its dealings with other institutions, such as Congress and the courts. The chapters of this book provide readers not only with comprehensive quantitative data on various aspects of the presidency, but also with information about change and continuity within the institutional presidency.

Changing Directions in Presidency Research

For more than two decades, presidency scholars have implored each other to engage in more rigorous, systematic forms of research. They have charged that the field is largely devoid of theory and have challenged each other to offer theoretical approaches to the topic that would direct such efforts. Researchers have denounced their own field as lagging behind other fields in political science (for example, the field of congressional studies) in adequately addressing questions through scientific explanation. Critics have charged that presidency research has been remiss in its development of theory, gathering of quantitative data, and presentation of statistical analyses across numerous presidents.

When these charges were first leveled in the 1970s and into the early 1980s, they were seemingly true. Many presidency scholars concentrated on questions about the personalities, power, and leadership of individual presidents. These concepts afforded incumbent-specific approaches to the study of the office that saw each president as different, bringing unique talents, foibles, and goals to the office and leaving with distinctive accomplishments and failures. From this perspective, the presidency was a composite of such heroic leaders as George Washington and Abraham Lincoln and their more feeble counterparts, such as James Buchanan and Franklin Pierce. No two presidents were alike. In effect, presidents were the presidency. To the extent that discussions of the office were offered, they were couched in the language of individual incumbents' power and leadership—the imperial presidency (too much power and malevolent leadership), the imperiled presidency (too little power and docile leadership), the impossible presidency (considerable power but docile leadership), and the impressive presidency (considerable power and benevolent leadership).

This political-actor perspective preempted systematic data analysis across presidents and hindered relevant generalizations, because presidents were scrutinized one at a time. The central theoretical question asked in much of this literature was how presidents differed in their decisions. Studies addressed the personality characteristics that most influenced decision making, the management styles presidents adopted to make their decisions, and the strategies they employed to convince others of the decisions' merits. Yet, such a perspective "promotes enormous complications in theory and research, opening a Pandora's box of individual motivation and behavior and orienting the field around causal mysteries that we are unlikely to solve" (Edwards, Kessel, and Rockman, 1993, 8). The question about how presidents differ in their decisions, if not the wrong question to ask, is surely too narrow a question that looks at the presidency through a fun house mirror—accentuating the sizes and shapes of the presidents, but leaving the actual office they hold a blur.

It is not surprising, then, that the answers scholars gave stressed variations among presidents. The analyses were often simply descriptions of events; qualitative case studies; or comparisons of case studies of single presidents based on anecdotes, personality sketches, and insiders' reminiscences. Many books included sequential chapters on presidents since Franklin Roosevelt, laying out how each officeholder shaped various aspects of the office.

Today, the charge of inadequate systematic research can no longer be leveled. Some scholars continue to address president-specific questions, but many now do so with the larger context of the presidency as an institution in mind (e.g., Hult and Walcott, 2004; Stuckey, 2004). Others have begun to ask questions that are inherently about the office, not solely about its occupants, using a wide array of theoretical approaches, research techniques, and data sets (e.g., Cameron, 2000; Mayer, 2002; Howell, 2003).

Asking New Questions

Presidency scholars have begun to ask questions that de-emphasize the uniqueness of individual presidents and focus instead on the presidency as an institution. Scholars are now asking how the institution of the presidency can affect political outcomes, including presidents' behavior. The answer researchers have given is that institutional regularities prompt all presidents, regardless of personality, leadership style, or ambition, to behave similarly in fundamental ways (Moe, 1985, 1994; Ragsdale, 1993; Rudalevige, 2002; Kumar, 2007; Wood, 2007). In addition, scholars are asking how the environment within which the presidency operates affects presidents' actions and public approval of their performances in office (Ostrom and Job, 1986; Brace and Hinckley, 1992; Mueller, 1994; Edwards, 2003). The conclusion they have reached is that political, social, and economic environmental constraints limit a president's latitude to make a difference as an individual. These lines of research consider presidential actions—whether they are legislative initiatives, vetoes, public appearances, civil rights commitments, or the use of military force—as the unit of analysis, rather than the president who is affecting the action. These questions are directing researchers' attention to the patterns that characterize the office rather than the idiosyncrasies of its occupants.

Consider as examples three regular patterns that scholars have found to characterize the institutional presidency. Perhaps the most widely known pattern is that the longer a president has been in office, the lower is his public approval. Although explanations of this pattern have differed sharply (cf. Mueller, 1970; Kernell, 1978), no one disputes the general trend in presidential popularity. This finding points to institutional continuities facing all presidents, regardless of their political party, election success, and policy accomplishments or lack thereof. A second pattern is that the smaller the number of initiatives a president undertakes in Congress, the higher is the president's legislative success (Ostrom and Simon, 1985; Edwards, 1990; Bond and Fleisher, 1992). This occurs regardless of the size of the president's party in Congress or the specific legislative initiatives considered. A third pattern is that presidential power in the use of military force expands; it never contracts (Howell, 2007; Savage, 2007; Rudalevige, 2006; see also Chapter 7). One president's actions in military affairs set a precedent for future presidents to expand presidential military efforts. This occurs regardless of which president is acting, which region of the world is involved, the size of the military effort, or its success or failure. There are certainly differences among presidents within these broad patterns. For instance, not all presidents begin their terms with approval ratings at or near the same level. Nonetheless, the universality of the downward trend in presidents' approval ratings is of great significance in understanding the institution of the presidency.

Looking for Answers

Scholars have obtained answers to their questions about the institutional presidency and its environment by gathering longitudinal data that illuminate the continuities in the way presidents behave. Moreover, because the unit of analysis is often a particular presidential action there is an underlying assumption that any one of these actions taken by one president can be compared to the same action taken by another president.

Thus, worthwhile data on the institutional presidency are emerging across time, spanning numerous individual presidencies. The data make comparisons across presidents more precise and generalizations about the institution more clear-cut. Researchers have become familiar with the wealth of publicly available data in the *Public Papers of the Presidents,* the *Code of Federal Regulations,* the *Budget of the United States,* the American Presidency Project (www.presidency.ucsb.edu), and other comprehensive sources that reveal the size and actions of the presidency. In addition, some scholars have gathered systematic data through extensive searches of material at presidential libraries. Although there is limited comparability in the data culled from one presidential library to the next, these data can nonetheless add to the picture of the presidency as an institution. Research using these sources dispels the infamous "$N = 1$" problem—one president in office at a time—and the complementary complaint that White House decision making is done privately. In addition, the systematic data on the presidency culled from these sources are increasingly being analyzed with more sophisticated and vigorous methodologies.

However, this progress in research can trigger tension among presidency scholars. Some continue to concentrate on finding out how individual presidents contribute to the presidency—What is George W. Bush really like? Others see George W. Bush as someone who will come and go; they consider that many of the factors that influence his success in Congress, his approval among the American public, and his policy achievements are not unique to him but general to the presidency. As George Edwards, John Kessel, and Bert Rockman have noted, "presidency research lacks a powerful consensus on appropriate methodology and theoretical approaches" (1991, 11). Yet, in many ways this lack of consensus has ensured progress toward more systematic and rigorous research.

A Less Elusive Executive

The two central goals of this book are to clarify the concept of institution as it applies to the presidency and to identify key statistical patterns characterizing the presidency as an institution. Presidency scholars, like researchers in political science generally, run the risk of overusing the term *institution* without truly understanding what it means. The term has become a handy buzz word that may well be added to the pool of other such terms that the discipline has seen come, and sometimes go, such as *power, system, inputs, outputs, role, culture,* and *rationality.* Often these terms are invoked to lend a theoretical framework to research that otherwise might be charged with stark empiricism. Adopted as a matter of convenience rather than as an element of theoretical rigor, writers employ their own commonsense definitions of the word, making it cover more and more situations and in so doing making it less and less helpful in distinguishing political phenomena.

The Study of Institutions

Across the large number of people writing about political institutions, there is little agreement on how the term should be conceptualized. Three different perspectives exist. One view sees institutions as "humanly devised constraints that shape human interaction" or "the rules of the game" (North, 1990, 3). According to this view, institutions include all rules, from informal norms and conventions, such as the seniority system in Congress, to formal constraints, such as constitutions. Such rules are in place as rational responses to collective action problems; the rules become agreements used to structure cooperation and reduce the costs of making decisions and carrying out other transactions. In contemporary social science, this perspective emerges from economics and has become the basis for what is called the "new institutionalism" in political science, especially current in the study of Congress.

Yet, the new institutionalism is not all that new. Ironically, its precursors are evident in early political science writings on the American presidency. Edward Corwin (1957), Pendleton Herring (1940), Louis Koenig (1944), and Clinton Rossiter (1960) foreshadow the current work with a focus on the constitutional foundations, powers, and precedents of the presidency—the rules by which the office developed. Although these scholars do not adopt notions of rationality, they nonetheless offer a traditional approach to institutionalism in political science.

Furthermore, this view of institutions rests on a slim conceptual reed. Kenneth Shepsle and Barry Weingast (1987), in a widely cited work that has been taken as an archetypical example of the new institutionalism, never define the term institution, but merely assume that their audience knows what it means. In response, Keith Krehbiel provides some help in identifying "'institutional foundations' (i.e., formal rules and precedents)" (1987, 929). Yet this parenthetical phrase is all that is offered.

References in economics are more definitive, but no more satisfying. Douglass North categorically distinguishes institutions (the rules) from organizations, which are the game and players (1990, 4–5). Thus, an organization cannot be an institution. This divorce of organization from institution prohibits the quite common explanation of an institution as a well-established social organization. From the economics viewpoint, entities such as schools, churches, universities, hospitals, legislatures, and executive offices cannot be considered institutions, although the rules by which they operate can.

A second view of institutions maintains that an institution is a stable organization that has established patterns of behavior over time that fulfill certain functions in society. Sociologists in the 1950s and 1960s identified institutions according to their lack of expendability, the creation of norms and routines, and maintenance of boundaries (Selznick, 1957; Eisenstadt, 1964). Institutions do not exist to resolve collective action problems; rather, they adapt self-images that are extensions of cultural and social expectations. Political scientists applied this concept to political organizations such as legislatures, cabinets, and political parties (Huntington, 1965; Polsby, 1968). Research using this perspective considered aspects of institutions such as autonomy (the independence of an organization from other social groupings), complexity (differentiation and multiplication of organizational subunits), coherence (consensus about the internal procedures of an organization), and adaptability (age of the organization and changes it has withstood).

A third view of institutions, which also emerged in sociology, is at once more narrow than the economics view and more broad than the old sociological view (Powell and DiMaggio, 1991). Today, sociologists, too, write of a new institutionalism, but their version directly counters that of economics and political science. The new institutionalism in sociology expressly rejects notions of rational choice as the basis for the formation and maintenance of institutions. According to this view, institutions are not formal and informal rules designed for the expedient reduction of decision costs. Instead, they are social relationships and actions that come to be taken for granted to the extent that they achieve rulelike status in social thought and action. These include such conventions as the handshake, marriage, attending college, the "No Smoking" sign, and the Nobel Prize (Meyer and Rowan, 1991). Indeed, "taken for grantedness" is a common, if curious, noun used by many in the field. Thus, institutions have cultural and symbolic, not rational, foundations.

The new institutionalism in sociology also broadens the traditional sociological attention to organizations by examining "organizational fields."

These are homogenous practices and arrangements found across a wide variety of similarly situated organizations. Such fields include the university, the corporation, the art museum, and the industry. They demonstrate similar characteristics and share a consensus about goals and boundaries of the field across a wide variety of specific organizations. For instance, the form and functions of universities are more alike than different in their approach to departmental units, tenure, the granting of degrees, and so on and thus are said to constitute a field (DiMaggio, 1991).

The Presidency as an Institution

The literature on the presidency shows no clear direction or choice among these three approaches to institutions. Presidency scholars mix and match views without necessarily recognizing their differences or even acknowledging their existence. Terry Moe adopts the traditional sociological view in a brief footnote and writes of institutions as regularized behavior patterns (1985, 236n). In later works (1993), he drops the sociological view in favor of rational choice institutionalism but does not explain why. Others retain the traditional sociological perspective (Burke, 1992; Pika, 1988; Hart, 1987; Wayne, 1978). Yet, elements of the new sociological perspective also creep into some of these writings. Although authors are seemingly unaware of the new institutionalism in sociology, they often consider the presidency as having characteristics of a bureaucracy, and thus of being part of a larger organizational field. Some of the confusion stems from the ambiguity of the three views. But the difficulty also rests with presidency scholars themselves who have not clearly articulated or agreed upon the dimensions of the presidency as an institution.

To help resolve these issues, this book considers the presidency as an institution from the traditional sociological view but also enlarges that view. The traditional sociological view defies the tendency of the new sociological perspective to be overly broad and label almost anything as an institution. Designating the handshake, the "No Smoking" sign, and the Nobel Prize as institutions confuses what may be more aptly considered symbols for institutions. The traditional sociological approach does not mistake the characteristics of an institution for the institution itself, a problem with the economics view. For instance, the use of the informal rule of seniority in Congress is indicative of Congress as an institution rather than seniority as an institution. The traditional sociological view permits the identification of two dimensions of an institution: organizational and behavioral. It recognizes the intuitive understanding already in place in much of the presidency literature that an organization imbued "with value beyond the technical requirements of the task at hand" is an institution (Selznick, 1957, 17). It also suggests that regular behavior patterns accompany, but are distinct from, the organizational dynamics.

Yet, the traditional sociological view falters in not fully recognizing a third dimension of institutions—structure. The organizational and behavioral dimensions of an institution do not simply come about on their own. Structural elements are the intrinsic, defining characteristics of the institution that provide the parameters within which the organization and institutional behavior occur. These structures are not so broad as to identify an organizational field; instead, they describe the most typical features of a single institution. For instance, there are certain elements that distinguish the American presidency from the German or French presidencies. The structures guiding the American office include quadrennial indirect elections, separation of powers, and the combination of head of state with policy actor. These structures establish the parameters within which the institutional organization and behavior occur. Thus, this book identifies three dimensions of the presidency as an institution: organizational, behavioral, and structural.

The organizational dimension reveals how an institution is fused with value as an end in itself. Applied to the presidency, it involves the routines, procedures, and units that comprise the Executive Office of the President. Although presidents often make marginal changes within the organization, the office is not reinvented each time a president arrives at the White House (see Chapter 6). Because of the tangible qualities of the organization, this dimension is especially important in juxtaposing the presidency as an institution against presidents as individuals.

The behavioral dimension involves the extent to which presidents faced with similar environmental circumstances respond in similar ways. Perhaps one of the most well-defined behavioral aspects of the contemporary presidency is the use of public persuasion. Scholars often concentrate on the uniqueness of individual presidents' public leadership—their speaking styles, how stiff or relaxed they are in public, the degree to which they are willing to meet the people. Yet, institutional behavior—in the form of major national addresses, news conferences, and ceremonial appearances—guides many of these individual actions. In addition, imagery attached to the office—that is, the image of the president as the one person in charge of the government and as the representative of the people—creates consistency in the way presidents present themselves to the public (see Chapter 4).

The structural dimension defines how the U.S. Constitution, historical precedents, and temporal orderings shape the presidency. Most fundamentally, the presidency is structured as an electoral and representative office, independent from the legislature. As an electoral office, the presidency runs on a four-year clock set by the most recent and the next presidential election. Time systematically defines how the office operates. Political resources and opportunities decrease as time moves further away from the election victory and the "honeymoon" ends (Light, 1991).

As a representative office, the presidency rests on a symbolic connection between the people and the president; the president is a symbol of the nation and is thereby identified with its achievements and misfortunes. As an independent office, the presidency reflects separation of powers. This independence has allowed the presidency to garner more power than the Framers originally envisioned, though the executive's gain has not necessarily been at the expense of Congress, which itself benefits from the separation of powers. These three dimensions—organizational, behavioral, and structural—define the manner in which the presidential institution has a life of its own.

Statistical Patterns of the Presidency

The statistical patterns revealed in this book show that the institution of the presidency shapes presidents as much as presidents, during their short tenures, shape the institution. Both the resources and constraints inherent in the institution make the actions of individual presidents far more similar than different to the actions of their immediate predecessors and successors. In addition, the institutional presidency may even act independently of presidents in making policy decisions or shaping presidents' public activities. While it is true that some presidents have fashioned significant innovations, such one-time reforms or pathbreaking decisions often become commonplace practices or precedents for future presidents and thus a part of the institution. This book attempts to place these president-specific changes within the context of an evolving presidency. It is also true that exogenous events in the national and international environment are important. These events may shape both presidents' actions and the institution itself. The data presented here provide the necessary foundation for fashioning explanations about the connections among the presidency, presidents, and the political environment. Readers will find three sets of statistical patterns in the book: institutional patterns, environmental patterns, and incumbent-specific patterns. Of course, data are not self-interpreting. Scholars may find other statistical patterns than those highlighted here. In either case, the data may allow them to pursue answers to questions they have not thought about in the past.

Institutional Continuity

The transition between administrations provides one of the strongest tests of the validity of institutional patterns. How can the presidency truly exist as an ongoing institution when, on January 20 following the election of a new president, virtually every important White House office changes occupants? The turnover is dramatic and takes place whether or not the successive executives belong to different political parties. Even when a president begins a second term, changes abound. A new chief establishes a new direction.

Still, the outlook of the new administration reflects past campaigns, administrations, and policies, all of which provide continuity. In addition, as broad new themes shape specific relationships among (new) individuals in (old) organizations, many arrangements and procedures persist from previous administrations. When one incumbent replaces another, the newcomer may well perpetuate established practices out of a need to respond quickly in a context of limited information and expertise.

The executive apparatus shows even more systematic continuity. Although members of the White House staff change with some frequency, the broader institution of the presidency is hardly recreated each time a new administration enters office. Many, if not all, top staffers change during a transition, but the career personnel stay. As an example, on January 6, 1977, the International Trade Commission recommended to President Gerald Ford that tariffs be placed on shoes imported from abroad. Ford decided not to act on the matter but instead left it to his successor. The day after Jimmy Carter took office, he received a memo from the National Security Council on shoe import quotas. On February 4, the Office of the United States Trade Representative—a unit within the Executive Office of the President charged with advising presidents on trade—provided Carter with a background memo. In both instances, action was being taken on material inherited from the Ford administration (see DiClerico, 1985, 248–249). This item on the national policy agenda continued to be addressed, regardless of who was president.

Yet, incumbent change surely remains prominent even amidst this continuity. Ultimately, the most appropriate way of viewing the change wrought by a new incumbent and administration is to see it as a structural cycle of the institution, not a feature of the presidential entourage. Quadrennial change is merely one of the regularly occurring patterns that constitute the presidency and help explain the behavior of old and new alike at the White House. While every president enters office determined to make a difference, students of the presidency are deceived if they think that this is a function of an individual president. Instead, it is much more reflective of the electoral and representative nature of the office. Election cycle change is actually a very regular and well-known aspect of the presidency—it inheres in the office, not in its incumbents.

Environmental Influences

The overall environment plays a role in establishing some of the most compelling patterns in the presidency. These patterns derive from the way national politics depends on exogenous events and conditions, such as wars, economic booms and busts, rising crime rates, hefty trade imbalances, and the collapse of long-standing governments abroad. Such circumstances are not wholly or even principally under presidents' control, although they are sometimes mistakenly assumed to be so. Herbert Hoover made this point when he said, "Once upon a time my political opponents honored me as possessing the fabulous intellectual and economic power by which I created a world-wide depression all by myself." Sharing Hoover's sentiments, William Howard Taft observed,

> There is a class of people that . . . visit the President with responsibility for everything that is done and that is not done. If poverty prevails where, in their judgment, it should not prevail, then the President is responsible. If other people are richer than they ought to be, the President is responsible. While the President's powers are broad, he cannot do everything. . . . This would be ludicrous if it did not sometimes take serious results. The President cannot make clouds to rain, he cannot make the corn to grow, he cannot make business to be good. (1916, 47–50)

In many ways, the success or failure attributed to individual presidents may well be the result of conditions in the broader social, political, and economic environment that make presidents look good and bad, or better and worse, than they would otherwise.

Incumbent Differences

President-specific dynamics comprise a third set of patterns derived from the data. General patterns take on recognizable forms across different administrations, though individual incumbents may give them distinct character. An example from Chapter 4 reveals that President Richard Nixon held significantly fewer news conferences than did other presidents. Another example from Chapter 5 indicates that President George W. Bush's public approval ratings started high, soared even higher, then dropped precipitously. A final example from Chapter 6 shows that President Ford sharply cut the size of the Executive Office of the President upon taking office.

Yet each of these incumbent-specific patterns must be placed in the larger context of the office. Nixon held fewer news conferences, but he did not abandon these sessions with the press because he could not. The practice of giving news conferences is an institutional feature of the presidency that a president—even Nixon, who bitterly distrusted the press—would stop only at his political peril. George W. Bush obtained the highest approval rating of any president after the terrorist bombings on September 11, 2001, yet the institutional pattern still caught up with him when public expectations went unmet on domestic and economic issues and the country soured on the Iraq War. President Ford drastically cut the size of the White House staff, but he did not cut its budget.

None of these examples are meant to suggest that the institution has some kind of magical power over individual incumbents. Rather, the institution represents an encompassing set of offices, procedures, and relationships within which presidents act and react and which help to guide their behavior.

Systematic Research on the Presidency

Although this book contains many statistics, data points, trend lines, and figures, this does not suggest that all research on the presidency should be quantitative or that all quantitative research is better than qualitative research. Indeed, not all questions worthy of being asked can be answered with quantitative data. Quantitative or qualitative work done shoddily reveals nothing. Quantitative and qualitative work done thoroughly can provide (and has provided) important insights into the office. It is surely possible for presidency scholars to develop theoretically driven, systematic analyses using either type of data. There is nothing intrinsically more rigorous, difficult, or informative about quantitative research relative to qualitative research (King, 1993; King, Keohane, Verba, 1994). But, ultimately, this book stands as a reminder that there is little room left in the study of the presidency for research based on unsystematic, albeit absorbing, anecdotes and passing observations. Researchers often masquerade such anecdotal evidence as systematically gathered and analyzed qualitative data, which it is not.

Anecdotal observation has at least two negative consequences. First, it leads observers to make misinformed judgments and statements. For example, the 1980 and 1984 elections were widely perceived as two of the largest presidential election victories ever. Accordingly, Democrats and Republicans alike believed that the American public supported Ronald Reagan's policies wholeheartedly. Although his 1984 victory was a substantial electoral college win, fully one-third of all election victories in this century were decided by larger popular vote margins (see Chapter 3). Moreover, two-thirds of all presidential elections in this century were decided by larger popular vote margins than Reagan's 1980 victory.

Second, anecdotal observation leaves scholars without a reliable basis for comparison and analysis. Presidential behavior, reporters' comments, newspaper editorials, presidents' biographies and autobiographies, and political arguments by members of Congress or the administration are impossible to evaluate adequately without knowledge of comparable situations and statistics. For example, commentators often overstated Carter's unpopularity, portraying him as unable to lead the country during trying times. In an equally overstated fashion, observers pointed to Reagan's exceptional popularity, dubbing him the "Teflon" president when his personal popularity remained seemingly untouched by the relative unpopularity of his political positions. Yet systematic analysis of the evidence reveals that these characterizations of the two presidents were erroneous. Data in Chapter 5 make clear that during the first two years of their terms, these two presidents had similar public approval ratings.

Thoroughgoing data analysis—whether quantitative or qualitative—of an individual president's term or across several presidents' terms alleviates these twin problems. Comparisons are routine and evaluations of the evidence are more reliable. Presidency watchers of all kinds have an interest in eliminating anecdotal observation to reduce the chasm between information about American presidents and information about the presidency. As more presidency scholars test theories and hypotheses with appropriate data, generalizations about the presidency become more numerous and more trustworthy. Many of these generalizations are already in place (Ragsdale, 1997). Such research provides the opportunity for cumulative scientific study that will move the field toward a consensus about how to ask new questions and away from past squabbles about the second-class status of the field.

Outline of the Book

The book is organized into ten chapters. Data in the chapters are presented in as long a time frame as possible. Chapter 1 offers a brief look at presidents from Washington to George W. Bush—their personal backgrounds and their political experience. The chapter reminds readers of who these men were and the significance of the eras in which they lived.

Chapters 2 and 3 consider how elections create structural aspects of the presidency as an institution. Chapter 2 offers a view of the presidential selection process, providing data on presidential nominating conventions beginning in 1832. It continues with an examination of the rise in importance of presidential primaries since 1912. Media coverage of recent nominations is also addressed, showing that what was once a heavily party-dominant task is now a much more candidate-driven process. Chapter 3 examines general election outcomes since 1789 and offers information on modern-day presidential campaigns.

Chapters 4 and 5 consider the nature of institutional behavior, first from the perspective of presidents' activities and then from the perspective of the public's reactions to these activities. Chapter 4 provides an analysis of presidents' public appearances since Calvin Coolidge as a form of institutional behavior. Chapter 5 offers public opinion data on presidents since Franklin Roosevelt that reveal a downward trend over time. The presidents' public institutional behavior may shape subsequent public behavior.

Chapters 6, 7, and 8 look at organization as a pivotal part of the presidency as an institution. Chapter 6 considers the size and shape of the office of the president, its budget, and the units within it since its inception in 1924. The chapter also examines the broad outlines of the executive branch and stresses that the organization of the presidency is not the same thing as the executive branch, nor is it in control of the executive branch. Chapters 7 and 8 look at the independent policymaking the presidency as an organization produces. Chapter 7 examines presidents' efforts in war and diplomacy. It highlights their use of military force, whether sanctioned by Congress or not, and the powerful precedents these military efforts have created for future presidents. The chapter also examines U.S. diplomatic efforts in the form of executive agreements and treaties. Chapter 8 considers the domestic and economic policymaking of the White House. It presents data on presidents' executive orders and their efforts at budget and tax policymaking.

The final two chapters examine relations between the presidency and the other institutions of government. The structural, behavioral, and organizational dimensions of the presidency are evident in relations between the presidency and Congress (Chapter 9) and between the presidency and the courts (Chapter 10). Chapter 9 inventories presidential requests to Congress and presidential positions on legislation before Congress since Dwight Eisenhower and notes vetoes taken since Washington. Chapter 10 depicts the judicial nominations of presidents and examines court rulings against presidents since Washington.

1

Presidents of the United States

- **Personal Backgrounds**
- **Careers**
- **Ratings of Presidents**

Can anyone grow up to be president, as the old adage suggests? The tables of this chapter present data with which to examine this question. Table 1-1 lists the presidents and vice presidents of the United States; Table 1-2 examines the personal backgrounds of the presidents; and Tables 1-3, 1-4, and 1-5 offer accounts of the presidents' political lives. The data reveal that the forty-two presidents of the United States have come from every conceivable set of circumstances. Apparently, it does not matter whether one is 5 feet, 4 inches (James Madison) or 6 feet, 4 inches tall (George Bush, Bill Clinton). It does not matter whether one goes to Ivy League schools such as Harvard (John Adams) or Yale (George Bush and George W. Bush) or to no school at all (George Washington). One can be young (John Tyler, John F. Kennedy, Clinton) or old (William H. Harrison, Dwight Eisenhower, Ronald Reagan). There have been presidents with no political experience (Zachary Taylor, Ulysses S. Grant) and presidents with lengthy political careers behind them (Lyndon Johnson, Gerald Ford). These differences would seem to lend credence to the political-actor perspective discussed in the introduction—namely, that no two presidents are alike, and they all arrive and leave the presidency via distinctive paths. The political-actor perspective contends that this uniqueness is worthy of study.

Yet, most of these characteristics do not have much to offer in our search to understand how presidents will act in office. Tables 1-6 and 1-7 look at the various ratings of presidents. The polls reveal considerable agreement among historians, political scientists, and other experts on the presidency as to who are the best presidents: Abraham Lincoln, Franklin Roosevelt, Washington, Thomas Jefferson, Theodore Roosevelt, and Woodrow Wilson. But beyond that, there is more divergence on how to evaluate presidential greatness, as seen by the standard deviations presented in the two tables. There is very little agreement among students of the presidency on how to rate Reagan, Herbert Hoover, and Andrew Johnson. The ratings also suggest that neither personal nor political characteristics are good predictors of success (as defined in the several polls). Nothing in the presidents' immediate personal or political backgrounds provides clues to their so-called greatness.

Table 1-8 considers American first ladies, who have acted as official hostesses for White House functions, served as the unofficial policy confidants of presidents, and conducted great humanitarian and community service work. Most first ladies have been the wives of the presidents. And, like their husbands, they come from all kinds of backgrounds, wealthy (Martha Washington) and not (Bess Truman), interested in politics (Eleanor Roosevelt) and not (Pat Nixon), although most have been well educated for the times in which they lived.

So are there any useful patterns to be observed? Three are most noteworthy. First, there is a clear bias in who has become (and can become) president. Anyone can become president who is *not* female, African American, Hispanic, Jewish, atheist, or openly homosexual. People who are not white men have run for the office over the years, beginning with suffragist Victoria Woodhall, who announced she was running for president before women even had the right to vote. But not until the 2008 race did a woman (former first lady and current New York senator Hillary Rodham Clinton) and an African American (Sen. Barack Obama of Illinois) have a credible shot at a party nomination. When Obama secured the Democratic nomination, he made history as the first African American to run as a major-party contender for president.

Second, Tables 1-6 and 1-7 reveal that several presidents who were judged "great" were in fact caught up in circumstances beyond their control—Lincoln faced the Civil War, Woodrow Wilson encountered World War I, and Franklin Roosevelt confronted the Great Depression and World War II. As noted in the introduction, it is important to consider the environment within which presidents act. Social, economic, and political events and conditions may force, as much as allow, presidents to behave boldly. A note of caution is also in order regarding interpretation. Greatness is surely in the eye of the beholder. Although the polls show agreement on the top four or five presidents, there is little consensus thereafter. A person's judgment of greatness varies depending on his or her own background, political interests, partisanship, and view of the office.

Finally, historical eras are important in studying individual presidents. As an example, drawn from Tables 1-3 and 1-4, the twentieth-century presidency attracts a particular type of office-seeker who is far different from that of the nineteenth century. Twentieth-century presidents are less likely to have served in Congress than those of the nineteenth century;

indeed, they are less likely to have had any lengthy political experience at all prior to running for office. Researchers should bear in mind that eighteenth- and nineteenth-century presidents and their twentieth-century counterparts are unlike, largely because the office they have held has radically changed over time (Ragsdale, 1993).

Before the twentieth century, the presidency operated under a doctrine of presidential restraint in which presidents did not take the lead in government but instead deferred to Congress. This view of presidential restraint closely followed the intent of the Framers—in the U.S. Constitution the chief executive is given a limited set of specified powers rather than any inherent executive authority. As such, it is no accident that twenty of the twenty-five presidents who entered office before 1900 were not activists. Only Washington, Jefferson, Jackson, Polk, and Lincoln are exceptions to this early rule of restraint. This is not because those twenty presidents were especially prosaic or unhappy men, unable to champion the office they held. Nor is it because the five other presidents were keenly charismatic, energetic, or intelligent. Instead, conceptions of the Constitution strongly restricted the institution in which all twenty-five served. On occasion, circumstances, such as the founding of government, the outbreak of war, or internal crises, have allowed presidents to move beyond the restrictions. Yet decades separated these precedents, and they did not create an overall pattern for future presidents.

At the opening of the twentieth century, ideas about the presidency and government changed. A theory of presidential activism replaced that of presidential restraint. Presidents should use their power to act, in Theodore Roosevelt's words, as "the steward of the people bound actively and affirmatively to do all he could for the people" (1913, 389). Since the twentieth century, the office has expanded presidents' activities far beyond what they were in the previous century. Thus, in thinking about presidents, it is important to consider the times in which they sought and held the office.

Table 1-1 U.S. Presidents and Vice Presidents, Washington to G.W. Bush

President (political party)	*President's term of service*	*Vice president*	*Vice president's term of service*
George Washington (F)	April 30, 1789–March 4, 1793	John Adams	April 30, 1789–March 4, 1793
George Washington (F)	March 4, 1793–March 4, 1797	John Adams	March 4, 1793–March 4, 1797
John Adams (F)	March 4, 1797–March 4, 1801	Thomas Jefferson	March 4, 1797–March 4, 1801
Thomas Jefferson (DR)	March 4, 1801–March 4, 1805	Aaron Burr	March 4, 1801–March 4, 1805
Thomas Jefferson (DR)	March 4, 1805–March 4, 1809	George Clinton	March 4, 1805–March 4, 1809
James Madison (DR)	March 4, 1809–March 4, 1813	George Clinton[a]	March 4, 1809–April 12, 1812
James Madison (DR)	March 4, 1813–March 4, 1817	Elbridge Gerry[a]	March 4, 1813–Nov. 23, 1814
James Monroe (DR)	March 4, 1817–March 4, 1821	Daniel D. Tompkins	March 4, 1817–March 4, 1821
James Monroe (DR)	March 4, 1821–March 4, 1825	Daniel D. Tompkins	March 4, 1821–March 4, 1825
John Quincy Adams (DR)	March 4, 1825–March 4, 1829	John C. Calhoun	March 4, 1825–March 4, 1829
Andrew Jackson (D)	March 4, 1829–March 4, 1833	John C. Calhoun[b]	March 4, 1829–Dec. 28, 1832
Andrew Jackson (D)	March 4, 1833–March 4, 1837	Martin Van Buren	March 4, 1833–March 4, 1837
Martin Van Buren (D)	March 4, 1837–March 4, 1841	Richard M. Johnson	March 4, 1837–March 4, 1841
William H. Harrison[a] (W)	March 4, 1841–April 4, 1841	John Tyler[c]	March 4, 1841–April 6, 1841
John Tyler (W)	April 6, 1841–March 4, 1845		
James K. Polk (D)	March 4, 1845–March 4, 1849	George M. Dallas	March 4, 1845–March 4, 1849
Zachary Taylor[a] (W)	March 4, 1849–July 9, 1850	Millard Fillmore[c]	March 4, 1849–July 10, 1850
Millard Fillmore (W)	July 10, 1850–March 4, 1853		
Franklin Pierce (D)	March 4, 1853–March 4, 1857	William R. King[a]	March 24, 1853–April 18, 1853
James Buchanan (D)	March 4, 1857–March 4, 1861	John C. Breckinridge	March 4, 1857–March 4, 1861
Abraham Lincoln (R)	March 4, 1861–March 4, 1865	Hannibal Hamlin	March 4, 1861–March 4, 1865
Abraham Lincoln[a] (R)	March 4, 1865–April 15, 1865	Andrew Johnson[c]	March 4, 1865–April 15, 1865
Andrew Johnson (R)	April 15, 1865–March 4, 1869		
Ulysses S. Grant (R)	March 4, 1869–March 4, 1873	Schuyler Colfax	March 4, 1869–March 4, 1873
Ulysses S. Grant (R)	March 4, 1873–March 4, 1877	Henry Wilson[a]	March 4, 1873–Nov. 22, 1875
Rutherford B. Hayes (R)	March 4, 1877–March 4, 1881	William A. Wheeler	March 4, 1877–March 4, 1881
James A. Garfield[a] (R)	March 4, 1881–Sept. 19, 1881	Chester A. Arthur[c]	March 4, 1881–Sept. 20, 1881

Chester A. Arthur (R)	Sept. 20, 1881–March 4, 1885		
Grover Cleveland (D)	March 4, 1885–March 4, 1889	Thomas A. Hendricks[a]	March 4, 1885–Nov. 25, 1885
Benjamin Harrison (R)	March 4, 1889–March 4, 1893	Levi P. Morton	March 4, 1889–March 4, 1893
Grover Cleveland (D)	March 4, 1893–March 4, 1897	Adlai E. Stevenson	March 4, 1893–March 4, 1897
William McKinley (R)	March 4, 1897–March 4, 1901	Garret A. Hobart[a]	March 4, 1897–Nov. 21, 1899
William McKinley[a] (R)	March 4, 1901–Sept. 14, 1901	Theodore Roosevelt[c]	March 4, 1901–Sept. 14, 1901
Theodore Roosevelt (R)	Sept. 14, 1901–March 4, 1905		
Theodore Roosevelt (R)	March 4, 1905–March 4, 1909	Charles W. Fairbanks	March 4, 1905–March 4, 1909
William H. Taft (R)	March 4, 1909–March 4, 1913	James S. Sherman[a]	March 4, 1909–Oct. 30, 1912
Woodrow Wilson (D)	March 4, 1913–March 4, 1917	Thomas R. Marshall	March 4, 1913–March 4, 1917
Woodrow Wilson (D)	March 4, 1917–March 4, 1921	Thomas R. Marshall	March 4, 1917–March 4, 1921
Warren G. Harding[a] (R)	March 4, 1921–Aug. 2, 1923	Calvin Coolidge[c]	March 4, 1921–Aug. 3, 1923
Calvin Coolidge (R)	Aug. 3, 1923–March 4, 1925		
Calvin Coolidge (R)	March 4, 1925–March 4, 1929	Charles G. Dawes	March 4, 1925–March 4, 1929
Herbert Hoover (R)	March 4, 1929–March 4, 1933	Charles Curtis	March 4, 1929–March 4, 1933
Franklin D. Roosevelt (D)	March 4, 1933–Jan. 20, 1937	John N. Garner	March 4, 1933–Jan. 20, 1937
Franklin D. Roosevelt (D)	Jan. 20, 1937–Jan. 20, 1941	John N. Garner	Jan. 20, 1937–Jan. 20, 1941
Franklin D. Roosevelt (D)	Jan. 20, 1941–Jan. 20, 1945	Henry A. Wallace	Jan. 20, 1941–Jan. 20, 1945
Franklin D. Roosevelt[a] (D)	Jan. 20, 1945–April 12, 1945	Harry S. Truman[c]	Jan. 20, 1945–April 12, 1945
Harry S. Truman (D)	April 12, 1945–Jan. 20, 1949		
Harry S. Truman (D)	Jan. 20, 1949–Jan. 20, 1953	Alben W. Barkley	Jan. 20, 1949–Jan. 20, 1953
Dwight D. Eisenhower (R)	Jan. 20, 1953–Jan. 20, 1957	Richard Nixon	Jan. 20, 1953–Jan. 20, 1957
Dwight D. Eisenhower (R)	Jan. 20, 1957–Jan. 20, 1961	Richard Nixon	Jan. 20, 1957–Jan. 20, 1961
John F. Kennedy[a] (D)	Jan. 20, 1961–Nov. 22, 1963	Lyndon B. Johnson[c]	Jan. 20, 1961–Nov. 22, 1963
Lyndon B. Johnson (D)	Nov. 22, 1963–Jan. 20, 1965		
Lyndon B. Johnson (D)	Jan. 20, 1965–Jan. 20, 1969	Hubert H. Humphrey	Jan. 20, 1965–Jan. 20, 1969
Richard Nixon (R)	Jan. 20, 1969–Jan. 20, 1973	Spiro T. Agnew	Jan. 20, 1969–Jan. 20, 1973
Richard Nixon[b] (R)	Jan. 20, 1973–Aug. 9, 1974	Spiro T. Agnew[b]	Jan. 20, 1973–Oct. 10, 1973
		Gerald R. Ford[c]	Dec. 6, 1973–Aug. 9, 1974
Gerald R. Ford[c] (R)	Aug. 9, 1974–Jan. 20, 1977	Nelson A. Rockefeller	Dec. 19, 1974–Jan. 20, 1977
Jimmy Carter (D)	Jan. 20, 1977–Jan. 20, 1981	Walter F. Mondale	Jan. 20, 1977–Jan. 20, 1981

(Table continues)

Table 1-1 *(Continued)*

President (political party)	*President's term of service*	*Vice president*	*Vice president's term of service*
Ronald Reagan (R)	Jan. 20, 1981–Jan. 20, 1985	George Bush	Jan. 20, 1981–Jan. 20, 1985
Ronald Reagan (R)	Jan. 20, 1985–Jan. 20, 1989	George Bush	Jan. 20, 1985–Jan. 20, 1989
George H. W. Bush (R)	Jan. 20, 1989–Jan. 20, 1993	Dan Quayle	Jan. 20, 1989–Jan. 20, 1993
Bill Clinton (D)	Jan. 20, 1993–Jan. 20, 1997	Albert Gore	Jan. 20, 1993–Jan. 20, 1997
Bill Clinton (D)	Jan. 20, 1997–Jan. 20, 2001	Albert Gore	Jan. 20, 1997–Jan. 20, 2001
George W. Bush (R)	Jan 20, 2001–Jan. 20, 2009	Richard Cheney	Jan. 20, 2001–Jan. 20, 2009

Source: Harold Stanley and Richard Niemi, *Vital Statistics on American Politics, 2007–2008* (Washington, D.C.: CQ Press, 2008), 253–255.

Note: D—Democrat; DR—Democratic-Republican; F—Federalist; R—Republican; W—Whig.

[a] Died in office.
[b] Resigned.
[c] Succeeded to the presidency.

Table 1-2 Personal Backgrounds of U.S. Presidents, Washington to G.W. Bush

President	*Date of birth*	*Place of birth*	*Date of death*	*Age at death*	*Higher education*	*Occupation*	*Number of children*	*Height in inches*
1. George Washington	Feb. 22, 1732	Va.	Dec. 14, 1799	67	None	Farmer/surveyor	0	74
2. John Adams	Oct. 30, 1735	Mass.	July 4, 1826	90	Harvard	Farmer/lawyer	5	67
3. Thomas Jefferson	April 13, 1743	Va.	July 4, 1826	83	William & Mary	Farmer/lawyer	6	75
4. James Madison	March 16, 1751	Va.	June 28, 1836	85	Princeton	Farmer	0	64
5. James Monroe	April 28, 1758	Va.	July 4, 1831	73	William & Mary	Farmer/lawyer	2	72
6. John Quincy Adams	July 11, 1767	Mass.	Feb. 23, 1848	80	Harvard	Lawyer	4	67
7. Andrew Jackson	March 15, 1767	S.C.	June 8, 1845	78	None	Lawyer	0	73
8. Martin Van Buren	Dec. 5, 1782	N.Y.	Jan. 18, 1862	71	None	Lawyer	4	66
9. William H. Harrison	Feb. 9, 1773	Va.	April 4, 1841	68	Hampden	Military	10	N/A
10. John Tyler	March 29, 1790	Va.	Jan. 18, 1862	71	William & Mary	Lawyer	15	72
11. James K. Polk	Nov. 2, 1795	N.C.	June 15, 1849	53	North Carolina	Lawyer	0	68
12. Zachary Taylor	Nov. 24, 1784	Va.	July 9, 1850	65	None	Military	6	68
13. Millard Fillmore	Jan. 7, 1800	N.Y.	March 8, 1874	74	None	Lawyer	2	69
14. Franklin Pierce	Nov. 23, 1804	N.H.	Oct. 8, 1869	64	Bowdoin	Lawyer	3	70
15. James Buchanan	April 23, 1791	Pa.	June 1, 1868	77	Dickinson	Lawyer	0	72
16. Abraham Lincoln	Feb. 12, 1809	Ky.	April 15, 1865	56	None	Lawyer	4	74
17. Andrew Johnson	Dec. 29, 1808	N.C.	July 31, 1875	66	None	Tailor	5	70
18. Ulysses S. Grant	April 27, 1822	Ohio	July 23, 1885	63	West Point	Military	4	68
19. Rutherford B. Hayes	Oct. 4, 1822	Ohio	Jan. 17, 1893	70	Kenyon	Lawyer	8	68
20. James A. Garfield	Nov. 19, 1831	Ohio	Sep. 19, 1881	49	Williams	Educator/lawyer	5	N/A
21. Chester A. Arthur	Oct. 5, 1829	Vt.	Nov. 18, 1886	57	Union	Lawyer	3	74
22. Grover Cleveland	March 18, 1837	N.J.	June 24, 1908	71	None	Lawyer	5	71
23. Benjamin Harrison	Aug. 20, 1833	Ohio	March 13, 1901	67	Miami (Ohio)	Lawyer	3	66
24. Grover Cleveland	March 18, 1837	N.J.	June 24, 1908	71	None	Lawyer	5	71
25. William McKinley	Jan. 29, 1843	Ohio	Sep. 14, 1901	58	Allegheny	Lawyer	2	67
26. Theodore Roosevelt	Oct. 27, 1858	N.Y.	Jan. 6, 1919	60	Harvard	Lawyer/author	6	70

(Table continues)

Table 1-2 *(Continued)*

	President	*Date of birth*	*Place of birth*	*Date of death*	*Age at death*	*Higher education*	*Occupation*	*Number of children*	*Height in inches*
27.	William H. Taft	Sep. 15, 1857	Ohio	March 8, 1930	72	Yale	Lawyer	3	72
28.	Woodrow Wilson	Dec. 28, 1856	Va.	Feb. 3, 1924	67	Princeton	Educator	3	71
29.	Warren G. Harding	Nov. 2, 1865	Ohio	Aug. 2, 1923	57	Ohio Central	Newspaper editor	0	72
30.	Calvin Coolidge	July 4, 1872	Vt.	Jan. 5, 1933	60	Amherst	Lawyer	2	70
31.	Herbert Hoover	Aug. 10, 1874	Iowa	Oct. 20, 1964	90	Stanford	Engineer	2	71
32.	Franklin D. Roosevelt	Jan. 30, 1882	N.Y.	April 12, 1945	63	Harvard	Lawyer	5	74
33.	Harry S. Truman	May 8, 1884	Mo.	Dec. 26, 1972	88	None	Clerk/Store owner	1	69
34.	Dwight D. Eisenhower	Oct. 14, 1890	Texas	March 28, 1969	78	West Point	Military	1	70
35.	John F. Kennedy	May 29, 1917	Mass.	Nov. 22, 1963	46	Harvard	Lawyer	2	72
36.	Lyndon B. Johnson	Aug 27, 1908	Texas	Jan. 22, 1973	64	Southwest Texas State Teachers' College	Educator	2	75
37.	Richard Nixon	Jan. 9, 1913	Calif.	Apr. 22, 1994	81	Whittier	Lawyer	2	72
38.	Gerald R. Ford	July 14, 1913	Neb.	Dec. 26, 2006	93	Michigan	Lawyer	4	72
39.	Jimmy Carter	Oct. 1, 1924	Ga.			Annapolis	Farmer/businessman	4	69
40.	Ronald Reagan	Feb. 6, 1911	Ill.	June 5, 2004	93	Eureka	Actor	4	74
41.	George H. W. Bush	June 12, 1924	Mass.			Yale	Businessman	6	76
42.	Bill Clinton	Aug. 19, 1946	Ark.			Georgetown	Lawyer	1	76
43.	George W. Bush	July 6, 1946	Conn.			Yale	Businessman	2	71

Sources: Adapted from *Guide to U.S. Elections*, 5th ed. (Washington, D.C.: CQ Press, 2005), vol. I, 809–815.

Note: N/A—Not available.

Table 1-3 Political Careers of U.S. Presidents Prior to Their Presidencies, Washington to G. W. Bush

President	*Party*	*Age at first political office*	*First political office/last political office*	*Years in Congress*	*Years as governor*	*Years as vice president*	*Age at becoming president*
1. George Washington	F	17	County surveyor/military general	2	0	0	57
2. John Adams	F	39	Highway surveyor/vice president	5	0	4	61
3. Thomas Jefferson	DR	26	State legislator/vice president	5	3	4	58
4. James Madison	DR	25	State legislator/secretary of state	15	0	0	58
5. James Monroe	DR	24	State legislator/secretary of state	7	4	0	59
6. John Quincy Adams	DR	27	Minister to Netherlands/secretary of state	0[a]	0	0	58
7. Andrew Jackson	D	21	Prosecuting attorney/U.S. Senate	4	0	0	62
8. Martin Van Buren	D	30	County surrogate/vice president	8	0	4	55
9. William H. Harrison	W	26	Territorial delegate/minister to Colombia	0	0	0	68
10. John Tyler	W	21	State legislator/vice president	12	2	0	51
11. James K. Polk	D	28	State legislator/governor	14	3	0	50
12. Zachary Taylor	W	—	None/military general	0	0	0	65
13. Millard Fillmore	W	28	State legislator/vice president	8	0	1	50
14. Franklin Pierce	D	25	State legislator/district attorney	9	0	0	48
15. James Buchanan	D	22	County prosecutor/minister to Great Britain	20	0	0	65
16. Abraham Lincoln	R	25	State legislator/U.S. House	2	0	0	52
17. Andrew Johnson	D	20	City alderman/vice president	14	4	0	57
18. Ulysses S. Grant	R	—	None/military general	0	0	0	47
19. Rutherford B. Hayes	R	36	City solicitor/governor	3	6	0	55
20. James A. Garfield	R	28	State legislator/U.S. Senate	18	0	0	50
21. Chester A. Arthur	R	31	State engineer/vice president	0	0	1	51
22. Grover Cleveland	D	26	District attorney/governor	0	2	0	48
23. Benjamin Harrison	R	24	City attorney/U.S. Senate	6	0	0	56

(Table continues)

Table 1-3 *(Continued)*

President	*Party*	*Age at first political office*	*First political office/last political office*	*Years in Congress*	*Years as governor*	*Years as vice president*	*Age at becoming president*
24. Grover Cleveland	D	26	District attorney / governor	0	2	0	53
25. William McKinley	R	26	Prosecuting attorney / governor	14	4	0	54
26. Theodore Roosevelt	R	24	State legislator / vice president	0	2	1	43
27. William H. Taft	R	24	Prosecuting attorney / secretary of war	0	0	0	52
28. Woodrow Wilson	D	54	Governor / governor	0	2	0	56
29. Warren G. Harding	R	35	State legislator / U.S. Senate	6	0	0	56
30. Calvin Coolidge	R	26	City council / vice president	0	2	3	51
31. Herbert Hoover	R	43	Relief administrator / secretary of commerce	0	0	0	55
32. Franklin D. Roosevelt	D	28	State legislator / governor	0	4	0	49
33. Harry S. Truman	D	38	County judge / vice president	10	0	0	61
34. Dwight D. Eisenhower	R	—	None / military general	0	0	0	63
35. John F. Kennedy	D	29	U.S. House / U.S. Senate	14	0	0	43
36. Lyndon B. Johnson	D	28	U.S. House / U.S. Senate	24	0	3	55
37. Richard Nixon	R	34	U.S. House / vice president	6	0	8	56
38. Gerald R. Ford	R	36	U.S. House / vice president	25	0	2	61
39. Jimmy Carter	D	38	Member, County Board of Education / governor	0	4	0	52
40. Ronald Reagan	R	55	Governor / governor	0	8	0	69
41. George H. W. Bush	R	42	U.S. House / vice president	4	0	8	64
42. Bill Clinton	D	30	State attorney general / governor	0	12	0	46
43. George W. Bush	R	48	Governor / governor	0	6	0	54

Sources: Adapted from *Presidential Elections Since 1789*, 4th ed. (Washington D.C.: Congressional Quarterly, 1987), 4; Norman Thomas, Joseph Pika, and Richard Watson, *The Politics of the Presidency*, rev. 6th ed. (Washington, D.C.: CQ Press, 2006), 139–140.

Note: D—Democrat; DR—Democratic-Republican; F—Federalist; W—Whig; R—Republican.

[a] Adams served in the U.S. House for six years after leaving the presidency.

Table 1-4 Presidents' Previous Public Positions, Washington to G. W. Bush

	Number of presidents holding position prior to presidency	
Position	Pre-1900 (25)	Post-1900 (18)
Vice president	7	7
Cabinet member	7	3
U.S. representative	13	5
U.S. senator	9	5
U.S. Supreme Court justice	0	0
Federal judge	0	1
Governor	11	8
State legislator	16	5
State judge, prosecutor	2	2
Mayor	2	1
Diplomat, ambassador	7	2
Military general	11	1

	Last public position held before presidency	
Position	Pre-1900 (25)	Post-1900 (18)
Vice president		
Succeeded to presidency	4	5
Won presidency in own right	3	2
Congress		
House	1	0
Senate	3	2
Appointive federal office		
Military general	3	1
Cabinet secretary	3	2
Ambassador	2	0
Other civilian	1	0
Governor	5	6

Source: Harold Stanley and Richard Niemi, *Vital Statistics on American Politics, 2007–2008* (Washington, D.C.: CQ Press, 2008), 258.

Table 1-5 Presidents Who Died in Office

President	*Year of death*	*Portion of term served (in months)*	*Age*	*Cause*
William H. Harrison	1841	1	68	Illness
Zachary Taylor	1850	16	65	Illness
Abraham Lincoln	1865	1	56	Assassination
James A. Garfield	1881	6	49	Assassination
William McKinley	1901	6	58	Assassination
Warren G. Harding	1923	29	57	Illness
Franklin D. Roosevelt	1945	1	63	Illness
John F. Kennedy	1963	35	46	Assassination

Source: Adapted from *Guide to U.S. Elections*, 5th ed. (Washington, D.C.: CQ Press, 2005), vol. I, 811–814.

Table 1-6 Ratings of U.S. Presidents, Washington to G. W. Bush

President	*Schlesinger 1948 poll rank*	*Schlesinger 1962 poll rank*	*1982 Murray-Blessing survey of 846 historians*	Chicago Tribune *1982 poll rank*
1. George Washington	2	2	3	3
2. John Adams	9	10	9	14 (tie)
3. Thomas Jefferson	5	5	4	5
4. James Madison	14	12	14	17
5. James Monroe	12	18	15	16
6. John Quincy Adams	11	13	16	19
7. Andrew Jackson	6	6	7	6
8. Martin Van Buren	15	17	20	18
9. William Henry Harrison	—	—	—	38
10. John Tyler	22	25	28	29
11. James K. Polk	10	8	12	11
12. Zachary Taylor	25	24	27	28
13. Millard Fillmore	24	26	29	31
14. Franklin Pierce	27	28	31	35
15. James Buchanan	26	29	33	36
16. Abraham Lincoln	1	1	1	1
17. Andrew Johnson	19	23	32	32
18. Ulysses S. Grant	28	30	35	30
19. Rutherford B. Hayes	13	14	22	22
20. James Garfield	—	—	—	33
21. Chester A. Arthur	17	21	26	24
22, 24. Grover Cleveland	8	11	17	13
23. Benjamin Harrison	21	20	23	25
25. William McKinley	18	15	18	10
26. Theodore Roosevelt	7	7	5	4
27. William Howard Taft	16	16	19	20
28. Woodrow Wilson	4	4	6	7
29. Warren G. Harding	29	31	36	37
30. Calvin Coolidge	23	27	30	27
31. Herbert Hoover	20	19	21	21
32. Franklin D. Roosevelt	3	3	2	2
33. Harry S. Truman	—	9	8	8
34. Dwight D. Eisenhower	—	22	11	9
35. John F. Kennedy	—	—	13	14 (tie)
36. Lyndon B. Johnson	—	—	10	12
37. Richard Nixon	—	—	34	34
38. Gerald R. Ford	—	—	24	23
39. Jimmy Carter	—	—	25	26
40. Ronald Reagan	—	—	—	—
41. George H. W. Bush	—	—	—	—
42. Bill Clinton	—	—	—	—
43. George W. Bush	—	—	—	—

(Table continues)

Table 1-6 *(Continued)*

President	*Siena 1982 poll rank*	*Siena 1990 poll rank*	*Siena 1994 poll rank*	*Ridings-McIver 1996 poll rank*
1. George Washington	4	4	4	3
2. John Adams	10	14	12	14
3. Thomas Jefferson	2	3	5	4
4. James Madison	9	8	9	10
5. James Monroe	15	11	15	13
6. John Quincy Adams	17	16	12	18
7. Andrew Jackson	13	9	11	8
8. Martin Van Buren	21	21	22	21
9. William Henry Harrison	26	35	28	35
10. John Tyler	34	33	34	34
11. James K. Polk	12	13	14	11
12. Zachary Taylor	29	34	33	29
13. Millard Fillmore	32	32	35	36
14. Franklin Pierce	35	36	37	37
15. James Buchanan	37	38	39	40
16. Abraham Lincoln	3	2	2	1
17. Andrew Johnson	38	39	40	38
18. Ulysses S. Grant	36	37	38	38
19. Rutherford B. Hayes	22	23	24	26
20. James Garfield	25	30	27	30
21. Chester A. Arthur	24	26	26	32
22, 24. Grover Cleveland	18	17	19	17
23. Benjamin Harrison	31	29	28	31
25. William McKinley	19	19	18	17
26. Theodore Roosevelt	5	5	3	5
27. William Howard Taft	20	20	21	24
28. Woodrow Wilson	6	6	6	6
29. Warren G. Harding	39	40	41	38
30. Calvin Coolidge	30	31	36	33
31. Herbert Hoover	27	28	29	24
32. Franklin D. Roosevelt	1	1	1	2
33. Harry S. Truman	7	7	7	7
34. Dwight D. Eisenhower	11	12	8	9
35. John F. Kennedy	8	10	10	15
36. Lyndon B. Johnson	14	15	13	12
37. Richard Nixon	28	25	23	32
38. Gerald R. Ford	23	27	32	27
39. Jimmy Carter	33	24	25	19
40. Ronald Reagan	16	22	20	26
41. George H. W. Bush	—	18	31	22
42. Bill Clinton	—	—	16	23
43. George W. Bush	—	—	—	—

Sources: Adapted from Harold Stanley and Richard Niemi, *Vital Statistics on American Politics, 2007–2008* (Washington, D.C.: CQ Press, 2008), 256–257; Siena Research Institute, Siena College, "Ranking U.S. Presidents and First Ladies," http://lw.siena.edu/sri/RankingUSPresidents/.

CSPAN 1999 poll rank	*Wall Street Journal 2000 poll rank*	*Siena 2002 poll rank*	*Wall Street Journal 2005 poll rank*	*Average*	*Standard deviation*
3	1	4	1	2.83	1.12
16	13	12	13	12.17	2.25
7	4	5	4	4.42	1.24
18	15	9	17	12.67	3.63
14	16	8	16	14.08	2.71
19	20	17	25	16.92	3.82
13	6	13	10	9.00	2.92
30	23	24	27	21.58	4.14
37	—	36	—	33.57 (7 rankings)	4.65
36	34	37	35	31.75	4.67
12	10	11	9	11.08	1.68
28	31	34	33	29.58	3.42
35	35	38	36	32.42	4.29
39	37	39	38	34.92	4.08
41	39	41	40	36.58	4.85
1	2	2	2	1.58	0.67
40	36	42	37	34.67	7.10
33	32	35	29	33.42	3.58
25	22	27	24	22.00	4.31
29	—	33	—	29.57 (7 rankings)	2.94
28	26	30	26	25.50	3.90
16	12	20	12	15.00	3.69
31	27	32	30	27.33	4.16
15	14	19	14	16.33	2.77
4	5	3	5	4.83	1.27
20	19	21	20	19.67	2.15
6	11	6	11	6.58	2.23
38	37	40	39	37.08	3.63
27	25	29	23	28.42	3.90
34	29	31	31	26.17	5.01
2	3	1	3	2.00	0.85
5	7	7	7	7.18 (11 rankings)	0.98
9	9	10	8	10.73 (11 rankings)	3.95
8	18	14	15	12.50 (10 rankings)	3.34
10	17	15	18	13.60 (10 rankings)	2.72
25	33	26	32	29.20 (10 rankings)	4.24
23	28	28	28	26.30 (10 rankings)	2.98
22	30	25	34	26.30 (10 rankings)	4.72
11	8	16	6	15.63 (8 rankings)	6.97
20	21	22	21	22.14 (7 rankings)	4.14
21	24	18	22	20.67 (6 rankings)	3.08
—	—	23	19	21.00 (2 rankings)	2.83

Note: The ratings are the results of polls of historians, political scientists, and other experts on the presidency. "—" indicates not rated.

Table 1-7 Presidents' Ratings from Best to Worst, Washington to G. W. Bush

President	*Average ranking*	*Standard deviation*
Abraham Lincoln	1.58	0.67
Franklin Roosevelt	2.00	0.85
George Washington	2.83	1.12
Thomas Jefferson	4.42	1.24
Theodore Roosevelt	4.83	1.27
Woodrow Wilson	6.58	2.23
Harry Truman	7.18	0.98
Andrew Jackson	9.00	2.92
Dwight Eisenhower	10.73	3.95
James K. Polk	11.08	1.68
John Adams	12.17	2.25
John Kennedy	12.50	3.34
James Madison	12.67	3.63
Lyndon Johnson	13.60	2.72
Ronald Reagan	13.88	6.97
James Monroe	14.08	2.71
Grover Cleveland	15.00	3.69
William McKinley	16.33	2.77
John Q. Adams	16.90	3.82
William Taft	19.67	2.15
Bill Clinton	20.67	3.08
George W. Bush	21.00	2.83
Martin Van Buren	21.58	4.14
Rutherford B. Hayes	22.00	4.31
George H. W. Bush	22.00	4.14
Chester Arthur	22.14	3.90
Herbert Hoover	25.50	5.01
Jimmy Carter	26.17	4.72
Gerald Ford	26.30	2.98
Benjamin Harrison	26.30	4.16
Calvin Coolidge	27.33	3.90
Richard Nixon	28.42	4.24
James Garfield	29.20	2.94
Zachary Taylor	29.57	3.42
John Tyler	29.58	4.67
Millard Fillmore	31.75	4.29
Ulysses S. Grant	32.41	3.58
William H. Harrison	33.42	4.65
Andrew Johnson	33.57	7.10
Franklin Pierce	34.92	4.08
James Buchanan	36.58	4.85
Warren Harding	37.33	3.63

Source: Table 1-6.

Table 1-8 American First Ladies

First lady	*First lady's term of service*	*President (political party)*	*Relation to president*
Martha Custis Washington	April 30, 1789–March 4, 1797	George Washington (F)	Wife
Abigail Smith Adams	March 4, 1797–March 4, 1801	John Adams (F)	Wife
Martha Jefferson Randolph	March 4, 1801–March 4, 1809	Thomas Jefferson (DR)	Daughter
Dolley Madison	March 4, 1809–March 4, 1817	James Madison (DR)	Wife
Elizabeth Kortright Monroe	March 4, 1817–March 4, 1825	James Monroe (DR)	Wife
Louisa Johnson Adams	March 4, 1825–March 4, 1829	John Quincy Adams (DR)	Wife
Emily Donalson	March 4, 1829–Dec. 19, 1836	Andrew Jackson (D)	Niece
Sarah Yorke Jackson	Nov. 26, 1834–March 4, 1837	Andrew Jackson (D)	Daughter-in-law
Angelica Singleton Van Buren	March 4, 1837–March 4, 1841	Martin Van Buren (D)	Wife
Jane Irwin Harrison	March 4, 1841–April 4, 1841	William H. Harrison (W)	Daughter-in-law
Letitia Christian Tyler	April 4, 1841–Sept. 10, 1842	John Tyler (W)	First wife (died in 1842)
Priscilla Cooper Tyler	Sept. 10, 1842–June 26, 2844	John Tyler (W)	Daughter-in-law
Julia Gardiner Tyler	June 26, 1844–March 4, 1845	John Tyler (W)	Second wife
Sarah Childress Polk	March 4, 1845–March 4, 1849	James K. Polk (D)	Wife
Margaret Mackall Smith Taylor	March 4, 1849–July 9, 1850	Zachary Taylor (W)	Wife
Abigail Powers Fillmore	July 10, 1850–March 4, 1853	Millard Fillmore (W)	Wife
Jane Means Appleton Pierce	March 4, 1853–March 4, 1857	Franklin Pierce (D)	Wife
Harriet Lane	March 4, 1857–March 4, 1861	James Buchanan (D)	Niece
Mary Todd Lincoln	March 4, 1861–April 15, 1865	Abraham Lincoln (R)	Wife
Eliza McCardle Johnson	April 15, 1865–March 4, 1869	Andrew Johnson (R)	Wife
Julie Dent Grant	March 4, 1869–March 4, 1877	Ulysses S. Grant (R)	Wife
Lucy Webb Hayes	March 4, 1877–March 4, 1881	Rutherford B. Hayes (R)	Wife
Lucretia Rudolph Garfield	March 4, 1881–Sept. 19, 1881	James A. Garfield (R)	Wife
Mary Arthur McElroy	Sept. 20, 1881–March 4, 1885	Chester A. Arthur (R)	Sister
Rose Cleveland	March 4, 1885–June 2, 1886	Grover Cleveland (D)	Sister
Frances Folsom Cleveland	June 2, 1886–March 4, 1889	Grover Cleveland (D)	Wife
Caroline Lavinia Scott Harrison	March 4, 1889–Oct. 25, 1892	Benjamin Harrison (R)	Wife (died in 1892)

(Table continues)

Table 1-8 *(Continued)*

First lady	*First lady's term of service*	*President (political party)*	*Relation to president*
Mary Harrison McKee	Oct. 25, 1892–March 4, 1893	Benjamin Harrison (R)	Daughter
Frances Folsom Cleveland	March 4, 1893–March 4, 1897	Grover Cleveland (D)	Wife
Ida Saxton McKinley	March 4, 1897–Sept. 14, 1901	William McKinley (R)	Wife
Edith Kermit Carrow Roosevelt	Sept. 14, 1901–March 4, 1905	Theodore Roosevelt (R)	Wife
Helen Herron "Nellie" Taft	March 4, 1905–March 4, 1913	William H. Taft (R)	Wife
Ellen Axson Wilson	March 4, 1913–Aug. 6, 1914	Woodrow Wilson (D)	First wife (died in 1914)
Edith Bolling Galt Wilson	Dec. 18, 1915–March 4, 1921	Woodrow Wilson (D)	Second wife
Florence Kling Harding	March 4, 1921–Aug. 2, 1923	Warren G. Harding (R)	Wife
Grace Goodhue Coolidge	Aug. 3, 1923–March 4, 1929	Calvin Coolidge (R)	Wife
Lou Henry Hoover	March 4, 1929–March 4, 1933	Herbert Hoover (R)	Wife
Anna Eleanor Roosevelt	March 4, 1933–April 12, 1945	Franklin D. Roosevelt (D)	Wife
Elizabeth Wallace "Bess" Truman	April 12, 1945–Jan. 20, 1953	Harry S. Truman (D)	Wife
Mamie Doud Eisenhower	Jan. 20, 1953–Jan. 20, 1961	Dwight D. Eisenhower (R)	Wife
Jacqueline Bouvier Kennedy	Jan. 20, 1961–Nov. 22, 1963	John F. Kennedy (D)	Wife
Claudia Taylor "Lady Bird" Johnson	Nov. 22, 1963–Jan. 20, 1969	Lyndon B. Johnson (D)	Wife
Thelma Ryan "Pat" Nixon	Jan. 20, 1969–Aug. 9, 1974	Richard Nixon (R)	Wife
Elizabeth Bloomer "Betty" Ford	Aug. 9, 1974–Jan. 20, 1977	Gerald R. Ford (R)	Wife
Rosalynn Smith Carter	Jan. 20, 1977–Jan. 20, 1981	Jimmy Carter (D)	Wife
Nancy Davis Reagan	Jan. 20, 1981–Jan. 20, 1989	Ronald Reagan (R)	Wife
Barbara Pierce Bush	Jan. 20, 1989–Jan. 20, 1993	George H. W. Bush (R)	Wife
Hillary Rodham Clinton	Jan. 20, 1993–Jan. 20, 2001	Bill Clinton (D)	Wife
Laura Welch Bush	Jan. 20, 2001–Jan. 20, 2009	George W. Bush (R)	Wife

Source: "First Ladies Gallery," www.whitehouse.gov/history/firstladies/.

Note: D—Democrat; DR—Democratic-Republican; F—Federalist; R—Republican; W—Whig.

2

Presidential Selection

- **Party Convention History**
- **Nomination Methods**
- **Primary Results**
- **Television Coverage of Primaries and Conventions**
- **Profile of Convention Delegates**
- **Party Convention Results**

The introduction outlined three dimensions of an institution: organization (the institution's routines, procedures, and units), behavior (its regular patterns of activity), and structure (its intrinsic, identifying characteristics). Each dimension distinguishes one institution from another and ensures that the institution is both taken for granted and indispensable. One of the central structural features of the presidential institution is periodic, regularly scheduled elections. These elections are held at four-year intervals, in races separate from those for the legislature, largely between two parties, and with the results determined indirectly by the electoral college. It is commonplace to discuss how these electoral peculiarities set up the rules by which the game is played, and thereby determine who wins and goes on to hold office. While one cannot argue against this almost tautological observation, the focus tends to fall on the victorious presidential candidates as individuals, highlighting their personal and political backgrounds and the techniques they used to master the game. However, this perspective misses how the elections themselves direct the presidency, no matter who is elected to the office.

This chapter examines a central feature of the electoral structure, one that helps shape the presidential institution: ambivalence toward political parties. There is a tendency to characterize Americans as antipathetic, rather than ambivalent, toward parties. Writers rush to quote George Washington, who once spoke of "the baneful effects of the spirit of party ... a spirit not to be encouraged" (quoted in Chambers, 1963, 6–7). Yet, such a characterization understates the practical need for parties in organizing voters, espousing policy positions, and staffing government; it also fails to appreciate the speed with which the parties developed, the longevity they have enjoyed, and the excitement they have generated in the voting public. This ambivalence is marked by both a spirited philosophical distrust of parties and a practical embrace of them. The electoral structure plainly sets up a governing institution that is wholly different from one in which other structural features are employed, such as a strong multiparty system. Furthermore, changes in these structural elements have guided how the institution has evolved.

Selecting the Nominees

Two basic features of the presidential nomination process—the method of selection and the role of the national nominating convention—permit an assessment of this characteristic ambivalence toward parties. Four distinct historical periods show evidence of ambivalence: (1) the congressional caucus period from 1800 to 1824, (2) the brokered convention period from 1828 to 1908, (3) the emergent primary period from 1912 to 1968, and (4) the media primary period from 1972 to the present.

The first nomination system was the simplest and most nationally party-dominant. Caucuses of members of Congress from the two principal parties—the Democratic-Republicans and the Federalists—met to select their presidential nominees, many of whom were former members of Congress. The selection process did not readily take into account the preferences of rank-and-file party members or the popular support of an outside candidate such as Andrew Jackson. The caucus system broke down in 1824 with the demise of the Federalist Party and the rise of factions among the Democratic-Republicans. Although the 1824 caucus named a candidate, William Crawford of Georgia, state legislatures disregarded this choice and supported three regional candidates instead.

During the brokered convention system, state and national conventions replaced the congressional caucus. State party leaders, wielding large blocs of delegates, competed with each other at the national nominating conventions. Tables 2-1 and 2-2 list ballots taken at the national conventions for the Democrats since 1832 and the Republicans since 1856, respectively. The nature of the brokered convention period is readily evident. On average, the Democrats required ten ballots to select their nominees; the Republicans required five. Prior to the Civil War, the Democrats had a particularly difficult time getting the southern and northern wings of the party to cooperate in selecting a nominee. This is revealed by the forty-nine ballots required to nominate Franklin Pierce and the seventeen needed to nominate James Buchanan.

The demands of the Progressive Era, which heralded a more open and democratic electoral process, led to the party primary period. In the primary, voters affiliated with a party cast their ballots directly to nominate delegates to the national party convention. The data in Table 2-3 permit an examination of the growth of presidential primaries. During this emergent primary period, less than half the states adopted primaries, which were often "beauty contests" or "advisory." In 1912 a dozen states adopted presidential primaries; in 1916 this number almost doubled and more than 50 percent of convention delegates for the two parties were selected in primaries. The movement stalled during World War I, and some states moved to repeal their presidential primary laws. During this period, delegates selected in the primaries were not pledged to a specific candidate, nor were the ballots cast by party voters binding on the party. This allowed room for negotiation between candidates and state party leaders, and brokered party politics continued. As Tables 2-1 and 2-2 indicate, the number of ballots needed to secure a nomination dropped by half, but multiple ballots were still frequent. The Democrats required an average of five ballots and the Republicans an average of two to select their nominees.[1]

The 1968 presidential election was the last time a candidate, Democrat Hubert Humphrey, secured a party nomination without running in a single primary. Relying on commitments from state party leaders, the method of Humphrey's nomination stood in stark contrast to the primary victories of Sen. Eugene McCarthy of Minnesota and Sen. Robert Kennedy of New York, before his assassination (see Table 2-7). Many Democrats were disturbed by the hollowness of the primaries in the nomination process. This led to Democratic Party reforms after the 1968 election that saw many states adopt primaries or open their caucuses and conventions to grass-roots supporters.

In the current media primary period, existing since 1972, primaries have become *the* road to the White House. The nomination is typified by one long, continuous primary covered ardently by the media, especially television. This began within the Democratic Party in 1972 as a reaction to the chaotic 1968 Chicago convention. A party commission, headed by Sen. George McGovern of South Dakota, revamped party rules to give primaries more influence; the Republicans soon followed suit. Compare the number of primaries in 1972 to that in 2008, thirty-six years later: the parties held twenty-three (Democrats) and twenty-two (Republicans) primaries in 1972, and in 2008 they held forty (Democrats) and forty-three (Republicans) primaries. This amounts to a roughly 75 percent increase in the number of states holding primaries for the Democrats and a near doubling for the Republicans. As seen in Table 2-3, in 2008 78 percent of the delegates from the Democratic Party and 86 percent of the delegates from the Republican Party were selected in primaries, including those held in the eleven largest states—California, New York, Texas, Pennsylvania, Illinois, Ohio, Florida, Michigan, New Jersey, North Carolina, and Georgia. As the importance of primaries has increased, the importance of national conventions has decreased. During this modern period the national conventions have merely ratified rather than determined the nominees of the parties, all of whom have been selected on the first ballot. Indeed, the Republicans have not taken a second ballot since 1948 and the Democrats have not taken a second ballot since 1952.

As one phase blurred into another, the ambivalence toward parties has endured. During each of the four periods, parties have been seen as both barriers against democracy and vehicles for democracy. These two views are in constant tension. When the congressional caucus was denounced as a "cabal," its demise left a void that state parties quickly filled with the appearance of greater openness and representation. But the appearance was largely just that. Although the state conventions were more broad based in membership than had been the "King Caucus," state party bosses nonetheless controlled the newly opened nominating conventions. The caucus was condemned as a barrier against democracy, while state conventions were touted as vehicles for democracy. Yet, party-boss control itself created a new and formidable barrier against democracy. Ambivalence toward parties continued. In the emergent primary period, party primaries were a novel democratic device, but state party leaders maintained control of the nomination process. The media primary period, which will be discussed in greater depth below, has heightened this ambivalence. The increasing preeminence of primaries, both in sheer numbers and in the intensity of media coverage, has diminished party control over the nomination and increased the importance of individual candidates. Still, parties retain importance in sponsoring the nomination process.

These four phases suggest that there has been a historical reconfiguration of the significance of political parties. While control of the nomination process by party elites has eroded, the system nevertheless demonstrates the persistence of American political parties. For more than 150 years, the Republican and Democratic Party labels have existed at national and state levels. Would-be presidents still must channel their hopes through the nomination process of one of the two main parties. It has been difficult for even an exceedingly well-financed, self-anointed, third-party candidate campaign to make inroads into the durability of the two major parties. In Leon Epstein's words, the key to the parties' persistence is their "permeability"—they are "readily entered by individuals and groups who want [their] electoral labels" (1986, 5).

Elements of the Media Primary

Primaries and Candidate Success

The next set of tables provides a closer look at several aspects of the media primary period. To begin, it is important to understand the most frequently used nomination methods:

- Caucus/convention. Party regulars meet and send delegates pledged to a candidate to the state party convention.
- Closed primary. Only those voters registered with a party may vote in that party's primary. They are voting for delegates pledged to represent a specific candidate at the national convention.
- Independent primary. Voters registered with a party and independents (those not registered with either party) may vote in the primary. Like the closed primary, voters are selecting delegates pledged to represent a specific candidate at the national convention.
- Open primary. Any registered voter may vote in the primary. This often leads to cross-over voting, when members of one party vote in the primary of the other party. As in the other two types of primaries, voters are selecting delegates pledged to represent a specific candidate at the national convention.

Table 2-4 shows that although primaries have become the preferred method of nomination, states have entertained a great deal of flexibility in switching from a caucus/convention system to a primary system from one election year to the next. In addition, states choose from among the three types of primaries: closed, independent, and open. For example, Kansas used the caucus/convention approach in 1976, switched to an independent primary in 1980, switched back to the caucus in 1984 and 1988, adopted an open primary in 1992 and continued with it in 1996, returned to the independent primary in 2000, and then went back to a caucus/convention system in 2004 and 2008. To make matters even more complex, some states give parties the option of selecting their own method of nomination rather than mandating a single method for all parties in the state.

Three observations emerge from Table 2-5, which aggregates the data from Table 2-4. First, while the number of states using the caucus/convention system declined from 1972 to 2008, the caucus system still accounts for 20 percent of the nominating processes used in the states. Second, closed primaries remain a popular device for parties to appeal to the party faithful and exclude voters from outside the parties. In 2008, fourteen primaries for either Democrats or Republicans were closed. Third, the numbers of independent and open primaries have risen, relative to the closed primary. In 2008 there were fifteen independent primaries and seventeen open primaries, exceeding the number of closed primaries. The rise of independent primaries marks parties' increasing recognition that there are many independents in the electorate who do not identify with either party. Open primaries also suggest parties' recognition that their candidates must appeal to a broad spectrum of the American electorate in order to win. These facts again stress ambivalence toward parties at work in the media primary era. The presence of the caucuses and the closed primaries maintain the integrity of the parties more than do open and independent primaries. At the same time, the rise in independent primaries indicates that the parties are permitting voters who are not affiliated with any party to help make the nomination decisions.

Table 2-6 shows that selection method makes a difference in who ultimately succeeds in a candidacy. To be sure, the differences between primaries and caucuses/conventions should not be overstated. In Everett Ladd's words, current party caucuses may be little more than "restrictive primaries" (1981, 34). Many enjoy large numbers of participants who differ from their primary counterparts only in that they spend several hours rather than several minutes casting their ballots. Nonetheless, caucuses and primaries create differences in candidates' strategies. Some candidates may spend considerable time devising plans to capture key primaries while avoiding caucuses; others may plan the reverse. Perhaps the clearest example of the caucus-primary difference occurred in the 2008 nomination cycle. On the Democratic side, Barack Obama won the Iowa caucuses in the first contest of 2008. He had a strong team of volunteers who were eager and well organized to go to caucus venues—high school gymnasiums, churches, and meeting halls. On the following Tuesday, Hillary Clinton won New Hampshire's independent primary. She spent considerably more money in New Hampshire than in Iowa, spent more time in the state, and had a message, particularly for women voters, that was more effective there. On the Republican side, Mike Huckabee, a little-known former governor of Arkansas, won the Iowa caucuses relying heavily on evangelical Christian supporters to get out on caucus night. In contrast, Sen. John McCain of Arizona won the New Hampshire primary, with Huckabee placing third. McCain relied on a broader base of Republican and independent voters who turned out in record numbers.

In theory, primaries should advance democracy; in practice, they simply sharpen candidate independence from the parties and its other members. A quick start is important because candidates are no longer building internal party coalitions. They have traded these party candidacies for their own media visibility, fundraising, campaign organization, and standing in public opinion polls, all of which take a great deal of time to develop. In 1972 and again in 1976 the eventual nominees—George

McGovern and Jimmy Carter—ran outside the established party and started campaigning nearly two years before the election. This has continued in recent elections. In 2008 many candidates of both parties started campaigning in 2006. When Fred Thompson, a former Tennessee senator, entered the Republican race for the White House on Labor Day 2007, many criticized his late entry strategy. The other candidates had long been on the campaign trail, spending money and time in various states.

Upon entering the media primary, candidate success is subject to the vagaries of "momentum" (Aldrich, 1980). The sequential arrangement of primaries creates a self-propelling campaign dynamic. Doing well in an early primary generates resources for subsequent primaries. These necessary resources include money, media coverage, endorsements, poll results, and campaign staffing. Doing poorly often shuts off the flow of resources. This creates the patterns evident in Tables 2-7 through 2-17: the importance of success in early primaries, the rapid winnowing of contenders, and the bolstering of candidates who emerge from being unknowns to being recognized as major contenders.

For primary states, the complement of momentum is "frontloading." States jockey for the earliest and best time slots to maximize media coverage of their races and maximize their impact on the final outcome. Several southern states in 1980 began to hold primaries simultaneously on the second Tuesday in March. By 1988 what became known as Super Tuesday was a regional fixture of the nominating process (Norrander, 1992). By 1992 several states had moved their primaries and caucuses to the week before Super Tuesday (dubbed Junior Tuesday) to dull the impact of the South and at the same time take part in the effort to narrow the field. Frontloading on Junior Tuesday and Super Tuesday is evident in Table 2-15, which shows that more than half the Republican delegates were decided on or before Super Tuesday in 2000. Yet, frontloading has evolved still further. In 2008 states competed more fervently for early time slots than at any time since 1972. This meant that several states, notably Michigan, attempted to preempt New Hampshire as the first primary of the season. Both parties invoked sanctions against the wayward states by refusing to accept a certain portion of their delegates at the conventions. The frontloading was equally evident in the importance of what became billed as "Super-Duper Tuesday," February 5, 2008. Gone were both Junior Tuesday and the once-southern, regional cast to Super Tuesday. In their places were twenty-one primaries or caucuses across an array of states, including California, Illinois, and New York, all on the same day. February 5 was, then, an all but national primary day in which the nominations for both parties were secured. This is a full month earlier than previous schedules for Super Tuesday, which typically happened in March.

Frontloading opens the nomination to a wider range of candidates, all of whom hope they can do well in at least one early contest. For instance,

Table 2-15 shows that in 2000 John McCain won the New Hampshire Republican primary on February 1; George W. Bush won Delaware on February 8 and South Carolina on February 19, while McCain came back to win Arizona and Michigan on February 22. Frontloading also closes the nomination by discouraging aspirants who do not do well early on and who therefore will not be considered a serious contender in later rounds. Gary Bauer and Steve Forbes withdrew from the 2000 race on February 1 and February 8, respectively. When McCain faltered in North Dakota, Virginia, and Washington, all on February 29, Bush was all but assured the nomination a week before his Super Tuesday victories on March 7.

Media Coverage

The growth of media coverage has matched the growth of primaries. Television, in particular, has the same effects on presidential selection as the primaries. It opens the nomination to a broader pool of hopeful candidates by providing lesser-known or unknown candidates the chance to gain instantaneous recognition among the party's electorate. But it rapidly closes the nomination to candidates who cannot afford the high price of television campaigning or lack the organization or the primary showings to get their message across. Journalists following the campaign become substitutes for the old party power-brokers—what they cover, how they cover it, and what they do not cover become major determinants of the outcome.

Table 2-18 shows that a considerable amount of coverage during the 1988 through 2004 primary seasons focused on the "horse race" element of these contests—who was ahead, who was behind, and who was going to win. The horse race consumed 83 percent of nomination coverage in 2000 and 67 percent in 2004. Tables 2-19 and 2-20 report positive television coverage of primary candidates in 2000 and 2004. However, positive television coverage is not per se a good indicator of the all-important momentum that helps determine the eventual nominee. For example, George W. Bush received increasingly less positive coverage as he advanced toward securing the Republican nomination in 2000.

Independent Partisanship

Primaries combine with media coverage to create an "independent partisanship" that typifies presidential candidacies.[2] Although many observers of presidential elections comment on the independence of presidential candidates, they neglect to recognize the continued importance of parties. Both words of the phrase—*independent* and *partisanship*—are equally significant. Independence dictates that candidates raise their own money, develop their own campaign strategies, take their own polls, hire their own media consultants and staff, and reach out to a network of volunteers on their own. As Richard Neustadt put it, "We have left the age of barons and entered the age of candidates. Its hallmarks are management by private firms, exposure through the tube, funding by direct-mail drives as well as fat-cats, and canvassing by zealous volunteers" (1975, 434).

Despite the independent nature of candidates' campaigns, candidates are still partisans, Republican or Democrat. The average Republican candidate continues to disagree with the average Democratic candidate on contentious issues in the campaign. The two appeal to different voters, and voters perceive the two parties differently. In addition, the candidates work hard to gather the support of party officials, officeholders, and fundraisers. So while the old-style party organization, brokers, and deals no longer hold sway, there are new-style party leaders who are often influential in determining which campaigns prosper and fail. Independent partisanship is a modern sign of the long-standing ambivalence toward political parties.

The End of Conventions?

Although parties themselves have not declined as much as some may think, party conventions have. The media primary has eliminated much of the importance of party conventions as venues for candidates' coalition-building. Conventions retain only nominal, and highly ceremonial, authority over the party's choice for president. As Tables 2-1 and 2-2 make clear, party nomination fights today do not occur on the floor of the convention. The extent to which party conventions are becoming less crucial in the nomination of presidents is also witnessed by the declining amount of television coverage they receive. Table 2-21 shows that in 1952 the networks dedicated 119 hours of coverage to the two parties' conventions; in 2004 they gave a scant 6 hours of coverage to the Democratic and Republican conventions.

Although the importance of the convention as a decision-making body has declined, it continues to reflect the party to the nation. Table 2-22 offers a profile of convention delegates since 1968. The parties, in varying degrees, have made an effort to open their conventions to a wider group of people. The number of women attending the Democratic and Republican conventions has increased. African Americans have become more prominent at the Democratic Party convention. Neither party, however, has done especially well in adding young people to its ranks of delegates.

The final tables in the chapter (Tables 2-23 through 2-31) document the balloting of the conventions from 1968 to 2004. Although all the nominations listed were won on the first ballot, the results reveal conflicts within the parties that the nominees have had to resolve to successfully begin the general election phase of the campaign and ultimately win the election. They also reveal the regional bases of some of the nominees' internal party support. Conventions, then, alert nominees to the intra-party challenges they face. This reinforces the independent partisanship of the presidential nominees. They come to the convention as their own candidates, but they leave it carrying many party bags.

Conclusion

This ongoing ambivalence toward parties, and its accompanying manifestations in primaries, media coverage, weakened national conventions, and independent partisanship, has a paradoxical effect on the presidency as an institution. The view of parties as barriers against democracy allows presidents to develop direct appeals to the American people. Presidents portray themselves as above party politics and freely criticize parties as key obstacles to national progress. This places great emphasis on presidents as individuals who are no longer attached to conventional party moorings. It casts the presidency as a plebiscitary office rather than a partisan one.

Still, partisanship remains central to the way the White House is run. Data in Chapter 4 indicate the number of partisan appearances presidents have made and data in Chapter 5 show the advantage presidents have received from people who identified with the president's party in public approval ratings. Data in Chapters 6 and 9 show that almost all people who have immediately surrounded the president have been of the president's party; more than 90 percent of presidential appointments to executive branch and judicial branch positions have also been partisan. Data in Chapter 8 reveal that policy solutions, especially on domestic and economic affairs, have a partisan cast; data in Chapter 9 demonstrate that presidents have been routinely more successful with their party in Congress than with the opposing party.

Thus, ambivalence toward parties in the nomination process is molded as a structural feature of the presidency. Contemporary presidents come to Washington as intensely independent politicians. They have their own campaign organizations, and many do not have strong ties to others in their party. Yet, while often having campaigned as being against status quo government, above party politics, and a Washington outsider, presidential candidates turned presidents face the nagging realization that they are now squarely in the midst of all three. In fact, their independence prompts work in the White House and in Congress to go forward in an intensely partisan fashion, acting as the glue that holds people together and defines the sides of an issue.

Notes

1. The Democratic number excludes the extraordinary 103 ballots taken to nominate John Davis in 1924.
2. The term was first used to apply to voters in Jack Dennis, "Political Independence in America, Part I: On Being an Independent Partisan Supporter," *British Journal of Political Science* 18 (March 1988): 77–109.

Table 2-1 Democratic National Conventions, 1832–2008

Year	*City*	*Date*	*Presidential nominee*	*Ballots* [a]
1832	Baltimore	May 21	Andrew Jackson	1
1835	Baltimore	May 20	Martin Van Buren	1
1840	Baltimore	May 5	Martin Van Buren	1
1844	Baltimore	May 27–29	James K. Polk	9
1848	Baltimore	May 22–26	Lewis Cass	4
1852	Baltimore	June 1–6	Franklin Pierce	49
1856	Cincinnati	June 2–6	James Buchanan	17
1860	Baltimore	June 18–23	Stephen A. Douglas	2
1864	Chicago	Aug. 29	George B. McClellan	1
1868	New York	July 4–11	Horatio Seymour	22
1872	Baltimore	July 9	Horace Greeley	1
1876	St. Louis	June 27–29	Samuel J. Tilden	2
1880	Cincinnati	June 22–24	Winfield S. Hancock	2
1884	Chicago	July 8–11	Grover Cleveland	2
1888	St. Louis	June 5	Grover Cleveland	1
1892	Chicago	June 21	Grover Cleveland	1
1896	Chicago	July 7	William J. Bryan	5
1900	Kansas City	July 4–6	William J. Bryan	1
1904	St. Louis	July 6–9	Alton S. Parker	1
1908	Denver	July 7–10	William J. Bryan	1
1912	Baltimore	June 25–July 2	Woodrow Wilson	46
1916	St. Louis	June 14–16	Woodrow Wilson	1
1920	San Francisco	June 28–July 6	James M. Cox	43
1924	New York	June 24–July 9	John W. Davis	103
1928	Houston	June 26–29	Alfred E. Smith	1
1932	Chicago	June 27–July 2	Franklin D. Roosevelt	4
1936	Philadelphia	June 23–27	Franklin D. Roosevelt	[b]
1940	Chicago	July 15–18	Franklin D. Roosevelt	1
1944	Chicago	July 19–21	Franklin D. Roosevelt	1
1948	Philadelphia	July 12–14	Harry S. Truman	1
1952	Chicago	July 21–26	Adlai E. Stevenson	3
1956	Chicago	Aug. 13–17	Adlai E. Stevenson	1
1960	Los Angeles	July 11–15	John F. Kennedy	1
1964	Atlantic City	Aug. 24–27	Lyndon B. Johnson	[b]
1968	Chicago	Aug. 26–29	Hubert H. Humphrey	1
1972	Miami Beach	July 10–13	George McGovern	1
1976	New York	July 12–15	Jimmy Carter	1
1980	New York	Aug. 11–14	Jimmy Carter	1
1984	San Francisco	July 16–19	Walter Mondale	1
1988	Atlanta	July 18–21	Michael Dukakis	1
1992	New York	July 13–16	Bill Clinton	1
1996	Chicago	Aug. 26–29	Bill Clinton	1
2000	Los Angeles	Aug. 14–17	Al Gore	1
2004	Boston	July 26–29	John Kerry	1
2008	Denver	Aug. 25–28	Barack Obama	1

Source: Adapted from *Guide to U.S. Elections*, 5th ed. (Washington, D.C.: CQ Press, 2005).

[a] Number of ballots required to select nominee.

[b] Acclamation.

Table 2-2 Republican National Conventions, 1856–2008

Year	*City*	*Date*	*Presidential nominee*	*Ballots* [a]
1856	Philadelphia	June 17–19	John C. Fremont	2
1860	Chicago	May 16–19	Abraham Lincoln	3
1864	Baltimore	June 7–8	Abraham Lincoln	1
1868	Chicago	May 20–21	Ulysses S. Grant	1
1872	Philadelphia	June 5–6	Ulysses S. Grant	1
1876	Cincinnati	June 14–16	Rutherford B. Hayes	7
1880	Chicago	June 2–8	James A. Garfield	36
1884	Chicago	June 3–6	James G. Blaine	4
1888	Chicago	June 19–25	Benjamin Harrison	8
1892	Minneapolis	June 7–10	Benjamin Harrison	1
1896	St. Louis	June 16–18	William McKinley	1
1900	Philadelphia	June 19–21	William McKinley	1
1904	Chicago	June 21–23	Theodore Rooosevelt	1
1908	Chicago	June 16–19	William H. Taft	1
1912	Chicago	June 18–22	William H. Taft	1
1916	Chicago	June 7–10	Charles E. Hughes	3
1920	Chicago	June 8–12	Warren G. Harding	10
1924	Cleveland	June 10–12	Calvin Coolidge	1
1928	Kansas City	June 12–15	Herbert Hoover	1
1932	Chicago	June 14–16	Herbert Hoover	1
1936	Cleveland	June 9–12	Alfred M. Landon	1
1940	Philadelphia	June 24–28	Wendell L. Willkie	6
1944	Chicago	June 24–28	Thomas E. Dewey	1
1948	Philadelphia	June 21–25	Thomas E. Dewey	3
1952	Chicago	July 7–11	Dwight D. Eisenhower	1
1956	San Francisco	Aug. 20–23	Dwight D. Eisenhower	1
1960	Chicago	July 25–28	Richard Nixon	1
1964	San Francisco	July 13–16	Barry Goldwater	1
1968	Miami Beach	Aug. 5–8	Richard Nixon	1
1972	Miami Beach	Aug. 21–22	Richard Nixon	1
1976	Kansas City	Aug. 16–19	Gerald R. Ford	1
1980	Detroit	July 14–17	Ronald Reagan	1
1984	Dallas	Aug. 20–23	Ronald Reagan	1
1988	New Orleans	Aug. 15–18	George H. W. Bush	1
1992	Houston	Aug. 17–20	George H. W. Bush	1
1996	San Diego	Aug. 12–15	Robert Dole	1
2000	Philadelphia	Aug. 12–15	George W. Bush	1
2004	New York City	Aug. 30–Sept. 1	George W. Bush	1
2008	St. Paul	Sept. 1–4	John McCain	1

Source: Adapted from *Guide to U.S. Elections*, 5th ed. (Washington, D.C.: CQ Press, 2005).

[a] Number of ballots required to select nominee.

Table 2-3 The Growth of Presidential Primaries, 1912–2008

	Democratic Party		*Republican Party*	
Year	Number of primaries	Percentage of delegates selected in primaries	Number of primaries	Percentage of delegates selected in primaries
1912	12	32.9	13	41.7
1916	20	53.5	20	58.9
1920	16	44.6	20	57.8
1924	14	35.5	17	45.3
1928	17	42.2	16	44.9
1932	16	40.0	14	37.7
1936	14	36.5	12	37.5
1940	13	35.8	13	38.8
1944	14	36.7	13	38.7
1948	14	36.3	12	36.0
1952	16	39.2	13	39.0
1956	19	41.3	19	43.5
1960	16	38.4	15	38.6
1964	16	41.4	17	45.6
1968	17	48.7	17	47.0
1972	23	66.5	23	58.2
1976	29	76.1	29	70.4
1980	33	81.1	35	78.0
1984	29	67.1	30	66.6
1988	35	81.4	37	80.7
1992	40	88.0	39	85.4
1996	37	70.9	39	85.9
2000	42	64.4	43	83.8
2004	36	83.2	33	56.9
2008	37	78.0	37	86.0

Sources: (1912–2004) Adapted from Harold Stanley and Richard Niemi, *Vital Statistics on American Politics, 2007–2008* (Washington, D.C.: CQ Press, 2008), 70; (2008) adapted from "CQ Politics 2008 Primary Guide," http://innovation.cq.com/primaries.

Note: Primaries include binding and nonbinding presidential preference primaries as well as primaries selecting national convention delegates only without indication of presidential preference. Number of primaries is based on the data in Table 2-4.

Table 2-4 Presidential Nomination Methods, by State, 1968–2008

State	*1968*	*1972*	*1976*	*1980*	*1984*	*1988*	*1992*	*1996*	*2000*	*2004*	*2008*
Alabama	CP	CP	OP	OP	IP	IP	IP	IP	OP	OP	OP
Alaska	CC	CC	CC	CC	CC	CC	CC	CC	CC	CC	CC
Arizona	CO-D/ CC-R	CC	CC	CC	CC	CC	CC	CC	CP	CP-D/ CC-R	CP-D/ CC-R
Arkansas	CC	CC	OP	OP-D/ CC-R	CC	OP	OP	OP	OP	OP	OP
California	CP	CP	CP	CP	CP	CP	CP	CP	CP	IP-D/ CP-R	IP-D/ CP-R
Colorado	CC	CC	CC	CC	CC	CC	OP	OP	OP	CC	CC
Connecticut	CC	CC	CC	CP	CP-D/ CC-R	CP	CP	CP	CP	CP	CP
Delaware	CC	CC	CC	CC	CC	CC	CC	CC-D/ CO-R	NB-D/ CC-R	CP-D/ CC-R	CP
Florida	CP	CP	CP	CP	CP	CP	CP	CP	CP	CP	CP
Georgia	CO-D/ CC-R	CC	OP	OP	IP	IP	IP	IP	OP	OP	OP-D/ IP-R
Hawaii	CC	CC	CC	CC	CC	CC	CC	CC	CC	CC	CC
Idaho	CC	CC	OP	CC-D/ OP-R	IP-D/ OP-R	NB-D/ OP-R	NB-D/ OP-R	NB-D/ OP-R	NB-D/ OP,CO-R	CC-D/ OP-R	CC-D/ OP-R
Illinois	CP	CP	OP	OP	CP	CP	CP	CP	OP-D/ CP,CO-R	OP	OP

(Table continues)

Table 2-4 *(Continued)*

State	*1968*	*1972*	*1976*	*1980*	*1984*	*1988*	*1992*	*1996*	*2000*	*2004*	*2008*
Indiana	OP	OP	OP	OP	IP	IP	IP	IP	OP-D/ OP,CO-R	OP	IP-D/ OP-R
Iowa	CC	CC	CC	CC	CC	CC	CC	CC	CC	CC	CC
Kansas	CC	CC	CC	IP	CC	CC	OP	OP	IP	CC	CC
Kentucky	CC	CC	CC	IP	CC	CP	CP	CP	CP	CP	CP
Louisiana	CO	CC	CC	CP	CP	CP	CP	CP-D/ CC-R	CP	CP	CP
Maine	CC	CC	CC	CC	CC	CC	CC	CC	IP	CC	CC
Maryland	CO-D/ CC-R	CP	CP	CP	CP	CP	CP	CP	CP-D/ IP-R	CP-D/ IP-R	CP-D/ IP-R
Massachusetts	IP	IP	IP	IP	IP	IP	IP	IP	IP	IP	IP
Michigan	CC	OP	OP	CC-D/ OP-R	CC	CC-D/ NB-R	CP	CC-D/ OP-R	CC-D/ OP-R	IP-D/ CC-R	IP-D/ OP-R
Minnesota	CC	CC	CC	CC	CC	CC	CC	CC	CC	CC	CC
Mississippi	CC	CC	CC	CC-D/ CP-R	CC	IP	IP	IP	OP	OP	OP
Missouri	CC/CO-D CC-R	CC	CC	CC	CC	IP	CC	CC	OP	OP	OP
Montana	CC	CC	OP	OP	OP	IP-D/ NB-R	OP-D/ NB-R	OP-D/ NB-R	OP-D/ NB-R	OP-D/ NB-R	OP

Nebraska	OP	OP	OP	OP	CP	CP	CP	IP	CP-D/ NB-R	CP-D/ NB-R	IP
Nevada	CC	CC	CP	CP	CC	CC	CC	CC	CC	CC	CC
New Hampshire	IP	IP	IP	IP	IP	IP	IP	IP	IP	IP	IP
New Jersey	IP	IP	IP	IP	CP	CP	CP	IP-D/ NB-R	IP-D/ CP-R	IP-D/ CP-R	IP
New Mexico	CC	CP	CC	CP	CP	CP	CP	CP	CP	CC-D/ CP-R	CC
New York	CO/CP	CO/CP	CP	CP	CP	CP	CP	CP	CP-D/ CP,CO-R	CP	IP-D/ CP-R
North Carolina	CC	CP	CP	CP	CP	CP	CP	CP-D/ IP-R	IP	CC	CP-D/ IP-R
North Dakota	CC	CC	CC	CC	CP	NB-D/ OP-R	NB-D/ OP-R	NB-D/ OP-R	CO	CC	CC
Ohio	OP	OP	OP	OP	IP	IP	IP	IP	OP	OP	IP
Oklahoma	CC	CC	CC	CC	CC	CP	CP	CP	CP	CP	CP
Oregon	CP	CP	CP	CP	CP	CP	CP	CP	CP	CP	CP
Pennsylvania	CO/CP	CP	CP	CP	CP	CP	CP	NB	CP-D/ CP,CO-R	CP-D/ CP,CO-R	CP
Rhode Island	CO-D/ CC-R	IP	IP	IP	IP	IP	IP	IP	IP	IP	IP
South Carolina	CC	CC	CC	CC	CC-D/ OP-R	CC	OP-D/ CC-R	CC-D/ OP-R	OP	OP-D/ CC-R	OP
South Dakota	CP	CP	CP	CP	CP	CP	CP	CP	CP	CP	CP

(Table continues)

Table 2-4 *(Continued)*

State	*1968*	*1972*	*1976*	*1980*	*1984*	*1988*	*1992*	*1996*	*2000*	*2004*	*2008*
Tennessee	CC	OP	OP	OP	IP	IP	IP	IP	OP	OP	OP
Texas	CC	CC	OP	CP	CC-D/ OP-R	IP	IP	IP	OP,CO-D/ OP-R	OP,CO-D/ OP-R	OP
Utah	CC	CC	CC	CC	CC	CC	CC	CC	IP	IP-D/ CC-R	IP-D/ CC-R
Vermont	CC	CC	NB	NB	NB	NB	NB	OP	OP	OP	OP
Virginia	CC	CC	CC	CC	CC	IP-D/ NB-R	CC	CC	CC-D/ OP-R	OP-D/ CC-R	OP
Washington	CO/ CC-D CC-R	CC	CC	CC	CC	CC	CP	CC-D CC/OP-R	NB-D/ CP,CC-R	CC	CC
West Virginia	CP	CP	CP	CP	CP	CP	CP-D/ IP-R	CP-D/ IP-R	CP	CP	IP
Wisconsin	OP	OP	OP	OP	NB-D/ OP-R	IP-D/ OP-R	IP-D/ OP-R	OP	OP	OP	OP
Wyoming	CC	CC	CC	CC	CC	CC	CC	CC	CC	CC	CC
District of Columbia	CP	CP	CP	CP	CP	CP	CP	CP	CC	CC	CC
Puerto Rico	CC	CC	CC	OP	IP-D/ CC-R	IP	IP	IP	IP	CC-D/ OP-R	CC-D/ OP-R

Sources: (1968–2004) Adapted from Harold Stanley and Richard Niemi, *Vital Statistics on American Politics, 2007–2008* (Washington, D.C.: CQ Press, 2008), 73–74; (2008) adapted from "CQ Politics Primary Guide," http://innovation.cq.com/primaries.

Note: CC—delegates chosen by local caucuses and state conventions; CO—delegates chosen by state party committee; CP—closed primary in which only voters registered to a party may vote in that party's primary; IP—independent primary in which voters registered to a party and independents may vote in that party's primary, but voters registered to other parties may not; OP—open primary in which any registered voter may vote, regardless of party affiliation; NB—nonbinding presidential primary (delegates are actually chosen by caucuses and conventions); D—Democrat; R—Republican.

Table 2-5 Types of Presidential Nomination Methods, 1968–2008

Method of selection[a]	*1968*	*1972*	*1976*	*1980*	*1984*	*1988*	*1992*	*1996*	*2000*	*2004*	*2008*
Caucus/convention	30	29	23	15	20	14	12	11	7	13	13
	4 (R)			1 (R)	2 (R)		1 (R)	2 (R)	2 (R)	6 (R)	2 (R)
				3 (D)	2 (D)	1 (D)		3 (D)	2 (D)	3 (D)	2 (D)
Party committee	1	0	0	0	0	0	0	1 (R)	1	0	0
									4 (R)	1 (R)	
	4 (D)								1 (D)	1 (D)	
Closed primary	10	13	11	15	16	18	19	12	11	9	9
				1 (R)					5 (R)	4 (R)	2 (R)
					1 (D)		1 (D)	3 (D)	4 (D)	5 (D)	3 (D)
Independent primary	3	4	4	6	8	12	11	12	8	3	7
							1 (R)	2 (R)	1 (R)	1 (R)	3 (R)
					2 (D)	3 (D)	1 (D)	1 (D)	1 (D)	4 (D)	5 (D)
Open primary	4	6	13	10	1	1	3	5	11	11	12
				2 (R)	4 (R)	3 (R)	3 (R)	5 (R)	5 (R)	3 (R)	4 (R)
				1 (D)			2 (D)	1 (D)	4 (D)	4 (D)	1 (D)
Nonbinding primary	0	0	1	1	1	1	1	1	0	0	0
						3 (R)	1 (R)	2 (R)	2 (R)	2 (R)	
					1 (D)	2 (D)	2 (D)	2 (D)	3 (D)		

Source: Collated from Table 2-4.

Note: Numbers denoted with (R) or (D)—Republican and Democrat, respectively—indicate states in which the two parties used different methods of selection. These are in addition to the number of states in which both parties adopted the same method. For example, in 1968 thirty states adopted the convention method and in four additional states only the Republicans used this method. Hence, in that year, there was a total of thirty-four states in which at least one party used the convention method. Total methods adopted in a given year may therefore exceed the number of states plus Puerto Rico and the District of Columbia.

[a] *Caucus/convention* denotes delegates chosen by local caucuses and state conventions; *party committee* denotes delegates chosen by state party committee; *closed primary* denotes contest in which only voters registered to a party may vote in that party's primary; *independent primary* denotes contest in which voters registered to a party and independents may vote in that party's primary, but voters registered to other parties may not; *open primary* denotes contest in which any registered voter may vote, regardless of party affiliation; *nonbinding primary* denotes nonbinding presidential primary—delegates are actually chosen by caucuses and conventions.

Table 2-6 Presidential Candidates' Delegate Strength from Caucus States and Primary States, 1968–2008

Year/candidate	*Caucus states*	*Primary states*	*Number of convention votes*	*Percentage of convention*
1968 Democratic convention				
Humphrey	80.20%	53.40%	1,760.25	67.10
McCarthy	12.10	34.40	601.00	22.90
McGovern	3.80	7.50	146.50	5.60
Others	4.00	4.70	114.25	4.40
Total	N = 1,346.00	N = 1,276.00	2,622.00	100.00
1968 Republican convention				
Nixon	59.60	43.20	692.00	51.90
Rockefeller	14.40	27.90	277.00	20.80
Reagan	11.20	16.40	182.00	13.70
Others	14.70	12.40	182.00	13.70
Total	N = 706.00	N = 627.00	1,333.00	100.00
1972 Democratic convention				
McGovern	41.00	64.90	1,715.40	56.90
Jackson	30.00	11.50	534.00	17.70
Wallace	7.30	15.50	385.70	12.80
Others	21.70	8.10	380.90	12.60
Total	N = 1,009.00	N = 2,007.00	3,016.00	100.00
1976 Republican convention				
Ford	44.90	55.90	1,187.00	52.50
Reagan	55.10	43.90	1,070.00	47.40
Others	0.00	0.10	2.00	0.10
Total	N = 693.00	N = 1,566.00	2,259.00	100.00
1980 Democratic convention				
Carter	71.00	60.80	2,123.00	63.70
Kennedy	24.30	38.60	1,150.50	34.50
Others	4.70	0.50	57.50	1.70
Total	N = 953.00	N = 2,378.00	3,331.00	100.00
1984 Democratic convention				
Mondale	56.30	55.60	2,191.00	55.90
Hart	29.60	31.20	1,200.50	30.60
Jackson	11.90	11.90	465.50	11.90
Others	2.30	1.30	66.00	1.70
Total	N = 1,460.00	N = 2,463.00	3,923.00	100.00
1988 Democratic convention				
Dukakis	62.60	71.50	2,876.25	69.90
Jackson	36.20	28.10	1,218.50	29.60
Others	1.20	0.40	23.00	0.60
Total	N = 766.75	N = 3,351.00	4,117.75	100.00

(Table continues)

Table 2-6 *(Continued)*

Year/candidate	*Caucus states*	*Primary states*	*Number of convention votes*	*Percentage of convention*
1992 Democratic convention				
Brown	10.90%	14.20%	596.00	13.90
Clinton	84.40	77.80	3,372.00	78.60
Tsongas	3.70	5.50	209.00	4.90
Others	1.00	2.50	111.00	2.60
Total	*N* = 514.00	*N* = 3,774.00	4,288.00	100.00
1996 Republican convention				
Dole	87.00	98.60	1,928.00	96.90
Buchanan	10.60	0.70	43.00	2.20
Others	2.40	0.80	19.00	1.00
Total	*N* = 293.00	*N* = 1,697.00	1,990.00	100.10
2008 Democratic convention				
Clinton	32.61	48.76	1,896.00	46.21
Edwards	0.62	0.06	6.00	0.15
Obama	66.77	51.19	2,201.00	53.64
Total	*N* = 647.00	*N* = 3,456.00	4,103.00	100.00
2008 Republican convention				
Huckabee	22.16	10.38	268.00	12.45
McCain	26.12	83.19	1,574.00	73.14
Paul	5.28	1.07	39.00	1.81
Romney	46.44	5.36	271.00	12.59
Total	*N* = 379.00	*N* = 1,773.00	2,512.00	100.00

Sources: (1968–2004) Adapted from *Guide to U.S. Elections,* 5th ed. (Washington, D.C.: CQ Press, 2005), vol. I, 668–671; (2008) adapted from "CQ Politics 2008 Primary Guide," http://innovation.cq.com/primaries.

Note: Shown are major presidential candidates with opposition. The table is based on first-ballot votes before switches. For 1984–1992, 2008, votes of Democratic superdelegates not chosen through caucuses or primaries are counted as if they were chosen by the delegate selection method in their state. States holding both primaries and caucuses are counted among primary states in these calculations. ("States" include all jurisdictions having delegates.)

Table 2-7 Leading Candidates in Presidential Primaries, 1968 (percent)

		Democrats					*Republicans*			
Date	*State*	Eugene McCarthy	Robert Kennedy	Hubert Humphrey	Lyndon Johnson	Others	Ronald Reagan	Richard Nixon	Nelson Rockefeller	Others
March 12	N.H.	41.9	—	—	49.6	8.5	—	77.6	10.8	11.6
April 2	Wis.	56.2	6.3	0.5	34.6	2.8	10.4	79.7	1.6	8.3
April 23	Pa.	71.7	11.0[a]	8.7[a]	3.6[a]	5.0	2.8[a]	59.7[a]	18.4[a]	19.1[a]
April 30	Mass.	49.3	27.6[a]	17.7[a]	2.8	2.7	1.7[a]	25.8[a]	30.0[a]	42.5[b]
May 7	D.C.	—	62.5[c]	37.5[c]	—	0.0	—	90.1[d]	[d]	9.9[d]
	Ind.	27.0	42.3	—	—	30.7[e]	—	100.0	—	0.0
	Ohio	—	—	—	—	100.0[f]	—	—	—	100.0[f]
May 14	Neb.	31.2	51.7	7.4	5.6	4.1	21.3	70.0	5.1[a]	3.6
	W. Va.	—	—	—	—	100.0[e]	—	—	—	100.0[g]
May 28	Fla.	28.7	—	—	—	71.3[h]	—	—	—	100.0[g]
	Ore.	44.0	38.0	3.3[a]	12.1	2.7	20.4	65.0	11.6[a]	3.0
June 4	Calif.	41.8	46.3	—	—	12.0[g]	100.0	—	—	0.0
	N.J.	36.1[a]	31.3[a]	20.3[a]	—	12.3	3.1[a]	81.1[a]	13.0[a]	2.8
	S.D.	20.4	49.5	—	30.0	0.0	—	100.0	—	0.0
June 11	Ill.	38.6	—	17.1	—	44.3[i]	7.1[a]	78.1[a]	9.7[a]	5.1[a]

Source: Adapted from *Guide to U.S. Elections,* 5th ed. (Washington, D.C.: CQ Press, 2005), vol. I, 363–365.

Note: Entries may not total 100 percent due to rounding. "—" indicates candidate did not enter primary.

[a] Write-in.
[b] John A. Volpe (Massachusetts) received 29.5 percent of the vote.
[c] Figures from the District of Columbia Board of Elections. No figures are available for vote for delegates to Republican convention.
[d] Prior to the primary, the District Republican organization agreed to divide the nine delegate votes, with six going to Rockefeller, according to the 1968 *Congressional Quarterly Almanac,* vol. 24.
[e] Roger D. Branigin (Indiana) received 30.7 percent of the vote.
[f] One candidate in each party's primary received 100 percent of the vote: in the Democratic primary, Stephen M. Young (Ohio); in the Republican primary, James A. Rhodes (Ohio).
[g] Unpledged delegates at large.
[h] George A. Smathers (Florida) received 46.1 percent of the vote, and 25.2 percent were unpledged delegates at large.
[i] Edward M. Kennedy (Massachusetts) received 33.7 percent of the vote.

Table 2-8 Leading Candidates in Presidential Primaries, 1972 (percent)

		Democrats					Republicans			
Date	*State*	Hubert Humphrey	George McGovern	George Wallace	Edmund Muskie	Others[a]	Richard Nixon	John Ashbrook	Paul McCloskey	Others[b]
March 7	N.H.	0.4[c]	37.1	0.2[c]	46.4	15.9	67.6	9.7	19.8	2.9
March 14	Fla.	18.6	6.2	41.6	8.9	24.8	87.0	8.8	4.2	0.0
March 21	Ill.	0.1[c]	0.3[c]	0.6[c]	62.6	36.4[d]	97.0[c]	0.5[c]	0.1[c]	2.4[c]
April 4	Wis.	20.7	29.6	22.0	10.3	17.4	96.9	0.9	1.3	0.8
April 25	Mass.	7.9	52.7	7.4	21.3	10.6	81.2	4.0	13.5	1.4
	Pa.	35.1	20.4	21.3	20.4	2.8	83.3[c]	—	—	16.8
May 2	D.C.[e]	—	—	—	—	100.0[f]	—	—	—	0.0
	Ind.	47.1	—	41.2	11.7	0.0	100.0	—	—	0.0
	Ohio	41.2	39.6	—	8.9	10.2	100.0	—	—	0.0
May 4	Tenn.	15.9	7.2	68.2	2.0	6.7	95.8	2.1	2.1	0.0
May 6	N.C.	—	—	50.3	3.7	45.9[g]	94.8	—	5.2	0.0
May 9	Neb.	34.3	41.3	12.4	3.6	8.3	92.4	2.6	4.6	0.4
	W. Va.	66.9	—	33.1	—	0.0	—	—	—	100.0[h]
May 16	Md.	26.8	22.4	38.7	2.4	9.8	86.2	5.8	8.0	0.0
	Mich.	15.7	26.8	51.0	2.4	4.1	95.5	—	2.9	1.6
May 23	Ore.	12.5	50.2	20.0	2.5	14.7	82.0	5.9	10.4	1.7
	R.I.	20.3	41.2	15.3	20.7	2.4	88.3	3.1	6.0	2.6
June 6	Calif.	38.6	43.5	7.5[c]	2.0	8.3	90.1	9.8	—	0.0
	N.J.	—	—	—	—	100.0[i]	—	—	—	100.0[h]
	N.M.	25.9	33.3	29.3	4.2	7.4	88.5	—	6.1	5.5
	S.D.	—	100.0	—	—	0.0	100.0	—	—	0.0

Source: Adapted from *Guide to U.S. Elections*, 5th ed. (Washington, D.C.: CQ Press, 2005), vol. I, 366–370.

(Table continues)

Table 2-8 *(Continued)*

Note: Entries may not total 100 percent due to rounding. "—" indicates candidate did not enter primary.

[a] In addition to scattered votes, "others" includes Patrick Paulsen, who received 1,211 votes in the New Hampshire primary.
[b] In addition to scattered votes, "others" includes Edward T. Coll, who received 280 votes in the New Hampshire primary and 589 votes in the Massachusetts primary.
[c] Write-in.
[d] Eugene McCarthy received 36.3 percent of the vote.
[e] No Republican primary was held in 1972.
[f] Walter E. Fauntroy (District of Columbia) received 71.8 percent of the vote.
[g] Terry Sanford (North Carolina) received 37.3 percent of the vote.
[h] Unpledged delegates at large.
[i] Shirley Chisholm (New York) received 66.9 percent of the vote; Sanford (North Carolina) received 33.1 percent of the vote.

Table 2-9 Leading Candidates in Presidential Primaries, 1976 (percent)

		Democrats					*Republicans*		
Date	*State*	Jimmy Carter	Frank Church	Morris Udall	George Wallace	Others	Gerald Ford	Ronald Reagan	Others
Feb. 24	N.H.	28.4	—	22.7	1.3[a]	37.7[b]	49.4	48.0	2.6
March 2	Mass.	13.9	—	17.7	16.7	49.6[c]	61.2	33.7	5.0
	Vt.	42.2	—	—	—	48.8[d]	84.0	15.2	0.0
March 9	Fla.	34.5	0.4	2.1	30.5	30.8[e]	52.8	47.2	0.0
March 16	Ill.	48.1	—	—	27.6	23.8	58.9	40.1	1.0
March 23	N.C.	53.6	—	2.3	34.7	9.1	52.4	45.9	1.7
April 6	Wis.	36.6	—	35.6	12.5	13.1	55.2	44.3	0.3
April 27	Pa.	37.0	—	18.7	11.3	31.8[f]	92.1	5.1	2.8
May 4	D.C.	39.7	—	26.0	—	1.6[g]	100.0[h]	—	0.0
	Ga.	83.4	0.5	1.9	11.5	1.4	37.1	68.3	0.0
	Ind.	68.0	—	—	15.2	16.9	48.7	51.3	0.0
May 11	Neb.	37.6	38.5	2.7	3.2	5.8	45.4	54.5	0.1
	W. Va.	—	—	—	11.0	[i]	56.8	43.2	0.0
May 18	Md.	37.1	—	5.5	4.1	53.3[j]	58.0	42.0	0.0
	Mich.	43.4	—	43.1	6.9	6.2	64.9	34.3	0.8
May 25	Ariz.	62.6	—	7.5	16.5	13.3	35.1	63.4	1.5
	Idaho	11.9	78.7	1.3	1.5	4.4	24.9	74.3	0.8
	Ky.	59.4	—	10.9	16.8	12.2	50.9	46.9	2.1
	Nev.	23.3	9.0	3.0	3.3	61.3[k]	28.8	66.3	5.0
	Ore.	26.7	33.6	2.7	1.3	27.3[l]	50.3	45.8	3.9
	Tenn.	77.6	2.4	3.7	10.9	5.3	49.8	49.1	1.1
	Mont.	24.6	59.4	6.3	3.4	6.3	34.6	63.1	2.2
June 1	R.I.	30.2	27.2	4.2	0.8	37.5	65.3	31.2	3.5
	S.D.	41.2	—	33.3	2.4	23.2	44.0	51.2	4.8
June 8	Calif.	20.5	7.4	5.0	3.0	64.1[m]	34.5	65.5	0.0
	N.J.	58.4	13.6	—	8.6	14.8	100.0[h]	—	0.0
	Ohio[n]	39.0	5.3	10.1	12.5	30.0[o]	55.2	44.8	0.0

(Table continues)

Table 2-9 (*Continued*)

Source: Adapted from *Guide to U.S. Elections,* 5th ed. (Washington, D.C.: CQ Press, 2005), vol. I, 371–376.

Note: Entries may not total 100 percent due to rounding. "—" indicates candidate did not enter primary.

[a] Write-in votes.
[b] Birch Bayh received 15.2 percent of the vote and Sargent Shriver received 8.2 percent of the vote.
[c] Henry M. Jackson received 22.3 percent of the vote.
[d] Shriver received 27.6 percent of the vote.
[e] Jackson received 23.9 percent of the vote.
[f] Jackson received 24.6 percent of the vote. Jackson suspended his campaign May 1.
[g] Uncommitted slate headed by delegate Walter E. Fauntroy received 21.6 percent of the vote; another uncommitted slate headed by Walter E. Washington received 11.1 percent.
[h] Ford unopposed.
[i] Robert C. Byrd received 89.0 percent of the vote. Byrd was also on the ballot in Florida, where he received 0.4 percent, and in Georgia, where he received 0.7 percent.
[j] Edmund G. Brown received 48.4 percent of the vote.
[k] Brown received 52.7 percent of the vote.
[l] Brown received 24.7 percent of the vote; these were write-in votes.
[m] Brown received 59.0 percent of the vote.
[n] Gertrude W. Donahey headed an at-large slate that received 4.0 percent.
[o] Brown received 15.2 percent of the vote.

Table 2-10 Leading Candidates in Presidential Primaries, 1980 (percent)

		Democrats				Republicans				
Date	*State*	Jimmy Carter	Edward Kennedy	Jerry Brown	Others	Ronald Reagan	George H. W. Bush	John Anderson	Howard Baker	Others
Feb. 17	P.R.	51.7	48.0	0.2	0.1	—	60.1	—	37.0	22.1
Feb. 26	N.H.	47.1	37.3	9.6	6.0	49.6	22.7	9.8	12.1	5.8
March 4	Mass.	28.7	65.1	3.5	2.7	28.8	31.0	30.7	4.8	4.7
	Vt.	73.1	25.5	0.1	1.3	30.1	21.7	29.0	12.3	6.9
March 8	S.C.	a	a	a	a	54.7	14.8	—	0.5	30.0
March 11	Fla.	60.7	23.2	4.9	11.2	56.2	30.2	9.2	1.0	3.4
	Ga.	88.0	8.4	1.9	1.7	73.2	12.6	8.4	0.4	5.4
	Ala.	81.6	13.2	4.0	1.2	69.7	25.9	0.9	0.9	2.6
March 18	Ill.	65.0	30.0	3.0	2.0	48.4	11.0	36.7	1.0	2.9
March 25	N.Y.	41.1	58.9	—	0.0	a	a	a	a	a
	Conn.	41.5	46.9	2.6	9.0	33.9	38.6	22.1	1.3	4.1
April 1	Wis.	56.2	30.1	11.8	1.9	40.2	30.4	27.4	0.4	1.6
	Kans.	56.6	31.6	4.9	6.9	63.0	12.6	18.2	1.3	4.9
April 5	La.	55.7	22.5	4.7	17.1	74.9	18.8	—	—	6.3
April 22	Pa.	45.4	45.7	2.3	6.6	42.5	50.5	2.1	2.5	2.4
May 3	Texas	55.9	22.8	2.6	18.7	51.0	47.4	—	—	1.6
May 6	Ind.	67.7	32.3	—	0.0	73.7	16.4	9.9	—	0.0
	N.C.	70.1	17.7	2.9	9.3	67.6	21.8	5.1	1.5	4.0
	D.C.	36.9	61.7	—	1.4	0.0	66.1	26.9	—	7.0
	Tenn.	75.2	18.1	1.9	4.8	74.1	18.1	4.5	—	3.3
May 13	Md.	47.5	38.0	3.0	11.5	48.2	40.9	9.7	—	1.2
	Neb.	46.9	37.6	3.6	11.9	76.0	15.3	5.8	—	2.9
May 20	Mich.	—	—	29.4	70.6	31.8	57.5	8.2	—	2.5
	Ore.	56.7	31.1	9.3	2.9	54.0	34.6	10.2	—	1.2
May 27	Ark.	60.1	17.5	—	22.4	a	a	a	a	a

(*Table continues*)

Table 2-10 (*Continued*)

		Democrats				*Republicans*				
Date	*State*	Jimmy Carter	Edward Kennedy	Jerry Brown	Others	Ronald Reagan	George H. W. Bush	John Anderson	Howard Baker	Others
	Idaho	62.0	22.0	4.0	12.0	82.3	4.0	9.7	—	4.0
	Ky.	66.9	23.0	—	10.1	82.4	7.2	5.1	—	5.3
	Nev.	37.6	28.8	—	33.6	83.0	6.5	—	—	10.5
June 3	Calif.	37.6	44.8	4.0	13.5	80.3	4.9	13.6	—	1.2
	Miss.	[a]	[a]	[a]	[a]	89.4	8.2	—	—	2.4
	Mont.	51.0	37.0	—	12.0	87.0	10.0	—	—	4.0
	N.J.	38.0	56.0	—	6.0	81.0	17.0	—	—	2.0
	N.M.	41.8	46.3	—	11.9	63.8	9.9	12.0	—	14.3
	Ohio	51.1	44.4	—	4.5	80.8	19.2	—	—	0.0
	R.I.	25.8	68.3	0.8	5.1	72.8	18.6	—	—	8.6
	S.D.	45.4	48.6	—	6.0	82.2	4.2	—	—	13.6
	W. Va.	62.2	37.8	—	0.0	83.6	14.1	—	—	2.3

Source: Adapted from *Guide to U.S. Elections,* 5th ed. (Washington, D.C.: CQ Press, 2005), vol. I, 377–383.

Note: Entries may not total 100 percent due to rounding. "—" indicates candidate did not enter primary.

[a] No primary was held.

Table 2-11 Leading Candidates in Presidential Primaries, 1984 (percent)

		Democrats				*Republicans*	
Date	*State*	Walter Mondale	Gary Hart	Jesse Jackson	Others[a]	Ronald Reagan[b]	Others[a]
Feb. 28	N.H.	27.9	37.3	5.3	29.5[c]	86.1	13.9
March 6	Vt.	20.0	70.0	7.8	2.2	98.7	1.3
March 13	Ala.	34.6	20.7	19.6	24.1	[d]	[d]
	Fla.	33.4	39.2	12.2	15.2	100.0	0.0
	Ga.	30.5	27.3	21.0	20.8	100.0	0.0
	Mass.	25.5	39.0	5.0	30.5[e]	89.5	10.5
	R.I.	34.5	45.0	8.7	11.8	90.7	9.3
March 18	P.R.	99.1	0.6	—	0.3	[d]	[d]
March 20	Ill.	40.4	35.2	21.0	3.4	99.9	0.1
March 27	Conn.	29.1	52.7	12.0	6.2	[d]	[d]
April 3	N.Y.	44.8	27.4	25.6	2.2	[d]	[d]
	Wis.	41.1	44.4	9.8	4.7	95.2	4.8
April 10	Pa.	45.1	33.3	16.0	5.6	99.3	0.7
May 1	D.C.	25.6	7.1	67.3	0.0	100.0	0.0
	Tenn.	41.0	29.1	25.3	4.6	90.9	9.1
May 5	La.	22.3	25.0	42.9	9.8	89.7	10.3
	Texas	[f]	[f]	[f]	[f]	96.5	3.5
May 8	Ind.	40.9	41.8	13.7	3.6	100.0	0.0
	Md.	42.5	24.3	25.5	7.7	100.0	0.0
	N.C.	35.6	30.2	25.4	8.8	[d]	[d]
	Ohio	40.3	42.0	16.4	1.3	100.0	0.0
May 15	Neb.	26.6	58.2	9.1	6.1	99.0	1.0
	Ore.	27.3	58.5	9.3	4.9	98.0	2.0
May 22	Idaho	30.1	58.0	5.7	6.2	92.2	7.8

(Table continues)

Table 2-11 *(Continued)*

		Democrats				*Republicans*	
Date	*State*	Walter Mondale	Gary Hart	Jesse Jackson	Others[a]	Ronald Reagan[b]	Others[a]
June 5	Calif.	35.3	38.9	18.4	7.4	100.0	0.0
	Mont.	5.9	9.0	1.1	84.0	92.4	7.6
	N.J.	45.1	29.7	23.6	1.6	100.0	0.0
	N.M.	36.1	46.7	11.8	5.4	94.9	5.1
	S.D.[d]	39.0	50.7	5.2	5.1	—	0.0
	W. Va.	53.8	37.3	6.7	2.2	91.8	8.2
	N.D.	2.8	85.1	0.2	11.9	100.0	0.0

Source: Adapted from *Guide to U.S. Elections*, 5th ed. (Washington, D.C.: CQ Press, 2005), vol. I, 384–389.

Note: Entries may not total 100 percent due to rounding. "—" indicates candidate did not enter primary.

[a] Includes uncommitted voters.
[b] Reagan won all 25 primaries with at least 86 percent of the vote in each.
[c] John Glenn received 12 percent of the vote, and George McGovern received 5 percent of the vote.
[d] No Republican primary was held.
[e] McGovern received 21 percent of the vote.
[f] No Democratic primary was held.

Table 2-12 Leading Candidates in Presidential Primaries, 1988 (percent)

		Democrats				Republicans			
Date	*State*	Michael Dukakis	Jesse Jackson	Albert Gore	Others[a]	George H.W. Bush	Bob Dole	Pat Robertson	Others[a]
Feb. 16	N.H.	35.8	7.8	6.8	49.7[b]	37.6	28.4	9.4	24.6
Feb. 23	S.D.	31.2	5.4	8.4	55.0[c]	18.6	55.2	19.6	6.5
March 1	Vt.	55.8	25.7	—	18.5	49.3	39.0	5.1	6.6
March 5	S.C.	d	d	d	d	48.5	20.6	19.1	11.8
March 8	Ala.	7.7	43.6	37.4	11.3	64.5	16.3	13.9	5.2
	Ark.	18.9	17.1	37.3	26.6	47.0	25.9	18.9	8.2
	Fla.	40.9	20.0	12.7	26.5	62.1	21.2	10.6	6.0
	Ga.	15.6	39.8	32.4	12.2	53.8	23.6	16.3	6.3
	Ky.	18.6	15.6	45.8	19.9	59.3	23.0	11.1	6.5
	La.	15.3	35.5	28.0	21.1	57.8	17.7	18.2	6.3
	Md.	45.6	28.7	8.7	16.9	53.3	32.4	6.4	7.9
	Mass.	58.6	18.7	4.4	18.3	58.5	26.3	4.5	10.7
	Miss.	8.3	44.4	33.3	14.1	66.0	16.9	13.5	3.6
	Mo.	11.6	20.2	2.8	65.5[e]	42.2	41.1	11.2	5.6
	N.C.	20.3	33.0	34.7	12.1	45.4	39.1	9.8	5.6
	Okla.	16.9	13.3	41.4	28.4	37.4	34.9	21.1	6.5
	R.I.	69.8	15.2	4.0	11.1	64.9	22.6	5.7	6.8
	Tenn.	3.4	20.7	72.3	3.6	60.0	21.6	12.6	5.8
	Texas	32.8	24.5	20.2	22.6	63.9	13.9	15.3	6.9
	Va.	22.0	45.1	22.3	9.6	53.3	26.0	13.7	7.0
March 15	Ill.	16.3	32.3	5.1	46.2[f]	54.7	36.0	6.8	2.5
March 20	P.R.	22.9	29.0	14.4	33.7	97.1	2.7	0.1	0.1
March 29	Conn.	58.1	28.3	7.7	5.9	70.6	20.2	3.1	6.2
April 5	Wis.	47.6	28.2	17.4	6.9	82.2	7.9	6.9	3.1
April 19	N.Y.	50.9	37.1	10.0	2.1	g	g	g	g

(Table continues)

Table 2-12 *(Continued)*

		Democrats				*Republicans*			
Date	*State*	Michael Dukakis	Jesse Jackson	Albert Gore	Others[a]	George H. W. Bush	Bob Dole	Pat Robertson	Others[a]
April 26	Penn.	66.5	27.3	3.0	3.3	79.0	11.9	9.1	0.0
May 3	D.C.	17.9	80.0	0.8	1.3	87.6	7.0	4.0	1.4
	Ind.	69.6	22.5	3.4	4.5	80.4	9.8	6.6	3.3
	Ohio	62.7	27.5	2.2	7.7	81.0	11.9	7.1	0.0
May 10	Neb.	62.9	25.7	1.5	9.8	68.0	22.3	5.1	4.9
	W. Va.	78.9	14.0	3.6	3.5	77.3	10.9	7.3	3.5
May 17	Ore.	56.8	38.1	1.4	3.6	72.9	17.9	7.7	1.5
May 24	Idaho	73.4	15.7	3.7	7.2	81.2	—	8.6	10.2
June 7	Calif.	60.8	35.2	1.8	2.2	82.9	12.9	4.2	0.0
	Mont.	68.7	22.1	1.8	7.3	73.0	19.4	0.0	7.5
	N.J.	63.2	32.9	2.8	1.1	100.0	—	—	0.0
	N.M.	61.0	28.1	2.5	8.4	78.2	10.5	6.0	5.3
June 14	N.D.	84.9	15.1	—	—	94.0	—	—	6.0

Sources: Democratic data adapted from *Congressional Quarterly Weekly Report*, July 9, 1988, 1894; Republican data adapted from *CQWR*, August 13, 1988, 2254.

Note: Entries may not total 100 percent due to rounding. "—" indicates candidate did not enter primary. Richard Gephardt withdrew from the Democratic race on March 28, Paul Simon on April 17, and Gore on April 21. Dole withdrew from the Republican race on March 29 and Robertson on May 16.

[a] Includes uncommitted voters.
[b] Gephardt received 19.8 percent of the vote and Simon received 17.1 percent of the vote.
[c] Gephardt received 43.5 percent of the vote.
[d] No Democratic primary was held.
[e] Gephardt received 57.8 percent of the vote.
[f] Simon received 42.3 percent of the vote.
[g] No Republican primary was held.

Table 2-13 Leading Candidates in Presidential Primaries, 1992 (percent)

		Democrats				*Republicans*		
Date	*State*	Bill Clinton	Paul Tsongas	Jerry Brown	Others[a]	George H. W. Bush	Patrick Buchanan	Others[a]
Feb. 18	N.H.	24.7	33.2	8.1	34.0	53.0	37.4	9.7
Feb. 25	S.D.	19.1	9.6	3.9	67.4[b]	69.3	—	30.7[c]
March 3	Colo.	26.9	25.6	28.8	18.8	67.5	30.0	2.5
	Ga.	57.2	24.0	8.1	10.7	64.3	35.7	0.0
	Md.	33.5	40.6	8.2	17.8	70.1	29.9	0.0
March 7	S.C.	62.9	18.3	6.0	12.8	66.9	25.7	7.4
March 10	Fla.	50.8	34.5	12.4	2.3	68.1	31.9	0.0
	La.	69.5	11.1	6.6	12.8	62.0	27.0	10.9
	Mass.	10.9	66.3	14.6	8.2	65.6	27.7	6.8
	Miss.	73.1	8.1	9.6	9.2	72.3	16.7	11.0
	Okla.	70.5	—	16.7	18.5	69.6	26.6	3.8
	R.I.	21.2	52.9	18.8	7.0	63.0	31.8	5.2
	Tenn.	67.3	19.4	8.0	5.2	72.5	22.2	5.1
	Texas	65.6	19.2	8.0	7.2	69.8	23.9	6.3
March 17	Ill.	51.6	25.8	14.6	7.9	76.4	22.5	1.2
	Mich.	50.7	16.6	25.8	6.9	67.2	25.0	7.8
March 24	Conn.	35.6	19.5	37.2	7.6	66.7	21.9	11.4
April 5	P.R.	95.6	0.1	1.6	2.6	99.2	0.4	0.4
April 7	Kan.	51.3	15.2	13.0	20.5	62.0	14.8	23.2
	Minn.	31.1	21.3	30.6	17.0	63.9	24.2	11.9
	N.Y.	40.9	28.6	26.2	4.2	d	d	d
	Wis.	37.2	21.8	34.5	6.5	75.6	16.3	8.2
April 28	Penn.	56.5	12.8	25.7	5.0	76.8	23.2	0.0
May 5	D.C.	73.8	10.4	7.2	8.5	81.5	18.5	0.0
	Ind.	63.3	12.2	21.5	3.0	80.1	19.9	0.0
	N.C.	64.1	8.3	10.4	17.2	70.7	19.5	9.8

(*Table continues*)

Table 2-13 *(Continued)*

		Democrats				*Republicans*		
Date	*State*	Bill Clinton	Paul Tsongas	Jerry Brown	Others[a]	George H. W. Bush	Patrick Buchanan	Others[a]
May 12	Neb.	45.5	7.1	21.0	19.2	81.4	13.5	5.2
	W. Va.	74.2	6.9	11.9	6.9	80.5	14.6	4.9
May 19	Ore.	45.3	10.5	31.4	12.7	67.1	19.0	14.0
	Wash.	42.0	12.8	23.1	22.1	67.0	10.2	22.8
May 26	Ark.	68.0	—	11.0	20.9	83.1	11.9	5.0
	Idaho	49.0	—	16.7	34.3	63.5	13.1	23.4
	Ky.	56.0	4.9	8.3	30.8	74.5	—	25.5
June 2	Ala.	68.2	—	6.8	25.0	74.3	7.6	18.1
	Calif.	47.5	7.4	40.2	5.0	73.6	26.4	0.0
	Mont.	46.9	10.8	18.5	23.9	71.6	11.8	16.6
	N.J.	59.2	11.1	19.5	10.2	77.5	15.0	7.5
	N.M.	52.8	6.3	16.9	24.1	63.8	9.1	27.1
	Ohio	61.2	10.6	19.0	9.2	83.2	16.8	27.1
June 9	N.D.	12.6[e]	—	—	87.4	83.4	—	16.6

Source: Democratic data adapted from *Congressional Quarterly Weekly Report*, July 4, 1992, 69; Republican data adapted from *CQWR*, August 8, 1992, 63.

Note: Entries may not total 100 percent due to rounding. "—" indicates candidate did not enter primary. Bob Kerrey withdrew from the Democratic race on March 5, Tom Harkin on March 9, and Paul Tsongas on March 19.

[a] Includes uncommitted voters.
[b] Kerrey received 40.2 percent of the vote and Harkin received 25.2 percent.
[c] All uncommitted delegates.
[d] No Republican primary was held.
[e] Clinton's votes were write-ins.

Table 2-14 Leading Candidates in Presidential Primaries, 1996 (percent)

		Republicans					Democrats
Date	*State*	Bob Dole	Pat Buchanan	Lamar Alexander	Malcolm Forbes Jr.	Others[a]	Bill Clinton
Feb. 20	N.H.	26.2	27.2	22.6	12.2	11.8	83.9
Feb. 24	Del.	27.2	18.7	13.3	32.7	8.1	90.3
Feb. 27	Ariz.	29.6	27.6	7.1	33.4	2.3	[b]
	N.D.	42.1	18.3	6.3	19.5	13.8	[b]
	S.D.	44.7	28.6	8.7	12.8	5.2	[b]
March 2	S.C.	45.1	29.2	10.4	12.7	2.7	[b]
March 3	P.R.	97.9	0.4	0.5	0.5	0.7	[b]
March 5	Colo.	43.6	21.5	9.8	20.8	4.3	88.9
	Conn.	54.4	15.1	5.4	20.1	5.0	[b]
	Ga.	40.6	29.1	13.6	12.7	4.0	100.0
	Maine	46.3	24.5	6.6	14.8	7.7	88.4
	Md.	53.3	21.1	5.5	12.7	7.4	84.2
	Mass.	47.7	25.2	7.5	13.9	5.6	87.1
	R.I.	64.4	2.6	19.0	0.9	13.1	89.1
	Vt.	40.3	16.7	10.6	15.6	16.8	96.5
March 12	Fla.	56.9	18.1	1.6	20.2	3.2	[b]
	La.	47.8	33.1	2.1	13.2	3.8	80.8
	Miss.	60.3	25.9	1.8	8.0	4.0	92.5
	Okla.	59.3	21.5	1.3	14.1	3.8	76.2
	Ore.	50.8	21.3	7.0	13.3	7.6	94.8
	Tenn.	51.2	25.2	11.3	7.7	4.6	88.9
	Texas	55.6	21.4	1.8	12.8	8.3	86.4
March 19	Ill.	65.1	22.7	1.5	4.9	5.8	96.2
	Mich.	50.6	33.9	1.5	5.1	9.0	[b]
	Ohio	66.4	21.5	2.0	6.0	4.0	92.6
	Wis.	52.3	33.8	1.9	5.6	6.4	97.6

(Table continues)

Table 2-14 (*Continued*)

		Republicans					*Democrats*
Date	*State*	Bob Dole	Pat Buchanan	Lamar Alexander	Malcolm Forbes Jr.	Others[a]	Bill Clinton
March 26	Calif.	66.1	18.4	1.8	7.5	6.3	92.8
	Nev.	51.9	15.2	2.3	19.2	11.4	[b]
	Wash.	63.1	20.9	1.3	8.6	6.0	98.5
April 23	Penn.	63.6	18.0	—	8.0	10.3	92.0
May 7	D.C.	75.5	9.5	—	—	15.0	98.2
	Ind.	70.6	19.4	—	9.9	0.0	100.0
	N.C.	71.5	13.0	2.7	4.1	8.6	80.6
May 14	Neb.	75.7	10.4	2.6	6.2	5.1	86.9
	W. Va.	68.8	16.3	2.9	4.9	7.1	86.5
May 21	Ark.	76.5	23.5	—	—	0.0	75.8
May 28	Idaho	62.3	22.3	—	—	15.4	87.7
	Ky.	73.8	8.1	3.2	3.3	11.5	76.8
June 4	Ala.	74.9	15.7	—	—	9.4	79.9
	Mont.	61.3	24.4	—	7.2	7.1	90.0
	N.J.	82.3	11.0	—	—	6.7	95.2
	N.M.	75.4	8.2	3.9	5.7	6.9	90.3

Source: Congressional Quarterly Weekly Report, March 9, 1996, 646; *Guide to the Republican National Convention*, supplement to *CQWR*, vol. 54, no. 31, 63–64.

Note: Entries may not total 100 percent due to rounding. "—" indicates candidate did not enter primary.

[a] Includes uncommitted voters.
[b] No Democratic primary was held.

Table 2-15 Leading Candidates in Presidential Primaries, 2000 (percent)

		Democrats			*Republicans*			
Date	*State*	Al Gore	Bill Bradley	Others[a]	George W. Bush	John McCain	Alan Keyes	Others[a]
Feb. 1	N.H.	49.7	45.6	4.7	30.4	48.5	6.4	14.7
Feb. 8	Del.	57.2	40.2	2.6	50.7	25.4	3.8	20.1
Feb. 19	S.C.	[b]	[b]	[b]	53.4	41.9	4.5	0.2
Feb. 22	Ariz.	77.9	18.9	3.2	35.7	60.0	3.6	0.7
	Mich.	0.0	0.0	100.0	43.1	51.0	4.6	1.3
Feb. 29	Va.	[b]	[b]	[b]	52.8	43.9	3.1	0.2
	Wash.	68.2	31.4	0.4	57.8	38.9	2.4	0.9
March 7	Calif.	81.2	18.2	0.6	60.6	34.7	4.0	0.7
	Conn.	55.4	41.5	3.1	46.8	48.7	3.3	1.2
	Ga.	83.8	16.2	0.0	66.9	27.8	4.6	0.7
	Maine	54.0	41.3	4.7	51.0	44.0	3.1	1.9
	Md.	67.3	28.5	4.2	56.2	36.2	6.7	0.9
	Mass.	59.9	37.3	2.8	31.8	64.7	2.5	1.0
	Mo.	64.6	33.6	1.8	57.9	35.3	5.7	1.1
	N.Y.	65.6	33.5	0.9	51.0	43.4	3.3	2.3
	Ohio	73.6	24.7	1.7	58.0	37.0	4.0	1.0
	R.I.	57.2	40.6	2.2	36.5	60.2	2.6	0.7
	Vt.	54.3	43.9	1.8	35.3	60.3	2.7	1.7
March 10	Colo.	71.4	23.3	5.3	64.7	27.1	6.6	1.6
	Utah	79.9	20.1	0.0	63.3	14.0	21.3	1.4
March 14	Fla.	81.8	18.2	0.0	73.8	19.9	4.6	1.7
	La.	73.6	19.9	6.5	83.6	8.9	5.7	1.8
	Miss.	89.6	8.6	1.8	87.9	5.4	5.6	1.1
	Okla.	68.7	25.4	5.9	79.1	10.4	9.3	1.2
	Tenn.	92.1	5.3	2.6	77.0	14.5	6.7	1.8

(Table continues)

Table 2-15 *(Continued)*

		Democrats			*Republicans*			
Date	*State*	Al Gore	Bill Bradley	Others[a]	George W. Bush	John McCain	Alan Keyes	Others[a]
	Texas	80.2	16.3	3.5	87.5	7.1	3.9	1.5
March 21	Ill.	84.3	14.2	1.5	67.4	21.5	9.0	2.1
April 3	Pa.	74.6	20.8	4.6	73.5	22.7	1.1	2.7
	Wis.	88.5	8.8	2.7	69.2	18.1	9.9	2.8
May 2	D.C.	95.9	0.0	4.1	72.8	24.4	—	2.8
	Ind.	74.9	21.9	3.2	81.2	18.8	0.0	0.0
	N.C.	70.4	18.3	11.3	78.6	10.9	7.9	2.6
May 9	Neb.	70.0	26.5	3.5	78.2	15.1	6.5	0.2
	W.Va.	72.0	18.4	9.6	79.6	12.9	4.8	2.7
May 16	Ore.	84.9	—	15.1	83.6	—	13.4	3.0
May 23	Ark.	78.5	0.0	21.5	80.2	0.0	19.8	0.0
	Idaho	75.7	0.0	24.3	73.5	0.0	19.1	7.4
	Ky.	71.3	14.7	14.0	83.0	6.3	4.7	6.0
June 6	Ala.	77.0	0.0	23.0	84.2	0.0	11.5	4.3
	Mont.	77.9	0.0	22.1	77.6	0.0	18.3	4.1
	N.J.	94.9	0.0	5.1	83.6	0.0	16.4	0.0
	N.M.	74.6	20.6	4.8	82.6	10.1	6.4	0.9
	S.D.	b	b	b	78.2	13.8	7.7	0.3

Source: Federal Campaign Commission, "Federal Elections 2000: Presidential Primary Election Results by State," www.fec.gov/pubrec/fe2000/2000presprim.htm.

Note: Entries may not total 100 percent due to rounding. "—" indicates candidate did not enter primary.

[a] Includes uncommitted voters.
[b] No Democratic primary was held.

Table 2-16 Leading Candidates in Presidential Primaries, 2004 (percent)

		Democrats				*Republicans*	
Date	*State*	John Kerry	John Edwards	Howard Dean	Others[a]	George W. Bush	Others[a]
Jan. 13	D.C.	—	—	42.6	57.4	[b]	[b]
Jan. 27	N.H.	38.4	12.1	26.3	23.2	79.8	20.2
Feb. 3	Ariz.	42.6	6.9	14.0	36.5	[b]	[b]
	Del.	50.4	11.0	10.4	28.2	[b]	[b]
	Mo.	50.6	24.6	8.7	16.1	95.1	4.9
	Okla.	26.8	29.5	4.2	39.5	90.0	10.0
	S.C.	29.8	45.1	4.8	20.3	[b]	[b]
Feb. 10	Tenn.	41.0	26.5	4.4	28.1	95.5	4.5
	Va.	51.5	26.6	7.0	14.9	[b]	[b]
Feb. 17	Wis.	39.6	34.3	18.2	7.9	99.1	0.9
Feb. 24	Utah	55.2	29.8	3.8	11.2	[b]	[b]
March 2	Calif.	64.4	19.8	4.2	11.6	100.0	0.0
	Conn.	58.3	23.7	4.0	14.0	[b]	[b]
	Ga.	46.8	41.4	1.8	10.0	100.0	0.0
	Md.	59.6	25.5	2.6	12.3	100.0	0.0
	Mass.	71.7	17.6	2.8	7.9	88.8	11.2
	N.Y.	61.2	20.1	2.9	15.8	[b]	[b]
	Ohio	51.8	34.1	2.5	11.6	100.0	0.0
	R.I.	71.2	18.6	4.0	6.2	84.9	15.1
	Vt.	31.6	6.2	53.6	8.6	96.7	3.3
March 9	Fla.	77.2	10.0	2.8	10.0	[b]	[b]
	La.	69.7	16.1	4.9	9.3	96.1	3.9
	Miss.	78.4	7.3	2.6	11.7	92.5	7.5
	Texas	67.1	14.3	4.8	13.8	100.0	0.0
March 16	Ill.	71.7	10.8	3.9	13.6	100.0	0.0

(Table continues)

Table 2-16 (*Continued*)

		Democrats				*Republicans*	
Date	*State*	John Kerry	John Edwards	Howard Dean	Others[a]	George W. Bush	Others[a]
April 27	Pa.	74.1	9.7	10.1	6.1	100.0	0.0
May 4	Ind.	72.8	11.2	6.8	9.2	100.0	0.0
May 11	Neb.	73.3	11.2	6.8	8.7	100.0	0.0
	W. Va.	69.2	13.4	4.2	13.2	100.0	0.0
May 18	Ariz.	66.6	—	—	33.4	97.1	2.9
	Ky.	60.1	14.5	3.6	21.8	92.5	7.5
	Ore.	78.6	—	—	21.4	94.9	5.1
May 25	Idaho	82.3	—	—	17.7	89.5	10.5
June 1	Ala.	75.0	—	—	25.0	92.8	7.2
	S.D.	82.3	0.0	5.7	12.0	b	b
June 6	N.M.	b	b	b	b	100.0	0.0
June 8	Mont.	68.0	9.1	0.0	22.9	94.4	5.6
	N.J.	92.3	0.0	0.0	7.7	100.0	0.0

Source: *Guide to U.S. Elections,* 5th ed. (Washington, D.C.: CQ Press, 2005), vol. I, 407–430.

Note: Entries may not total 100 percent due to rounding. "—" indicates candidate did not enter primary.

[a] Includes uncommitted voters.
[b] No primary was held.

Table 2-17 Leading Candidates in Presidential Primaries, 2008 (percent)

		Democrats				*Republicans*			
Date	*State*	Hillary Clinton	John Edwards	Barack Obama	Others[a]	Mike Huckabee	John McCain	Mitt Romney	Others[a]
Jan. 8	N.H.	39.1	16.9	36.5	7.5	11.2	37.1	31.6	20.0
Jan. 15	Mich.	55.3	0.0	0.0	44.7	16.1	29.7	38.9	15.3
Jan. 19, 26	S.C.	36.5	17.6	55.4	0.3	29.9	33.2	15.1	21.7
Jan. 29	Fla.	49.7	14.4	33.0	3.3	13.5	36.0	31.1	19.4
Feb. 5	Ala.	41.7	1.5	55.8	1.0	40.7	37.2	18.2	3.9
	Ariz.	50.5	5.3	42.1	2.1	9.0	47.4	34.1	9.4
	Ark.	69.7	1.9	26.6	1.9	60.3	20.4	13.6	5.8
	Calif.	51.9	4.0	42.5	1.7	11.5	42.1	34.4	12.0
	Ct.	46.6	1.0	50.7	1.7	7.0	52.1	33.0	7.9
	Del.	42.3	1.3	53.1	3.4	15.3	45.0	32.5	7.0
	Ga.	31.1	1.7	66.4	0.8	34.0	31.6	30.2	4.3
	Ill.	32.9	1.9	64.6	0.7	16.5	47.4	28.7	7.1
	Mass.	56.2	1.6	40.8	1.4	3.9	41.0	51.3	3.9
	Mo.	48.0	2.0	49.2	0.8	31.5	33.0	29.3	6.3
	N.J.	53.8	1.3	44.0	1.0	8.2	55.4	28.4	8.0
	N.Y.	57.4	1.1	39.9	1.6	10.8	51.2	27.8	10.2
	Okla.	54.8	10.2	31.2	3.8	33.1	36.8	24.9	5.4
	Tenn.	53.8	4.5	40.5	1.3	34.5	31.8	23.6	10.0
	Utah	39.2	2.8	56.6	1.4	2.9	5.4	89.6	0.7
	Dem. Abroad	33.0	0.0	67.0	0.0	b	b	b	b
Feb. 9	La.	35.6	3.4	57.4	3.6	43.2	41.9	6.3	8.6
Feb. 12	D.C.	24.0	0.3	75.2	0.6	16.6	67.7	6.0	9.7
	Md.	36.7	1.3	59.7	1.0	29.1	55.1	6.3	9.5
	Va.	35.4	0.5	63.6	0.4	40.7	50.1	3.6	5.6

(Table continues)

Table 2-17 (*Continued*)

		Democrats				*Republicans*			
Date	*State*	Hillary Clinton	John Edwards	Barack Obama	Others[a]	Mike Huckabee	John McCain	Mitt Romney	Others[a]
Feb. 19	Wis.	40.7	0.6	58.1	0.3	36.9	54.8	2.0	6.3
Feb. 24	P.R.	[b]	[b]	[b]	[b]	5.0	91.0	—	4.0
March 4	Ohio	54.3	1.7	44.0	0.0	30.6	59.9	3.3	6.1
	R.I.	58.5	0.6	40.4	0.6	21.6	64.8	4.4	9.2
	Texas	50.9	1.0	47.4	0.7	37.8	51.2	2.0	9.0
	Vt.	38.6	1.3	59.4	0.7	14.2	72.2	4.3	9.1
March 11	Miss.	37.0	0.9	60.8	1.2	12.5	78.9	1.5	7.1
April 22	Pa.	54.6	—	45.4	0.0	11.3	72.8	—	15.9
May 3	Guam	49.9	—	50.1	0.0	[b]	[b]	[b]	[b]
May 6	Ind.	50.7	—	49.3	0.0	10.0	77.6	4.8	7.7
	N.C.	41.5	—	56.2	2.2	12.1	73.6	[b]	14.3
May 13	W. Va.	67.0	7.3	25.7	0.0	10.3	76.0	4.4	9.2
May 20	Ky.	65.5	2.0	29.9	2.6	8.3	72.3	4.7	14.7
	Ore.	41.2	—	58.8	0.0	—	84.9	—	15.1
Feb. 24	P.R.	68.4	—	31.6	0.0	[b]	[b]	[b]	[b]
June 3	Mont.	41.2	—	56.4	2.3	[b]	[b]	[b]	[b]
	N.M.	[a]	[b]	[b]	[b]	—	86.0	—	14.0
	S.D.	55.3	—	44.7	0.0	7.1	70.1	3.2	19.5

Source: http://politics.nytimes.com/election-guide/2008/primaries/democraticprimaries/index.html.

Note: Entries may not total 100 percent due to rounding. "—" indicates candidate did not enter primary / South Carolina held its Republican primary Jan. 19; the Democratic primary was Jan. 26.

[a] Includes uncommitted voters.
[b] No primary was held.

Table 2-18 Content of Television News Coverage of Primary Campaigns, 1988–2004

Time period	*News content* Candidate character	Policy issues	Horse race[a]	*Total number of news stories*[b]
Preelection year				
1987	48%	19%	33%	258
1991	33	47	20	211
1995	14	44	42	485
Pre–New Hampshire				
Jan. 1–Feb. 16, 1988	38	22	39	238
Jan. 1–Feb. 17, 1992	35	43	22	190
Jan. 1–Feb. 11, 1996	18	42	40	192
Jan. 1–23, 2000	21	39	53	126
New Hampshire				
Feb. 16, 1988	22	7	70	108
Feb. 18, 1992	31	18	51	104
Feb. 19, 1996	33	25	42	98
Jan. 31, 2000	30	22	86	77
Super Tuesday				
March 8, 1988	23	18	58	130
March 10, 1992	17	22	62	76
March 11, 1996	13	18	70	48
March 6, 2000	25	24	95	127
Midwest				
March–May 1988	8	10	82	148
March–May 1992	40	21	40	54
March 1996	10	30	60	23
New York				
April 19, 1988	22	22	56	59
April 7, 1992	45	28	28	131
California				
June 7, 1988	15	43	41	123
June 2, 1992	31	39	30	273
March 26, 1996	12	52	36	34
Primary total				
1988	29	20	50	1,064
1992	33	36	31	1,039
1996	16	39	45	1,019
2000	N/A	22	78	550
2004	N/A	18	77	356

Sources: (1987–1988) Adapted from Harold Stanley and Richard Niemi, *Vital Statistics on American Politics,* 3d ed. (Washington, D.C.: CQ Press, 1992), 63; (1991–1992) adapted from Stanley and Niemi, *Vital Statistics on American Politics,* 4th ed. (Washington, D.C.: CQ Press, 1994), 63; (1995–1996) adapted from Stanley and Niemi, *Vital Statistics on American Politics, 1997–1998* (Washington, D.C.: CQ Press, 1998), 175; (2000, 2004) adapted from Stanley and Niemi, *Vital Statistics on American Politics, 2005–2006* (Washington, D.C.: CQ Press, 2006),

(Table continues)

Table 2-18 *(Continued)*

Note: Data are derived from content analysis conducted by the Center for Media and Public Affairs of the ABC, CBS, and NBC evening news broadcasts. For 2000, data not available for preelection year, Midwest, New York, and California. For 2004, only summary data available. N/A—not available.

[a] News stories in which focus was on who was leading—or trailing—in the polls.
[b] The count is news statements, not stories. More than one statement can be found in a story.

Table 2-19 Positive Television News Coverage of Presidential Candidates, 2000 Primaries

Party/candidate	*1999 (1/1–12/31)*	*Pre-Iowa*	*New Hampshire*	*South Carolina*	*Michigan*	*Super Tuesday (3/3–3/9)*
Democrats						
Al Gore	61	48	28	38	[a]	40
Bill Bradley	52	68	42	65	[a]	57
Republicans						
George W. Bush	61	48	54	50	41	44
Elizabeth Dole	76	—	—	—	—	—
Malcolm Forbes	67	[a]	[a]	[a]	—	—
John McCain	60	[a]	58	55	60	48

Source: Harold Stanley and Richard Niemi, *Vital Statistics on American Politics, 2001–2002* (Washington, D.C.: CQ Press, 2001), 190.

Note: Entries are the percentage of positive television news stories calculated from the total of all clearly positive and negative stories aired on the ABC, CBS, and NBC evening news broadcasts. Based on content analysis conducted by the Center for Media and Public Affairs. "Horse race" assessments are excluded. "—" indicates no stories.

[a] Fewer than ten assessments made.

Table 2-20 Positive Television News Coverage of Presidential Candidates, 2004 Primaries (percent)

Party/candidate	*Nomination (1/1–3/1)*	*Pre-conventions (3/2–7/25)*
Democrats		
John Kerry	36	15
John Edwards	39	29
Howard Dean	21	6
Ramsey Clark	24	[a]
Republican		
George W. Bush	12	8
Independent		
Ralph Nader	7	6

Source: Harold Stanley and Richard Niemi, *Vital Statistics on American Politics, 2005–2006* (Washington, D.C.: CQ Press, 2006), 184.

Note: Entries are the percentage of positive television news stories calculated from the total of all clearly positive and negative stories aired on the ABC, CBS, and NBC evening news broadcasts. Based on a content analysis conducted by the Center for Media and Public Affairs.

[a] Fewer than fifteen assessments made.

Table 2-21 Television Coverage and Viewership of National Party Conventions, 1952–2004

Year/party	*Audience rating*[a]	*Average hours viewed by household*	*Network hours telecast*[b]
1952			
Republicans	N/A	10.5	57.5
Democrats	N/A	13.1	61.1
1956			
Republicans	N/A	6.4	22.8
Democrats	N/A	8.4	37.6
1960			
Republicans	N/A	6.2	25.5
Democrats	N/A	8.3	29.3
1964			
Republicans	N/A	7.0	36.5
Democrats	N/A	6.4	23.5
1968			
Republicans	28.5%	6.5	34.0
Democrats	26.4	8.5	39.1
1972			
Republicans	18.3	3.5	19.8
Democrats	23.4	5.8	36.7
1976			
Republicans	25.2	6.3	29.5
Democrats	31.5	5.2	30.4
1980			
Republicans	27.0	3.8	22.7
Democrats	21.6	4.4	24.1
1984			
Republicans	23.4	1.9	11.9
Democrats	19.2	2.5	12.9
1988			
Republicans	19.8	2.2	12.6
Democrats	18.3	2.3	12.8
1992			
Republicans	22.0	N/A	7.3
Democrats	20.5	N/A	8.0
1996			
Republicans	16.7	N/A	5.0
Democrats	17.2	N/A	4.5
2000			
Republicans	13.9	N/A	5.2
Democrats	15.3	N/A	5.3
2004			
Republicans	15.3	N/A	3.0
Democrats	14.3	N/A	3.0

Source: Harold Stanley and Richard Niemi, *Vital Statistics on American Politics, 2007–2008* (Washington, D.C.: CQ Press, 2008), 199.

Note: N/A—not available.

Table 2-21 (*Continued*)

---

[a] Percentage of television households viewing the convention during an average minute. Through 1988, based on viewing of ABC, CBS, and NBC; for 1992 and 1996, based on viewing the three networks plus PBS and CNN; for 2000, the three networks plus PBS, CNN, Fox News, and MSNBC; for 2004, the three networks plus CNN, Fox News, and MSNBC.
[b] Number of hours during which one or more of ABC, CBS, or NBC was broadcasting the convention.

Table 2-22 Profile of National Party Convention Delegates, 1968–2004 (percent)

	1968		*1972*		*1976*		*1980*		*1984*		*1988*		*1992*		*1996*		*2000*		*2004*	
	D	*R*	*D*	*R*	*D*	*R*	*D*	*R*	*D*	*R*	*D*	*R*	*D*	*R*	*D*	*R*	*D*	*R*	*D*	*R*
Women	13	16	40	29	33	31	49	29	49	44	48	33	50	43	53	46	48	35	50	43
Black	5	2	15	4	11	3	15	3	18	4	23	4	18	5	17	3	19	4	18	6
Under thirty	3	4	22	8	15	7	11	5	8	4	4	3	5	N/A	6	2	4	3	7	4
Lawyer	28	22	12	N/A	16	15	13	15	17	14	16	17	12	N/A	10	11	9	9	N/A	N/A
Teacher	8	2	11	N/A	12	4	15	4	16	6	14	5	9	N/A	9	2	7	N/A	N/A	N/A
Union member	N/A	N/A	16	N/A	21	3	27	4	25	4	25	3	28	N/A	24	4	31	4	25	3
Attending first convention	67	66	83	78	80	78	87	84	78	69	65	68	62	N/A	61	56	51	54	57	55
Protestant	N/A	N/A	42	N/A	47	73	47	72	49	71	50	69	49	N/A	47	62	47	63	43	65
Catholic	N/A	N/A	26	N/A	34	18	37	22	29	22	30	22	31	N/A	30	25	31	27	32	26
Jewish	N/A	N/A	9	N/A	9	3	8	3	8	2	7	2	9	N/A	6	3	8	2	8	2
Liberal	N/A	N/A	N/A	N/A	40	3	46	2	48	1	43	0	47	1	43	0	36	1	41	1
Moderate	N/A	N/A	N/A	N/A	47	45	42	36	42	35	43	35	44	32	48	27	56	34	52	33
Conservative	N/A	N/A	N/A	N/A	8	48	6	58	4	60	5	58	5	63	5	70	5	63	3	63
Median age	49	49	42	N/A	43	48	44	49	43	51	46	51	46	N/A	N/A	521	51	53	N/A	N/A

Source: Harold Stanley and Richard Niemi, *Vital Statistics on American Politics, 2007–2008* (Washington, D.C.: CQ Press, 2008), 80.

Note: D—Democrat; R—Republican; N/A—not available.

Table 2-23 The 1968 National Political Party Conventions

	Democratic first ballot[a]					Republican first ballot[b]			
State	Total votes	Hubert Humphrey	Eugene McCarthy	George McGovern	Channing Phillips	Total votes	Richard Nixon	Nelson Rockefeller	Ronald Reagan
Alabama	32	23.0	0.0	0.0	0.0	26	14	0	12
Alaska	22	17.0	2.0	3.0	0.0	12	11	1	0
Arizona	19	14.5	2.5	2.0	0.0	16	16	0	0
Arkansas	33	30.0	2.0	0.0	0.0	18	0	0	0
California	174	14.0	91.0	51.0	17.0	86	0	0	86
Colorado	35	16.5	10.0	5.5	3.0	18	14	3	1
Connecticut	44	35.0	8.0	0.0	1.0	16	4	12	0
Delaware	22	21.0	0.0	0.0	0.0	12	9	3	0
Florida	63	58.0	5.0	0.0	0.0	34	32	1	1
Georgia	43	19.5	13.5	1.0	3.0	30	21	2	7
Hawaii	26	26.0	0.0	0.0	0.0	14	0	0	0
Idaho	25	21.0	3.5	0.5	0.0	14	9	0	5
Illinois	118	112.0	3.0	3.0	0.0	58	50	5	3
Indiana	63	49.0	11.0	2.0	1.0	26	26	0	0
Iowa	46	18.5	19.5	5.0	0.0	24	13	8	3
Kansas	38	34.0	1.0	3.0	0.0	20	0	0	0
Kentucky	46	41.0	5.0	0.0	0.0	24	22	2	0
Louisiana	36	35.0	0.0	0.0	0.0	26	19	0	7
Maine	27	23.0	4.0	0.0	0.0	14	7	7	0
Maryland	49	45.0	2.0	2.0	0.0	26	18	8	0
Massachusetts	72	2.0	70.0	0.0	0.0	34	0	34	0
Michigan	96	72.5	9.5	7.5	6.5	48	4	0	0
Minnesota	52	38.0	11.5	0.0	2.5	26	9	15	0
Mississippi	24	9.5	6.5	4.0	2.0	20	20	0	0
Missouri	60	56.0	3.5	0.0	0.5	24	16	5	3

(*Table continues*)

Table 2-23 (*Continued*)

	Democratic first ballot[a]					Republican first ballot[b]			
State	Total votes	Hubert Humphrey	Eugene McCarthy	George McGovern	Channing Phillips	Total votes	Richard Nixon	Nelson Rockefeller	Ronald Reagan
Montana	26	23.5	2.5	0.0	0.0	14	11	0	3
Nebraska	30	15.0	6.0	9.0	0.0	16	16	0	0
Nevada	22	18.5	2.5	1.0	0.0	12	9	3	0
New Hampshire	26	6.0	20.0	0.0	0.0	8	8	0	0
New Jersey	82	62.0	19.0	0.0	1.0	40	18	0	0
New Mexico	26	15.0	11.0	0.0	0.0	14	8	1	5
New York	190	96.5	87.0	1.5	2.0	92	4	88	0
North Carolina	59	44.5	2.0	0.5	0.0	26	9	1	16
North Dakota	25	18.0	7.0	0.0	0.0	8	5	2	1
Ohio	115	94.0	18.0	2.0	0.0	58	2	0	0
Oklahoma	41	37.5	2.5	0.5	0.5	22	14	1	7
Oregon	35	0.0	35.0	0.0	0.0	18	18	0	0
Pennsylvania	130	103.8	21.5	2.5	1.5	64	22	41	1
Rhode Island	27	23.5	2.5	0.0	0.0	14	0	14	0
South Carolina	28	28.0	0.0	0.0	0.0	22	22	0	0
South Dakota	26	2.0	0.0	24.0	0.0	14	14	0	0
Tennessee	51	49.5	0.5	1.0	0.0	28	28	0	0
Texas	104	100.5	2.5	0.0	1.0	56	41	0	15
Utah	26	23.0	2.0	0.0	1.0	8	2	0	0
Vermont	22	8.0	6.0	7.0	0.0	12	9	3	0
Virginia	54	42.5	5.5	0.0	2.0	24	22	2	0
Washington	47	32.5	8.5	6.0	0.0	24	15	3	6
West Virginia	38	34.0	3.0	0.0	0.0	14	11	3	0
Wisconsin	59	8.0	49.0	1.0	1.0	30	30	0	0
Wyoming	22	18.5	3.5	0.0	0.0	12	12	0	0

Canal Zone[c]	5	4.0	0.0	1.0	0.0	0	0	0	0
District of Columbia	23	2.0	0.0	0.0	21.0	9	6	3	0
Guam	5	5.0	0.0	0.0	0.0	0	0	0	0
Puerto Rico	8	8.0	0.0	0.0	0.0	5	0	5	0
Virgin Islands	5	5.0	0.0	0.0	0.0	3	2	1	0
Total[d]	2,622	1,759.25	601.0	146.5	67.5	1,333	692	277	182

Source: Adapted from *Guide to U.S. Elections,* 5th ed. (Washington, D.C.: Congressional Quarterly, 2005), vol. I, 650–651.

[a] Other candidates: Dan K. Moore, 17.5 (12 in North Carolina, 3 in Virginia, 2 in Georgia, 0.5 in Alabama); Edward M. Kennedy, 12.75 (proceedings record, 12.5) (3.5 in Alabama, 3 in Iowa, 3 in New York, 1 in Ohio, 1 in West Virginia, 0.75 in Pennsylvania, 0.5 in Georgia); Paul Bryant, 1.5 (Alabama); George Wallace, 0.5 (Alabama); James H. Gray, 0.5 (Georgia). Not voting, 15 (3 in Alabama, 3 in Georgia, 2 in Mississippi, 1 in Arkansas, 1 in California, 1 in Delaware, 1 in Louisiana, 1 in Rhode Island, 1 in Vermont, 1 in Virginia).
[b] Other candidates: James A. Rhodes, 55 (Ohio); George Romney, 50 (44 in Michigan, 6 in Utah); Clifford P. Case, 22 (New Jersey); Frank Carlson, 20 (Kansas); Winthrop Rockefeller, 18 (Arkansas); Hiram L. Fong, 14 (Hawaii); Harold Stassen, 2 (1 in Minnesota, 1 in Ohio); John V. Lindsay, 11 (Minnesota).
[c] There were no Republican delegates from the Canal Zone.
[d] Democrats assign fractions of delegates to candidates; Republicans do not.

Table 2-24 The 1972 National Political Party Conventions

	Democratic first ballot[a]						Republican first ballot		
State	Total votes	George McGovern	Jesse Jackson	George Wallace	Shirley Chisholm	Terry Sanford	Total votes	Richard Nixon	Paul McCloskey
Alabama	37	9.00	1.00	24.0	0.00	1.0	18	18	0
Alaska	10	6.50	3.25	0.0	0.00	0.0	12	12	0
Arizona	25	21.00	3.00	0.0	0.00	1.0	18	18	0
Arkansas	27	1.00	1.00	0.0	0.00	0.0	18	18	0
California	271	0.00	0.00	0.0	0.00	0.0	96	96	0
Colorado	36	27.00	0.00	0.0	7.00	0.0	20	20	0
Connecticut	51	30.00	20.00	0.0	0.00	1.0	22	22	0
Delaware	13	5.85	6.50	0.0	0.65	0.0	12	12	0
Florida	81	2.00	0.00	75.0	2.00	0.0	40	40	0
Georgia	53	14.50	14.50	11.0	12.00	1.0	24	24	0
Hawaii	17	6.50	8.50	0.0	1.00	0.0	14	14	0
Idaho	17	12.50	2.50	0.0	2.00	0.0	14	14	0
Illinois	170	119.00	30.50	0.5	4.50	2.0	58	58	0
Indiana	76	26.00	20.00	26.0	1.00	0.0	32	32	0
Iowa	46	35.00	0.00	0.0	3.00	4.0	22	22	0
Kansas	35	20.00	10.00	0.0	2.00	1.0	20	20	0
Kentucky	47	10.00	35.00	0.0	0.00	2.0	24	24	0
Louisiana	44	10.25	10.25	3.0	18.50	2.0	20	20	0
Maine	20	5.00	0.00	0.0	0.00	0.0	8	8	0
Maryland	53	13.00	0.00	38.0	2.00	0.0	26	26	0
Massachusetts	102	102.00	0.00	0.0	0.00	0.0	34	34	0
Michigan	132	50.50	7.00	67.0	3.00	1.0	48	48	0
Minnesota	64	11.00	0.00	0.0	6.00	0.0	26	26	0
Mississippi	25	10.00	0.00	0.0	12.00	3.0	14	14	0
Missouri	73	24.50	48.50	0.0	0.00	0.0	30	30	0
Montana	17	16.00	0.00	0.0	1.00	0.0	14	14	0
Nebraska	24	21.00	3.00	0.0	0.00	0.0	16	16	0
Nevada	11	5.75	5.25	0.0	0.00	0.0	12	12	0

New Hampshire	18	10.80	5.40	0.0	0.00	0.0	14	14	0
New Jersey	109	89.00	11.50	0.0	4.00	1.5	40	40	0
New Mexico	18	10.00	0.00	8.0	0.00	0.0	14	13	1
New York	278	263.00	9.00	0.0	6.00	0.0	88	88	0
North Carolina	64	0.00	0.00	37.0	0.00	27.0	32	32	0
North Dakota	14	8.40	2.80	0.7	0.70	0.0	12	12	0
Ohio	153	77.00	39.00	0.0	23.00	3.0	56	56	0
Oklahoma	39	10.50	23.50	0.0	1.00	4.0	22	22	0
Oregon	34	34.00	0.00	0.0	0.00	0.0	18	18	0
Pennsylvania	182	81.00	86.50	2.0	9.50	1.0	60	60	0
Rhode Island	22	22.00	0.00	0.0	0.00	0.0	8	8	0
South Carolina	32	6.00	10.00	6.0	4.00	6.0	22	22	0
South Dakota	17	17.00	0.00	0.0	0.00	0.0	14	14	0
Tennessee	49	0.00	0.00	33.0	10.00	0.0	26	26	0
Texas	130	54.00	23.00	48.0	4.00	0.0	52	52	0
Utah	19	14.00	1.00	0.0	0.00	3.0	14	14	0
Vermont	12	12.00	0.00	0.0	0.00	0.0	12	12	0
Virginia	53	33.50	4.00	1.0	5.50	9.0	30	30	0
Washington	52	0.00	52.00	0.0	0.00	0.0	24	24	0
West Virginia	35	16.00	14.00	1.0	0.00	4.0	18	18	0
Wisconsin	67	55.00	3.00	0.0	5.00	0.0	28	28	0
Wyoming	11	3.30	6.05	0.0	1.10	0.0	12	12	0
Canal Zone	3	3.00	0.00	0.0	0.00	0.0	[b]	[b]	[b]
District of Columbia	15	13.50	1.50	0.0	0.00	0.0	9	9	0
Guam	3	1.50	1.50	0.0	0.00	0.0	3	3	0
Puerto Rico	7	7.00	0.00	0.0	0.00	0.0	5	5	0
Virgin Islands	3	1.00	1.50	0.0	0.50	0.0	3	3	0
Total[c]	3,016	1,728.35	525.00	381.7	151.95	77.5	1,348	1,347	1

Source: Adapted from *Guide to U.S. Elections*, 5th ed. (Washington, D.C.: Congressional Quarterly, 2005), vol. I, 651–654.

[a] Other candidates: Humphrey, 66.7 (46 in Minnesota, 4 in Ohio, 4 in Wisconsin, 3 in Michigan, 2 in Indiana, 2 in Pennsylvania, 2 in Florida, 1 in Utah, 1 in Colorado, 1 in Hawaii, 0.7 in North Dakota); Mills, 33.8 (25 in Arkansas, 3 in Illinois, 3 in New Jersey, 2 in Alabama, 0.55 in Wyoming, 0.25 in Alaska); Muskie, 24.3 (15 in Maine, 5.5 in Illinois, 1.8 in New Hampshire, 1 in Texas, 1 in Colorado); Kennedy, 12.7 (4 in Iowa, 3 in Illinois, 2 in Ohio, 1 in Kansas, 1 in Indiana, 1 in Tennessee, 0.7 in North Dakota); Hays, 5 (Ohio); McCarthy, 2 (Illinois); Mondale, 1 (Kansas); Clark, 1 (Minnesota); not voting, 5 (Tennessee).

[b] There were no Republican delegates from the Canal Zone.

[c] Democrats assign fractions of delegates to candidates; Republicans do not.

Table 2-25 The 1976 National Political Party Conventions

	Democratic first ballot						Republican first ballot		
State	Total votes	Jimmy Carter	Morris Udall	Jerry Brown	Ellen McCormack	Others[a]	Total votes	Gerald Ford	Ronald Reagan
Alabama	35	30.0	0.0	0.0	0	5.0	37	0	37
Alaska	10	10.0	0.0	0.0	0	0.0	19	17	2
Arizona	25	6.0	19.0	0.0	0	0.0	29	2	27
Arkansas	26	25.0	1.0	0.0	0	0.0	27	10	17
California	280	73.0	2.0	205.0	0	0.0	167	0	167
Colorado	35	15.0	6.0	11.0	0	3.0	31	5	26
Connecticut	51	35.0	16.0	0.0	0	0.0	35	35	0
Delaware	12	10.5	0.0	1.5	0	0.0	17	15	2
Florida	81	70.0	0.0	1.0	0	10.0	66	43	23
Georgia	50	50.0	0.0	0.0	0	0.0	48	0	48
Hawaii	17	17.0	0.0	0.0	0	0.0	19	18	1
Idaho	16	16.0	0.0	0.0	0	0.0	21	4	17
Illinois	169	164.0	1.0	2.0	1	1.0	101	86	14
Indiana	75	72.0	0.0	0.0	0	3.0	54	9	45
Iowa	47	25.0	20.0	1.0	0	1.0	36	19	17
Kansas	34	32.0	2.0	0.0	0	0.0	34	30	4
Kentucky	46	39.0	2.0	0.0	0	5.0	37	19	18
Louisiana	41	18.0	0.0	18.0	0	5.0	41	5	36
Maine	20	15.0	5.0	0.0	0	0.0	20	15	5
Maryland	53	44.0	6.0	3.0	0	0.0	43	43	0
Massachusetts[b]	104	65.0	21.0	0.0	2	16.0	43	28	15
Michigan	133	75.0	58.0	0.0	0	0.0	84	55	29
Minnesota	65	37.0	2.0	1.0	11	14.0	42	32	10
Mississippi[c]	24	23.0	0.0	0.0	0	0.0	30	16	14
Missouri	71	58.0	4.0	2.0	7	0.0	49	18	31
Montana	17	11.0	2.0	0.0	0	4.0	20	0	20
Nebraska	23	20.0	0.0	3.0	0	0.0	25	7	18
Nevada	11	3.0	0.0	6.5	0	1.5	18	5	13
New Hampshire	17	15.0	2.0	0.0	0	0.0	21	18	3
New Jersey	108	108.0	0.0	0.0	0	0.0	67	63	4
New Mexico	18	14.0	4.0	0.0	0	0.0	21	0	21
New York	274	209.5	56.5	4.0	0	4.0	154	133	20

North Carolina[d]	61	56.0	0.0	0.0	0	3.0	54	25	29
North Dakota	13	13.0	0.0	0.0	0	0.0	18	11	7
Ohio	152	132.0	20.0	0.0	0	0.0	97	91	6
Oklahoma	37	32.0	1.0	0.0	0	4.0	36	0	36
Oregon	34	16.0	0.0	10.0	0	8.0	30	16	14
Pennsylvania	178	151.0	21.0	6.0	0	0.0	103	93	10
Rhode Island	22	14.0	0.0	8.0	0	0.0	19	19	0
South Carolina	31	28.0	0.0	1.0	0	2.0	36	9	27
South Dakota	17	11.0	5.0	0.0	0	1.0	20	9	11
Tennessee	46	45.0	0.0	0.0	0	1.0	43	21	22
Texas	130	124.0	0.0	4.0	0	2.0	100	0	100
Utah	18	10.0	0.0	5.0	0	3.0	20	0	20
Vermont	12	5.0	4.0	3.0	0	0.0	18	18	0
Virginia	54	48.0	6.0	0.0	0	0.0	51	16	35
Washington	53	36.0	11.0	3.0	0	3.0	38	7	31
West Virginia	33	30.0	1.0	0.0	0	2.0	28	20	8
Wisconsin	68	29.0	25.0	0.0	1	13.0	45	45	0
Wyoming	10	8.0	1.0	1.0	0	0.0	17	7	10
Canal Zone	3	3.0	0.0	0.0	0	0.0	[e]	[e]	[e]
Democrats Abroad	3	2.5	0.0	0.5	0	0.0	0	0	0
District of Columbia	17	12.0	5.0	0.0	0	0.0	14	14	0
Guam	3	3.0	0.0	0.0	0	0.0	4	4	0
Puerto Rico	22	22.0	0.0	0.0	0	0.0	8	8	0
Virgin Islands	3	3.0	0.0	0.0	0	0.0	4	4	0
Total[f]	3,008	2,238.5	329.5	300.5	22	114.5	2,259	1,187	1,070

Source: Adapted from *Guide to U.S. Elections,* 5th ed. (Washington, D.C.: Congressional Quarterly, 2005), vol. I, 655–656.

[a] Other votes: George Wallace, 57 (Alabama 5, Florida 10, Illinois 1, Indiana 3, Kentucky 5, Louisiana 5, Massachusetts 11, North Carolina 3, South Carolina 2, Tennessee 1, Texas 1, Wisconsin 10); Frank Church, 19 (Colorado 3, Montana 4, Nevada 1, Oregon 8, Utah 1, Washington 2); Hubert Humphrey, 10 (Minnesota 9, South Dakota 1); Henry M. Jackson, 10 (Massachusetts 2, New York 4, Washington 1, Wisconsin 3); Fred Harris, 9 (Massachusetts 2, Minnesota 4, Oklahoma 3); Milton J. Shapp, 2 (Massachusetts 1, Utah 1). Receiving one vote each: Robert C. Byrd (West Virginia); Cesar Chavez (Utah); Leon Jaworski (Texas); Barbara C. Jordan (Oklahoma); Edward M. Kennedy (Iowa); Jennings Randolph (West Virginia); Fred Stover (Minnesota). In addition, a Nevada delegate cast one-half vote for nobody.

[b] Massachusetts passed when it was first called and cast its vote at the end of the ballot.

[c] One abstention.

[d] Two abstentions.

[e] There were no Republican delegates from the Canal Zone.

[f] Democrats assign fractions of delegates to candidates; Republicans do not. The Republican total also includes 1 vote for Elliot Richardson (New York) and one not voting (Illinois).

Table 2-26 The 1980 National Political Party Conventions

	Democratic first ballot[a]				Republican first ballot				
State	Total votes	Jimmy Carter	Edward Kennedy	Other[b]	Total votes	Ronald Reagan	John Anderson	George H. W. Bush	Other
Alabama	45	43.0	2.0	0.0	27	27	0	0	0
Alaska	11	8.4	2.6	0.0	19	19	0	0	0
Arizona	29	13.0	16.0	0.0	28	28	0	0	0
Arkansas	33	25.0	6.0	2.0	19	19	0	0	0
California	306	140.0	166.0	0.0	168	168	0	0	0
Colorado	40	27.0	10.0	3.0	31	31	0	0	0
Connecticut	54	26.0	28.0	0.0	35	35	0	0	0
Delaware	14	10.0	4.0	0.0	12	12	0	0	0
Florida	100	75.0	25.0	0.0	51	51	0	0	0
Georgia	63	62.0	0.0	0.0	36	36	0	0	0
Hawaii	19	16.0	2.0	0.0	14	14	0	0	0
Idaho	17	9.0	7.0	1.0	21	21	0	0	0
Illinois	179	163.0	16.0	0.0	102	81	21	0	0
Indiana	80	53.0	27.0	0.0	54	54	0	0	0
Iowa	50	31.0	17.0	2.0	37	37	0	0	0
Kansas	37	23.0	14.0	0.0	32	32	0	0	0
Kentucky	50	45.0	5.0	0.0	27	27	0	0	0
Louisiana	51	50.0	1.0	0.0	31	31	0	0	0
Maine	22	11.0	11.0	0.0	21	21	0	0	0
Maryland	59	34.0	24.0	1.0	30	30	0	0	0
Massachusetts	111	34.0	77.0	0.0	42	33	9	0	0
Michigan	141	102.0	38.0	0.0	82	67	0	13	1[c]
Minnesota	75	41.0	14.0	20.0	34	33	0	0	1
Mississippi	32	32.0	0.0	0.0	22	22	0	0	0
Missouri	77	58.0	19.0	0.0	37	37	0	0	0
Montana	19	13.0	6.0	0.0	20	20	0	0	0
Nebraska	24	14.0	10.0	0.0	25	25	0	0	0
Nevada	12	8.1	3.9	0.0	17	17	0	0	0

New Hampshire	19	10.0	9.0	0.0	22	22	0	0	0
New Jersey	113	45.0	68.0	0.0	66	66	0	0	0
New Mexico	20	10.0	10.0	0.0	22	22	0	0	0
New York	282	129.0	151.0	2.0	123	121	0	0	0
North Carolina	69	66.0	3.0	0.0	40	40	0	0	0
North Dakota	14	5.0	7.0	2.0	17	17	0	0	0
Ohio	161	89.0	72.0	0.0	77	77	0	0	0
Oklahoma	42	36.0	3.0	2.0	34	34	0	0	0
Oregon	39	26.0	13.0	0.0	29	29	0	0	0
Pennsylvania	185	95.0	90.0	0.0	83	83	0	0	0
Rhode Island	23	6.0	17.0	0.0	13	13	0	0	0
South Carolina	37	37.0	0.0	0.0	25	25	0	0	0
South Dakota	19	9.0	10.0	0.0	22	22	0	0	0
Tennessee	55	51.0	4.0	0.0	32	32	0	0	0
Texas	152	108.0	38.0	5.0	80	80	0	0	0
Utah	20	11.0	4.0	5.0	21	21	0	0	0
Vermont	12	5.0	7.0	0.0	19	19	0	0	0
Virginia	64	59.0	5.0	0.0	51	51	0	0	0
Washington	58	36.0	22.0	0.0	37	36	1	0	0
West Virginia	35	21.0	10.0	2.0	18	18	0	0	0
Wisconsin	75	48.0	26.0	1.0	34	28	6	0	0
Wyoming	11	8.0	3.0	0.0	19	19	0	0	0
Democrats Abroad	4	1.5	2.0	0.5	—	—	—	—	—
District of Columbia	19	12.0	5.0	0.0	14	14	0	0	0
Guam	4	4.0	0.0	0.0	4	4	0	0	0
Puerto Rico	41	21.0	20.0	0.0	14	14	0	0	0
Virgin Islands	4	4.0	0.0	0.0	4	4	0	0	0
Total[d]	3,331	2,123.0	1,150.5	48.5	1,994	1,939	37	13	1

Source: Adapted from *Guide to U.S. Elections*, 5th ed. (Washington, D.C.: Congressional Quarterly, 2005), vol. I, 657–658.

[a] Other votes: uncommitted, 10 (3 in Texas, 2 in Colorado, 2 in North Dakota, 1 in Arkansas, 1 in Maryland, and 1 in Idaho); William Proxmire, 10 (Minnesota); Scott M. Matheson 5 (Utah); Koryne Horbal, 5 (Minnesota); Ronald V. Dellums, 2.5 (2 in New York, 0.5 from Democrats Abroad). Receiving 2 votes each were: John C. Culver (Iowa); Warren Spannaus (Minnesota); Alice Tripp (Minnesota); Kent Hance (Texas); Robert C. Byrd (West Virginia). Receiving 1 vote each

(*Table continues*)

Table 2-26 *(Continued)*

were: Dale Bumpers (Arkansas); Edmund S. Muskie (Colorado); Walter F. Mondale (Minnesota); Hugh L. Carey (Oklahoma); Tom Steed (Oklahoma); Edmund G. Brown, Jr. (Wisconsin). Also 5 not voting and 4 absent.

[b] At the conclusion of the roll call, Delaware switched to 14 for Carter and none for Kennedy. Iowa switched to 33 for Carter and 17 for Kennedy. Totals after switches: Carter, 2,129; Kennedy, 1,146.5. The votes received by other candidates did not change. After the switches, Carter was nominated by acclamation following a motion to that effect by the Massachusetts delegation.

[c] One vote for Anne Armstrong. Four not voting.

[d] Democrats assign fractions of delegates to candidates; Republicans do not.

Table 2-27 The 1984 National Political Party Conventions

	Democratic first ballot						
State	Total votes	Walter Mondale	Gary Hart	Jesse Jackson	Others[a]	Abstained[b]	*Republican first ballot: Ronald Reagan (total)*
Alabama	62	39	13.0	9.0	1	0	38
Alaska	14	9	4.0	1.0	0	0	18
Arizona	40	20	16.0	2.0	0	2	32
Arkansas	42	26	9.0	7.0	0	0	29
California	345	95	190.0	33.0	0	27	176
Colorado	51	1	42.0	1.0	0	7	35
Connecticut	60	23	36.0	1.0	0	0	35
Delaware	18	13	5.0	0.0	0	0	19
Florida	143	82	55.0	3.0	0	2	82
Georgia	84	40	24.0	20.0	0	0	37
Hawaii	27	27	0.0	0.0	0	0	14
Idaho	22	10	12.0	0.0	0	0	21
Illinois	194	114	41.0	39.0	0	0	92
Indiana	88	42	38.0	8.0	0	0	52
Iowa	58	37	18.0	2.0	1	0	37
Kansas	44	25	16.0	3.0	0	0	32
Kentucky	63	51	5.0	7.0	0	0	37
Louisiana	69	26	19.0	24.0	0	0	41
Maine	27	13	13.0	0.0	1	0	20
Maryland	74	54	3.0	17.0	0	0	31
Massachusetts	116	59	49.0	5.0	3	0	52
Michigan	155	96	49.0	10.0	0	0	77
Minnesota	86	63	3.0	4.0	16	0	32
Mississippi	43	26	4.0	13.0	0	0	30
Missouri	86	55	14.0	16.0	0	0	47
Montana	25	11	13.0	1.0	0	0	20

(*Table continues*)

Table 2-27 (*Continued*)

	Democratic first ballot						
State	Total votes	Walter Mondale	Gary Hart	Jesse Jackson	Others[a]	Abstained[b]	*Republican first ballot: Ronald Reagan (total)*
Nebraska	30	12	17.0	1.0	0	0	24
Nevada	20	9	10.0	1.0	0	0	22
New Hampshire	22	12	10.0	0.0	0	0	22
New Jersey	122	115	0.0	7.0	0	0	64
New Mexico	28	13	13.0	2.0	0	0	24
New York	285	156	75.0	52.0	0	0	136
North Carolina	88	53	19.0	16.0	0	0	53
North Dakota	18	10	5.0	1.0	2	0	18
Ohio	175	84	80.0	11.0	0	0	89
Oklahoma	53	24	26.0	3.0	0	0	35
Oregon	50	16	31.0	2.0	0	0	32
Pennsylvania	195	177	0.0	18.0	0	0	97
Rhode Island	27	14	12.0	0.0	0	0	14
South Carolina	48	16	13.0	19.0	0	0	35
South Dakota	19	9	10.0	0.0	0	0	19
Tennessee	76	39	20.0	17.0	0	0	46
Texas	200	119	40.0	36.0	2	0	109
Utah	27	8	19.0	0.0	0	0	26
Vermont	17	5	8.0	3.0	0	1	19
Virginia	78	34	18.0	25.0	0	0	50
Washington	70	31	36.0	3.0	0	0	44
West Virginia	44	30	14.0	0.0	0	0	19
Wisconsin	89	58	25.0	6.0	0	0	46
Wyoming	15	7	7.0	0.0	0	1	18
American Samoa[c]	6	6	0.0	0.0	0	0	—
Democrats Abroad	5	3	1.5	0.5	0	0	—
District of Columbia	19	5	0.0	14.0	0	0	14
Guam	7	7	0.0	0.0	0	0	4

Latin America[c]	5	5	0.0	0.0	0	0	—
Puerto Rico	53	53	0.0	0.0	0	0	14
Virgin Islands	6	4	0.0	2.0	0	0	4
Total[d]	3,923	2,191	1,200.5	465.5	26	40	2,235

Source: Adapted from *Guide to U.S. Elections*, 5th ed. (Washington, D.C.: Congressional Quarterly, 2005), vol. I, 659–660.

[a] Other votes: Alabama, 1 for Martha Kirkland; Iowa, 1 for George McGovern; Maine, 1 for Joseph R. Biden, Jr.; Massachusetts, 3 for McGovern; Minnesota, 16 for Thomas F. Eagleton; North Dakota, 2 for Eagleton; Texas, 2 for John Glenn.
[b] This figure does not include the following absences: Florida, 1; Missouri, 1; New York, 2; Oregon, 1; Rhode Island, 1; Texas, 3; and Virginia, 1.
[c] American Samoa and Latin America did not have any Republican delegates.
[d] Democrats assign fractions of delegates to candidates; Republicans do not.

Table 2-28 The 1988 National Political Party Conventions

	Democratic first ballot					
State	Total votes[a]	Michael Dukakis	Jesse Jackson	Others	Abstained	*Republican first ballot: George H. W. Bush (total)*
Alabama	65	37	28	0	0	38
Alaska	17	9	7	1	0	19
Arizona	43	28	14	0	0	33
Arkansas	48	31	11	0	1	27
California	363	235	122	0	0	175
Colorado	55	37	18	0	0	36
Connecticut	63	47	16	0	0	35
Delaware	19	9	7	2	1	17
Florida	154	116	35	0	0	82
Georgia	94	50	42	0	0	48
Hawaii	28	19	8	0	0	20
Idaho	24	20	3	0	0	22
Illinois	200	138	57	0	0	92
Indiana	89	70	18	0	0	51
Iowa	61	49	12	0	0	37
Kansas	45	30	15	0	0	34
Kentucky	65	59	6	0	0	38
Louisiana	76	41	33	1	0	41
Maine	29	17	12	0	0	22
Maryland	84	59	25	0	0	41
Massachusetts	119	99	19	0	0	52
Michigan	162	80	80	0	2	77
Minnesota	91	57	29	3	0	31
Mississippi	47	19	26	0	0	31
Missouri	88	50	37	0	0	47
Montana	28	22	5	0	0	20
Nebraska	30	22	8	0	0	25
Nevada	23	16	5	0	0	20

New Hampshire	22	22	0	0	0	23
New Jersey	126	107	19	0	0	64
New Mexico	30	22	8	0	0	26
New York	292	194	97	0	0	136
North Carolina	95	58	35	0	0	54
North Dakota	22	17	3	0	2	16
Ohio	183	136	46	0	1	88
Oklahoma	56	52	4	0	0	36
Oregon	54	35	18	0	0	32
Pennsylvania	202	179	23	0	0	96
Rhode Island	28	24	3	0	1	21
South Carolina	53	22	31	0	0	37
South Dakota	20	19	1	0	0	18
Tennessee	84	63	20	0	0	45
Texas	211	135	71	1	4	111
Utah	28	25	3	0	0	26
Vermont	20	9	9	1	0	17
Virginia	86	42	42	0	2	50
Washington	77	50	27	0	0	41
West Virginia	47	47	0	0	0	28
Wisconsin	91	65	25	0	0	47
Wyoming	18	14	4	0	0	18
American Samoa	6	6	0	0	0	[b]
Democrats Abroad	9	8	1	0	0	—
District of Columbia	25	7	18	0	0	14
Guam	4	4	0	0	0	4
Puerto Rico	57	49	8	0	0	14
Virgin Islands	5	0	5	0	0	4
Total	4,162	2,876	1,219	9	14	2,277

Source: (Democratic data) *Congressional Quarterly Weekly Report,* July 23, 1988, 2033; (Republican data) *Guide to U.S. Elections*, 5th ed. (Washington, D.C.: Congressional Quarterly, 2005), vol. I, 662–663.

[a] Figures may not add to totals due to absences.
[b] There were no Republican delegates from American Samoa.

Table 2-29 The 1992 National Political Party Conventions

	Democratic first ballot					Republican first ballot			
State	Total votes	Bill Clinton	Jerry Brown	Paul Tsongas	Others/ Abstentions	Total votes	George H. W. Bush	Patrick Buchanan	Others/ Abstentions
Alabama	67	67	0	0	0	38	38	0	0
Alaska	18	18	0	0	0	19	19	0	0
Arizona	49	23	12	14	0	37	37	0	0
Arkansas	48	48	0	0	0	27	27	0	0
California	406	211	160	0	35	201	201	0	0
Colorado	58	26	19	13	0	37	31	5	1
Connecticut	66	45	21	0	0	35	35	0	0
Delaware	21	17	3	1	0	19	19	0	0
Florida	167	141	3	15	8	97	97	0	0
Georgia	96	96	0	0	0	52	52	0	0
Hawaii	28	24	2	0	2	14	14	0	0
Idaho	26	22	0	1	3	22	22	0	0
Illinois	195	155	9	29	2	85	85	0	0
Indiana	93	73	20	0	0	51	51	0	0
Iowa	59	55	2	0	2	23	23	0	0
Kansas	44	43	0	0	1	30	30	0	0
Kentucky	64	63	0	0	1	35	35	0	0
Louisiana	75	75	0	0	0	38	38	0	0
Maine	31	14	13	4	0	22	22	0	0
Maryland	85	83	0	2	0	42	42	0	0
Massachusetts	119	109	6	1	3	38	35	1	2
Michigan	159	120	35	0	4	72	72	0	0
Minnesota	92	61	8	2	21	32	32	0	0
Mississippi	46	46	0	0	0	34	34	0	0
Missouri	92	91	1	0	0	47	47	0	0
Montana	24	21	2	0	1	20	20	0	0
Nebraska	33	24	9	0	0	24	24	0	0
Nevada	27	23	4	0	0	21	21	0	0

New Hampshire	24	17	0	7	0	23	0	0	23
New Jersey	126	102	24	0	0	60	60	0	0
New Mexico	34	30	3	0	1	25	25	0	0
New York	290	155	67	64	4	100	100	0	0
North Carolina	99	95	1	0	3	57	57	0	0
North Dakota	22	18	0	19	4	17	17	0	0
Ohio	178	144	34	0	0	83	83	0	0
Oklahoma	58	56	2	0	0	34	34	0	0
Oregon	57	38	19	0	0	23	23	0	0
Pennsylvania	194	139	43	4	8	91	90	1	0
Rhode Island	58	57	0	0	1	15	15	0	0
South Carolina	54	54	0	0	0	36	36	0	0
South Dakota	21	21	0	0	0	19	19	0	0
Tennessee	85	85	0	0	0	45	34	11	0
Texas	232	204	4	20	4	121	121	0	0
Utah	29	20	9	0	0	27	27	0	0
Vermont	21	14	7	0	0	19	19	0	0
Virginia	97	94	3	0	0	55	55	0	0
Washington	84	49	18	14	3	35	35	0	0
West Virginia	41	41	0	0	0	18	18	0	0
Wisconsin	94	46	30	18	0	35	35	0	0
Wyoming	19	18	1	0	0	20	20	0	0
American Samoa	5	5	0	0	0	4	4	0	0
Democrats Abroad	9	9	0	0	0	—	—	—	—
District of Columbia	31	31	0	0	0	14	14	0	0
Guam	4	4	0	0	0	4	4	0	0
Puerto Rico	58	57	0	0	1	14	14	0	0
Virgin Islands	5	5	0	0	0	4	4	0	0
Total	4,288	3,372	596	209	111	2,210	2,166	18	26

Sources: (Democratic data) *Congressional Quarterly Weekly Report*, July 25, 1992, 2220; (Republican data) *CQWR*, Aug. 22, 1992, 2582.

Table 2-30 The 1996 National Political Party Conventions

State	Democratic first ballot: Bill Clinton (total)	Republican first ballot				
		Total votes	Bob Dole	Patrick Buchanan	Others	Abstained
Alabama	66	40	40	0	0	0
Alaska	19	19	16	0	0	3
Arizona	52	39	37	0	0	2
Arkansas	47	20	16	0	0	4
California	424	165	165	0	0	0
Colorado	58	27	27	0	0	0
Connecticut	67	27	27	0	0	0
Delaware	21	12	12	0	0	0
District of Columbia	33	14	14	0	0	0
Florida	178	98	98	0	0	0
Georgia	91	42	42	0	0	0
Hawaii	30	14	14	0	0	0
Idaho	23	23	19	0	0	4
Illinois	193	69	69	0	0	0
Indiana	88	52	52	0	0	0
Iowa	56	25	25	0	0	0
Kansas	42	31	31	0	0	0
Kentucky	61	26	26	0	0	0
Louisiana	71	30	17	10	3	0
Maine	32	15	15	0	0	0
Maryland	88	32	32	0	0	0
Massachusetts	114	37	37	0	0	0
Michigan	156	57	52	5	0	0
Minnesota	92	33	33	0	0	0
Mississippi	47	33	33	0	0	0
Missouri	93	36	24	11	1	0

Montana	24	14	14	0	0	0
Nebraska	34	24	24	0	0	0
Nevada	26	14	14	0	0	0
New Hampshire	26	16	16	0	0	0
New Jersey	122	48	48	0	0	0
New Mexico	34	18	18	0	0	0
New York	289	102	102	0	0	0
North Carolina	99	58	58	0	0	0
North Dakota	22	18	17	0	0	1
Ohio	172	67	67	0	0	0
Oklahoma	52	38	38	0	0	0
Oregon	57	23	18	5	0	0
Pennsylvania	195	73	73	0	0	0
Rhode Island	32	16	16	0	0	0
South Carolina	51	37	37	0	0	0
South Dakota	22	18	18	0	0	0
Tennessee	83	38	37	0	0	1
Texas	229	123	121	2	0	0
Utah	31	28	27	1	0	0
Vermont	22	12	12	0	0	0
Virginia	97	53	53	0	0	0
Washington	90	36	27	9	0	0
West Virginia	43	18	18	0	0	0
Wisconsin	93	36	36	0	0	0
Wyoming	19	20	20	0	0	0
American Samoa	6	4	4	0	0	0
Guam	6	4	4	0	0	0
Puerto Rico	58	14	14	0	0	0
Virgin Islands	4	4	4	0	0	0
Total	4,289	1,990	1,928	43	4	15

Source: Congressional Quarterly, *Guide to the Republican National Convention,* supplement to *Congressional Quarterly Weekly Report,* Aug. 3, 1996.

Table 2-31 The 2000 and 2004 National Political Party Conventions

	2000		2004	
	Democratic first ballot[a]	*Republican first ballot*	*Democratic first ballot*	*Republican first ballot*
State	Al Gore	George W. Bush	John Kerry	George W. Bush
Alabama	64	44	62	48
Alaska	19	23	17	29
Arizona	55	30	64	52
Arkansas	47	24	47	35
California	435	162	441	173
Colorado	61	40	50	50
Connecticut	67	25	62	30
Delaware	22	12	23	18
Florida	186	80	201	112
Georgia	92	54	98	69
Hawaii	33	14	17	20
Idaho	23	28	23	32
Illinois	190	74	186	73
Indiana	88	55	81	55
Iowa	57	25	57	31
Kansas	42	35	41	39
Kentucky	58	31	57	46
Louisiana	73	29	71	45
Maine	33	14	28	21
Maryland	95	31	99	39
Massachusetts	118	37	121	44
Michigan	157	58	155	61
Minnesota	91	34	85	41

Mississippi	48	33	40	38
Missouri	92	35	88	57
Montana	24	23	21	28
Nebraska	32	30	31	35
Nevada	29	17	32	33
New Hampshire	29	17	26	32
New Jersey	124	54	116	52
New Mexico	35	21	37	24
New York	294	101	284	102
North Carolina	103	62	102	67
North Dakota	22	19	22	23
Ohio	170	69	159	1
Oklahoma	52	38	47	41
Oregon	58	24	56	31
Pennsylvania	191	78	178	75
Rhode Island	33	14	32	21
South Carolina	52	37	55	46
South Dakota	22	22	22	27
Tennessee	81	37	85	55
Texas	231	124	232	138
Utah	29	29	28	36
Vermont	22	12	22	18
Virginia	95	56	98	64
Washington	94	37	88	41
West Virginia	42	18	39	30
Wisconsin	93	37	87	40
Wyoming	18	22	19	28
American Samoa	6	4	6	9
Democrats Abroad	9	—	9	—
District of Columbia	33	15	39	19
Guam	6	4	5	9

(Table continues)

Table 2-31 *(Continued)*

	2000		2004	
	Democratic first ballot[a]	*Republican first ballot*	*Democratic first ballot*	*Republican first ballot*
State	Al Gore	George W. Bush	John Kerry	George W. Bush
Puerto Rico	58	14	56	23
Virgin Islands	6	4	6	9
Total	4,339	2,066	4,253[b]	2,508[c]

Source: *Guide to U.S. Elections,* 5th ed. (Washington, D.C.: CQ Press, 2005), vol. 1, 668–671.

[a] Bill Bradley "freed" his delegates the day before the convention.
[b] Total delegate count was 4,322; 43 voted present, 26 abstained.
[c] Total delegate count was 2,509; 1 delegate did not vote.

3
Presidential Elections

- **National Popular and Electoral Votes for President**
- **Third Parties**
- **Electoral College Anomalies**
- **Popular and Electoral Votes by State**
- **Turnout**
- **Voters' Perceptions of Candidates**
- **Television Coverage of Presidential Candidates**
- **Public Opinion Polls on Presidential Candidates**
- **Campaign Contributions**

Chapter 2 discussed how periodic elections are a structural element of the presidency. It examined how ambivalence toward parties (a philosophical distrust of political parties in tandem with a practical embrace of them) has helped create an independent-partisan institution. This institution is at once plebiscitary, emphasizing the success and failure of individual incumbents, and tied to parties, shaping political strategies and policy solutions along party lines. This chapter continues the discussion by focusing on the general election. It considers how seemingly mundane details of elections, and the loftier claims of democracy upon which they rest, structure the way the presidency operates.

Textbooks matter of factly describe the defining characteristics of American presidential elections—four-year intervals, a two-party system, separate executive and legislative elections, and results determined by the electoral college. These features are so obvious that they are often not recognized as relevant to the design of the presidential institution. Yet, each contributes to the way the presidential campaign is fought, how the general election is won, and the kind of electoral office that results.

A more keenly philosophical issue asserts that elections grant citizens the ability to control government. Equally important, they permit office-seekers and officeholders to claim themselves representatives of the people by characterizing their election victories as mandates from the citizenry. Candidates since Thomas Jefferson have claimed that election success allows the president to wield power, having "unite[d] in himself the confidence of the whole people" (Ford, 1892–1899, 8:26). This democratic promise intertwines with the ambivalence toward parties to highlight individual candidates and campaign imagery.

This chapter is divided into two parts. First, it examines how election details, the promise of democracy, and ambivalence toward parties have affected presidential election results since the early republic. The historical perspective permits an assessment of how these three factors have changed and how they have altered the presidency as an institution. Second, it outlines how these same three factors shape specific elements of contemporary campaigns—namely, imagery, issues, the media, polling, and money.

Elections and Reelections

Although only one person is elected president, presidential elections contain three distinct sets of results: the national popular vote, the national electoral college vote, and the state-by-state outcomes. While each can reveal a different pattern of results, the differences are not as remarkable as sometimes assumed. In addition, while ballots for president are being counted, results are also being tallied in congressional elections, which may strengthen or weaken the president's political position. Finally, turnout results can affect who wins and how effectively that person will be able to govern.

The Popular Vote

Table 3-1 presents the popular and electoral college results of presidential elections from 1789 to 2004. A glance down the popular vote column reveals the extent to which the presidency has been a strongly competitive two-party office. Since 1824, when popular votes were first cast, presidents have won with an average of 51.3 percent of the vote. The table also reveals the remarkable longevity of the two major parties. The Democrats fielded candidates as early as 1828; the Republicans emerged in 1856, and although they did not capture the White House, they fostered the collapse of the Whig Party. From 1856 to 2004 Republicans have won twenty-three presidential elections; Democrats have won fifteen. The White House has swung from one party to the other eighteen times. In races in the twentieth and early twenty-first centuries, from 1904 to 2004, Republicans garnered fourteen victories and Democrats twelve, and the White House changed hands ten times.[1]

There has been, however, a noticeable decline in competitiveness between the nineteenth century (the twenty elections from 1824 to 1900) and the twentieth and early twenty-first centuries (the twenty-six elections from 1904 to 2004). Nineteenth-century presidents won with an average of 49 percent of the popular vote as third parties captured votes regionally. While no nineteenth-century candidate captured more than 56 percent of the popular vote, the *average* popular vote tally from 1904 to 2004 has been 53 percent. Indeed, as amplified in Table 3-2, in ten of the twenty elections from 1824 to 1900, presidents were elected with less than 50 percent of the vote. The oft-cited period of Republican Party dominance after the Civil War looks much less robust when considered in relation to the popular election results during that period: Rutherford B. Hayes, James A. Garfield, and Benjamin Harrison were all minority presidents, and Grover Cleveland stole the office from the Republicans on two separate occasions, in both cases with a minority of the popular vote. In contrast, only eight of the twenty-six elections since 1904 have seen presidential candidates win with a minority of the popular vote.

As detailed in Table 3-3, winning candidates of the nineteenth century held on average a 6 percentage point advantage over their nearest rival. Victorious twentieth- and early twenty-first-century candidates have held nearly a 12 percentage point advantage over their chief opponent. Competition was particularly diminished during the twentieth century when seated incumbents have sought reelection. In the ten instances in which victorious presidential candidates received at least 55 percent of the vote, seven involved seated incumbents. Two recent exceptions are Bill Clinton, who won his second term with only 49.2 percent of the popular vote, and George W. Bush, who was reelected in 2004 with 50.7 percent of the popular vote.

Data in Table 3-4 show that at no time have third-party candidates had a major influence on the race. Only twelve third-party candidates, who ran in just eleven presidential elections from 1824 to 2000, have received at least 10 percent of the popular vote. In the last two decades, only independent candidate H. Ross Perot has surpassed the 10 percent plateau. In 1992 he garnered 19 percent of the vote, but in 1996 he was less of a factor in the election and tallied only slightly more than 8 percent of the vote. In 2000 many blamed Ralph Nader's Green Party candidacy for Al Gore's defeat in Florida, yet Nader only received 2.7 percent of the national vote.

Electoral Votes

Electoral college results amplify this decline in competitiveness. Built in to the electoral college is a mathematical bias that skews the results away from the popular vote. Since all states but Maine have adopted a winner-take-all provision in calculating the relationship between popular and electoral votes, victorious presidential candidates have always received a larger percentage of electoral votes than popular votes (see Table 3-1). In fact, over the entire time period from 1824 to 2004, winning presidential candidates have averaged a 22 percentage point advantage in their electoral vote result compared with their popular vote result (see Table 3-3). The most dramatic example of this was in 1912 when Woodrow Wilson won only 41.8 percent of the national popular vote, but received 81.9 percent of the national electoral vote. The skewed results imply a larger public mandate for the new president than in fact truly exists. Many new presidents have, indeed, capitalized on this, even though the popular vote is a much more accurate reflection of the country's decision. For instance, in the early days of his administration, Ronald Reagan continually talked of the large mandate he had to expand the military and cut other federal programs by winning 90.9 prcent of the electoral college vote when, in fact, he had won only 50.7 percent of the popular vote.The electoral college structure also can create situations in which the popular vote winner is not actually elected president. The winner-take-all approach requires that a candidate merely receive one more popular vote in a state than any other candidate to gain all of its electoral votes. Due to population differences among the states, it is mathematically possible for a candidate to be elected with a majority of the electoral votes but without a majority of the popular vote. As shown in Table 3-5, this has happened four times in the forty-six elections held since 1824, when popular votes began to be counted: in 1824, 1876, 1888, and 2000.

At the end of balloting in the four-way race of 1824, Andrew Jackson held more popular and electoral college votes than any other candidate, although he had a majority of neither. The Constitution requires that the winner must obtain a majority of electoral votes, so the race was cast into the House of Representatives, which decided in favor of Jackson's rival, John Quincy Adams. This led to Jackson's supporters charging that the election had been stolen under a "corrupt bargain" arranged in the House.

In the initial count of the votes in 1876, Democrat Samuel Tilden obtained a majority of the popular vote and held more electoral college votes than Republican Rutherford Hayes. But Republicans challenged the electoral college votes in three Southern states—Florida, Louisiana, and South Carolina—and a lone elector in Oregon. Since neither candidate held a majority of electoral college votes, the race was again given to the House of Representatives. After bitter partisan wrangling, the House established an Electoral Commission made up of members of the House, Senate, and Supreme Court that ultimately decided in favor of Hayes. The suspicion at the time was that Hayes won the election in exchange for the end of Reconstruction in the South.

In 1888 Grover Cleveland won a majority of the popular vote by 90,596 votes, but Benjamin Harrison earned a majority of the electoral college votes and was thereby elected president. Cleveland won his revenge in 1892 when he defeated Harrison in both the popular and electoral college results.

In the 2000 election—112 years later—Democratic candidate Al Gore won the popular vote by more than 500,000 votes. However, the electoral college majority hinged on results in Florida, which were so close that a mandatory recount was ordered. The Supreme Court heard arguments on whether the recount should go forward. Voting 5–4 in *Bush v. Gore,* the Court decided that the recount be halted and the election results as they stood certified. Bush led Florida by 527 votes and captured its 25 electoral college votes, and with them the presidency.

Table 3-6 shows a final oddity of the electoral college process: electors who have failed to cast their votes for the candidate for whom they were legally bound to vote. This occurred most recently in 2004, when an unknown elector in Minnesota cast a ballot for John Edwards, the Democratic vice presidential candidate, rather than Al Gore. However, none of these instances altered the outcomes of the elections.

The peculiarities of the electoral college system, then, are real. The mathematical bias built into the electoral college through winner-take-all calculations surfaces in every election, even when the popular and electoral college winners are the same. They permit presidents to claim mandates when the mandates may be more apparent than real. They also create more serious problems when a winner becomes a loser and a loser becomes president. These possibilities, though infrequent, raise significant questions about the electoral college as a democratic institution. In each of the four instances when a mismatch occurred, it led to bitter political disputes with consequences for the voters, the parties, and the government. Despite this, there has been no systematic effort to reform the electoral college, not even after the 2000 controversy. There is little incentive for the winning party to acknowledge the flaws of the electoral college and so reform efforts tend not to gain traction.

State and Demographic Results

Changes in competitiveness are also evident in the states. Table 3-7 details the parties' strength in capturing states in presidential elections from 1789 to 2004. Tables 3-8 through 3-12 provide a more detailed breakdown of the popular vote from 1968 to 2004. They reveal how few states have been truly competitive during the several political eras (see Table 3-7, in particular). Instead, they have swung over time. For example, Massachusetts shifted from a Republican stronghold in the 1896–1928 period to being a Democratic stronghold thereafter. Southern states have also shifted. They were consistently Democratic during the 1932–1964 period, but have shifted in favor of the Republican Party in the most recent elections. The percentages at the bottom of Table 3-7 show that the parties' dominance of states has increased in the latter part of the twentieth century and early twenty-first century. During the period from 1968 to 2004 the Republicans captured all the states 66 percent of the time, compared to capturing 59 and 58 percent of the states, respectively, during the two periods from 1860 to 1892 and 1896 to 1928.

Tables 3-13 through 3-17 present data on state electoral votes from 1968 to 2004. The constitutional provision that the president must receive a majority of the electoral college vote provides candidates with a convenient road map they must follow to win. Candidates must target large-population states, with high numbers of electoral votes, in which their party is competitive. As is readily apparent in Tables 3-13 through 3-17, from 1968 to 2004 the victorious presidential candidate captured these states 86 percent of the time. The candidate who will ultimately succeed and the campaign themes on which that candidate runs must be effective in these highly populated states. The electoral college, then, indirectly makes the presidency an institution that follows the population and demographic shifts of the country.

Congressional Outcomes

Constitutionally separate executive and legislative elections create an electoral prize that makes presidential candidates, and ultimately presidents, a unique focus of national politics. Yet these separate congressional elections can also create a problem for presidents, whose party fortunes in one or both chambers of Congress may not match their own electoral strength. Matters invariably worsen at the midterm, when the president's party has lost congressional seats in every election (except 1934, 1998, and 2002) since the Civil War. Table 3-18 shows how well the president's party fared in House elections from 1824 to 2006, and when it faced divided government (a time in which a majority of one or both houses was not of the president's party). Congressional competition has not diminished with the decline in presidential competitiveness. The president's party captured 52 percent of the vote in the nineteenth century and has captured 52 percent of the vote in the twentieth and early twenty-first centuries. The strength of incumbency, which has been documented as a significant component of congressional voting, may insulate the parties from decline (Garand and Gross, 1984).[2] Presidents have faced divided government thirty-nine times in one or both houses—twenty-three times in the twentieth and early twenty-first centuries, sixteen times in the nineteenth century. Divided government typically has occurred first in congressional midterm elections and then continued into subsequent presidential election years. Only since 1968 has divided government emerged in presidential election years and continued through midterm election years. A comparison of Tables 3-1 and 3-18 reveals that the most competitive period in American party history was between 1876 and 1896, when minority-elected presidents and divided government were exceedingly common (see also Table 8-1, which examines the actual seats won by the parties in the House and Senate).

Turnout

Turnout determines the results of both presidential and congressional races. Turnout declined in the twentieth century in presidential elections, and, more notably, in midterm congressional elections. Considerable debate exists, however, about whether turnout in the nineteenth century was truly at high levels or whether corruption and party maneuvers before the introduction of the Australian (i.e., confidential) ballot made turnout appear to be much higher than it was (Burnham, 1965; Rusk, 1970). Presidential election turnout increased steadily after women were given the right to vote in 1920, dropped off in the 1940s, reached its peak in the 1960s, and tapered off through the 1990s, but has increased again since 2000. As seen in Figure 3-1, turnout varies by region. Turnout in the South has been consistently lower, sometimes dramatically so, than turnout in the rest of the country. Only recently has southern turnout risen, while turnout in the rest of the nation has leveled off. Tables 3-19 through 3-22 reveal the variation in turnout by state in presidential election years in greater detail.

Elections and Institutions over Time

Historical statistics on presidential elections indicate both underlying continuity and fundamental change in outcomes between the nineteenth and the twentieth and early twenty-first centuries. The two major parties continue to battle for the White House with relative equality. Even when one party has not held the White House for several terms, it ultimately has managed to take it back. Divided government has bedeviled presidents with regularity during the two centuries. Yet, the election winner, regardless of party, has gained a much larger popular vote margin since the twentieth century than that achieved in the nineteenth century. As the ambivalence toward parties has intensified, the focus of the democratic promise has shifted from party elites to the candidates themselves. Presidential and congressional outcomes diverge, not only because presidential candidates are running as independent partisans, but because congressional candidates are as well. Final election results are more likely to reflect momentum shifts that favor one candidate at the expense of another as the end of a campaign approaches. All these factors lead to a more personal victory and, consequently, a more personal office.

Elements of the Campaign

Most statistical data about campaigns are available only for the contemporary period, thus historical changes in presidential campaigns are more difficult to gauge than are changes in the actual election outcomes. Contemporary campaigns involve five key components: imagery, issues, media, polling, and money.

Candidate Imagery

Arguably, the central feature of modern presidential campaigns is candidate imagery. Candidates spend much of their campaign efforts developing images to which voters will be attracted—impressionistic accounts of who the candidate is and the kinds of personal credentials he or she has. Presidential candidates attempt to display the qualities of a good president in their personal characteristics and in their ability to empathize with the voters. Citizens' perceptions of candidate characteristics and citizens' emotional responses to candidates are depicted in Tables 3-23 and 3-24, respectively. The data make clear that citizens indeed evaluate candidates differently. For instance, Table 3-23 shows that individuals in 1984 considered Ronald Reagan far more inspiring, and a stronger leader, than Walter Mondale. In general, the winning candidate is perceived to have more favorable personal characteristics than the losing candidate. The one exception was in 2004, when people perceived John Kerry as more favorable or equally favorable to George W. Bush on dimensions of intelligence, honesty, knowledge, and caring. Bush, however, bested Kerry on being a strong leader. Not surprisingly, nonincumbents have stirred much less intense emotion than incumbents in the four races examined. Table 3-24 reveals that in 2004 George W. Bush angered a majority of people (56.1 percent), while Kerry angered relatively few (31.4 percent).

Issue Positions

Issues are important in presidential campaigns as well, although one must be careful in ascertaining whether what a candidate calls an issue is really that. Many "issues" are little more than emotional, symbolic themes, often intentionally vague, designed as extensions of the candidate's image and intended to resonate among as many voters as possible: "It's Morning in America" (Reagan in 1984), "Patriotism" (George H.W. Bush in 1988), "Change" (Bill Clinton in 1992), "Family Values" (George W. Bush in 1992), and "Change We Can Believe in" (Barack Obama, 2008) are examples of such pseudo issues. More traditional policy-oriented issues are discussed as well and may influence the vote. Figure 3-2 shows that voters in 2004 clearly saw George W. Bush as the candidate best able to handle terrorism and conflict in Iraq, while John Kerry was perceived as better suited to deal with health care and little difference was seen between the candidates on the economy.

Media Coverage

Media coverage of campaigns affects how candidates are able to emphasize certain personal characteristics, emotional themes, and substantive issues. Table 3-25 presents data on television news coverage of the general election campaigns of 1988 through 2004. Coverage of candidate character, policy issues, and the horse race varies considerably from one election year to the next. Not unexpectedly, close contests—1992, 2000, and 2004, for example—reflect more coverage of the horse race, who is ahead and who will win. Stories about candidates' personalities are typically more frequent than those about policy issues. Table 3-26 examines the extent of positive coverage of candidates in the 1988 through 2004 general election periods. It would be difficult to predict who would win the races based on this rather erratic positive news coverage. In 1992 George H.W. Bush received only mildly positive coverage throughout the general election period. Clinton received glowing coverage prior to the Republican convention, but thereafter positive coverage declined, except during the debates. Judging from the data, even odds could have been laid on Bush and Clinton during the final weeks of the campaign. From the period of the Republican convention onward, Perot received far more positive coverage than either of the two major-party candidates. In 2000 coverage of George W. Bush started out positive but fell off as the race grew closer; in contrast, his coverage started out more negative in 2004 but ended up quite positive.

Public Opinion Polls

Public opinion polls are another central ingredient to presidential election campaigns. Table 3-27 examines the fluctuation in public opinion throughout the general election period for elections from 1948 to 2004. In twelve of the fifteen races, the front-runner in the earliest poll ultimately won the race. Only the 1960, 1980, and 1992 elections proved exceptions. Almost all front-runners found their initial poll advantages narrowed by Election Day, with the exception of Richard Nixon in 1972, Reagan in 1984, and Clinton in 1996, whose election support actually grew from the first poll trial heats.

Table 3-28 permits an assessment of who voted for whom, as revealed in the popular vote results by several demographic groupings. The table shows how the national popular vote is the aggregation of considerable variation among key groups. For instance, the so-called gender gap can be seen in the 1952, 1956, 1976, 1980, 1984, 1996, 2000, and 2004. In the last three elections, women have been much more likely to support the Democratic candidate, while men preferred the Republican. Racial differences are also quite apparent, with Democratic candidates typically receiving much higher support than Republican candidates from nonwhites.

Campaign Money

Fundraising is an important aspect of any election in America. The overall expenditures of Republican and Democratic presidential candidates in general elections since 1996 appear in Table 3-29. In most of these years Republican expenditures were higher than Democratic expenditures, although both parties exhibited increases up until 1964. At that point, the Republican Party began spending more than twice the amount spent by the Democrats. In 1972, during the Nixon-McGovern campaign, the Republicans spent nearly triple the amount spent by the Democrats. In response to this gap, and also in reaction to Watergate, Congress approved public funding of presidential campaigns in the Federal Election Campaign Act of 1974. Implementation of this law in 1976 brought about equality between the parties in expenditures for presidential campaigns by providing candidates the opportunity to receive federal matching funds if they stayed under various funding limits. Table 3-30 outlines the limits for candidates in presidential primary and general elections, for the parties' conventions, and for parties' efforts outside the conventions, including voter registration drives, polling, and advertising.

As a comparison of Table 3-29 and 3-30 makes clear, the campaign spending limits have not limited campaign spending in American presidential elections. In 1996 candidates began opting out of accepting federal matching funds during the primary period. Republican candidate billionaire Steve Forbes started the precedent. George W. Bush took no matching funds in either 2000 or 2004; he was joined by Democratic candidate John Kerry in 2004. In 2008 Hillary Clinton and Barack Obama, leading Democratic contenders, and Rudy Giuliani and Mitt Romney, Republican contenders, all declined federal matches for the primaries, and Obama also opted out of federal funds during the general election campaign—the first (but unlikely to be the last) candidate to do this. By doing so, candidates are free to raise as much money as they can privately. In addition, other organizations have maneuvered around federal limits through independent expenditures and multiple party organizations and political action committees—the campaign spending arms of interest groups.

Campaigns over Time

Modern presidential campaigns are theatrical, candidate-centric affairs. Although systematic data do not exist about the campaigns of the nineteenth century (and the early twentieth century), there is evidence that these earlier campaigns were theater of a different sort (Schlesinger, 1973a). They, too, were fought on the basis of imagery, but it was party, not candidate, imagery. For instance, in one of the earliest party imagery elections, the election of 1840, the Whigs presented themselves as the party of the log cabin and hard cider. They then made their presidential candidate, the well-to-do, successful Gen. William Henry Harrison, fit the party image. Harrison's simple life and love of cider became legendary (Lorant, 1951). Nineteenth-century campaigns were fought on the basis of issues as well, but presidential and congressional candidates did not advance their own themes and position papers. Instead, they held to their parties' positions on such matters as the national bank, tariffs, the national debt, and western land. No doubt the news coverage of campaigns in the nineteenth century was extensive, but it was reported in party-line papers. The news did not travel fast, nor was it nationally focused, making it difficult for momentum shifts to sweep the country (Rubin, 1981). The absence of public opinion polls made any momentum shifts that did occur difficult to detect. Campaign money was significant in the nineteenth century, but it was money that the parties, not the candidates, spent on developing party slogans, celebrations, rallies, newspaper circulation, and turnout.

Today, by contrast, imagery, issues, media coverage, polls, and money are unabashedly used to direct the voters' attention to individual candidates. A candidate's image may in fact magnify any mistakes made during the campaign. Dukakis's ride in a tank wearing an out-sized helmet and George Bush's comment that he was not aware of how the deficit affected individual lives attest to this. George W. Bush's difficulty in coming up with the names of various foreign leaders during the 2000 campaign helped shape an image of foreign policy inexperience that Bush did not shake as he entered the White House. Only the events of September 11 and their aftermath recreated Bush's image as a powerful foreign policy player. However, successful candidates can claim a public mandate grounded in such carefully crafted images. Invoking the promise of democracy, they can assert a strong mandate to govern in the name of the people, allowing them greater leeway to advance policy aims, but saddling them with a greater burden to succeed.

Conclusion

From the statistical descriptions of presidential nominations and elections two central features of the contemporary presidential institution have emerged. First, imagery is an important component of the institution. Candidate images blur into the image of a single executive who is the most powerful, unique, visible, and important political figure in the country, if not the world. This single executive image proceeds from the notion of the president as the only official elected by the entire country, and thus the truest representative of the people (Ragsdale, 1993). The president is a symbol of the nation, embodying America, its unity, values, and mission in the world. The chief executive is the one person in charge of the government, the nation's principal problem-solver who personally attempts to resolve intractable problems that mere mortals have failed to alleviate.

This personalization of the institution encourages an immediate and ongoing evaluation of its primary occupant. In an almost daily plebiscite, presidents are subject to the latest poll results, media assessments of their policy success and administrative competence, and constant speculations about their personal habits and tastes. In addition, the imagery becomes a part of the way in which the national policy debate is shaped. It is not simply a discussion of the issues, but of the way presidents present themselves as well. Do they convey sufficient competence, concern, trust, patriotism, or even anger? Can they convince the public that they are on the right side of a policy question and that it is the opposition that is misguided? The horse race continues even after the president has won the election.

A second feature of the contemporary presidential institution is an ongoing ambivalence toward parties. Party appears to matter both more and less to the presidency than it once did. Party influence endures in part because it has become the lone reliable arbiter of policy disputes. Party provides some order to the muddle of views held by independent partisans in the White House and on Capitol Hill. Republicans still line up against Democrats. The intensity of the partisan debate is witnessed in perennial strife over presidential appointments. During the Reagan and Bush years, congressional Democrats conducted a proxy war against the White House over the Supreme Court nominations of Robert Bork and Clarence Thomas and the nomination of former senator John Tower to become secretary of defense. During the Clinton administration, Republicans returned fire by attacking nominees Zöe Baird and Lani Guinier. In 1993 President Clinton further demonstrated the power of partisanship by constructing a Democrats-only coalition to pass the budget. After the 1994 election, the first Republican-controlled Congress since the 1950s further heightened partisanship. Speaker of the House Newt Gingrich touting the Republicans' Contract with America forced the Clinton White House into confrontations and government shutdowns. One of the hallmarks of the George W. Bush presidency was taking positions and pushing legislation for the conservative Republican "base." When Democrats regained control of the House and Senate in the 2006 midterm election, they began a series of investigations into presidential war power and the Iraq War that had not been seriously considered under the Republican Congress. However, party influence has waned because journalists, public opinion polls, and campaign fund-raising strategies have replaced party brokers in deciding who has momentum in the nomination process and who is likely to be the front-runner going into the general election.

The tension between public imagery and partisanship presents twenty-first century presidents with a sharp irony. They win the office with larger victory margins and are more salient national figures than their nineteenth-century counterparts. Yet the mandate that has placed them above party leaves them isolated from other politicians, both of their own party and of the opposition's. Current party politics deepens the irony. It is not uncommon for members of the president's party to attack the president in public debate and private negotiation. At the same time, presidents are still able to cut deals and settle policy issues through party. Contemporary presidential elections offer this baffling maze to presidents, many of whom have had little experience in Washington or even in government of any kind. These elections, with their peculiarities of state-by-state calculations and popular and electoral vote differences, still remain deeply entrenched structures of the presidential institution and direct how presidents act within it.

Notes

1. The election of 1900 is considered a nineteenth-century election for two reasons. First, it marked the reelection of William McKinley, who was first elected in 1896 and was a president steeped in the earlier century. Second, electoral votes were calculated from state population figures from the 1890 census, not the 1900 census.
2. Table 3-18 examines only party competitiveness; it does not consider incumbent-challenger competitiveness in congressional races. Although there is considerable debate on how to measure incumbent electoral strength, research indicates that this strength has increased and thus dampened candidate competition (Garand and Gross, 1984; Alford and Brady, 1993).

Table 3-1 Major-Party Popular and Electoral Votes for President, 1789–2004

Year	Number of states	Total popular vote[a]	Total electoral votes	Winning candidate	Percentage of popular vote received by winning candidate[a]	Electoral votes received by winning candidate		Losing candidate	Percentage of popular vote received by losing candidate[a]	Electoral votes received by losing candidate	
						(N)	(%)			(N)	(%)
1789	10	—	69	Washington (F)	—	69	100.0	[b]	—	[b]	[b]
1792	15	—	135	Washington (F)	—	132	97.7	[b]	—	[b]	[b]
1796	16	—	139	J. Adams (F)	—	71	51.1	Jefferson (DR)	—	68	48.9
1800	16	—	137	Jefferson (DR)	—	73	53.3	J. Adams (F)	—	65	47.4
1804	17	—	176	Jefferson (DR)	—	162	92.0	Pinckney (F)	—	14	8.0
1808	17	—	176	Madison (DR)	—	122	69.3	Pinckney (F)	—	47	26.7
1812	18	—	218	Madison (DR)	—	128	58.7	Clinton (F)	—	89	40.8
1816	19	—	221	Monroe (DR)	—	183	82.8	King (F)	—	34	15.4
1820	24	—	235	Monroe (DR)	—	231	98.3	J. Q. Adams (I)	—	1	0.4
1824	24	365,833	261	J. Q. Adams (I)	30.9	84	32.2	Jackson (D)	41.3	99	37.9
1828	24	1,148,018	261	Jackson (D)	56.0	178	68.2	J. Q. Adams (NR)	43.6	83	31.8
1832	24	1,293,973	288	Jackson (D)	54.2	219	76.0	Clay (NR)	37.4	49	17.0
1836	26	1,503,534	294	Van Buren (D)	50.8	170	57.8	W. Harrison (W)	36.6	73	24.8
1840	26	2,411,808	294	W. Harrison (W)	52.8	234	79.6	Van Buren (D)	46.8	60	20.4
1844	26	2,703,659	275	Polk (D)	49.5	170	61.8	Clay (W)	48.1	105	38.2
1848	30	2,879,184	290	Taylor (W)	47.3	163	56.2	Cass (D)	42.5	127	43.8
1852	31	3,161,830	296	Pierce (D)	50.8	254	85.8	Scott (W)	43.9	42	14.2
1856	31	4,054,647	296	Buchanan (D)	45.3	174	58.8	Fremont (R)	33.1	114	38.5
1860	33	4,685,561	303	Lincoln (R)	39.8	180	59.4	Douglas (D)	29.5	12	4.0
1864	36	4,031,887	234	Lincoln (R)	55.0	212	90.6	McClellan (D)	45.0	21	9.0
1868	37	5,722,440	294	Grant (R)	52.7	214	72.8	Seymour (D)	47.3	80	27.2
1872	37	6,467,679	366	Grant (R)	55.6	286	78.1	Greeley (D)	43.8	[c]	[c]
1876	38	8,413,101	369	Hayes (R)	48.0	185	50.1	Tilden (D)	51.0	184	49.9
1880	38	9,210,420	369	Garfield (R)	48.3	214	58.0	Hancock (D)	48.2	155	42.0
1884	38	10,049,754	401	Cleveland (D)	48.5	219	54.6	Blaine (R)	48.2	182	45.3
1888	38	11,383,320	401	B. Harrison (R)	47.8	233	58.1	Cleveland (D)	48.6	168	42.0
1892	44	12,056,097	444	Cleveland (D)	46.1	277	62.4	B. Harrison (R)	43.0	145	32.7
1896	45	13,935,738	447	McKinley (R)	51.0	271	60.6	Bryan (D)	46.7	176	39.4

1900	45	13,970,470	447	McKinley (R)	51.7	292	65.3	Bryan (D)	45.5	155	34.7
1904	45	13,518,964	476	T. Roosevelt (R)	56.4	336	70.6	Parker (D)	37.6	140	29.4
1908	46	14,882,734	483	Taft (R)	51.6	321	66.5	Bryan (D)	43.0	162	33.5
1912	48	15,040,963	531	Wilson (D)	41.8	435	81.9	Taft (R)	23.2	8	1.5
1916	48	18,535,022	531	Wilson (D)	49.2	277	52.2	Hughes (R)	46.1	254	47.8
1920	48	26,753,786	531	Harding (R)	60.3	404	76.1	Cox (D)	34.2	127	23.9
1924	48	29,075,959	531	Coolidge (R)	54.1	382	71.9	David (D)	28.8	136	25.6
1928	48	36,790,364	531	Hoover (R)	58.2	444	83.6	Smith (D)	40.8	87	16.4
1932	48	39,749,382	531	F. Roosevelt (D)	57.4	472	88.9	Hoover (R)	39.6	59	11.1
1936	48	45,642,303	531	F. Roosevelt (D)	60.8	523	98.4	Landon (R)	36.5	8	1.5
1940	48	49,840,443	531	F. Roosevelt (D)	54.7	449	84.6	Willkie (R)	44.8	82	15.4
1944	48	47,974,819	531	F. Roosevelt (D)	53.3	432	81.4	Dewey (R)	45.9	99	18.6
1948	48	48,692,442	531	Truman (D)	49.5	303	57.1	Dewey (R)	45.1	189	35.6
1952	48	61,551,118	531	Eisenhower (R)	55.1	442	83.2	Stevenson (D)	44.4	89	16.8
1956	48	62,025,372	531	Eisenhower (R)	57.4	457	86.1	Stevenson (D)	42.0	73	13.7
1960	50	68,828,960	537	Kennedy (D)	49.7	303	56.4	Nixon (R)	49.5	219	40.8
1964[d]	50	70,641,104	538	L. Johnson (D)	61.1	486	90.3	Goldwater (R)	38.5	52	9.9
1968	50	73,203,370	538	Nixon (R)	43.4	301	55.9	Humphrey (D)	42.7	191	35.5
1972	50	77,727,590	538	Nixon (R)	60.7	520	96.7	McGovern (D)	37.5	17	3.2
1976	50	81,555,889	538	Carter (D)	50.1	297	55.2	Ford (R)	48.0	240	44.6
1980	50	86,515,221	538	Reagan (R)	50.7	489	90.9	Carter (D)	41.0	49	9.1
1984	50	92,652,793	538	Reagan (R)	58.8	525	97.6	Mondale (D)	40.6	13	2.4
1988	50	91,584,820	538	G.H.W. Bush (R)	53.4	426	79.2	Dukakis (D)	45.6	111	20.6
1992	50	104,425,014	538	Clinton (D)	43.0	370	68.8	G.H.W. Bush (R)	37.4	168	31.2
1996	50	96,273,262	538	Clinton (D)	49.2	379	70.4	Dole (R)	40.7	159	29.6
2000	50	105,396,627	538	G. W. Bush (R)	47.9	271	50.4	Gore (D)	48.4	266	49.4
2004	50	122,295,345	538	G. W. Bush (R)	50.7	286	53.2	Kerry (D)	48.3	251	46.7

Source: Guide to U.S. Elections, 5th ed. (Washington, D.C.: CQ Press, 2005), vol. I, A4.

Note: Only the top two vote-getters are listed. For significant third-party contenders, see Table 3-4. F—Federalist; DR—Democratic-Republican; I—Independent Democrat-Republican; NR—National Republican; W—Whig; D—Democrat; R—Republican.

[a] Reliable data on the popular vote are not available before 1824. Calculations based on all votes cast for major and minor party candidates.
[b] Washington ran unopposed in 1789 and 1792.
[c] Horace Greeley, the Democratic candidate, died between the popular vote and the meeting of the electoral college. The 66 Democratic electors split their votes among several candidates, including 3 votes cast for Greeley that Congress refused to count.
[d] The Twenty-third Amendment provided for three electoral college votes for the District of Columbia, beginning with the 1964 election.

Table 3-2 Candidates Who Won Presidency Without Popular Vote Majorities, 1824–2004

Year	*Candidate*	*Percentage of popular vote received*	*Percentage of electoral vote received*
1824	J. Q. Adams (I)	30.9	32.2
1844	Polk (D)	49.5	61.8
1848	Taylor (W)	47.3	56.2
1856	Buchanan (D)	45.3	58.8
1860	Lincoln (R)	39.8	59.4
1876	Hayes (R)	48.0	50.1
1880	Garfield (R)	48.3	58.0
1884	Cleveland (D)	48.5	54.6
1888	B. Harrison (R)	47.8	58.1
1892	Cleveland (D)	46.1	62.4
1912	Wilson (D)	41.8	81.9
1916	Wilson (D)	49.2	52.2
1948	Truman (D)	49.5	57.1
1960	Kennedy (D)	49.7	56.4
1968	Nixon (R)	43.4	55.9
1992	Clinton (D)	43.0	68.8
1996	Clinton (D)	49.2	70.4
2000	G. W. Bush (R)	47.9	50.5

Source: Adapted from *Guide to U.S. Elections*, 5th ed. (Washington, D.C.: CQ Press, 2005).

Note: Reliable data on the popular vote not available before 1824. Calculations based on all votes cast for major and minor party candidates. I—Independent Democratic-Republican; D—Democrat; W—Whig; R—Republican.

Table 3-3 Comparison of Popular and Electoral Vote Mandates, 1824–2004

Year	*Winning candidate*	*Percentage of popular vote received*[a]	*Popular vote advantage*[b]	*Percentage of electoral vote received*	*Electoral vote advantage*[b]	*Percentage difference between electoral votes and popular votes*
1824	J. Q. Adams (I)	30.9	–10.4	32.2	–5.7	1.3
1828	Jackson (D)	56.0	12.4	68.2	36.4	12.2
1832	Jackson (D)	54.2	16.8	76.0	59.0	21.8
1836	Van Buren (D)	50.8	14.2	57.8	33.0	7.0
1840	W. Harrison (W)	52.9	6.1	79.6	59.2	26.7
1844	Polk (D)	49.5	1.4	61.8	23.6	12.3
1848	Taylor (W)	47.3	4.8	56.2	12.4	8.9
1852	Pierce (D)	50.8	6.9	85.8	71.6	35.0
1856	Buchanan (D)	45.3	12.2	58.8	20.3	13.5
1860	Lincoln (R)	39.9	10.4	59.4	55.4	19.5
1864	Lincoln (R)	55.1	10.2	90.6	81.6	35.5
1868	Grant (R)	52.7	5.4	72.8	45.6	20.1
1872	Grant (R)	55.6	11.8	78.1	66.0	22.5
1876	Hayes (R)	48.0	–3.0	50.1	0.2	2.1
1880	Garfield (R)	48.3	0.1	58.0	16.0	9.7
1884	Cleveland (D)	48.9	0.7	54.6	9.2	5.7
1888	B. Harrison (R)	47.8	–0.8	58.1	16.2	10.3
1892	Cleveland (D)	46.0	3.0	62.4	29.7	16.4
1896	McKinley (R)	51.1	5.3	60.6	21.2	9.5
1900	McKinley (R)	51.7	6.2	65.3	30.6	13.6
1904	T. Roosevelt (R)	56.4	18.8	70.6	41.2	14.2
1908	Taft (R)	51.6	8.6	66.5	33.0	14.9
1912	Wilson (D)	41.8	18.6	81.9	80.4	40.1
1916	Wilson (D)	49.2	3.1	52.2	4.4	3.0
1920	Harding (R)	60.3	26.1	76.1	52.2	15.8

(Table continues)

Table 3-3 *(Continued)*

Year	*Winning candidate*	*Percentage of popular received*[a]	*Popular vote advantage*[b]	*Percentage of electoral received*	*Electoral vote advantage*[b]	*Percentage difference between electoral votes and popular votes*
1924	Coolidge (R)	54.0	25.2	71.9	46.3	17.9
1928	Hoover (R)	58.2	17.4	83.6	67.2	25.4
1932	F. Roosevelt (D)	57.4	17.8	88.9	77.8	31.5
1936	F. Roosevelt (D)	60.8	24.3	98.5	97.0	37.7
1940	F. Roosevelt (D)	54.7	9.9	84.6	69.2	29.9
1944	F. Roosevelt (D)	53.4	7.5	81.4	62.8	28.0
1948	Truman (D)	49.5	4.4	57.1	21.5	7.6
1952	Eisenhower (R)	54.9	10.5	83.2	66.4	28.3
1956	Eisenhower (R)	57.4	15.4	86.1	72.4	28.7
1960	Kennedy (D)	49.7	0.2	56.4	15.6	6.7
1964	L. Johnson (D)	61.1	22.6	90.3	80.6	29.2
1968	Nixon (R)	43.4	0.7	55.9	20.4	12.5
1972	Nixon (R)	60.7	23.2	96.7	93.5	36.0
1976	Carter (D)	50.1	2.1	55.2	10.6	5.1
1980	Reagan (R)	50.7	9.7	90.9	81.8	40.2
1984	Reagan (R)	58.8	18.2	97.6	95.2	38.8
1988	G.H.W. Bush (R)	53.4	7.8	79.2	58.6	25.8
1992	Clinton (D)	43.0	5.6	68.8	37.6	25.8
1996	Clinton (D)	49.2	8.5	70.4	40.8	21.2
2000	G.W. Bush (R)	47.9	–0.5	50.4	1.0	2.5
2004	G.W. Bush (R)	50.7	2.4	53.2	6.5	2.5

Source: Adapted from *Guide to U.S. Elections*, 5th ed. (Washington, D.C.: CQ Press, 2005), vol. I, 674–719, 759–804.

Note: I—Independent Democratic-Republican; D—Democrat; W—Whig; R—Republican.

[a] Based on all votes cast for major and minor party candidates.
[b] Percentage point difference between winner and nearest rival.

Table 3-4 Significant Third-Party Presidential Candidates, 1824–2004

Year	*Candidate*	*Party*	*Percentage of popular vote received*	*Electoral votes received*
1824	Henry Clay	Democratic-Republican	13	37
	William Crawford	Democratic-Republican	11	41
1836	Hugh White	Whig	10	26
1848	Martin Van Buren	Free Soil	10	0
1856	Millard Fillmore	Whig-American	22	8
1860	John Breckinridge	Southern Democrat	18	72
	John Bell	Constitutional Union	13	39
1912	Theodore Roosevelt	Progressive	27	88
1924	Robert LaFollette	Progressive	17	13
1968	George Wallace	American Independent	14	46
1992	H. Ross Perot	Independent	19	0

Source: Adapted from *Guide to U.S. Elections*, 5th ed. (Washington, D.C.: CQ Press, 2005), vol. I, 720–731.

Note: Only candidates who received at least 10 percent of the popular vote are listed. No significant third-party candidate prior to 1824.

Table 3-5 Electoral College Anomalies, 1789–2004

Year	*Candidate*	*Percentage of popular vote received*[a]	*Percentage of electoral vote received*	*Winner*
1800[b]	J. Adams	—	65	Jefferson
	Jefferson	—	73	
	Burr	—	73	
1824[c]	J. Q. Adams	31	32	J. Q. Adams
	Jackson	41	38	
1876[d]	Hayes	48	50	Hayes
	Tilden	51	50	
1888	Cleveland	49	42	B. Harrison
	B. Harrison	48	48	
2000	Gore	48	49	G. W. Bush
	G. W. Bush	48	50	

Source: Guide to U.S. Elections, 5th ed. (Washington, D.C.: CQ Press, 2005), vol. I, 738.

[a] Reliable data on the popular vote not available before 1824.
[b] Jefferson was elected by the House of Representatives.
[c] Adams was elected by the House of Representatives after a four-way race.
[d] The returns from Florida, Louisiana, Oregon, and South Carolina were disputed. Congress, in joint session, declared Hayes the winner.

Table 3-6 Faithless Electors, 1789–2004

Year	*Elector*	*State*	*Elected to vote for*	*Voted for*
1796	Unknown	Pennsylvania	John Adams	Thomas Jefferson
1820	Unknown	New Hampshire	James Monroe	John Quincy Adams
1948	Preston Parks	Tennessee	Harry Truman	Strom Thurmond
1956	W. F. Turner	Alabama	Adlai Stevenson	Walter E. Jones
1960	Henry D. Irwin	Oklahoma	Richard Nixon	Harry F. Byrd
1968	Dr. Lloyd W. Bailey	North Carolina	Richard Nixon	George C. Wallace
1972	Roger L. McBride	Virginia	Richard Nixon	John Hospers
1976	Mike Padden	Washington	Gerald Ford	Ronald Reagan
1988	Margaret Leach	West Virginia	Michael Dukakis	Lloyd Bentsen
2000	Barbara Lett-Simmons	District of Columbia	Al Gore	vote withheld
2004	Anonymous[a]	Minnesota	John Kerry	John Edwards

Source: Adapted from *Guide to U.S. Elections*, 5th ed. (Washington, D.C.: CQ Press, 2005), vol. I, 735.

[a] In 2004 an anonymous Kerry elector in Minnesota gave his or her secret ballot to John Edwards.

Table 3-7 Party Winning Presidential Election, by State, 1789–2004

State	*1789–1824*			*1828–1856*			*1860–1892*			*1896–1928*			*1932–1964*			*1968–2004*		
	D	F	O	D	R	O	D	R	O	D	R	O	D	R	O	D	R	O
Alabama	2	0	0	8	0	0	6	2	0	9	0	0	7	1	1	1	8	1
Alaska	—	—	—	—	—	—	—	—	—	—	—	—	1	1	0	0	10	0
Arizona	—	—	—	—	—	—	—	—	—	2	3	0	5	4	0	1	9	0
Arkansas	—	—	—	6	0	0	6	1	0	9	0	0	9	0	0	3	6	1
California	—	—	—	2	0	0	2	7	0	1	7	1	6	3	0	4	6	0
Colorado	—	—	—	—	—	—	0	4	1	5	4	0	4	5	0	1	9	0
Connecticut	2	8	0	2	6	0	4	5	0	1	8	0	5	4	0	5	5	0
Delaware	2	8	0	2	6	0	7	1	1	1	8	0	5	4	0	5	5	0
Florida	—	—	—	2	1	0	4	3	1	8	1	0	6	3	0	2	8	0
Georgia	8	2	0	5	3	0	7	0	1	9	0	0	8	1	0	3	6	1
Hawaii	—	—	—	—	—	—	—	—	—	—	—	—	2	0	0	8	2	0
Idaho	—	—	—	—	—	—	—	—	1	4	5	0	6	3	0	0	10	0
Illinois	2	0	0	8	0	0	1	8	0	1	8	0	7	2	0	4	6	0
Indiana	3	0	0	6	2	0	3	6	0	1	8	0	3	6	0	0	10	0
Iowa	—	—	—	2	1	0	0	9	0	1	8	0	4	5	0	4	6	0
Kansas	—	—	—	—	—	—	0	7	1	3	6	0	3	6	0	0	10	0
Kentucky	8	1	0	2	6	0	8	0	1	6	3	0	7	2	0	3	7	0
Louisiana	4	0	0	6	2	0	5	1	1	9	0	0	6	2	1	3	6	1
Maine	2	0	0	5	3	0	0	9	0	1	8	0	1	8	0	5	5	0
Maryland	4	6	0	1	6	1	7	1	1	4	5	0	6	3	0	7	3	0
Massachusetts	3	7	0	0	8	0	0	9	0	2	7	0	7	2	0	8	2	0
Michigan	—	—	—	4	2	0	0	9	0	0	8	1	5	4	0	8	2	0
Minnesota	—	—	—	—	—	—	0	9	0	0	8	1	7	2	0	9	1	0
Mississippi	2	0	0	7	1	0	5	1	1	9	0	0	6	1	2	1	8	1

(Table continues)

Table 3-7 *(Continued)*

	1789–1824			*1828–1856*			*1860–1892*			*1896–1928*			*1932–1964*			*1968–2004*		
State	D	F	O	D	R	O	D	R	O	D	R	O	D	R	O	D	R	O
Missouri	—	—	—	8	0	0	7	2	0	4	5	0	8	1	0	3	7	0
Montana	—	—	—	—	—	—	0	1	0	4	5	0	6	3	0	1	9	0
Nebraska	—	—	—	—	—	—	0	7	0	4	5	0	3	6	0	0	10	0
Nevada	—	—	—	—	—	—	1	6	1	5	4	0	7	2	0	2	8	0
New Hampshire	4	6	0	6	2	0	0	9	0	2	7	0	4	5	0	3	7	0
New Jersey	5	5	0	3	5	0	7	2	0	1	8	0	6	3	0	4	6	0
New Mexico	—	—	—	—	—	—	—	—	—	2	3	0	7	2	0	3	7	0
New York	6	3	0	5	3	0	4	5	0	1	8	0	6	3	0	7	3	0
North Carolina	8	1	0	5	3	0	5	2	1	8	1	0	9	0	0	1	9	0
North Dakota	—	—	—	—	—	—	—	—	—	2	7	0	3	6	0	0	10	0
Ohio	6	0	0	4	4	0	0	9	0	2	7	0	5	4	0	3	7	0
Oklahoma	—	—	—	—	—	—	—	—	—	4	2	0	6	3	0	0	10	0
Oregon	—	—	—	—	—	—	1	8	0	1	8	0	5	4	0	5	5	0
Pennsylvania	8	2	0	6	2	0	0	9	0	0	8	1	5	4	0	6	4	0
Rhode Island	4	5	0	2	6	0	0	9	0	2	7	0	7	2	0	8	2	0
South Carolina	8	2	0	6	0	2	4	3	1	9	0	0	7	1	1	1	9	0
South Dakota	—	—	—	—	—	—	0	1	0	1	7	1	3	6	0	0	10	0
Tennessee	8	0	0	3	5	0	6	1	1	7	2	0	6	3	0	3	7	0
Texas	—	—	—	3	0	0	7	0	0	8	1	0	7	2	0	2	8	0
Utah	—	—	—	—	—	—	—	—	—	2	7	0	6	3	0	0	10	0
Vermont	6	3	0	7	1	0	0	9	0	0	9	0	1	8	0	4	6	0
Virginia	8	2	0	8	0	0	5	1	1	8	1	0	6	3	0	0	10	0
Washington	—	—	—	—	—	—	0	1	0	2	6	1	6	3	0	6	4	0
West Virginia	—	—	—	—	—	—	5	3	0	1	8	0	8	1	0	6	4	0
Wisconsin	—	—	—	2	1	0	1	8	0	1	7	1	5	4	0	6	4	0

Wyoming	—	—	—	—	—	—	0	1	0	3	6	0	5	4	0	0	10	0
District of Columbia[a]	—	—	—	—	—	—	—	—	—	—	—	—	1	0	0	10	0	0
Total[b]	113 (65%)	61 (35%)	0	136 (62%)	79 (36%)	3 (1%)	118 (37%)	189 (59%)	15 (5%)	170 (40%)	244 (58%)	7 (2%)	274 (63%)	158 (36%)	5 (1%)	159 (33%)	336 (66%)	5 (1%)

Source: Guide to U.S. Elections, 5th ed. (Washington, D.C.: CQ Press, 2005), vol. I, 750–804.

Note: D—The Democratic-Republican party from 1796 to 1820 and in 1828, the Jackson faction in 1824, and the Democratic party in 1832 and later; F—Federalists from 1789 to 1816, Independent Democratic-Republicans in 1820, and the J.Q. Adams faction in 1824; R—National Republicans in 1828 and 1832, Whigs from 1836 to 1852, and the Republican party in 1856 and later; O—others (third-party) parties. Southern Democrats in 1860 are counted as Democratic. "—" indicates that the state was not yet admitted to the Union.

[a] Residents of the District of Columbia received the presidential vote in 1961.
[b] Fewer total votes for a given state within a party system indicate admission of the state during the party system or nonvoting in certain southern states in 1864, 1868, and 1872.

Table 3-8 Percentage of Popular Votes for President, by State, 1968 and 1972

	1968				*1972*		
State	Richard M. Nixon (R)	Hubert H. Humphrey (D)	George C. Wallace (AI)	Others	Richard M. Nixon (R)	George S. McGovern (D)	Others
Alabama	14.0	18.8	65.8	1.4	48.8	47.5	3.7
Alaska	45.3	42.7	12.1	0.0	58.1	34.6	7.3
Arizona	54.8	35.0	9.6	0.6	61.6	30.4	8.0
Arkansas	30.8	30.4	38.9	0.0	68.9	30.7	0.4
California	47.8	44.7	6.7	0.7	55.0	41.5	3.5
Colorado	50.5	41.3	7.5	0.7	62.6	34.6	2.9
Connecticut	44.3	49.5	6.1	0.1	58.6	40.1	1.4
Delaware	45.1	41.6	13.3	0.0	59.6	39.2	1.2
Florida	40.5	30.9	28.5	0.0	71.9	27.8	0.3
Georgia	30.4	26.8	42.8	0.0	75.3	24.7	0.3
Hawaii	38.7	59.8	1.5	0.0	62.5	37.5	0.0
Idaho	56.8	30.7	12.6	0.0	64.2	26.0	9.7
Illinois	47.1	44.2	8.5	0.3	59.0	40.3	0.5
Indiana	50.3	38.0	11.5	0.3	66.1	33.3	0.5
Iowa	53.0	40.8	5.7	0.5	57.6	40.5	1.9
Kansas	54.8	34.7	10.2	0.3	67.7	29.5	2.9
Kentucky	43.8	37.7	18.3	0.3	63.4	34.8	6.3
Louisiana	23.5	28.2	48.3	0.0	66.0	28.6	5.4
Maine	43.1	55.3	1.6	0.0	61.5	38.5	0.0
Maryland	41.9	43.6	14.5	0.0	61.3	37.4	1.4
Massachusetts	32.9	63.0	3.7	0.4	45.2	54.2	0.6
Michigan	41.5	48.2	10.0	0.4	56.2	41.8	2.0
Minnesota	41.5	54.0	4.3	0.2	51.6	46.1	2.4
Mississippi	13.5	23.0	63.5	0.0	78.2	19.6	2.2
Missouri	44.9	43.7	11.4	0.0	62.3	37.7	0.3
Montana	50.6	41.6	7.3	0.5	57.9	37.9	4.2
Nebraska	59.8	31.8	8.4	0.0	70.5	29.5	0.0
Nevada	47.5	39.3	13.3	0.0	63.7	36.3	0.0

New Hampshire	52.1	43.9	3.8	0.2	64.0	34.9	1.2
New Jersey	46.1	44.0	9.1	0.8	61.6	36.8	1.7
New Mexico	51.9	39.8	7.9	0.5	61.1	36.6	2.4
New York	44.3	49.8	5.3	0.6	58.5	40.3	0.3
North Carolina	39.5	29.2	31.3	0.0	69.5	28.9	1.7
North Dakota	55.9	38.2	5.8	0.1	62.1	35.8	2.1
Ohio	45.2	43.0	11.8	0.0	59.6	38.1	2.3
Oklahoma	47.7	32.0	20.3	0.0	73.7	24.0	2.3
Oregon	49.8	43.8	6.1	0.3	52.5	42.3	5.3
Pennsylvania	44.0	47.6	8.0	0.4	59.1	39.1	1.7
Rhode Island	31.8	64.0	4.1	0.1	53.0	46.8	0.2
South Carolina	38.1	29.6	32.3	0.0	70.8	27.7	1.5
South Dakota	53.3	42.0	4.8	0.0	54.2	45.5	0.3
Tennessee	37.9	28.1	34.0	0.0	67.7	29.8	2.5
Texas	39.9	41.1	19.0	0.0	66.2	33.3	0.6
Utah	56.5	37.1	6.4	0.1	67.6	26.4	6.0
Vermont	52.8	43.5	3.2	0.6	62.7	36.6	0.9
Virginia	43.4	32.5	23.6	0.5	67.8	30.1	2.1
Washington	45.2	47.3	7.4	0.2	56.9	38.6	4.5
West Virginia	40.8	49.6	9.6	0.0	63.6	36.4	0.0
Wisconsin	47.9	44.3	7.6	0.3	53.4	43.7	2.9
Wyoming	55.8	35.5	8.7	0.0	69.0	30.5	0.5
District of Columbia	18.2	81.8	0.0	0.0	21.6	78.1	0.3
Average	43.4	42.7	13.5	0.3	60.7	37.5	1.8

Source: Adapted from *Guide to U.S. Elections*, 5th ed. (Washington, D.C.: CQ Press, 2005), vol. I, 710–711.

Note: R—Republican; D—Democrat; AI—American Independent.

Table 3-9 Percentage of Popular Votes for President, by State, 1976 and 1980

	1976				*1980*			
State	Jimmy Carter (D)	Gerald R. Ford (R)	Eugene J. McCarthy (I)	Others	Ronald Reagan (R)	Jimmy Carter (D)	John Anderson (I)	Others
Alabama	55.7	42.6	0.0	1.6	48.8	47.5	1.2	2.5
Alaska	35.7	57.9	0.0	6.5	54.3	26.4	7.0	12.3
Arizona	39.8	56.4	2.6	1.2	60.6	28.2	8.8	2.4
Arkansas	65.0	34.9	0.1	0.1	48.1	47.5	2.7	1.7
California	47.6	49.3	0.7	2.3	52.7	35.9	8.6	2.8
Colorado	42.6	54.0	2.4	1.0	55.1	31.1	11.0	2.8
Connecticut	46.9	52.1	0.3	0.8	48.2	38.5	12.2	1.1
Delaware	52.0	46.6	1.0	0.4	47.2	44.8	6.9	1.1
Florida	51.9	46.6	0.8	0.7	55.5	38.5	5.2	0.8
Georgia	66.7	33.0	0.1	0.2	41.0	55.8	2.2	1.0
Hawaii	50.6	48.1	0.0	1.3	42.9	44.8	10.6	1.7
Idaho	36.8	59.3	0.3	3.5	66.4	25.2	6.2	2.2
Illinois	48.1	50.1	1.2	0.6	49.7	41.7	7.3	1.3
Indiana	45.7	53.3	0.0	1.0	56.0	37.7	5.0	1.3
Iowa	48.5	49.5	1.6	0.5	51.3	38.6	8.8	1.3
Kansas	44.9	52.5	1.4	1.2	57.8	33.3	7.0	1.9
Kentucky	52.8	45.6	0.6	1.1	49.1	47.6	2.4	0.9
Louisiana	51.7	46.0	0.5	1.8	51.2	45.8	1.7	1.3
Maine	48.1	48.9	2.3	0.8	45.6	42.3	10.2	1.9
Maryland	52.8	46.7	0.3	0.2	44.2	47.1	7.8	0.9
Massachusetts	56.1	40.4	2.6	0.9	41.9	41.7	15.2	1.2
Michigan	46.4	51.8	1.3	0.4	49.0	42.5	7.0	1.5
Minnesota	54.9	42.0	1.8	1.3	42.6	46.5	8.5	2.4
Mississippi	49.6	47.7	0.5	2.3	49.4	48.1	1.3	1.2
Missouri	51.1	47.5	1.2	0.2	51.2	44.3	3.7	0.8
Montana	45.4	52.8	0.0	1.8	56.8	32.4	8.1	2.7

Nebraska	38.5	59.2	1.5	0.8	65.5	26.0	7.0	1.4
Nevada	45.8	50.2	0.0	4.1	62.5	26.9	7.1	3.5
New Hampshire	43.5	54.7	1.2	0.6	57.7	28.4	12.9	1.0
New Jersey	47.9	50.1	1.1	0.9	52.0	38.6	7.9	1.5
New Mexico	48.1	50.5	0.3	1.2	54.9	36.7	6.5	1.9
New York	51.9	47.5	0.1	0.6	46.7	44.0	7.5	1.8
North Carolina	55.2	44.2	0.0	0.5	49.3	47.2	2.9	0.6
North Dakota	45.8	51.6	1.0	1.6	64.2	26.3	7.8	1.7
Ohio	48.9	48.7	1.4	1.0	51.5	40.9	5.9	1.7
Oklahoma	48.7	50.0	1.3	0.0	60.5	35.0	3.3	1.2
Oregon	47.6	47.8	3.9	0.7	48.3	38.7	9.5	3.5
Pennsylvania	50.4	47.7	1.1	0.8	49.6	42.5	6.4	1.5
Rhode Island	55.4	44.1	0.1	0.5	37.2	47.7	14.4	0.7
South Carolina	56.2	43.1	0.0	0.7	49.4	48.2	1.6	0.8
South Dakota	48.9	50.4	0.0	0.7	60.5	31.7	6.5	1.3
Tennessee	55.9	42.9	0.3	0.8	48.7	48.4	2.2	0.7
Texas	51.1	48.0	0.5	0.4	55.3	41.4	2.5	0.8
Utah	33.6	62.4	0.7	3.2	72.8	20.6	5.0	1.6
Vermont	43.1	54.4	2.1	0.4	44.4	38.4	14.9	2.3
Virginia	48.0	49.3	0.0	2.8	53.0	40.3	5.1	1.6
Washington	46.1	50.0	2.4	1.5	49.7	37.3	10.6	2.4
West Virginia	58.0	41.9	0.0	0.0	45.3	49.8	4.3	0.6
Wisconsin	49.4	47.8	1.7	1.2	47.9	43.2	7.1	1.8
Wyoming	39.8	59.3	0.4	0.5	62.6	28.0	6.8	2.6
District of Columbia	81.6	16.5	0.0	1.9	13.4	74.8	9.3	2.4
Average	50.1	48.0	0.9	1.0	50.7	41.0	6.6	1.7

Source: Adapted from *Guide to U.S. Elections*, 5th ed. (Washington, D.C.: CQ Press, 2005), vol. I, 712–713.

Note: D—Democrat; R—Republican; I—Independent.

Table 3-10 Percentage of Popular Votes for President, by State, 1984 and 1988

	1984			*1988*		
State	Ronald Reagan (R)	Walter Mondale (D)	Others	George H. W. Bush (R)	Michael Dukakis (D)	Others
Alabama	60.5	38.3	1.2	59.2	39.9	0.9
Alaska	66.6	29.9	3.5	59.7	36.2	4.1
Arizona	66.4	32.5	1.1	60.0	38.8	1.2
Arkansas	60.5	38.3	1.2	56.4	42.2	1.4
California	57.5	41.3	1.2	51.1	47.6	1.3
Colorado	63.4	35.1	1.5	53.1	45.3	1.6
Connecticut	60.7	38.8	0.5	52.0	46.9	1.1
Delaware	59.8	39.9	0.3	55.9	43.5	0.6
Florida	65.3	34.7	0.0	60.9	38.5	0.6
Georgia	60.2	39.8	0.0	59.7	39.5	0.8
Hawaii	55.1	43.8	1.1	44.7	54.3	1.0
Idaho	72.4	26.4	1.2	62.1	36.0	1.9
Illinois	56.2	43.3	0.5	50.7	48.6	0.7
Indiana	61.7	37.7	0.6	59.8	39.7	0.5
Iowa	53.3	45.9	0.8	44.5	54.7	0.8
Kansas	66.3	32.6	1.1	55.8	42.5	1.7
Kentucky	60.0	39.4	0.6	55.5	43.9	0.6
Louisiana	60.8	38.2	1.0	54.3	44.1	1.6
Maine	60.8	38.8	0.4	55.3	43.9	0.8
Maryland	52.5	47.0	0.5	51.1	48.2	0.7
Massachusetts	51.2	48.4	0.4	45.4	53.2	1.4
Michigan	59.2	40.2	0.6	53.5	45.7	0.8
Minnesota	49.5	49.7	0.8	45.9	52.9	1.2
Mississippi	61.9	37.4	0.7	59.9	39.1	1.0
Missouri	60.0	40.0	0.0	51.8	47.9	0.3
Montana	60.5	38.2	1.3	52.1	46.2	1.7
Nebraska	70.6	28.8	0.6	60.1	39.2	0.7
Nevada	65.8	32.0	2.2	58.9	37.9	3.2

New Hampshire	68.6	30.9	0.5	62.5	36.3	1.2
New Jersey	60.1	39.2	0.7	56.2	42.6	1.2
New Mexico	59.7	39.2	1.1	51.9	46.9	1.2
New York	53.8	45.8	0.4	47.5	51.6	0.9
North Carolina	61.9	37.9	0.2	58.0	41.7	0.3
North Dakota	64.8	33.8	1.4	56.0	43.0	1.0
Ohio	58.9	40.1	1.0	55.0	44.1	0.9
Oklahoma	68.6	30.7	0.7	57.9	41.3	0.8
Oregon	55.9	43.7	0.4	46.6	51.3	2.1
Pennsylvania	53.3	46.0	0.7	50.7	48.4	0.9
Rhode Island	51.8	47.9	0.3	43.9	55.7	0.4
South Carolina	63.6	35.6	0.8	61.5	37.6	0.9
South Dakota	63.0	36.5	0.5	52.9	46.5	0.6
Tennessee	57.8	41.6	0.6	57.9	41.5	0.6
Texas	63.6	36.1	0.3	56.0	43.3	0.7
Utah	74.5	24.7	0.8	66.2	32.0	1.8
Vermont	57.9	40.8	1.3	51.1	47.6	1.3
Virginia	62.3	37.1	0.6	59.7	39.2	1.1
Washington	55.8	42.9	1.3	48.5	50.0	1.5
West Virginia	55.1	44.6	0.3	47.5	52.2	0.3
Wisconsin	54.3	45.1	0.8	47.8	51.4	0.8
Wyoming	70.5	28.2	1.2	60.5	38.0	1.5
District of Columbia	13.7	85.4	0.9	14.3	82.6	3.1
Average	58.8	40.6	0.6	53.4	45.6	1.0

Source: Adapted from *Guide to U.S. Elections*, 5th ed. (Washington, D.C.: CQ Press, 2005), vol. I, 714–715.

Note: R—Republican; D—Democrat.

Table 3-11 Percentage of Popular Votes for President, by State, 1992 and 1996

	1992				*1996*			
State	Bill Clinton (D)	George H. W. Bush (R)	Ross Perot	Others	Bill Clinton (D)	Bob Dole (R)	Ross Perot	Others
Alabama	40.9	47.6	10.8	0.6	43.2	50.1	6.0	0.7
Alaska	30.3	39.5	28.4	1.8	33.3	50.8	10.9	5.0
Arizona	36.5	38.5	23.8	1.2	46.5	44.3	8.0	1.2
Arkansas	53.2	35.5	10.4	0.9	53.7	36.8	7.9	1.6
California	46.0	32.6	20.6	0.8	51.1	38.2	7.0	3.7
Colorado	40.1	35.9	23.3	0.7	44.4	45.8	6.6	3.2
Connecticut	42.2	35.8	21.6	0.4	52.8	34.7	10.0	2.5
Delaware	43.5	35.3	20.4	0.7	51.8	36.6	10.6	1.0
Florida	39.0	40.9	19.8	0.3	48.0	42.3	9.1	0.5
Georgia	43.5	42.9	13.3	0.3	45.8	47.0	6.4	0.8
Hawaii	48.1	36.7	14.2	1.0	56.9	31.6	7.6	3.8
Idaho	28.4	42.0	27.0	2.5	33.6	52.2	12.7	1.5
Illinois	48.6	34.3	16.6	0.4	54.3	36.8	8.0	0.8
Indiana	36.8	42.9	19.8	0.5	41.6	47.1	10.5	0.8
Iowa	43.3	37.3	18.7	0.7	50.3	39.9	8.5	1.3
Kansas	33.7	38.9	27.0	0.4	36.1	54.3	8.6	1.0
Kentucky	44.6	41.3	13.7	0.4	45.8	44.9	8.7	0.6
Louisiana	45.6	41.0	11.8	1.6	52.0	39.9	6.9	1.1
Maine	38.8	30.4	30.4	0.4	51.6	30.8	14.2	3.4
Maryland	49.8	35.6	14.2	0.4	54.3	38.3	6.5	1.0
Massachusetts	47.5	29.0	22.7	0.7	61.5	28.1	8.9	1.6
Michigan	43.8	36.4	19.3	0.6	51.7	38.5	8.7	1.1
Minnesota	43.5	31.9	24.0	0.7	51.1	35.0	11.8	2.2
Mississippi	40.8	49.7	8.7	0.8	44.1	49.2	5.8	0.9
Missouri	44.1	33.9	21.7	0.3	47.5	41.2	10.1	1.2
Montana	37.6	35.1	26.1	1.1	41.3	44.1	13.6	1.1
Nebraska	29.4	46.6	23.6	0.4	35.0	53.7	10.5	0.9
Nevada	37.4	34.7	26.2	1.7	43.9	42.9	9.5	3.7

New Hampshire	38.9	37.6	22.6	0.9	49.3	39.4	9.7	1.6
New Jersey	43.0	40.6	15.6	0.9	53.7	35.9	8.5	1.9
New Mexico	45.9	37.3	16.1	0.6	49.2	41.9	5.8	3.2
New York	49.7	33.9	15.7	0.6	59.5	30.6	8.0	1.9
North Carolina	42.7	43.4	13.7	0.2	44.0	48.7	6.7	0.6
North Dakota	32.2	44.2	23.1	0.5	40.1	46.9	12.2	0.7
Ohio	40.2	38.3	21.0	0.5	47.4	41.0	10.7	1.0
Oklahoma	34.0	42.6	23.0	0.3	40.4	48.3	10.8	0.5
Oregon	42.5	32.5	24.2	0.8	47.2	39.1	8.8	5.0
Pennsylvania	45.1	36.1	18.2	0.5	49.2	40.0	9.6	1.3
Rhode Island	47.0	29.0	23.2	0.8	59.7	26.8	11.2	2.3
South Carolina	39.9	48.0	11.5	0.6	44.0	49.8	5.6	0.7
South Dakota	37.1	40.7	21.8	0.4	43.0	46.5	9.7	0.8
Tennessee	47.1	42.4	10.1	0.4	48.0	45.6	5.6	0.8
Texas	37.1	40.6	22.0	0.3	43.8	48.8	6.7	0.7
Utah	24.7	43.4	27.3	4.6	33.3	54.4	10.0	2.3
Vermont	46.1	30.4	22.8	0.7	53.4	31.1	12.0	3.6
Virginia	40.6	45.0	13.6	0.8	45.1	47.1	6.6	1.1
Washington	43.4	32.0	23.7	1.0	49.8	37.3	8.9	3.9
West Virginia	48.4	35.4	15.9	0.3	51.5	36.8	11.3	0.5
Wisconsin	41.1	36.8	21.5	0.6	48.8	38.5	10.4	2.4
Wyoming	34.0	39.6	25.6	0.9	36.8	49.8	12.3	1.1
District of Columbia	84.6	9.1	4.3	2.0	85.2	9.3	1.9	3.5
Average	43.0	37.4	18.9	0.6	49.2	40.7	8.4	1.7

Source: Guide to U.S. Elections, 5th ed. (Washington, D.C.: CQ Press, 2005), vol. I, 716–717.

Note: R—Republican; D—Democrat; I—Independent.

Table 3-12 Percentage of Popular Votes for President, by State, 2000 and 2004

	2000				*2004*		
State	George W. Bush (R)	Al Gore (D)	Ralph Nader (I)	Others	George W. Bush (R)	John Kerry (D)	Others
Alabama	56.5	41.6	1.1	0.9	62.5	36.8	0.7
Alaska	58.6	27.7	10.1	3.6	61.1	35.5	3.4
Arizona	51.0	44.7	3.0	1.3	54.9	44.4	0.7
Arkansas	51.3	45.9	1.5	1.3	54.3	44.5	1.2
California	41.7	53.4	3.8	1.1	44.4	54.3	1.3
Colorado	50.8	42.4	5.3	1.5	51.7	47.0	1.3
Connecticut	38.4	55.9	4.4	1.3	43.9	54.3	1.8
Delaware	41.9	55.0	2.5	0.6	45.8	53.3	0.9
Florida	48.8	48.8	1.6	0.8	52.1	47.1	0.8
Georgia	54.7	43.0	0.5	1.8	58.0	41.4	0.6
Hawaii	37.5	55.8	5.9	0.8	45.3	54.0	0.7
Idaho	67.2	27.6	2.5	2.7	68.4	30.3	1.3
Illinois	42.6	54.6	2.2	0.6	44.5	54.8	0.7
Indiana	56.6	41.0	0.8	1.6	59.9	39.3	0.8
Iowa	48.2	48.5	2.2	1.1	49.9	49.2	0.9
Kansas	58.0	37.2	3.4	1.4	62.0	36.6	1.4
Kentucky	56.5	41.4	1.5	0.6	59.6	39.7	0.7
Louisiana	52.6	44.9	1.2	1.3	56.7	42.2	1.1
Maine	44.0	49.1	5.7	1.2	44.6	53.6	1.8
Maryland	40.3	56.5	2.7	0.5	42.9	55.9	1.2
Massachusetts	32.5	59.8	6.4	1.3	36.8	61.9	1.3
Michigan	46.1	51.3	2.0	0.6	47.8	51.2	1.0
Minnesota	45.5	47.9	5.2	1.4	47.6	51.1	1.3
Mississippi	57.6	40.7	0.8	0.9	59.5	39.8	0.7
Missouri	50.4	47.1	1.6	0.9	53.3	46.1	0.6

Montana	58.4	33.4	5.9	2.3	59.1	38.6	2.3
Nebraska	62.2	33.3	3.5	1.0	65.9	32.7	1.4
Nevada	49.5	46.0	2.5	2.0	50.5	47.9	1.6
New Hampshire	48.1	46.8	3.9	1.2	48.9	50.2	0.9
New Jersey	40.3	56.1	3.0	0.6	46.2	52.9	0.9
New Mexico	47.8	47.9	3.6	0.7	49.8	49.0	1.2
New York	35.2	60.2	3.6	1.0	40.1	58.4	1.5
North Carolina	56.0	43.2	0.0	0.8	56.0	43.6	0.4
North Dakota	60.7	33.1	3.3	2.9	62.9	35.5	1.6
Ohio	50.0	46.4	2.5	1.1	50.8	48.7	0.5
Oklahoma	60.3	38.4	0.0	1.3	65.6	34.4	0.0
Oregon	46.5	47.0	5.0	1.5	47.2	51.3	1.5
Pennsylvania	46.4	50.6	2.1	0.9	48.4	50.9	0.7
Rhode Island	31.9	61.0	6.1	1.0	38.7	59.4	1.9
South Carolina	56.8	40.9	1.5	0.8	58.0	40.9	1.1
South Dakota	60.3	37.6	0.0	2.1	59.9	38.4	1.7
Tennessee	51.1	47.3	1.0	0.6	56.8	42.5	0.7
Texas	59.3	38.0	2.2	0.5	61.1	38.2	0.7
Utah	66.8	26.3	4.7	2.2	71.5	26.0	2.5
Vermont	40.7	50.6	6.9	1.8	38.8	58.9	2.3
Virginia	52.5	44.4	2.2	0.9	53.7	45.5	0.8
Washington	44.6	50.2	4.1	1.1	45.6	52.8	1.6
West Virginia	51.9	45.6	1.6	0.9	56.1	43.2	0.7
Wisconsin	47.6	47.8	3.6	1.0	49.3	49.7	1.0
Wyoming	67.8	27.7	2.1	2.4	68.9	29.1	2.0
District of Columbia	9.0	85.2	5.2	0.6	9.3	89.2	1.5
Total	47.9	48.4	2.7	1.0	50.7	48.3	1.0

Source: Guide to U.S. Elections, 5th ed. (Washington, D.C.: CQ Press, 2005), vol. I, 718–719.

Note: R—Republican; D—Democrat; I—Independent.

Table 3-13 Electoral Votes, by State, 1968

State	*Electoral votes*	*1968 winner*
Alabama	10	W
Alaska	3	N
Arizona	5	N
Arkansas	6	W
California[a]	40	N
Colorado	6	N
Connecticut	8	H
Delaware	3	N
Florida[a]	14	N
Georgia	12	W
Hawaii	4	H
Idaho	4	N
Illinois[a]	26	N
Indiana[a]	13	N
Iowa	9	N
Kansas	7	N
Kentucky	9	N
Louisiana	10	W
Maine	4	H
Maryland	10	H
Massachusetts[a]	14	H
Michigan[a]	21	H
Minnesota	10	H
Mississippi	7	W
Missouri	12	N
Montana	4	N
Nebraska	5	N
Nevada	3	N
New Hampshire	4	N
New Jersey[a]	17	N
New Mexico	4	N
New York[a]	43	H
North Carolina[a]	13	N[b]
North Dakota	4	N
Ohio[a]	26	N
Oklahoma	8	N
Oregon	6	N
Pennsylvania[a]	29	H
Rhode Island	4	H
South Carolina	8	N
South Dakota	4	N
Tennessee	11	N
Texas[a]	25	H
Utah	4	N
Vermont	3	N
Virginia	12	N
Washington	9	H

(Table continues)

Table 3-13 *(Continued)*

State	*Electoral votes*	*1968 winner*
West Virginia	7	H
Wisconsin	12	N
Wyoming	3	N
District of Columbia	3	H
Total votes	538	
Number of votes needed to win	270	
Winner (votes)		N (301)
Number of large states won		7

Source: Adapted from *Guide to U.S. Elections*, 5th ed. (Washington, D.C.: CQ Press, 2005), vol. I, 795.

Note: W—George Wallace; N—Richard Nixon; H—Hubert Humphrey.

[a] One of twelve states with highest number of electoral votes. Total votes from these states add to 281.
[b] One electoral vote went to Wallace.

Table 3-14 Electoral Votes, by State, 1972, 1976, and 1980

State	*Electoral votes*	*1972 winner*	*1976 winner*	*1980 winner*
Alabama	9	N	C	R
Alaska	3	N	F	R
Arizona	6	N	F	R
Arkansas	6	N	C	R
California[a]	45	N	F	R
Colorado	7	N	F	R
Connecticut	8	N	F	R
Delaware	3	N	C	R
Florida[a]	17	N	C	R
Georgia	12	N	C	C
Hawaii	4	N	C	C
Idaho	4	N	F	R
Illinois[a]	26	N	F	R
Indiana[a]	13	N	F	R
Iowa	8	N	F	R
Kansas	7	N	F	R
Kentucky	9	N	C	R
Louisiana	10	N	C	R
Maine	4	N	F	R
Maryland	10	N	C	C
Massachusetts[a]	14	M	C	R
Michigan[a]	21	N	F	R
Minnesota	10	N	C	C
Mississippi	7	N	C	R
Missouri	12	N	C	R
Montana	4	N	F	R
Nebraska	5	N	F	R
Nevada	3	N	F	R
New Hampshire	4	N	F	R
New Jersey[a]	17	N	F	R
New Mexico	4	N	F	R
New York[a]	41	N	C	R
North Carolina[a]	13	N	C	R
North Dakota	3	N	F	R
Ohio[a]	25	N	C	R
Oklahoma	8	N	F	R
Oregon	6	N	F	R
Pennsylvania[a]	27	N	C	R
Rhode Island	4	N	C	C
South Carolina	8	N	C	R
South Dakota	4	N	F	R
Tennessee	10	N	C	R
Texas[a]	26	N	C	R
Utah	4	N	F	R
Vermont	3	N	F	R
Virginia	12	N[b]	F	R

(Table continues)

Table 3-14 *(Continued)*

State	*Electoral votes*	*1972 winner*	*1976 winner*	*1980 winner*
Washington	9	N	F[c]	R
West Virginia	6	N	C	C
Wisconsin	11	N	C	R
Wyoming	3	N	F	R
District of Columbia	3	M	C	C
Total votes	538			
Number of votes needed to win	270			
Winner (votes)		N (520)	C (297)	R (489)
Number of large states won		11	7	12

Source: Adapted from *Guide to U.S. Elections*, 5th ed. (Washington, D.C.: CQ Press, 2005), vol. I, 796–798.

Note: N—Richard Nixon; C—Jimmy Carter; R—Ronald Reagan; F—Gerald Ford; M—George McGovern.

[a] One of twelve states with highest number of electoral votes. Total votes from these states add to 285.
[b] One electoral vote went to John Hospers.
[c] One electoral vote went to Reagan.

Table 3-15 Electoral Votes, by State, 1984 and 1988

State	*Electoral votes*	*1984 winner*	*1988 winner*
Alabama	9	R	B
Alaska	3	R	B
Arizona	7	R	B
Arkansas	6	R	B
California[a]	47	R	B
Colorado	8	R	B
Connecticut	8	R	B
Delaware	3	R	B
Florida[a]	21	R	B
Georgia[a]	12	R	B
Hawaii	4	R	D
Idaho	4	R	B
Illinois[a]	24	R	B
Indiana[a]	12	R	B
Iowa	8	R	D
Kansas	7	R	B
Kentucky	9	R	B
Louisiana	10	R	B
Maine	4	R	B
Maryland	10	R	B
Massachusetts[a]	13	R	D
Michigan[a]	20	R	B
Minnesota	10	M	D
Mississippi	7	R	B
Missouri	11	R	B
Montana	4	R	B
Nebraska	5	R	B
Nevada	4	R	B
New Hampshire	4	R	B
New Jersey[a]	16	R	B
New Mexico	5	R	B
New York[a]	36	R	D
North Carolina[a]	13	R	B
North Dakota	3	R	B
Ohio[a]	23	R	B
Oklahoma	8	R	B
Oregon	7	R	D
Pennsylvania[a]	25	R	B
Rhode Island	4	R	D
South Carolina	8	R	B
South Dakota	3	R	B
Tennessee	11	R	B
Texas[a]	29	R	B
Utah	5	R	B
Vermont	3	R	B
Virginia[a]	12	R	B

(Table continues)

Table 3-15 *(Continued)*

State	*Electoral votes*	*1984 winner*	*1988 winner*
Washington	10	R	D
West Virginia	6	R	D[b]
Wisconsin	11	R	D
Wyoming	3	R	B
District of Columbia	3	M	D
Total votes	538		
Number of votes needed to win	270		
Winner (votes)		R (525)	B (426)
Number of large states won		14	12

Source: Adapted from *Guide to U.S. Elections*, 5th ed. (Washington, D.C.: CQ Press, 2005), vol. I, 799–800.

Note: R—Ronald Reagan; B—George H. W. Bush; M—Walter Mondale; D—Michael Dukakis.

[a] One of fourteen states with highest number of electoral votes. Total votes from these states add to 303.
[b] One electoral vote went to Lloyd Bentsen.

Table 3-16 Electoral Votes, by State, 1992 and 1996

State	*Electoral votes*	*1992 winner*	*1996 winner*
Alabama	9	B	D
Alaska	3	B	D
Arizona	8	B	C
Arkansas	6	C	C
California[a]	54	C	C
Colorado	8	C	D
Connecticut	8	C	C
Delaware	3	C	C
Florida[a]	25	B	C
Georgia[a]	13	C	D
Hawaii	4	C	C
Idaho	4	B	D
Illinois[a]	22	C	C
Indiana	12	B	D
Iowa	7	C	C
Kansas	6	B	D
Kentucky	8	C	C
Louisiana	9	C	C
Maine	4	C	C
Maryland	10	C	C
Massachusetts	12	C	C
Michigan[a]	18	C	C
Minnesota	10	C	C
Mississippi	7	B	D
Missouri	11	C	C
Montana	3	C	D
Nebraska	5	B	D
Nevada	4	C	C
New Hampshire	4	C	C
New Jersey[a]	15	C	C
New Mexico	5	C	C
New York[a]	33	C	C
North Carolina[a]	14	B	D
North Dakota	3	B	D
Ohio[a]	21	C	C
Oklahoma	8	B	D
Oregon	7	C	C
Pennsylvania[a]	23	C	C
Rhode Island	4	C	C
South Carolina	8	B	D
South Dakota	3	B	D
Tennessee	11	C	C
Texas[a]	32	B	D
Utah	5	B	D
Vermont	3	C	C
Virginia[a]	13	B	D

(Table continues)

Table 3-16 *(Continued)*

State	*Electoral votes*	*1992 winner*	*1996 winner*
Washington	11	C	C
West Virginia	5	C	C
Wisconsin	11	C	C
Wyoming	3	B	D
District of Columbia	3	C	C
Total votes	538		
Number of votes needed to win	270		
Winner (votes)		C (370)	C (379)
Number of large states won		8	8

Sources: (1992) Bureau of the Census, *Statistical Abstract of the United States 1993* (Washington, D.C.: Government Printing Office, 1993), 264; (1996) *Congressional Quarterly Weekly Report,* Nov. 9, 1996, 3192.

Note: B—George H. W. Bush; D—Dole; C—Bill Clinton.

[a] One of twelve states with highest number of electoral votes. Total votes from these states add to 283.

Table 3-17 Electoral Votes, by State, 2000 and 2004

State	*Electoral votes 2000*	*2000 winner*	*Electoral votes 2004*	*2004 winner*
Alabama	9	B	9	B
Alaska	3	B	3	B
Arizona	8	B	10	B
Arkansas	6	B	6	B
California[a]	54	G	55	K
Colorado	8	B	9	B
Connecticut	8	G	7	K
Delaware	3	G	3	K
Florida[a]	25	B	27	B
Georgia[a]	13	B	15	B
Hawaii	4	G	4	K
Idaho	4	B	4	B
Illinois[a]	22	G	21	K
Indiana	12	B	11	B
Iowa	7	G	7	B
Kansas	6	B	6	B
Kentucky	8	B	8	B
Louisiana	9	B	9	B
Maine	4	G	4	K
Maryland	10	G	10	K
Massachusetts	12	G	12	K
Michigan[a]	18	G	17	K
Minnesota	10	G	10	K
Mississippi	7	B	6	B
Missouri	11	B	11	B
Montana	3	B	3	B
Nebraska	5	B	5	B
Nevada	4	B	5	B
New Hampshire	4	B	4	K
New Jersey[a]	15	G	15	K
New Mexico	5	G	5	B
New York[a]	33	G	31	K
North Carolina[a]	14	B	15	B
North Dakota	3	B	3	B
Ohio[a]	21	B	20	B
Oklahoma	8	B	7	B
Oregon	7	G	7	K
Pennsylvania[a]	23	G	21	K
Rhode Island	4	G	4	K
South Carolina	8	B	8	B
South Dakota	3	B	3	B
Tennessee	11	B	11	B
Texas[a]	32	B	34	B
Utah	5	B	5	B
Vermont	3	G	3	K
Virginia[a]	13	B	13	B

(Table continues)

Table 3-17 *(Continued)*

State	*Electoral votes 2000*	*2000 winner*	*Electoral votes 2004*	*2004 winner*
Washington	11	G	11	K
West Virginia	5	B	5	B
Wisconsin	11	G	10	K
Wyoming	3	B	3	B
District of Columbia	3	G	3	K
Total votes	538		538	
Number of votes needed to win	270		270	
Winner (votes)		B (271)		B (286)
Number of large states won		6		6

Source: Guide to U.S. Elections, 5th ed. (Washington, D.C.: CQ Press, 2005), vol. I, 803–804.

Note: B—George W. Bush; G—Al Gore; K—John Kerry.

[a] One of twelve states with highest number of electoral votes. Total votes from these states add to 283.

Table 3-18 Representation of the President's Party in the Two-Party House Vote, 1824–2006

Year	*President's party*	*Percentage of House vote*[a]	*Unified or Divided Government*
1824	DR	58	UG
1826	DR	61	DG
1828	D	44	UG
1830	D	53	UG
1832	D	55	UG
1834	D	54	UG
1836	D	52	UG
1838	D	54	UG
1840	W	54	UG
1842	W	45	DG-H
1844	D	51	UG
1846	D	53	DG-H
1848	W	48	DG
1850	W	45	DG
1852	D	54	UG
1854	D	80	DG-H
1856	D	70	UG
1858	D	69	DG-H
1860	R	57	UG
1862	R	63	UG
1864	R	64	UG
1866	D	59	UG
1868	R	56	UG
1870	R	53	UG
1872	R	55	UG
1874	R	53	DG-H
1876	R	49	DG-H
1878	R	45	DG
1880	R	49	U
1882	R	43	DG-H
1884	D	47	DG-S
1886	D	44	DG-S
1888	R	49	DG-H
1890	R	45	DG-H
1892	D	53	UG
1894	D	45	DG
1896	R	48	UG
1898	R	46	UG
1900	R	50	UG
1902	R	48	UG
1904	R	53	UG
1906	R	49	UG
1908	R	48	UG
1910	R	46	DG-H
1912	D	61	UG
1914	D	57	UG
1916	D	55	UG
1918	D	54	DG
1920	R	56	UG

(Table continues)

Table 3-18 *(Continued)*

Year	*President's party*	*Percentage of House vote*[a]	*Unified or Divided Government*
1922	R	47	UG
1924	R	51	UG
1926	R	51	UG
1928	R	51	UG
1930	R	46	DG-H
1932	D	62	UG
1934	D	64	UG
1936	D	63	UG
1938	D	60	UG
1940	D	59	UG
1942	D	57	UG
1944	D	58	UG
1946	D	54	DG
1948	D	58	UG
1950	D	57	UG
1952	R	47	UG
1954	R	42	DG
1956	R	44	DG
1958	R	38	DG
1960	D	59	UG
1962	D	55	UG
1964	D	59	UG
1966	D	52	UG
1968	R	48	DG
1970	R	44	DG
1972	R	48	DG
1974	R	42	DG
1976	D	57	UG
1978	D	54	UG
1980	R	48	DG-H
1982	R	47	DG-H
1984	R	48	DG-H
1986	R	45	DG
1988	R	46	DG
1990	R	44	DG
1992	D	51	UG
1994	D	49	DG
1996	D	49	DG
1998	D	48	DG
2000	R	49	DG
2002	R	50	DG-S
2004	R	49	UG
2006	R	46	DG

Source: Clerk of the House of Representatives, Election Information, http://clerk.house.gov/member_info/electionInfo.

Note: DR—Democratic-Republican; D—Democrat; W—Whig; R—Republican; UG—unified government: a majority of congressional seats held by the president's party; DG—divided government; DG-H—divided government in the House; DG-S—divided government in the Senate.

[a] The tally is the percentage of the two-party House vote representing the president's party.

Figure 3-1 State Turnout in Presidential Elections, by Region, 1920–2004

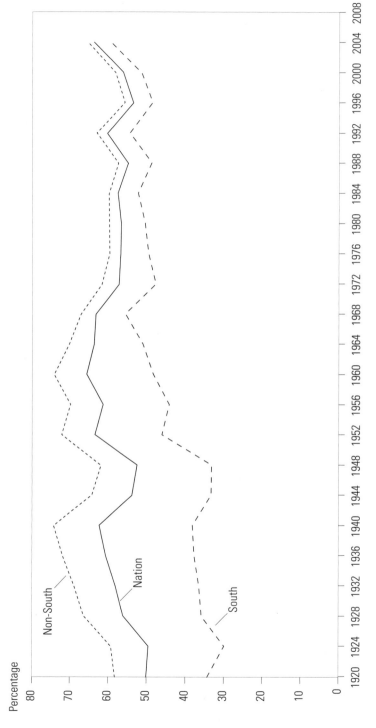

Source: Adapted from Jerrold G. Rusk, *A Statistical History of the American Electorate* (Washington, D.C.: CQ Press, 2001), 52.

Table 3-19 State Voter Turnout in Presidential Elections, by State, 1824–1876 (percent)

State	*1824*	*1828*	*1832*	*1836*	*1840*	*1844*	*1848*	*1852*	*1856*	*1860*	*1864*	*1868*	*1872*	*1876*
Alabama	49.1	52.6	31.5	64.9	89.7	81.3	71.5	46.5	72.1	79.2	[a]	74.0	79.5	72.9
Arkansas	—	—	—	28.8	67.7	62.2	54.1	46.8	58.1	76.7	[a]	40.9	68.1	65.6
California	—	—	—	—	—	—	—	84.7	85.8	72.1	60.7	59.5	59.6	81.6
Colorado	—	—	—	—	—	—	—	—	—	—	—	—	—	[b]
Connecticut	16.7	28.7	46.6	52.3	75.6	76.3	66.2	64.3	70.5	60.4	65.2	69.0	72.6	86.1
Delaware	—	—	67.1	69.5	82.8	84.7	78.7	72.4	74.7	74.6	74.0	76.8	73.3	73.3
Florida	—	—	—	—	—	—	63.5	54.6	71.9	74.1	[a]	[b]	76.9	90.8
Georgia	—	35.6	32.0	64.3	88.2	93.2	89.6	55.8	82.5	83.5	[a]	68.0	55.1	63.3
Illinois	24.1	52.2	46.1	43.3	85.9	76.6	70.7	64.8	72.4	80.5	69.6	77.7	75.0	87.3
Indiana	37.1	68.9	72.8	69.4	86.4	84.7	78.2	80.2	88.3	89.4	83.5	93.7	87.3	97.2
Iowa	—	—	—	—	—	—	61.0	53.7	82.2	81.2	63.1	73.6	77.5	90.1
Kansas	—	—	—	—	—	—	—	—	—	—	37.0	50.1	76.7	64.6
Kentucky	25.4	70.7	74.0	60.8	74.3	80.4	73.6	63.3	73.7	69.8	40.6	63.8	63.8	78.0
Louisiana	—	36.3	21.5	19.2	39.4	44.9	47.3	44.4	48.9	53.4	[a]	71.4	76.6	78.4
Maine	17.6	42.6	67.5	37.7	81.7	67.3	63.1	55.3	70.5	62.0	69.4	67.1	57.9	71.9
Maryland	50.1	69.7	55.7	67.5	84.5	80.4	74.4	70.0	75.1	74.6	55.0	65.8	74.9	82.3
Massachusetts	32.2	27.7	43.4	42.8	65.6	59.0	53.0	45.1	55.6	51.4	49.1	50.8	58.5	71.7
Michigan	—	—	—	34.8	84.9	79.4	73.8	71.3	81.1	80.1	68.7	78.3	71.6	87.9
Minnesota	—	—	—	—	—	—	—	—	—	75.0	57.7	70.8	87.1	89.4
Mississippi	40.0	56.5	27.2	64.2	88.2	88.1	86.3	64.9	80.5	86.6	[a]	[c]	70.8	78.8
Missouri	19.8	53.5	15.5	34.9	74.1	74.3	58.8	42.8	51.0	64.4	34.0	42.7	66.8	76.1
Nebraska	—	—	—	—	—	—	—	—	—	—	—	46.5	48.5	56.8
Nevada	—	—	—	—	—	—	—	—	—	—	89.1	57.1	76.0	96.1
New Hampshire	17.9	74.5	70.3	38.1	87.4	65.5	61.4	58.9	79.7	73.8	77.3	75.3	80.5	89.1
New Jersey	33.2	70.8	68.9	69.2	80.5	81.4	73.0	68.3	69.8	74.9	69.0	77.1	81.5	95.4
New York	—	67.4	70.3	58.7	76.0	72.2	59.7	61.5	64.3	67.1	68.5	75.3	80.9	91.6
North Carolina	40.3	54.7	30.5	52.7	83.7	79.2	71.3	65.6	65.8	70.2	[a]	84.7	71.9	89.7
Ohio	34.8	75.9	73.9	75.5	84.5	83.6	77.6	75.4	76.5	81.6	81.9	85.2	84.2	93.8

(Table continues)

Table 3-19 *(Continued)*

State	*1824*	*1828*	*1832*	*1836*	*1840*	*1844*	*1848*	*1852*	*1856*	*1860*	*1864*	*1868*	*1872*	*1876*
Oregon	—	—	—	—	—	—	—	—	—	86.8	89.7	92.4	66.6	74.2
Pennsylvania	18.9	54.6	50.7	51.5	77.5	75.7	73.2	68.6	74.1	70.3	76.9	80.5	67.8	81.5
Rhode Island	12.4	17.5	26.0	23.8	33.6	38.7	30.2	42.1	45.9	43.5	45.2	34.7	40.6	50.8
South Carolina	d	d	d	d	d	d	d	d	d	d	d	73.4	60.4	89.4
Tennessee	27.0	49.7	27.9	55.3	89.6	89.9	83.8	73.0	78.6	80.5	a	40.2	65.7	74.3
Texas	—	—	—	—	—	—	72.3	39.1	62.5	61.7	a	c	56.2	53.8
Vermont	—	54.0	50.2	52.7	73.7	65.5	59.9	52.7	60.2	52.5	63.8	67.2	68.6	81.2
Virginia	11.6	27.7	31.1	35.4	54.7	54.6	48.0	63.9	67.6	70.5	a	c	66.2	77.2
West Virginia	—	—	—	—	—	—	—	—	—	—	38.1	52.4	61.2	83.5
Wisconsin	—	—	—	—	—	—	58.4	62.6	81.5	79.0	68.8	80.0	81.6	96.4
United States	28.2	51.9	47.9	50.7	76.4	73.6	66.6	60.4	70.7	71.9	63.8	67.2	69.9	80.1

Source: Adapted from Jerrold G. Rusk, *A Statistical History of the American Electorate* (Washington, D.C.: CQ Press, 2001), tables 3-23, 3-24.

Note: "—" indicates state was not yet admitted to the Union. Turnout is measured as the total number of votes cast divided by the voting-eligible population.

[a] Confederate states did not participate in the 1864 election.
[b] Florida (in 1868) and Colorado (in 1876) cast three Republican electoral votes through its legislature rather than by popular vote.
[c] Mississippi, Texas, and Virginia did not participate in the 1868 election.
[d] South Carolina chose its electors through its legislature until 1868.

Table 3-20 State Voter Turnout in Presidential Elections, by State, 1880–1932 (percent)

State	*1880*	*1884*	*1888*	*1892*	*1896*	*1900*	*1904*	*1908*	*1912*	*1916*	*1920*	*1924*	*1928*	*1932*
Alabama	58.9	54.2	56.6	68.4	51.8	38.8	24.2	21.6	22.7	24.0	20.6	13.5	19.1	17.7
Arizona	—	—	—	—	—	—	—	—	39.6	47.7	46.8	40.8	41.6	48.5
Arkansas	60.2	60.0	65.4	55.6	51.8	41.2	33.9	40.4	31.0	39.9	21.3	15.3	20.9	21.8
California	74.4	74.4	81.4	76.7	76.1	69.8	58.8	55.6	44.7	56.9	47.2	49.1	55.8	61.1
Colorado	64.3	61.0	68.2	61.6	69.7	74.0	70.0	65.0	58.8	60.0	56.0	62.0	67.4	74.3
Connecticut	87.7	83.3	86.6	85.4	83.3	79.7	80.4	76.2	71.5	74.2	57.8	57.3	72.3	70.7
Delaware	81.7	75.7	69.0	80.6	78.9	81.8	81.9	86.2	83.5	84.5	75.1	68.5	75.3	76.3
Florida	86.3	82.8	78.2	35.5	40.0	29.8	24.0	26.1	23.6	33.4	28.3	16.9	32.5	30.4
Georgia	49.3	41.1	37.6	53.7	35.6	24.4	24.0	22.4	19.1	23.9	10.6	11.5	15.7	16.5
Idaho	—	—	—	63.7	76.2	75.0	64.6	66.0	60.0	67.6	62.3	64.6	64.4	74.0
Illinois	89.4	85.4	85.1	88.1	96.9	89.9	80.5	81.5	75.6	68.3	60.4	64.0	73.1	74.4
Indiana	96.8	93.8	95.6	91.5	97.6	94.7	92.6	93.4	81.0	84.9	73.1	70.6	74.7	78.8
Iowa	86.8	95.5	89.5	89.3	95.6	89.2	81.0	81.8	78.7	78.2	65.4	69.3	69.5	69.1
Kansas	79.3	84.1	96.5	87.1	87.6	89.5	76.7	81.3	75.1	65.9	58.0	63.9	65.5	70.7
Kentucky	72.5	69.1	80.7	73.9	89.3	87.1	77.7	84.0	74.6	82.6	71.9	61.0	67.7	67.4
Louisiana	50.9	51.7	49.7	45.1	35.5	21.7	15.5	19.7	19.3	21.5	14.1	12.4	20.1	23.0
Maine	85.1	73.0	71.5	63.3	63.0	55.0	49.4	53.1	63.6	65.8	47.0	44.8	60.2	66.3
Maryland	78.8	90.1	85.3	80.4	87.3	85.9	69.6	70.8	64.9	68.3	52.3	41.0	56.7	51.2
Massachusetts	71.6	72.2	69.5	71.6	67.3	64.1	64.4	62.2	62.2	63.3	53.3	56.5	73.8	69.3
Michigan	85.2	78.6	92.7	83.6	95.3	89.0	78.7	75.7	69.7	73.0	55.7	53.6	56.1	61.8
Minnesota	87.2	80.2	90.2	77.3	86.0	76.7	64.1	65.9	60.9	64.7	59.5	61.9	68.5	66.1
Mississippi	49.7	48.5	44.1	18.4	22.0	17.0	15.5	16.4	15.1	20.0	9.4	12.0	15.2	13.7
Missouri	77.6	76.7	81.7	77.2	88.1	82.6	74.2	78.9	74.0	80.4	67.1	63.2	69.1	70.9
Montana	—	—	—	77.7	75.2	75.5	63.5	59.9	61.0	70.0	61.4	59.0	64.8	69.9
Nebraska	72.9	73.6	82.8	72.4	80.4	86.6	75.8	84.2	74.3	81.0	55.7	63.7	71.3	71.8
Nevada	84.5	65.8	73.3	69.1	68.7	71.4	55.8	84.1	63.4	70.7	61.0	54.9	60.6	70.7
New Hampshire	91.5	86.8	90.2	86.1	78.2	83.9	81.5	80.8	78.4	78.1	67.5	67.4	77.7	77.5

(Table continues)

Table 3-20 *(Continued)*

State	*1880*	*1884*	*1888*	*1892*	*1896*	*1900*	*1904*	*1908*	*1912*	*1916*	*1920*	*1924*	*1928*	*1932*
New Jersey	96.3	88.3	90.4	89.2	87.8	85.9	83.5	82.2	69.2	71.4	59.6	60.8	75.5	72.0
New Mexico	—	—	—	—	—	—	—	—	55.7	74.2	62.3	60.3	57.5	67.0
New York	92.5	88.7	91.7	85.4	83.9	84.6	83.2	79.5	72.1	71.9	56.4	56.1	67.8	65.7
North Carolina	82.6	86.1	86.0	78.5	85.7	70.2	46.0	51.9	46.5	51.5	44.6	35.9	43.1	44.0
North Dakota	—	—	—	69.3	71.0	81.5	70.8	74.5	59.8	75.9	70.2	63.7	72.3	74.4
Ohio	93.6	92.8	91.6	85.9	95.1	91.0	82.8	87.4	75.0	77.1	62.6	57.7	66.8	65.4
Oklahoma	—	—	—	—	—	—	—	68.7	55.6	58.8	48.3	47.3	50.5	54.3
Oregon	81.2	77.3	72.0	77.4	85.1	65.4	53.2	52.7	58.2	61.2	52.4	55.1	57.3	60.4
Pennsylvania	84.6	79.6	81.3	75.2	82.4	75.0	74.3	71.8	64.6	64.1	42.7	45.8	62.5	53.1
Rhode Island	50.7	50.6	56.7	66.1	60.5	56.2	63.3	62.3	62.8	66.6	57.9	66.2	68.8	71.6
South Carolina	83.1	42.9	35.0	28.9	26.2	18.0	18.5	20.5	14.7	17.5	8.6	6.4	8.5	12.3
South Dakota	—	—	—	77.2	86.1	94.5	80.0	75.7	69.4	74.0	56.6	59.4	71.9	76.8
Tennessee	74.4	73.2	79.2	64.0	71.4	56.6	47.7	48.1	45.0	46.7	35.4	23.3	25.7	26.5
Texas	65.8	77.3	74.5	75.3	86.6	60.3	29.2	32.8	30.4	34.4	21.6	25.1	23.9	26.5
Utah	—	—	—	—	79.6	84.2	77.6	71.8	65.5	75.2	69.6	69.3	72.5	79.0
Vermont	79.1	69.2	71.0	60.4	67.1	57.9	52.7	52.7	62.6	64.5	45.3	51.3	66.8	66.6
Virginia	63.7	81.7	83.1	75.3	70.9	59.6	27.6	27.4	25.7	26.7	19.4	18.1	24.0	22.1
Washington	—	—	—	68.7	63.7	64.9	59.3	56.7	49.8	54.1	52.4	51.0	56.0	63.6
West Virginia	82.5	86.3	94.0	89.7	93.4	91.4	89.1	86.9	83.1	83.1	71.7	75.2	76.4	81.8
Wisconsin	89.7	94.0	92.7	87.3	95.5	86.5	80.8	77.5	68.5	70.3	52.2	57.3	63.8	65.0
Wyoming	—	—	—	46.4	50.6	51.0	50.5	51.7	50.3	55.0	53.7	70.3	67.5	73.6
United States	77.4	74.9	76.9	71.2	73.8	69.1	61.1	62.3	56.9	60.9	50.1	49.5	56.0	58.0

Source: Adapted from Jerrold G. Rusk, *A Statistical History of the American Electorate* (Washington, D.C.: CQ Press, 2001), tables 3-24, 3-25.

Note: "—" indicates state was not yet admitted to the Union. Turnout is measured as the total number of votes cast divided by the voting-eligible population.

Table 3-21 State Voter Turnout in Presidential Elections, by State, 1936–1984 (percent)

State	*1936*	*1940*	*1944*	*1948*	*1952*	*1956*	*1960*	*1964*	*1968*	*1972*	*1976*	*1980*	*1984*
Alabama	18.8	18.9	15.0	12.6	24.2	27.7	31.2	36.2	53.1	43.4	47.0	49.3	51.2
Alaska	—	—	—	—	—	—	46.1	46.8	53.5	47.5	53.0	59.7	67.8
Arizona	49.0	57.0	42.0	45.1	54.1	48.6	56.0	57.9	51.4	48.3	47.1	46.9	48.1
Arkansas	17.2	18.2	19.3	21.9	36.9	38.0	41.2	51.4	54.3	48.2	51.9	52.1	53.5
California	64.6	73.4	64.7	62.6	69.8	66.0	70.8	69.5	65.2	62.8	54.6	55.5	57.3
Colorado	74.9	79.7	67.7	64.2	72.6	69.7	72.5	69.2	65.9	60.2	59.7	58.1	59.7
Connecticut	74.6	77.2	73.3	70.2	80.6	77.4	80.1	74.5	71.9	68.5	65.5	64	64.1
Delaware	79.8	79.4	67.2	69.1	79.2	73.6	74.5	70.4	69.7	62.8	59.2	55.9	56.5
Florida	31.2	40.9	33.7	34.4	48.6	44.9	51.8	53.7	55.7	50.6	52.2	52.9	53.0
Georgia	17.7	17.7	17.6	21.4	31.5	29.8	30.5	45.4	47.7	37.4	42.4	42.2	43.0
Hawaii	—	—	—	—	—	—	59.6	59.0	60.1	53.2	51.3	48.3	49.2
Idaho	71.6	77.0	64.8	63.6	78.9	75.9	81.5	76.2	73.0	63.9	61.8	69.6	63.2
Illinois	81.6	82.4	74.5	69.7	75.7	73.0	77.4	74.3	71.1	63.9	61.9	60.5	60.9
Indiana	78.6	81.1	71.6	67.0	75.7	73.9	77.4	72.7	71.0	61.2	60.7	58.4	56.9
Iowa	73.5	75.5	64.2	62.2	75.5	74.0	76.9	70.9	69.3	64.2	64.3	63.5	64.1
Kansas	76.4	75.1	62.1	64.8	71.6	67.5	70.6	64.3	64.4	59.9	59.4	57.8	59.0
Kentucky	59.9	59.5	51.8	47.9	56.1	57.5	59.4	55.0	55.3	48.1	48.8	50.4	52.1
Louisiana	26.0	27.3	24.1	27.1	40.2	36.1	45.0	47.5	55.4	44.3	49.0	54.5	59.1
Maine	64.5	65.0	57.1	48.6	62.9	62.6	74.6	66.5	67.7	61.4	65.7	66.1	66.1
Maryland	58.1	57.2	47.0	41.5	57.5	55.1	58.1	55.5	56.0	50.6	51.0	51.9	52.9
Massachusetts	75.8	78.7	70.6	70.7	77.1	75.6	79.0	72.6	69.8	64.0	64.3	61.9	60.9
Michigan	62.0	66.6	63.3	55.1	68.2	71.8	74.1	68.1	67.0	60.5	60.1	61.3	58.4
Minnesota	69.6	72.3	62.7	65.2	72.2	68.9	77.8	75.1	73.6	69.2	72.3	71.4	69.8
Mississippi	14.4	14.7	15.0	16.0	23.8	21.0	25.5	34.2	53.4	44.3	48.7	52.5	53.9
Missouri	77.2	74.4	62.1	60.8	71.6	68.9	72.1	66.0	64.0	57.6	57.9	59.5	58.6
Montana	70.6	72.2	58.7	61.8	71.4	71.7	72.1	71.1	68.8	68.0	64.6	66.1	68.7
Nebraska	75.5	75.4	67.7	57.7	71.4	67.6	71.9	67.4	60.9	56.8	57.1	57.5	58.0
Nevada	68.0	75.6	64.5	63.5	69.8	67.0	62.8	61.9	57.8	50.6	43.8	44.1	42.3

(Table continues)

Table 3-21 *(Continued)*

State	*1936*	*1940*	*1944*	*1948*	*1952*	*1956*	*1960*	*1964*	*1968*	*1972*	*1976*	*1980*	*1984*
New Hampshire	77.7	79.6	73.1	69.6	78.9	75.4	81.6	73.7	70.9	64.9	58.2	58.9	54.3
New Jersey	74.9	76.1	68.7	62.4	72.2	70.2	74.3	71.9	68.6	61.8	60.5	58.1	61.0
New Mexico	67.4	66.6	48.7	53.4	60.6	57.2	63.0	63.8	61.0	58.5	54.9	52.8	55.3
New York	72.4	75.7	70.4	64.2	71.1	69.6	70.3	67.7	62.9	59.2	54.2	51.7	56.0
North Carolina	47.4	42.7	38.0	35.5	51.4	47.5	53.7	52.3	54.7	42.9	43.4	44.2	48.3
North Dakota	77.9	78.4	61.1	60.9	74.8	71.2	79.0	73.2	70.1	68.6	68.5	65.7	67.3
Ohio	71.8	75.4	66.7	58.1	69.5	66.8	72.1	66.4	64.1	57.9	56.0	56.2	58.7
Oklahoma	56.4	60.6	52.8	52.5	68.5	61.5	64.0	63.1	61.1	56.9	55.2	53.6	57.1
Oregon	62.4	67.1	58.2	56.2	69.5	71.5	73.4	68.9	66.9	62.8	61.6	63.2	63.2
Pennsylvania	72.5	67.6	59.5	55.6	66.2	65.7	71.4	67.8	65.7	56.5	55.1	52.8	55.3
Rhode Island	77.9	75.6	64.6	65.4	79.6	74.2	77.5	71.7	68.1	62.5	61.4	61.7	58.8
South Carolina	12.5	10.1	9.8	12.8	29.1	24.7	30.6	39.1	46.9	38.4	40.9	41.3	41.8
South Dakota	78.7	81.5	60.0	63.3	74.1	74.7	78.6	75.5	72.8	69.5	65.0	67.8	65.2
Tennessee	30.1	30.7	28.2	28.7	44.7	46.0	50.4	52.0	54.0	43.6	49.0	49.4	50.1
Texas	24.3	30.3	28.3	28.2	43.5	38.4	42.8	45.2	49.4	45.9	47.7	47.8	52.8
Utah	77.4	83.1	74.7	75.4	82.6	77.8	81.5	80.2	78.1	70.5	68.5	67	65.0
Vermont	68.4	66.8	56.7	54.2	66.8	67.3	74.4	68.8	64.8	61.8	56.7	59.3	61.5
Virginia	22.9	22.1	22.2	21.8	29.9	32.0	33.6	42.0	51.0	45.1	48.3	49.1	52.5
Washington	66.2	70.6	66.7	62.7	71.0	71.2	74.0	69.4	67.0	64.4	60.0	60	60.2
West Virginia	84.9	83.0	65.5	65.7	76.2	74.7	77.8	73.9	70.7	62.8	57.8	53.3	53.8
Wisconsin	68.9	72.4	65.5	59.4	72.1	68.0	74.1	69.7	67.1	63.0	67.3	68.6	64.8
Wyoming	73.4	74.8	63.1	59.3	72.3	67.6	74.7	74.9	66.1	64.9	57.4	55.1	59.3
District of Columbia	—	—	—	—	—	—	—	41.5	37.0	31.4	34.0	37	45.4
United States	60.4	62.1	53.8	52.3	63.4	61.2	64.9	63.3	63.0	57.1	56.5	56.6	57.4

Source: Adapted from Jerrold G. Rusk, *A Statistical History of the American Electorate* (Washington, D.C.: CQ Press, 2001), tables 3-25, 3-26.

Note: "—" indicates state not yet admitted to the Union, or, for the District of Columbia, not yet able to vote for president. Turnout is measured as the number of votes cast divided by the voting-eligible population.

Table 3-22 State Voter Turnout in Presidential Elections, by State, 1988–2004 (percent)

State	*1988*	*1992*	*1996*	*2000*	*2004*
Alabama	47.3	55.5	48.1	51.3	58.3
Alaska	57.7	67.6	58.7	68.3	72.8
Arizona	48.7	54.9	46.3	45.6	57.9
Arkansas	48.8	54.2	48.4	47.5	54.7
California	55.7	60.2	53.2	55.2	60.5
Colorado	59.6	63.3	56.0	58.5	68.9
Connecticut	60.8	67.2	58.7	61.3	66.1
Delaware	52.1	56.9	50.3	58.4	65.6
Florida	48.9	56.0	53.2	54.2	66.8
Georgia	40.3	47.5	43.1	46.1	56.8
Hawaii	48.1	48.3	45.8	43.9	50.7
Idaho	60.8	66.2	60.3	56.6	63.5
Illinois	57.1	62.5	52.7	56.8	61.4
Indiana	54.1	55.9	49.9	50.1	56.0
Iowa	59.9	65.8	58.7	61.6	70.8
Kansas	56.2	64.0	58.0	56.6	64.5
Kentucky	49.2	53.7	47.8	51.7	60.9
Louisiana	55.6	59.9	58.3	55.8	61.1
Maine	62.9	74.2	64.7	68.1	73.7
Maryland	51.0	56.8	50.0	55.0	65.2
Massachusetts	60.8	62.8	57.2	60.6	65.2
Michigan	55.3	62.9	55.0	60.0	67.9
Minnesota	67.6	73.0	65.8	69.8	77.8
Mississippi	51.9	52.8	45.9	49.0	56.2
Missouri	56.3	62.5	54.8	58.0	67.0
Montana	64.4	69.2	64.2	62.0	65.9
Nebraska	58.4	63.8	56.9	57.2	64.3
Nevada	44.1	53.6	41.1	46.6	56.6
New Hampshire	57.7	64.9	58.1	63.2	71.7
New Jersey	57.1	60.7	55.6	56.8	64.9
New Mexico	52.3	53.3	48.5	48.9	58.4
New York	52.7	56.5	52.6	55.0	58.6
North Carolina	44.4	51.1	46.5	50.3	59.5
North Dakota	64.7	66.5	56.6	60.7	67.9
Ohio	55.7	61.4	55.2	56.8	68.1
Oklahoma	52.0	60.1	50.4	50.1	59.7
Oregon	59.7	68.9	60.8	63.8	71.0
Pennsylvania	51.0	55.3	50.2	53.9	64.0
Rhode Island	56.1	62.5	54.9	55.1	60.0
South Carolina	39.9	45.8	41.3	47.4	54.3
South Dakota	63.5	66.6	61.6	58.2	70.5
Tennessee	45.9	52.9	47.7	49.7	57.7
Texas	49.6	52.4	44.4	48.8	53.9
Utah	62.6	65.0	51.3	54.3	61.8
Vermont	60.4	68.9	59.5	65.4	66.9
Virginia	50.0	55.3	49.9	54.6	64.7
Washington	55.7	63.3	57.3	61.1	68.0
West Virginia	48.3	50.4	45.9	46.5	54.4
Wisconsin	62.5	69.9	58.6	67.0	76.7
Wyoming	55.9	62.0	61.9	60.9	66.3
District of Columbia	42.2	52.0	45.6	50.0	58.4
United States	54.63	60.10	53.44	55.9	63.5

Source: (1988–1996) Adapted from Jerrold G. Rusk, *A Statistical History of the American Electorate* (Washington, D.C.: CQ Press, 2001), table 3-27; (2000, 2004) updated by the author with original data from the Clerk of the House of Representatives and the *Statistical Abstract of the United States.*

Table 3-23 Personal Characteristics of Major-Party Candidates, 1980–2004 (percent)

	1980		*1984*		*1988*	
Characteristic	Jimmy Carter (D)	Ronald Reagan (R)	Walter Mondale (D)	Ronald Reagan (R)	Michael Dukakis (D)	George H. W. Bush (R)
Intelligent	—	—	79.5	80.9	82.1	75.3
Compassionate	—	—	68.9	57.2	65.0	55.5
Decent	—	—	83.1	81.1	79.2	82.1
Inspiring	35.1	45.8	29.3	56.9	44.7	36.6
Knowledgeable	73.2	67.1	74.8	74.4	75.9	79.2
Moral	78.2	65.9	74.2	77.3	69.1	69.9
Strong leadership	35.1	55.0	43.0	69.1	51.0	50.0
Cares about people	—	—	56.0	45.1	56.9	45.1
Honest	—	—	—	—	—	—

Source: Calculated by the author from the American National Election Studies, www.electionstudies.org.

Note: Entries are the percentage of respondents indicating that the characteristic fits the candidate "well" or "extremely well." "—" indicates question not asked.

Table 3-24 Emotional Responses to Major-Party Presidential Candidates, 1980–2004 (percent)

	1980		*1984*		*1988*	
Emotion	Jimmy Carter (D)	Ronald Reagan (R)	Walter Mondale (D)	Ronald Reagan (R)	Michael Dukakis (D)	George H. W. Bush (R)
Anger	63.4	23.7	29.8	47.7	28.6	24.7
Fear	23.4	28.0	17.3	24.1	20.7	14.7
Hope	60.1	48.0	41.0	60.3	41.3	39.0
Pride	49.3	31.3	30.3	55.4	28.3	33.0

Source: Calculated by the author from the American National Election Studies, www.electionstudies.org.

Note: Entries are the percentage of respondents indicating that they have felt that emotion toward a candidate, based on valid responses.

1992		1996		2000		2004	
Bill Clinton (D)	George H. W. Bush (R)	Bill Clinton (D)	Bob Dole (R)	Al Gore (D)	George W. Bush (R)	John Kerry (D)	George W. Bush (R)
82.2	80.7	88.4	—	85.8	75.7	85.1	60.5
71.5	58.0	69.3	—	—	—	—	—
46.0	57.9	—	—	—	—	—	—
55.4	39.1	52.7	36.8	—	—	—	—
78.1	81.2	83.7	83.7	84.4	70.2	79.7	58.9
43.9	77.4	39.2	78.5	74.7	73.4	68.3	68.7
54.9	55.3	60.1	60.0	58.2	65.9	51.9	64.5
60.3	34.8	57.8	42.4	58.7	46.3	57.0	45.9
—	—	42.8	69.2	72.7[a]	77.4[a]	75.0[a]	67.6[a]

[a]Question wording changes to: "Do you feel the candidate is dishonest?" Coding reflects those who disagree with the statement.

1992		1996		2000		2004	
Bill Clinton (D)	George H. W. Bush (R)	Bill Clinton (D)	Bob Dole (R)	Al Gore (D)	George W. Bush (R)	John Kerry (D)	George W. Bush (R)
25.3	51.2	52.7	34.6	29.2	27.2	31.4	56.1
23.5	40.0	32.3	24.6	18.6	23.3	22.8	43.9
50.8	48.0	58.7	36.1	47.7	43.3	46.5	55.4
23.7	56.3	50.6	38.7	34.1	30.4	34.6	61.1

Figure 3-2 Voter Perceptions of Candidates' Handling of Issues, 2004

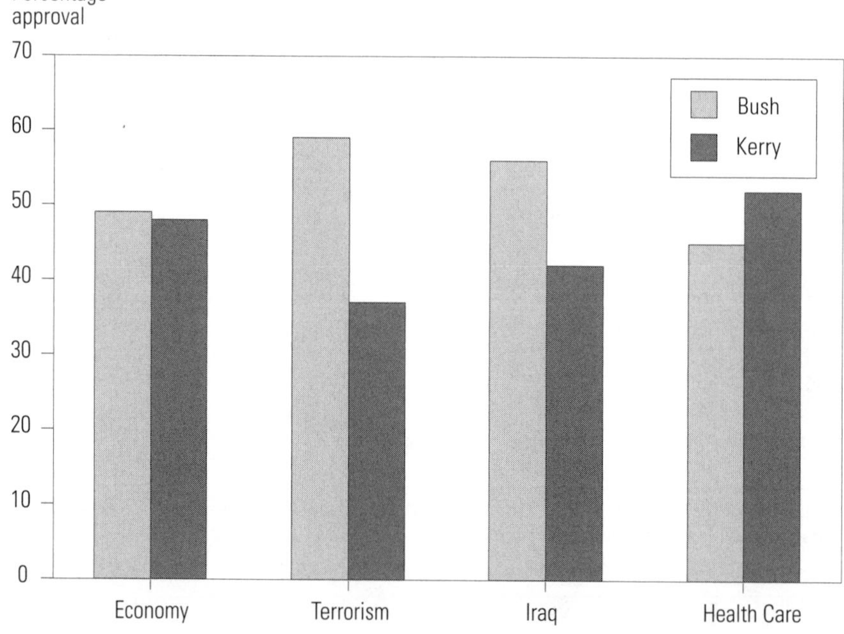

Source: Calculated by the author from the American National Election Studies, www.electionstudies.org.

Table 3-25 Content of Television News Coverage of General Elections, 1988–2004

Time period	*News content* Candidate character	Policy issues	Horse race[a]	*Total number of news stories*[b]
Convention period				
Before first convention				
June 8–July 21, 1988 (Dem.)	1	0	0	248
June 3–July 10, 1992 (Dem.)	34	49	17	247
June 1–Aug. 9, 1996 (Rep.)	24	63	13	282
2000	N/A	N/A	N/A	
March 2-July 25, 2004	16	29	31	8,518
First convention				
1988	N/A	N/A	N/A	
July 11–July 19, 1992 (Dem.)	48	30	22	185
Aug. 10–18, 1996 (Rep.)	33	34	33	188
July 31-Aug. 3, 2000	N/A	16	38	72
2004	N/A	N/A	N/A	
Second convention				
1988	N/A	N/A	N/A	
Aug. 15–23, 1992 (Rep.)	25	50	25	138
Aug. 24–Sept. 1, 1996 (Dem.)	50	27	23	151
Aug. 14-Aug. 17, 2000	N/A	23	56	46
2004	N/A	N/A	N/A	
Total convention period				
July 22–Aug. 18, 1988	43	38	18	200
July 11–Aug. 23, 1992	36	45	19	505
Aug. 10–Sept. 1, 1996	43	30	27	379
July 31-Aug. 17, 2000	N/A	20	47	118
July 26-Sept. 2, 2004	24	30	22	4,657
General election period				
Pre-debates				
1988	N/A	N/A	N/A	
Aug. 24–Oct. 10, 1992	34	38	28	443
Sept. 2–Oct. 5, 1996	50	33	17	197
Sept. 4-Oct. 2, 2000	N/A	51	62	154
Sept. 3-Sept. 29, 2004	15	33	26	3,767
Debates				
Aug. 19–Oct. 13, 1988	49	38	14	480
Oct. 11–Oct. 19, 1992	25	23	52	124
Oct. 6–Oct. 16, 1996	24	45	31	98
Oct. 3-Oct. 17, 2000	N/A	51	62	154

(Table continues)

Table 3-25 *(Continued)*

Time period	*News content* Candidate character	Policy issues	Horse race[a]	*Total number of news stories*[b]
Sept. 30-Oct. 10, 2004	14	35	26	2,417
Final days				
Oct. 14–Nov. 7, 1988	35	33	33	309
Oct. 20–Nov. 2, 1992	28	28	44	239
Oct. 17–Nov. 4, 1996	32	36	32	188
Oct. 18-Nov. 6, 2000	N/A	32	80	391
Oct. 14-Nov. 2, 2004	13	34	42	3,901
Total general election period				
1988	46	36	19	1,237
1992	33	28	27	1,558
1996	40	34	26	862
2000	N/A	33	83	1,130
2004	18	26	46	34,696

Sources: (1988) Adapted from Harold Stanley and Richard Niemi, *Vital Statistics on American Politics,* 3d ed. (Washington, D.C.: Congressional Quarterly, 1988), 63; (1992) *Vital Statistics,* 4th ed. (Washington, D.C.: Congressional Quarterly, 1994), 63; (1996) *Vital Statistics, 1997–1998* (Washington, D.C.: Congressional Quarterly, 1998), 175; (2000) *Vital Statistics, 2001–2002* (Washington, D.C.: CQ Press, 2002), 181–182; (2004) *Vital Statistics, 2007–2008* (Washington, D.C.: CQ Press, 2008), 190–191.

Note: Data are derived from content analysis of the ABC, CBS, and NBC evening news broadcasts conducted by the Center for Media and Public Affairs. N/A—not available.

[a] News stories in which the focus is on who is leading or trailing in the polls.
[b] 2004 entries are based on statements rather than stories.

Table 3-26 Positive Television News Coverage of Presidential and Vice Presidential Candidates during the General Election, 1988–2004

	Election year							
	1988		1992			1996		
Time period	*G. H. W. Bush/ Quayle (R)*	*Dukakis/ Bentsen (D)*	*G. H. W. Bush/ Quayle (R)*	*Clinton/ Gore (D)*	*Perot/ Stockdale (I)*	*Dole/ Kemp (R)*	*Clinton/ Gore (D)*	*Perot (I)*
Nomination	63/—	43/82	32/22	50/100	42/—	44/76	64/—	—
First party convention	39/—	64/73	46/29	67/79	33/—	72/76	27/25	31
Pre–second party convention	—/—	24/100	34/35	32/50	60/—	55/71	51/—	75
Second party convention	—/—	29/88	47/75	31/50	75/—	40/50	57/92	—
Pre-debates	—/—	—/—	32/42	35/70	41/—	46/75	40/71	50
Debates	26/42	30/53	34/50	47/45	62/53	44/42	40/—	—
Post-debates	36/25	38/96	34/—	36/—	49/—	50/—	39/—	36

	Election year			
	2000[a]		2004	
Time period	*G. W. Bush (R)*	*Gore (D)*	*G. W. Bush/Cheney (R)*	*Kerry/Edwards (D)*
Nomination	50	43	12/4	35/39
First party convention	—	67	8/12	15/29
Pre–second party convention	44	67	—	—
Second party convention	44	67	13/8	19/18
Pre-debates	39	43	24	27
Debates	38	30	12	8
Post-debates	41	42	27	46

(Table continues)

Table 3-26 *(Continued)*

Sources: (1988) Adapted from Harold Stanley and Richard Niemi, *Vital Statistics on American Politics,* 3d ed. (Washington, D.C.: Congressional Quarterly, 1988), 71; (1992) *Vital Statistics,* 4th ed. (Washington, D.C.: CQ Press, 1992), 71; (1996) *Vital Statistics, 1997–1998* (Washington, D.C.: 1998), 185; (2000) *Vital Statistics, 2001–2002* (Washington, D.C.: 2002), 190; (2004) *Vital Statistics, 2007–2008* (Washington, D.C.: 2006), 188–189.

Note: In 1988 and 1992 the Democrats held the first convention, while in 1996 the Republicans held the first convention. Entries are the percentage of positive television news stories calculated from the total of all clearly positive and negative stories aired on ABC, CBS, and NBC evening news broadcasts. Data are derived from content analysis of the network news broadcasts conducted by the Center for Media and Public Affairs. "—" indicates not available; R—Republican; D—Democrat; I—Independent.

[a] No information obtained for running mates in 2000.

Table 3-27 Election Year Presidential Preferences, 1948–2004 (percent)

Year/candidate	*First poll of year*	*First poll after conventions*	*Early October*	*Final survey*	*Election results*
1948					
Truman (D)[a]	46 (+5)	37	40	45	50 (+5)
Dewey (R)	41	48 (+11)	46 (+6)	50 (+5)	45
1952					
Eisenhower (R)	59 (+28)	50 (+7)	53 (+12)	51 (+2)	55 (+11)
Stevenson (D)	31	43	41	49	44
1956					
Eisenhower (R)[a]	61 (+26)	52 (+11)	51 (+10)	60 (+19)	57 (+15)
Stevenson (D)	35	41	41	41	42
1960					
Kennedy (D)	43	44	49 (+3)	51 (+2)	50 (+0.2)
Nixon (R)	48 (+5)	50 (+6)	46	49	50
1964					
L. Johnson (D)[a]	75 (+57)	65 (+36)	64 (+35)	64 (+28)	61 (+23)
Goldwater (R)	18	29	29	36	38
1968					
Nixon (R)	43 (+9)	43 (+12)	43 (+12)	43 (+1)	43 (+.7)
Humphrey (D)	34	31	31	42	43
Wallace (AIP)	9	19	20	15	14
1972					
Nixon (R)[a]	53 (+19)	64 (+34)	60 (+26)	62 (+24)	61 (+23)
McGovern (D)	34	30	34	38	38
1976					
Carter (D)	47 (+5)	51 (+15)	47 (+2)	48	50 (+2)
Ford (R)[a]	42	36	45	49 (+1)	48
1980					
Carter (D)[a]	62 (+29)	39 (+1)	44 (+4)	44	41
Reagan (R)	33	38	40	47 (+3)	51 (+10)
Anderson (I)		13	9	8	7
1984					
Reagan (R)[a]	48 (+1)	55 (+15)	56 (+17)	59 (+18)	59 (+18)
Mondale (D)	47	40	39	41	41
1988					
G.H.W. Bush (R)	52 (+12)	48 (+4)	49 (+6)	53 (+11)	54 (+8)
Dukakis (D)	40	44	43	42	46
1992					
G.H.W. Bush (R)[a]	53 (+15)	42	35	37	37
Clinton (D)	38	52 (+10)	52 (+17)	49 (+12)	43 (+6)
Perot	—	—	7	14	19
1996					
Clinton (D)[a]	43 (+4)	55 (+21)	55 (+21)	52 (+11)	49 (+8)
Dole (R)	39	34	34	41	41
Perot	16	6	6	7	9

(Table continues)

Table 3-27 *(Continued)*

Year/candidate	*First poll of year*	*First poll after conventions*	*Early October*	*Final survey*	*Election results*
2000					
G. W. Bush (R)	52 (+9)	46	49 (+8)	48 (+2)	48
Gore (D)	43	47 (+1)	41	46	48 (+0.5)
Nader (Green)	—	3	2	4	3
2004					
G. W. Bush (R)[a]	55 (+12)	52 (+7)	49	49	51 (+3)
Kerry (D)	43	45	49	49	48
Nader (I)	—	1	1	1	0.4

Source: Harold Stanley and Richard Niemi, *Vital Statistics on American Politics, 2005–2006* (Washington, D.C.: CQ Press, 2006), 128.

Note: "—" indicates not included in survey question. D—Democrat; R—Republican; AIP—American Independent Party; I—Independent.

[a] Incumbent.

Table 3-28 Demographic Groups' Support of Presidential Candidates, 1952–2004 (percent)

		Sex		*Race*		*Age*			*Education*			*Region*			
Election	*Vote*	Men	Women	White	Non-white	Under 30	30–49	50+	Grade school	High school	College	East	Midwest	South	West
1952															
Stevenson	45	47	42	43	79	51	47	39	52	45	34	45	42	51	42
Eisenhower	55	53	58	57	21	49	53	61	48	55	66	55	58	49	58
1956															
Stevenson	42	45	39	41	61	43	45	39	50	42	31	40	41	49	43
Eisenhower	58	55	61	59	39	57	55	61	50	58	69	60	59	51	57
1960															
Kennedy	50	52	49	49	68	54	54	46	55	52	39	53	48	51	49
Nixon	50	49	51	51	32	45	46	54	45	48	61	47	52	49	51
1964															
L. Johnson	61	60	62	59	94	64	63	59	66	62	52	68	61	52	60
Goldwater	39	40	38	41	6	36	37	41	34	38	48	32	39	48	40
1968															
Humphrey	43	41	45	38	85	47	44	41	52	42	37	50	44	31	44
Nixon	43	43	43	47	12	38	41	47	33	43	15	43	47	36	49
Wallace	14	16	12	15	3	15	15	12	15	15	9	7	9	33	7
1972															
McGovern	38	37	38	32	87	48	33	36	49	34	37	42	40	29	41
Nixon	62	63	62	68	13	52	67	64	51	66	63	58	60	71	59

(Table continues)

Table 3-28 *(Continued)*

		Sex		*Race*		*Age*			*Education*			*Region*			
Election	*Vote*	Men	Women	White	Non-white	Under 30	30–49	50+	Grade school	High school	College	East	Midwest	South	West
1976															
Carter	51	53	48	46	85	53	48	52	58	54	42	51	48	54	46
Ford	49	45	51	52	15	45	49	48	55	46	41	47	50	45	51
1980															
Carter	41	38	44	36	86	47	38	41	54	43	35	43	41	44	35
Reagan	51	53	49	56	10	41	52	54	42	51	53	47	51	52	54
Anderson	7	7	6	7	2	11	8	4	3	5	10	9	7	3	9
1984															
Mondale	41	36	45	41	82	40	40	41	51	43	39	46	42	37	40
Reagan	59	64	55	59	18	60	60	59	49	57	61	54	58	63	60
1988															
Dukakis	46	44	48	41	82	49	45	37	55	46	42	51	47	40	46
G.H.W. Bush	54	56	52	59	18	51	55	63	45	54	58	49	53	60	54
1992															
Clinton	43	41	46	39	77	40	42	46	56	40	43	47	44	38	45
G.H.W. Bush	38	37	38	41	11	37	37	39	28	38	40	35	34	45	35
Perot	19	22	16	20	12	23	21	15	16	22	17	20	17	22	18
1996															
Clinton	50	45	54	46	82	54	49	50	58	52	47	60	46	44	51
Dole	41	44	39	45	12	30	41	45	27	34	45	31	45	46	43
Perot	9	11	7	9	6	16	10	5	15	14	8	9	9	10	6

2000															
Gore	50	45	53	43	87	47	45	53	55	52	46	55	48	45	48
G.W. Bush	50	52	45	55	9	47	53	45	42	46	51	42	49	54	47
Nader		3	2	3	4	6	2	2	3	2	3	3	3	1	5
2004															
Kerry	48	44	52	43	83	60	43	50	—	54	43	58	48	43	48
G.W. Bush	51	56	48	57	17	40	57	50	—	46	57	42	52	57	52

Sources: (1952–1996) *Gallup Poll Monthly*, November 1996, 17–20; (2000, 2004) Alec Gallup and Frank Newport, eds., *The Gallup Poll Public Opinion 2004* (New York: Rowman and Littlefield, 2006), 442–443.

Note: Estimates from actual election results. "—" indicates not available.

Table 3-29 Presidential Campaign Receipts, 1996–2004 (in millions)

	1996		*2000*		*2004*	
Primary campaigns						
	Clinton	$42.5	G. W. Bush	$95.5	G. W. Bush	$269.6
	Dole	44.9	Gore	48.1	Kerry	234.6
	All others	160.9	All others	208.0	All others	169.7
General election campaigns						
	Major-party grants	123.6	Major-party grants	135.2	Major-party grants	149.2
	Clinton legal/accounting	4.2	Bush legal/accounting	9.0	Bush legal/accounting	12.2
	Dole legal/accounting	3.5	Gore legal/accounting	11.5	Kerry legal/accounting	8.9
	Perot grant	29.0	Reform grant	12.6		
Conventions						
	Major-party grants	24.7	Major-party grants	27.0	Major-party grants	29.8
	Convention (Dem.)	20.4	Convention (Dem.)	29.3	Convention (Dem.)	56.8
	Convention (Rep.)	24.2	Convention (Rep.)	70.8	Convention (Rep.)	85.7
			Reform grant	2.5		
Total		$478.0		$649.5		$1,016.5

Source: Federal Election Commission Press Office, www.fec.gov/press/press2005/20050203pressum/presbigpic.xls.

Table 3-30 Spending Limits in Presidential Elections, 1976–2004 (in millions)

Year	*Candidate primary election*[a]	*Candidate general election*[b]	*Party convention*[c]	*Party general election*[d]
1976	$10.9	$21.8	$2.2	$3.2
1980	14.7	29.4	4.4	4.6
1984	20.2	40.4	8.1	6.9
1988	27.7	46.1	9.2	8.3
1992	33.1	55.2	10.6	10.3
1996	30.9	61.8	12.4	12.0
2000	40.5	67.6	13.5	13.7
2004	44.8	74.6	14.9	16.2
2008	42.1	84.1	16.8	19.2

Sources: (1976–1984) U.S. Federal Election Commission, *Annual Report, 1984 and 1985;* (1988) Federal Election Commission press release, February 5, 1988, and Federal Election Commission, *Annual Report, 1988;* (1992) Federal Election Commission press release, January 30, 1992, and February 12, 1992; (1996, 2000, 2004, 2008) Federal Election Commission, www.fec.gov, www.fec.gov/pages/brochures/pubfund.shtml, www.fec.gov/press/press2000/preslimits2000.htm, www.fec.gov/press/bkgnd/fund.shtml, www.fec.gov/pages/brochures/pubfund_limits_2004.shtml, www.fec.gov/pages/brochures/pubfund_limits_2008.shtml.

[a] The amount of money candidates may spend during the primary season if they accept matching federal campaign funds.
[b] The amount of money candidates may spend during the general election season if they accept matching federal campaign funds.
[c] The amount of money the parties may spend on their conventions when receiving matching federal campaign funds.
[d] The amount of money the parties may spend during the general election when receiving matching federal campaign funds.

4

Public Appearances

- **Major Presidential Speeches**
- **News Conferences**
- **Press Secretaries**
- **Foreign Travel**
- **Minor Policy Speeches**
- **Ceremonial Appearances**
- **Partisan Appearances**

In Chapters 2 and 3 periodic elections were identified as one of the key structural components of the institution of the presidency. As a structural component, elections contribute to two interrelated behavioral features of the presidency: the presentation of public imagery and the perpetual campaign. Ambivalence toward parties, which is an established feature of both the nomination process and the general election, poses a contradiction between a belief in the usefulness of parties and a disdain for their factional features. This disdain draws attention toward individual candidates and the images they convey and away from their party affiliations, a process that is reinforced by the promise of democracy as candidates proclaim themselves representatives of the people. Presidential elections thus personalize the presidency and make imagery one of its cornerstones. Presidents advance the image of a single executive who is the most powerful, unique, important, and visible person in politics. This image portrays the president as the one who is in charge of government, the person who can identify the central problems of the nation and offer solutions to these problems. Partisanship remains a strong component of presidential elections and continues to direct presidential behavior, but it is far less vivid than the single executive image.

Public imagery is one of the most deceptive behavioral components of the presidency because it places inordinate attention on presidents as individuals. Personal trivia become public imperatives. News stories and street corner conversations cover presidents' favorite foods, their families and their pets, their temperaments and their habits. The hallmark of the imagery is the uniqueness of each president, which is captured anew each time another president is elected. Consequently, people do not recognize that the imagery itself is a feature of the institution and not a profile of individual presidents.

To convey the imagery, presidents conduct a perpetual campaign of public appearances. By one estimate, contemporary chief executives have spent one-third of their time in office making public appearances (Kernell, 1984, 243). Roderick Hart calculates that from 1945 to 1985, presidents appeared in public nearly 10,000 times (1987, xix). Here, too, there is a tendency to focus on the differences between the presidents making the appearances.

Scholars, journalists, and members of the public are apt to point to presidents' speaking styles and accents, how comfortable they look before the cameras, and the way they deliver messages. The data analyzed in this chapter, however, suggest that attention to such differences is at best misleading. The perpetual campaign is institutional behavior that shows different individuals facing similar circumstances and engaging in similar behavior. The presidents, despite their differences, become interchangeable actors playing the same part. This chapter considers presidents' public appearances as a part of the perpetual campaign. Chapter 5 follows with an examination of public approval of presidents as an evaluative measure of their performances in this campaign and elsewhere.

National Appearances

With the advent of radio and television, presidents have become more public figures than they were in the nineteenth century. In the earlier period, one of the chief events of a president's term in office was to make a grand tour throughout the country to, in the words of James Monroe, "quicken and symbolize national identity" (Ketcham, 1984, 125–126). They would travel through major cities where thousands of cheering people would greet them. In contrast, modern presidents appear before millions of people via radio or television in what are truly national appearances. These appearances are of three principal types: major addresses and news conferences, both of which are broadcast live, and travel abroad, during which presidents portray themselves as envoys of the United States. These appearances bring attention to the presidency and make its occupant appear closely tied to the people.

Major National Addresses

Tables 4-1 through 4-3 provide a compilation of major national presidential addresses since the time of Calvin Coolidge.[1] Indeed, the use of major addresses began with Coolidge, who, although nicknamed "Silent Cal," cultivated a large radio audience. As the *New York Times* noted in 1927, Coolidge had "spoken directly to more people than any other chief executive addressed in a lifetime." A major radio broadcaster of the day observed, "The people always want to listen to the President [Coolidge], because they know he always has something to say and there always is real food for thought in his remarks" (*New York Times,* Sept. 4, 1927, 11).

These major addresses—delivered to a national audience during evening listening hours—are the most fully developed form of institutional public behavior and arguably the most important. In these addresses presidents announce decisions to go to war, inform the nation of international crises, discuss urgent economic travails, and outline their visions for the nation's future. The news media perceive these addresses as having such import that they receive coverage both before and after the president speaks. Because regular programming is preempted, large audiences hear them. Consequently, the speeches create a symbolic connection between presidents and the public more dramatically than any other type of public appearance. In so doing, they augment the single executive image as public and media attention turn toward the president.

As Table 4-2 shows, the number of major national speeches made by Presidents Coolidge to George W. Bush has been strikingly consistent and relatively infrequent at less than five per year (or roughly one national address every three months). Herbert Hoover made the fewest speeches (11), and Ronald Reagan, in his second term, made the most (27). This pattern is all the more significant considering that it transcends the development of different forms of mass media—from early radio for Coolidge to satellite television and the Internet for George W. Bush. The limited use of major addresses by each of the presidents maximizes the impact of the speeches and minimizes problems of overexposure (Ragsdale, 1984).

Presidential News Conferences

Table 4-4 examines news conferences held by presidents from Coolidge to George W. Bush. These news conferences involve all formal exchanges with reporters during which a written transcript of questions asked is kept. News conferences are a long-standing, frequently used institutional activity. Begun by Theodore Roosevelt on an informal, irregular basis and transformed by Woodrow Wilson into a formal, twice-weekly event, Presidents Warren G. Harding, Coolidge, and Hoover continued to use the press conference, although all required reporters' questions to be submitted in writing in advance. Franklin Roosevelt eliminated this requirement, and it has never resurfaced. President Harry S. Truman moved the news conference from the Oval Office, where it had traditionally been held, to an auditorium to better accommodate the expanding size of the White House press corps. During the Eisenhower administration the television networks began to film the press conferences, and many of them have been carried live since the Kennedy years (Cornwell, 1966; Grossman and Kumar, 1981).

This brief history reveals three phases in the development of the news conference as institutional behavior. First, the actions of Theodore Roosevelt and Woodrow Wilson created a presidential-press relationship that quickly became institutional behavior for presidents and members of the press corps alike. Subsequent presidents with far more limited views of the presidency than either Theodore Roosevelt or Wilson maintained these conferences as an official forum from which presidents could disseminate their version of the news. The spontaneous give-and-take of the press conference, which Theodore Roosevelt and Wilson initiated and Franklin Roosevelt resurrected, has contributed a second key element to the institutional behavior for both presidents and the press. To be sure, presidents have often complained of "flabby and dumb" questions, while the press has often protested evasive and overly rehearsed answers. Yet, the extemporaneous exchange offers both sides the opportunity to capture the public's attention in ways the more staged news conferences did not. Finally, live coverage has brought the exchange directly to the public, creating a more vivid forum for the presentation of the single executive image. Presidents can demonstrate how much they are in control of facts, figures, and certain contentious members of the press. The importance of presidents' relations with the press has also prompted all presidents since Hoover to designate a press secretary to help maintain communication (see Table 4-5).

Table 4-4 identifies two distinct periods in the use of news conferences. Presidents from Coolidge through Truman averaged five news conferences per month. In contrast, presidents from Dwight Eisenhower to George W. Bush gave slightly more than one press conference per month. This shift to fewer conferences may be the result of the introduction of television into the news conference format. With increased visibility attached to these press exchanges, presidents may have become reluctant to hold the sessions too often. The tables also reveal that individual variations during this period are not as unique as popular commentary would suggest. Many have said that Richard Nixon hid from the press because he sorely disliked them and that Ronald Reagan stayed away from news conferences because he might bumble into an off-the-cuff mistake. The data show that both presidents averaged fewer than one press conference per month during their terms. Yet neither abandoned the practice of holding news conferences altogether. If they had, they would have been criticized for violating expected institutional behavior. Furthermore, the data also indicate that other presidents, notably Gerald Ford, Jimmy Carter, Bill Clinton in his second term, and George W. Bush in his first term averaged only slightly more than one news conference per month. The limited use of news conferences since Eisenhower is a pattern that transcends the mere individual profiles of Nixon and Reagan. Despite the drop in the formal number of news conferences, presidents are never far away from the press. Beginning with President Reagan, presidents began making remarks to the press either in the press room or coming or going from the White House. While not official press conferences, these remarks nonetheless give the president exposure to the press and also permit the press to gather information from the president.

Foreign Travel

Presidents also travel and make appearances outside the United States. Table 4-6 shows the number of days of travel and the number of appearances made at foreign locales by Presidents Truman through George W. Bush. Presidents' foreign appearances have been at moderate levels since 1945. Foreign travel reflects an interplay between environmental changes, specifically technological advances in air transportation, and institutional behavior. To occur with any regularity at all, these trips depend on the ease and speed of air travel. But fast planes are not the only ingredient in understanding this behavior. Table 4-6 reveals that recent presidents have gone abroad more frequently. Beginning with the presidency of George Bush, presidents have tended to travel more outside the country than did earlier presidents. During his second term, Clinton traveled more outside the United States than any other president. George W. Bush also conducted extensive foreign travel. Criticized early in his term for not having been abroad and for being unfamiliar with the names of several heads of state, the younger Bush compensated with numerous foreign trips.

Foreign travel can also prompt criticism. When presidents spend too much time outside the country, they may be accused of paying inadequate attention to domestic problems. George Bush, who traveled abroad more than any other president since Truman, faced this charge during his term, in particular after the Persian Gulf War, when many people felt the president should turn his attention to domestic affairs. Instead, Bush made several trips to Europe, Japan, and the Persian Gulf, and in so doing may have violated one of the parameters of institutional behavior regarding the frequency of foreign travel. In general, presidents traveling abroad act as chief of state and are interested in capitalizing on this role at home. The image of the single executive representing the entire nation before the world is a powerful one, especially when used with some degree of restraint.

Group Appearances

Presidents' perpetual campaigns continue in their appearances before groups in Washington and at sites throughout the country.[2] Presidents strive to construct nationwide support by obtaining constituent group approval in addition to appealing to the public as a whole. Collectively, these groups often take on the characteristics of the broader American middle class. Presidents appeal to group identities but attempt to create a larger picture of groups working together for the common good. As an illustration, consider this passage from Reagan's inaugural address: "Our concern must be for a special interest group that has been too long neglected. It knows no sectional boundaries or ethnic and racial divisions, and it crosses party lines. It is made of men and women who raise our food, patrol our streets, man our mines and factories, teach our children, keep our homes and heal us when we're sick—professionals, industrialists, shopkeepers, clerks, cabbies, and truck drivers. They are in short, 'We the people,' this breed called Americans." Presidents engage in two types of group activities: minor policy speeches and symbolic appearances in Washington, D.C., and across the country.

Minor Policy Speeches

Table 4-7 shows minor presidential speeches made from Hoover to George W. Bush. These speeches involve substantive policy recommendations or proposals made to a specific group or in a certain forum. Often given at university commencements or various labor, business, or professional association conventions, presidents use their remarks to outline concrete policy proposals. These speeches are usually as specific in discussing a national problem as are major addresses, but they are shorter and not nationally broadcast. They can be used by a president to promote positions before groups who may be most supportive of the ideas conveyed. Less often, presidents go before hostile groups to promote cooperation. In some instances, presidents may actually seek to antagonize hostile groups and thereby cause other groups to coalesce behind the presidential position. Since the success of presidents' policy efforts in part rests on their ability to draw together a coalition of diverse groups, these minor addresses are important in allowing presidents to tailor remarks to specific audiences. Compared with major national addresses, these targeted appeals can be given with greater frequency and may succeed or fail in ways that major addresses to the entire public would not.

Table 4-7 reveals that presidents since Hoover have made on average some 10 minor speeches annually. The data reveal two distinct periods in the delivery of minor speeches. Presidents from Hoover to Nixon delivered on average 6 minor speeches in a year, while presidents since Ford have made 16 minor speeches annually. President Clinton gave more minor speeches than any other president. He gave 48 minor speeches in 1997 alone, which is equal to the total for Eisenhower in his second term and Kennedy combined. By comparison, George W. Bush has given far fewer minor speeches than his predecessors, his numbers more resembling those of presidents before Ford. This appears to be because of the all-consuming nature of the Iraq War in Bush's presidency. Bush gave many speeches about the war, but offered no policy pronouncements in them. Lacking policy measures, these speeches could not be counted as minor speeches.

The overall increase in the later period may reflect a change in the presidency's approach to groups. The White House became more organized and strategic with respect to specific group interests during the Ford and Carter presidencies (Ragsdale, 1993). The Carter administration created the Office of Public Liaison to expand White House relations with key interest groups. This office and other efforts to court interest groups expanded in subsequent administrations.

Symbolic Appearances In and Out of Washington

Presidents engage in ceremonial appearances as a key form of institutional behavior that allows them to show their symbolic connection to the American people. Examples include bill signings, the greeting of foreign guests, the honoring of a group or individual, and the commemoration of a historical or seasonal event. Some of these appearances border on the trivial, for example, when a president congratulates the baseball team winning the World Series. But they demonstrate the importance of the president's role as chief of state domestically, just as foreign travel demonstrates it abroad. These appearances offer presidents the opportunity to project an image of caring and concern to the nation as a whole through television and newspaper coverage. Indeed, many of the ceremonial appearances are designed specifically for the broader national audience, rather than the immediate one. These ceremonial appearances occur in Washington, D.C., and at locales across the United States.

As shown in Table 4-8, presidents make numerous appearances before various groups in and around Washington. Presidents Hoover through Eisenhower made relatively few Washington appearances, an average of 24 annually. This is contrasted to the period since Kennedy, in which presidents have appeared before groups at the White House and elsewhere in Washington an average of 178 times annually—nearly a five-fold increase over the previous period. Nixon stands out as having made relatively few Washington appearances during the latter period. He particularly minimized public exposure during the Vietnam War and Watergate. Instead, Nixon relied on major addresses to the nation in which he presented his case without confronting specific groups.

Presidents also make appearances at locations outside of Washington, D.C. (see Table 4-9). These U.S. appearances are largely ceremonial. Presidents travel to a particular community to commemorate a local event, meet civic groups and local leaders, or survey damage caused by natural disasters. The trend observed for Washington appearances repeats itself for U.S. public appearances. Hoover through Eisenhower made far fewer U.S. appearances (an average of 12 per year) than did presidents since John F. Kennedy (an average of 64 per year). Presidents Clinton and George W. Bush have exceeded their predecessors in the number of U.S. appearances. Some of these appearances help presidents achieve an image as a strong, caring national leader and others detract from that. Perhaps no better example of this juxtaposition was with George W. Bush who made several trips to New York City and to ground zero after the World Trade Center bombings in New York City on September 11, 2001. Bush looked heroic but humble as he stood alongside the firefighters and volunteers combing the rubble. In contrast, after Hurricane Katrina, Bush made several visits to the storm-wrecked area but had difficulty conveying that he grasped the depths of the devastation in New Orleans or was ready to do what it took to rebuild the city.

Partisan Appearances

The national and group approaches are supplemented by a third type of appeal in which presidents act as party leaders. They do so in ways that nonetheless maintain the popular conception of the office. The party becomes the vehicle through which presidents satisfy the public. By this logic, democracy is best served by the competitive exchange of ideas between the parties. Presidents pursue a course of public appearances that include meetings with party leaders, fund-raisers and rallies for party candidates, and gatherings of party workers. But presidents also continue to suggest on other occasions that they are nonpartisan and thereby maintain the uneasy balance in the ambivalence toward parties.

As Tables 4-10 and 4-11 show, presidents not surprisingly make roughly three times more partisan appearances during election years. The number of partisan appearances increased dramatically beginning with Ford, who made some 400 political appearances in little more than two years. Presidents from Hoover to Nixon made on average 15 political appearances a year, while presidents since Ford have made 66 partisan appearances a year. Presidents' use of these partisan appearances is not affected by their own election campaigns as party outsiders. Presidents Carter, Reagan, and Clinton, each of whom built their candidacies at least partly outside the traditional structure of the parties and against Washington party elites, nevertheless made significant numbers of party appearances.

The Mix of Public Activity

One final way of considering public appearances involves presidents' total domestic public activity. Table 4-12 is a compilation of presidents' major speeches, news conferences, minor addresses, Washington appearances, and U.S. appearances. The table is amplified by Figure 4-1, which depicts the annual rate of domestic appearances, taken separately and together. Partisan political appearances have been excluded because they involve presidents in activities of a nonofficial nature. Foreign appearances also do not figure in this tally because presidents often travel abroad for reasons other than public exposure back home (that is, matters of summitry, diplomacy, or war). The remaining items thus provide an overall measure of the level of presidents' official activity within the United States. Consistent with several earlier tables, the figure reveals two time periods: Hoover through Eisenhower were far less active than presidents since Kennedy, who have made an average of almost one public appearance per day.

Conclusion

The data in this chapter reveal two important features of institutional behavior. First, presidents' public appearances are more alike than different. One may be tempted to analyze a chief executive's overtures to the public on a personal level and thereby concentrate on the uniqueness of a president—his specific contributions, style of communication, speaking skills, mannerisms, likability, and personality. The single executive image allows presidents to advance their own unique identities. Calvin Coolidge is not Lyndon Johnson, and Lyndon Johnson is not Bill Clinton. Yet the public behavior sponsored by the single executive image says that indeed Coolidge is Johnson, and Johnson is Clinton. Contemporary presidents actively engage in all forms of public appearances. Even Eisenhower, who was the least active of the presidents studied, made seven domestic appearances per month. Presidents Coolidge, Johnson, and Clinton, with seemingly little in common, each gave five major addresses per year.

This similitude defies conventional wisdom about individual presidents and their unique public styles. Presidents such as Kennedy and Reagan, who were viewed as eloquent speakers, made no more major speeches than presidents such as Nixon and Carter, who were viewed as awkward speakers. Of course, this does not directly address the level of success achieved by presidents in making their public appearances. But evidence shows that presidents gain similar advantages no matter what their styles or personal skills (Ragsdale, 1984; Brace and Hinckley, 1992; Ragsdale, 1997). Institutional behavior overshadows individual differences.

Second, institutional behavior ineluctably changes over time. The similarities witnessed in a group of presidents do not imply that their behavior is fixed. Over the time period studied, the perpetual campaign became a much more intensive part of presidents' activities in office. Although Nixon creates something of an exception to the rule, presidents since Kennedy have been increasingly active. There is no evidence of a saturation point—a point at which presidents cannot physically add just one more public appearance into a day, week, or year. If anything, Presidents Clinton and George W. Bush appear more active publicly than the earlier presidents. Yet, it is too soon to tell whether their behavior marks the beginning of a third distinct period, one in which the president's schedule of public appearances is all but frenetic.

The change in the perpetual campaign from the 1940s and 1950s to the 1960s and thereafter has apparently resulted from the interconnection of four factors, three within the political environment—television, public opinion polling, and group interests—and the fourth, a structural element of the presidency—election campaigns.

The advent of television has created a medium through which presidents can receive extensive coverage of each public appearance, from the most significant national addresses down to the celebratory meeting with a national spelling bee champion. Captured live and on evening news broadcasts, presidents enter Americans' living rooms daily in a form of mediated intimacy. The White House can strategically plan this intimacy based on the results of public opinion polls, which are conducted much more frequently now than in the past. The White House can gather information on how the public evaluates presidential performance. The perpetual campaign may counter slipping poll results. Interest groups, always at the core of American government, are more numerous and may well be more entrenched today than during any earlier period (Schlozman and Tierney, 1986). The perpetual campaign allows presidents to court as many groups as possible.

Joined to these three environmental factors is what presidents have learned about the intensity of campaigning from their election contests. They become familiar, if not comfortable, with particular types of appearances delivered at a feverish pace. They know the importance of television, polls, and meetings with organized groups. In addition, they apply one of the campaign's most critical lessons: election campaigners never really know whether bumper stickers, billboards, television advertisements, debates, or direct mail work. Instead, they assume that trying every technique for which they have money and energy will pay off and at least not backfire.

This combination of factors makes increases in the perpetual campaign all but self-fulfilling. Like the earnest campaigners, presidents assume that the more appearances they make, the better off they will be in their ability to influence, increase, or maintain public support overall, among key groups within the public as well as key segments of their political party. As all presidents follow a similar logic, the number of public appearances will steadily increase over time. How successful the campaign is remains an open question. Evidence indicates that presidents from Truman to Reagan did not gain public approval from public appearances made, other than major national addresses (Ragsdale, 1993). Presidents may be applauded by the groups or regions targeted in their appeals, but their overall national approval level is not affected. Other patterns of public approval, more fully discussed in Chapter 5, indirectly confirm this finding. Recent presidents (such as Ford and Reagan) who were publicly quite active actually have lower average approval than their less active predecessors (such as Eisenhower and Kennedy) (see Table 5-1).

When people are asked the question, "What do American presidents do on the job?" they think of critical decisions on such matters as military strategy, domestic legislation, budget allocations, and international diplomacy. Yet, the tables in this chapter reveal how presidents engage in a perpetual campaign of public appearances that consumes ever more of their time.

Notes

1. Throughout this chapter major addresses and news conferences are calculated beginning with Coolidge while other forms of appearances, such as foreign travel, minor speeches, Washington appearances, and U.S. appearances, are calculated beginning with Truman. The earlier period, from Coolidge to Roosevelt, is not comparable to the more contemporary period with respect to these latter types of appearances, many of which were designed expressly for television coverage. The series starts, then, just as radio coverage of events is merging into television coverage.
2. In this chapter groups are defined broadly to include local communities, organized interests, and other less entrenched associations of individuals representing such associations.

Table 4-1 Description of Major Presidential Speeches by President, Coolidge to G. W. Bush, II

President	*Speech*
Coolidge	
Feb. 23, 1924	George Washington address
April 15, 1924	Daughters of the American Revolution
April 23, 1924	Associated Press luncheon
May 11, 1924	Better homes movement
May 31, 1924	Memorial Day at Arlington Cemetery
Sept. 2, 1924	Labor leaders at White House
Oct. 24, 1924	Foreign and domestic policy
Jan. 27, 1925	Budget Bureau
March 5, 1925	Inaugural address
April 19, 1925	Chicago World's Fair
April 21, 1925	Daughters of the American Revolution
May 31, 1925	Memorial Day at Arlington Cemetery
June 23, 1925	Business organization of government
Feb. 23, 1926	National Education Association
April 20, 1926	Daughters of the American Revolution
June 1, 1926	Memorial Day at Arlington Cemetery
Nov. 12, 1926	World Court
Feb. 23, 1927	Washington's Birthday
June 11, 1927	Memorial Day at Arlington Cemetery
Aug. 11, 1927	Mount Rushmore dedication
April 17, 1928	Daughters of the American Revolution
May 31, 1928	Gettysburg, Pennsylvania
Nov. 12, 1928	Armistice Day
Dec. 5, 1928	Budget message to Congress
Hoover	
March 4, 1929	Inaugural address
Sept. 18, 1929	Peace efforts and arms reduction
Dec. 3, 1929	State of the Union
Dec. 1, 1930	Economy
Dec. 2, 1930	State of the Union
Jan. 22, 1931	Drought relief
Oct. 18, 1931	Employment
Dec. 2, 1931	State of the Union
March 6, 1932	Hoarding money
Oct. 16, 1932	Community funds relief
Dec. 6, 1932	State of the Union
F. Roosevelt, I	
March 4, 1933	Inaugural address
March 12, 1933	Fireside chat—banking
May 7, 1933	Fireside chat—recovery
July 24, 1933	Fireside chat—recovery
Oct. 22, 1933	Fireside chat—recovery
Jan. 3, 1934	State of the Union
June 28, 1934	Fireside chat—economy
Sept. 30, 1934	Fireside chat—recovery
Jan. 4, 1935	State of the Union
April 28, 1935	Fireside chat—faith in government

(Table continues)

Table 4-1 (*Continued*)

President	*Speech*
F. Roosevelt, I (continued)	
Jan. 3, 1936	State of the Union
Sept. 6, 1936	Fireside chat—drought, conserving soil and water
F. Roosevelt, II	
Jan. 20, 1937	Inaugural address
March 9, 1937	Fireside chat—reorganizing the judiciary
Oct. 12, 1937	Fireside chat—legislation in Congress
Jan. 3, 1938	State of the Union
April 14, 1938	Fireside chat—economic conditions
June 24, 1938	Fireside chat—Democratic candidates
Aug. 15, 1938	Social security program
Jan. 4, 1939	State of the Union
Sept. 3, 1939	Fireside chat—war in Europe
Jan. 3, 1940	State of the Union
April 15, 1940	World order—against terror and hatred
May 26, 1940	Fireside chat—time to build defenses
Dec. 29, 1940	Fireside chat—national security
F. Roosevelt, III	
Jan. 20, 1941	Inaugural address
May 27, 1941	Fireside chat—extended national emergency
Sept. 1, 1941	Fireside chat—assist in every way
Sept. 11, 1941	Fireside chat—nation cannot be passive
Dec. 9, 1941	Fireside chat—declaration of war with Japan
Jan. 6, 1942	State of the Union
Feb. 23, 1942	Fireside chat—progress of war
April 28, 1942	Fireside chat—progress of war
Sept. 7, 1942	Fireside chat—cost of living and progress of war
Oct. 12, 1942	Fireside chat—reports on the home front
Jan. 7, 1943	State of the Union
May 2, 1943	Fireside chat—seizure of coal mines
July 28, 1943	Fireside chat—progress of war
Sept. 8, 1943	Fireside chat—war loan drive
Dec. 24, 1943	Fireside chat—Teheran & Cairo conferences
Jan. 11, 1944	State of the Union
June 5, 1944	Fireside chat—fall of Rome
June 12, 1944	Fireside chat—progress of war
Oct. 5, 1944	Right to vote for everyone
F. Roosevelt, IV	
Jan. 6, 1945	State of the Union
Truman, I	
April 16, 1945	State of the Union
April 25, 1945	United Nations Conference
May 8, 1945	Surrender of Germany
Aug. 9, 1945	Potsdam conference
Sept. 1, 1945	Surrender of Japan
Oct. 30, 1945	Wages and prices during reconversion
Jan. 3, 1946	Status of reconversion
Jan. 21, 1946	State of the Union

Table 4-1 *(Continued)*

President	*Speech*
Truman, I (continued)	
April 19, 1946	World hunger
May 24, 1946	Railroad strike emergency
June 29, 1946	Price controls
Oct. 14, 1946	Lifting price controls
Jan. 6, 1947	State of the Union
June 20, 1947	Veto of Taft-Hartley Act
Oct. 29, 1947	Special session of Congress
Jan. 7, 1948	State of the Union
April 14, 1948	Savings bonds
Truman, II	
Jan. 20, 1949	Inaugural address
July 13, 1949	National economy
Jan. 4, 1950	State of the Union
July 19, 1950	Korean War
Sept. 1, 1950	Korean War
Sept. 9, 1950	Signing of the Defense Production Act
Dec. 15, 1950	Declares national emergency (Korea)
Jan. 8, 1951	State of the Union
April 11, 1951	Korean War: Relieves MacArthur of command
June 14, 1951	Need to extend inflation controls
Nov. 7, 1951	International arms reduction
Jan. 9, 1952	State of the Union
March 6, 1952	Mutual security program
April 8, 1952	Steel mills (nation)
June 19, 1952	Steel mills (Congress)
Eisenhower, I	
Jan. 20, 1953	Inaugural address
Feb. 2, 1953	State of the Union
April 16, 1953	World peace
May 19, 1953	National security costs
June 3, 1953	Report with the cabinet
July 26, 1953	Korean armistice signed
Aug. 6, 1953	Achievements of the administration and the Eighty-third Congress
Jan. 4, 1954	Administration purposes and accomplishments
Jan. 7, 1954	State of the Union
March 15, 1954	Tax program
April 15, 1954	National goals and problems
Aug. 23, 1954	Achievements of the Eighty-third Congress
Jan. 6, 1955	State of the Union
July 15, 1955	Departure for the Geneva conference
July 25, 1955	Return from Geneva
Feb. 29, 1956	Decision on second term
April 16, 1956	Farm bill veto
Aug. 3, 1956	DDE and Dulles on Suez
Oct. 31, 1956	Middle East, Eastern Europe
Jan. 5, 1957	Middle East (Congress)
Jan. 10, 1957	State of the Union

(Table continues)

Table 4-1 *(Continued)*

President	*Speech*
Eisenhower, II	
Jan. 21, 1957	Inaugural address
Feb. 20, 1957	Middle East and United Nations
May 14, 1957	Government costs
May 21, 1957	Mutual security programs
Sept. 24, 1957	Desegregation in Little Rock
Nov. 7, 1957	National security (advances in technology)
Nov. 13, 1957	National security
Dec. 23, 1957	Report on NATO conference in Paris
Jan. 9, 1958	State of the Union
March 16, 1959	West Berlin and Soviet challenges to peace
Aug. 6, 1959	Labor bill needed
Sept. 10, 1959	Report on European trip
Dec. 3, 1959	Departure on goodwill trip to Europe, Asia, Africa
Jan. 7, 1960	State of the Union
Feb. 21, 1960	South America departure
March 8, 1960	South America return
May 25, 1960	Events in Paris
Jan. 17, 1961	Farewell address
Kennedy	
Jan. 20, 1961	Inaugural address
Jan. 30, 1961	State of the Union
May 25, 1961	National problems and needs
June 6, 1961	Return from Europe
July 25, 1961	Crisis in Berlin
Jan. 11, 1962	State of the Union
March 2, 1962	Nuclear testing and disarmament
Aug. 13, 1962	National economy
Sept. 30, 1962	Situation at the University of Mississippi
Oct. 22, 1962	Cuban missile crisis
Jan. 14, 1963	State of the Union
May 12, 1963	Racial strife in Birmingham
June 11, 1963	Civil rights
July 26, 1963	Nuclear Test Ban Treaty
Sept. 18, 1963	Nuclear Test Ban Treaty
L. Johnson[a]	
Nov. 27, 1963	Joint session
Jan. 8, 1964	State of the Union
Feb. 26, 1964	Tax bill signing
April 9, 1964	Moratorium on railroad labor dispute
July 2, 1964	Civil rights signing
Oct. 18, 1964	Events in Russia, China, Great Britain
Jan. 4, 1965	State of the Union
Jan. 20, 1965	Inaugural address
March 15, 1965	American hopes and goals
May 2, 1965	Dominican Republic situation
Aug. 30, 1965	Postponement of steel industry shutdown
Sept. 3, 1965	Announcement of steel settlement

Table 4-1 *(Continued)*

President	*Speech*
L. Johnson[a] (continued)	
Jan. 12, 1966	State of the Union
Jan. 10, 1967	State of the Union
July 24, 1967	Detroit riot (authorization of federal troops)
July 27, 1967	Civil disorder
Jan. 17, 1968	State of the Union
Jan. 26, 1968	North Korea
March 31, 1968	Vietnam; will not run
April 5, 1968	Martin Luther King assassination
June 5, 1968	Robert Kennedy assassination
Oct. 31, 1968	Bombing halt
Jan. 14, 1969	State of the Union
Nixon, I	
Jan. 20, 1969	Inaugural address
May 14, 1969	Vietnam War
Aug. 8, 1969	Domestic programs (family assistance plan, revenue sharing)
Nov. 3, 1969	Vietnam War
Dec. 15, 1969	Vietnam War (troop reductions)
Jan. 22, 1970	State of the Union
April 20, 1970	Vietnam War (troop reductions)
April 30, 1970	Cambodian invasion
June 3, 1970	Report on Cambodian invasion
June 17, 1970	Economic policy
Oct. 10, 1970	Vietnam War (peace initiatives)
Jan. 22, 1971	State of the Union
April 7, 1971	Vietnam War (general)
Aug. 15, 1971	Economic policy (wage-price freeze)
Sept. 9, 1971	Economic stabilization
Oct. 7, 1971	Economic stabilization (post-freeze)
Jan. 20, 1972	State of the Union
Jan. 25, 1972	Peace plan
Feb. 28, 1972	China
March 16, 1972	Busing
April 16, 1972	Vietnam
May 8, 1972	Vietnam
June 1, 1972	Return from Soviet Union
Nixon, II	
Jan. 20, 1973	Inaugural address
Jan. 23, 1973	Paris peace accord
March 29, 1973	Vietnam and domestic problems
April 30, 1973	Watergate
June 13, 1973	Price controls
Aug. 15, 1973	Watergate
Oct. 12, 1973	Ford as vice president
Nov. 7, 1973	Energy shortage
Nov. 25, 1973	Energy policy
Jan. 30, 1974	State of the Union
April 29, 1974	Taxes

(Table continues)

Table 4-1 *(Continued)*

President	*Speech*
Nixon, II (continued)	
July 3, 1974	Return from Soviet Union
July 25, 1974	Inflation, economy
Ford	
Aug. 9, 1974	Remarks on taking oath of office
Aug. 12, 1974	Address to joint session of Congress
Sept. 8, 1974	Nixon pardon
Oct. 8, 1974	Economic policy (Whip Inflation Now program)
Jan. 13, 1975	Energy and the economy
Jan. 15, 1975	State of the Union
March 29, 1975	Signing of tax reduction bill
April 10, 1975	U.S. foreign policy
May 27, 1975	Energy programs
Oct. 6, 1975	Federal tax and spending reductions
Jan. 19, 1976	State of the Union
Jan. 12, 1977	State of the Union
Carter	
Jan. 20, 1977	Inaugural address
Feb. 2, 1977	Report to the American people
April 18, 1977	Energy plan
April 20, 1977	Address to Congress on energy plan
Nov. 8, 1977	Update on energy plan
Jan. 19, 1978	State of the Union
Feb. 1, 1978	Panama Canal treaties (benefits of)
Sept. 18, 1978	Camp David Summit on Middle East
Oct. 24, 1978	Anti-inflation program
Jan. 23, 1979	State of the Union
April 5, 1979	Energy (decontrol of oil prices)
June 18, 1979	Report on Vienna Summit and SALT II
July 15, 1979	National goals
Oct. 1, 1979	Soviet troops in Cuba and SALT II
Jan. 4, 1980	Soviet invasion of Afghanistan
Jan. 23, 1980	State of the Union
April 25, 1980	Hostage rescue attempt
Reagan, I	
Jan. 20, 1981	Inaugural address
Feb. 5, 1981	Economy
Feb. 18, 1981	Program for economic recovery (Congress)
April 28, 1981	Economic recovery (Congress)
July 27, 1981	Tax reduction
Sept. 24, 1981	Economic recovery
Jan. 26, 1982	State of the Union
April 29, 1982	Federal budget
Aug. 16, 1982	Tax and budget legislation
Sept. 1, 1982	Middle East
Sept. 20, 1982	Lebanon
Oct. 13, 1982	Economy
Nov. 22, 1982	Arms reduction and deterrence

Table 4-1 *(Continued)*

President	*Speech*
Reagan, I (continued)	
Jan. 25, 1983	State of the Union
March 23, 1983	National security
April 27, 1983	Central America
Sept. 5, 1983	Soviet attack on Korean airline
Oct. 27, 1983	Lebanon, Grenada
Jan. 25, 1984	State of the Union
May 9, 1984	Central America
Reagan, II	
Jan. 21, 1985	Inaugural address
Feb. 6, 1985	State of the Union
April 24, 1985	Federal budget and deficit reduction
May 28, 1985	Tax reform
Nov. 14, 1985	U.S.-Soviet summit in Geneva
Nov. 21, 1985	U.S.-Soviet summit in Geneva
Jan. 28, 1986	Explosion of space shuttle *Challenger*
Feb. 4, 1986	State of the Union
Feb. 26, 1986	National security
March 16, 1986	Nicaragua
April 14, 1986	Air strike against Libya
June 14, 1986	Nicaragua
July 4, 1986	Independence Day
Sept. 14, 1986	Drug abuse
Oct. 13, 1986	Iceland meetings with Gorbachev
Nov. 13, 1986	Iran-contra controversy
Dec. 2, 1986	Iran-contra controversy
Jan. 27, 1987	State of the Union
March 4, 1987	Iran-contra controversy
June 15, 1987	Venice economic summit, arms control, and deficit
Aug. 12, 1987	Iran-contra controversy
Dec. 10, 1987	U.S.-Soviet summit
Jan. 25, 1988	State of the Union
Feb. 2, 1988	Nicaragua
Jan. 11, 1989	Farewell address
G. H. W. Bush	
Jan. 20, 1989	Inaugural address
Feb. 9, 1989	State of the Union
Sept. 5, 1989	Drug abuse
Nov. 22, 1989	Thanksgiving address
Dec. 20, 1989	Panama
Jan. 31, 1990	State of the Union
Sept. 11, 1990	Federal budget and Persian Gulf crisis
Oct. 2, 1990	Federal budget
Jan. 16, 1991	Allied air attacks in Persian Gulf
Jan. 29, 1991	State of the Union
Feb. 23, 1991	Allied ground offensive in Persian Gulf
Feb. 26, 1991	Suspension of allied combat in Persian Gulf
March 6, 1991	Cessation of conflict in Persian Gulf
Sept. 27, 1991	Nuclear weapons reduction

(Table continues)

Table 4-1 *(Continued)*

President	*Speech*
G.H.W. Bush (continued)	
Jan. 28, 1992	State of the Union
May 1, 1992	Los Angeles riots
Clinton, I	
Jan. 20, 1993	Inaugural address
Feb. 15, 1993	Economic program
Feb. 17, 1993	Administration goals
Aug. 3, 1993	Economic program
Sept. 22, 1993	Health care reform
Jan. 25, 1994	State of the Union
Sept. 15, 1994	Haiti
Sept. 18, 1994	Haiti
Oct. 18, 1994	Iraq
Dec. 15, 1994	Middle Class Bill of Rights
Jan. 24, 1995	State of the Union
June 13, 1995	Budget plan
Nov. 27, 1995	Peace agreement in Bosnia
Jan. 23, 1996	State of the Union
Clinton, II	
Jan. 20, 1997	Second inaugural address
Feb. 4, 1997	State of the Union
Jan. 27, 1998	State of the Union
Aug. 17, 1998	Testimony before Grand Jury on Monica Lewinsky
Aug. 20, 1998	Military Action in Afghanistan and Sudan
Dec. 16, 1998	Military strikes in Iraq begin
Dec. 19, 1998	Completion of Iraq air strikes
Jan. 19, 1999	State of the Union
March 24, 1999	Air strikes against Serbian targets
June 10, 1999	Military-technical agreement on Kosovo
Jan. 27, 2000	State of the Union
Jan. 18, 2001	Farewell address
G.W. Bush, I	
Jan. 20, 2001	Inaugural address
Feb. 27, 2001	Address to Congress on administrative goals (State of the Union)
Aug. 9, 2001	Stem cell research
Sept. 11, 2001	Terrorist attacks
Sept. 20, 2001	U.S. response to terrorist attacks
Oct. 7, 2001	Strikes against al Qaeda and Taliban in Afghanistan
Nov. 8, 2001	Homeland security
Jan. 29, 2002	State of the Union
June 6, 2002	Proposed Homeland Security Department
Sept. 11, 2002	First anniversary Sept. 11, 2001, attacks
Oct. 7, 2002	Threat of Iraq
Jan. 28, 2003	State of the Union
March 17, 2003	Situation in Iraq
March 19, 2003	Iraq War (fighting begins)
May 1, 2003	Iraq address on aircraft carrier (fighting ends)

Table 4-1 *(Continued)*

President	*Speech*
G.W. Bush, I (continued)	
Sept. 7, 2003	Iraq War
Dec. 14, 2003	Capture of Saddam Hussein
Jan. 20, 2004	State of the Union
G. W. Bush, II[b]	
Jan. 20, 2005	Second inaugural
Feb. 2, 2005	State of the Union
June 28, 2005	Iraq War
July 19, 2005	John Roberts nomination as chief justice
Sept. 15, 2005	Hurricane Katrina relief
Dec. 18, 2005	Iraq War
Jan. 31, 2006	State of the Union
May 15, 2006	Immigration reform
Sept. 11, 2006	Sept. 11, 2001, anniversary, War on Terror
Jan. 10, 2007	Iraq War
Jan. 23, 2007	State of the Union
Sept. 13, 2007	Iraq War

Sources: Coded and calculated by the author from: (Coolidge) H. Quint and R. Farrell, *The Talkative President* (Amherst: University of Massachusetts Press, 1964), and various issues of the *New York Times;* (F. Roosevelt) successive volumes of *The Public Papers of Franklin Roosevelt* (Washington, D.C.: Government Printing Office); (Hoover, Truman through Clinton) successive volumes of *The Public Papers of the Presidents* (Washington, D.C.: Government Printing Office); (George W. Bush) www.gpoaccess.gov/pubpapers/index.html.

[a] Includes full term from Nov. 1963 to Jan. 1969.
[b] Through 2007 only.

Table 4-2 Major Presidential Speeches, by Term, Coolidge to G.W. Bush, II

	All speeches			*Discretionary speeches*[a]		
President	Total	Yearly average	Average interval between speeches (months)	Total	Yearly average	Average interval between speeches (months)
Coolidge	24	4.8	4.8	23	5.8	4.6
Hoover	11	2.2	4.4	6	1.5	8.0
F. Roosevelt, I	12	3.0	4.0	8	2.0	6.0
F. Roosevelt, II	13	3.3	3.7	9	2.3	5.3
F. Roosevelt, III	19	4.8	2.5	15	3.8	3.2
F. Roosevelt, IV	1	—	—	0	—	—
Truman, I	17	3.4	2.8	13	3.3	3.7
Truman, II	15	3.8	3.2	11	2.8	4.4
Eisenhower, I	21	5.3	2.3	16	4.0	3.0
Eisenhower, II	20	5.0	2.5	16	4.0	3.0
Kennedy	15	5.0	2.3	11	3.7	3.2
L. Johnson[b]	23	4.6	2.7	15	3.0	4.2
Nixon, I	23	5.8	2.1	19	4.8	2.5
Nixon, II	13	8.1	1.5	11	5.5	1.8
Ford	12	5.2	2.4	8	4.0	3.5
Carter	17	4.3	2.8	13	3.3	3.7
Reagan, I	20	5.0	2.4	16	4.0	3.0
Reagan, II	27	6.8	1.8	22	5.5	2.2
G.H.W. Bush	17	4.3	2.8	12	3.0	4.0
Clinton, I	14	3.5	3.4	10	2.5	4.8
Clinton, II	12	3.0	4.0	7	1.8	6.9
G.W. Bush, I	18	4.5	4.0	13	3.3	3.7
G.W. Bush, II[c]	12	4.0	4.0	8	2.7	4.5

Total	376			282		
Average		4.5	3.0		3.5	4.1

Sources: Coded and calculated by the author from (Coolidge) H. Quint and R. Farrell, *The Talkative President* (Amherst: University of Massachusetts Press, 1964), and various issues of the *New York Times*; (F. Roosevelt) successive volumes of *The Public Papers of Franklin Roosevelt* (Washington, D.C.: Government Printing Office); (Hoover and Truman through Clinton) successive volumes of *The Public Papers of the Presidents* (Washington, D.C.: Government Printing Office); (G. W. Bush) www.gpoaccess.gov/pubpapers/indx.html.

Note: "Major speeches" are defined as live nationally televised and broadcast addresses to the country that preempt all major network programming. They include inaugural addresses, State of the Union messages, other addresses to joint sessions of Congress delivered during prime time, and prime-time addresses to the nation.

[a] Excludes inaugural addresses and State of the Union messages.
[b] Includes full term from Nov. 1963 to Jan. 1969.
[c] Through 2007 only.

Table 4-3 Major Presidential Speeches, by Subject Category, Coolidge to G. W. Bush, II

	General		*Foreign*		*Economic*		*Domestic*		
President	*N*	*%*	*N*	*%*	*N*	*%*	*N*	*%*	*Total*
Coolidge	12	50	2	8	4	17	6	25	24
Hoover	6	55	1	9	3	27	1	9	11
F. Roosevelt, I	4	33	0	0	5	42	3	25	12
F. Roosevelt, II	4	31	4	31	4	31	1	7	13
F. Roosevelt, III	5	26	11	58	2	10	1	5	19
F. Roosevelt, IV	1	100	0	0	0	0	0	0	1
Truman, I	4	24	5	29	5	29	3	18	17
Truman, II	4	27	7	47	2	13	2	13	15
Eisenhower, I	10	47	8	38	1	5	2	10	21
Eisenhower, II	5	25	12	60	0	0	3	15	20
Kennedy	5	33	6	40	1	7	3	20	15
L. Johnson[a]	10	43	4	17	3	13	6	26	23
Nixon, I	4	17	13	57	4	17	2	9	23
Nixon, II	3	23	2	15	5	38	3	23	13
Ford	5	42	1	8	5	42	1	8	12
Carter	6	35	6	35	5	29	0	0	17
Reagan, I	4	20	8	40	8	40	0	0	20
Reagan, II	6	22	14	52	2	7	5	19	27
G. H. W. Bush	5	29	6	35	1	6	5	29	17
Clinton, I	5	36	4	29	4	29	1	7	14
Clinton, II	6	50	5	42	0	0	1	8	12
G. W. Bush, I	9	50	8	44	0	0	1	6	18
G. W. Bush, II[b]	5	42	4	33	0	0	3	25	12
Total	128		131		64		53		376
Average percent		36		33		18		14	

Sources: Coded and calculated by the author from (Coolidge) H. Quint and R. Farrell, *The Talkative President* (Amherst: University of Massachusetts Press, 1964), and various issues of the *New York Times*; (F. Roosevelt) successive volumes of *The Public Papers of Franklin Roosevelt* (Washington, D.C.: Government Printing Office); (Hoover and Truman through Clinton) successive volumes of *The Public Papers of the Presidents* and *Weekly Compilations of Presidential Documents* (Washington, D.C.: Government Printing Office); (G. W. Bush) www.gpoaccess.gov/pubpapers/index.html.

Note: Foreign policy subjects include diplomacy, summitry, treaties, and war. Economic policy includes the economy and energy. Domestic policy involves civil rights, civil protests, riots, social welfare, education, agriculture, and domestic political matters such as Watergate. General policy encompasses two or more of the three types. For example, G. W. Bush speeches on the Sept. 11, 2001, terrorist attacks and homeland security are coded as general, since they encompass both domestic security and foreign policy concerns. Percentages may not add to 100 due to rounding.

[a] Includes full term from Nov. 1963 to Jan. 1969.
[b] Through 2007 only.

Table 4-4 Presidential News Conferences, by Year, Coolidge to G. W. Bush, II

Coolidge	
1924	92
1925	88
1926	79
1927	80
1928	68
Total	407
Yearly average	81
Monthly average	6.8
Hoover	
1929	78
1930	86
1931	62
1932–33	42
Total	268
Yearly average	67
Monthly average	5.6
F. Roosevelt, I	
1933	81
1934	73
1935	59
1936	67
Total	280
Yearly average	70
Monthly average	5.8
F. Roosevelt, II	
1937	73
1938	86
1939	84
1940	89
Total	332
Yearly average	83
Monthly average	6.9
F. Roosevelt, III	
1941	78
1942	66
1943	58
1944	54
Total	256
Yearly average	64
Monthly average	5.3
F. Roosevelt, IV	
1945	13
Total	13
Yearly average	—
Monthly average	3.1
Truman, I	
1945	36
1946	46
1947	33
1948	27
Total	142
Yearly average	36
Monthly average	3.0
Truman, II	
1949	47
1950	39
1951	39
1952	35
Total	160
Yearly average	40
Monthly average	3.3
Eisenhower, I	
1953	23
1954	33
1955	19
1956	24
Total	99
Yearly average	25
Monthly average	2.1
Eisenhower, II	
1957	26
1958	21
1959	31
1960	16
Total	94
Yearly average	24
Monthly average	2.0
Kennedy	
1961	19
1962	27
1963	19
Total	65
Yearly average	22
Monthly average	1.9
L. Johnson[a]	
1963–64	33
1965	17
1966	41
1967	22
1968	19
Total	132

Table 4-4 *(Continued)*

L. Johnson (continued)	
Yearly average	26
Monthly average	2.1
Nixon, I	
1969	8
1970	6
1971	9
1972	7
Total	30
Yearly average	8
Monthly average	0.6
Nixon, II	
1973	7
1974	2
Total	9
Yearly average	5
Monthly average	0.5
Ford	
1974	7
1975	19
1976	15
Total	41
Yearly average	19
Monthly average	1.4
Carter	
1977	22
1978	19
1979	12
1980	6
Total	59
Yearly average	15
Monthly average	1.2
Reagan, I	
1981	6
1982	6
1983	7
1984	4
Total	23
Yearly average	6
Monthly average	0.5
Reagan, II	
1985	5
1986	7
1987	3
1988	4
Total	19
Yearly average	5
Monthly average	0.4
G. H. W. Bush	
1989	31
1990	31
1991	47
1992	22
Total	131
Yearly average	33
Monthly average	2.7
Clinton, I	
1993	28
1994	44
1995	27
1996	19
Total	118
Yearly average	30
Monthly average	2.5
Clinton, II	
1997	21
1998	13
1999	18
2000	8
Total	58
Yearly average	15
Monthly average	1.5
G. W. Bush, I	
2001	16
2002	12
2003	16
2004	10
Total	54
Yearly average	14
Monthly average	1.1
G. W. Bush, II[b]	
2005	16
2006	29
2007	25
Total	70
Yearly average	23
Monthly average	1.9

Table 4-4 *(Continued)*

Sources: Coded and calculated by the author from: (Coolidge-Clinton) successive volumes of *The Public Papers of the Presidents* (Washington, D.C.: Government Printing Office); (G. W. Bush) www.gpoaccess.gov/pubpapers/index.html.

Note: Excludes interviews, call-ins, and informal remarks made to mark trip arrivals and departures.

[a] Includes full term from Nov. 1963 to Jan. 1969.
[b] Through 2007 only.

Table 4-5 White House Press Secretaries, Hoover to G. W. Bush

Press secretary	*President*	*Years*	*Background*
George Akerson	Hoover	1929–1931	Reporter
Theodore G. Joslin	Hoover	1931–1933	AP reporter
Stephen T. Early	F. Roosevelt	1933–1945	AP, UPI reporter
Charles Ross	Truman	1945–1950	Reporter
Joseph H. Short	Truman	1950–1952	Reporter
Roger Tubby	Truman	1952–1953	Journalist
James C. Hagerty	Eisenhower	1953–1961	Reporter
Pierre E. Salinger	Kennedy	1961–1963	Investigative writer
Pierre E. Salinger	L. Johnson	1963–1964	Investigative writer
George Reedy	L. Johnson	1964–1965	UPI reporter
Bill Moyers	L. Johnson	1965–1967	Associate director of Peace Corps
George Christian	L. Johnson	1967–1969	Reporter
Ronald L. Ziegler	Nixon	1969–1974	Advertising
Jerald F. terHorst	Ford	1974	Bureau chief, newspaper
Ron H. Nessen	Ford	1974–1977	Journalist
Jody L. Powell	Carter	1977–1981	Advertising
James Brady[a]	Reagan	1981–1989	Campaign aide
Larry Speakes	Reagan	1981–1987	Reporter
Marlin Fitzwater	Reagan	1987–1989	Government information aide
Marlin Fitzwater	G. H. W. Bush	1989–1992	Government information aide
Dee Dee Myers	Clinton	1993–1994	Campaign aide
Michael McCurry	Clinton	1994–1998	State Department press aide
Joe Lockhart	Clinton	1998–2000	Reporter
Jake Siewert	Clinton	2000–2001	Communications director
Ari Fleisher	G. W. Bush	2001–2003	Congressional press secretary
Scott McClellan	G. W. Bush	2003–2006	Campaign aide
Tony Snow	G. W. Bush	2006–2007	Reporter
Dana Perino[b]	G. W. Bush	2007–	Reporter/public affairs

Source: Congressional Quarterly's Guide to the Presidency, ed. Michael Nelson (Washington, D.C.: Congressional Quarterly, 1989), 733; updated by the author.

[a] Although Brady was severely wounded in the 1981 presidential assassination attempt, his title remained press secretary until 1989. Speakes's title was assistant to the president and principal deputy press secretary, while Fitzwater's was assistant to the president for press relations. Fitzwater became White House press secretary in the Bush administration.
[b] As of 2007 only.

Table 4-6 Foreign Appearances by President, Truman, I to G. W. Bush, II

			Yearly average	
President	*Days of travel*	*Number of appearances*	Days	Appearances
Truman, I	10	7	3	2
Truman, II	0	0	0	0
Eisenhower, I	3	7	1	2
Eisenhower, II	50	115	13	29
Kennedy	28	77	9	26
L. Johnson[a]	29	55	6	11
Nixon, I	35	108	9	27
Nixon, II	17	25	9	14
Ford	30	63	14	29
Carter	52	69	13	17
Reagan, I	36	82	9	21
Reagan, II	48	51	12	13
G. H. W. Bush	86	113	24	29
Clinton, I	72	129	18	32
Clinton, II	144	255	36	64
G. W. Bush, I	70	111	18	28
G. W. Bush, II[b]	57	118	19	39

Source: Coded and calculated by the author from: (Truman through Clinton, I) successive volumes of *The Public Papers of the Presidents* (Washington, D.C.: Government Printing Office); (Clinton, II through G. W. Bush, II) *The Public Papers of the Presidents,* as found in the American Presidency Project at www.presidency.ucsb.edu.

Note: Foreign appearances are defined as the total number of appearances made by a president during travel outside the United States. An appearance includes formal remarks, toasts to other heads of state, airport greetings, remarks to reporters, and remarks to American citizens who reside in the host country.

[a] Includes full term from Nov. 1963 to Jan. 1969.
[b] Through 2007 only.

Table 4-7 Minor Presidential Speeches, by Year, Hoover to G.W. Bush, II

Hoover	
1929	3
1930	3
1931	1
1932/1933	3
Total	10
Yearly average	2.5
Monthly average	0.2
F. Roosevelt, I	
1933	1
1934	1
1935	1
1936	1
Total	4
Yearly average	1
Monthly average	0.08
F. Roosevelt, II	
1937	2
1938	1
1939	1
1940	0
Total	4
Yearly average	1
Monthly average	0.08
F. Roosevelt, III/IV	
1941	0
1942	0
1943	1
1944/1945	0
Total	1
Yearly average	0.25
Monthly average	0.02
Truman, I	
1945	4
1946	0
1947	1
1948	0
Total	5
Yearly average	1
Monthly average	0.1
Truman, II	
1949	8
1950	13
1951	9
1952	9
Total	39
Yearly average	10
Monthly average	0.8
Eisenhower, I	
1953	5
1954	2
1955	2
1956	2
Total	11
Yearly average	3
Monthly average	0.2
Eisenhower, II	
1957	5
1958	7
1959	2
1960	4
Total	18
Yearly average	5
Monthly average	0.4
Kennedy	
1961	6
1962	7
1963	17
Total	30
Yearly average	10
Monthly average	0.9
L. Johnson[a]	
1963–64	11
1965	9
1966	11
1967	4
1968	14
Total	49
Yearly average	10
Monthly average	0.8
Nixon, I	
1969	5
1970	6
1971	10
1972	4
Total	25
Yearly average	6
Monthly average	0.5
Nixon, II	
1973	12
1974	10
Total	22
Yearly average	12
Monthly average	1.1

Table 4-7 *(Continued)*

Ford	
1974	5
1975	36
1976	36
Total	77
Yearly average	35
Monthly average	2.7
Carter	
1977	21
1978	15
1979	22
1980	24
Total	82
Yearly average	21
Monthly average	1.7
Reagan, I	
1981	11
1982	27
1983	19
1984	21
Total	78
Yearly average	20
Monthly average	1.6
Reagan, II	
1985	6
1986	2
1987	7
1988	1
Total	16
Yearly average	4
Monthly average	0.3
G.H.W. Bush	
1989	9
1990	2
1991	7
1992	2
G.H.W. Bush (continued)	
Total	20
Yearly average	5
Monthly average	0.4
Clinton, I	
1993	26
1994	23
1995	33
1996	28
Total	110
Yearly average	28
Monthly average	2.3
Clinton, II	
1997	48
1998	12
1999	14
2000	7
Total	81
Yearly average	20
Monthly average	1.7
G.W. Bush, I	
2001	9
2002	10
2003	7
2004	1
Total	27
Yearly average	7
Monthly average	0.6
G.W. Bush, II[b]	
2005	3
2006	3
2007	1
Total	7
Yearly average	2
Monthly average	0.2

Source: Coded and calculated by the author from: (Hoover through Clinton, I) successive volumes of *The Public Papers of the Presidents* (Washington, D.C.: Government Printing Office); (Clinton, II through G.W. Bush, II) *The Public Papers of the Presidents,* as found in The American Presidency Project at www.presidency.ucsb.edu.

[a] Includes full term from Nov. 1963 to Jan. 1969.
[b] Through 2007 only.

Table 4-8 Public Appearances in Washington, D.C., by Year, Hoover to G. W. Bush, II

Hoover	
1929	11
1930	28
1931	16
1932/1933	24
Total	79
Yearly average	20
Monthly average	1.6
F. Roosevelt, I	
1933	10
1934	11
1935	9
1936	11
Total	41
Yearly average	10
Monthly average	0.9
F. Roosevelt, II	
1937	6
1938	7
1939	11
1940	6
Total	30
Yearly average	7.5
Monthly average	0.6
F. Roosevelt, III/IV	
1941	11
1942	9
1943	11
1944	8
1945	1
Total	40
Yearly average	10
Monthly average	0.8
Truman, I	
1945	5
1946	14
1947	12
1948	8
Total	39
Yearly average	10
Monthly average	0.8
Truman, II	
1949	63
1950	34
1951	87
1952	69
Total	253
Yearly average	63
Monthly average	5.3
Eisenhower, I	
1953	31
1954	45
1955	28
1956	20
Total	124
Yearly average	31
Monthly average	2.6
Eisenhower, II	
1957	34
1958	28
1959	57
1960	44
Total	163
Yearly average	41
Monthly average	3.4
Kennedy	
1961	110
1962	168
1963	139
Total	417
Yearly average	139
Monthly average	11.9
L. Johnson[a]	
1963–64	273
1965	192
1966	177
1967	197
1968	199
Total	1,038
Yearly average	208
Monthly average	17.0

Table 4-8 *(Continued)*

Nixon, I	
1969	146
1970	99
1971	76
1972	47
Total	368
Yearly average	92
Monthly average	7.7
Nixon, II	
1973	88
1974	34
Total	122
Yearly average	68
Monthly average	6.1
Ford	
1974	68
1975	173
1976	202
Total	443
Yearly average	201
Monthly average	15.3
Carter	
1977	204
1978	168
1979	156
1980	189
Total	717
Yearly average	179
Monthly average	15.0
Reagan, I	
1981	170
1982	185
1983	252
1984	206
Total	813
Yearly average	203
Monthly average	17.0
Reagan, II	
1985	139
1986	137
1987	182
1988	175
Total	633
Reagan, II (continued)	
Yearly average	158
Monthly average	13.2
G. H. W. Bush	
1989	181
1990	189
1991	218
1992	145
Total	733
Yearly average	183
Monthly average	15.3
Clinton, I	
1993	184
1994	209
1995	213
1996	193
Total	799
Yearly average	200
Monthly average	16.6
Clinton, II	
1997	194
1998	200
1999	225
2000	213
Total	832
Yearly average	208
Monthly average	17.3
G. W. Bush, I	
2001	274
2002	190
2003	143
2004	135
Total	742
Yearly average	186
Monthly average	15.5
G. W. Bush, II[b]	
2005	206
2006	247
2007	152
Total	605
Yearly average	202
Monthly average	16.8

Source: Coded and calculated by the author from: (Hoover through Clinton, I) successive volumes of *The Public Papers of the Presidents* (Washington, D.C.: Government Printing Office); (Clinton, II through G. W. Bush, II) *The Public Papers of the Presidents,* as found in The American Presidency Project at www.presidency.ucsb.edu.

[a] Includes full term from Nov. 1963 to Jan. 1969.
[b] Through 2007 only.

Table 4-9 U.S. Public Appearances, by Year, Hoover to G.W. Bush, II

Hoover	
1929	5
1930	5
1931	14
1932/1933	6
Total	30
Yearly average	7.5
Monthly average	0.6
F. Roosevelt, I	
1933	8
1934	17
1935	13
1936	48
Total	86
Yearly average	21.5
Monthly average	1.8
F. Roosevelt, II	
1937	15
1938	23
1939	8
1940	9
Total	55
Yearly average	13.8
Monthly average	1.1
F. Roosevelt, III/IV	
1941	7
1942	2
1943	2
1944	8
1945	0
Total	19
Yearly average	3.8
Monthly average	0.4
Truman, I	
1945	5
1946	7
1947	6
1948	17
Total	35
Yearly average	9
Monthly average	0.7
Truman, II	
1949	8
1950	26
1951	9
Truman, II (continued)	
1952	10
Total	53
Yearly average	13
Monthly average	1.1
Eisenhower, I	
1953	16
1954	30
1955	22
1956	7
Total	75
Yearly average	19
Monthly average	1.6
Eisenhower, II	
1957	7
1958	10
1959	5
1960	21
Total	43
Yearly average	11
Monthly average	0.9
Kennedy	
1961	15
1962	41
1963	41
Total	97
Yearly average	32
Monthly average	2.8
L. Johnson[a]	
1963–64	83
1965	31
1966	56
1967	32
1968	36
Total	244
Yearly average	49
Monthly average	3.9
Nixon, I	
1969	39
1970	46
1971	61
1972	20
Total	166
Yearly average	42
Monthly average	3.5

Table 4-9 *(Continued)*

Nixon, II	
1973	19
1974	19
Total	38
Yearly average	21
Monthly average	1.9
Ford	
1974	20
1975	77
1976	86
Total	183
Yearly average	83
Monthly average	6.3
Carter[b]	
1977	35
1978	42
1979	40
1980	55
Total	172
Yearly average	43
Monthly average	3.6
Reagan, I	
1981	19
1982	65
1983	103
1984	73
Total	260
Yearly average	65
Monthly average	5.4
Reagan, II	
1985	33
1986	20
1987	45
1988	35
Total	133
Yearly average	33
Monthly average	2.7
G. H. W. Bush	
1989	69
1990	58
1991	70
1992	58
Total	255
Yearly average	64
Monthly average	5.3
Clinton, I	
1993	80
1994	108
1995	134
1996	88
Total	330
Yearly average	83
Monthly average	6.9
Clinton, II	
1997	82
1998	95
1999	121
2000	127
Total	425
Yearly average	106
Monthly average	8.85
G. W. Bush, I	
2001	125
2002	153
2003	92
2004	86
Total	456
Yearly average	114
Monthly average	9.5
G. W. Bush, II[c]	
2005	106
2006	111
2007	71
Total	288
Yearly average	96
Monthly average	8

Source: Coded and calculated by the author from: (Hoover through Clinton, I) successive volumes of *The Public Papers of the Presidents* (Washington, D.C.: Government Printing Office); (Clinton, II through G. W. Bush, II) *The Public Papers of the Presidents,* as found in The American Presidency Project at www.presidency.ucsb.edu.

[a] Includes full term from Nov. 1963 to Jan. 1969.
[b] Does not include series of "town meetings" begun early in term.
[c] Through 2007 only.

Table 4-10 Political Appearances, by Year, Hoover to G.W. Bush, II

Hoover	
1929	0
1930	0
1931	0
1932/1933	31
Total	31
F. Roosevelt, I	
1933	0
1934	0
1935	0
1936	57
Total	57
F. Roosevelt, II	
1937	0
1938	0
1939	1
1940	8
Total	9
F. Roosevelt, III/IV	
1941	0
1942	0
1943	0
1944	10
1945	0
Total	10
Truman, I	
1945	0
1946	2
1947	1
1948	82
Total	85
Truman, II	
1949	14
1950	6
1951	6
1952	62
Total	88
Eisenhower, I	
1953	8
1954	17
1955	5
1956	36
Total	66
Eisenhower, II	
1957	3
1958	16
1959	2
1960	24
Total	45
Kennedy	
1961	7
1962	33
1963	9
Total	49
L. Johnson[a]	
1963–64	98
1965	4
1966	8
1967	7
1968	14
Total	131
Nixon, I	
1969	12
1970	39
1971	5
1972	46
Total	102
Nixon, II	
1973	2
1974	9
Total	11
Ford	
1974	34
1975	44
1976	331
Total	409
Carter	
1977	13
1978	51
1979	21
1980	149
Total	234
Reagan, I	
1981	23
1982	35
1983	22
1984	126
Total	206

Table 4-10 *(Continued)*

Reagan, II		Clinton, II	
1985	17	1997	76
1986	48	1998	108
1987	9	1999	86
1988	49	2000	201
Total	123	Total	471
G. H. W. Bush		G. W. Bush, I	
1989	21	2001	10
1990	73	2002	84
1991	14	2003	56
1992	250	2004	225
Total	358	Total	375
Clinton, I		G. W. Bush, II[b]	
1993	11	2005	10
1994	47	2006	59
1995	15	2007	9
1996	170	Total	78
Total	243		

Source: Coded and calculated by the author from: (Hoover through Clinton, I) successive volumes of *The Public Papers of the Presidents* (Washington, D.C.: Government Printing Office); (Clinton, II through G. W. Bush, II) *The Public Papers of the Presidents,* as found in The American Presidency Project at www.presidency.ucsb.edu.

[a] Includes full term from Nov. 1963 to Jan. 1969.
[b] Through 2007 only.

Table 4-11 Political Appearances in Election and Nonelection Years, Hoover to G. W. Bush, II

President	*Total*	*Election year*[a]	*Nonelection year*
Hoover	31	31	0
F. Roosevelt, I	57	57	0
F. Roosevelt, II	9	8	0
F. Roosevelt, III/IV	10	10	0
Truman, I	85	84	1
Truman, II	88	68	20
Eisenhower, I	66	53	13
Eisenhower, II	45	40	5
Kennedy	49	33	16
L. Johnson[b]	131	120	11
Nixon, I	102	85	17
Nixon, II	11	9	2
Ford	409	365	44
Carter	234	200	34
Reagan, I	206	161	45
Reagan, II	123	97	26
G. H. W. Bush	358	323	35
Clinton, I	243	170	24
Clinton, II	471	433	38
G. W. Bush, I	375	309	66
G. W. Bush, II[c]	78	59	19

Source: Coded and calculated by the author from: (Hoover through Clinton, I) successive volumes of *The Public Papers of the Presidents* (Washington, D.C.: Government Printing Office); (Clinton, II through G. W. Bush, II) *The Public Papers of the Presidents,* as found in The American Presidency Project at www.presidency.ucsb.edu.

Note: A political appearance is defined as any appearance before an expressly partisan political group or for an expressly partisan purpose.

[a] Average of midterm congressional election years and presidential election year.
[b] Includes full term from Nov. 1963 to Jan. 1969.
[c] Through 2007 only.

Table 4-12 Level of Public Activities of Presidents, Hoover to G. W. Bush, II

President	*Total activities*	*Yearly average*	*Monthly average*
Hoover	398	100	8.3
F. Roosevelt, I	423	106	8.8
F. Roosevelt, II	434	109	9.0
F. Roosevelt, III/IV	336	84	6.5
Truman, I	248	62	5.2
Truman, II	520	130	10.8
Eisenhower, I	330	83	6.9
Eisenhower, II	338	85	7.0
Kennedy	658	219	18.8
L. Johnson[a]	1,463	293	24.0
Nixon, I	634	159	13.2
Nixon, II	204	113	10.2
Ford	756	344	26.0
Carter	1,047	262	22.0
Reagan, I	1,194	299	24.9
Reagan, II	852	213	18.0
G. H. W. Bush	1,244	311	26.0
Clinton, I	1,371	343	28.5
Clinton, II	1,949	487	40.6
G. W. Bush, I	1,697	424	35.4
G. W. Bush, II[b]	1,096	365	30.4

Source: Coded and calculated by the author from: (Hoover through Clinton, I) successive volumes of *The Public Papers of the Presidents* (Washington, D.C.: Government Printing Office); (Clinton, II through G. W. Bush, II) *The Public Papers of the Presidents,* as found in The American Presidency Project at www.presidency.ucsb.edu.

Note: Public activities are defined as including all domestic public appearances by a president, including major speeches, news conferences, minor speeches, Washington appearances, and U.S. appearances but not political appearances.

[a] Includes full term from Nov. 1963 to Jan. 1969.
[b] Through 2007 only.

Figure 4-1 Presidents' Domestic Public Appearances, Hoover to G.W. Bush, II (yearly averages)

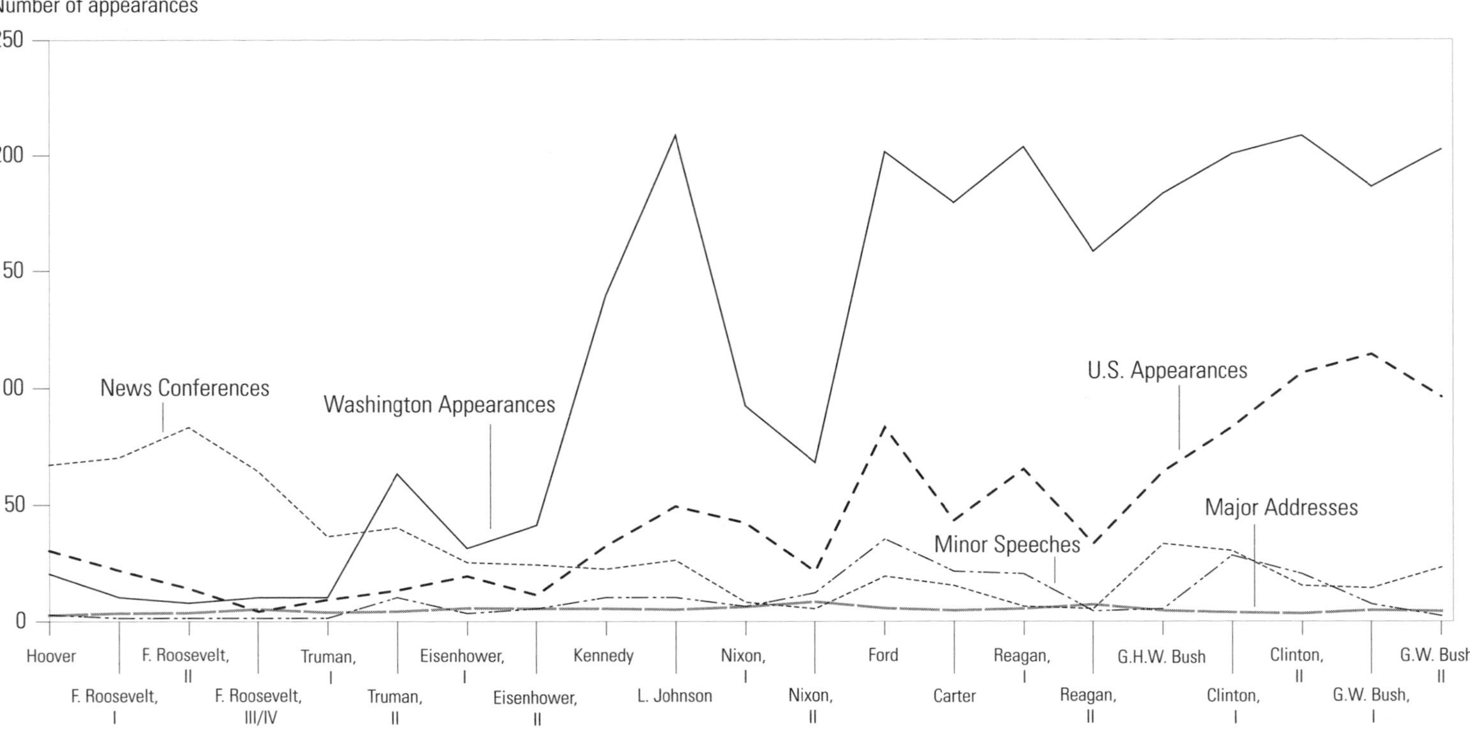

Sources: Coded and calculated by the author from: (Roosevelt) successive volumes of *The Public Papers of Franklin Roosevelt* (Washington, D.C.: Government Printing Office); (Hoover, Truman through Clinton) successive volumes of *The Public Papers of the Presidents* (Washington, D.C.: Government Printing Office); (G.W. Bush) www.gpoaccess.gov/pubpapers/index.html.

5

Public Opinions

- **National Presidential Approval**
- **Approval by Party, Region, and Demographic Characteristics**
- **Presidents' Handling of the Economy and Foreign Affairs**
- **The Public's Most Important Problem**
- **Public Confidence in Major Institutions**

The previous chapter analyzed how presidents' public appearances form one type of institutional behavior. This chapter poses another critical test of the extent to which the presidency is an institution: How does the public evaluate the performances of individual presidents? If these public evaluations are president-specific, that is, if they respond uniquely to the decisions of the president and the events that occur during his term, then relations between the president and the public do not have a significant institutional component.

Americans surely wish to believe that their evaluations of presidents are uniquely personal, both with respect to the individual making the judgment and to the particular president who is being judged. But when public evaluations reveal identifiable patterns across presidents, with the public responding alike to similar types of presidential activities and environmental circumstances, then they in fact constitute another form of institutional behavior.

This chapter is divided into three parts. First, it analyzes presidential approval over time; second, it considers approval among various political, demographic, and economic clusters of people within the population; and, finally, it compares public evaluations of presidents on domestic policy with evaluations of presidents on foreign policy.[1] The corresponding data help determine the type of institutional behavior patterns that may be observable within the public.

Approval over Time

Presidential popularity or approval is the longest available time series on American public opinion. Since 1937 the Gallup poll organization has asked scientifically selected samples of Americans the question, "Do you approve or disapprove of the way [the incumbent] is handling his job as president?" Critics have rightly raised concerns about the question's wording. It is unclear how people respond to the term *job.* What elements of the president's job are they judging? Are they actually judging the job itself or personal characteristics of the president that they use as a substitute barometer for job performance? Despite these legitimate complaints, the poll results are considered to be among the few reliable political "facts" known about presidents. The president's popularity rating is one number that national politicians know without hesitation. When presidential popularity rises (or drops) abruptly, the shift is widely reported in the news media, discussed in Washington, and applauded (or lamented) at the White House.

When the Clinton White House was faced with allegations in January 1998 that the president may have had an affair with an intern and that steps were taken to cover it up, two things were clear about the importance of public opinion polls. First, Bill Clinton's approval ratings did not drop in the midst of the initial tumult. Indeed, his approval ratings actually rose by eight points after he delivered a strong State of the Union message a week after the allegations first surfaced. This suggests that the Gallup question is actually a job performance measure (as intended) and not a substitute for overall approval of the president as a person. Second, poll results were closely monitored in and out of the White House to detect signs of the erosion of public support. Gallup took five national opinion samples within thirteen days—January 16, 23, 24, 25, and 28—to capture public opinion shifts.

As shown in Tables 5-1 and 5-2, presidential popularity follows a generally uniform time trend: popularity starts high, drops, and then moves up slightly toward the end of the term (Stimson, 1976; Brace and Hinckley, 1992). As Table 5-3 and Figure 5-1 indicate, several presidents since Franklin Roosevelt have escaped this pattern: Roosevelt himself, who had consistently high approval ratings, especially after the start of World War II; Dwight D. Eisenhower, whose first-term popularity started high and stayed high; Bill Clinton, whose second-term popularity also remained high; and George H. W. Bush, whose popularity started moderately high, soared during the Persian Gulf War, and then plummeted. By contrast, George W. Bush's approval ratings started moderately high in his first term, soared after the September 11, 2001, attacks, and then more gradually dropped. The younger Bush's second term pattern fits the general pattern more closely.

Presidents typically arrive at the White House with relatively high levels of approval. Table 5-3 shows that Presidents Harry S. Truman, Dwight D. Eisenhower, Lyndon Johnson, Gerald Ford, and George W. Bush in his second term received the highest approval rating for their entire terms during their first month in office. It took Bill Clinton until August 1996, when his approval rating reached 60 percent, to exceed the 58 percent approval rating he attained in his first month in office. Presidents John F. Kennedy, Richard Nixon, Jimmy Carter, and Ronald Reagan all found their high point within their first four months in office. Thus, although these presidents varied considerably in the activities they undertook at the outset of their terms and later, public approval nevertheless followed a similar course for each president.

Figure 5-1 examines presidential popularity over time in greater detail. There are three phases to the overall pattern: the honeymoon, disillusionment, and forgiveness. A honeymoon of relatively high public approval characterizes the first phase, typically lasting six months to one year. During this time, the public explores the personal profiles of the presidents and their families. This is also the time during which presidents may announce major policy initiatives without having yet begun the battles on Capitol Hill to bring their proposals to fruition, battles that they may not win. During this phase presidents come closest to matching the single executive image—the image of the president as a powerful, unique, important, and visible official, and the one who is in charge of government.

Honeymoons are of varying durations. Ford's honeymoon ended after three months when he pardoned Nixon. His approval ratings plummeted twenty-one points, from 71 percent upon taking office to just 50 percent in October 1974. Bill Clinton's honeymoon may have actually ended even before his inauguration. Controversies surrounding his promise to lift the ban on gays in the military and his nomination of Zöe Baird to become attorney general dampened the public's approval of the president-elect. Other honeymoons ended more gradually. Johnson's popularity eroded slowly as pessimism about Vietnam grew. His popularity averaged 63 percent during 1965, but by May 1966 had dipped to the 50 percent mark.

The disillusionment phase emerges as a gap between public expectations and presidential performance arises (Sigelman and Knight, 1983). Presidents are judged on how well they have lived up to expectations people associate with the presidency, the performance of past presidents, and the promises made during the election campaign. Reagan, dubbed by the press the "Teflon President" because problems encountered by his administration never seemed to stick to him personally, was perceived as able to satisfy public expectations to an extent that other presidents had not been able to match. Reagan's honeymoon seemed never to completely end. Yet, Reagan did not escape the disillusionment phase. Reagan's popularity during his first three years in office was nearly identical to Carter's. Both Carter and Reagan saw their honeymoons fade toward the end of their first year; both faced disillusionment over the next two years with deepening economic woes—Carter's primarily inflation, Reagan's primarily unemployment. Although Reagan may have projected a more comfortable image than Carter, he was no more a "Teflon President" than was his predecessor.

Disillusionment was undoubtedly a factor in the sharp decline in George H. W. Bush's approval ratings, as people felt that his administration did not turn its attention to economic problems at home after the Persian Gulf War. James Baker, then secretary of state, commented after the victory in the Gulf: "When you have 90 percent approval, you can do whatever you damn well please." But this was actually a miscalculation. The American people judged the first Bush administration for its inaction and Bush's approval ratings tumbled. Similarly, his son George W. Bush's approval ratings suffered as the war in Iraq continued. The White House contributed to this disillusionment through its own image-making attempts when on May 3, 2003, Bush arrived on the U.S.S. *Abraham Lincoln* aircraft carrier by Navy jet, wearing a full flight suit and proclaimed: "In the Battle of Iraq, the United States and our allies have prevailed," as a banner announcing "Mission Accomplished" fluttered behind him. The second Bush White House set expectations that it failed to meet in the months and years after this event as the war, its costs, and its casualties mounted.

Forgiveness may occur in the fourth year of the term as presidents enjoy slight increases in popularity. People respond to the upcoming election and discover that the president's opponent is mortal, too. Or, if the president is leaving office, people conclude that he was not so bad after all. Table 5-3 reveals that even Presidents Carter and George H. W. Bush, who lost their reelection bids, saw their approval ratings rise slightly in the months nearing or even after the election. For example, Bush's approval rating reached its lowest point, 32 percent, in July 1992, but his popularity rebounded to 43 percent in November 1992 after he had been defeated for reelection.

These data provide evidence of institutional behavior in the way the public judges presidents. Certainly it is difficult to conceptualize the public as a part of an institution behaving in ways specific to that institution. Despite writers' use of the term *the public* as a proper noun, they are, in fact, referring to an unwieldy mixture of millions of people of varied backgrounds who all think differently. Yet the breadth of these differences is actually compelling evidence that public opinion is a form of institutional behavior. This vast array of people, with little in common, all evaluate presidents favorably early in the term, increasingly less favorably as the term progresses, and then with an upswing in opinion at term's end. This holds true even among different categories of individuals within the population. The expectations that people have of presidents, drawn in large measure from the single executive image, become the centerpiece of this institutional behavior—the glue, as it were, that holds millions of opinions together.

The Carter-Reagan comparison described above offers a good example of the public's institutional behavior. Despite differences in personal styles, specific events, and ongoing conditions that unfolded during their first three years in office, popularity ratings for Carter and Reagan evolved in a similar way. Even President George H. W. Bush's exceptional approval ratings held some elements of the overall institutional pattern. His term began with 57 percent approval (one percentage point less than the inaugural rating for President Clinton). It then peaked at 89 percent at the end of the Persian Gulf War in February 1991, a rating never before seen since polling began in the 1930s. After the war, however, Bush's approval followed the familiar downward trend. His approval dropped fifty-eight percentage points in a single year to 41 percent by February 1992 and then rose slightly at the close of his term to 49 percent approval. Similarly, his son's approval soared to 90 percent after 9/11, the highest figure ever recorded for an American president, toppling his father's record rating. George W. Bush's approval ratings continued to be high throughout the balance of 2001 and much of 2002. They received a boost again at the outset of the Iraq War in March 2003 but dropped steadily thereafter. By mid-2004, they were consistently below 50 percent. From September 2001 to October 2004, the younger Bush suffered an approval drop of 43 percentage points. The poll numbers then improved somewhat in the weeks immediately prior to the 2004 election and Bush's victory. (Chapter 7 presents an analysis of public opinion on presidents' war efforts.)

Social Categories and Presidential Approval

Attention to presidents' overall approval ratings presents a picture of national public opinion that can be decidedly misleading. Too often press commentaries on the latest poll results and scholarly studies of presidential approval treat the nation as a monolith. Yet various segments of the population are not likely to uniformly approve of a president. The analysis below permits an examination of variations across political, demographic, and economic breakdowns of the population on the basis of party identification, region, income, race, gender, age, and education.

Party, Region, and Income Differences

Tables 5-4 and 5-5 present a breakdown of public approval by party identification, region, and income on a quarterly basis and averaged annually and over a term, respectively. Not surprisingly, the tables show that citizens are far more likely to approve of a president of their own party than one of the other party. Indeed, this generalization holds on average for every quarter since 1953. In addition, unlike the public's general attachment to party, this partisan aspect of presidential approval has not weakened over time. Partisan differences between Republicans and Democrats, while never small, increased beginning with Reagan. Although the partisan gap in approval lessened somewhat with George H. W. Bush, it grew again with Clinton and George W. Bush. Party differences of opinion about the younger Bush lessened in his second term as Republicans increasingly turned against him because of the Iraq War.

It is also apparent that Republican presidents generally command higher approval among their partisans than do Democratic presidents. The natural advantage Democratic presidents have as a result of larger numbers of Democratic Party identifiers in the population may be partly canceled by Republicans' stronger approval for their party's presidents. These party differences are an indicator of the ambivalence toward parties that confront American presidents. Although they may disparage parties as ugly roadblocks to national progress, Americans nonetheless use party affiliation as a convenient and powerful device by which to evaluate presidents' performances.

Tables 5-4 and 5-5 also reveal that regional variation in presidential approval is far less striking than party differences. The principal contrast appears to be between the South and the other regions of the country. Four Republican presidents—Nixon, Reagan, George H. W. Bush, and George W. Bush—generally received stronger approval in the South than in the rest of the nation. Each developed a "southern strategy," an approach originated by Nixon to gain Republican inroads in the predominantly Democratic South. The South became a much more competitive, increasingly Republican, region. Carter, a southerner, did as well as Nixon in the region; Clinton, another southerner, did not. George W. Bush, the former governor of Texas, continually did better in the South throughout his presidency. But even so, his support declined dramatically from 71 percent in 2002 to 39 percent in 2007.

The two tables show that Democratic presidents receive higher approval ratings from the poor than from the wealthy; for Republican presidents, the pattern is reversed. For most quarters and all presidents, this difference is quite noticeable. The income gap was largest during Reagan's term.

Demographic and Education Differences

Tables 5-6 through 5-9 consider differences based on three key demographic categories—race, gender, and age. In addition, Tables 5-8 and 5-9 examine approval across different levels of education. Democratic presidents, especially Clinton, have received much higher approval from nonwhites than Republican presidents. Nonwhites gave especially low marks to Presidents Nixon and Reagan. The so-called gender gap is much less distinct. The results show no evidence of systematic differences between men and women in presidents' approval ratings. However, they show a dramatic difference in men's and women's ratings of Reagan and George W. Bush. Men's approval of Reagan was on average nine percentage points higher than women's in his first term and eight percentage points higher in his second term. Bush's ratings were on average seven percentage points higher for men than for women. This gap remained in his second term even as his popularity dropped for both groups.

Tables 5-8 and 5-9 examine public approval broken down by age and education. Age differences were most distinct for Kennedy, Reagan (in his second term), and George H. W. Bush, all of whom were favored more by younger people than older people. There is very little age group difference for Clinton or George W. Bush. The data also dispel two common impressions about young Americans' views of presidents: Despite Vietnam, Johnson was not disliked by younger Americans, and only during his second term was Reagan more popular with younger people than older people. Among the young, Reagan's first term approval rating of 50 percent equaled that for Carter and was slightly lower than the 51 percent received by Clinton and the 52 percent rceived by Ford. Age differences were far less distinct than education differences. Approval of Republican presidents generally increased from the lowest to the highest levels of education. Three Democratic presidents—Kennedy, Johnson, and Carter—showed very slight differences in the opposite direction. They were somewhat more popular among those with limited education than those with at least some college training.

Social Groups and Approval Over Time

The tables not only permit an analysis of the differences among political, demographic, and economic categories in the population, but they also reveal the overall time trend of declining presidential popularity over the course of a term observed for the nation as a whole. This is acutely evident across each of the several social category breakdowns—party, region, income, race, gender, age, and education. Although levels of approval vary sharply across subgroups, the overall direction of approval starts as high as it is ever likely to be, falls, and then rebounds slightly at the end of a president's term.

Policy and Office Approval

Public approval measures are a generic barometer of public reactions to presidents. They do not capture any specific judgments citizens may have about the way in which a president handles certain policy areas or their impressions of the office of the presidency. Table 5-10 presents public approval of presidents' handling of the economy and foreign policy since the 1970s. Americans judged Reagan and Clinton equally competent in the two areas in their first terms, while Carter and George H. W. Bush were rated more highly in foreign affairs than on the economy. After the terrorist attacks on the United States on September 11, 2001, the public rated George W. Bush more favorably on foreign affairs than domestic affairs, but by the end of his first term people perceived his handling of domestic and foreign affairs fairly similarly and lower than earlier ratings. During his second term in the midst of the Iraq War, people were somewhat more likely to approve his domestic job performance than his foreign policy efforts, but not dramatically so. The data are not sufficient to characterize two types of presidencies—one foreign, the other domestic—a distinction that has long been debated in studies of presidents' relations with Congress.

In survey answers respondents have identified what they believed to be the most important national problem for each year since 1935 (Table 5-11). These national problems, which have primarily involved war and economic difficulties, are usually ones that presidents are expected to solve. War has been the sole major concern twenty-three times since 1935 and the economy twenty-five times. Since 1945, citizens have also been asked which political party they believed would best be able to handle the national problem they identified in these surveys. Table 5-12 shows that respondents have tended to place their faith more heavily in Democrats, regardless of whether they held the White House or not. These patterns are seemingly related to partisanship in the citizenry. The larger percentage of people who identify with the Democratic Party may be positively predisposed toward believing that that party will better be able to solve the nation's problems.

The final table in the chapter, Table 5-13, reveals the low level of confidence people have in the presidency as an office. Confidence in the White House dropped significantly in the wake of the Watergate scandal. Indeed, the percentage of the public having a great deal of confidence in the White House did not rise above 20 percent until Carter's inauguration.

Public confidence dropped again during the latter part of Carter's term. Not surprisingly, confidence was renewed at the time of the Persian Gulf War, but declined to more typical levels thereafter. Confidence again rebounded after the events of September 11, 2001, and at the start of the Iraq War, but by 2007 confidence in the White House had fallen to levels last seen during the Iran-contra scandal of the Reagan administration. Indeed, confidence fell more dramatically during the George W. Bush administration than during any other administration. Confidence in the White House was at 58 percent in 2002, but 19 percent in 2007—a drop of 39 percentage points. Compared with other institutions in American society, the White House generally enjoys less of the public's confidence than the Supreme Court, although usually more than Congress. This, too, is a behavioral component of the institution that may account for the predictable drop in presidents' approval ratings.

Conclusion

Presidents' popularity with the public as a whole and among key demographic and political groups exhibits an inexorable downward trend over the course of a term. Presidents come into office enjoying their highest levels of popularity, but that popularity quickly erodes. This has been true of presidents who presided over robust economies, had dramatic successes in international diplomacy, conducted popular military interventions, and won reelection. This decline is evident even among a president's most ardent supporters. Presidents can engage in activities to temporarily boost their popularity—major national addresses, legislative victories, and dramatic foreign policy successes (Ragsdale, 1984; Brace and Hinckley, 1992). But the time trend does not alter and is certainly an institutional pattern of the presidency. The clash between presidents' institutional behavior, in the form of public appearances, and the public's institutional response means that large numbers of public appearances will not ensure a high level of popularity.

The downward trend in approval constrains the behavior of presidents. It sets off a stopwatch that presidents must heed. They know that they can count on the benefit of public approval with any degree of certainty only during their first year in office. Thereafter, national and international events, over which presidents may or may not have some control, and presidents' own accomplishments may boost their support, but only temporarily.

Approval may also constrain presidential behavior in another way. Presidents may consciously design certain policy decisions or the timing of decisions with approval ratings in mind (Brace and Hinckley, 1992).

Thus, they juggle the demands of government with their level of popularity. There is no evidence, however, that this type of manipulation has paid off, as presidents' popularity still starts high and finishes low. Since presidents cannot ever fully live up to the single executive image, no matter how they frame and time their decisions, the erosion of popularity is all but inevitable.

The social category differences that are observed across presidents are underpinned by party. People typically found in Democratic electoral coalitions—nonwhites, the poor, the less-educated—continue to be relatively strong supporters of Democratic presidents throughout their terms in office. Similarly, people who are typically part of Republican electoral coalitions—whites, those with higher incomes, and the better-educated—continue to support Republican presidents throughout their terms in office. Part of the institutional profile of the presidency is its partisan nature and the polarizing effects of that partisanship. This is not only revealed in these data and the electoral data from Chapters 2 and 3, but will also be evident in Chapter 8, which examines presidential relations with Congress. Although presidents like to portray themselves as presidents of all the people, these data reveal how difficult it is for a president to convert people who are not among the electoral supporters of the chief executive's party.

Separate from the interplay of party and social categories, one incumbent-specific portrait of polarization stands out. Across each of the social category breakdowns examined in these data—party, income, race, gender, age, and education—Reagan's approval is consistently at the extremes for opposing subpopulations: high for whites, low for nonwhites, high for the wealthy, low for the poor. There seems to be little middle ground in Reagan's approval patterns, and this accentuates the typical party differences that other presidents encounter. For Reagan, polarization was not simply a feature of party but also a matter of his own political agenda and people's reactions to it.

Individual presidents may make some degree of difference in their dealings with the public, but such independent efforts are largely overshadowed by the time trend and social category differences that do not depend on who the president is, but rather at what point he is in his term and what party affiliation he holds.

Note

1. The Gallup time series begins with Franklin Roosevelt, as recorded in Table 5-3. Other analyses in the chapter begin with Truman, for whom polling data were more regularly available. Demographic and political breakdowns in approval are available only since Eisenhower. Data on economic and foreign policy approval are available beginning with Nixon.

Table 5-1 Presidential Approval, by Month since Inauguration, Truman to G. W. Bush (percent)

Month	Percentage approving[a]										
	Truman[b]	Eisenhower	Kennedy	L. Johnson	Nixon	Ford	Carter	Reagan	G. H. W. Bush	Clinton	G. W. Bush[c]
1st	—	—	—	—	59	71	—	51	55	58	—
2nd	—	67	72	74	60	50	71	55	63	59	62
3rd	—	74	73	76	62	54	72	60	56	52	53
4th	—	73	83	80	60	48	63	67	58	55	62
5th	—	74	74	76	62	42	64	68	63	44	56
6th	87	—	72	75	63	38	63	58	70	46	52
7th	—	73	75	74	63	39	67	60	67	44	56
8th	—	74	76	74	62	37	66	60	64	56	55
9th	—	61	79	—	58	39	59	52	70	48	90
10th	82	65	77	—	56	51	51	56	60	48	88
11th	75	59	79	—	67	52	56	54	70	54	87
12th	—	69	78	—	59	—	57	49	71	58	86
13th	63	71	79	70	64	46	52	47	80	53	84
14th	49	67	78	69	56	45	50	47	73	51	82
15th	51	66	80	70	53	44	48	46	74	48	79
16th	—	68	78	69	56	41	41	44	67	51	77
17th	—	61	71	69	59	39	43	45	65	46	77
18th	43	62	69	64	54	46	42	44	69	43	76
19th	—	75	66	70	55	48	39	41	63	41	71
20th	—	63	68	66	55	50	43	42	76	42	65
21st	33	66	63	66	51	48	48	42	67	44	68
22nd	—	61	62	64	58	47	49	42	54	45	63
23rd	34	57	74	63	57	45	50	43	54	41	65
24th	35	70	76	65	52	—	51	41	63	47	61
25th	48	70	74	62	57	—	43	35	83	47	60

(Table continues)

Table 5-1 *(Continued)*

	Percentage approving[a]										
Month	Truman[b]	Eisenhower	Kennedy	L. Johnson	Nixon	Ford	Carter	Reagan	G. H. W. Bush	Clinton	G. W. Bush[c]
26th	—	73	70	63	50	—	37	40	80	42	57
27th	63	66	67	61	50	—	42	41	82	44	71
28th	57	70	65	56	50	—	40	41	82	51	70
29th	65	68	64	57	50	53	32	46	76	42	64
30th	55	67	61	54	49	—	29	47	76	47	61
31st	61	72	61	51	48	—	29	42	72	48	58
32nd	—	71	63	48	50	—	32	43	71	46	59
33rd	55	71	56	56	49	—	30	48	74	48	50
34th	—	—	58	47	52	—	31	46	66	46	53
35th	54	78	58	46	49	—	38	53	65	53	50
36th	54	75	—	44	50	—	54	54	50	51	63
37th	50	77	—	49	50	—	58	55	50	46	49
38th	—	75	—	44	52	—	55	55	47	53	51
39th	—	73	—	46	53	—	39	54	41	52	53
40th	36	69	—	45	54	—	39	52	42	56	52
41st	39	71	—	45	62	—	38	54	41	53	47
42nd	39	73	—	49	57	—	31	54	38	52	48
43rd	—	70	—	45	—	—	33	52	29	58	48
44th	—	67	—	51	—	—	32	54	39	53	49
45th	—	—	—	47	—	—	37	57	36	55	54
46th	—	—	—	39	—	—	—	58	34	54	48
47th	—	75	—	38	62	—	31	61	43	58	55
48th[d]	—	79	—	38	59	—	34	59	49	58	49
49th	69	73	—	41	67	—	—	64	—	62	51
50th	—	72	—	42	65	—	—	60	—	57	52

51st	57	65	—	46	58	—	—	56	—	59	45
52nd	—	64	—	49	48	—	—	52	—	54	48
53rd	50	63	—	41	44	—	—	55	—	57	48
54th	57	65	—	36	44	—	—	58	—	55	46
55th	—	63	—	50	39	—	—	63	—	55	44
56th	—	59	—	41	36	—	—	65	—	60	45
57th	51	59	—	39	33	—	—	60	—	61	45
58th	—	57	—	40	27	—	—	63	—	59	41
59th	—	58	—	35	31	—	—	65	—	61	38
60th	—	—	—	42	29	—	—	63	—	56	43
61st	45	58	—	43	26	—	—	64	—	69	43
62nd	37	54	—	—	25	—	—	—	—	66	38
63rd	37	48	—	43	26	—	—	63	—	66	37
64th	—	54	—	44	26	—	—	62	—	63	34
65th	41	54	—	—	26	—	—	68	—	64	33
66th	37		—	—	28	—	—	64	—	60	37
67th	46	58	—	—	24	—	—	63	—	65	40
68th	43	56	—	—	24	—	—	61	—	62	42
69th	35	54	—	—		—	—	61	—	66	44
70th	41	57	—	—	—	—	—	63	—	66	37
71st	—	52	—	—	—	—	—	—	—	66	33
72nd	33	57	—	—	—	—	—	48	—	65	35
73rd	36	57	—	—	—	—	—	49	—	67	36
74th	26	59	—	—	—	—	—		—	66	37
75th	28	58	—	—	—	—	—	47	—	64	34
76th	24	60	—	—	—	—	—	48	—	60	36
77th	24	64	—	—	—	—	—	—	—	53	33
78th	25	62	—	—	—	—	—	53	—	57	32
79th	29	61	—	—	—	—	—	49	—	64	31
80th	31	67	—	—	—	—	—	49	—	60	32
81st	32	66	—	—	—	—	—	—	—	60	36
82nd	29	67	—	—	—	—	—	51	—	59	32

(Table continues)

Table 5-1 *(Continued)*

	Percentage approving[a]										
Month	Truman[b]	Eisenhower	Kennedy	L. Johnson	Nixon	Ford	Carter	Reagan	G.H.W. Bush	Clinton	G.W. Bush[c]
83rd	23	65	—	—	—	—	—	—	—	59	31
84th	—	77	—	—	—	—	—	49	—	57	—
85th	25	66	—	—	—	—	—	49	—	57	—
86th	22	64	—	—	—	—	—	—	—	57	—
87th	—	65	—	—	—	—	—	51	—	62	—
88th	28	62	—	—	—	—	—	50	—	59	—
89th	27	65	—	—	—	—	—	48	—	57	—
90th	32	57	—	—	—	—	—	51	—	55	—
91st	29	63	—	—	—	—	—	54	—	59	—
92nd	—	61	—	—	—	—	—	53	—	62	—
93rd	—	65	—	—	—	—	—	54	—	62	—
94th	32	58	—	—	—	—	—	51	—	58	—
95th	—	59	—	—	—	—	—	57	—	63	—
96th	32	59	—	—	—	—	—	63	—	66	—
Average	43	65	71	54	50	47	46	53	61	55	53

Source: Adapted from presidential approval ratings found at www.ropercenter.uconn.edu.

Note: The question was: "Do you approve or disapprove of the way [the incumbent] is handling his job as president?" "—" indicates not available.

[a] In months in which more than one approval poll was conducted, the last results of the month are presented.
[b] Beginning in 1945.
[c] Through 2007 only.
[d] End of first term for those presidents elected to office.

Table 5-2 Presidential Approval Average, by Year of Term, Truman to G. W. Bush (percent)

Year	Truman	Eisenhower	Kennedy	L. Johnson	Nixon	Ford	Carter	Reagan	G. H. W. Bush	Clinton	G. W. Bush[a]
(First rating)	87	67	72	74	59	71	71	51	55	58	62
1st	81	69	76	76	61	47	63	58	65	52	68
2nd	44	66	72	67	56	45	46	44	67	46	72
3rd	57	71	63	54	50	53	36	45	73	47	60
4th	41	73	—	45	56	—	39	55	49	54	50
5th	57	63	—	42	43	—	—	60	—	58	46
6th	40	55	—	43	26	—	—	62	—	65	38
7th	28	65	—	—	—	—	—	49	—	61	34
8th	28	62	—	—	—	—	—	53	—	60	—
(Last rating)	32	59	58	44	24	53	34	63	49	66	36

Source: Adapted from Table 5-1.

Note: "—" indicates not available.

[a] Through 2007 only.

Table 5-3 Aggregate Public Approval, F. Roosevelt, II to G.W. Bush, II (percent)

President/date	*Approve*	*Disapprove*	*No opinion*
F. Roosevelt, II			
Aug. 4, 1937	60	40	N/A
Oct. 30, 1937	63	37	N/A
May 22, 1938	54	46	N/A
May 29, 1938	54	46	N/A
July 4, 1938	52	40	7
Aug. 12, 1938	53	41	6
Aug. 18, 1938	50	44	7
Sept. 25, 1938	52	37	11
Oct. 3, 1938	54	38	8
Oct. 10, 1938	50	43	7
Oct. 19, 1938	52	41	7
Nov. 7, 1938	54	46	N/A
Nov. 16, 1938	56	45	N/A
Nov. 24, 1938	55	39	6
Dec. 4, 1938	53	38	9
Dec. 25, 1938	58	42	N/A
Jan. 9, 1939	58	42	N/A
Jan. 12, 1939	55	38	7
Jan. 22, 1939	59	37	4
Feb. 24, 1939	51	39	10
March 4, 1939	56	37	8
March 10, 1939	56	39	6
March 23, 1939	56	38	5
April 2, 1939	54	40	7
April 8, 1939	53	40	8
April 21, 1939	55	41	4
May 4, 1939	56	36	9
May 12, 1939	57	38	5
May 28, 1939	55	37	9
June 9, 1939	55	38	7
June 18, 1939	52	42	6
July 1, 1939	54	39	7
July 19, 1939	55	38	7
July 28, 1939	53	41	7
Aug. 10, 1939	57	43	N/A
Aug. 18, 1939	48	43	8
Sept. 1, 1939	54	37	9
Sept. 13, 1939	61	39	N/A
Sept. 21, 1939	50	36	14
Sept. 24, 1939	58	36	5
Oct. 5, 1939	65	35	N/A
Oct. 20, 1939	57	36	7
Oct. 26, 1939	63	37	N/A
Nov. 10, 1939	59	35	6
Nov. 17, 1939	56	38	6
Dec. 2, 1939	57	35	8
Dec. 14, 1939	55	38	8
Dec. 24, 1939	58	35	7

Table 5-3 *(Continued)*

President/date	*Approve*	*Disapprove*	*No opinion*
F. Roosevelt, II (continued)			
Jan. 13, 1940	64	36	N/A
Jan. 21, 1940	59	35	7
Feb. 2, 1940	61	34	5
Feb. 8, 1940	64	36	N/A
Feb. 22, 1940	60	35	5
March 15, 1940	59	35	7
March 27, 1940	54	40	7
April 5, 1940	56	38	6
April 11, 1940	57	36	7
May 18, 1940	65	28	7
June 1, 1940	61	32	7
June 27, 1940	58	36	6
Jan. 11, 1941	64	26	9
Feb. 16, 1941	68	26	6
Feb. 28, 1941	69	26	5
F. Roosevelt, III			
March 9, 1941	68	26	6
March 21, 1941	68	25	7
April 10, 1941	69	25	6
April 27, 1941	62	32	7
May 8, 1941	72	24	4
May 31, 1941	72	22	6
June 9, 1941	72	23	5
June 26, 1941	68	24	8
July 24, 1941	70	24	7
July 31, 1941	66	25	9
Aug. 7, 1941	73	20	7
Sept. 19, 1941	70	24	5
Nov. 27, 1941	73	20	8
Jan. 8, 1942	84	19	7
Jan. 25, 1942	84	10	6
Feb. 25, 1942	79	14	8
March 12, 1942	78	13	9
April 17, 1942	78	13	9
May 1, 1942	81	12	7
June 11, 1942	80	14	6
July 1, 1942	79	13	8
Aug. 15, 1942	70	16	14
Aug. 27, 1942	77	15	8
Sept. 5, 1942	75	19	6
Oct. 29, 1942	70	20	10
Nov. 21, 1942	72	19	9
Jan. 9, 1943	75	15	10
Jan. 29, 1943	75	17	8
March 26, 1943	72	19	9
Dec. 1943	66	24	10
March 1, 1944[a]	69	22	8

(Table continues)

Table 5-3 *(Continued)*

President/date	*Approve*	*Disapprove*	*No opinion*
F. Roosevelt, III (continued)			
June 1, 1944[a]	69	21	9
Aug. 1, 1944[a]	70	25	5
Dec. 1, 1944[a]	72	22	6
Truman, I			
June 1, 1945	87	3	10
Oct. 5, 1945	82	9	9
Nov. 2, 1945	75	14	11
Jan. 5, 1946	63	22	15
Feb. 28, 1946	49	38	13
March 29, 1946	51	33	16
June 1, 1946	45	42	13
June 14, 1946	43	45	12
Sept. 13, 1946	33	52	15
Nov. 15, 1946	34	53	13
Dec. 13, 1946	35	47	18
Jan. 17, 1947	48	39	13
March 14, 1947	60	23	17
March 28, 1947	63	21	16
April 25, 1947	57	25	18
May 23, 1947	65	24	11
June 20, 1947	55	31	14
July 4, 1947	61	28	12
Sept. 12, 1947	55	29	16
Nov. 28, 1947	54	33	13
Jan. 2, 1948	50	34	17
April 9, 1948	36	50	14
May 28, 1948	39	47	14
June 18, 1948	39	46	16
Truman, II			
Jan. 7, 1949	69	17	14
March 6, 1949	57	24	19
May 2, 1949	50	32	18
June 11, 1949	57	26	17
Sept. 3, 1949	46	38	16
Sept. 25, 1949	51	31	18
Jan. 8, 1950	45	40	15
Feb. 26, 1950	37	44	19
May 4, 1950	41	38	21
June 4, 1950	37	47	16
July 9, 1950	46	40	15
July 30, 1950	39	45	16
Aug. 20, 1950	43	32	25
Sept. 17, 1950	35	47	18
Oct. 1, 1950	35	50	15
Oct. 8, 1950	43	36	21
Oct. 21, 1950	41	46	14
Dec. 3, 1950	33	53	13

Table 5-3 *(Continued)*

President/date	*Approve*	*Disapprove*	*No opinion*
Truman, II (continued)			
Jan. 1, 1951	36	49	15
Feb. 4, 1951	26	60	14
March 4, 1951	27	59	14
March 26, 1951	28	57	15
April 16, 1951	24	55	20
May 19, 1951	24	63	12
June 16, 1951	25	59	16
July 8, 1951	29	54	17
Aug. 3, 1951	31	57	12
Sept. 21, 1951	32	54	14
Oct. 14, 1951	29	55	16
Nov. 11, 1951	23	61	16
Jan. 6, 1952	23	67	9
Jan. 20, 1952	25	62	13
Feb. 9, 1952	22	65	13
April 13, 1952	28	59	13
May 11, 1952	27	59	13
May 30, 1952	31	59	10
June 15, 1952	32	58	10
July 13, 1952	29	59	13
Oct. 3, 1952	33	55	13
Oct. 9, 1952	32	55	13
Dec. 11, 1952	32	56	11
Eisenhower, I			
Feb. 1, 1953	68	7	25
Feb. 22, 1953	67	8	25
March 28, 1953	74	8	18
April 19, 1953	73	10	16
May 9, 1953	74	10	16
July 4, 1953	69	15	16
July 25, 1953	73	13	14
Aug. 15, 1953	74	14	12
Sept. 12, 1953	61	20	19
Oct. 9, 1953	65	19	16
Nov. 1, 1953	61	26	13
Nov. 19, 1953	59	25	16
Dec. 11, 1953	69	22	9
Jan. 9, 1954	71	19	10
Jan. 28, 1954	70	17	13
Feb. 25, 1954	67	21	12
March 19, 1954	66	22	12
April 8, 1954	68	21	11
May 2, 1954	60	22	18
May 21, 1954	61	24	15
June 12, 1954	62	24	14
July 2, 1954	65	21	14
July 16, 1954	75	20	5

(Table continues)

Table 5-3 *(Continued)*

President/date	*Approve*	*Disapprove*	*No opinion*
Eisenhower, I (continued)			
Aug. 5, 1954	67	19	14
Aug. 26, 1954	63	24	13
Sept. 16, 1954	66	21	13
Oct. 15, 1954	61	26	13
Nov. 11, 1954	57	23	20
Dec. 2, 1954	69	23	8
Dec. 31, 1954	70	18	12
Jan. 20, 1955	70	17	13
Feb. 10, 1955	73	15	12
March 3, 1955	71	17	12
March 24, 1955	66	21	13
April 14, 1955	70	14	16
May 12, 1955	68	16	16
June 3, 1955	70	16	14
June 24, 1955	67	15	18
July 14, 1955	72	18	10
Aug. 4, 1955	76	11	13
Aug. 25, 1955	71	16	13
Sept. 15, 1955	71	16	13
Nov. 17, 1955	78	13	9
Dec. 8, 1955	75	13	12
Jan. 6, 1956	76	12	12
Jan. 26, 1956	77	14	9
Feb. 16, 1956	75	15	10
March 8, 1956	72	18	10
March 29, 1956	73	17	10
April 19, 1956	69	19	12
May 10, 1956	69	17	14
May 31, 1956	71	19	10
June 15, 1956	73	18	9
July 12, 1956	70	20	10
Aug. 3, 1956	67	19	13
Nov. 22, 1956	75	15	10
Dec. 14, 1956	79	11	10
Eisenhower, II			
Jan. 17, 1957	73	14	13
Feb. 7, 1957	72	16	12
Feb. 28, 1957	72	17	11
March 15, 1957	65	20	15
April 6, 1957	67	21	12
April 25, 1957	64	23	13
May 17, 1957	62	23	15
June 6, 1957	64	22	14
June 27, 1957	63	23	14
July 18, 1957	65	22	13
Aug. 8, 1957	63	20	17
Aug. 29, 1957	59	23	18
Sept. 19, 1957	59	26	15

Table 5-3 *(Continued)*

President/date	*Approve*	*Disapprove*	*No opinion*
Eisenhower, II (continued)			
Oct. 10, 1957	57	27	16
Nov. 7, 1957	58	27	15
Jan. 2, 1958	60	30	10
Jan. 24, 1958	58	27	15
Feb. 14, 1958	54	33	13
March 6, 1958	51	33	16
March 27, 1958	48	36	16
April 16, 1958	54	31	15
May 7, 1958	53	32	15
May 28, 1958	54	31	15
July 10, 1958	52	32	16
July 30, 1958	58	27	15
Aug. 20, 1958	56	27	17
Sept. 10, 1958	57	29	14
Sept. 24, 1958	54	28	18
Oct. 15, 1958	57	27	16
Nov. 7, 1958	52	30	18
Dec. 3, 1958	57	32	11
Jan. 7, 1959	57	27	16
Feb. 4, 1959	59	26	15
March 4, 1959	58	26	16
April 2, 1959	62	23	15
April 29, 1959	60	24	16
May 29, 1959	64	21	15
June 25, 1959	62	23	16
July 23, 1959	61	26	13
Aug. 20, 1959	67	20	13
Sept. 18, 1959	66	20	14
Oct. 16, 1959	67	19	14
Nov. 12, 1959	65	21	14
Dec. 3, 1959	67	18	15
Dec. 10, 1959	77	15	8
Jan. 6, 1960	66	19	15
Feb. 4, 1960	64	22	14
March 2, 1960	64	22	14
March 30, 1960	65	22	13
April 28, 1960	62	22	16
May 26, 1960	65	22	13
June 16, 1960	61	24	15
June 30, 1960	57	27	16
July 16, 1960	49	33	18
July 30, 1960	63	26	11
Aug. 11, 1960	63	24	13
Aug. 25, 1960	61	28	11
Sept. 9, 1960	58	28	14
Sept. 28, 1960	65	26	9
Oct. 18, 1960	58	31	11
Nov. 17, 1960	59	26	15
Dec. 8, 1960	59	28	13

(Table continues)

Table 5-3 *(Continued)*

President/date	*Approve*	*Disapprove*	*No opinion*
Kennedy			
Feb. 10, 1961	72	6	22
March 10, 1961	73	7	20
April 6, 1961	78	6	16
April 28, 1961	83	5	12
May 4, 1961	77	9	14
May 17, 1961	75	10	15
May 28, 1961	74	11	15
June 23, 1961	71	14	15
July 27, 1961	75	12	13
Aug. 24, 1961	76	12	12
Sept. 21, 1961	79	10	11
Oct. 19, 1961	77	12	10
Nov. 17, 1961	79	9	12
Dec. 7, 1961	78	11	12
Jan. 11, 1962	79	10	11
Feb. 18, 1962	78	11	10
March 8, 1962	80	12	9
April 6, 1962	77	13	10
May 3, 1962	74	16	10
May 31, 1962	71	19	10
June 28, 1962	69	19	12
July 26, 1962	66	23	11
Aug. 23, 1962	68	20	13
Sept. 20, 1962	63	22	16
Oct. 19, 1962	62	25	14
Nov. 16, 1962	74	14	12
Dec. 13, 1962	76	13	11
Jan. 11, 1963	74	14	12
Feb. 7, 1963	70	18	12
March 8, 1963	67	20	13
April 4, 1963	66	21	13
May 2, 1963	64	25	12
May 8, 1963	65	23	12
May 23, 1963	64	24	12
June 21, 1963	61	26	13
July 18, 1963	61	27	12
Aug. 15, 1963	63	26	11
Sept. 12, 1963	56	30	14
Oct. 11, 1963	58	29	13
Nov. 8, 1963	58	30	12
L. Johnson[b]			
Dec. 5, 1963	78	2	20
Dec. 12, 1963	74	4	22
Jan. 2, 1964	77	5	18
Jan. 30, 1964	76	8	16
Feb. 13, 1964	74	9	18
Feb. 28, 1964	80	9	11

Table 5-3 *(Continued)*

President/date	*Approve*	*Disapprove*	*No opinion*
L. Johnson[b] (continued)			
March 13, 1964	78	9	13
March 27, 1964	76	12	13
April 24, 1964	75	11	14
May 6, 1964	75	10	15
May 22, 1964	74	13	13
June 4, 1964	74	12	14
June 11, 1964	74	14	12
June 25, 1964	74	15	11
Nov. 20, 1964	70	19	11
Dec. 11, 1964	69	18	13
Jan. 7, 1965	71	15	14
Jan. 28, 1965	70	15	15
Feb. 19, 1965	69	18	14
March 11, 1965	68	18	14
March 18, 1965	69	21	10
April 2, 1965	67	22	11
April 23, 1965	64	22	14
May 13, 1965	70	18	12
June 4, 1965	69	19	12
June 24, 1965	66	21	13
July 16, 1965	66	20	14
Aug. 5, 1965	65	22	13
Aug. 27, 1965	64	25	11
Sept. 16, 1965	63	24	13
Oct. 8, 1965	66	21	13
Oct. 29, 1965	65	22	13
Nov. 18, 1965	62	22	15
Dec. 11, 1965	63	27	11
Dec. 31, 1966	59	24	17
Jan. 21, 1966	61	27	12
Feb. 10, 1966	56	34	10
March 3, 1966	58	28	14
March 24, 1966	57	28	15
April 14, 1966	54	33	13
May 5, 1966	46	34	20
May 19, 1966	50	33	17
June 16, 1966	48	39	13
July 8, 1966	56	31	14
July 29, 1966	51	38	10
Aug. 18, 1966	47	39	14
Sept. 8, 1966	46	39	15
Oct. 1, 1966	44	42	14
Oct. 21, 1966	44	41	15
Nov. 10, 1966	49	35	16
Dec. 8, 1966	44	47	9
Jan. 7, 1967	47	37	16
Jan. 26, 1967	46	37	16
Feb. 16, 1967	45	42	13

(Table continues)

Table 5-3 *(Continued)*

President/date	*Approve*	*Disapprove*	*No opinion*
L. Johnson[b] (continued)			
March 9, 1967	45	41	14
March 30, 1967	46	38	16
April 19, 1967	49	37	15
May 11, 1967	45	40	16
June 2, 1967	44	39	16
June 22, 1967	51	35	14
July 13, 1967	47	39	14
Aug. 3, 1967	40	47	13
Aug. 24, 1967	39	48	13
Sept. 14, 1967	38	48	14
Oct. 6, 1967	38	51	12
Oct. 27, 1967	41	49	10
Nov. 16, 1967	42	46	12
Dec. 7, 1967	46	41	13
Jan. 4, 1968	49	39	13
Feb. 1, 1968	41	47	12
Feb. 22, 1968	41	48	10
March 10, 1968	36	52	12
April 4, 1968	50	38	12
May 2, 1968	46	43	11
May 23, 1968	41	45	14
June 13, 1968	43	45	13
June 26, 1968	39	47	13
July 18, 1968	40	47	13
Aug. 7, 1968	35	52	13
Sept. 26, 1968	42	51	7
Nov. 9, 1968	43	44	13
Dec. 5, 1968	44	43	12
Jan. 1, 1969	49	38	14
Nixon, I			
Jan. 23, 1969	59	5	35
Feb. 20, 1969	60	6	34
March 12, 1969	66	8	26
March 27, 1969	62	10	27
April 10, 1969	60	12	28
May 1, 1969	62	15	23
May 15, 1969	65	12	23
May 22, 1969	62	15	23
June 19, 1969	63	16	21
July 10, 1969	58	22	20
July 24, 1969	63	21	16
Aug. 14, 1969	62	20	18
Sept. 11, 1969	60	23	16
Sept. 17, 1969	58	23	18
Oct. 2, 1969	58	24	18
Oct. 17, 1969	56	29	15
Nov. 12, 1969	67	19	14

Table 5-3 *(Continued)*

President/date	*Approve*	*Disapprove*	*No opinion*
Nixon, I (continued)			
Dec. 12, 1969	59	23	18
Jan. 2, 1970	61	22	17
Jan. 15, 1970	63	23	14
Jan. 30, 1970	64	24	12
Feb. 27, 1970	56	27	17
March 13, 1970	54	34	12
March 18, 1970	53	30	17
April 17, 1970	56	31	13
April 29, 1970	57	32	11
May 21, 1970	59	29	12
June 18, 1970	54	31	14
July 9, 1970	61	28	11
July 31, 1970	55	32	14
Aug. 25, 1970	55	31	14
Sept. 11, 1970	57	30	13
Sept. 25, 1970	51	31	18
Oct. 9, 1970	58	28	15
Nov. 13, 1970	57	30	13
Dec. 3, 1970	52	34	14
Jan. 8, 1971	57	34	10
Feb. 19, 1971	50	37	14
March 11, 1971	50	37	13
April 2, 1971	49	38	13
April 23, 1971	50	38	12
May 14, 1971	49	35	15
June 4, 1971	49	37	15
June 25, 1971	48	39	13
July 15, 1971	50	36	13
Aug. 27, 1971	49	39	13
Oct. 8, 1971	52	38	10
Oct. 29, 1971	49	37	14
Dec. 10, 1971	50	37	13
Jan. 7, 1972	50	39	11
Feb. 4, 1972	52	37	11
March 3, 1972	56	32	12
March 24, 1972	53	36	11
April 28, 1972	54	37	9
May 26, 1972	62	30	8
June 16, 1972	59	30	11
June 23, 1972	57	33	10
Nov. 10, 1972	62	28	10
Dec. 8, 1972	59	30	11
Jan. 12, 1973	51	37	12
Nixon, II			
Jan. 26, 1973	67	25	8
Feb. 16, 1973	65	25	10

(Table continues)

Table 5-3 *(Continued)*

President/date	*Approve*	*Disapprove*	*No opinion*
Nixon, II (continued)			
March 30, 1973	58	34	9
April 6, 1973	54	36	10
April 27, 1973	48	40	12
May 4, 1973	45	42	13
May 11, 1973	44	45	10
June 1, 1973	43	43	14
June 22, 1973	44	45	11
July 6, 1973	39	49	12
Aug. 3, 1973	31	57	11
Aug. 17, 1973	36	54	9
Sept. 7, 1973	34	56	10
Sept. 21, 1973	33	59	8
Oct. 5, 1973	30	57	13
Oct. 19, 1973	27	60	13
Nov. 2, 1973	27	63	10
Nov. 30, 1973	31	59	10
Dec. 7, 1973	29	60	11
Jan. 4, 1974	23	55	22
Jan. 18, 1974	26	64	10
Feb. 1, 1974	28	59	13
Feb. 8, 1974	27	63	10
Feb. 22, 1974	25	63	11
March 8, 1974	26	62	11
March 29, 1974	26	65	9
April 12, 1974	25	62	13
April 19, 1974	26	60	14
May 3, 1974	25	58	17
May 10, 1974	25	62	14
May 17, 1974	26	61	13
May 31, 1974	28	61	12
June 21, 1974	25	61	13
June 28, 1974	28	58	14
July 12, 1974	24	63	14
Aug. 2, 1974	24	66	10
Ford			
Aug. 16, 1974	71	3	26
Sept. 9, 1974	66	13	21
Sept. 27, 1974	50	28	22
Oct. 11, 1974	52	29	19
Oct. 18, 1974	54	29	18
Nov. 8, 1974	47	33	20
Nov. 15, 1974	48	32	20
Dec. 6, 1974	42	41	17
Jan. 10, 1975	37	39	24
Jan. 31, 1975	38	43	18
Feb. 28, 1975	39	45	16
March 7, 1975	39	45	17
March 28, 1975	37	43	20

Table 5-3 *(Continued)*

President/date	*Approve*	*Disapprove*	*No opinion*
Ford (continued)			
April 4, 1975	44	37	20
April 18, 1975	39	46	15
May 2, 1975	40	43	17
May 30, 1975	51	33	16
June 27, 1975	52	34	15
Aug. 1, 1975	45	36	18
Aug. 15, 1975	46	37	17
Sept. 12, 1975	45	38	17
Oct. 3, 1975	47	37	16
Oct. 17, 1975	47	40	13
Oct. 31, 1975	44	44	12
Nov. 21, 1975	41	46	13
Dec. 5, 1975	46	37	17
Dec. 12, 1975	39	45	15
Jan. 2, 1976	46	42	12
Jan. 23, 1976	45	45	10
Jan. 30, 1976	46	40	14
Feb. 27, 1976	48	38	14
March 19, 1976	50	36	14
April 9, 1976	48	40	12
May 21, 1976	47	38	15
June 11, 1976	45	40	15
Dec. 10, 1976	53	32	15
Carter			
Feb. 4, 1977	66	8	26
Feb. 18, 1977	71	9	20
March 4, 1977	70	9	21
March 15, 1977	75	9	16
March 25, 1977	72	10	18
April 1, 1977	67	14	19
April 15, 1977	63	18	19
April 29, 1977	63	18	18
May 6, 1977	66	19	15
May 20, 1977	64	19	17
June 3, 1977	63	19	18
June 17, 1977	63	18	19
July 8, 1977	62	22	16
July 22, 1977	67	17	16
Aug. 5, 1977	60	23	17
Aug. 19, 1977	66	16	18
Sept. 9, 1977	54	29	17
Sept. 30, 1977	59	24	17
Oct. 14, 1977	55	29	16
Oct. 21, 1977	54	30	16
Oct. 28, 1977	51	31	18
Nov. 4, 1977	55	30	15
Nov. 18, 1977	56	30	14

(Table continues)

Table 5-3 *(Continued)*

President/date	*Approve*	*Disapprove*	*No opinion*
Carter (continued)			
Dec. 9, 1977	57	27	16
Jan. 6, 1978	55	27	18
Jan. 20, 1978	52	28	20
Feb. 10, 1978	47	34	19
Feb. 24, 1978	50	33	17
March 3, 1978	49	33	18
March 10, 1978	50	35	15
March 31, 1978	48	39	13
April 14, 1978	40	44	16
April 28, 1978	41	42	17
May 5, 1978	41	43	16
May 19, 1978	43	43	14
June 2, 1978	44	41	15
June 16, 1978	42	42	16
July 7, 1978	40	41	19
July 21, 1978	39	44	17
Aug. 4, 1978	39	44	17
Aug. 11, 1978	40	43	17
Aug. 18, 1978	43	41	16
Sept. 8, 1978	42	42	16
Sept. 15, 1978	45	40	15
Sept. 22, 1978	48	34	18
Oct. 27, 1978	49	36	15
Nov. 10, 1978	52	36	12
Dec. 1, 1978	50	34	16
Dec. 8, 1978	51	34	15
Jan. 5, 1979	50	36	14
Jan. 19, 1979	43	41	16
Feb. 2, 1979	42	42	16
Feb. 23, 1979	37	46	16
March 2, 1979	39	48	13
March 16, 1979	47	39	14
March 23, 1979	42	44	14
April 6, 1979	40	46	14
May 3, 1979	37	49	14
May 18, 1979	32	53	15
June 1, 1979	29	56	15
June 22, 1979	29	57	14
June 29, 1979	28	59	13
July 13, 1979	29	58	13
Aug. 3, 1979	32	53	15
Aug. 10, 1979	33	55	12
Aug. 17, 1979	32	54	14
Sept. 7, 1979	30	55	15
Sept. 28, 1979	33	54	13
Oct. 5, 1979	29	58	13
Oct. 12, 1979	31	55	14
Nov. 2, 1979	32	55	13
Nov. 16, 1979	38	49	13

Table 5-3 *(Continued)*

President/date	*Approve*	*Disapprove*	*No opinion*
Carter (continued)			
Nov. 30, 1979	51	37	12
Dec. 7, 1979	54	35	11
Jan. 4, 1980	56	33	11
Jan. 25, 1980	58	32	10
Feb. 1, 1980	55	36	9
Feb. 29, 1980	52	38	10
March 7, 1980	43	45	12
March 28, 1980	39	51	10
April 11, 1980	39	50	11
May 2, 1980	43	47	10
May 16, 1980	38	51	11
May 30, 1980	38	52	10
June 13, 1980	32	56	12
June 27, 1980	31	58	11
July 11, 1980	33	55	12
Aug. 15, 1980	32	55	13
Sept. 12, 1980	37	55	8
Nov. 21, 1980	31	56	13
Dec. 5, 1980	34	55	11
Reagan, I			
Jan. 30, 1981	51	13	36
Feb. 13, 1981	55	18	27
March 13, 1981	60	24	16
April 3, 1981	67	18	15
April 10, 1981	67	19	14
May 8, 1981	68	21	11
June 5, 1981	59	28	13
June 19, 1981	59	29	12
June 26, 1981	58	30	12
July 17, 1981	60	29	11
July 24, 1981	56	30	14
July 31, 1981	60	28	12
Aug. 14, 1981	60	29	11
Sept. 18, 1981	52	37	11
Oct. 2, 1981	56	35	9
Oct. 30, 1981	53	35	12
Nov. 13, 1981	49	40	11
Nov. 20, 1981	54	37	9
Dec. 11, 1981	49	41	10
Jan. 8, 1982	49	40	11
Jan. 22, 1982	47	42	11
Feb. 5, 1982	47	43	10
March 12, 1982	46	45	9
April 2, 1982	45	46	9
April 23, 1982	43	47	10
April 30, 1982	44	46	10
May 14, 1982	45	44	11

(Table continues)

Table 5-3 *(Continued)*

President/date	*Approve*	*Disapprove*	*No opinion*
Reagan, I (continued)			
June 11, 1982	45	45	10
June 25, 1982	44	46	10
July 23, 1982	42	46	12
July 30, 1982	41	47	12
Aug. 13, 1982	41	49	10
Aug. 27, 1982	42	46	12
Sept. 17, 1982	42	48	10
Oct. 15, 1982	42	48	10
Nov. 5, 1982	43	47	10
Nov. 19, 1982	43	47	10
Dec. 10, 1982	41	50	9
Jan. 14, 1983	37	54	9
Jan. 21, 1983	37	53	10
Jan. 28, 1983	35	56	9
Feb. 25, 1983	40	50	10
March 11, 1983	41	49	10
April 15, 1983	41	49	10
April 29, 1983	43	46	11
May 13, 1983	43	45	12
May 20, 1983	46	43	11
June 10, 1983	43	45	12
June 24, 1983	47	44	9
July 22, 1983	42	47	11
July 29, 1982	44	42	14
Aug. 5, 1983	44	46	10
Aug. 12, 1983	43	45	12
Aug. 19, 1983	43	46	11
Sept. 9, 1983	47	42	11
Sept. 16, 1983	48	42	10
Oct. 7, 1983	45	44	11
Oct. 21, 1983	49	41	10
Nov. 18, 1983	53	37	10
Dec. 9, 1983	54	38	8
Jan. 13, 1984	52	38	10
Jan. 27, 1984	55	37	8
Feb. 10, 1984	56	36	9
March 16, 1984	54	39	8
April 6, 1984	54	37	9
May 3, 1983	52	37	11
May 18, 1984	54	38	8
June 6, 1984	55	33	12
June 22, 1984	54	36	10
June 29, 1984	53	37	10
July 6, 1984	53	36	11
July 13, 1984	55	35	10
July 27, 1984	52	37	11
Aug. 10, 1984	54	38	8
Sept. 7, 1984	57	36	7

Table 5-3 *(Continued)*

President/date	*Approve*	*Disapprove*	*No opinion*
Reagan, I (continued)			
Sept. 21, 1984	57	36	7
Sept. 28, 1984	54	35	11
Oct. 26, 1984	58	33	9
Nov. 9, 1984	61	31	8
Nov. 30, 1984	62	30	8
Dec. 7, 1984	59	32	9
Jan. 11, 1985	62	29	9
Reagan, II			
Jan. 25, 1985	64	28	8
Feb. 15, 1985	60	31	9
March 8, 1985	56	37	7
April 12, 1985	52	37	11
May 17, 1985	55	37	8
June 7, 1985	58	32	10
July 12, 1985	63	28	9
Aug. 13, 1985	65	26	9
Aug. 16, 1985	57	32	11
Sept. 13, 1985	60	30	10
Oct. 11, 1985	63	29	8
Nov. 1, 1985	62	28	10
Nov. 11, 1985	65	24	11
Dec. 6, 1985	63	29	8
Jan. 10, 1986	64	27	9
March 7, 1986	63	26	11
April 11, 1986	62	29	9
May 16, 1986	68	23	9
June 6, 1986	61	29	10
June 9, 1986	64	26	10
July 11, 1986	63	28	9
Aug. 8, 1986	61	27	12
Sept. 12, 1986	61	25	14
Oct. 24, 1986	63	29	8
Dec. 4, 1986	47	44	9
Jan. 16, 1987	48	43	9
Feb. 27, 1987	40	53	7
March 5, 1987	46	46	8
March 14, 1987	47	44	9
April 10, 1987	48	43	9
June 5, 1987	47	44	9
June 8, 1987	53	40	7
July 10, 1987	49	43	8
Aug. 7, 1987	45	41	14
Aug. 24, 1987	49	42	9
Oct. 23, 1987	51	41	8
Dec. 4, 1987	49	41	10
Jan. 8, 1988	50	41	9
Jan. 22, 1988	49	40	11

(Table continues)

Table 5-3 *(Continued)*

President/date	*Approve*	*Disapprove*	*No opinion*
Reagan, II (continued)			
March 4, 1988	50	42	8
March 8, 1988	51	37	12
April 8, 1988	50	39	11
May 13, 1988	48	43	9
June 10, 1988	51	39	10
June 24, 1988	48	40	12
July 1, 1988	51	35	14
July 15, 1988	54	36	10
Aug. 19, 1988	53	37	10
Sept. 25, 1988	54	37	9
Oct. 21, 1988	51	38	11
Nov. 11, 1988	57	35	8
Dec. 27, 1988	63	29	8
G.H.W. Bush			
Jan. 24, 1989	51	6	43
Jan. 27, 1989	55	12	33
Feb. 24, 1989	61	12	28
Feb. 28, 1989	63	13	24
March 10, 1989	56	16	28
April 10, 1989	58	16	26
May 4, 1989	56	22	22
May 15, 1989	63	18	20
June 8, 1989	70	14	16
July 6, 1989	67	18	14
Aug. 10, 1989	69	19	12
Aug. 15, 1989	64	18	18
Sept. 7, 1989	70	17	13
Sept. 22, 1989	67	19	15
Oct. 5, 1989	68	20	12
Oct. 13, 1989	60	23	18
Nov. 2, 1989	70	17	13
Nov. 9, 1989	70	17	13
Dec. 7, 1989	71	20	9
Jan. 4, 1990	80	11	9
Feb. 8, 1990	73	16	11
Feb. 15, 1990	73	16	11
March 8, 1990	68	18	14
March 15, 1990	74	15	11
April 5, 1990	68	16	16
April 19, 1990	67	17	16
May 4, 1990	66	21	14
May 17, 1990	65	20	15
June 7, 1990	69	17	14
June 15, 1990	69	17	14
July 6, 1990	63	24	13
July 9, 1990	60	24	16
July 19, 1990	60	25	15
Aug. 3, 1990	74	16	10

Table 5-3 *(Continued)*

President/date	*Approve*	*Disapprove*	*No opinion*
G. H. W. Bush (continued)			
Aug. 9, 1990	74	16	10
Aug. 16, 1990	75	16	9
Aug. 23, 1990	76	16	8
Aug. 30, 1990	74	17	9
Sept. 10, 1990	76	16	8
Sept. 14, 1990	72	17	10
Sept. 21, 1990	67	22	11
Sept. 27, 1990	68	20	13
Oct. 3, 1990	66	25	9
Oct. 11, 1990	56	33	11
Oct. 18, 1990	53	37	10
Oct. 25, 1990	55	36	10
Nov. 1, 1990	58	32	10
Nov. 8, 1990	58	34	8
Nov. 15, 1990	54	33	13
Nov. 29, 1990	61	29	10
Dec. 6, 1990	58	33	9
Dec. 8, 1990	67	16	17
Dec. 13, 1990	63	30	7
Jan. 3, 1991	58	31	11
Jan. 11, 1991	64	25	11
Jan. 17, 1991	82	12	6
Jan. 19, 1991	82	12	6
Jan. 23, 1991	83	13	4
Jan. 26, 1991	74	18	8
Jan. 30, 1991	82	15	3
Feb. 7, 1991	79	18	3
Feb. 14, 1991	80	14	6
Feb. 21, 1991	80	13	7
Feb. 28, 1991	89	8	3
March 7, 1991	87	8	5
March 14, 1991	86	9	5
March 21, 1991	84	10	6
March 28, 1991	82	11	7
April 4, 1991	83	12	5
April 11, 1991	77	13	10
April 25, 1991	76	15	9
May 2, 1991	74	19	7
May 16, 1991	77	15	8
May 23, 1991	76	16	8
May 30, 1991	74	17	9
June 13, 1991	71	19	10
June 26, 1991	72	22	6
July 11, 1991	72	21	7
July 18, 1991	70	21	9
July 25, 1991	71	21	8
Aug. 8, 1991	71	22	7
Aug. 23, 1991	74	18	8

(Table continues)

Table 5-3 *(Continued)*

President/date	*Approve*	*Disapprove*	*No opinion*
G. H. W. Bush (continued)			
Aug. 29, 1991	69	22	9
Sept. 5, 1991	70	21	9
Sept. 13, 1991	68	22	10
Sept. 26, 1991	66	25	9
Oct. 3, 1991	65	27	8
Oct. 10, 1991	66	28	6
Oct. 17, 1991	66	26	8
Oct. 24, 1991	62	29	9
Oct. 31, 1991	59	33	8
Nov. 7, 1991	56	36	8
Nov. 14, 1991	56	36	8
Nov. 21, 1991	52	39	9
Dec. 5, 1991	52	42	6
Dec. 12, 1991	50	41	9
Jan. 3, 1992	46	47	7
Jan. 16, 1992	46	48	6
Jan. 31, 1992	47	48	5
Feb. 6, 1992	44	48	8
Feb. 19, 1992	39	47	14
Feb. 28, 1992	41	53	6
March 11, 1992	41	47	12
March 20, 1992	41	49	10
March 26, 1992	42	51	7
April 9, 1992	39	54	7
April 20, 1992	42	48	10
May 7, 1992	42	51	7
May 18, 1992	41	52	7
June 4, 1992	37	56	7
June 12, 1992	37	55	8
June 26, 1992	38	55	7
July 24, 1992	32	59	9
July 31, 1992	29	60	11
Aug. 8, 1992	35	58	7
Aug. 21, 1992	40	54	6
Aug. 31, 1992	39	54	7
Sept. 11, 1992	39	55	6
Sept. 17, 1992	36	54	10
Oct. 1, 1992	34	56	10
Oct. 12, 1992	34	56	10
Nov. 20, 1992	43	46	11
Dec. 4, 1992	49	47	4
Dec. 18, 1992	49	41	10
Jan. 8, 1993	56	37	7
Clinton, I			
Jan. 24, 1993	58	20	22
Jan. 29, 1993	54	30	16
Feb. 12, 1993	51	34	15
Feb. 26, 1993	59	29	12

Table 5-3 *(Continued)*

President/date	*Approve*	*Disapprove*	*No opinion*
Clinton, I (continued)			
March 12, 1993	53	34	13
March 29, 1993	52	37	11
April 22, 1993	55	37	8
May 10, 1993	45	44	11
May 21, 1993	44	46	10
June 5, 1993	38	49	14
June 18, 1993	39	50	11
June 29, 1993	46	47	7
July 9, 1993	45	48	7
July 19, 1993	41	49	10
Aug. 8, 1993	44	48	8
Aug. 23, 1993	44	47	9
Sept. 10, 1993	47	42	11
Sept. 13, 1993	46	43	11
Sept. 24, 1993	56	36	8
Oct. 8, 1993	50	42	8
Oct. 13, 1993	47	44	8
Oct. 28, 1993	48	45	7
Nov. 2, 1993	48	45	7
Nov. 15, 1993	50	43	7
Nov. 19, 1993	48	43	9
Dec. 4, 1993	52	38	10
Dec. 17, 1993	54	40	6
Jan. 6, 1994	54	38	8
Jan. 15, 1994	54	38	8
Jan. 28, 1994	58	35	7
Feb. 26, 1994	53	41	6
March 7, 1994	50	42	8
March 11, 1994	50	41	9
March 25, 1994	52	41	7
March 28, 1994	51	42	7
April 16, 1994	51	41	8
April 22, 1994	48	44	8
May 20, 1994	51	42	7
June 3, 1994	46	47	7
June 11, 1994	49	44	7
June 25, 1994	44	47	9
July 1, 1994	43	48	9
July 15, 1994	42	49	9
Aug. 8, 1994	43	48	9
Aug. 15, 1994	39	52	9
Sept. 6, 1994	39	54	7
Sept. 20, 1994	44	51	5
Sept. 23, 1994	44	51	5
Oct. 7, 1994	42	52	6
Oct. 18, 1994	41	52	7
Oct. 22, 1994	48	46	6
Nov. 2, 1994	46	46	8

(Table continues)

Table 5-3 *(Continued)*

President/date	*Approve*	*Disapprove*	*No opinion*
Clinton, I (continued)			
Nov. 28, 1994	43	49	8
Dec. 2, 1994	42	50	8
Dec. 16, 1994	42	53	5
Dec. 28, 1994	40	52	8
Jan. 16, 1995	47	45	8
Feb. 3, 1995	49	44	7
Feb. 10, 1995	47	39	14
Feb. 24, 1995	42	48	10
March 17, 1995	46	45	9
March 27, 1995	44	47	9
April 1, 1995	51	40	10
April 17, 1995	46	45	9
April 21, 1995	51	39	10
May 5, 1995	47	39	15
May 11, 1995	51	42	7
May 19, 1995	42	41	18
June 5, 1995	47	42	11
July 7, 1995	48	42	10
July 14, 1995	47	40	13
July 20, 1995	46	44	10
July 28, 1995	48	36	15
Aug. 11, 1995	46	44	10
Aug. 25, 1995	46	43	11
Sept. 14, 1995	44	44	12
Sept. 22, 1995	48	44	8
Oct. 5, 1995	46	42	12
Oct. 19, 1995	49	40	11
Nov. 6, 1995	52	41	7
Nov. 17, 1995	53	38	9
Dec. 15, 1995	51	44	5
Jan. 5, 1996	42	49	9
Jan. 12, 1996	46	47	7
Jan. 26, 1996	52	42	6
Feb. 12, 1996	49	41	10
Feb. 23, 1996	53	40	7
March 1, 1996	52	32	16
March 8, 1996	54	37	9
March 15, 1996	52	39	9
April 9, 1996	54	40	6
April 23, 1996	56	37	7
May 9, 1996	55	39	6
May 28, 1996	53	38	9
June 18, 1996	58	37	5
June 27, 1996	52	42	6
July 18, 1996	57	35	8
July 26, 1996	58	35	7
Aug. 5, 1996	57	36	7
Aug. 16, 1996	52	39	9

Table 5-3 *(Continued)*

President/date	*Approve*	*Disapprove*	*No opinion*
Clinton, I (continued)			
Aug. 23, 1996	53	39	8
Aug. 30, 1996	60	33	7
Sept. 7, 1996	60	31	9
Sept. 14, 1996	53	26	21
Sept. 17, 1996	55	25	20
Oct. 1, 1996	58	34	8
Oct. 21, 1996	58	35	7
Oct. 26, 1996	54	36	10
Nov. 21, 1996	58	35	7
Dec. 9, 1996	58	34	8
Jan. 3, 1997	58	35	7
Jan. 10, 1997	62	31	7
Clinton, II			
Jan. 30, 1997	60	31	9
Feb. 24, 1997	57	33	10
March 24, 1997	59	35	6
April 11, 1997	54	37	9
April 18, 1997	54	37	9
May 6, 1997	57	35	8
May 30, 1997	57	35	8
June 26, 1997	55	36	9
July 25, 1997	58	34	8
Aug. 9, 1997	59	26	15
Aug. 12, 1997	61	32	7
Aug. 22, 1997	60	34	6
Sept. 6, 1997	61	28	11
Sept. 25, 1997	58	33	9
Oct. 3, 1997	55	36	9
Oct. 27, 1997	59	32	9
Nov. 6, 1997	59	31	10
Nov. 21, 1997	61	30	9
Dec. 18, 1997	56	36	8
Jan. 6, 1998	59	32	9
Jan. 16, 1998	60	30	10
Jan. 21, 1998	62	29	8
Jan. 28, 1998	67	28	5
Jan. 30, 1998	69	28	3
Feb. 13, 1998	66	30	4
Feb. 20, 1998	66	29	5
March 16, 1998	67	29	4
March 20, 1998	66	28	6
April 1, 1998	67	28	5
April 17, 1998	63	31	6
May 8, 1998	64	31	5
June 5, 1998	60	34	6
June 22, 1998	60	33	6
July 7, 1998	61	34	5

(Table continues)

Table 5-3 *(Continued)*

President/date	*Approve*	*Disapprove*	*No opinion*
Clinton, II (continued)			
July 13, 1998	63	31	6
July 29, 1998	65	31	4
Aug. 7, 1998	64	32	4
Aug. 10, 1998	65	30	5
Aug. 17, 1998	62	32	6
Aug. 18, 1998	66	29	5
Aug. 20, 1998	61	34	5
Aug. 21, 1998	60	35	5
Sept. 1, 1998	62	33	5
Sept. 10, 1998	60	37	3
Sept. 11, 1998	62	35	3
Sept. 12, 1998	63	35	2
Sept. 13, 1998	64	34	3
Sept. 14, 1998	63	35	2
Sept. 20, 1998	60	34	6
Sept. 21, 1998	66	31	3
Sept. 23, 1998	66	31	3
Oct. 6, 1998	63	34	3
Oct. 9, 1998	65	32	3
Oct. 29, 1998	66	30	4
Nov. 13, 1998	66	31	3
Nov. 19, 1998	66	30	4
Nov. 20, 1998	66	30	4
Dec. 4, 1998	66	30	4
Dec. 12, 1998	64	34	2
Dec. 15, 1998	63	33	4
Dec. 19, 1998	73	25	2
Dec. 28, 1998	64	34	2
Jan. 6, 1999	63	34	3
Jan. 8, 1999	67	30	3
Jan. 15, 1999	69	29	2
Jan. 22, 1999	69	29	2
Jan. 27, 1999	67	31	2
Feb. 4, 1999	65	33	3
Feb. 12, 1999	68	30	3
Feb. 19, 1999	66	30	4
Feb. 26, 1999	66	31	3
March 5, 1999	68	28	4
March 12, 1999	62	35	3
March 19, 1999	64	33	3
March 30, 1999	64	32	4
April 6, 1999	59	35	6
April 13, 1999	60	36	4
April 26, 1999	60	36	5
April 30, 1999	60	36	4
May 7, 1999	60	35	5
May 23, 1999	53	42	5
June 4, 1999	60	35	5

Table 5-3 *(Continued)*

President/date	*Approve*	*Disapprove*	*No opinion*
Clinton, II (continued)			
June 11, 1999	60	36	4
June 25, 1999	57	41	2
July 13, 1999	59	37	4
July 16, 1999	58	38	4
July 22, 1999	64	31	5
Aug. 3, 1999	60	35	4
Aug. 16, 1999	59	36	5
Aug. 24, 1999	60	35	6
Sept. 10, 1999	60	38	2
Sept. 23, 1999	59	38	3
Sept. 29, 1999	60	34	5
Oct. 8, 1999	56	39	5
Oct. 21, 1999	59	36	5
Nov. 4, 1999	58	38	4
Nov. 18, 1999	59	36	5
Dec. 9, 1999	56	41	3
Dec. 20, 1999	57	36	7
Jan. 7, 2000	63	35	2
Jan. 13, 2000	59	37	4
Jan. 17, 2000	62	35	3
Jan. 25, 2000	64	32	4
Feb. 4, 2000	63	33	4
Feb. 14, 2000	62	34	4
Feb. 25, 2000	57	39	4
March 10, 2000	63	34	3
March 17, 2000	56	39	5
March 30, 2000	62	34	4
April 28, 2000	59	39	2
May 5, 2000	57	36	7
May 18, 2000	57	37	6
June 22, 2000	55	40	5
July 6, 2000	59	36	5
July 14, 2000	59	37	4
Aug. 4, 2000	57	40	3
Aug. 11, 2000	58	39	3
Aug. 18, 2000	71	22	7
Aug. 29, 2000	62	35	3
Sept. 29, 2000	62	35	3
Oct. 6, 2000	58	37	5
Nov. 13, 2000	63	33	4
Dec. 2, 2000	60	35	5
Dec. 15, 2000	66	32	2
Jan. 5, 2001	65	31	4
Jan. 10, 2001	66	29	5
G.W. Bush, I			
Feb. 1, 2001	57	25	18
Feb. 9, 2001	57	25	18

(Table continues)

Table 5-3 *(Continued)*

President/date	*Approve*	*Disapprove*	*No opinion*
G. W. Bush, I (continued)			
March 5, 2001	63	22	15
March 9, 2001	58	29	13
March 26, 2001	53	29	18
April 6, 2001	59	30	11
April 20, 2001	62	29	9
May 7, 2001	53	33	14
June 8, 2001	55	35	10
June 11, 2001	55	33	12
June 28, 2001	52	34	13
July 10, 2001	50	43	8
July 19, 2001	56	33	11
Aug. 3, 2001	55	35	10
Aug. 10, 2001	57	35	8
Aug. 16, 2001	57	34	9
Sept. 21, 2001	90	6	4
Oct. 5, 2001	87	10	3
Oct. 11, 2001	89	8	3
Oct. 19, 2001	88	9	3
Nov. 2, 2001	87	9	4
Nov. 8, 2001	87	9	4
Nov. 26, 2001	87	8	5
Dec. 6, 2001	86	10	4
Dec. 14, 2001	86	11	3
Jan. 25, 2002	84	13	3
Feb. 4, 2002	82	14	4
Feb. 8, 2002	82	14	4
March 1, 2002	81	14	5
March 4, 2002	77	18	5
March 8, 2002	80	14	6
March 22, 2002	79	17	4
April 5, 2002	76	19	5
April 8, 2002	75	20	5
April 22, 2002	77	17	6
April 29, 2002	77	20	3
May 6, 2002	76	19	5
May 20, 2002	76	17	7
May 28, 2002	77	17	6
June 3, 2002	70	23	7
June 7, 2002	74	18	8
June 17, 2002	74	20	6
June 21, 2002	73	21	6
June 28, 2002	76	19	5
July 5, 2002	76	18	6
July 9, 2002	73	21	6
July 22, 2002	69	24	7
July 26, 2002	69	26	5
July 29, 2002	71	23	6
Aug. 5, 2002	68	26	6

Table 5-3 *(Continued)*

President/date	*Approve*	*Disapprove*	*No opinion*
G. W. Bush, I (continued)			
Aug. 19, 2002	65	28	7
Sept. 2, 2002	66	29	5
Sept. 5, 2002	66	30	4
Sept. 13, 2002	70	26	4
Sept. 20, 2002	66	30	4
Sept. 23, 2002	68	26	6
Oct. 3. 2002	67	28	5
Oct. 14, 2002	62	31	7
Oct. 21, 2002	67	28	5
Oct. 31, 2002	63	29	8
Nov. 8, 2002	68	27	5
Nov. 11, 2002	66	26	8
Dec. 5, 2002	64	29	7
Dec. 9, 2002	63	32	5
Dec. 16, 2002	63	33	4
Dec. 19, 2002	61	32	7
Jan. 3, 2003	63	32	5
Jan. 10, 2003	58	37	5
Jan. 13, 2003	61	34	5
Jan. 20, 2003	58	36	6
Jan. 23, 2003	60	36	4
Jan. 31, 2003	61	35	4
Feb. 3, 2003	59	35	6
Feb. 17, 2003	58	37	5
Feb. 24, 2003	57	37	6
March 3, 2003	57	37	6
March 14, 2003	58	38	4
March 22, 2003	71	25	4
March 29, 2003	71	26	3
April 4, 2003	70	27	3
April 7, 2003	69	26	5
April 14, 2003	71	24	5
April 22, 2003	70	26	4
May 5, 2003	69	28	3
May 19, 2003	66	30	4
May 30, 2003	64	32	4
June 27, 2003	61	36	3
July 7, 2003	62	34	4
Aug. 25, 2003	59	37	4
Sept. 8, 2003	52	43	5
Sept. 19, 2003	50	47	3
Oct. 6, 2003	55	42	3
Oct. 10, 2003	56	40	4
Oct. 24, 2003	53	42	5
Nov. 3, 2003	54	43	3
Nov. 10, 2003	51	45	4
Nov. 14, 2003	50	47	3
Dec. 5, 2003	55	43	2

(Table continues)

Table 5-3 *(Continued)*

President/date	*Approve*	*Disapprove*	*No opinion*
G. W. Bush, I (continued)			
Dec. 11, 2003	56	41	3
Jan. 2, 2004	60	35	5
Jan. 9, 2004	59	38	3
Jan. 12, 2004	53	44	3
Jan. 29, 2003	49	48	3
Feb. 6, 2004	52	44	4
Feb. 9, 2004	51	46	3
Feb. 16, 2004	51	46	3
March 5, 2004	49	48	3
March 8, 2004	50	47	3
March 26, 2004	53	44	3
April 5, 2004	52	45	3
April 16, 2004	52	45	3
May 2, 2004	49	48	3
May 7, 2004	46	51	3
May 21, 2004	47	49	4
June 3, 2004	49	49	2
June 21, 2004	48	49	3
July 8, 2004	47	49	4
July 30, 2004	48	49	4
Aug. 9, 2004	51	46	3
Aug. 23, 2004	49	47	4
Sept. 3, 2004	52	46	2
Sept. 13, 2004	52	45	3
Sept. 24, 2004	54	44	2
Oct. 1, 2004	50	48	2
Oct. 11, 2004	47	46	7
Oct. 14, 2004	51	47	2
Oct. 22, 2004	51	46	3
Oct. 29, 2004	51	46	3
Nov. 7, 2004	53	44	3
Nov. 19, 2004	55	42	3
Dec. 5, 2004	53	44	3
Dec. 17, 2004	49	46	5
Jan. 3, 2005	52	44	4
Jan. 7 2005	52	44	4
Jan 14, 2005	51	46	3
G. W. Bush, II[c]			
Feb. 2, 2005	57	40	3
Feb. 7, 2005	49	48	3
Feb. 21, 2005	51	45	4
Feb. 25, 2005	52	45	3
March 7, 2005	52	44	4
March 18, 2005	52	44	4
March 21, 2005	45	49	6
April 1, 2005	48	48	4
April 2, 2005	50	45	5

Table 5-3 *(Continued)*

President/date	*Approve*	*Disapprove*	*No opinion*
G. W. Bush, II[c] (continued)			
April 4, 2005	50	45	5
April 18, 2005	48	49	3
April 29, 2005	48	49	3
May 20, 2005	46	50	4
May 23, 2005	48	47	5
June 6, 2005	47	49	4
June 16, 2005	47	51	2
June 24, 2005	45	53	2
June 29, 2005	46	51	3
July 7, 2005	49	48	3
July 22, 2005	49	48	3
July 25, 2005	44	51	5
Aug. 5, 2005	45	51	4
Aug. 8, 2005	45	51	4
Aug. 28, 2005	45	52	3
Sept. 8, 2005	46	51	3
Sept. 12, 2005	45	52	3
Sept. 16, 2005	40	58	2
Sept. 26, 2005	45	50	5
Oct. 13, 2005	39	58	3
Oct. 21, 2005	42	55	3
Oct. 24, 2005	41	56	3
Oct. 28, 2005	41	56	3
Nov. 7, 2001	40	55	5
Nov. 11, 2005	37	60	3
Nov. 17, 2005	38	57	5
Dec. 5, 2005	43	52	5
Dec. 9, 2005	42	55	3
Dec. 16, 2005	41	56	3
Dec. 19, 2005	43	53	4
Jan. 6, 2006	43	54	3
Jan. 9, 2006	43	53	4
Jan. 20, 2006	43	54	4
Feb. 6, 2006	42	55	4
Feb. 9, 2006	39	56	4
Feb. 28, 2006	38	60	2
March 10, 2006	36	60	4
March 13, 2006	37	59	5
April 7, 2006	37	60	3
April 10, 2006	36	59	5
April 28, 2006	34	63	3
May 5, 2006	31	65	5
May 8, 2006	33	61	6
June 1, 2006	36	57	6
June 9, 2006	38	56	6
June 23, 2006	37	60	3
July 6, 2006	40	55	5
July 21, 2006	37	59	4

(Table continues)

Table 5-3 *(Continued)*

President/date	*Approve*	*Disapprove*	*No opinion*
G. W. Bush, II[c] (continued)			
July 28, 2006	40	56	4
Aug. 7, 2006	37	59	4
Aug. 18, 2006	42	54	4
Sept. 7, 2006	39	56	5
Sept. 15, 2006	44	51	5
Oct. 6, 2006	37	59	4
Oct. 9, 2006	37	57	6
Oct. 20, 2006	37	58	4
Nov. 2, 2006	38	56	6
Nov. 9, 2006	33	62	4
Jan. 5, 2007	37	59	4
Jan. 12, 2007	34	63	4
Jan. 15, 2007	36	61	3
Feb. 1, 2007	32	65	4
Feb. 9, 2007	37	59	3
March 2, 2007	33	63	4
March 11, 2007	35	61	4
March 23, 2007	34	62	4
April 2, 2007	38	58	4
April 13, 2007	36	60	4
May 4, 2007	34	63	3
June 1, 2007	32	62	6
June 11, 2007	32	65	3
July 6, 2007	29	66	5
July 12, 2007	31	63	6
Aug. 3, 2007	34	62	4
Aug. 13, 2007	32	63	5
Sept. 7, 2007	33	62	5
Oct. 4, 2007	32	64	4
Oct. 12, 2007	32	64	3
Nov. 2, 2007	31	64	5
Nov. 11, 2007	32	61	7

Source: Roper Center Public Opinion Archives at www.ropercenter.uconn.edu/. All results are from the Gallup poll unless otherwise noted.

Note: Percentages may not total 100 prcent due to rounding.

[a] Polls conducted by the Organization of Public Opinion Research.
[b] Full term from Nov. 23, 1963, through Jan. 19, 1969.
[c] Through 2007 only.

Figure 5-1 Popularity Trends, Truman to G. W. Bush

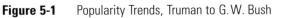

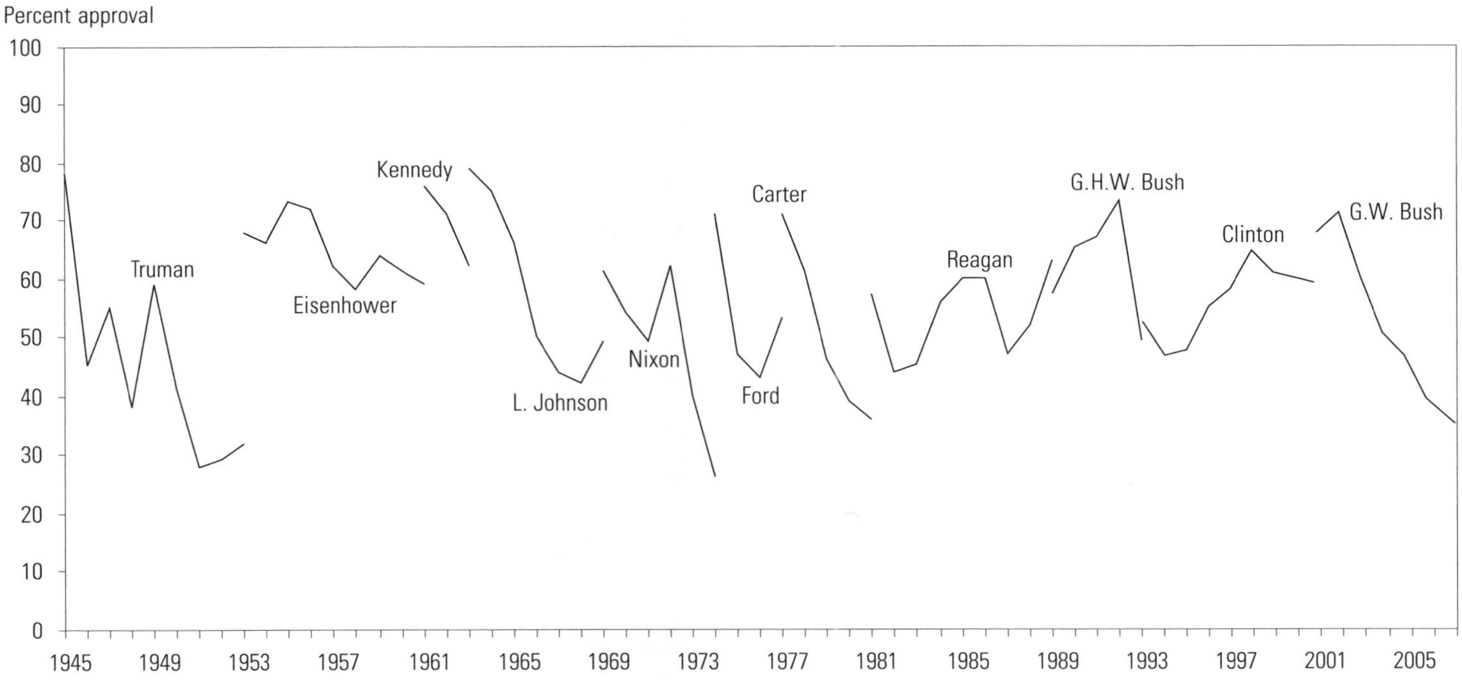

Source: Adapted from Table 5-2.

Table 5-4 Quarterly Presidential Approval, by Party, Region, and Income, Eisenhower, I to G. W. Bush, II (average percent per quarter)

	Party			*Region*				*Income*[a]		
President/year/quarter	Rep.	Dem.	Ind.	East	Midwest	South	West	High	Middle	Low
Eisenhower, I										
1953/1	85	60	69	71	70	70	69	—	—	—
1953/2	88	64	74	73	74	74	74	—	—	—
1953/3	88	57	68	70	70	66	73	—	—	—
1953/4	87	47	64	66	64	61	64	—	—	—
1954/1	90	53	72	67	70	70	69	—	—	—
1954/2	86	46	66	63	63	61	69	—	—	—
1954/3	87	51	70	67	69	64	70	—	—	—
1954/4	87	50	68	64	64	65	66	—	—	—
1955/1	90	55	73	68	70	68	75	—	—	—
1955/2	90	54	70	67	70	66	74	—	—	—
1955/3	90	57	76	74	73	67	77	—	—	—
1955/4	92	62	80	80	79	69	79	—	—	—
1956/1	94	58	78	78	74	69	76	—	—	—
1956/2	92	53	73	76	71	65	69	—	—	—
1956/3	92	49	73	73	67	65	70	—	—	—
1956/4	95	62	80	80	79	69	79	—	—	—
Eisenhower, II										
1957/1	90	55	75	75	71	67	71	—	—	—
1957/2	85	47	65	68	64	58	65	—	—	—
1957/3	84	44	65	68	64	58	65	—	—	—
1957/4	84	40	59	65	62	54	62	—	—	—
1958/1	83	36	56	59	57	47	54	—	—	—
1958/2	81	34	55	59	56	44	56	—	—	—
1958/3	82	39	57	59	56	49	58	—	—	—

1958/4	84	36	56	61	59	42	57	—	—	—
1959/1	85	42	60	63	60	50	60	—	—	—
1959/2	88	47	64	65	63	56	66	—	—	—
1959/3	88	49	68	68	67	58	66	—	—	—
1959/4	90	55	71	70	68	66	74	—	—	—
1960/1	90	48	68	68	66	59	67	—	—	—
1960/2	87	45	67	67	65	53	61	—	—	—
1960/3	86	41	64	62	60	54	59	—	—	—
1960/4	89	40	58	61	60	56	60	—	—	—
Kennedy										
1961/1	56	85	68	74	72	70	75	—	—	—
1961/2	59	88	72	79	78	70	77	—	—	—
1961/3	60	87	73	79	78	70	79	—	—	—
1961/4	59	88	76	80	80	74	78	—	—	—
1962/1	63	90	75	79	81	77	78	—	—	—
1962/2	50	86	71	76	74	68	75	—	—	—
1962/3	39	82	63	68	65	59	67	—	—	—
1962/4	46	87	67	75	73	62	72	—	—	—
1963/1	48	84	68	76	72	63	69	—	—	—
1963/2	40	80	59	71	67	52	65	—	—	—
1963/3	39	75	54	69	63	43	64	—	—	—
1963/4	31	79	55	68	61	45	59	—	—	—
L. Johnson[b]										
1963/4	73	80	71	76	79	71	80	—	—	—
1964/1	67	84	72	80	78	72	76	—	—	—
1964/2	61	84	68	81	77	65	73	—	—	—
1964/3	—	—	—	—	—	—	—	—	—	
1964/4	47	85	63	80	72	58	71	—	—	—
1965/1	60	79	72	76	74	64	68	68	76	70
1965/2	51	77	62	79	70	52	63	65	71	67
1965/3	50	77	57	71	67	60	66	64	68	67
1965/4	46	76	60	75	64	51	59	65	66	64
1966/1	40	73	47	66	59	45	61	58	59	53

(Table continues)

Table 5-4 *(Continued)*

	Party			*Region*				*Income*[a]		
President/year/quarter	Rep.	Dem.	Ind.	East	Midwest	South	West	High	Middle	Low
L. Johnson[b] (continued)										
1966/2	33	65	44	59	51	43	48	48	54	52
1966/3	32	67	47	61	51	43	50	52	54	49
1966/4	28	66	40	62	46	40	43	47	48	53
1967/1	25	62	40	55	46	40	42	43	46	49
1967/2	29	61	41	52	46	39	49	46	46	47
1967/3	25	56	37	48	42	34	43	41	42	41
1967/4	25	60	35	49	39	35	44	41	42	41
1968/1	26	57	31	46	39	38	44	38	45	46
1968/2	32	61	39	55	46	39	43	46	49	44
1968/3	24	51	31	43	37	32	36	34	38	45
1968/4	29	59	35	50	43	33	43	41	45	42
Nixon, I										
1969/1	80	51	60	56	64	63	63	67	62	57
1969/2	83	49	58	63	60	63	64	66	64	58
1969/3	82	49	61	60	62	64	62	63	63	57
1969/4	83	49	63	59	64	66	60	67	60	59
1970/1	84	42	62	56	59	64	58	67	60	56
1970/2	81	42	61	55	55	63	59	64	56	53
1970/3	82	40	56	53	55	55	58	58	53	52
1970/4	82	39	55	55	52	61	55	60	55	49
1971/1	80	37	54	52	51	54	49	59	52	43
1971/2	80	34	48	48	48	53	46	52	50	43
1971/3	81	38	49	52	51	54	47	58	53	46
1971/4	85	34	45	52	45	52	47	54	48	43
1972/1	81	35	53	50	50	57	49	56	51	45

1972/2	88	43	62	59	56	68	51	63	59	53
1972/3	88	43	61	58	58	66	50	64	58	59
1972/4	88	44	60	57	60	65	50	66	58	56
Nixon, II										
1973/1	90	49	70	64	65	71	62	71	66	58
1973/2	75	29	47	41	45	51	42	52	42	39
1973/3	63	20	36	36	35	39	33	52	46	39
1973/4	54	17	27	24	29	36	28	31	27	27
1974/1	54	13	26	21	28	32	23	27	25	25
1974/2	51	14	26	22	26	31	27	30	24	25
1974/3	50	13	22	20	21	30	25	27	23	23
Ford										
1974/3	71	56	61	67	76	68	72	76	69	65
1974/4	68	37	49	46	50	47	48	53	47	42
1975/1	61	29	37	35	40	39	38	42	38	33
1975/2	66	37	51	47	47	48	48	54	47	33
1975/3	65	37	46	44	48	45	47	54	42	40
1975/4	63	31	43	39	47	42	41	46	41	35
1976/1	66	35	50	40	47	47	51	51	44	38
1976/2	68	35	49	41	49	50	49	52	42	42
1976/3	74	37	52	45	54	52	50	—	—	—
1976/4	80	40	54	49	58	54	51	—	—	—
Carter										
1977/1	56	81	70	67	67	72	63	73	72	66
1977/2	48	72	62	65	62	63	65	64	62	62
1977/3	47	73	61	63	64	63	60	64	62	60
1977/4	40	66	53	55	54	58	56	56	56	56
1978/1	34	60	53	53	55	55	47	48	51	54
1978/2	25	53	38	43	39	44	37	33	43	44
1978/3	20	52	36	40	38	40	44	40	47	52
1978/4	31	63	52	52	53	54	50	51	51	60
1979/1	24	55	43	47	38	46	42	44	43	41

(Table continues)

Table 5-4 *(Continued)*

	Party			*Region*				*Income*[a]		
President/year/quarter	Rep.	Dem.	Ind.	East	Midwest	South	West	High	Middle	Low
Carter (continued)										
1979/2	20	43	33	33	33	38	34	30	36	38
1979/3	19	36	24	25	25	34	26	25	28	31
1979/4	28	48	36	—	—	—	—	—	—	—
1980/1	42	65	50	56	55	63	47	54	55	57
1980/2	28	57	35	42	43	53	36	52	44	48
1980/3	14	48	20	28	30	42	25	50	33	38
1980/4	14	49	30	28	35	38	36	33	31	43
Reagan, I										
1981/1	80	39	57	52	56	57	55	65	54	39
1981/2	89	49	66	62	66	66	64	74	64	47
1981/3	85	42	60	55	60	60	60	72	58	40
1981/4	84	33	53	50	53	52	51	61	47	31
1982/1	82	27	50	45	48	48	49	57	45	32
1982/2	79	24	47	44	46	44	45	56	43	30
1982/3	76	21	44	42	44	39	42	55	41	28
1982/4	79	22	44	39	44	40	48	55	41	29
1983/1	67	19	41	37	39	35	38	48	37	27
1983/2	78	26	49	45	44	45	50	57	46	29
1983/3	83	30	52	48	50	50	50	61	54	37
1983/4	87	33	54	50	55	55	51	64	61	44
1984/1	86	33	56	52	54	61	53	70	66	43
1984/2	85	32	58	52	51	54	59	71	58	45
1984/3	89	32	61	54	55	60	56	70	60	44
1984/4	92	32	63	56	60	65	52	70	62	43

Reagan, II										
1985/1	88	39	61	57	64	64	63	71	68	51
1985/2	87	24	55	50	54	57	59	65	59	44
1985/3	90	39	68	63	67	72	56	74	70	53
1985/4	90	39	63	67	55	62	66	70	66	56
1986/1	88	40	60	61	61	65	65	73	65	56
1986/2	88	51	70	69	67	68	67	78	70	56
1986/3	88	44	65	66	61	64	64	69	67	54
1986/4	74	24	45	45	48	47	50	—	—	—
1987/1	80	23	49	49	47	48	50	59	50	34
1987/2	76	24	50	44	48	54	45	53	49	41
1987/3	78	28	48	50	50	50	45	58	45	36
1987/4	78	21	51	43	47	54	50	57	48	36
1988/1	81	28	51	46	51	57	50	—	—	—
1988/2	—	—	—	—	—	—	—	—	—	—
1988/3	78	29	49	49	48	54	59	56	47	48
1988/4	87	24	55	51	54	58	49	63	54	42
G. H. W. Bush										
1989/1	69	38	47	47	48	57	53	56	44	48
1989/2	81	42	51	58	60	62	50	65	55	50
1989/3	83	59	66	66	72	71	67	73	68	66
1989/4	87	49	66	68	63	70	69	74	72	61
1990/1	93	64	75	75	77	81	76	85	78	71
1990/2	86	51	63	59	66	71	64	71	60	60
1990/3	86	58	66	69	68	73	66	78	71	61
1990/4	—	—	—	—	—	—	—	—	—	—
1991/1	95	72	80	80	82	84	83	87	86	77
1991/2	94	63	74	72	75	83	75	85	80	65
1991/3	88	61	66	69	72	70	73	79	72	67
1991/4	80	37	57	57	58	67	57	67	62	52
1992/1	71	21	38	42	41	46	42	50	44	36
1992/2	68	18	36	38	40	43	42	42	42	38
1992/3	70	13	30	32	35	37	40	42	36	32
1992/4	75	19	38	40	43	45	39	49	44	34

(Table continues)

Table 5-4 *(Continued)*

	Party			*Region*				*Income*[a]		
President/year/quarter	Rep.	Dem.	Ind.	East	Midwest	South	West	High	Middle	Low
Clinton, I										
1993/1	28	82	51	63	53	51	57	52	53	61
1993/2	23	75	35	50	52	45	47	44	49	53
1993/3	24	73	43	53	50	44	42	41	48	52
1993/4	24	77	46	54	51	46	50	47	49	52
1994/1	28	78	54	59	54	51	54	48	55	59
1994/2	24	77	46	59	47	47	48	49	52	50
1994/3	17	76	40	47	48	39	42	35	45	47
1994/4	14	77	46	55	48	44	46	38	45	52
1995/1	19	74	42	48	44	40	47	38	42	51
1995/2	20	75	50	55	47	46	48	43	48	54
1995/3	21	76	44	55	44	42	46	37	45	55
1995/4	21	79	50	53	53	44	52	48	50	55
1996/1	21	81	55	60	49	51	52	51	50	60
1996/2	23	82	52	59	56	50	52	49	53	59
1996/3	24	90	58	65	58	59	54	55	58	65
1996/4	22	88	51	60	55	54	58	53	56	59
Clinton, II										
1997/1	35	86	51	62	63	54	56	50	57	65
1997/2	26	82	52	62	48	52	56	51	55	58
1997/3	27	86	57	58	58	56	61	52	57	65
1997/4	—	—	—	—	—	—	—	—	—	—
1998/1	37	88	59	66	55	56	57	55	57	60
1998/2	32	88	58	72	57	58	54	52	59	66
1998/3	38	85	60	—	—	—	—	—	—	—
1998/4	41	91	69	78	72	69	74	69	71	76

1999/1	35	91	69	—	—	—	—	—	—	—
1999/2	—	—	—	—	—	—	—	—	—	—
1999/3	—	—	—	—	—	—	—	—	—	—
1999/4	—	—	—	—	—	—	—	—	—	—
2000/1	35	87	67	—	—	—	—	—	—	—
2000/2	—	—	—	—	—	—	—	—	—	—
2000/3[c]	37	91	63	68	65	67	69	47	60	71
2000/4	—	—	—	—	—	—	—	—	—	—
G. W. Bush, I										
2001/1	89	32	55	57	57	64	47	—	—	—
2001/2	90	29	52	47	57	54	52	64	—	37
2001/3	90	41	59	56	59	66	44	61	—	55
2001/4	98	79	85	—	—	—	—	—	—	—
2002/1	97	67	72	—	—	—	—	—	—	—
2002/2	96	57	72	—	—	—	—	—	—	—
2002/3	96	49	66	62	72	71	69	72	72	63
2002/4	93	41	61	—	—	—	—	—	—	—
2003/1	92	36	56	56	58	55	46	—	—	—
2003/2	94	41	64	—	—	—	—	—	—	—
2003/3	91	27	54	—	—	—	—	—	—	—
2003/4	89	24	43	—	—	—	—	—	—	—
2004/1	90	19	50	—	—	—	—	—	—	—
2004/2	91	16	43	—	—	—	—	—	—	—
2004/3[c]	90	13	43	44	55	54	47	58	50	47
2004/4[d]	92	13	45	39	48	56	46	52	56	41
G. W. Bush, II[e]										
2005/1	90	18	43	47	53	57	48	55	54	45
2005/2	88	16	39	—	—	—	—	—	—	—
2005/3	86	15	38	34	37	42	36	43	39	35
2005/4	83	10	32	36	43	47	46	51	45	33
2006/1	82	10	30	36	42	48	45	51	44	33
2006/2	76	9	26	26	32	40	31	39	33	25
2006/3	82	10	32	30	38	44	36	41	41	29

(Table continues)

Table 5-4 *(Continued)*

	Party			*Region*				*Income*[a]		
President/year/quarter	Rep.	Dem.	Ind.	East	Midwest	South	West	High	Middle	Low
G. W. Bush, II[e] (continued)										
2006/4	81	8	30	29	33	45	38	44	38	26
2007/1	79	9	27	—	—	—	—	—	—	—
2007/2	74	7	28	31	37	40	33	41	38	26
2007/3	72	7	26	—	—	—	—	—	—	—
2007/4	67	7	27	26	29	39	31	40	30	27

Sources: (1953–1964) George Edwards III and George Gallup, *Presidential Approval* (Baltimore: Johns Hopkins University Press, 1989), reprinted by permission of the Johns Hopkins University Press; (1965–1976) compiled from *The Gallup Public Opinion Index,* periodic volumes; (1977–1984) author's analysis of original Gallup surveys; (1988–1996) *Gallup Poll Monthly,* successive volumes; (1997–2007) George Gallup, *The Gallup Poll* (Lanham, Md.: Rowman and Littlefield), successive volumes, 1997–2007, http://brain.gallup.com and www.gallup.com, unless otherwise noted.

Note: Each number is the average of all Gallup polls for which the breakdowns were reported for that quarter. "—" indicates not available.

[a] Gallup provides respondents with a series of family-income categories for self-placement. These have been collapsed into three broad classifications of low, middle, and high income. The income categories reported by Gallup that were at or below the family poverty line, as taken from census data, constitutes the low-income category. Gallup breakdowns that ranged around the national mean income, again as reported by the census, represent the middle-income classification. Finally, incomes that fell into the highest brackets specified by Gallup make up the high-income category.
[b] Includes full term from Nov. 1963 to Jan. 1969.
[c] American National Election Study results.
[d] Pew Research Center for the People and the Press results.
[e] Through 2007 only.

Table 5-5 Annual and Term Average of Presidential Approval Ratings, by Party, Region, and Income, Eisenhower, I to G.W. Bush, II

	Party				*Region*					*Income*[a, b]			
President/year	Rep.	Dem.	Ind.	Difference[c]	East	Midwest	South	West	Difference[d]	High	Middle	Low	Difference[e]
Eisenhower, I													
1953	87	57	69	30	70	70	68	70	2	—	—	—	
1954	88	50	69	38	65	67	65	69	2	—	—	—	
1955	91	57	75	34	72	73	68	76	6	—	—		
1956	93	56	76	37	77	73	67	74	7	—	—	—	
Average	90	55	72	35	71	70	67	72	4				
Eisenhower, II													
1957	86	47	66	39	69	65	59	66	7	—	—	—	
1958	83	36	56	47	60	57	46	56	12	—	—	—	
1959	88	48	66	40	67	65	58	67	8	—	—		
1960	88	44	64	44	65	63	56	62	8	—	—	—	
Average	86	44	63	42	65	62	54	63	9				
Kennedy													
1961	59	87	72	–28	78	77	71	77	6	—	—	—	
1962	50	86	69	–36	75	73	67	73	7	—	—	—	
1963	40	80	59	–40	71	66	51	64	16	—	—		
Average	49	84	67	–35	75	72	63	72	10	—	—	—	
L. Johnson													
1963/1964	62	83	69	–21	79	77	67	75	10				
1965	52	77	63	–25	75	69	57	64	12	66	70	67	
1966	33	68	45	–35	62	52	43	51	12	51	54	52	–1
1967	26	60	38	–34	51	43	37	45	9	43	44	45	–2
1968	28	57	34	–29	49	41	36	42	8	40	44	44	–4
Average	40	69	50	–29	63	56	48	55	10	50	53	52	–2

(Table continues)

Table 5-5 *(Continued)*

	Party				*Region*					*Income* [a, b]			
President/year	Rep.	Dem.	Ind.	Difference[c]	East	Midwest	South	West	Difference[d]	High	Middle	Low	Difference[e]
Nixon, I													
1969	82	50	61	32	60	63	64	62	–2	66	62	58	8
1970	82	41	59	41	55	55	61	58	–5	62	56	53	9
1971	82	36	49	46	51	49	53	47	–4	56	51	44	12
1972	86	41	59	45	56	56	64	50	–10	62	57	53	9
Average	83	42	57	41	55	56	61	54	–6	62	56	52	10
Nixon, II													
1973	71	29	45	42	41	44	49	41	–7	52	45	41	11
1974	52	13	25	39	21	25	31	25	–7	28	24	24	4
Average	61	21	35	40	31	34	40	33	–6	40	35	33	7
Ford													
1974	70	47	55	23	57	63	58	60	2	65	58	54	11
1975	64	34	44	30	41	46	44	44	0	49	42	35	14
1976	72	37	51	35	44	52	51	50	–2	52	43	40	12
Average	68	39	50	29	47	54	51	51	0	55	48	43	12
Carter													
1977	48	73	62	–25	63	62	64	61	–2	64	63	61	3
1978	28	57	45	–29	47	46	48	45	–2	43	48	53	–10
1979	23	46	34	–23	35	32	39	34	–5	33	36	37	–4
1980	25	55	34	–30	39	41	49	36	–10	47	41	47	0
Average	31	58	44	–27	46	45	50	44	–5	47	47	49	–2
Reagan, I													
1981	85	41	59	44	55	59	59	58	–2	68	56	39	29
1982	79	24	46	55	43	46	43	46	2	56	43	30	26

1983	79	27	49	52	45	47	46	47	0	58	50	34	24
1984	88	32	59	56	54	55	59	55	–4	70	62	44	26
Average	83	31	53	52	49	52	52	51	–1	63	52	37	26
Reagan, II													
1985	89	35	62	54	59	60	64	61	–4	70	66	51	19
1986	85	40	60	45	60	59	61	62	–1	73	67	55	18
1987	78	24	50	54	47	48	52	48	–4	57	48	37	20
1988	82	27	52	55	49	51	56	53	–5	60	51	45	15
Average	83	32	56	51	54	55	58	56	–3	65	58	47	18
G. H. W. Bush													
1989	80	47	58	33	60	61	65	60	–5	67	60	56	11
1990	88	58	68	30	68	70	75	69	–6	78	70	64	14
1991	89	58	69	31	70	72	76	72	–5	80	75	65	15
1992	71	18	36	53	38	40	43	41	–3	46	42	35	11
Average	82	45	58	37	59	61	65	60	–5	68	62	55	13
Clinton, I													
1993	25	77	44	–52	55	52	47	49	5	46	50	55	–9
1994	21	77	47	–56	55	49	45	48	6	43	49	52	–9
1995	20	76	47	–56	53	47	43	48	6	42	46	54	–12
1996	23	85	54	–62	61	55	54	54	3	52	54	61	–9
Average	22	79	48	–57	56	51	47	50	5	46	50	55	–9
Clinton, II													
1997	29	85	53	–56	61	56	54	58	4	51	56	63	–12
1998	37	88	62	–51	72	61	61	62	4	59	62	67	–8
1999	35	91	69	–56	—	—	—	—		—	—	—	—
2000	36	89	65	–53	68	65	67	69	0	47	60	71	–24
Average	34	88	62	–54	67	61	61	63	3	52	60	67	–15
G. W. Bush, I													
2001	92	45	63	47	53	58	61	48	–8	63		46	17

(Table continues)

Table 5-5 *(Continued)*

	Party				*Region*					*Income*[a, b]			
President/year	Rep.	Dem.	Ind.	Difference[c]	East	Midwest	South	West	Difference[d]	High	Middle	Low.	Difference[e]
G. W. Bush, I (continued)													
2002	95	54	67	41	62	72	71	69	–3	72	72	63	9
2003	92	32	54	60	56	58	55	46	–2	—	—	—	—
2004	91	15	45	76	42	52	55	47	–8	55	53	44	11
Average	92	37	57	55	53	60	61	52	–6	63	63	51	12
G. W. Bush, II													
2005	87	15	38	72	39	44	49	43	–7	50	46	38	12
2006	80	9	30	71	30	36	44	38	–9	44	39	28	16
2007	73	8	27	65	29	33	40	32	–9	41	34	27	14
Average	80	10	32	70	33	38	44	38	–8	45	40	31	14

Source: Adapted from Table 5-4.

Note: "—" indicates not available.

[a] Gallup provides respondents with a series of family income categories for self-placement. These have been collapsed into three broad classifications of low, middle, and high income. The income categories reported by Gallup that were at or below the family poverty line, as taken from census data, constitutes the low-income category. Gallup breakdowns that ranged around the national mean income, again as reported by the census, represent the middle-income classification. Finally, incomes that fell into the highest brackets specified by Gallup make up the high-income category.

[b] Data on income from 1953–1964 are not available.

[c] Entries are the differences in approval ratings between Republicans and Democrats.

[d] Entries are the differences in approval ratings between non-South (average of East, Midwest, and West) and the South.

[e] Entries are the differences in approval ratings between high and low income groups.

Table 5-6 Quarterly Presidential Approval, by Race and Sex, Eisenhower, I to G. W. Bush, II (average percent per quarter)

	Race		*Sex*	
President/year/quarter	White	Nonwhite[a]	Men	Women
Eisenhower, I				
1953/1	71	56	71	69
1953/2	75	57	74	73
1953/3	69	56	68	70
1953/4	65	49	62	65
1954/1	70	54	69	69
1954/2	65	48	62	64
1954/3	68	56	67	68
1954/4	65	56	65	64
1955/1	71	58	70	70
1955/2	69	63	70	68
1955/3	73	64	73	72
1955/4	77	71	75	78
1956/1	76	65	74	75
1956/2	72	60	70	72
1956/3	70	60	68	70
1956/4	77	73	78	76
Eisenhower, II				
1957/1	72	60	70	72
1957/2	63	55	63	64
1957/3	62	55	60	63
1957/4	56	68	59	56
1958/1	54	54	52	56
1958/2	54	50	51	56
1958/3	56	50	54	57
1958/4	56	46	54	56
1959/1	59	48	58	59
1959/2	64	50	62	60
1959/3	65	60	64	66
1959/4	70	61	68	70
1960/1	66	56	63	67
1960/2	64	47	61	62
1960/3	62	50	58	62
1960/4	61	44	58	60
Kennedy				
1961/1	72	77	73	72
1961/2	74	80	76	75
1961/3	76	80	79	75
1961/4	77	84	80	76
1962/1	79	82	78	80
1962/2	71	86	73	73
1962/3	64	86	66	65
1962/4	69	85	71	70
1963/1	68	85	70	70
1963/2	61	85	63	65

(Table continues)

Table 5-6 (*Continued*)

	Race		Sex	
President/year/quarter	White	Nonwhite[a]	Men	Women
Kennedy (continued)				
1963/3	56	87	57	62
1963/4	54	87	57	60
L. Johnson[b]				
1963/4	76	76	77	75
1964/1	76	81	77	76
1964/2	72	86	75	73
1964/3	—	—	—	—
1964/4	68	95	72	68
1965/1	67	89	70	69
1965/2	65	86	68	66
1965/3	61	90	65	64
1965/4	60	85	64	62
1966/1	55	82	59	57
1966/2	48	74	51	48
1966/3	47	78	52	48
1966/4	43	71	47	44
1967/1	43	66	48	44
1967/2	46	66	49	46
1967/3	39	67	41	40
1967/4	40	61	44	41
1968/1	41	63	41	42
1968/2	42	60	45	43
1968/3	35	58	39	38
1968/4	42	71	45	43
Nixon, I				
1969/1	60	50	60	58
1969/2	66	38	64	62
1969/3	63	42	62	60
1969/4	62	33	63	57
1970/1	64	30	62	56
1970/2	60	26	60	54
1970/3	59	27	57	55
1970/4	58	29	59	52
1971/1	54	31	55	49
1971/2	52	25	50	48
1971/3	53	26	49	50
1971/4	53	23	52	49
1972/1	56	25	55	51
1972/2	61	34	60	56
1972/3	—	—	—	—
1972/4	66	27	64	59
Nixon, II				
1973/1	64	31	62	59
1973/2	51	20	47	47
1973/3	37	14	35	34

Table 5-6 *(Continued)*

President/year/quarter	*Race*		*Sex*	
	White	Nonwhite[a]	Men	Women
Nixon, II (continued)				
1973/4	31	12	29	28
1974/1	29	9	27	26
1974/2	29	11	27	26
1974/3	26	9	25	23
Ford				
1974/3	64	51	62	63
1974/4	51	30	47	50
1975/1	41	22	37	39
1975/2	48	25	45	45
1975/3	47	29	44	46
1975/4	46	25	44	44
1976/1	49	30	48	47
1976/2	49	33	46	47
1976/3	—	—	—	—
1976/4	58	27	53	54
Carter				
1977/1	70	76	71	70
1977/2	64	66	64	64
1977/3	61	66	63	60
1977/4	54	62	55	55
1978/1	49	58	50	50
1978/2	41	54	42	42
1978/3	41	52	42	42
1978/4	49	61	50	54
1979/1	42	51	43	43
1979/2	32	41	31	34
1979/3	37	39	31	32
1979/4	39	45	39	40
1980/1	50	56	50	51
1980/2	37	39	35	39
1980/3	31	51	32	36
1980/4	30	55	29	36
Reagan, I				
1981/1	60	22	59	52
1981/2	69	23	67	59
1981/3	63	19	63	52
1981/4	58	18	57	48
1982/1	53	13	57	44
1982/2	50	15	49	40
1982/3	46	14	46	37
1982/4	47	14	47	39
1983/1	42	13	42	34
1983/2	48	18	48	34
1983/3	50	14	50	39
1983/4	55	18	56	46

(Table continues)

Table 5-6 *(Continued)*

	Race		*Sex*	
President/year/quarter	White	Nonwhite[a]	Men	Women
Reagan, I (continued)				
1984/1	59	19	59	50
1984/2	58	21	58	50
1984/3	60	18	59	51
1984/4	66	24	64	57
Reagan, II				
1985/1	65	32	63	58
1985/2	60	23	58	51
1985/3	65	34	66	58
1985/4	67	35	67	60
1986/1	67	35	68	60
1986/2	67	37	70	58
1986/3	66	36	65	59
1986/4	55	32	56	50
1987/1	50	21	49	43
1987/2	53	24	53	46
1987/3	51	21	54	42
1987/4	53	23	55	45
1988/1	53	23	56	44
1988/2	53	25	54	45
1988/3	57	25	59	48
1988/4	61	29	62	52
G.H.W. Bush				
1989/1	58	50	60	54
1989/2	63	49	64	59
1989/3	71	57	75	66
1989/4	72	57	71	67
1990/1	78	62	79	72
1990/2	69	58	69	66
1990/3	71	45	73	63
1990/4	61	28	62	53
1991/1	82	55	86	78
1991/2	77	53	77	72
1991/3	73	55	72	68
1991/4	53	40	56	46
1992/1	45	29	45	41
1992/2	43	25	39	42
1992/3	38	19	39	33
1992/4	45	23	44	40
Clinton, I				
1993/1	53	77	55	56
1993/2	45	73	44	51
1993/3	45	65	45	49
1993/4	46	73	47	52
1994/1	51	71	53	55

Table 5-6 *(Continued)*

President/year/quarter	*Race*		*Sex*	
	White	Nonwhite[a]	Men	Women
Clinton, I (continued)				
1994/2	46	71	50	50
1994/3	41	64	42	45
1994/4	44	72	48	47
1995/1	41	62	41	47
1995/2	46	67	48	50
1995/3	43	68	44	51
1995/4	48	71	48	54
1996/1	48	75	49	56
1996/2	51	72	51	56
1996/3	56	84	58	60
1996/4	52	81	55	58
Clinton, II				
1997/1	56	76	58	59
1997/2	50	81	50	59
1997/3	54	78	57	59
1997/4[c]	—	—	63	61
1998/1	54	78	59	57
1998/2	57	79	59	61
1998/3	—	—	59	66
1998/4	70	86	65	79
1999/1	—	—	—	—
1999/2	—	—	—	—
1999/3	—	—	—	—
1999/4	—	—	—	—
2000/1	—	—	—	—
2000/2	—	—	—	—
2000/3[d]	62	81	67	68
2000/4	—	—	55	58
G. W. Bush, I				
2001/1	61	35	64	50
2001/2	58	48	58	47
2001/3	62	34	62	52
2001/4	—	—	94	63
2002/1	—	—	77	70
2002/2	74	57	75	70
2002/3	72	54	64	67
2002/4	—	—	75	70
2003/1	58	42	57	58
2003/2	69	50	62	64
2003/3	—	—	67	57
2003/4	—	—	67	57
2004/1	65	20	58	56
2004/2	61	28	51	45
2004/3[d]	57	28	56	47
2004/4[e]	55	22	53	45

(Table continues)

Table 5-6 *(Continued)*

	Race		Sex	
President/year/quarter	White	Nonwhite[a]	Men	Women
G. W. Bush, II				
2005/1	56	22	53	51
2005/2	47	29	—	—
2005/3	44	18	39	38
2005/4 [e]	48	27	47	40
2006/1	47	15	47	40
2006/2	36	26	35	31
2006/3	42	22	42	34
2006/4	41	19	41	34
2007/1	40	19	40	32
2007/2	32	13	—	—
2007/3	—	—	—	—
2007/4	36	8	35	29

Sources: (1953–1988) George Edwards III and George Gallup, *Presidential Approval* (Baltimore: Johns Hopkins University Press, 1989), reprinted by permission of the Johns Hopkins University Press; (1989–1996) successive volumes of *Gallup Poll Monthly*; (1997–2007) George Gallup, *The Gallup Poll* (Lanham, Md.: Rowman and Littlefield), successive volumes, 1997–2007, http://brain.gallup.com, and www.gallup.com, unless otherwise noted.

Note: Each number is the average of all Gallup polls for which the breakdowns were reported for that quarter. "—" indicates not available.

[a] Includes African Americans, Mexican Americans, Native Americans, and Asian Americans.
[b] Includes full term from Nov. 1963 to Jan. 1969.
[c] *Newsweek* poll results.
[d] American National Election Study results.
[e] Pew Research Center for the People and the Press results.

Table 5-7 Annual and Average Presidential Approval, by Race and Sex, Eisenhower, I to G. W. Bush, II (average percent)

	Race			Sex		
President/year	White	Nonwhite[a]	Difference[b]	Men	Women	Difference[c]
Eisenhower, I						
1953	70	55	15	69	69	0
1954	67	54	13	66	66	0
1955	73	64	9	72	72	0
1956	74	65	9	73	73	0
Average	71	59	12	70	70	0
Eisenhower, II						
1957	63	60	3	63	64	–1
1958	55	50	5	53	56	–3
1959	65	55	10	63	64	–1
1960	63	49	14	60	63	–3
Average	62	53	9	60	62	–2
Kennedy						
1961	75	80	–5	77	75	2
1962	71	85	–14	72	72	0
1963	60	86	–26	62	64	–2
Average	68	84	–16	70	70	0
L. Johnson						
1963/1964	73	85	–12	75	73	2
1965	63	88	–25	67	65	2
1966	48	76	–28	52	49	3
1967	42	65	–23	46	43	3
1968	40	63	–23	43	42	1
Average	53	75	–22	57	54	3
Nixon, I						
1969	63	41	22	62	59	3
1970	60	28	32	60	54	6
1971	53	26	27	52	49	3
1972	61	29	32	60	55	5
Average	59	31	28	58	55	3
Nixon, II						
1973	46	19	27	43	42	1
1974	28	10	18	26	25	1
Average	37	15	22	35	34	1
Ford						
1974	58	41	17	55	57	–2
1975	46	25	21	43	44	–1
1976	52	30	22	49	49	0
Average	52	32	20	49	50	–1

(Table continues)

Table 5-7 *(Continued)*

	Race			*Sex*		
President/year	White	Nonwhite[a]	Difference[b]	Men	Women	Difference[c]
Carter						
1977	62	68	–5	63	62	1
1978	45	56	–11	46	47	–1
1979	38	44	–7	36	37	–1
1980	37	50	–13	37	41	–4
Average	45	55	–9	45	47	–2
Reagan, I						
1981	63	21	42	62	53	9
1982	49	14	35	50	40	10
1983	49	16	33	49	38	11
1984	61	21	40	60	52	8
Average	55	18	38	55	46	9
Reagan, II						
1985	64	31	33	64	57	7
1986	64	35	29	65	57	8
1987	52	22	30	53	44	9
1988	56	26	31	58	47	11
Average	59	28	31	60	51	9
G. H. W. Bush						
1989	66	53	13	68	62	6
1990	70	48	22	71	64	7
1991	71	51	21	73	66	7
1992	43	24	19	42	39	3
Average	62	44	18	63	58	5
Clinton, I						
1993	47	72	–25	48	52	–4
1994	46	70	–24	48	49	–1
1995	45	67	–23	45	51	–6
1996	52	78	–26	53	58	–5
Average	47	72	–24	49	52	–3
Clinton, II						
1997	53	78	–25	57	60	–3
1998	60	81	–21	61	66	–5
1999	—	—	—	—	—	—
2000	62	81	–19	61	63	–2
Average	59	80	–22	60	63	–3
G. W. Bush, I						
2001	60	39	21	70	53	17
2002	73	56	18	71	69	2

Table 5-7 *(Continued)*

	Race			*Sex*		
President/year	White	Nonwhite[a]	Difference[b]	Men	Women	Difference[c]
G. W. Bush, I (continued)						
2003	64	46	18	63	59	4
2004	60	25	35	55	48	7
Average	64	41	23	65	57	8
G. W. Bush, II						
2005	49	24	25	46	43	3
2006	42	21	21	41	35	6
2007	36	13	23	38	31	7
Average	42	19	23	42	36	6

Source: Adapted from Table 5–6.

[a] Includes African Americans, Mexican Americans, Native Americans, and Asian Americans.
[b] Entries are the differences in approval ratings between whites and nonwhites.
[c] Entries are the differences in approval ratings between men and women.

Table 5-8 Quarterly Presidential Approval, by Age and Education, Eisenhower, I to G.W. Bush, II (average percent per quarter)

	Age			*Education*			
President/year/quarter	18–29	30–49	50 and over	Grade school	High school	College	Postgraduate
Eisenhower, I							
1953/1	71	68	71	64	72	78	—
1953/2	73	73	74	66	76	85	—
1953/3	71	69	69	62	72	72	—
1953/4	65	63	64	57	65	70	—
1954/1	70	66	71	63	69	76	—
1954/2	62	61	67	57	65	72	—
1954/3	67	66	69	65	68	74	—
1954/4	64	63	67	58	66	72	—
1955/1	69	69	71	63	71	79	—
1955/2	67	68	71	65	69	77	—
1955/3	73	72	73	66	74	81	—
1955/4	78	76	78	73	78	80	—
1956/1	76	73	75	69	76	81	—
1956/2	73	70	72	66	72	78	—
1956/3	72	68	69	64	69	75	—
1956/4	79	76	78	73	79	79	—
Eisenhower, II							
1957/1	73	71	69	66	72	74	—
1957/2	69	64	61	60	65	68	—
1957/3	65	61	60	57	62	68	—
1957/4	61	57	58	53	58	64	—
1958/1	58	53	55	60	55	59	—
1958/2	56	52	54	47	54	61	—
1958/3	57	54	56	53	56	61	—

1958/4	59	56	54	52	56	60	—
1959/1	61	56	61	53	59	66	—
1959/2	64	61	63	56	64	69	—
1959/3	68	64	64	57	67	73	—
1959/4	71	68	69	62	71	77	—
1960/1	69	64	65	57	68	72	—
1960/2	63	62	61	58	63	67	—
1960/3	62	59	62	58	61	64	—
1960/4	62	57	60	54	61	63	—
Kennedy							
1961/1	77	75	68	71	72	76	—
1961/2	79	78	70	73	77	72	—
1961/3	80	79	72	75	78	73	—
1961/4	82	80	74	77	81	76	—
1962/1	87	80	74	77	81	76	—
1962/2	81	76	67	74	75	66	—
1962/3	77	69	58	65	67	62	—
1962/4	78	73	65	69	74	64	—
1963/1	79	74	63	68	73	67	—
1963/2	71	67	57	63	67	59	—
1963/3	67	62	54	60	61	57	—
1963/4	69	61	53	59	60	53	—
L. Johnson[a]							
1963/4	77	75	68	69	72	66	—
1964/1	81	76	76	75	77	79	—
1964/2	76	76	72	73	75	74	—
1964/3	—	—	—	—	—	—	—
1964/4	68	73	68	74	71	65	—
1965/1	71	71	68	69	72	66	—
1965/2	70	69	65	66	68	66	—
1965/3	72	64	62	64	67	61	—
1965/4	68	65	59	63	64	60	—
1966/1	61	59	56	60	58	54	—

(Table continues)

Table 5-8 *(Continued)*

	Age			*Education*			
President/year/quarter	18–29	30–49	50 and over	Grade school	High school	College	Postgraduate
L. Johnson[a] (continued)							
1966/2	54	52	46	51	50	48	—
1966/3	55	52	46	51	51	48	—
1966/4	48	44	46	49	46	38	—
1967/1	45	45	46	47	46	43	—
1967/2	49	48	46	45	48	48	—
1967/3	43	41	40	41	41	39	—
1967/4	40	44	41	40	44	40	—
1968/1	36	41	44	46	42	36	—
1968/2	42	45	44	44	44	44	—
1968/3	36	38	40	42	38	36	—
1968/4	44	43	45	47	45	36	—
Nixon, I							
1969/1	61	59	58	53	60	64	—
1969/2	65	63	62	57	63	70	—
1969/3	64	61	59	53	63	65	—
1969/4	61	59	61	52	61	66	—
1970/1	59	59	59	51	59	67	—
1970/2	58	58	55	48	57	65	—
1970/3	53	57	57	52	56	58	—
1970/4	53	56	57	51	57	57	—
1971/1	50	51	53	45	51	59	—
1971/2	45	51	50	46	50	50	—
1971/3	45	49	54	48	50	53	—
1971/4	47	52	52	42	50	57	—
1972/1	49	55	54	44	53	60	—

1972/2	54	56	59	54	58	61	—
1972/3	—	—	—	—	—	—	—
1972/4	56	61	64	59	62	62	—
Nixon, II							
1973/1	55	62	64	55	62	61	—
1973/2	43	49	47	42	48	48	—
1973/3	32	33	38	31	35	38	—
1973/4	24	28	39	34	33	35	—
1974/1	23	25	30	27	26	27	—
1974/2	22	26	30	27	26	28	—
1974/3	20	24	26	21	24	26	—
Ford							
1974/3	64	61	62	58	60	70	—
1974/4	51	48	47	42	49	53	—
1975/1	40	38	37	29	37	46	—
1975/2	45	45	44	37	44	54	—
1975/3	50	46	41	32	44	58	—
1975/4	48	46	39	35	44	50	—
1976/1	50	46	46	40	47	52	—
1976/2	50	48	45	40	46	52	—
1976/3	—	—	—	—	—	—	—
1976/4	56	47	56	45	52	59	—
Carter							
1977/1	75	71	67	67	71	73	—
1977/2	69	65	60	60	62	71	—
1977/3	67	62	56	55	60	67	—
1977/4	60	55	50	52	54	57	—
1978/1	55	50	47	52	49	49	—
1978/2	48	40	39	45	41	41	—
1978/3	46	40	41	46	42	39	—
1978/4	53	50	51	56	51	49	—
1979/1	53	49	47	51	49	52	—

(Table continues)

Table 5-8 *(Continued)*

	Age			*Education*			
President/year/quarter	18–29	30–49	50 and over	Grade school	High school	College	Postgraduate
Carter (continued)							
1979/2	37	31	31	35	32	35	—
1979/3	33	31	31	34	31	31	—
1979/4	41	37	40	42	39	39	—
1980/1	52	49	51	53	50	50	—
1980/2	40	34	37	40	37	35	—
1980/3	37	31	35	41	35	29	—
1980/4	38	28	33	38	35	26	—
Reagan, I							
1981/1	54	58	54	36	57	62	—
1981/2	62	66	72	47	63	71	—
1981/3	57	60	56	41	57	66	—
1981/4	52	54	51	38	52	60	—
1982/1	47	49	47	32	47	55	—
1982/2	44	46	44	35	42	54	—
1982/3	43	42	40	32	40	50	—
1982/4	41	43	43	29	41	51	—
1983/1	40	39	43	24	37	48	—
1983/2	42	46	43	32	42	53	—
1983/3	46	45	43	31	42	54	—
1983/4	49	52	50	40	48	56	—
1984/1	55	56	52	40	52	61	—
1984/2	56	56	51	36	51	62	—
1984/3	55	57	52	41	52	61	—
1984/4	62	60	59	45	57	65	—
1985/1	66	59	57	43	59	66	—

1985/2	58	57	50	36	51	63	—
1985/3	65	63	57	42	60	67	—
1985/4	66	64	60	47	62	69	—
1986/1	67	66	59	51	61	69	—
1986/2	68	67	58	44	63	69	—
1986/3	69	65	54	44	61	67	—
1986/4	56	54	48	48	54	59	—
1987/1	50	48	41	35	44	50	—
1987/2	53	52	48	40	49	51	—
1987/3	52	49	42	37	44	53	—
1987/4	55	51	45	44	48	53	—
1988/1	54	49	48	41	49	53	—
1988/2	54	48	47	43	48	51	—
1988/3	60	53	48	41	52	56	—
1988/4	59	58	54	50	55	59	—
G. H. W. Bush							
1989/1	54	50	50	41	53	58	—
1989/2	63	60	49	41	56	62	—
1989/3	70	70	68	64	70	74	—
1989/4	70	72	72	68	71	71	—
1990/1	73	75	71	63	74	78	—
1990/2	68	68	62	57	67	71	—
1990/3	63	66	53	46	61	70	—
1990/4	53	63	46	45	52	61	—
1991/1	73	74	76	75	76	70	—
1991/2	84	84	78	72	83	84	—
1991/3	73	74	66	64	75	68	—
1991/4	60	54	37	50	50	47	—
1992/1	54	41	35	34	42	46	—
1992/2	46	43	37	39	40	43	—
1992/3	39	31	28	27	35	40	—
1992/4	44	43	43	36	39	50	—

(Table continues)

Table 5-8 *(Continued)*

	Age			*Education*			
President/year/quarter	18–29	30–49	50 and over	Grade school	High school	College	Postgraduate
Clinton, I							
1993/1[b]	60	54	54	—	52	56	57
1993/2	55	48	45	—	39	42	44
1993/3	47	48	49	—	51	51	58
1993/4	51	49	50	—	51	55	61
1994/1	54	54	53	—	54	54	60
1994/2	50	51	49	—	50	47	50
1994/3	46	43	44	—	42	37	37
1994/4	50	47	48	—	42	41	47
1995/1	44	41	47	—	47	44	48
1995/2	49	50	49	—	53	50	51
1995/3	47	45	49	—	46	48	50
1995/4	50	48	56	—	52	50	50
1996/1	53	50	55	—	55	51	51
1996/2	51	53	57	—	56	52	60
1996/3	50	59	58	—	61	58	56
1996/4	58	58	54	—	59	57	57
Clinton, II				—			
1997/1	61	59	57	—	60	57	63
1997/2	55	56	53	—	53	58	56
1997/3	64	57	57	—	59	57	58
1997/4	—	—	—	—	—	—	—
1998/1	58	60	57	—	63	53	69
1998/2	59	64	57	—	64	58	57
1998/3	59	62	66	—	—	—	—
1998/4	71	71	75	—	75	67	76

1999/1	—	—	—	—	—	—	—
1999/2	—	—	—	—	—	—	—
1999/3	—	—	—	—	—	—	—
1999/4	—	—	—	—	—	—	—
2000/1	—	—	—	—	—	—	—
2000/2	—	—	—	—	—	—	—
2000/3[c]	67	60	58	75	70	60	68
2000/4	—	—	—	—	—	—	—
G.W. Bush, I				—			
2001/1	—	—	—	—	—	—	—
2001/2	—	—	—	—	—	—	—
2001/3	55	59	52	—	—	—	—
2001/4	84	89	89	—	—	—	—
2002/1	—	—	—	—	—	—	—
2002/2	63	64	60	—	—	—	—
2002/3	69	73	67	—	—	—	—
2002/4	—	—	—	—	—	—	—
2003/1[d]	52	55	51	18	50	55	52
2003/2	64	61	60	—	—	—	—
2003/3	53	56	50	—	51	52	43
2003/4	51	60	50	—	—	—	—
2004/1	57	66	54	—	57	56	48
2004/2	44	49	45	—	48	47	44
2004/3[c]	38	52	50	38	55	51	39
2004/4	40	49	52	—	—	—	—
G.W. Bush, II							
2005/1	46	55	51	—	52	54	43
2005/2	—	—	—	—	—	—	—
2005/3[e]	33	39	41	40	39	40	—
2005/4	39	44	44	—	42	46	39
2006/1	39	46	42	—	40	49	37
2006/2	28	35	33	—	30	39	30
2006/3	31	41	38	—	36	41	30

(Table continues)

Table 5-8 *(Continued)*

	Age			*Education*			
President/year/quarter	18–29	30–49	50 and over	Grade school	High school	College	Postgraduate
G. W. Bush, II (continued)							
2006/4	29	41	36	—	41	38	33
2007/1	33	38	35	—	34	39	33
2007/2	—	—	—	—	—	—	—
2007/3	—	—	—	—	—	—	—
2007/4	27	35	32	—	30	36	27

Sources: (1953–1988) George Edwards III and George Gallup, *Presidential Approval* (Baltimore: Johns Hopkins University Press, 1989), reprinted by permission of the Johns Hopkins University Press; (1989–1996) successive volumes of *Gallup Poll Monthly*; (1997–2007) George Gallup, *The Gallup Poll* (Lanham, Md.: Rowman and Littlefield), successive volumes, 1997–2007, http://brain.gallup.com, and www.gallup.com, unless otherwise noted.

Note: Figures are the average of all Gallup polls for which the breakdowns were reported for that quarter. "—" indicates not available.

[a] Includes full term from Nov. 1963 to Jan. 1969.
[b] Due to a change in Gallup survey techniques in 1993, grade school data no longer available and postgraduate data becomes available.
[c] American National Election Study results.
[d] Harris Poll results.
[e] Pew Research Center for the People and the Press results.

Table 5-9 Annual and Term Average Approval, by Age and Education, Eisenhower, I to G. W. Bush, II (average percent)

	Age				*Education*				
President/year	18–29	30–49	50 and over	Difference[a]	Grade school	High School	College	Postgraduate	Difference[b]
Eisenhower, I									
1953	70	68	70	0	62	71	76	—	–5
1954	66	64	69	–3	61	67	74	—	–7
1955	72	71	73	–1	67	73	79	—	–6
1956	75	72	74	1	68	74	78	—	–4
Average	71	69	71	0	64	71	77	—	–6
Eisenhower, II									
1957	67	63	62	5	59	64	69	—	–5
1958	58	54	55	3	53	55	60	—	–5
1959	66	62	64	2	57	65	71	—	–6
1960	64	61	62	2	57	63	67	—	–4
Average	64	60	61	3	56	62	67	—	–5
Kennedy									
1961	80	78	71	9	74	77	74	—	3
1962	81	75	66	15	71	74	67	—	7
1963	72	66	57	15	63	65	59	—	6
Average	77	73	65	13	69	72	67	—	5
L. Johnson									
1963/1964	76	75	71	5	73	74	71	—	3
1965	70	67	64	6	66	68	63	—	5
1966	55	52	49	6	53	51	47	—	4
1967	44	45	43	1	43	45	43	—	2

(Table continues)

Table 5-9 *(Continued)*

	Age				*Education*				
President/year	18–29	30–49	50 and over	Difference[a]	Grade school	High School	College	Postgraduate	Difference[b]
L. Johnson (continued)									
1968	40	42	43	–3	45	42	38	—	4
Average	57	56	54	3	56	56	52	—	4
Nixon, I									
1969	63	61	60	3	54	62	66	—	–4
1970	60	58	57	3	55	59	59	—	–0
1971	47	51	52	–5	45	50	55	—	–5
1972	53	57	59	–6	52	58	61	—	–3
Average	56	57	57	–1	52	57	60	—	–3
Nixon, II									
1973	39	43	47	–8	41	45	46	—	–1
1974	22	25	29	–7	25	25	27	—	–2
Average	30	34	38	–8	33	35	36	—	–1
Ford									
1974	58	55	55	3	50	55	62	—	–7
1975	46	44	40	6	33	42	52	—	–10
1976	52	47	49	3	42	48	54	—	–6
Average	52	48	48	4	42	48	56	—	–8
Carter									
1977	68	63	58	10	59	62	67	—	–5
1978	51	45	45	6	50	46	45	—	1
1979	41	37	37	4	41	38	39	—	–1
1980	42	36	39	3	43	39	35	—	4
Average	50	45	45	5	48	46	46	—	0

Reagan, I									
1981	56	60	58	–2	41	57	65	—	–8
1982	44	45	44	0	32	43	53	—	–10
1983	44	46	45	–1	32	42	53	—	–11
1984	48	50	49	–1	35	47	57	—	–10
Average	48	50	49	–1	35	47	57	—	–10
Reagan, II									
1985	64	61	56	8	42	58	66	—	–8
1986	65	63	55	10	47	60	66	—	–6
1987	53	50	44	9	39	46	52	—	–6
1988	57	52	49	8	44	51	55	—	–4
Average	60	56	51	9	43	54	60	—	–6
G. H. W. Bush									
1989	64	63	60	4	54	63	66	—	–3
1990	64	68	58	6	53	64	70	—	–6
1991	73	72	64	9	65	71	67	—	4
1992	46	40	36	10	34	39	45	—	–6
Average	62	61	54	8	51	59	62	—	–3
Clinton, I									
1993	53	50	50	3	—	48	51	55	–3
1994	50	49	49	1	—	47	45	49	2
1995	48	46	50	–2	—	50	48	50	2
1996	53	55	56	–3	—	58	55	56	3
Average	51	50	51	0	—	51	50	52	1
Clinton, II									
1997	60	57	56	4	—	57	57	—	0
1998	62	64	64	–2	—	67	59	—	8
1999	—	—	—	—	—	—	—	—	—
2000	67	60	58	9	75	70	60	68	10
Average	63	61	59	4	75	65	59	68	6

(Table continues)

Table 5-9 *(Continued)*

	Age				*Education*				
President/year	18–29	30–49	50 and over	Difference[a]	Grade school	High School	College	Postgraduate	Difference[b]
G.W. Bush, I									
2001	70	74	71	–1	—	—	—	—	—
2002	66	69	64	2	—	—	—	—	—
2003	55	58	53	2	18	51	54	48	–3
2004	45	54	50	–5	38	53	51	44	2
Average	59	64	59	0	28	52	52	46	0
G.W. Bush, II									
2005	39	46	45	–6	40	44	47	41	–3
2006	32	41	37	–5	—	37	42	33	–5
2007	30	37	34	–4	—	32	38	30	–6
Average	34	41	39	–5	40	38	42	35	–4

Source: Adapted from Table 5-8.

[a] Entries are the difference in approval ratings between young (18–29) and old (50 and over) age groups.
[b] Entries are the difference in approval ratings between high school graduates and college graduates.

Table 5-10 Public Approval of Presidents' Handling of the Economy and Foreign Policy, Nixon to G. W. Bush, II (percent)

	Economy[a]			*Foreign policy*[b]		
President/date	Approve	Disapprove	Don't know / no opinion	Approve	Disapprove	Don't know / no opinion
Nixon[c]						
June 21, 1974	—	—	—	54	32	14
Ford[c]						
Nov. 8, 1974	32	48	20	—	—	—
Jan. 31, 1975	29	57	14	—	—	—
April 18, 1975	30	59	11	—	—	—
Average	30					
Carter[c]						
May 1977	47	53	—	—	—	—
June 1977	44	56	—	—	—	—
July 1977	41	59	—	48	52	—
Aug. 1977	39	61	—	—	—	—
Sept. 1977	35	65	—	32	68	—
Oct. 1977	32	68	—	38	62	—
Nov. 1977	33	67	—	38	62	—
Dec. 1977	34	66	—	42	58	—
Jan. 1978	28	72	—	43	57	—
Feb. 1978	27	73	—	38	62	—
April 1978	22	78	—	29	71	—
June 1978	21	79	—	25	75	—
July 1978	16	84	—	22	78	—
Aug. 1978	16	84	—	22	78	—
Sept. 1978	22	78	—	56	44	—
Nov. 1978	23	77	—	47	53	—

(Table continues)

Table 5-10 *(Continued)*

	Economy [a]			*Foreign policy* [b]		
President/date	Approve	Disapprove	Don't know/ no opinion	Approve	Disapprove	Don't know/ no opinion
Carter[c] (continued)						
Dec. 1978	27	73	—	46	54	—
Feb. 1979	22	78	—	37	63	—
March 1979	16	84	—	45	55	—
Average	29			38		
Reagan, I						
Feb. 13, 1981	—	—	—	51	16	33
March 13, 1981	56	32	12	53	29	18
April 10, 1981	60	29	11	—	—	—
May 8, 1981	58	31	11	—	—	—
June 26, 1981	51	40	9	—	—	—
Aug. 14, 1981	53	35	12	—	—	—
Sept. 25, 1981	59	34	7	—	—	—
Oct. 1, 1981	53	37	9	—	—	—
Oct. 9, 1981	—	—	—	63	30	7
Oct. 30, 1981	45	43	12	—	—	—
Nov. 13, 1981	40	50	10	—	—	—
Nov. 17, 1981	46	46	8	—	—	—
Dec. 11, 1981	41	50	9	—	—	—
Jan. 8, 1982	41	51	8	—	—	—
Jan. 22, 1982	46	46	8	52	33	15
Feb. 5, 1982	38	53	9	44	38	18
Feb. 17, 1982	38	57	5	40	41	19
March 3, 1982	42	53	5	45	43	12

March 12, 1982	56	32	12	36	44	20
March 18, 1982	43	52	5	43	45	12
April 2, 1982	38	56	6	36	45	19
April 21, 1982	44	51	5	53	34	14
April 30, 1982	37	55	8	43	37	20
May 24, 1982	40	53	7	46	35	19
June 11, 1982	35	58	7	45	36	19
Aug. 17, 1982	40	55	5	—	—	—
Sept. 9, 1982	41	52	7	50	35	15
Sept. 24, 1982	40	55	5	43	45	13
Oct. 5, 1982	41	51	9	44	39	17
Oct. 15, 1982	36	56	8	38	39	23
Dec. 7, 1982	38	58	5	45	33	22
Jan. 14, 1983	29	64	7	36	41	23
Jan. 18, 1983	38	58	5	45	33	22
Feb. 25, 1983	43	54	3	—	—	—
April 8, 1983	42	54	4	—	—	—
April 15, 1983	29	64	7	32	44	24
Aug. 19, 1983	37	54	9	31	46	23
Nov. 18, 1983	48	46	6	46	41	13
Jan. 13, 1984	48	43	9	38	49	13
Feb. 10, 1984	49	44	7	40	46	14
May 3, 1984	48	46	6	42	44	14
May 18, 1984	49	43	8	37	48	15
Nov. 9, 1984	—	—	—	50	35	15
Nov. 30, 1984	57	36	7	—	—	—
Average	44			44		
Reagan, II						
Jan. 11, 1985	51	41	8	52	33	15
March 3, 1985	51	44	5	45	39	16
May 17, 1985	47	47	8	43	45	12
July 12, 1985	53	39	8	50	37	13

(Table continues)

Table 5-10 *(Continued)*

President/date	*Economy*[a] Approve	Disapprove	Don't know/ no opinion	*Foreign policy*[b] Approve	Disapprove	Don't know/ no opinion
Reagan, II (continued)						
Oct. 11, 1985	48	44	8	—	—	—
Jan. 10, 1986	53	38	9	50	34	16
April 11, 1986	50	40	10	52	35	13
July 11, 1986	49	43	8	51	35	14
Dec. 4, 1986	50	45	5	34	57	9
Jan. 16, 1987	—	—	—	33	57	10
April 10, 1987	42	53	5	33	57	10
June 8, 1987	48	49	3	37	57	6
Aug. 24, 1987	46	49	5	34	57	9
March 8, 1988	40	53	7	41	48	11
July 1, 1988	43	51	6	54	35	11
Average	48			44		
G. H. W. Bush						
March 10, 1989	52	27	21	62	15	23
Nov. 2, 1989	40	51	9	65	21	14
July 6, 1990	40	53	7	62	26	12
Oct. 11, 1990	30	65	5	61	29	10
March 7, 1991	37	—	—	79	—	—
March 28, 1991	37	56	7	79	11	10
June 27, 1991	36	58	6	64	28	8
July 25, 1991	34	59	7	71	19	10
Aug. 8, 1991	36	59	5	74	20	6
Aug. 23, 1991	36	—	—	74	—	—

Sept. 13, 1991	32	—	—	70	—	—
Oct. 3, 1991	29	64	7	70	25	5
Oct. 24, 1991	28	—	—	68	—	—
Dec. 5, 1991	22	73	—	64	30	—
Jan. 3, 1992	24	—	—	64	—	—
Jan. 31, 1992	22	—	—	65	—	—
Feb. 28, 1992	21	—	—	55	—	—
May 7, 1992	20	76	—	52	43	—
Average	32			67		
Clinton, I						
Feb. 12, 1993	45	35	20	53	22	25
March 29, 1993	49	42	9	55	30	15
April 22, 1993	43	50	7	53	34	13
May 21, 1993	35	59	6	44	43	12
June 18, 1993	36	56	8	48	36	16
June 29, 1993	35	59	6	56	33	11
July 9, 1993	34	60	6	49	38	13
Aug. 8, 1993	38	57	5	46	44	10
Aug. 23, 1993	38	53	9	48	39	13
Sept. 10, 1993	39	50	11	46	36	18
Sept. 24, 1993	47	45	8	55	32	13
Oct. 8, 1993	43	48	9	40	52	8
Nov. 2, 1993	37	57	6	34	57	9
Nov. 19, 1993	43	50	7	41	49	10
Dec. 4, 1993	47	46	7	45	44	11
Jan. 6, 1994	49	45	6	45	43	12
Jan. 15, 1994	46	47	7	54	36	10
Jan. 28, 1994	53	40	7	52	37	11
Feb. 26, 1994	48	48	4	51	40	9
March 7, 1994	51	42	7	51	38	11
April 22, 1994	45	48	7	39	51	10
May 20, 1994	50	45	5	37	52	11

(Table continues)

Table 5-10 *(Continued)*

President/date	*Economy* [a] Approve	Disapprove	Don't know/ no opinion	*Foreign policy* [b] Approve	Disapprove	Don't know/ no opinion
Clinton, I (continued)						
June 3, 1994	47	46	7	39	50	11
June 11, 1994	49	45	6	44	45	11
June 25, 1994	43	48	9	34	52	14
July 15, 1994	36	57	7	33	60	7
Aug. 15, 1994	42	49	9	34	52	14
Sept. 6, 1994	43	52	5	34	57	9
Sept. 23, 1994	40	55	5	40	55	5
Oct. 18, 1994	38	57	5	—	—	—
Oct. 22, 1994	42	53	5	—	—	—
Nov. 2, 1994	43	51	6	49	44	7
Dec. 2, 1994	43	50	7	44	46	10
Jan. 16, 1995	47	48	5	44	49	7
Feb. 3, 1995	46	49	5	44	45	11
June 5, 1995	42	49	9	49	51	9
July 7, 1995	41	52	7	44	44	12
July 20, 1995	47	46	7	37	54	9
Oct. 19, 1995	44	49	7	43	44	13
Dec. 15, 1995	47	45	8	46	48	6
Jan. 12, 1996	44	52	4	48	46	6
March 15, 1996	46	49	5	49	45	6
June 27, 1996	49	44	7	52	38	10
Aug. 23, 1996	54	40	6	53	40	7
Nov. 21, 1996	53	36	11	54	39	7
Average	44			45		

Clinton, II						
Feb. 24, 1997	56	36	8	46	34	20
March 24, 1997	57	35	8	51	35	14
May 6, 1997	59	33	8	50	38	12
Nov. 21, 1997	64	28	8	55	35	10
Jan. 23, 1998	73	22	5	57	34	9
Jan. 24, 1998	70	25	5	58	32	10
Jan. 25, 1998	69	25	6	62	29	9
April 17, 1998	73	20	7	63	31	6
June 5, 1998	71	22	7	57	36	7
June 22, 1998	69	24	7	53	36	11
July 7, 1998	71	24	5	56	34	10
Jan. 15, 1999	81	15	4	64	32	4
March 19, 1999	80	12	8	60	30	10
March 30, 1999	78	16	6	54	40	6
April 6, 1999	73	18	9	55	38	7
April 26, 1999	72	22	6	50	43	7
June 4, 1999	74	20	6	55	40	5
May 18, 2000	65	30	5	51	40	9
July 16, 2000	57	35	8	51	35	14
Oct. 9, 2000	56	36	8	46	34	20
Average	68			55		
G. W. Bush, I						
Feb. 1, 2001	53	27	20	46	21	33
March 9, 2001	55	32	13	52	27	21
April 20, 2001	55	38	7	56	31	13
May 18, 2001	51	41	8	55	35	10
July 10, 2001	54	36	10	54	33	13
Oct. 5, 2001	72	23	5	81	14	5
Nov. 2, 2001	71	24	5	—	—	—
Jan. 25, 2002	64	30	6	83	14	3

(Table continues)

Table 5-10 *(Continued)*

	Economy [a]			*Foreign policy* [b]		
President/date	Approve	Disapprove	Don't know/ no opinion	Approve	Disapprove	Don't know/ no opinion
G. W. Bush, I (continued)						
Feb. 4, 2002	66	30	4	79	16	5
March 1, 2002	64	31	5	78	17	5
March 22, 2002	65	29	6	71	22	7
April 5, 2002	60	33	7	70	24	7
May 20, 2002	61	29	10	70	23	7
June 28, 2002	63	33	4	66	27	7
July 5, 2002	58	36	6	71	25	4
July 26, 2002	52	43	5	63	30	7
Oct. 21, 2002	49	44	7	58	35	7
Nov. 8, 2002	55	39	6	59	36	5
Dec. 9, 2002	49	47	4	59	35	6
Jan. 3, 2003	49	47	4	60	35	5
Jan. 10, 2003	48	47	5	53	42	5
Jan. 23, 2003	46	49	5	50	45	5
Jan. 31, 2003	47	48	5	57	39	4
Feb. 3, 2003	44	52	4	49	46	5
March 14, 2003	44	52	4	53	43	4
March 24, 2003	52	42	6	65	30	4
March 29, 2003	49	47	4	64	31	5
April 14, 2003	49	45	6	65	31	4
May 5, 2003	53	44	3	68	30	2
June 12, 2003	48	48	4	58	39	3
July 7, 2003	48	50	2	55	42	3
July 18, 2003	45	51	4	54	41	5

July 25, 2003	46	51	3	54	42	4
Aug. 25, 2003	45	52	3	55	42	3
Sept. 8, 2003	45	53	2	52	45	3
Oct. 6, 2003	42	55	3	49	49	2
Nov. 3, 2003	47	50	3	46	50	4
Dec. 5, 2003	48	49	3	53	43	4
Jan. 2, 2004	54	43	3	58	39	3
Jan. 29, 2004	43	54	3	46	51	3
Feb. 9, 2004	45	52	3	46	52	2
March 26, 2004	42	55	3	—	—	—
April 16, 2004	46	52	2	—	—	—
May 2, 2004	41	56	3	42	53	5
May 7, 2004	41	56	3	47	49	4
June 3, 2004	41	58	1	44	51	5
June 21, 2004	47	50	3	—	—	—
Aug. 9, 2004	46	51	3	44	51	5
Sept. 24, 2004	49	48	3	49	48	3
Oct. 14, 2004	46	51	3	—	—	—
Nov. 7, 2004	47	51	2	47	50	3
Average	51			59		
G. W. Bush, II						
Jan. 7, 2005	50	48	2	47	49	4
Feb. 4, 2005	50	47	3	51	44	5
Feb. 7, 2005	45	52	3	45	52	3
Feb. 25, 2005	48	49	3	50	46	4
April 1, 2005	41	55	4	—	—	—
April 29, 2005	43	53	4	45	49	6
May 20, 2005	40	58	2	44	51	5
June 24, 2005	41	55	4	43	52	5
Aug. 28, 2005	38	60	2	38	58	4
Sept. 8, 2005	39	58	3	37	59	4
Sept. 16, 2005	35	63	2	38	58	4

(Table continues)

Table 5-10 *(Continued)*

	Economy [a]			*Foreign policy* [b]		
President/date	Approve	Disapprove	Don't know/ no opinion	Approve	Disapprove	Don't know/ no opinion
G. W. Bush, II (continued)						
Nov. 11, 2005	37	61	2	37	59	4
Dec. 9, 2005	40	58	2	42	53	5
Dec. 16, 2005	41	56	3	39	57	4
Jan. 20, 2006	39	56	4	—	—	—
Feb. 6, 2006	40	56	4	39	55	6
Feb. 28, 2006	40	57	3	—	—	—
April 7, 2006	39	58	4	—	—	—
April 28, 2006	34	64	2	33	62	5
June 9, 2006	39	57	4	39	53	8
July 21, 2006	39	59	3	38	56	6
Aug. 18, 2006	39	57	4	39	55	6
Oct. 6, 2006	40	55	5	—	—	—
Jan. 5, 2007	45	51	4	34	61	4
Jan. 12, 2007	45	51	4	36	60	5
Feb. 1, 2007	41	56	3	31	65	4
March 23, 2007	41	55	4	33	63	4
May 4, 2007	39	58	3	35	60	5
Aug. 13, 2007	35	61	4	29	65	6
Average	41			39		

Sources: (Nixon and Ford) Adapted from various volumes of *Gallup Opinion Index*; (Carter through G. H. W. Bush) adapted from various issues of the *Gallup Report* and *Gallup Poll Monthly*; (Clinton) adapted from http://brain.gallup.com; (George W. Bush) adapted from www.gallup.com/poll/1726/Presidential-Ratings-Issues-Approval.aspx.

Note: "—" indicates question not asked. No data available for 1976 and 1980.

[a] Question asked was: (Nixon and Carter) "How would you rate [incumbent] on his handling of the economy—excellent, pretty good, only fair, or poor?" (Reagan through Clinton) "Do you approve or disapprove of the way [incumbent] is handling the nation's economy?"

[b] Question asked was: (Nixon and Carter) "How would you rate [incumbent] on his handling of foreign policy—excellent, pretty good, only fair, or poor?" (Reagan through G. W. Bush) "Do you approve or disapprove of the way [incumbent] is handling foreign affairs?"

[c] Approval is the percentage who rated [incumbent] excellent or pretty good in each policy area.

Table 5-11 The Public's Most Important Problem, 1935–2007

Year	*Problem*
1935	Unemployment
1936	Unemployment
1937	Unemployment
1938	Keeping out of war
1939	Keeping out of war
1940	Keeping out of war
1941	Keeping out of war, winning war
1942	Winning war
1943	Winning war
1944	Winning war
1945	Winning war
1946	High cost of living
1947	High cost of living, labor unrest
1948	Keeping peace
1949	Labor unrest
1950	Labor unrest
1951	Korean War
1952	Korean War
1953	Keeping peace
1954	Keeping peace
1955	Keeping peace
1956	Keeping peace
1957	Race relations, keeping peace
1958	Unemployment, keeping peace
1959	Keeping peace
1960	Keeping peace
1961	Keeping peace
1962	Keeping peace
1963	Keeping peace, race relations
1964	Vietnam, race relations
1965	Vietnam, race relations
1966	Vietnam
1967	Vietnam, high cost of living
1968	Vietnam
1969	Vietnam
1970	Vietnam
1971	Vietnam, high cost of living
1972	Vietnam
1973	High cost of living, Watergate
1974	High cost of living, Watergate, energy crisis
1975	High cost of living, unemployment
1976	High cost of living, unemployment
1977	High cost of living, unemployment
1978	High cost of living, energy problems
1979	High cost of living, energy problems
1980	High cost of living, unemployment
1981	High cost of living, unemployment
1982	Unemployment, high cost of living

Table 5-11 *(Continued)*

Year	*Problem*
1983	Unemployment, high cost of living
1984	Unemployment, fear of war
1985	Fear of war
1986	Unemployment
1987	Fear of war
1988	Economy in general
1989	Drugs
1990	Economy in general
1991	Economy in general
1992	Economy in general
1993	Economy in general
1994	Crime / violence
1995	Crime / violence
1996	Budget deficit
1997	Crime / violence
1998	Crime / violence, ethical / moral / religious decline
1999	Crime / violence
2000	Crime / violence, education, ethical / moral / religious decline
2001	Education, economy in general
2002	Economy in general, terrorism, fear of war
2003	Economy in general
2004	War in Iraq
2005	War in Iraq
2006	War in Iraq
2007	War in Iraq

Sources: (1935–1984) Adapted from *Gallup Report,* Oct. 1984, 22; (1985–1996) adapted from various issues of *Gallup Poll Monthly*; (1997–2007) "Gallup Update: Iraq Remains Top Problem Facing the Nation" Sept. 21, 2007, at http://brain.gallup.com.

Table 5-12 The Party Best Able to Handle the Most Important Problem, 1945–2007 (percent)

Year	*Month*	*Republican*	*Democratic*	*Uncommitted*
1945	Aug.	23	48	29
1946	Aug.	35	34	31
1948	April	32	28	40
1950	Sept.	19	27	54
1956	Oct.	33	25	42
1958	Feb.	19	40	41
1958	March	23	39	38
1959	Feb.	26	34	40
1959	March	26	41	33
1959	Oct.	27	29	44
1960	March	24	32	44
1960	July	23	36	41
1960	Aug.	35	36	29
1960	Oct.	27	29	44
1962	April	16	40	44
1962	Sept.	17	33	50
1963	April	17	36	47
1963	Oct.	23	49	28
1964	March	16	39	45
1964	May	16	40	44
1964	July	25	38	37
1964	Oct.	23	49	28
1965	June	16	37	47
1965	Aug.	16	36	48
1965	Oct.	17	34	49
1965	Dec.	17	38	45
1966	May	22	29	49
1966	Sept.	21	28	51
1967	Nov.	30	28	42
1968	May	28	30	42
1968	July	31	27	42
1968	Sept.	37	25	38
1968	Oct.	34	29	37
1970	Feb.	27	25	48
1970	Aug.	19	31	50
1970	Oct.	21	30	49
1971	June	20	30	50
1971	Aug.	18	35	47
1971	Dec.	22	32	46
1972	May	28	34	38
1972	Oct.	39	29	32
1974	Jan.	15	39	46
1974	June	16	38	46
1974	Aug.	20	38	42
1974	Sept.	13	39	48
1974	Oct.	18	39	43
1975	Feb.–March	14	42	44

Table 5-12 *(Continued)*

Year	*Month*	*Republican*	*Democratic*	*Uncommitted*
1975	Oct.	15	42	43
1976	Jan.	18	40	42
1976	April	18	39	43
1976	Oct.	23	43	34
1977	Oct.	14	38	48
1978	Feb.	19	35	46
1978	April	22	32	46
1978	July	19	33	48
1978	Sept.	20	34	46
1978	Oct.	21	31	48
1979	Feb.	23	29	48
1979	March	23	29	48
1979	May	21	31	48
1979	Aug.	20	30	50
1979	Oct.	25	33	42
1980	Jan.	21	34	45
1980	March	28	32	40
1980	July	30	27	43
1980	Sept.	35	32	33
1980	Oct.	40	31	29
1981	Jan.–Feb.	39	20	41
1981	May	36	21	43
1981	Oct.	32	29	39
1982	Jan.	30	34	36
1982	April	25	35	40
1982	June	28	35	37
1982	Aug.	26	35	39
1982	Oct.	29	41	30
1983	April	20	41	39
1983	July	24	38	38
1983	Nov.	28	35	37
1984	Feb.	30	32	38
1984	June	33	35	32
1985	Jan.	39	29	24
1985	Oct.	32	32	23
1986	July	33	36	21
1987	April	29	37	34
1988	Sept.	38	33	29
1989	—	—	—	—
1990	Oct.	30	29	41
1991	March	40	27	41
1992	March	34	40	26
1993	Jan.	29	45	26
1993	Sept.	31	37	32
1994	Jan.	31	39	30
1994	July	39	32	29
1994	Aug.	38	37	22

(Table continues)

Table 5-12 *(Continued)*

Year	*Month*	*Republican*	*Democratic*	*Uncommitted*
1994	Oct.	41	37	22
1995	Jan.	42	32	26
1996	May	40	44	16
1996	July	37	41	22
1997	Jan.	33	43	24
1998	April	40	42	18
1998	Aug.	44	43	13
1999	—	—	—	—
2000	—	—	—	—
2001	Jan.	37	39	22
2002	July	39	36	26
2003	—	—	—	—
2004	Jan.	39	46	15
2004	Sept.	47	44	9
2005	Jan.	41	41	18
2005	Sept.	39	40	21
2006	Sept.	34	49	16
2007	Sept.	30	47	22

Sources: (1945–1984) Adapted from *Gallup Report,* July 1984, 21; (1985–1996) adapted from various issues of *Gallup Poll Monthly;* (1997–2007) "Gallup Update: Iraq Remains Top Problem Facing the Nation," Sept. 21, 2007, at http://brain.gallup.com.

Note: "—" indicates not available. No data available for 1947, 1949, 1951–1955, 1957, 1961, 1969, and 1973.

Table 5-13 Confidence in Leaders of Major Institutions, 1966–2007 (percent)

		Major institution									
Date	*Survey organization*	White House[a]	Congress	Supreme Court	Medicine	Education	Military	Organized religion	Companies	Press	Organized labor
Feb. 1966	Harris	41	42	50	72	61	62	41	55	29	22
Jan. 1967[b]	Harris	37	41	40	60	56	56	40	47	26	20
Aug. 1971	Harris	23	19	23	61	37	27	27	27	18	14
Oct. 1972[b]	Harris	27	21	28	48	33	36	29	27	18	15
March 1973	NORC	29	24	32	54	37	32	35	29	23	16
Sept. 1973	Harris	19	30	33	58	44	40	36	30	30	20
Dec. 1973	Harris	13	17	—	60	46	—	29	28	28	16
March 1974	NORC	14	17	33	60	49	40	44	31	26	18
Aug. 1974	Harris	28	18	40	49	39	34	32	22	25	17
Sept. 1974	Harris	18	16	35	48	39	31	32	16	26	18
March 1975	NORC	13	13	31	50	31	35	24	19	24	10
April 1975	Harris	13	14	29	43	36	24	32	20	26	14
Aug. 1975	Harris	16	12	28	54	37	30	36	20	28	18
March 1976	Harris	16	18	32	—	—	36	—	22	21	—
March 1976	NORC	14	14	35	54	38	39	31	22	28	12
Jan. 1977	Harris	23	16	29	42	37	28	29	20	18	14
March 1977	NORC	28	19	36	52	41	36	40	27	25	15
Nov. 1977	Harris	23	15	31	55	41	31	34	23	19	15
March 1978	NORC	13	13	28	46	28	30	31	22	20	11
Aug. 1978	Harris	14	10	29	42	41	29	34	22	23	15
Feb. 1979	Harris	17	18	28	30	33	29	20	18	28	10
March 1980	NORC	12	9	25	52	30	28	35	27	22	15
Nov. 1980	Harris	17	18	27	34	36	28	22	16	19	14
Sept. 1981	Harris	24	16	29	37	34	28	22	16	16	12
March 1982	NORC	19	13	31	45	33	31	32	23	18	12

Table 5-13 *(Continued)*

		Major institution									
Date	*Survey organization*	White House[a]	Congress	Supreme Court	Medicine	Education	Military	Organized religion	Companies	Press	Organized labor
Nov. 1982	Harris	20	13	25	32	30	31	20	18	14	8
March 1983	NORC	13	10	27	52	29	29	28	24	13	8
Nov. 1983	Harris	23	20	33	35	36	35	22	18	19	10
March 1984	NORC	19	13	35	52	29	37	32	32	17	9
Nov. 1984	Harris	42	28	35	43	40	45	24	19	18	12
1985	Gallup	—	39	56	—	48	61	66	31	35	28
1986	Gallup	—	41	54	—	49	63	57	28	37	29
1987	Gallup	—	—	52	—	50	61	61	—	31	26
1988	Gallup	—	35	56	—	49	58	59	25	36	26
1989	Gallup	—	32	46	—	43	63	52	—	—	—
1990	Gallup	—	24	47	—	45	68	56	25	39	27
March 1991	Gallup	72	30	48	—	44	85	59	26	32	25
Oct. 1991	Gallup	50	18	39	—	35	69	56	22	32	22
1993	Gallup	43	18	44	34	39	68	53	22	31	26
1994	Gallup	38	18	42	36	34	64	54	26	29	26
1995	Gallup	45	21	44	41	40	64	57	21	32	26
1996	Gallup	39	20	45	42	38	66	57	24	34	25
1997	Gallup	49	22	50	38	40	59	55	28	35	23
1998	Gallup	53	28	50	40	40	64	58	30	34	26
1999	Gallup	49	26	50	40	36	68	58	29	33	28
2000	Gallup	42	26	46	39	37	66	56	30	37	25
2001	Gallup	48	27	50	40	38	66	60	28	35	26
2002	Gallup	58	29	50	38	38	78	45	20	35	26
2003	Gallup	55	29	47	44	40	82	50	22	33	28

2004	Gallup	52	30	47	44	40	75	53	26	30	31
2005	Gallup	44	22	41	42	37	74	53	21	28	24
2006	Gallup	33	19	40	38	37	73	52	17	30	24
2007	Gallup	25	23	34	30	33	69	46	18	22	19

Sources: (1966–1984) Adapted from *Public Opinion*, April/May 1985, 8; (1985–2007) "Confidence in Institutions," at http://brain.gallup.com; George Gallup, *The Gallup Poll Public Opinion 1997* (Wilmington, Del.: Scholarly Resources, 1998), 129.

Note: NORC—National Opinion Research Center. The question for NORC and Harris was: "As far as the people *running* various institutions are concerned, would you say you have a great deal of confidence, only some confidence, or hardly any confidence at all in them?" Figures are percentage of respondents answering "a great deal." The Gallup question was: "How much confidence do you have in [the institution]—a great deal, quite a lot, some, or very little?" Figures are percentage of respondents answering "a great deal" and "quite a lot." "—" indicates question not asked. No data available for 1968–1970.

[a] "White House" (Harris), "Executive Branch" (NORC), and "the presidency" (Gallup).
[b] Electoral participants only.

6

Presidential Organization and the Executive Branch

- **Executive Office of the President**
- **Units of the George W. Bush White House**
- **Chiefs of Staff**
- **Executive Departments and Agencies**
- **Executive Nominations**
- **Presidential Appointments**
- **Senate Action**

Chapters 2 and 3 considered elections as a structural element of the presidency. Chapters 4 and 5 analyzed public appearances and public opinion as behavioral elements of the institution. This chapter and the next two examine the organizational aspects of the presidency. The current chapter details the size and shape of the organization, while Chapters 7 and 8 consider how the organization makes decisions pertaining to foreign and domestic policy. There is perhaps no better or more tangible evidence of the institutional nature of the presidency than the large, ongoing, decentralized organization that surrounds presidents. Currently consisting of some 40 units, 1,700 people, and a budget of $389 million, its design clarifies the extent to which the institution has a life of its own and presidents are merely one, albeit important, player among many.

Presidents must respond to the dual problems of organization and administration in defining the executive office. Chief executives organize information and communication so that they can elicit the best advice possible for decision making. They also attempt to coordinate and control the activities of government and thereby administer the decisions that have been made. This chapter outlines three strategies that presidents have used to address these challenges: control of the bureaucratic administration surrounding the president, cultivation of intimacy among the president's immediate advisers, and attention to political representativeness in appointments to executive departments and agencies. Unhappily, data on the last two strategies are not as readily available as data on the first. This imbalance in the empirical record does not imply any imbalance in the presidents' proportionate use of the three.

The Bureaucratic Administration

According to Max Weber, the first strategy, aimed at managing the presidential bureaucracy, involves "the exercise of control on the basis of knowledge" (1947, 339). The key words are *control* and *knowledge.* The advisory staff, which is put in place to obtain information, is also used to control subsequent decisions. The staff acts primarily on the basis of what Weber calls "rational-legal authority." Established, universal rules guide the behavior of individuals who occupy offices and gain legitimized status from their official positions. This strategy suggests the need for a staff of experts who can act as both presidential advisers and administrative officers.

The first outlines of the bureaucratic administrative approach emerged as presidents sought advice and used the administrative skills of their cabinet members, who had specific spheres of competence and occupied offices established by law (Fenno, 1959). However, the cabinet's role was always severely limited by its partisan character. Because of this, a full-fledged bureaucratic administrative strategy evolved in the White House beginning in the 1920s and was permanently fixed there in 1939 when three important changes in the makeup of the presidency as a collective office occurred: (1) the Executive Office of the President (EOP), which serves as an official staff arm for presidents, was created; (2) the Bureau of the Budget (BOB) was transferred from the Treasury Department to the executive office; and (3) the White House Office (WHO) was formally organized within the EOP.

Each of these changes led to the establishment of "rational-legal" authority on impersonal terms—the offices and spheres of competence were present regardless of who worked within them and who was president. During the ensuing years, the organization of the executive office followed three central patterns of establishment.[1] First, boundaries were defined between the executive office as an organization and other executive departments and agencies. Second, the complexity of the organization increased as more functions became internally separated and more functions were added to the office. Third, universalistic and automatic modes of decision making were implemented within the EOP, especially at the BOB, which was reorganized and renamed the Office of Management and Budget (OMB) in 1970.

Organizational Boundaries

The organizational integrity of the executive office hinges on two key parameters: personnel size and budget resources. Table 6-1 and Figure 6-1 present data on the initial size of the executive staff, its expansion, and its eventual relative stability.[2] Tables 6-2 through 6-4 and Figure 6-2 examine the growth in expenditures for the White House organization.

Boundaries do not appear haphazardly but result from the various incentives and interests within the political institutions involved. Growth in the number of employees and in the budgets of the organizational presidency have had three main sources: presidential initiatives, congressional initiatives, and joint presidential-congressional efforts.

Presidential Initiatives. One of the principal sources of growth in the organizational presidency has been presidential efforts to develop and coordinate programs from the executive office. Presidents have used the executive office, and more narrowly the WHO, as visible organizational centers for their efforts. Presidents' initiatives are apparent in the statistics shown in Table 6-1 on the growth of the EOP and the units within it. Unevenness of growth over time, especially in the early period of these offices, stemmed partly from presidential responses to unpredictable changes in the political and policy environments. Franklin Roosevelt sought to coordinate both domestic and military efforts of American involvement in World War II through the EOP, which employed nearly 200,000 people in 1943 at the height of the war. The White House supervised various war establishment units, including the Office of War Mobilization, the Office for Emergency Management, the Board of Economic Warfare, the Office of Price Administration, and the Selective Service System.

Several other presidential initiatives were more the results of presidents' own interests rather than the vagaries of political events. Harry S. Truman dismantled the wartime executive office but increased the size of the WHO nearly fourfold. This increase was meant to provide a base for policy interests that Truman wished to pursue in the form of an annual presidential legislative program (Moe, 1985, 251; Hess, 1976, 44–58). "Responsiveness, however, can breed dependency" (Helmer, 1981, 63), and the size of the WHO never decreased after Truman's early expansion.

The next large increase in the size of the WHO occurred in 1971, when Richard Nixon attempted to control federal departments from the White House (Nathan, 1983). Contrary to popular belief about the dramatic growth of the office, Nixon's doubling of the number of employees in the WHO, while substantial, was notably less than the fourfold increase by Truman. "It is [also] a common misconception to regard the current EOP as the legacy of the Nixon period" (Helmer, 1981, 61). In fact, as the figures in Table 6-1 make clear, the greatest expansion of the total EOP in the post–World War II period occurred in 1958 under Dwight D. Eisenhower and in

1966 under Lyndon B. Johnson. Eisenhower pursued some restructuring and additions to the management responsibilities of the EOP (Berman, 1979, 58–63). Johnson tried to centralize programs of the Great Society in the White House (Moe, 1985, 253–254). The executive office under Nixon was on average no larger than it was under Johnson after 1966.

The size of the executive office was reduced only once in the postwar period. In the aftermath of Watergate, Gerald Ford decreased the EOP by 67 percent, eliminating some of the agencies and councils established during the Nixon years. In the process, he did not reduce the size of the WHO or the OMB. Indeed, both increased slightly by comparison with their counterparts during the Nixon administration. Although presidents since Ford have proclaimed that they will cut the size of the White House, as an example for the rest of the government, they have been only marginally successful in their efforts. The size of the EOP has been roughly stable since Ford. It decreased only 7 percent from the Ford to the Carter administration and another 7 percent from the Carter to the Reagan administration. The size of the EOP during the George H. W. Bush administration returned to where it stood under Jimmy Carter, and during the Clinton administration it was only slightly smaller. In the George W. Bush administration, the size of the executive office again increased somewhat, averaging above the 1,700 employee mark for both terms and thereby erasing the small decline in size that had occurred under Clinton. However, the size of the executive office still has not gone above 1,800 employees since the George H. W. Bush administration, and it has not dropped below 1,550 employees since Ronald Reagan's tenure. There is thus a fairly narrow band within which the size of the office has fluctuated for the past thirty years.

Presidential initiatives need not be as dramatic as the staff increases and decreases noted above. As Table 6-1 shows, increases in the BOB/ OMB were consistently incremental after boosts by Franklin Roosevelt, who added 453 staff members to this office in the 1939–1943 period. Although presidential scholars often note that the OMB was reorganized and enlarged after 1970 (Moe, 1985, 256), the analysis here indicates that personnel increased only 17 percent from 1970 to 1971, considerably less than the largest increase of 96 percent from 1940 to 1941.

Congressional Initiatives. Despite its name, many units of the EOP were the creation of Congress and some were either not sought by presidents or actually opposed by them. Congress contributed to the growth of the office because it desired policy coordination from a central agency. Efforts by Congress to enlarge and consolidate the executive office are evident from the data in Table 6-1. The Council of Economic Advisers (CEA) was created by congressional passage of the Employment Act of 1946, which gave the president the responsibility to "use all practicable means ... to promote maximum employment, production, and purchasing power"

(60 U.S. Statutes 24, February 20, 1946). The CEA has decreased somewhat in size since it was founded (37 people in 1949, 24 in 2007). The National Security Act of 1947, which gave presidents responsibility for coordinating national defense and foreign policy, also gave presidents a committee of advisers—the National Security Council (NSC). Unlike the CEA, the NSC has increased in size as a result of presidential initiative. Most notably, for a short period under Eisenhower (1958–1960) policy formation and implementation were separated into two boards in the NSC staff system, and hence the council size increased. A second increase occurred in 1970 when Nixon instructed Henry Kissinger, his newly named head of the NSC, to reestablish an "Eisenhower NSC system" (Kissinger, 1979). The NSC was later reduced in size somewhat during the Carter administration and remained roughly constant until small reductions were made under Clinton. During the George W. Bush administration, the NSC staff size grew again to levels more typical of Reagan and George H. W. Bush, with roughly 60 employees.

Presidents, however, have not always appreciated congressional initiatives taken to enlarge the executive office. The Council on Environmental Quality, established by Congress in 1969, was actively resisted by Nixon, even though he later called it one of his accomplishments (Hess, 1976, 124).

Congress, of course, is at a disadvantage in establishing presidential agencies. Congressional initiatives are ultimately translated by presidents as they see fit, and chief executives have considerable flexibility in making as much or as little as they desire of the offices provided. In addition, Congress is usually unable to reclaim authority in a policy area once it has established the executive apparatus.

Joint Efforts of Presidents and Congress. Presidents and Congress have also combined efforts to establish firmer boundaries for the executive office and units within it. In addition to creating more units with more personnel, the two branches have increased the budgets for the existing organizational units. Table 6-2 shows the average expenditures of the executive office and selected units within it. Table 6-3 presents annual appropriation and expenditure figures for the WHO and the total executive office. Table 6-4 lists similar figures for other key units of the EOP. A comparison of Table 6-1 with Tables 6-2 through 6-4 shows that the number of personnel assigned to the executive offices and the amounts of money spent in running these offices are quite different. The staff of the EOP has grown by 47 percent since 1949, whereas expenditures have increased nearly forty-eight times during the same years. Even calculated in constant dollars, the executive office budget shows more than a 400 percent increase.[3] This growth is largely explained by budget increases in just two units—the WHO and the BOB/OMB. The budget of the former increased forty times in current dollars (and tripled in constant dollars) since 1949, while its staff size grew more moderately—by 85 percent. As the table shows, the overall budget of the Executive Office ballooned in Franklin Roosevelt's third and fourth terms and during the second term of George W. Bush. In both instances, the presidents placed large war apparatus under the supervision of the Executive Office of the President. This was designed to have more firm presidential control over the funds being spent on efforts in World War II and the Iraq War, respectively. As Table 6-4 indicates, the budget of the BOB/OMB grew twenty-two times in current dollars (and almost doubled in constant dollars), but it actually posted a 1 percent decrease in staff over the same period. The budget growth of these two units helps to illuminate some of the anomalies between the two sets of figures. Johnson's efforts to coordinate the Great Society, for instance, left the expenditures of the EOP virtually unchanged but increased the money spent by the BOB. Ford's personnel cutbacks in 1975 were countered by increases in expenditures during 1975 and 1976, with the largest increases observed in the money allotted for the WHO and the OMB. The budget figures presented in Table 6-4 also show that the reorganization of the OMB was accompanied by budgetary expansion (a 58 percent increase from 1970 to 1972), although not personnel expansion.

Perhaps most intriguing, these budgetary figures indicate that relatively few attempts were made by presidents since Johnson to work with less money. Figure 6-2 displays the budget growth in real dollars for the total executive office, the WHO, and the BOB/OMB since 1924. Presidents may reduce the number of personnel for the total executive office, as Ford did, or for any one agency in the executive office, but they do not tamper with the overall budgets of these units. Carter and Reagan achieved modest decreases in the budgets for the three offices, which were reversed during the George H. W. Bush administration. While President Clinton touted the shrinking of the White House during his administration, he did so only in personnel—not in budget allocations, which steadily increased (even taking inflation into account).

Presidents and Congresses by and large accept the work of their predecessors, which is etched in the institutional history of the organization. A rare case in which a president actually attempted to dismantle an organization occurred when Reagan sought to curtail funds for the Council on Environmental Quality. Yet, with pressure from Congress and citizens' groups, Reagan's efforts at budget cutting were not fully successful. During his term of office, as Table 6-4 reveals, there was a tug-of-war between congressional appropriations and presidential expenditures for the council. Congress from 1981 to 1984 authorized more money than the council actually spent. Ironically, in 1985 the council's expenditures more than quadrupled, although its budget authority was somewhat curtailed by Reagan. By 1996 the council's budget authority had returned to the same level observed in the final year of the Carter administration, as though Reagan's attack on the agency had never taken place.

Beyond the day-to-day running of the executive office, presidents have requested and Congress has approved discretionary funds that can be used to meet emergencies both at home and abroad. As shown in Table 6-5, the "funds appropriated to the president" were first authorized toward the end of World War II so President Truman could target monies to countries especially hard hit by the war. These funds continued thereafter to permit presidents to provide strategic assistance during the cold war. Truman gave aid to Greece and Turkey before the Marshall Plan got under way. He also funneled monies to South Korea separate from funds spent directly on the Korean War. Eventually, funds appropriated to the president became a highly institutionalized feature of the presidential budget, routinely funding various international assistance programs, including ones for the North Atlantic Treaty Organization and the United Nations. Long-standing agencies, including the U.S. Agency for International Development, the Peace Corps, and the Alliance for Progress, were also funded out of these monies.

Various domestic programs have also been sponsored with these funds, including the Appalachian Regional Development Programs, disaster relief efforts, and federal drug control programs. Indeed, during the Johnson administration, the Office of Economic Opportunity and the War on Poverty were run through these funds.

By the 1990s funds appropriated to the president were so firmly associated with established programs that presidents had little of the flexibility that was originally intended. So, President Clinton's administration separated the international assistance funds from funds for "unanticipated needs," to offer the president new maneuverability. Continuing in this vein, President George W. Bush requested appropriations of more than $13 billion for an "Emergency Response Fund" in 2001 after the terrorist attacks of September 11, to meet exigencies from future terrorist activities. Strangely, only $88 million was expensed from this fund in 2002, and it has not been touched since, despite the administration's expressed focus on combating terrorism. Although presidents have long used special funds to facilitate the government's domestic disaster relief efforts, the George W. Bush administration neither used nor asked for additional unanticipated needs funds in the aftermath of Hurricane Katrina. However, attention has been devoted to relief abroad. As Table 6-5 also shows, in 2003 George W. Bush separately requested the establishment of the Iraq Relief and Reconstruction Fund, which contained initial appropriations of $20.7 billion for rebuilding projects. The White House first granted these funds to the Defense Department and, after 2004, to the Special Inspector General for Iraq Reconstruction.

Organizational Complexity

Greater size typically means greater complexity. The larger an organization, the more likely internal differentiation will occur. In many ways the internal complexity of an office reflects the complexity of the environment. Presidents attempt to satisfy disparate policy goals and policy groups by creating special offices or councils within the EOP. These special offices need not last long; they exist to allow presidents to exhibit their concern about a particular problem or group. Table 6-6 depicts the organizational units of the executive office since its creation in 1939. Although the core of offices in the EOP remains well established today, other units, such as the Permanent Advisory Committee on Government Organizations (1953–1961), have come and gone within and across presidential administrations. Not surprisingly, every president wants to put his own stamp on the EOP, either by adding, subtracting, renaming, or combining units.

George W. Bush was no exception, and in 2002 he proposed to Congress the consolidation of various units in the EOP for budget purposes. This action, approved by Congress in the 2002 appropriations act covering the Executive Office of the President, combined the Council of Economic Advisers, the National Security Council, the Office of Policy and Development, and the Office of Administration into a single unit called "the White House." These units heretofore had been treated as separate entities with separable budget lines. Indeed, despite the new budget measure, they continued to be separate, distinct entities within the executive office. Oddly, other long-standing, central units of the executive office—the Office of Management and Budget, the Council on Environmental Quality, the Office of National Drug Control Policy, the Office of Science and Technology Policy, and the Office of the United States Trade Representative—remained as named budget entities outside "the White House" umbrella. The justification for this reorganization was "consolidation and financial realignment for the Executive Office" and was planned to "give the President maximum flexibility in allocating resources and staff in support of his office; ... allow the President to address emergent national needs; produce greater economies of scale and other efficiencies in procuring goods and services; and enhance accountability for performance."[4]

While efficiency and accountability may have been the stated goals, one consequence of this move has been increased difficulty in tracking the budgets of the key units now huddled under "the White House" banner in the federal budget. The Budget of the United States now provides only estimates of expenses for the individual units within "the White House" for the next fiscal year. It no longer presents the actual expenses for the units or the budget authority granted to them, even though the units continue to operate quite separately from one another. Notably, the Budget of the United States now makes it impossible to track the budget authority and expenditures of the National Security Council, its new Counter-terrorism Directorate, and the Office of Homeland Security in the White House Office.

Despite this reporting change, the Department of Treasury, which is responsible under other laws for providing exact accountings of all units of the federal government, continues to track the actual budget authority and expenses of these specific units. Although obfuscated by the Bush budgets, it is still possible to track the appropriations and expenditures of these units through the Treasury data, which are presented in Tables 6-3 and 6-4.

Another indicator of complexity is depicted in Table 6-7, which lists the George W. Bush administration roster of twelve offices in the EOP. Table 6-8 lists the twenty-nine units of the WHO. The level of specialization, especially in the WHO, is striking.

Another way of examining complexity is to consider the manner in which members of the WHO moved from generalist to specialist positions over time. Table 6-9 shows that the number of White House staff members who held defined roles has increased dramatically since 1939. From 1939 to 1943, more than 80 percent of the staff had no functional title. By the late 1970s and the 1980s, more than 90 percent of the staff had functional roles. The final column of the table reports the number of self-identified subunits in the WHO. The number jumped sharply in 1975, from 6 to 30; it remained relatively stable through the Clinton administration. The George W. Bush administration reports far fewer total staff positions than previous administrations, even though the actual numbers of top staff have not declined. In other words, during the George W. Bush years, the lists of top White House staff are not as comprehensive as they were in all previous administrations. Still, the number of staff with functional titles remains high.

Automatic Decisions

The OMB engages in five types of automatic procedures in handling the high volume of presidential business: budget clearance, adopted in 1924; executive order clearance, adopted in 1936; legislative clearance, adopted in 1924; enrolled bill clearance, adopted in 1938; and a relatively recent innovation: administrative clearance, adopted in 1981. (These procedures are discussed in more detail in Chapters 8 and 9.)

Budget clearance procedures require all departments and agencies of the federal government to submit their budget requests to the OMB for approval. Similarly, legislative clearance procedures require departments and agencies to submit their legislative proposals to the OMB. All department or agency initiatives must be "in accord with the president's program" before they are sent to Capitol Hill. The OMB also screens executive orders, many of which are submitted to the White House by departments and agencies, before presidents sign them.

Enrolled bill procedures involve the OMB's examination of legislation that has passed Congress and awaits the president's signature. Given that some 900 pieces of legislation are passed by Congress each year, presidents are unlikely to be familiar with many of them. Departments in the executive branch make recommendations to the OMB, which in turn advises the White House as to whether the president should sign a given bill; presidents only involve themselves in the process when most of the work has already been done.

Administrative clearance involves a system by which the OMB reviews administrative rule making. The clearance process arose from precedents set by Nixon, Ford, and Carter and was formally codified by Reagan in Executive Order No. 12291. The Office of Information and Regulatory Affairs within the OMB screens various rules and regulations drafted by departments and agencies. Each agency must provide a "regulatory impact analysis" of final regulations, justifying costs, benefits, and possible alternatives (West and Cooper, 1985). The OMB then determines, on the basis of these analyses, whether the rules are consistent with the White House criteria. If they are, they are designated as "consistent without change." If they are not, the rules are returned to the agency in one of two ways. First, the OMB may issue a "prompt letter" designating the rules as "consistent with change." This requires the agency to act on specific modifications requested by the OMB in the prompt letter. Second, the OMB may issue a "return letter" which asserts that the rule has failed to meet OMB standards and expressly returns the rule to the agency for significant reworking. Table 6-10 summarizes OMB action on these administrative rules. Although most of the regulations are approved by the OMB, any intervention by the office is significant. As seen in the table, the number of rules that require some change based on OMB clearance has increased significantly since the Reagan codification. Indeed, the rules that receive "consistent with change" designations reached their highest levels ever during the George W. Bush administration—more than 70 percent of agency rules required modifications based on OMB instructions in 2007, up from less than 5 percent in 1981. The OMB review process has expanded in other ways since 1981. Originally, OMB only examined rules and regulations to determine if they were "economically significant" rules that have an annual effect on the economy of at least $100 million or "adversely affect in a material way the economy." The economic significance reviews are captured in Table 6-11. Like the previous table, Table 6-11 shows the increasing activism on the part of the OMB. The number of rules designated as having economic significance has steadily increased since 1981. In addition, OMB has expanded its oversight beyond economic significance to include impact on state and local governments, Indian tribal governments, other federal agencies, small businesses, energy supply, production, consumption, and risk assessment. The increasing organizational diffusion and standard operating procedures of the OMB are reflected in its budgeting, as well as its legislative and rule-making tasks.

Size and Permanence

In sum, the most significant outcome of the bureaucratic administration strategy is the magnitude and scope of the presidential entourage. This feature produces considerable institutional continuity across presidential administrations. Presidents find dismantling entrenched organizational/administrative units quite difficult, and it is usually either not worth the effort or not in their best interest to do so.

Presidents' Intimates

A second strategy by which presidents may gain knowledge and control involves personal intimacy—engaging those with whom the executives are familiar. This strategy reflects a desire among all heads of state, not just American presidents, to surround themselves with individuals who are personally loyal. As Aristotle wrote, "It is already the practice of kings to make themselves many eyes and ears and hands and feet. For they make colleagues of those who are friends of themselves and their governments" (1943, 165). Thus, the knowledge is not expertise, as it is in the bureaucratic administration approach, but intimacy. As Frederic Malek, an adviser on personnel for Nixon commented, "You don't get the best people. You get the people you know" (1978, 64).

Apart from the broad organizational units, presidents have always relied on small groups of loyal advisers. This partly reflects presidents' inability to interact easily with the large White House staff and their desire to seek advice on key decisions from a manageable group of loyalists. These personal advisers often reflect idiosyncrasies associated with a given president, in contrast to the established procedures and organizations within the executive office that extend from one president to the next.

An examination of the backgrounds of presidents' immediate advisers reveals that there are many similarities between presidents and their advisers. People nicknamed John F. Kennedy's intimates the "Irish mafia"; they included Kenneth O'Donnell, Lawrence O'Brien, and Robert Kennedy. Johnson brought Texans Walter Jenkins, Bill Moyers, and Jack Valenti to the White House. Nixon invited Californians H. R. Haldeman and John Ehrlichman and longtime friend John Mitchell. Ford relied on many former colleagues in Congress, including Sen. Robert Griffin of Michigan, former Wisconsin representative Melvin Laird, and Rep.

Richard Cheney of Wyoming. Carter was identified with a contingent of Georgians who came to Washington, including Bert Lance, Charles Kirbo, and Hamilton Jordan. Reagan looked to longtime friends and Californians such as William French Smith, William Clark, Edwin Meese, and Michael Deaver. George H. W. Bush relied on friends from the presidential campaign—John Sununu, governor of New Hampshire, and James Baker, a member of the Reagan administration. Clinton's so-called Arkansas Mafia included boyhood friend and first chief of staff Thomas "Mac" McLarty, Deputy White House Counsel Vincent Foster, and senior adviser Bruce Lindsay. George W. Bush selected Karl Rove and Karen Hughes as key White House aides, both of whom he had worked with when governor of Texas. Andrew Card Jr., who had been his father's deputy chief of staff, also became Bush's chief of staff. Table 6-12 lists the people who have held the position of White House chief of staff since 1932.

Presidents' advisers are likely to differ from members of the larger executive office, both in their outlook and their values. Presidents and their intimates often make decisions on long-range plans and more crisis-oriented issues concerning domestic, foreign, and military affairs. Yet, scholars too often concentrate on the decisions made by this small group, as though this was the only decision-making group worthy of study. They overlook that many of the decisions of the president and his closest advisers depend on information, positions, and decisions provided by the larger presidential organization. In addition, the organizational apparatus that surrounds each president and his advisers makes thousands of decisions that are attributed to the president, although he and his advisers know little about them.

Political Representation and the Executive Branch

Presidents also pursue a third strategy: political representativeness. Individuals are chosen on the basis of their political backgrounds—their partisan affiliations or ties to specific social groups. These presidential appointees are of a different sort from those chosen through the intimacy strategy. Most obviously, presidents reward members of their own party with positions in the government, or presidents select enthusiasts with a policy outlook similar to their own. Presidents also select as appointees representatives from particular social groups, including women, racial and ethnic minorities, and people from specific geographic regions.

Presidents most often invoke this option in the appointment of people to key policymaking positions in the executive departments and agencies. Presidents are nominally "in charge" of the executive branch, but they do not control it. Table 6-13, which details the size of executive departments and independent agencies, illustrates why contemporary presidents find it so difficult to wield any real clout over executive departments and why "infiltration" of departments and agencies with party supporters is not easily accomplished.

Since the "spoils system" appointments made by Andrew Jackson, presidents have appointed numerous individuals on the basis of partisan or ideological persuasion as a way of leaving their imprint "on the vast executive apparatus upon which the effective management of [their] programs depends" (Brown 1982, 282). Table 6-14 shows the full scope of presidential appointments that require Senate approval. Most of them involve the commissioning of officers in the armed services, which are not only pro forma appointments but also pro forma confirmations. The total number of nominations handled by the Senate peaked in 1981 at more than 100,000 and began to decline as the size of the military shrank with the end of the cold war. Of the total nominations, the number that represents highly placed policy executives is small. As Table 6-15 shows, presidents since Kennedy have on average made some 700 major appointments to such positions as department secretaries, undersecretaries, assistant secretaries, agency heads, and ambassadors. Although presidents have entered office pledging not to increase the number of political executives, they have either failed in that effort or actually found it appropriate to expand the number of political appointees. Presidents Reagan and George W. Bush both campaigned on the need for smaller government. Nevertheless, by Reagan's second term, the number of political executives in the administration was the same as the number under Carter. Clinton, too, said he would streamline the federal executive and in his first term did make fewer appointments than those made by his immediate predecessor, George H. W. Bush. However, by the end of Clinton's second term, the number of political executives was at the highest level ever. The number of appointments continued to grow under George W. Bush despite his assertion that he "ran on making sure that we don't grow the size of government." In fact, in his first term the number of political appointees requiring Senate confirmation increased by nearly 500 over those in Clinton's second term. He also expanded the number of "Schedule C" political appointees, who are hired without congressional approval. Their numbers grew from 1,229 at the start of his administration in 2001 to 1,640 by 2007.[5]

Presidents have considerable leeway in making cabinet appointments, as Table 6-16 shows. The Senate rarely rejects a cabinet nomination. However, this leeway cannot be equated with control of the appointment process. Presidents cannot know whom to appoint to all positions. Their reliance on party and ideology as qualifications for employment offers no guarantee that the right person will be found for the job. Beyond the problem of knowing those hired, presidents face another difficulty in controlling their administrations: political executives, whether or not they come from the president's party, tend not to stay in government very long. The mean service of senior executives during the George W. Bush administration, which prided itself on loyalty and continuity, was still just two years, the average for all presidents since Truman.

Conclusion

The three strategies—bureaucratic administration, personal intimacy, and political representation—are distinct yet often overlap. In the simplest terms, the bureaucratic strategy says, "Get the best people possible"; the intimacy strategy says, "Get the people you know best"; and the representation approach says, "Get people from the party and interest groups." The people presidents select following each of the three strategies may be the same—for instance, the president may appoint as national security adviser a party stalwart who is a longtime friend and an expert on foreign policy. In addition, the goal of each strategy is identical: to centralize organizational and administrative control in the White House. Separately and together, however, the strategies result in wholly decentralized mechanisms for decision making. Appointees to departments and agencies are both physically and bureaucratically distant from presidents. Experts on the White House staff are not much closer. Even personal intimates of presidents sometimes feign ignorance of presidential involvement or their own involvement in controversial decisions and give the impression that decisions were made elsewhere.

Chief executives are confronted with a keen dilemma. They seek singular control of information and policy decisions but are forced to work through a *collective* apparatus. The pastiche of staffs, interests, and loyalties makes it difficult for presidents to gain either the information or the control they seek. The problem presidents face is that they do not control the collective organization, although the collectivity has considerable control over many of their decisions. "When those subject to bureaucratic control seek to escape the influence of the existing bureaucratic apparatus, this is normally possible only by creating an organization of their own which is equally subject to the process of bureaucratization" (Weber, 1947, 338).

The WHO, as a specific unit within the larger executive office, thus symbolizes presidents' power. It was established to give presidents immediate information and advice on pressing national problems that could not readily be obtained from the larger executive office. But this immediacy has vanished with the emergence of a bureaucracy of more than 400 people. In common parlance, presidents "have administrations," but they, in fact, administer much less than does the broad organizational unit of the executive office. Through the organizational diffusion of the presidency, "the president" and "his administration" have become more independent from each other and less interdependent.

The problem of control seems inherently unsolvable. Presidents could not control cabinet departments, so they increased the size of the EOP. Because the EOP was itself too big and too diverse to control, presidents then expanded the WHO. The single individual in the Oval Office can personally supervise only a limited number of people, organizations, offices, agencies, goals, desires, plans, and programs, and this number cannot be expanded by reorganization or reallocation of control. The growth of the executive office (or any office) adds an inertial feature to the institution, emphasizing its separateness from other established organizations. As Terry Moe has noted, "organizations have their own routines, their own agendas, their own norms, their own ways of coding and interpreting the world" (1985, 240). Presidents, too, must learn to play by these organizational rules.

Notes

1. This discussion is adapted from Polsby (1968, 144–168). Polsby uses the term *institutionalization* to denote the process of establishing fixed procedures for decision making, routines and sanctions for hiring and firing, and the establishment of official positions within an organization. Because this book describes the institution of the presidency and not just the institutionalization of its administrative component, the term is avoided here.
2. Tables 6-1 through 6-4 and Figures 6-1 and 6-2 begin with President Calvin Coolidge since his is the first full term with available data from the budget of the United States on presidential staff expenditures. Note also that, although the White House staff was formally designated the White House Office in 1939, Tables 6-2 through 6-4 use this term for all presidents listed.
3. This is calculated using 2003 expenditures prior to the large spending campaign to fund the war in Iraq. This provides a more appropriate picture of the spending increases for the executive office as an organization.
4. Budget of the United States, Appendix, Executive Office of the President, Fiscal Year 2003, 927, at www.gpoaccess.gov/usbudget/fy03/index.html.
5. U.S. House, Committee on Government Reform, Minority Staff Special Investigation Division, May 2006, "The Growth of Political Appointees in the Bush Administration," 1, at http: //oversight.house.gov/Documents/20060503 160909-97328.pdf. Federal Register Part IV Office of Personnel Management Excepted Service; Consolidated Listing of Schedules A, B, and C Exceptions; Notice. October 23, 2007, 60160–60183, at www.access.gpo.gov/su_docs/fedreg/ a071023c.html.

Table 6-1 Size of Executive Office of the President, Coolidge to G. W. Bush, II

President/year	*Number of units*	*Total executive staff*	*White House Office*	*Bureau of Budget/ OMB*	*National Security Council*	*Council of Economic Advisers*	*Council of Environmental Quality*	*All others*
Coolidge								
1924	1	133	38	—	—	—	—	—
1925	1	133	38	—	—	—	—	—
1926	1	137	37	—	—	—	—	—
1927	1	141	37	—	—	—	—	—
1928	1	135	37	—	—	—	—	—
Average		136	37					
Hoover								
1929	1	131	36	—	—	—	—	—
1930	1	139	36	—	—	—	—	—
1931	1	114	37	—	—	—	—	—
1932	1	109	37	—	—	—	—	—
Average		123	37					
F. Roosevelt, I								
1933	1	110	50	—	—	—	—	60
1934	1	107	49	—	—	—	—	58
1935	1	97	44	—	—	—	—	53
1936	1	98	44	—	—	—	—	54
Average		103	47				—	56
F. Roosevelt, II								
1937	1	100	45	—	—	—	—	55
1938	1	105	45	—	—	—	—	60
1939	6	631	45	103	—	—	—	483
1940	6	647	63	156	—	—	—	428
Average		371	47	130			—	257

(Table continues)

Table 6-1 *(Continued)*

President/year	*Number of units*	*Total executive staff*	*White House Office*	*Bureau of Budget/ OMB*	*National Security Council*	*Council of Economic Advisers*	*Council of Environmental Quality*	*All others*
F. Roosevelt, III								
1941	6	21,428	53	305	—	—	—	21,070[a]
1942	5	86,817	49	459	—	—	—	86,309[a]
1943	4	194,194	51	556	—	—	—	193,587[a]
1944	4	182,833	50	546	—	—	—	182,237[a]
Average		121,318	51	467				120,801[a]
F. Roosevelt/Truman								
1945	3	174,138	61	565	—	—	—	173,512[a]
Truman, I								
1946	4	95,068	61	718	—	—	—	94,289[a]
1947	6	43,232	293	562	—	—	—	42,377[a]
1948	6	1,118	210	561	19	43	—	285
Average		46,472	188	614				45,650[a]
Truman, II								
1949	6	1,167	223	512	17	37	—	381
1950	6	1,256	295	520	17	36	—	388
1951	8	1,219	259	522	19	41	—	378
1952	9	1,434	245	498	23	34	—	634
Average		1,269	256	513	19	37		445
Eisenhower, I								
1953	9	1,376	248	457	24	34	—	613
1954	7	1,175	266	419	28	26	—	436

1955	7	1,167	290	438	28	35	—	370
1956	8	1,196	374	430	27	31	—	334
Average		1,229	295	436	27	32		438
Eisenhower, II								
1957	8	1,218	387	442	26	31	—	332
1958	10	2,660	394	440	64	28	—	1,734
1959	9	2,631	405	437	65	34	—	1,696
1960	9	2,919	446	434	65	32	—	1,942
Average		2,357	408	438	55	31		1,426
Kennedy								
1961	7	2,838	411	485	56	35	—	1,851
1962	8	1,676	467	497	44	44	—	626
1963	9	1,659	388	510	39	38	—	684
Average		2,058	422	497	46	39		1,054
L. Johnson[b]								
1964	10	1,542	349	520	43	42	—	588
1965	11	2,849	333	524	38	46	—	1,908
1966	12	4,683	295	583	37	53	—	3,672
1967	12	4,813	272	653	38	55	—	3,795
1968	12	5,306	273	594	35	78	—	4,326
Average		3,839	304	575	38	55		2,858
Nixon								
1969	14	5,167	344	582	46	53	—	4,142
1970	15	4,742	311	633	75	59	32	3,632
1971	17	5,360	660	656	83	59	54	3,777
1972	17	5,639	596	703	81	70	57	4,132
1973	15	4,804	542	637	82	53	56	3,434
Average		5,142	491	642	73	59	50	3,823

(Table continues)

Table 6-1 *(Continued)*

President/year	*Number of units*	*Total executive staff*	*White House Office*	*Bureau of Budget/ OMB*	*National Security Council*	*Council of Economic Advisers*	*Council of Environmental Quality*	*All others*
Nixon/Ford								
1974	15	5,751	583	688	85	42	61	4,292
Ford								
1975	13	1,910	625	699	89	40	61	422
1976	15	1,899	541	724	95	39	69	431
Average		1,905	583	712	92	40	65	427
Carter								
1977	12	1,716	464	709	73	38	49	383
1978	11	1,613	371	602	74	33	49	484
1979	11	1,818	408	637	74	23	48	646
1980	11	1,886	406	616	69	35	49	711
Average		1,758	412	641	73	82	49	556
Reagan, I								
1981	11	1,683	394	677	67	34	16	495
1982	11	1,596	366	612	60	40	12	506
1983	11	1,621	384	611	60	33	11	522
1984	12	1,595	374	603	64	29	13	512
Average		1,624	380	626	63	34	13	509
Reagan, II								
1985	12	1,549	362	569	61	32	11	514
1986	12	1,519	363	543	67	33	11	502
1987	12	1,514	361	513	67	35	11	527
1988	12	1,645	362	532	61	33	12	645
Average		1,557	362	539	64	33	11	547

G.H.W. Bush								
1989	12	1,589	363	527	66	33	10	590
1990	14	1,680	374	515	68	40	15	668
1991	14	1,782	384	548	65	33	23	729
1992	14	1,855	400	561	54	31	27	782
Average		1,727	380	538	63	34	19	692
Clinton, I								
1993	14	1,776	445	561	51	31	22	666
1994	13	1,577	381	544	49	29	6	568
1995	12	1,555	387	522	44	28	16	558
1996	12	1,559	382	524	44	30	17	562
Average		1,617	399	538	47	29	15	589
Clinton, II								
1997	12	1,590	396	507	43	28	17	599
1998	12	1,602	389	505	41	27	19	621
1999	12	1,632	389	523	40	27	19	634
2000	12	1,658	396	511	42	30	21	658
Average	12	1,623	393	512	42	28	19	629
G.W. Bush, I								
2001	12	1,624	375	513	46	31	18	641
2002	12	1,695	407	502	61	33	22	670
2003	12	1,701	409	494	58	28	21	691
2004	13	1,792	413	513	61	29	21	755
Average	12	1,704	401	506	57	30	21	688
G.W. Bush, II[c]								
2005	12	1,693	396	480	62	26	19	710
2006	12	1,698	399	479	60	24	17	719
2007	12	1,719	413	472	64	24	18	728
Average	12	1,703	403	477	62	25	18	718

(Table continues)

Table 6-1 *(Continued)*

Sources: (1924–1988) Bureau of the Census, *Statistical Abstract of the United States 1924–1988* (Washington, D.C.: Government Printing Office, 1924–1988); Executive Office of the President, *The Budget of the United States 1924–1998* (Washington, D.C.: Government Printing Office, 1924–1998); (1989–1996) Office of Personnel Management, *Federal Civilian Workforce Statistics* (Washington, D.C.: Government Printing Office, 1994–1996); (1997–2007) Office of Personnel Management, "Employment and Trends Table 9," www.opm.gov/feddata/html/empt.asp.

Note: The Bureau of Budget moved to the executive office from the Treasury Department in 1939 and was reorganized and renamed the Office of Management and Budget in 1970. The National Security Council was created in 1947, the Council of Economic Advisers in 1946, and the Council of Environmental Quality in 1969. The "All others" category includes personnel for maintenance and grounds, which ranges from sixty people in the 1930s to eighty people in the 1980s. Remaining employees have some tie to White House policy units.

[a] Includes war establishment units.
[b] Includes full term from Nov. 1963 to Jan. 1969.
[c] Through 2007 only.

Figure 6-1 Number of Employees in the Executive Office of the President, Office of Management and Budget, and White House Office, Coolidge to G.W. Bush

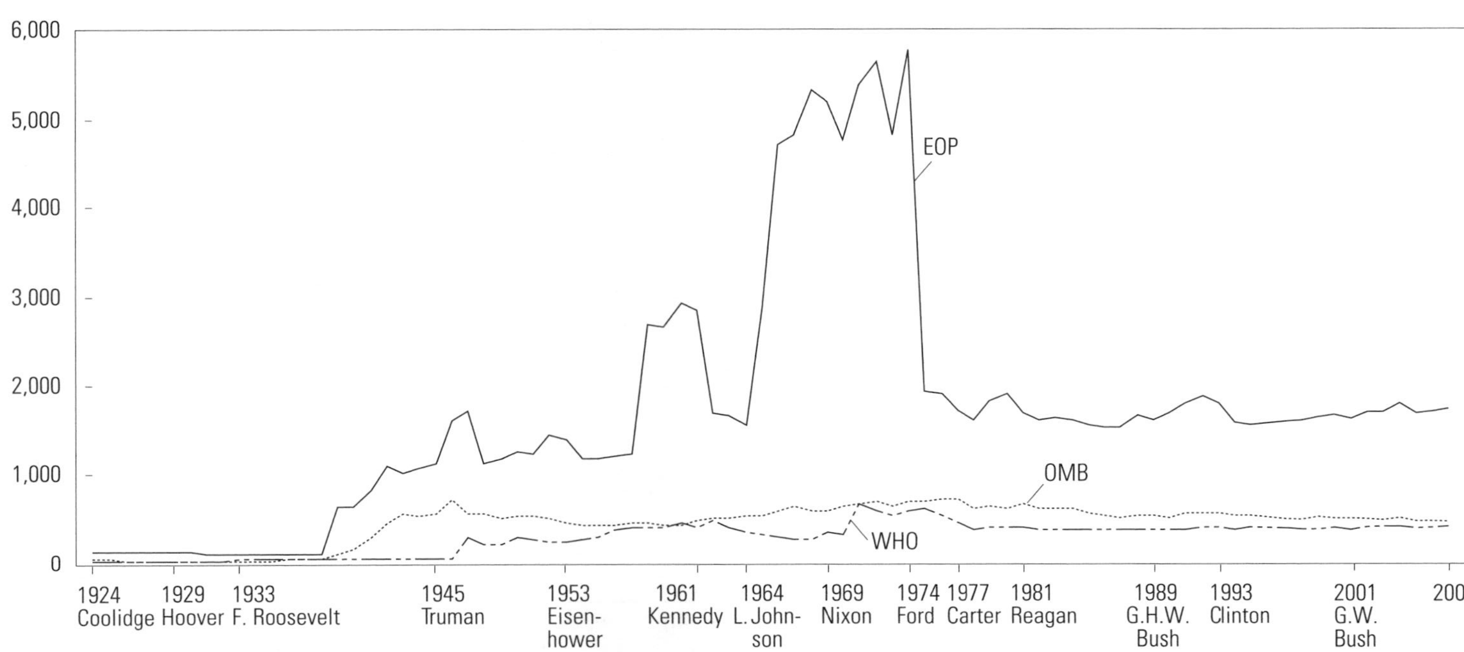

Source: Lyn Ragsdale and John J. Theis, "The Institutionalization of the American Presidency, 1924–1992," *American Journal of Political Science* 41 (October 1997): 121–139, updated by the author.

Note: Employees in war establishment units from 1941 to 1946 have been excluded. Prior to 1970, the Office of Management and Budget was known as the Bureau of the Budget.

Table 6-2 Average Expenditures for Selected Units in the Executive Office of the President, by Term, Coolidge to G. W. Bush, II (in millions of current dollars)

President	*Executive Office total*	*White House Office*	*Bureau of Budget/OMB*	*National Security Council*	*Council of Economic Advisers*	*Council of Environmental Quality*
Coolidge	.501	.391	—	—	—	—
Hoover	.506	.317	—	—	—	—
F. Roosevelt, I	.403	.264	—	—	—	—
F. Roosevelt, II	1.503	.291	.519	—	—	—
F. Roosevelt, III/IV	1,465.980	.407	2.007	—	—	—
Truman, I	196.030	.969	3.403	—	.230	—
Truman, II	8.556	1.537	3.338	.105	.308	—
Eisenhower, I	9.226	2.121	3.398	.203	.277	—
Eisenhower, II	49.216	3.541	4.314	.595	.361	—
Kennedy	40.383	3.854	5.463	.594	.534	—
L. Johnson[a]	26.120	3.882	7.888	.619	.693	—
Nixon, I	42.115	7.660	14.123	1.620	1.152	1.635
Nixon, II	57.614	11.458	19.491	2.485	1.462	2.334
Ford	86.024	15.792	23.457	2.907	1.522	2.958
Carter	80.733	17.309	29.632	3.246	1.956	3.750
Reagan, I	101.593	19.421	34.841	3.618	2.068	.301
Reagan, II	112.328	24.483	38.637	4.450	2.329	1.147
G. H. W. Bush	164.966	31.033	47.635	5.209	2.915	1.875
Clinton, I	211.758	38.898	55.708	6.416	3.379	1.889
Clinton, II	289.539	47.316	57.228	6.844	3.383	2.389
G. W. Bush, I	388.050	54.109	65.633	7.883	3.965	2.641
G. W. Bush, II	5,353.684	49.312	71.824	9.443	3.652	2.933

Source: Adapted from Tables 6-3 and 6-4.

Note: The Bureau of the Budget moved to the executive office from the Treasury Department in 1939 and was reorganized and renamed the Office of Management and Budget in 1970. The National Security Council was created in 1947, the Council of Economic Advisers in 1946, and the Council of Environmental Quality in 1969.

[a] Includes full term from Nov. 1963 to Jan. 1969.

Table 6-3 Budget Authority and Outlays for White House Staff, Coolidge to G.W. Bush, II (in millions of current dollars)

	Total Executive Office		*White House Office*	
President/year	Budget authority	Outlays	Budget authority	Outlays
Coolidge				
1924	.574	.451	.475	.324
1925	.657	.412	.558	.311
1926	.502	.439	.452	.333
1927	.819	.613	.709	.496
1928	.438	.590	.334	.489
Hoover				
1929	.437	.487	.335	.360
1930	.653	.605	.487	.289
1931	.425	.507	.290	.331
1932	.475	.425	.290	.288
F. Roosevelt, I				
1933	.392	.369	.267	.255
1934	.369	.359	.249	.248
1935	.442	.458	.268	.279
1936	.437	.425	.294	.275
F. Roosevelt, II				
1937	.515	.502	.294	.278
1938	.511	.479	.301	.293
1939	2.531	2.371	.304	.287
1940	2.810	2.661	.402	.304
F. Roosevelt, III				
1941	3.896	10.219	.396	.343
1942	440.762	239.019	.398	.366
1943	1,722.539	1,646.903	.399	.416
1944	2,970.258	2,760.787	.377	.437
F. Roosevelt/Truman				
1945	1,223.701	2,672.974	.429	.473
Truman, I				
1946	657.022	446.364	.418	.507
1947	133.573	133.400	.959	.915
1948	6.692	8.327	1.028	1.486
Truman, II				
1949	9.948	7.997	1.245	1.271
1950	10.736	8.407	1.525	1.495
1951	9.339	8.710	1.736	1.587
1952	9.817	9.108	2.034	1.795
Eisenhower, I				
1953	9.350	8.936	2.108	1.860
1954	9.395	9.493	1.950	1.780

(Table continues)

Table 6-3 *(Continued)*

	Total Executive office		*White House Office*	
President/year	Budget authority	Outlays	Budget authority	Outlays
Eisenhower, I (continued)				
1955	8.533	8.535	2.045	1.957
1956	10.395	9.938	3.283	2.885
Eisenhower, II				
1957	10.715	10.399	3.525	3.370
1958	51.029	75.074	3.583	3.535
1959	55.297	55.788	3.702	3.672
1960	63.140	55.604	2.521	3.585
Kennedy				
1961	71.780	69.042	3.906	3.864
1962	26.507	28.993	4.145	4.007
1963	23.601	23.113	4.195	3.691
L. Johnson[a]				
1964	24.972	22.904	4.380	4.067
1965	26.444	24.018	4.380	4.112
1966	26.282	27.416	4.505	3.786
1967	29.307	27.767	4.605	3.671
1968	31.011	28.495	4.659	3.722
Nixon				
1969	32.066	30.889	4.924	4.577
1970	38.403	36.355	6.690	6.468
1971	49.958	47.127	10.109	8.623
1972	60.113	54.087	11.092	10.971
1973	93.369	49.164	11.517	11.635
Nixon/Ford				
1974	97.252	66.064	11.924	11.280
Ford				
1975	75.646	92.823	16.617	15.543
1976[b]	69.258	79.224	17.013	16.041
Carter				
1977	78.149	73.387	17.412	17.236
1978	77.687	74.568	16.665	16.822
1979	81.763	79.590	17.413	16.159
1980	100.334	95.386	19.191	19.017
Reagan, I				
1981	103.121	95.635	21.528	21.078
1982	92.817	94.675	19.902	19.953
1983	101.371	94.186	22.115	20.766
1984	109.064	95.317	23.436	15.885
Reagan, II				
1985	115.715	111.261	25.439	24.306
1986	107.736	107.345	23.835	23.192
1987	117.999	109.422	24.824	25.059
1988	125.093	121.282	26.426	25.374

Table 6-3 *(Continued)*

	Total Executive Office		*White House Office*	
President/year	Budget authority	Outlays	Budget authority	Outlays
G. H. W. Bush				
1989	128.976	123.980	27.950	27.276
1990	292.351	157.406	30.232	29.329
1991	190.000	193.000	33.000	32.000
1992	226.000	185.478	35.000	35.527
Clinton, I				
1993	242.582	195.400	42.795	40.186
1994	232.029	221.585	38.754	39.774
1995	188.183	229.045	40.193	36.661
1996	208.000	201.000	40.193	39.000
Clinton, II				
1997	217.000	221.000	40.000	39.000
1998	246.000	237.000	51.449	45.843
1999	718.631	416.463	52.251	51.050
2000	281.183	283.692	52.493	53.372
G. W. Bush, I				
2001[c]	13,345.176	280.189	53.560	52.010
2002	373.661	495.716	54.611	57.243
2003[d]	2,579.272	388.246	50.385	49.088
2004	18,760.497	3,309.087	68.760	58.094
G. W. Bush, II				
2005	405.257	7,724.958	61.044	55.281
2006	340.078	5,379.000	53.292	44.767
2007	389.000	2,957.095	48.759	47.887

Source: (1924–1996) U.S. Executive Office of the President, *The Budget of the United States 1924–1998* (Washington, D. C.: Government Printing Office, 1924–1998); (1997–2007) U.S. Treasury, Financial Management Service, "Combined Statement of Receipts, Outlays, and Balances," http://fms.treas.gov/annualreport.

Note: Figures for the White House Office include the salaries of the president and vice president. Figures for the total Executive Office include the budget for the White House mansion and grounds. All funds are those allocated and spent during the fiscal year ending June 30.

[a] Includes full term from Nov. 1963 to Jan. 1969.
[b] Transition quarter excluded from figures for this year. In 1976 the beginning of the fiscal year was changed from July 1 to October 1. A transition quarter (July 1–Sept. 30, 1976) was used. It belonged to neither fiscal year 1976 nor fiscal 1977.
[c] After the Sept. 11, 2001, attacks, $13.04 billion was appropriated to the Executive Office of the President as emergency response funds. $88 million were expended in 2002; no other funds have been expended to date.
[d] In 2003 and 2004, $2.48 billion and $18.44 billion, respectively, were appropriated for the Iraqi Relief and Reconstruction Fund (IRRF) which is held in the Executive Office of the President. Outlays from the IRRF have been expended since 2003: $580 million in 2003; $3.01 billion in 2004; 7.34 billion in 2005; $5.1 billion in 2006; $2.3 billion in 2007.

Table 6-4 Budget Authority and Outlays for Key Executive Office Units, F. Roosevelt, II to G.W. Bush, II (in millions of current dollars)

	Bureau of Budget/OMB		*National Security Council*		*Council of Economic Advisers*		*Council on Environmental Quality*	
President/year	BA	O	BA	O	BA	O	BA	O
F. Roosevelt, II								
1939	.481	.397	—	—	—	—	—	—
1940	.671	.640	—	—	—	—	—	—
F. Roosevelt, III								
1941	.836	.945	—	—	—	—	—	—
1942	1.315	1.512	—	—	—	—	—	—
1943	1.982	2.126	—	—	—	—	—	—
1944	2.601	2.818	—	—	—	—	—	—
F. Roosevelt / Truman								
1945	2.956	2.633	—	—	—	—	—	—
Truman, I								
1946	3.037	3.278	—	—	—	—	—	—
1947	3.762	3.598	—	—	.275	.148	—	—
1948	3.377	3.334	—	.052	.350	.311	—	—
Truman, II								
1949	3.281	3.261	.200	.113	.310	.319	—	—
1950	3.300	3.191	.200	.099	.300	.283	—	—
1951	3.377	3.225	.160	.121	.300	.286	—	—
1952	3.608	3.676	.160	.139	.342	.345	—	—

Eisenhower, I								
1953	3.461	3.442	.155	.154	.225	.243	—	—
1954	3.412	3.260	.220	.202	.302	.234	—	—
1955	3.889	3.310	.215	.204	.341	.304	—	—
1956	3.559	3.580	.244	.253	.329	.328	—	—
Eisenhower, II								
1957	3.935	3.853	.248	.252	.366	.340	—	—
1958	4.340	4.157	.711	.613	.375	.339	—	—
1959	4.551	4.615	.759	.767	.393	.383	—	—
1960	4.665	4.632	.792	.746	.395	.382	—	—
Kennedy								
1961	5.426	5.260	.817	.794	.436	.421	—	—
1962	5.517	5.304	.554	.503	.584	.506	—	—
1963	5.872	5.825	.550	.485	.601	.675	—	—
L. Johnson[a]								
1964	6.500	6.636	.575	.515	.615	.613	—	—
1965	7.307	7.089	.627	.608	.697	.655	—	—
1966	8.104	7.627	.738	.731	.675	.613	—	—
1967	8.913	9.063	.664	.601	.790	.731	—	—
1968	9.500	9.024	.664	.639	.858	.854	—	—
Nixon								
1969	9.674	10.050	.811	.668	1.130	1.020	—	—
1970	11.676	12.141	1.860	1.418	1.187	1.188	.350	—
1971	14.785	15.100	2.182	2.171	1.233	1.234	1.500	1.378
1972	18.311	19.200	2.424	2.221	2.112	1.166	2.300	1.891
1973	18.544	19.581	2.762	2.437	1.369	1.498	2.550	2.310
Nixon/Ford								
1974	18.271	19.400	2.802	2.532	1.414	1.425	2.466	2.358

(Table continues)

Table 6-4 *(Continued)*

	Bureau of Budget/OMB		*National Security Council*		*Council of Economic Advisers*		*Council on Environmental Quality*	
President/year	BA	O	BA	O	BA	O	BA	O
Ford								
1975	21.735	21.910	2.900	2.621	1.600	1.468	2.500	2.735
1976[b]	23.592	25.004	3.052	3.192	1.621	1.575	3.236	3.181
Carter								
1977	29.153	26.536	3.270	2.965	1.873	1.833	3.300	3.780
1978	30.371	29.299	3.315	3.039	2.018	2.024	2.854	1.267
1979	31.919	29.788	3.525	3.451	2.042	1.822	3.026	4.251
1980	33.431	32.907	3.645	3.527	2.102	2.145	3.126	5.702
Reagan, I								
1981	36.022	35.123	3.839	3.268	2.205	1.975	2.542	.906
1982	35.896	36.722	3.557	3.488	1.985	2.103	1.957	.936
1983	34.987	32.531	4.064	3.852	2.177	2.048	.926	.827
1984	37.311	34.987	4.497	3.864	2.464	2.144	1.475	.348
Reagan, II								
1985	38.852	39.754	4.605	4.454	2.560	2.170	.700	1.830
1986	37.237	36.810	4.428	4.235	2.202	2.306	.670	1.159
1987	39.033	37.306	4.612	4.369	2.370	2.375	.803	.408
1988	41.300	40.676	5.000	4.743	2.500	2.463	.826	1.191
G. H. W. Bush								
1989	41.993	41.871	5.100	4.959	2.787	2.715	.850	.769
1990	46.943	44.372	5.335	5.352	2.865	2.834	1.465	1.175
1991	51.000	53.000	6.000	5.000	3.000	3.000	2.000	3.000
1992	55.000	51.297	6.185	5.523	3.345	3.109	2.525	2.554

Clinton, I								
1993	56.039	54.753	6.118	6.173	3.428	3.323	2.56	2.148
1994	56.539	56.933	6.648	6.193	3.420	3.574	.675	.537
1995	58.000	55.573	6.872	6.648	3.474	3.180	2.000	2.436
1996	57.240	55.573	7.000	6.648	3.542	3.439	3.020	2.436
Clinton, II								
1997	56.000	56.000	7.000	7.000	3.000	3.000	2.000	2.000
1998	57.440	49.209	6.648	6.741	3.542	3.371	2.500	2.048
1999	60.541	59.252	6.798	6.941	3.666	3.445	2.675	2.746
2000	63.256	64.452	6.970	6.692	3.825	3.716	2.816	2.763
G. W. Bush, I								
2001	68.635	63.505	7.149	6.701	4.101	3.668	2.894	2.219
2002	71.357	72.095	7.488	7.557	4.208	4.495	2.972	2.546
2003	62.240	62.490	7.770	10.079	3.739	3.819	3.011	2.755
2004	66.763	64.442	10.489	7.196	4.475	3.876	3.219	3.043
G. W. Bush, II[c]								
2005	67.864	67.535	8.860	9.443	4.008	3.730	3.258	3.144
2006	76.161	72.556	8.618	9.715	4.000	3.774	2.677	2.694
2007	76.714	75.381	8.684	9.170	4.032	3.451	2.698	2.962

Source: (1939–1996) U.S. Executive Office of the President, *The Budget of the United States 1939–1998* (Washington, D.C.: Government Printing Office, 1939–1998; (1997–2008) U.S. Treasury Department, Financial Management Service, "Combined State of Receipts, Outlays, and Balances," http://fms.treas.gov/annualreport.

Note: The Bureau of the Budget was moved to the White House from the Treasury Department in 1939. It was reorganized and renamed the Office of Management and Budget in 1970. The Council of Economic Advisers was designated in 1946, with funding beginning in 1947. The National Security Council, authorized in 1947, did not expend funds until 1948. Funding for the Council of Environmental Quality began in 1970. BA—budget authority, O—outlays.

[a] Includes full term from Nov. 1963 to Jan. 1969.
[b] Transition quarter excluded from figures for the year. In 1976 the beginning of the fiscal year was changed from July 1 to Oct. 1. A transition quarter (July 1–Sept. 30, 1976) was used. It belonged to neither fiscal 1976 nor fiscal 1977.
[c] Through 2007 only.

Figure 6-2 Expenditures by the Executive Office of the President, Office of Management and Budget, and White House Office, Coolidge to G.W. Bush (in millions of constant dollars)

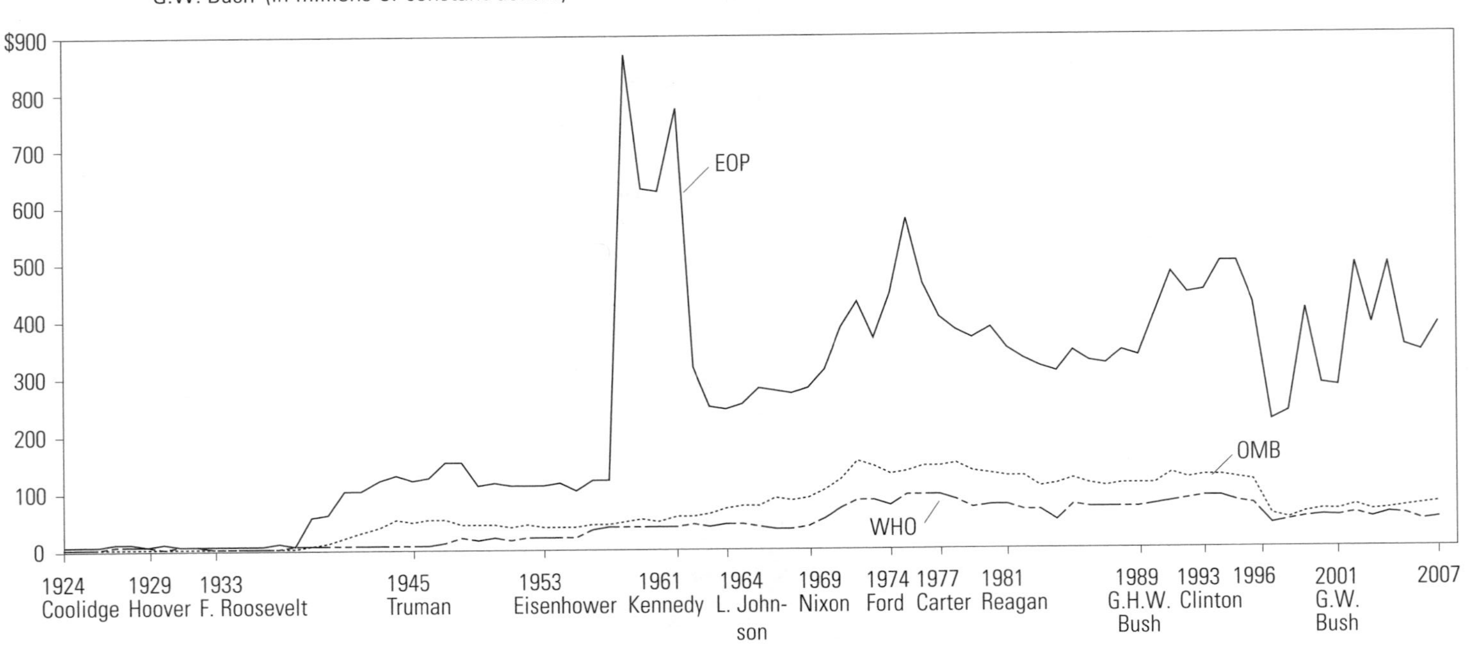

Source: Lyn Ragsdale and John J. Theis, "The Institutionalization of the American Presidency, 1924–1992," *American Journal of Political Science* 41 (October 1997): 121–139, updated by the author.

Notes: Data calculated in constant (real) dollars using 1967 as the base. This procedure takes into account the inflation rate for the periods, thereby discounting the budget figures. To obtain the constant dollar figures, the budget values are divided by the consumer price index for the period. Expenditures for war establishment units from 1941 to 1946 have been excluded. Prior to 1970, the Office of Management and Budget was known as the Bureau of the Budget. Expenditures for war establisment units from 1941 to 1946 and the Iraq Reconstruction Fund from 2004 to 2007 have been excluded.

Table 6-5 "Funds Appropriated to the President" (in millions of current dollars)

	Foreign assistance		*Unanticipated needs/ Emergency Response Fund*		*Iraq Relief*		*Total*	
President/year	Budget authority	Outlays	Budget authority	Outlays	Budget authority	Outlays	Budget authority	Outlays
Truman, I								
1945	1,223.00	0.00	—	—	—	—	1,223.00	0.00
1946	657.00	5.00	—	—	—	—	657.00	5.00
1947	134.00	47.00	—	—	—	—	134.00	47.00
1948	1,363.00	164.00	—	—	—	—	1,363.00	164.00
Truman, II								
1949	5,764.00	4,044.00	—	—	—	—	5,764.00	4044.00
1950	4,786.00	3,627.00	—	—	—	—	4,786.00	3627.00
1951	8,121.00	4,158.00	—	—	—	—	8,121.00	4158.00
1952	7,385.00	4,983.00	—	—	—	—	7,385.00	4983.00
Eisenhower, I								
1953	1,907.00	5,783.00	—	—	—	—	1,907.00	5783.00
1954	4,729.00	5,282.00	—	—	—	—	4,729.00	5282.00
1955	4,400.00	4,381.00	—	—	—	—	4,400.00	4381.00
1956	4,500.00	4,473.00	—	—	—	—	4,500.00	4473.00
Eisenhower, II								
1957	4,100.00	4,110.00	—	—	—	—	4,100.00	4110.00
1958	4,100.00	4,081.00	—	—	—	—	4,100.00	4081.00
1959	1,780.00	1,776.00	—	—	—	—	1,780.00	1776.00
1960	1,780.00	1,756.00	—	—	—	—	1,780.00	1756.00
Kennedy								
1961	1,990.00	1,882.00	—	—	—	—	1,990.00	1882.00
1962	4,170.00	3,443.00	1.00	.72	—	—	4,171.00	3,443.72
1963	5,663.00	3,968.00	1.00	.39	—	—	5,664.00	3,968.39

(Table continues)

Table 6-5 *(Continued)*

	Foreign assistance		*Unanticipated needs/ Emergency Response Fund*		*Iraq Relief*		*Total*	
President/year	Budget authority	Outlays	Budget authority	Outlays	Budget authority	Outlays	Budget authority	Outlays
L. Johnson								
1964	3,329.00	4,119.00	1.00	.51	—	—	3,330.00	4,119.51
1965	5,835.00	4,307.00	1.00	.94	—	—	5,836.00	4,307.94
1966	5,895.00	4,324.00	1.00	.05	—	—	5,896.00	4,324.05
1967	5,428.00	4,872.00	1.00	.25	—	—	5,429.00	4,872.25
1968	4,542.00	4,913.00	1.00	.12	—	—	4,543.00	4,913.12
Nixon, I								
1969	4,875.00	4,967.00	1.00	.15	—	—	4,876.00	4,967.15
1970	4,980.00	4,774.00	1.00	.85	—	—	4,981.00	4,774.85
1971	5,426.00	4,452.00	1.00	.27	—	—	5,427.00	4,452.27
1972	7,518.00	4,276.00	1.00	.46	—	—	7,519.00	4,276.45
Nixon, II								
1973	6,593.00	3,733.00	1.00	.01	—	—	6,594.00	3,733.01
1974	12,430.00	3,329.00	1.00	.44	—	—	12,431.00	3,329.43
Ford								
1975	8,725.00	3,988.00	1.00	.34	—	—	8,726.00	3,988.34
1976	10,566.00	3,525.00	1.00	.37	—	—	10,567.00	3,525.37
Carter								
1977	4,639.00	2,487.00	1.25	.89	—	—	4,640.25	2,487.89
1978	7,528.00	4,450.00	1.00	.15	—	—	7,529.00	4,450.15
1979	7,272.00	3,757.00	1.00	1.03	—	—	7,273.00	3,758.03
1980	12,457.00	7,523.00	1.45	.83	—	—	12,458.45	7,523.82

Reagan, I								
1981	14,662.00	7,010.00	1.00	.18	—	—	14,663.00	7,010.18
1982	8,550.00	6,073.00	1.00	.23	—	—	8,551.00	6,073.23
1983	3,332.00	5,492.00	1.00	.28	—	—	3,333.00	5,492.28
1984	15,603.00	8,480.00	1.00	.37	—	—	15,604.00	8,480.37
Reagan, II								
1985	20,363.00	11,858.00	1.00	.16	—	—	20,364.00	11,858.16
1986	10,708.00	11,041.00	1.00	.26	—	—	10,709.00	11,041.25
1987	13,001.00	10,406.00	1.00	.58	—	—	13,002.00	10,406.58
1988	11,655.00	7,252.00	1.00	.44	—	—	11,656.00	7,252.44
G. H. W. Bush								
1989	10,951.00	4,291.00	1.00	.11	—	—	10,952.00	4,291.11
1990	12,408.00	10,086.00	1.00	.02	—	—	12,409.00	10,086.02
1991	15,728.00	11,723.00	1.00	0.00	—	—	15,729.00	11,723.00
1992	13,437.00	11,109.00	1.00	0.00	—	—	13,438.00	11,109.00
Clinton, I								
1993	24,660.00	11,527.00	1.00	0.00	—	—	24,661.00	11,527.00
1994	9,567.00	10,511.00	4.25	.08	—	—	9,571.25	10,511.08
1995	14,907.00	11,161.00	1.00	1.00	—	—	14,908.00	11,162.00
1996	10,178.00	9,716.00	1.00	0.00	—	—	10,179.00	9,716.00
Clinton, II								
1997	8,463.00	10,191.00	0.00	0.00	—	—	8,463.00	10,191.00
1998	7,107.00	9,001.00	1.00	0.00	—	—	7,108.00	9,001.00
1999	27,438.00	10,059.00	144.00	153.00	—	—	27,582.00	10,212.00
2000	14,059.00	12,084.00	1.00	1.00	—	—	14,060.00	12,085.00
G. W. Bush, I								
2001	11,405.00	11,767.00	13,040.00	88.00	—	—	24,445.00	11,767.00
2002	14,441.00	13,309.00	14,219.00	139.00	—	—	28,660.00	13,448.00
2003	18,465.00	13,466.00	1.00	0.00	2,250.00	58.00	20,716.00	13,524.00
2004	15,621.00	13,738.00	1.00	0.00	18,421.00	3,006.00	34,043.00	16,744.00

(Table continues)

Table 6-5 *(Continued)*

	Foreign assistance		*Unanticipated needs/ Emergency Response Fund*		*Iraq Relief*		*Total*	
President/year	Budget authority	Outlays	Budget authority	Outlays	Budget authority	Outlays	Budget authority	Outlays
G. W. Bush, II								
2005	18,264.00	15,034.00	71.00	28.00	0.00	7,338.00	18,335.00	22,400.00
2006	18,722.00	13,945.00	1.00	4.00	0.00	7,004.00	18,723.00	20,953.00
2007	18,622.00	16,754.00	12.00	1.00	0.00	2,001.00	18,634.00	18,756.00

Source: (1945–1961) *Statistical Abstract of the United States,* annual volumes found at www.census.gov/compendia/statab/past_years.html; (1962–1984) *Budget of the United States,* annual volumes, fttp://fraser.stlouis.fed.org/publications/usbudget; (1985–2007) *Budget of the United States, FY 2008,* Public Budget Database, www.whitehouse.gov/omb/budget/fy2008, and U.S. Department of Treasury, Financial Management Service, "Monthly Treasury Bulletin," http://fms.treas.gov/bulletin/backissues.html.

Note: "—" indicates funding program did not exist.

Table 6-6 Units in the Executive Office of the President, 1939–2008

Unit	*President*	*Duration*
White House Office	F. Roosevelt	1939–
Council on Personnel Administration	F. Roosevelt	1939–1940
Office of Government Reports	F. Roosevelt	1939–1942
Liaison Office for Personnel Management	F. Roosevelt	1939–1943
National Resources Planning Board	F. Roosevelt	1939–1943
Bureau of the Budget[a]	F. Roosevelt	1939–1970
Office of Emergency Management	F. Roosevelt	1940–1954
Committee for Congested Production Areas	F. Roosevelt	1943–1944
War Refugee Board	F. Roosevelt	1944–1945
Council of Economic Advisers	Truman	1946–
National Security Council	Truman	1947–
National Security Resources Board	Truman	1947–1953
Telecommunications Adviser to the President	Truman	1951–1953
Office of Director of Mutual Security	Truman	1951–1954
Office of Defense Mobilization	Truman	1952–1959
Permanent Advisory Committee on Government Organizations	Eisenhower	1953–1961
Operations Coordinating Board	Eisenhower	1953–1961
President's Board of Consultants on Foreign Intelligence Activities	Eisenhower	1956–1961
Office of Civil and Defense Mobilization	Eisenhower	1958–1962
National Aeronautics and Space Council	Eisenhower	1958–1973
President's Foreign Intelligence Advisory Board	Kennedy	1961–1977
Office of Emergency Planning	Kennedy	1962–1969
Office of Science and Technology	Kennedy	1962–1973
Office of Special Representative for Trade Negotiations	Kennedy	1963–
Office of Economic Opportunity	Johnson	1964–1975
Office of Emergency Preparedness	Johnson	1965–1973
National Council on Marine Resources and Engineering Development	Johnson	1966–1971
Council on Environmental Quality	Nixon	1969–
Council for Urban Affairs	Nixon	1969–1970
Office of Intergovernmental Relations	Nixon	1969–1973
Domestic Policy Council/Domestic Policy Staff[b]	Nixon	1970–1978
Office of Management and Budget	Nixon	1970–
Office of Telecommunications Policy	Nixon	1970–1977
Council on International Economic Policy	Nixon	1971–1977
Office of Consumer Affairs	Nixon	1971–1973
Special Action Office for Drug Abuse Prevention	Nixon	1971–1975
Federal Property Council	Nixon	1973–1977
Council on Economic Policy	Nixon	1973–1974
Energy Policy Office	Nixon	1973–1974
Council on Wage and Price Stability	Nixon	1974–1981
Energy Resource Council	Nixon	1974–1977
Office of Science and Technology Policy	Ford	1976–
Intelligence Oversight Board	Ford	1976–1993
Office of Administration	Carter	1977–

(*Table continues*)

Table 6-6 *(Continued)*

Unit	*President*	*Duration*
Office of Drug Abuse Policy	Carter	1977–1978
Office of Policy Development	Carter	1978–
Office of Private Sector Initiatives	Reagan	1981–1989
President's Foreign Intelligence Advisory Board	Reagan	1982–
National Critical Materials Council	Reagan	1984–1993
Office of National Drug Control Policy	G.H.W. Bush	1989–
Office of National Service	G.H.W. Bush	1989–1994
National Space Council	G.H.W. Bush	1990–1993
Points of Light Foundation	G.H.W. Bush	1990–1993
National Economic Council	Clinton	1993–
President's Council on Sustainable Development	Clinton	1993–2001
National Partnership Council	Clinton	1993–
Domestic Policy Council	Clinton	1993–
Office of National AIDS Policy	Clinton	1995–
Office of Women's Initiatives and Outreach	Clinton	1995–2001
President's Critical Infrastructure Protection Board	Clinton	1998–2002
White House Office of Faith-Based and Community Initiatives	G. W. Bush	2001–
Office of Strategic Initiatives and External Affairs	G. W. Bush	2001–
Office of Homeland Security/Homeland Security Council	G. W. Bush	2001–
USA Freedom Corps	G. W. Bush	2002–
Office of Global Communications	G. W. Bush	2003–
Privacy and Civil Liberties Oversight Board	G. W. Bush	2004–

Source: (1939–1979) Adapted from Thomas Cronin, *The State of the Presidency,* 2d ed. (Boston: Little, Brown, 1980), Table A.3, 386; (1980–1993) *U.S. Government Manual;* (1994–2008) *U.S. Government Manual,* www.whitehouse.gov, www.usa.gov.

Note: This list does not include short-term advisory commissions, study councils, and cabinet-level coordinating committees. Also excluded is the Central Intelligence Agency, which since 1947 has been formally part of the Executive Office of the President but in practice operates as an independent agency.

[a] Became the Office of Management and Budget in 1970.
[b] Unit currently in operation as the Office of Policy Development.

Table 6-7 Executive Office of the President, G. W. Bush, II

Council of Economic Advisers
Council on Environmental Quality
National Security Council
Office of Administration
Office of Management and Budget
Office of National Drug Control Policy
Office of Policy Development
Office of the Vice President
Office of Science and Technology Policy
Office of the United States Trade Representative
President's Foreign Intelligence Advisory Board
White House Office

Sources: www.whitehouse.gov; www.usa.gov; www.fms.treas.gov.

Table 6-8 Units of the White House Office, G. W. Bush, 2008

Domestic Policy Council
Homeland Security Council/Office of Homeland Security
National Economic Council
Office of the Cabinet Liaison
Office of the Chief of Staff
Office of Communications
Office of Faith-Based and Community Initiatives
Office of the First Lady
Office of Intergovernmental Affairs
Office of Legislative Affairs
Office of National AIDS Policy
Office of Political Affairs
Office of Presidential Advance
Office of Presidential Correspondence
Office of Public Liaison
Office of Speechwriting
Office of Strategic Initiatives and External Affairs
Presidential Personnel Office
Presidential Scheduling Office
Privacy and Civil Liberties Oversight Board
Travel Office
USA Freedom Corps
Visitors Office
White House Counsel
White House Fellows Office
White House Management Office
White House Military Office
White House Personnel Office
White House Photo Office

Source: www.whitehouse.gov/government/off-descrp.html.

Table 6-9 Top Level Staff Not Assigned to Specific White House Office Subunits, 1939–2007

Year	*Total staff listed*[a]	*Total number unassigned*[b]	*Percent unassigned*	*Number of subunits*[c]
1939	8	7	87.5	1
1940	9	7	77.8	1
1941	9	7	77.8	1
1942	11	9	81.8	1
1943	13	11	84.6	1
1944	13	10	76.9	2
1945	14	9	64.2	3
1946	17	11	64.6	5
1947	16	8	50.0	6
1948	—	—	—	—
1949	—	—	—	—
1950	18	10	55.6	6
1951	17	9	52.9	6
1952	18	10	55.6	6
1953	29	14	48.3	11
1954	32	13	40.6	12
1955	41	23	56.1	15
1956	—	—	—	—
1957	47	25	53.2	13
1958	45	24	53.3	13
1959	49	22	44.9	13
1960	49	22	44.9	13
1961	26	11	42.3	9
1962	29	14	48.3	6
1963	28	13	46.4	9
1964	29	14	48.3	8
1965	25	12	48.0	9
1966	26	13	50.0	7
1967	26	11	42.3	8
1968	27	12	44.9	6
1969	46	21	45.6	11
1970	57	28	49.1	15
1971	49	23	46.9	14
1972	52	25	48.1	13
1973	40	22	55.0	5
1974	47	32	68.1	6
1975	64	9	14.1	30
1976	60	8	13.3	30
1977	80	4	5.0	34
1978	75	7	9.3	31
1979	78	8	10.3	29
1980	84	9	10.7	31
1981	58	7	12.1	19
1982	78	6	7.7	28

Table 6-9 *(Continued)*

Year	*Total staff listed*[a]	*Total number unassigned*[b]	*Percent unassigned*	*Number of subunits*[c]
1983	92	6	6.5	28
1984	90	6	6.7	30
1985	79	3	3.8	32
1986	84	4	4.8	33
1987	82	5	6.1	35
1988	82	4	4.9	34
1989	84	4	4.8	36
1990	87	5	5.7	35
1991	86	4	4.7	35
1992	90	4	4.4	36
1993	82	2	2.4	34
1994	120	2	1.6	39
1995	116	3	2.5	40
1996	90	3	3.3	33
1997	97	2	2.1	32
1998	110	5	4.5	35
1999	121	3	2.5	36
2000	116	4	3.4	33
2001	84	5	6.0	29
2002	78	4	5.1	32
2003	75	3	4.0	29
2004	44	2	4.5	23
2005	36	3	8.3	24
2006	34	3	8.8	25
2007	34	3	8.8	23

Sources: Lyn Ragsdale and John J. Theis, "The Institutionalization of the American Presidency, 1924–1992," *American Journal of Political Science* 41 (October 1997): 121–139, updated by the author from *U.S. Government Manual, 1998–2007,* www.gpoaccess.gov/gmanual/index.html.

Note: "—" indicates not available.

[a] Total number of individuals listed under the heading of White House Office in the *U.S. Government Manual.*

[b] Refers to those individuals listed with the title: Special Assistant to the President, Deputy Assistant to the President, Assistant to the President, Counselor to the President, Senior Adviser, or Special Consultant to the President. These individuals have no specific functional area linked to their title.

[c] Refers to the number of subunits, as reported by the White House.

Table 6-10 Office of Management and Budget Review of Agency Rules, 1981–2007

OMB decision[a]	*1981*	*1982*	*1983*	*1984*	*1985*
Consistent without change					
Number	2,435	2,218	2,044	1,644	1,566
Percentage	87.27	84.11	82.31	77.84	70.76
Consistent with change					
Number	136	271	314	321	510
Percentage	4.87	10.27	12.64	15.19	23.04
Withdrawn by agency					
Number	50	31	40	52	67
Percentage	1.79	1.17	1.61	2.46	3.02
Returned for consideration/ sent improperly					
Number	92	71	34	59	41
Percentage	3.29	2.68	1.36	2.78	1.84
Suspended					
Number	0	0	0	0	0
Percentage	—	—	—	—	—
Emergency, statutory, or judicial deadline					
Number	38	36	51	35	28
Percentage	1.35	1.36	2.04	1.64	1.26
Exempt from executive review					
Number	39	10	0	1	1
Percentage	1.39	0.37	—	0.04	0.04
Total regulations	2,790	2,637	2,483	2,112	2,213

1986	*1987*	*1988*	*1989*	*1990*	*1991*	*1992*	*1993*	*1994*
1,373	1,632	1,671	1,638	1,533	1,595	1,474	1,459	444
68.30	70.53	70.80	73.78	71.73	63.21	64.47	67.33	53.42
461	547	519	431	412	685	593	509	310
22.93	23.63	21.99	19.41	19.27	27.15	25.94	23.49	37.30
56	60	57	61	54	70	105	130	36
2.78	2.59	2.41	2.74	2.52	2.77	4.59	5.99	4.33
34	15	30	29	24	30	22	19	10
1.68	0.65	1.26	1.30	1.12	1.17	0.95	0.88	1.20
0	0	0	15	58	68	50	10	0
—	—	—	0.67	2.71	2.69	2.18	0.46	—
86	60	81	45	54	75	42	40	31
4.26	2.59	3.42	2.02	2.52	2.96	1.83	1.84	3.73
0	0	2	1.0	2	0	0	0	0
—	—	0.08	0.04	0.09	—	—	—	—
2,010	2,314	2,360	2,220	2,137	2,523	2,286	2,167	831

(*Table continues*)

Table 6-10 *(Continued)*

OMB decision[a]	*1995*	*1996*	*1997*	*1998*	*1999*
Consistent without change					
Number	329	210	189	176	185
Percentage	53.06	41.42	37.42	36.13	31.51
Consistent with change					
Number	242	261	283	289	365
Percentage	39.03	51.47	56.03	59.34	62.18
Withdrawn by agency					
Number	32	26	26	15	18
Percentage	5.16	5.12	5.14	3.08	3.06
Returned for consideration/ sent improperly					
Number	4	1	5	3	6
Percentage	0.64	0.19	0.98	0.61	1.02
Suspended					
Number	0	0	0	0	0
Percentage	—	—	—	—	—
Emergency, statutory, or judicial deadline					
Number	13	9	2	4	13
Percentage	2.09	1.77	0.38	0.82	2.21
Exempt from executive review					
Number	0	0	0	0	0
Percentage	—	—	—	—	—
Total regulations	620	507	505	487	587

Source: General Services Administration, Office of Management and Budget Review Counts, at www.reginfo.gov (successive years).

Note: "—" indicates not available. Percentages may not total to 100 percent due to rounding.

[a] OMB decides whether a particular rule is consistent with Executive Order 12291. The order mandates that all agencies and departments must supply proper justification of the cost and necessity for their rules.

2000	*2001*	*2002*	*2003*	*2004*	*2005*	*2006*	*2007*
200	197	212	217	187	165	159	117
34.3	28.14	31.68	30.34	29.82	27.00	26.50	21.42
352	319	363	431	393	400	415	393
60.37	45.57	54.26	60.27	62.67	65.46	69.16	71.97
23	154	51	49	41	40	22	35
3.94	22.00	7.62	6.85	6.53	6.54	3.66	6.41
1	20	6	8	5	6	4	1
0.17	2.85	0.88	1.10	0.78	0.97	0.66	0.18
0	0	0	0	0	0	0	0
—	—	—	—	—	—	—	—
7	10	37	10	1	0	0	0
1.19	1.42	5.52	1.38	0.15	—	—	—
0	0	0	0	0	0	0	0
—	—	—	—	—	—	—	—
583	700	669	715	627	611	600	546

Table 6-11 Office of Management and Budget Review Decisions on Matters of Economic Significance, Reagan, I to G.W. Bush, II

						Average Review time (in days)	
President/year	*Reviews with economic significance*	*Percentage*	*Reviews without economic significance*	*Percentage*	*Total*	Economic significance	No economic significance
Reagan, I							
1981	60	2.15	2,730	97.85	2,790	12	9
1982	79	3.00	2,558	97.00	2,637	12	12
1983	63	2.54	2,420	97.46	2,483	28	15
1984	60	2.84	2,052	97.16	2,112	31	22
Reagan, II							
1985	59	2.67	2,154	97.33	2,213	65	27
1986	74	3.68	1,936	96.32	2,010	30	24
1987	70	3.02	2,245	96.98	2,315	44	25
1988	82	3.47	2,278	96.53	2,360	51	32
G.H.W. Bush							
1989	79	3.56	2,141	96.44	2,220	64	28
1990	82	3.84	2,055	96.16	2,137	57	27
1991	142	5.63	2,381	94.37	2,523	39	29
1992	121	5.29	2,165	94.71	2,286	44	39
Clinton, I							
1993	106	4.89	2,061	95.11	2,167	53	42
1994	134	16.13	697	83.87	831	33	30
1995	74	11.94	546	88.06	620	41	35
1996	74	14.60	433	85.40	507	39	42

Clinton, II							
1997	81	16.04	424	83.96	505	47	54
1998	73	14.99	414	85.01	487	33	50
1999	86	14.65	501	85.35	587	51	53
2000	92	15.78	491	84.22	583	60	62
G.W. Bush, I							
2001	111	15.86	589	84.14	700	46	60
2002	100	14.95	569	85.05	669	44	46
2003	101	14.13	614	85.87	715	42	50
2004	85	13.56	542	86.44	627	35	55
G.W. Bush, II							
2005	82	13.42	529	86.58	611	39	59
2006	71	11.83	529	88.17	600	34	59
2007	80	14.65	466	85.35	546	49	64

Source: General Services Administration, Office of Management and Budget Review Counts, at www.reginfo.gov/public/do/eoCountsSearch.

Table 6-12 Chiefs of Staff, F. Roosevelt to G. W. Bush

President	*Chief of Staff*	*Years*
F. Roosevelt	none	—
Truman	John R. Stedman[a]	1946–1952
Eisenhower	Sherman Adams[a]	1953–1958
	Wilton Persons[a]	1958–1961
Kennedy	none	—
L. Johnson	none	—
Nixon	H. R. Haldeman	1969–1973
	Alexander M. Haig	1973–1974
Ford	Donald Rumsfeld	1974–1975
	Richard M. Cheney	1975–1977
Carter	Hamilton Jordan	1979–1980
	Jack Watson	1980–1981
Reagan	James A. Baker III	1981–1985
	Donald T. Regan	1985–1987
	Howard H. Baker Jr.	1987–1988
	Kenneth Duberstein	1988–1989
G. H. W. Bush	John H. Sununu	1989–1991
	Samuel Skinner	1991–1992
	James A. Baker III	1992–1993
Clinton	Thomas F. McLarty III	1993–1994
	Leon Panetta	1994–1997
	Erskine Bowles	1997–1998
	John Podesta	1998–2001
G. W. Bush	Andrew H. Card Jr.	2001–2006
	Joshua B. Bolten	2006–

Source: Michael Nelson, ed., *Congressional Quarterly's Guide to the Presidency* (Washington, D.C.: Congressional Quarterly, 1989); updated by the author.

[a] These aides carried the title of "assistant" rather than "chief of staff."

Table 6-13 Size of Executive Departments and Various Independent Agencies for Selected Years

		Paid civilian employees			
Executive department	*Year established*	1980	1990	2000	2007
Agriculture	1889	126,139	122,594	104,466	106,879
Commerce[a]	1913	48,563	69,920	47,657	40,870
Defense[b]	1947	960,116	1,034,152	676,268	677,705
Education	1980	7,364	4,771	4,734	4,231
Energy	1977	21,557	17,731	15,692	14,723
Health and Human Services[c]	1980	155,662	123,959	62,605	62,116
Homeland Security	2002	—	—	—	156,800
Housing and Urban Development	1965	16,964	13,596	10,319	9,755
Interior	1849	77,357	77,679	73,818	76,221
Justice	1870	56,327	83,932	125,970	107,191
Labor	1913	23,400	17,727	16,040	16,445
State	1789	23,497	25,288	27,983	35,157
Transportation	1966	72,361	67,364	63,598	53,641
Treasury	1789	124,663	158,655	143,508	109,564
Veterans Affairs[d]	1989	228,285	248,174	219,547	250,058
Total departments		1,942,255	2,065,542	1,592,205	1,721,356
Select independent agencies					
Board of Governors, Federal Reserve System	1913	1,498	1,525	2,372	1,873
Environmental Protection Agency	1970	14,715	17,123	18,036	18,309
Equal Employment Opportunity Commission	1961	3,515	2,880	2,780	2,185
Federal Communications Commission	1934	2,244	1,778	1,965	1,832
Federal Deposit Insurance Corporation	1933	3,520	17,641	6,958	4,636
Federal Trade Commission	1914	1,846	988	1,019	1,131
General Services Administration	1949	37,654	20,277	14,334	12,128
National Aeronautics and Space Administration	1958	23,714	24,872	18,819	18,443
National Labor Relations Board	1935	2,936	2,263	2,054	1,732

(Table continues)

Table 6-13 *(Continued)*

Executive department	*Year established*	*Paid civilian employees*			
		1980	1990	2000	2007
National Science Foundation	1950	1,394	1,318	1,247	1,371
Nuclear Regulatory Commission	1974	3,283	3,353	2,858	3,725
Office of Personnel Management[e]	1883	8,280	6,636	3,780	5,305
Railroad Retirement Board	1934	1,795	1,772	1,176	998
Securities and Exchange Commission	1935	2,056	2,302	2,955	3,628
Small Business Administration	1953	5,804	5,128	4,150	4,314
Smithsonian Institution	1846	4,403	5,092	5,065	4,902
Social Security Administration[f]	1934	—	—	64,474	63,996
Tennessee Valley Authority	1933	51,714	28,392	13,145	12,110
U.S. Postal Service	1971	660,014	816,886	860,726	747,986
All Others		363,413	129,015	91,324	81,615
Total independent agencies		1,102,156	999,894	1,050,900	929,950
Total federal government employees		3,044,411	3,065,436	2,643,105	2,651,306

Sources: (1980) U.S. Department of Commerce, *Statistical Abstract of the United States 1987* (Washington, D.C.: Government Printing Office, 1987); (1990, 2000) U.S. Department of Commerce, *Statistical Abstract of the United States 2007*, "Federal Civilian Employment by Branch and Agency: 1990–2006," www.census.gov/compendia/statab/cats/federal_govt_finances_employment/federal_civilian_employment.html; (2007) Office of Personnel Management, "Employment and Trends Table 9," www.opm.gov/feddata/html/2007/july/table9.asp.

Note: "—" indicates not available.

[a] Originally the Department of Commerce and Labor, established in 1903 and split in 1913.
[b] Originally the Department of War, established in 1789.
[c] Originally the Department of Health, Education, and Welfare, established in 1953.
[d] Originally Veterans Administration.
[e] Originally U.S. Civil Service Commission, renamed Office of Personnel Management in 1979.
[f] Separated from the Department of Health and Human Services as an independent agency in 1995.

Table 6-14 Total Executive Nominations Submitted for Senate Confirmation, Truman, I to G. W. Bush, II

	Presidential action		*Senate action*		
President/year	Submitted	Withdrawn	Confirmed	Unconfirmed[a]	Rejected
Truman, I					
1945	11,056	11	10,966	77	2
1946	25,966	6	25,585	375	0
1947	40,557	132	39,855	570	0
1948	26,084	21	14,941	11,122	0
Truman, II					
1949	55,311	39	54,869	401	2
1950	25,699	6	25,590	99	4
1951	20,636	5	20,435	196	0
1952	26,284	40	26,069	173	2
Eisenhower, I					
1953	23,542	31	23,419	92	0
1954	45,916	12	45,143	761	0
1955	40,686	15	39,897	771	3
1956	43,487	23	42,797	667	0
Eisenhower, II					
1957	45,114	33	44,620	416	0
1958	59,079	21	58,691	367	0
1959	46,934	6	46,371	556	1
1960	44,542	22	43,528	992	0
Kennedy					
1961	50,770	1,271	48,961	538	0
1962	52,079	8	51,780	291	0
1963	67,456	21	66,603	832	0
L. Johnson[b]					
1964	54,734	15	53,598	1,121	0
1965	55,765	13	54,576	1,176	0
1966	67,254	160	66,289	805	0
1967	69,254	19	69,082	153	0
1968	50,977	15	49,149	1,813	0
Nixon					
1969	73,159	477	72,635	46	1
1970	61,305	10	61,162	132	1
1971	50,499	6	48,855	1,638	0
1972	66,554	5	66,054	495	0
1973	68,080	10	66,817	1,253	0
Nixon/Ford					
1974	66,304	4/46[c]	64,437	1,816	0

(Table continues)

Table 6-14 *(Continued)*

	Presidential action		*Senate action*		
President/year	Submitted	Withdrawn	Confirmed	Unconfirmed[a]	Rejected
Ford					
1975	75,039	6/236[c]	71,276	3,521	0
1976	60,263	15	60,102	146	0
Carter					
1977	74,659	61	65,631	8,967	0
1978	62,850	5	59,099	3,746	0
1979	86,212	8	84,859	1,345	0
1980	69,929	10	69,806	113	0
Reagan, I					
1981	106,620	33	105,284	1,295/8[c]	0
1982	79,648	22	79,562	47/7[c]	0
1983	56,041	2	55,536	26/477[c]	0
1984	41,852	2	41,743	107	0
Reagan, II					
1985	59,643	8	55,918	3,677/34[c]	0
1986	39,971	8	39,893	70	0
1987	51,929	10	46,404	5,494/20[c]	1
1988	42,758	13	41,317	428	0
G. H. W. Bush					
1989	48,434	34	45,585	2,762/52[c]	1
1990	44,934	14	42,493	5,189	0
1991	45,369	12	45,180	167/10[c]	0
1992	31,077	12	30,619	589	0
Clinton, I					
1993	42,339	1,078	38,676	2,572/13[c]	0
1994	35,045	2	37,446	169	0
1995	48,279	11	40,535	7,724/9[c]	0
1996	26,211	11	33,176	748	0
Clinton, II					
1997	25,828	13	25,576	239	0
1998	20,225	27	20,302	133	0
1999	23,640	12	22,468	1,160	0
2000	22,162	13	22,512	787	0
G. W. Bush, I					
2001	26,570	69	25,091	1,410	0
2002	23,045	10	23,633	193	0
2003	28,423	13	21,580	6,830	0
2004	24,420	26	27,047	26	0
G. W. Bush, II[d]					
2005	27,686	18	25,942	1,726	0
2006	28,169	22	29,603	203	0
2007	22,454	25	20,939	1,490	0

Table 6-14 *(Continued)*

Source: (1945–1996) Successive volumes of U.S. Congress, *Executive Proceedings of the Senate* (Washington, D.C.: Government Printing Office); (1997–2007) "Resume of Congressional Activity," *Congressional Record—Daily Digest*, www.senate.gov.

[a] Those nominations returned to the president or not acted upon before Senate adjournment and carried over to the next session.
[b] Includes full term from Nov. 1963 to Jan. 1969.
[c] Second figure indicates number of nominations that failed confirmation at adjournment under Senate rules. No final action was taken on the nominations, and they were not carried over to the next session.
[d] Through 2007 only.

Table 6-15 Presidential Appointments Confirmed by Senate, Kennedy to G. W. Bush, II

President/year	*Executive Office*	*Cabinet departments*	*Ambassadors*	*Independent agencies*	*Total*
Kennedy					
1961	6	120	12	51	189
1962	8	49	12	30	99
1963	6	31	13	45	95
Total	20	200	37	126	383
L. Johnson					
1964	5	28	10	24	67
1965	11	69	20	40	140
1966	10	46	22	29	107
1967	5	56	21	30	112
1968	4	37	20	46	107
Total	35	236	93	169	533
Nixon					
1969	10	160	51	48	269
1970	7	28	8	27	70
1971	7	38	4	42	91
1972	2	36	8	20	66
1973	5	109	21	39	174
1974	1	38	9	18	66
Total	32	409	101	194	736
Ford					
1974	3	16	6	20	45
1975	4	73	18	55	150
1976	4	52	9	36	101
Total	11	141	33	111	296
Carter					
1977	16	177	37	63	293
1978	4	53	16	46	119
1979	7	59	29	35	130
1980	2	48	5	23	78
Total	29	337	87	167	620
Reagan, I					
1981	13	180	28	75	296
1982	4	31	9	56	100
1983	3	51	13	39	106
1984	3	40	6	24	73
Total	23	302	56	194	575
Reagan, II					
1985	12	88	49	55	204
1986	5	74	40	42	161
1987	3	58	38	29	128
1988	3	64	39	21	127
Total	23	284	166	147	620

Table 6-15 *(Continued)*

President/year	*Executive Office*	*Cabinet departments*	*Ambassadors*	*Independent agencies*	*Total*
G. H. W. Bush					
1989	18	172	66	34	290
1990	5	57	40	52	154
1991	13	77	43	153	286
1992	3	38	24	45	110
Total	39	344	173	284	840
Clinton, I					
1993	18	209	66	28	321
1994	3	47	37	100	187
1995	8	39	51	27	125
1996	3	19	30	29	81
Total	32	314	184	184	714
Clinton, II					
1997	11	134	85	119	349
1998	5	82	46	74	207
1999	5	98	57	122	282
2000	0	54	34	58	146
Total	21	368	222	373	984
G. W. Bush, I					
2001	18	381	104	106	609
2002	3	121	33	117	274
2003	10	123	50	180	363
2004	1	56	54	94	205
Total	32	681	241	497	1451
G. W. Bush, II					
2005	12	173	75	110	370
2006	5	109	38	133	285
2007	3	97	52	77	229
Total	20	379	165	320	884

Sources: (Kennedy through Reagan, I) Successive volumes of *Congressional Quarterly Almanac* (Washington, D.C.: Congressional Quarterly); (Reagan, II through Clinton, I) successive volumes of *Journal of the Executive Proceedings of the Senate*; (Clinton, II through G. W. Bush, II) "Presidential Nominations," http://thomas.loc.gov.

Table 6-16 Presidential Cabinet Nominations Rejected or Withdrawn

Nominee	*Position*	*President*	*Date*	*Vote*
Lucius Stockton	secretary of war	Adams	Jan. 16,1801	withdrawn
Henry Dearborn	secretary of war	Madison	March 2, 1815	withdrawn
Roger B. Taney	secretary of Treasury	Jackson	June 23, 1834	18–28
Caleb Cushing	secretary of Treasury	Tyler	March 3, 1843	19–27
Caleb Cushing	secretary of Treasury	Tyler	March 3, 1843	10–27
Caleb Cushing	secretary of Treasury	Tyler	March 3, 1843	2–29
David Henshaw	secretary of navy	Tyler	Jan. 15, 1844	6–34
James M. Porter	secretary of war	Tyler	Jan. 30, 1844	3–38
James S. Green	secretary of Treasury	Tyler	June 15, 1844	[a]
Edwin D. Morgan	secretary of Treasury	Lincoln	Feb. 13, 1865	withdrawn
Thomas Ewing Sr.	secretary of war	A. Johnson	Feb. 22, 1868	held in committee
Henry Stanbery	attorney general	A. Johnson	June 2, 1868	11–29
Benjamin Bristow	attorney general	Grant	Jan. 8, 1874	withdrawn
Charles B. Warren	attorney general	Coolidge	March 10, 1925	39–41
Charles B. Warren	attorney general	Coolidge	March 16, 1925	39–46
Lewis L. Strauss	secretary of commerce	Eisenhower	June 19, 1959	46–49
Robert C. Wood	secretary of housing and urban development	L. Johnson	Jan. 9, 1969	held in committee
John Tower	secretary of defense	G.H.W. Bush	March 9, 1989	47–53
Zoe E. Baird	attorney general	Clinton	Jan. 26, 1993	withdrawn
Anthony Lake	CIA director	Clinton	April 18, 1997	withdrawn
Hershel Gober	secretary of veterans affairs	Clinton	Oct. 27, 1997	withdrawn
Linda Chavez	secretary of labor	G.W. Bush	Jan. 9, 2001	withdrawn
Bernard Kerik	secretary of homeland security	G.W. Bush	Dec. 10, 2004	withdrawn

Source: U.S. Senate, Art and History Home, "Nominations," "Chapter 10: Cabinet Nominations Rejected or Withdrawn," www.senate.gov/artandhistory/history/common/briefing/Nominations.htm#10.

Note: Data current through 2007.

[a] Not recorded.

7

Presidents in War and Diplomacy

- **Types of Wars**
- **The Costs of War**
- **Presidents' Military Funding Decisions**
- **Treaties and Executive Agreements**

"The President shall be Commander in Chief of the Army and Navy of the United States, and of the Militia of the several States, when called into the actual Service of the United States. . . ." A single sentence in the U.S. Constitution gives presidents their responsibilities in times of war. The Framers intended the sentence to be concise and descriptive, offering the president a title of "Commander in Chief," something that they saw George Washington fitting perfectly. In the Framers' view, the real war power rested with Congress with its authority to "declare war." Nevertheless, they also worked to limit legislative power, scratching out the word "make" for the word "declare." The word "make" was expressly dropped to avoid any interpretations that would permit the United States to be the aggressor, signaling that it should only declare war if provoked. It should and would react defensively.

Early presidents adhered to the rules of the Constitution. Thomas Jefferson wrote that the president "was unauthorized by the Constitution without the sanction of Congress to go beyond the line of defense" (quoted in Schlesinger Jr., 1973b, 22). Andrew Jackson, pondering the annexation of Texas, referred the question to Congress in 1836 because he said it was a decision "probably leading to war" and thus the proper subject for "that body by whom war can only be declared and by whom all the provisions for sustaining its perils must be furnished" (Richardson, 1897, IV: 1485). James Buchanan advised that "without the authority of Congress, the President cannot fire a hostile gun in any case except to repel the attacks of an enemy" (Richardson, 1897, VII: 3101).

Today, however, there is little left of the original intent of the Framers. Presidents have crafted their own war power. It is a power they use in big and small ways that range from sending hundreds of thousands of troops into battle for many years to sending a few hundred marines to help evacuate American citizens in unsafe areas around the globe. Presidents have successively set precedents that push congressional power and checks and balances to the periphery. Congress's power to declare war is all but a nullity. Instead, in some instances, presidents have requested war resolutions with ever more sweeping language as political insurance for their military involvements. In other instances, they have taken action independently of Congress, in effect giving themselves permission to use military forces by embroidering the commander-in-chief clause. Presidents have cornered Congress's "power of the purse"—its ability to appropriate and not appropriate funds—by suggesting that the safety of the troops would be compromised if monies were not forthcoming. Presidents have ignored at their convenience the War Powers Resolution, passed by Congress in 1973 to recapture some of its lost ground; it requires presidents to notify Congress when they commit troops abroad. And Congress itself has delegated powers to presidents before, during, and after wars, which presidents have used to maximize their control over military involvements. As James Madison sardonically observed to Thomas Jefferson in 1798, "the History of all Govts demonstrates that the Ex. is the branch of power most interested in war, and most prone to it" (Hunt, 1906, 6: 312–313).

At its most basic, presidents' self-defined war power involves their ability to unilaterally commit American troops anywhere in the world. This has been done primarily under the guise of defensive efforts to protect American lives and interests. Successive presidents have expanded the definition of defense. Defensive wars were once conducted to repel actual attacks against Americans. But today, defensive actions include not only imminent or possible attacks against Americans, but actual, imminent, and possible attacks against American interests. As the United States grew as a world power, especially after World War I, almost any event in the world could be construed as affecting American interests. And as the concept of "national security" enlarged after World War II in the depths of the Cold War, the language of justification for acting defensively grew ever broader, larger, and louder. This expansive view of national security has grown further still following the attacks of September 11, 2001. Since terrorists often act covertly, without a government sponsor, and can be anywhere at any time, presidents can justify efforts in the name of national security in much deeper and all-encompassing ways than the Cold War presidents would ever have imagined.

Presidents' war power illuminates four central features of presidential policymaking that exist regardless of the type of policy. As will be seen in this and the next chapter, these generalizations also hold for presidents' diplomacy, domestic agenda setting, and economic plans. First, presidents engage in independent policymaking. They do so with few constraints from the other branches of government. Much of presidential war power has been devised by presidents successfully building on the work of their predecessors. While in other areas of policymaking, presidents often seek to do the opposite of their immediate predecessors, especially if they are from the opposing party, there is no such strategy in the creation and expansion of war power. One president's precedent, even one which rests on inaccurate interpretations of previous presidents' decisions or historic events, becomes ripe for enlargement, not retraction, by the next president.

Second, presidents personally conduct these war efforts, directing actions in real-time and utilizing available intelligence to set strategy. President Franklin D. Roosevelt had nightly briefings on how the war in Europe and Asia was going delivered to his bedside table. President Richard Nixon selected the actual targets used in the secret bombing missions in Cambodia in 1969 and 1970. President George W. Bush received hourly briefings as American forces hunted down and captured Saddam Hussein. More than in many other policy areas, presidents take on military involvements as their own challenges. Although relying on the advice of members of the White House staff, the Departments of Defense and State, and the Central Intelligence Agency, presidents interject their own decision-making capabilities, worldviews, and degrees of risk.

Third, the presidency as an institution is also heavily involved in these independent policy efforts. Presidents do not go to war alone. There are considerable incentives for presidents' advisers and the various government departments and agencies to put their stamp on the decisions of military involvements. Often these involvements lead to fierce competition among various agencies to claim responsibility for tasks that are relevant to the missions of multiple departments. Tape recordings reveal the competition between Secretary of Defense Robert McNamara and Secretary of State Dean Rusk over the appropriate strategy to deal with Russian ships loaded with missiles entering Cuban waters during the Cuban missile crisis (May and Zelikow, 1997). In 1979, National Security Adviser Zbigniew Brzezinski planned the helicopter rescue attempt of U.S. hostages held in Iran down to the number of helicopters, but he and President Jimmy Carter failed to discuss the plans with Secretary of State Cyrus Vance, who resigned in protest after the mission failed. In the Iraq War, there was a long-running dispute between Secretary of State Condoleezza Rice and Secretary of Defense Donald Rumsfeld over whether mistakes had been made in conduct of the war.

Finally, policy complexity defines the environment within which presidents engage in these independent policy efforts. Although presidents might well conclude that with all the power at their disposal, military efforts will go smoothly and inevitably toward an American victory, history has shown otherwise. The environment within which presidents make decisions is chaotic and unpredictable, and presidents often lack the information they might need to sort out what is happening. As a consequence, presidents often adopt a "go for broke" strategy—to spend whatever it takes to "win the war" (Ragsdale, 2008). In embracing this strategy, several presidents have failed to recognize the possibility that the war was badly executed from the outset, nullifying the impact that additional funding could have in securing victory.

This chapter is organized in four parts. First, it considers different types of presidential military involvements: wars declared by Congress, wars that receive congressional authorization but are not formally declared, and involvements entered into by the president using his independent power as commander in chief. According to a Congressional Research Service report, there have been some 271 instances of American use of force across these three categories from 1798 to 2007 (Congressional Research Service, "Instances of Use of U.S. Armed Forces Abroad," 2007). There have been 5 declared wars, 14 congressionally authorized wars, and 252 presidential uses of force conducted independently of explicit congressional authorization. The chapter then examines the costs of major wars in casualties, money, and public opinion support. Third, the chapter discusses presidents' military funding decisions outside the congressional appropriations process. Finally, the chapter examines presidential diplomacy and efforts at conducting peaceful relations with other nations.

Declared Wars

Some people wonder whether a war is legitimate if it has not been officially declared, but presidents have spent little time pondering this question. Table 7-1 lists the 11 declarations associated with the 5 officially declared wars in American history: the War of 1812, the Mexican-American War, the Spanish-American War, World War I, and World War II. In each of these instances, the declarations indicated that the state of war "has been thrust upon the United States." In addition, each declaration contained language similar to that given President Woodrow Wilson as America entered World War I: the president is "authorized and directed to employ the entire naval and military forces of the United States and the resources of the Government to carry on war against [the Government of the enemy nation(s)]; and to bring the conflict to a successful termination, all of the resources of the country are hereby pledged by the Congress of the United States" (Congressional Research Service, "Declarations of War and

Authorizations for the Use of Military Force, 2003, 4). The authorization in declared wars is therefore sweeping and broad. It permits presidents to employ the "entire" armed forces and pledges "all" the resources of the United States. Thus, even with Congress involved in the war, presidents are indeed independent policymakers as the events of the war unfold.

How were these wars "thrust upon the United States?" In each case, the impetus was a direct attack on Americans. The War of 1812 erupted as evidence emerged that the British were supplying arms to Native Americans for battles over their lands with frontiersmen. The British also seized American ships and put their crews into the service of the British navy. As the Americans saw it, these were direct attacks on American citizens and sufficient grounds for war.

In 1846, Mexican troops killed eleven Americans who were part of a patrol sent to protect newly annexed Texas. Andrew Jackson's prediction a decade earlier that Texas annexation would "probably lead to war" was correct. President James Polk requested that Congress declare war on May 11, 1846, stating that Mexico had "invaded our territory and shed American blood upon the American soil." Congress did so on May 13.

In 1898, the U.S.S. *Maine,* stationed in Havana to lend support to Cuba's struggle for independence from Spain, exploded and sank, killing 260 men. Although there were conflicting reports on whether the explosion was caused by an internal malfunction or a Spanish submarine mine, American war sentiment pitched. Two months after the *Maine* incident, President William McKinley, reluctant to go to war, and members of Congress fashioned an ultimatum asking Spain to end its hold over Cuba. When Spain declared war on the United States because of the ultimatum, the United States followed suit and declared war on Spain.

Although the United States maintained its official neutrality for three years during World War I from 1914 to 1917, President Wilson eventually pushed for a declaration of war against Germany when German submarines sank seven American merchant ships. As additional impetus, the British disclosed a telegram they had intercepted, known as the infamous Zimmerman telegram, in which the Germans invited the Mexicans to enter the war on their side with the promise that Germany would help Mexico regain Texas, Arizona, and New Mexico from the United States.

The most clear-cut attack occurred on December 7, 1941, when the Japanese bombed U.S. naval ships in Pearl Harbor, Hawaii, leaving thousands of sailors dead, two ships sunk, three others badly damaged, and most of the aircraft stationed on the island destroyed. There was little disagreement about what to do next. The isolation to which the United States had returned after World War I abruptly ended and Franklin Roosevelt, never an isolationist, asked Congress for a declaration of war, first against Japan and then against Germany.

The Precedent of the Spanish-American War

The five instances are similar as each president asked Congress for a declaration of war based on provocation against American lives, sovereignty, or interests. Yet the justification for the Spanish-American War, particularly as expressed in the ultimatum, was unique and became important as a precedent for future presidents for three distinct reasons. First, although the sinking of the *Maine* led to public outcry against the Spanish, it was not McKinley's or Congress's primary reason for war. The long-standing interest of the United States was to aid Cuba's pursuit of independence. Both the ultimatum and the declaration of war asserted for the first time that it was part of America's "interests" to see another nation free. The resolution held that "the people of the Island of Cuba are, of right ought to be, free and independent." Thus, the American government took its very first stand on notions of democracy in the context of another country's fight. Today we might think little of American intervention on behalf of protecting democracy because it has happened numerous times in countries such as Iraq, Vietnam, Korea, El Salvador, Panama, Nicaragua, the Dominican Republic, Philippines, and Chile. But the Spanish-American War was the first of such efforts.

Second, the resolution went further, forcefully stating that "it is the duty of the United States to demand, and the Government of the United States does hereby demand, that the Government of Spain at once relinquish its authority and government in the Island of Cuba." Here, also for the first time, the United States commanded that a sovereign country conform to its policy regarding another country. Although, of course, Cuba was off the coast of Florida, it was certainly not principally an American matter what Spain resolved with Cuba.

Third, the resolution provided presidents enviable power. It proclaimed that "the President of the United States be, and he hereby is, directed and empowered to use the entire land and naval forces of the United States, and to call into the actual service of the United States the militia of the several states, to such extent as may be necessary to carry these resolutions into effect." These words, written in the ultimatum resolution, not the declaration of war, gave McKinley the ability to use the "entire" armed forces to do whatever was "necessary." This became the gold standard for presidential authority for most of the twentieth century until the Persian Gulf War, when, as discussed below, it expanded further.

In the end, the United States decisively won the war against Spain—acquiring the Philippines, Puerto Rico, Guam, and not annexing Cuba, but holding it as a protectorate. The language passed by Congress justifying the war stood as an unswerving guide for the United States' conduct in the twentieth century. The ultimatum resolution combined with the military victory gave the United States the "right" to intervene in other countries' affairs as the guardian of and a crusader for democracy. The American victory put the United States on the world stage as a country to be reckoned with. Together these gave American presidents a new platform from which to assert their independent power in military affairs and greatly increased the policy complexity they found in exercising it, as more and more places around the world, about which the United States knew little, came under the umbrella of "American interest."

Congressional Authorization of Military Force

In fourteen other instances, presidents have requested lesser congressional authorizations, rather than formal declarations of war. These cases, depicted in Table 7-2, began when John Adams sought legislation from Congress to protect U.S. commercial ships that were routinely being seized by French naval vessels. Congress passed legislation to "more effectually protect the Commerce and Coasts of the United States" (Congressional Research Service, "Declarations of War," 2003). The language of the authorization was narrow—targeting only the French Navy—and specific—the capture of its vessels. The other authorizations of the nineteenth century also reflected this specificity.

Ironically, there is a nearly a one-hundred-year gap between the last request for authorization in the nineteenth century, made by James Buchanan in the fight against Paraguay, and the first request of the twentieth century, made by Dwight Eisenhower, who sought congressional authorization for possible American military action to protect Formosa (now Taiwan) from mainland Communist China. During those one hundred years, there was considerable expansion of presidential power, the American military, and American national security interests. The requests to Congress during the twentieth and twenty-first centuries are far more sweeping than those of the earlier period and each set a precedent for the next. In addition, while the nineteenth-century presidents viewed their efforts to secure congressional authorization as mandatory, later presidents viewed congressional authorizations as discretionary—a matter of political expediency. Thus, although contemporary presidents seek congressional approval, they do so firmly believing in their own independent policymaking abilities.

As listed in Table 7-2, there are four authorizations beginning with Eisenhower's Formosa request that are of particular note, setting specific examples for future presidents: contingent war, all but declared war, a United Nations war, and preemptive war.

Contingent War

In the Formosa instance, Eisenhower asked for contingency authorization—in advance, in case it became necessary to act. He noted before asking for congressional authorization that "authority for some of the actions which might be required would be inherent in the authority of the Commander in Chief" but a congressional resolution would publicly "establish" this authority (Schlesinger, 1973b, 159–160). The resolution stated that the president was "authorized to employ the Armed Forces as he deems necessary" to defend Formosa. Although, as matters unfolded, Eisenhower did not actually invoke the authority, the precedent was set. The Formosa resolution granted the president carte blanche to decide when American troops should be used. Congress gave before-the-fact approval for the possible use of force with no knowledge of the specific situation under which the hostilities might begin. This contingency approval was also used in 2001 after the September 11 attacks. Congress authorized the president to "use all necessary and appropriate force against those nations, organizations, or persons he determines planned, authorized, committed or aided the terrorist attacks." Congress did not identify the nations, organization, or persons in question, leaving that up to the president.

All But Declared War

On August 7, 1964, North Vietnamese gunboats attacked two American destroyers in the Gulf of Tonkin. Although American involvement in the Vietnam War had been slowly increasing for years, President Lyndon Johnson used the provocation to ask Congress to authorize a resolution that read: "Congress approves and supports the determination of the President, as Commander in Chief, to take all necessary measures to repel any armed attack against the forces of the United States and to prevent further aggression." Johnson wryly commented in 1967, "We did not think the resolution was necessary to what we did and what we're doing." Johnson nonetheless used what became known as the Gulf of Tonkin Resolution as justification and political insurance for expanding the war through 1968. Similar in its sweep to the ultimatum resolution prior to the Spanish-American War, the White House and the Congress treated the Gulf of Tonkin Resolution as all but a declaration of war. Indeed, when antiwar members of Congress sought to repeal the resolution several times, it was with the expressed intent that this would somehow delegitimize the war. When Nixon entered office, he forcefully opposed the repeal in 1969 but reversed his stance in 1970, saying that U.S. war efforts were never based on the resolution, but on the constitutional authority given the president as commander in chief.

United Nations War

At the outset of the Persian Gulf War, George H. W. Bush received congressional authorization to use "all available means, after January 15, 1991, to uphold and implement all relevant Security Council resolutions and to restore international peace and security to the area" after Iraqi president Saddam Hussein invaded Kuwait. When asked if he needed such congressional authorization, Bush, like Eisenhower and Johnson before him, said matter-of-factly, "I don't think I need it." Indeed, Bush had already sent some 350,000 U.S. forces to the Persian Gulf region. Bush believed he did not need congressional permission for two reasons: one, the commander in chief clause itself, and two, the United States was acting as part of a broader United Nations mission, similar to that during the Korean War (see below). But the resolution was nevertheless important as a convenient statement of presidential power. The use of the language "all available means" was more embracing than "all necessary measures." Many "available" tools of war may not be "necessary" to achieve victory. The United Nations had backed the war in the latter part of 1990 in a series of resolutions, making this the United Nations' war. So, the U.S. war effort was part of a larger international effort and this, in effect, gave the president even more justification for conducting the war however he saw fit.

Preemptive War

In the Iraq War, President George W. Bush sought and was granted permission to engage in a preemptive war against Hussein's regime to prevent the use of weapons of mass destruction that were said to be in the Hussein government's possession. On October 16, 2002, Congress passed a joint resolution giving the president the authority to use U.S. armed forces "as he determines to be necessary and appropriate" to "defend the national security of the United States against the continuing threat posed by Iraq." Although the word "defend" was used in the resolution, it marked the first time that an American president proceeded to enter a purely offensive, rather than defensive, war, because of a "threat" posed by another country. There was no immediate provocation from the Iraqi government as there had been in its 1990 invasion of Kuwait. Instead, the justification for the war was that Iraq might at any time foment a surprise attack.

The logic of the Bush administration brings to mind arguments by two members of the House of Representatives—a past and future president, John Quincy Adams and Abraham Lincoln—at the time of the Mexican-American War. Although the stated reasons for war were the death of American patrol members and Mexico's own war declaration, many in Congress objected to what they saw as President Polk's provocation of Mexico. Sending American soldiers to the disputed border between Texas and Mexico meant that American troops were likely to cross into Mexican territory. And some people, including Adams and Lincoln, viewed this as an offensive, rather than defensive, effort. Those defending Polk argued that it was necessary for American forces to cross into Mexico in an attempt to prevent Mexico from going to war and invading Texas. Adams strenuously objected to the "irreversible precedent that the President of the United States has but to declare that War exists, with any nation upon Earth, by the act of that Nation's Government, and the War is essentially declared" (Bemis, 1956, 499). Lincoln concurred: "Allow the President to invade a neighboring nation, whenever he shall deem it necessary to repel an invasion ... and you allow him to make war at pleasure. [If the] President should choose to say he thinks it necessary to invade Canada to prevent the British from invading us, how could you stop him? ... You may say to him 'I see no probability of the British invading us' but he will say to you 'be silent; I see it, if you don't' " (Basler, 1953, 1: 451–452).

Congress's authorization of the Iraq War is the most categorically sweeping precedent in American history. It gives the president the authority to use U.S. armed forces "as he determines to be necessary and appropriate" to "defend the national security of the United States against the continuing threat posed by Iraq." This language is groundbreaking in three ways. First, it permits the president to use the American military as he deems "necessary and appropriate." This all but deeds away any responsibility or power of the Congress to oversee the war. The addition of the word "appropriate," like the word "available" in the 1990 resolution, broadens the president's power beyond that granted in previous authorizations. A president may deem many things "appropriate" that are not actually "necessary." Second, the president is authorized to stop a "continuing threat," not an actual provocation. As Lincoln's words note, the president can be quite creative in defining such a threat. Third, although the resolution notes United Nations Security Council resolutions as further justification for the effort, there were no resolutions that immediately preceded the U.S. invasion of Iraq. Instead, the congressional resolution cites U.N. language from the Persian Gulf War nearly a decade before. So, this was not a United Nations war in the way in which the Korean War or the Persian Gulf War had been.

Bush's preemptive war precedent sets the stage for the future. There is little doubt given the history of the presidency that future presidents will embrace the use of "necessary and appropriate" means to "stop a continuing threat" to create another justification for future military involvement. And it is quite possible that the next time, presidents will not return to Congress for additional permission but merely rely on the Bush precedent as sufficient grounds for their own efforts. Presidents' independent policymaking efforts in military affairs are now at their most far reaching.

And the extent of this power is not only a reflection of the complex policy environment in which presidents have found themselves, but they have actually increased that complexity.

Independent Presidential Military Involvements

As shown in Table 7-3, American presidents have engaged the military in a variety of situations without requesting congressional authorization. This reveals, at its most fundamental, presidents' independent policy-making. As summarized in Table 7-4, presidents have entered 248 military involvements unilaterally. Many of these, notably in the nineteenth century, were naval missions to quell pirate raids on U.S. merchant ships or the landings of marines to help protect American lives and interests caught in the midst of civil unrest in countries far from the United States. Presidents such as John Tyler, Zachary Taylor, Millard Fillmore, and James Buchanan, surely not known for their expansive views of presidential power, saw these as police actions not directed against sovereign nations in many cases and, therefore, not requiring congressional attention. The efforts, thus, were conducted immediately and exclusively under the guise of the commander-in-chief power. Other instances, especially after World War II, involved many more troops sent to protect American interests against communism or other threats. Two instances noted in the table stand out as the benchmarks for presidents' independent use of American forces and the creation of their own independent war power: Abraham Lincoln's at the outset of the Civil War and Harry Truman's decision to go to war in Korea.

The most important early precedent was, of course, Lincoln's at the outbreak of the Civil War when Southern gunboats fired on Fort Sumter in Charleston, South Carolina, one of four remaining Union-held forts in the heart of the Confederacy. Learning of the attack, Lincoln found Congress out of session. He chose not to call them back until Independence Day, some twelve weeks later. During the interim, he expanded the army and navy, called out state militias, spent $2 million from the Treasury without congressional appropriation, blockaded southern ports, closed post offices to "treasonable correspondences," suspended the writ of habeas corpus in several locations, and ordered the arrest and military detention of suspected traitors. Congress authorized none of these actions at the time, although approved some of them after the fact. Instead, Lincoln issued executive orders and proclamations to proceed.

Lincoln's rationale was that a presidential war power emerged from the combination of several constitutional powers: the presidential oath that required that the president "preserve, protect, and defend the Constitution," the "take care clause" that states that the president "shall take Care that the Laws be faithfully executed," and the Commander in Chief clause about which Lincoln observed, "I suppose I have a right to take any measure which may best subdue the enemy." The Supreme Court and Congress later ratified most, although not all, of Lincoln's actions and thus presidential war power in extraordinary circumstances was set. Lincoln's actions should *not* have set the stage for future presidents' efforts, because the extraordinary circumstances within which Lincoln found himself were unlikely to be repeated. Yet all subsequent presidents have relied on Lincoln's amalgam war power.

The most significant modern precedent is President Truman's decision to enter the Korean War without congressional authorization. Although there was discussion within the Truman White House that the president should make the request of Congress, he ultimately chose not to. Truman boldly proclaimed in a press conference: "Under the President's constitutional powers as Commander in Chief of the Armed Forces he has the authority to send troops anywhere in the world. That power has been recognized repeatedly by the Congress and the courts." When asked by a reporter whether he needed congressional permission, Truman replied acerbically, "I do not have to unless I want to. But of course I am polite, and I usually always consult them" (*Public Papers of the Presidents,* June 11, 1951). The clarity and sweep of Truman's words and his complete disregard for congressional approval became a hotly debated position at the time. As the war dragged on and became increasingly unpopular, many felt it would have been wise for Truman to have Congress's initial backing.

As for future presidents, the Truman precedent has been important in opposing ways. The political backlash against Truman's decision not to seek congressional approval led Eisenhower, Johnson, George H. W. Bush, and George W. Bush to seek it, even though they said they did not need such approval because of Truman's decision (see Table 7-2). In many other circumstances, presidents have used the Truman precedent in its purest form to "send troops anywhere in the world." Since Vietnam, presidents have ordered troops into various trouble spots such as El Salvador, Honduras, Libya, Panama, Grenada, Bosnia, Kosovo, and Somalia, citing Truman and not formally seeking congressional authorization.

War Powers Resolution

Experts on both the presidency and Congress have long wondered why Congress has been so willing, indeed at times eager, to hand over such a vast, creative war power to presidents. In part this has been a matter of sequencing. Presidents can easily get the upper hand by the mere fact that troops are in harm's way. Once there, it is difficult for Congress not to provide funds to support the troops. Congress attempted to reassert its own role in war making with the War Powers Resolution of 1973. The resolution, passed over President Nixon's veto, requires that the president "in every possible instance shall consult with Congress before introducing United States Armed Forces into hostilities or into situations where imminent involvement in hostilities is clearly indicated." The president must then submit a report to Congress within forty-eight hours after committing the troops, describing the reasons and the constitutional authority for the action. Once the notification has been given, a clock starts ticking. The president has sixty days to complete the military mission, although he may request a thirty-day extension. The operation, however, must be completed in the ninety-day period unless Congress declares war or supplies specific authorization. Although the War Powers Resolution looks good on paper, every president since Gerald Ford has steadfastly denied its constitutionality. The Supreme Court has equally consistently refused to rule on the matter.

What the War Powers Resolution has accomplished is that presidents have begun to routinely notify Congress of their use of troops. Presidents do not, of course, concede any power to put troops in place, keep troops in place, or move them somewhere else by doing so. They view their limited adherence to the act as a matter of polite communication and always report it as "consistent with" the War Powers Resolution, rather than formally invoking the act. On June 11, 1951, well before the War Powers Resolution, Truman summed up this presidential approach: "I don't ask their permission, I just consult them" (*Public Papers of the Presidents,* June 11, 1951). Table 7-5 examines the 123 instances in which presidents have notified the Congress "consistent with" the reporting requirements of the War Powers Resolution. In another 17 times, the president did not notify Congress, even though troops were committed to an area of conflict.

The Costs of War

As many presidents have discovered, wars are costly, whether they are long or short, involve many troops or only a few, or have been based on congressional authorization or not. These costs are a reflection of the policy complexity attached to many military involvements, which by their very nature involve high degrees of uncertainty and risk. It is difficult for presidents and their advisers to predict how things will turn out and how quickly an endpoint can be achieved. War costs can be considered in four ways: length, lives, money, and public approval. Table 7-6 examines the length, casualties, and money spent on America's major wars. The Vietnam War was the longest war, World War II was the most deadly, and the Iraq War has been the most expensive. Table 7-7 considers in greater detail the costs of the wars in Iraq and Afghanistan.

Figure 7-1 considers the public's support of American war efforts in Korea, Vietnam, and Iraq. The three wars started with Americans believing in their merits. At the outset of the Korean War, Americans universally believed that the war was appropriate. This changed dramatically when China entered the war in October 1950. Public approval for the Vietnam War started lower than that for Korea and dropped further. Support for the Iraq War started at levels more similar to those for Korea but moved consistently downward. Since December 2005, a majority of Americans have believed that the Iraq War was a mistake.

Presidential Funding Efforts

In addition to the use of military force, presidents have adopted several other techniques to enhance their independent policy role in military affairs. In the Foreign Assistance Act of 1961, Congress granted presidents discretion for the funding of various military operations and foreign assistance projects. The law provided that a president may use special funding authorities without prior congressional approval when a president determines that the effort "is vital to the security of the United States" (for full details, see U.S. General Accounting Office, 1985). This is known as a presidential determination (or presidential finding). Determinations grant presidents the authority to meet emergencies or respond to situations in which formal foreign assistance agreements are not possible. The determinations directly involve independent presidential policymaking. They also reveal the ways in which the presidency as an institution is involved in these efforts. Although the president signs the determinations, their actual language and the initial impetus for them typically begin in the State Department. In some instances, the determinations are crafted in the Executive Office of the President by members of the National Security Council staff.

Table 7-8 documents the total number of general presidential determinations from John F. Kennedy to George W. Bush. Beginning with Nixon's second term, general determinations became a relatively frequent device for both direct military support and nonmilitary support for economic, humanitarian, and disaster relief. They increased somewhat during the George H. W. Bush administration and the early years of Clinton's first term. Much of this increase was due to determinations giving aid to countries in the Persian Gulf. President George W. Bush has also made similar numbers of determinations in the midst of the antiterror campaign and the Iraq War.

Three specific types of determinations that have been excluded from Table 7-8 are waivers, transfers, and drawdowns. As shown in Table 7-9, the waiver is the most frequently used of these and provides for funds "without regard to any conditions as to eligibility contained in this [Foreign Assistance] Act, when the President determines that such use is important to the security of the United States" (U.S. General Accounting Office, 1985, 29). The conditions being waived are time limits, usage limits, currency requirements, and war status limitations on the funds. Waiver authority was used to undertake military operations in Laos, Vietnam, and Cambodia. These efforts would have been prohibited by the Foreign Assistance Act had waivers not been invoked. President George W. Bush has used the waiver authority more than any other president. Indeed, in 2007, Bush issued the two largest waivers ever: one for $1.05 billion and another for $643 million for economic support for Iraq. His administration has also issued waivers on matters related to antiterrorism, trade, and democracy promotion in various countries other than Iraq.

A second form of special funding authority is the transfer. This allows presidents, again without approval from Congress, to transfer up to 10 percent of the funds under one provision of several foreign assistance acts to another provision of any other assistance act "whenever the President determines it to be necessary" (U.S. General Accounting Office, 1985, 24). As Table 7-10 shows, these transfers have amounted to more than $634 million between various foreign assistance accounts.

Presidents also have the "drawdown authority," which allows presidents to provide equipment, spare parts, and services from the Department of Defense to a foreign government without congressional or other budgetary authorization or appropriations. A president may draw down U.S. military stock or equipment once he has determined that the security of the United States is at stake. After the equipment has been sent, presidents are authorized to replace or reimburse the Defense Department for the stocks and services that have been drawn down. Subsequent foreign assistance appropriations provide for replacements and reimbursements. One of the most infamous uses of the drawdown authority was the secret shipment of arms to Iran by the Reagan administration. As Table 7-11 shows, the George W. Bush administration has used the drawdown authority to send $725 million in equipment and other materiel to Afghanistan to aid its antiterror efforts. This is the largest amount ever sent to a single country, considerably more than the drawdowns made by Presidents Johnson, Nixon, and Ford to aid Vietnam and Cambodia.

Presidential Diplomacy

In addition to exercising their war power, presidents engage in diplomatic efforts that also reveal the four dimensions of policymaking: independent effort, personal attention, institutional control, and policy complexity. In diplomatic affairs, presidents have considerable free rein. Since the tenure of George Washington they have been considered, in the words of then representative John Marshall, later chief justice of the United States, as the "sole organ of the nation" in foreign affairs. Presidents often become personally involved in diplomatic efforts. Presidents during the Cold War eagerly engaged in summitry with the Soviet Union. Richard Nixon pored over briefing books before his historic trip to China. Jimmy Carter personally negotiated a peace settlement between Israel and Egypt. Yet at the same time, the State Department runs much of presidential diplomacy. There are ongoing enterprises in the State Department that occur year after year, regardless of who is president, and reflect the institutional nature of American foreign policy efforts. Finally, the policy environment in diplomacy is just as complex as it is in war. There are numerous competing interests both within the United States and across the world on what to do next and who should be an ally or an enemy.

Presidents' diplomacy depends on two principal types of international agreements: treaties, which constitutionally require approval of the Senate by a two-thirds vote, and executive agreements, which require no congressional action. Executive agreements, which presidents simply sign into effect, are often used for relatively routine matters (for example, to enable nations to exchange postal services and to fix the tax status of foreign nationals in the United States and of American citizens abroad). However, executive agreements may significantly shape American foreign policy. Actions affected by executive agreements have included the annexation of Texas and Hawaii, initiatives taken by the United States prior to the Japanese bombing of Pearl Harbor at the outset of World War II, the initiation and termination of U.S. involvement in the Korean War, and key escalations during the Vietnam War (Margolis, 1986). The Supreme Court has maintained that executive agreements have the same force in law as treaties (*United States v. Pink,* 315 U.S. 203, 1942).

Treaties and executive agreements have been recorded and aggregated from 1789 to 2004. Table 7-12 indicates the total number of international agreements issued from the time of Washington through Harry S. Truman's first administration, while Table 7-13 records the number of international agreements from Truman's second term through the end of George W. Bush's first term. As Table 7-12 shows, both treaties and executive agreements increased dramatically beginning with the McKinley administration as a result of the Spanish-American War. Theodore Roosevelt continued to expand the use of international agreements, most significantly during his second term.

A second sharp rise in the number of international agreements accompanied U.S. involvement in World War II and the postwar emergence of the United States as a superpower. The war years brought a dramatic increase in executive foreign policy activity as agreements were signed on all war fronts from Africa to the Soviet Union. This major environmental shock did more to encourage use of executive agreements than any president's isolated decisions, although the foreign policy strategies of Franklin Roosevelt and Truman were certainly contributing factors (Schlesinger, 1973). Setting the stage for American involvement in the war, Roosevelt sold American destroyers to the British by executive agreement, without congressional approval. Foreign policy activity grew still more during Truman's second term, with U.S. involvement in the Korean War and the undertaking of the Marshall Plan (see Table 7-13). Presidents since Truman have made, on average, more than 1,000 agreements over the course of their terms in office. Figure 7-2 summarizes the changes in the numbers of treaties and executive agreements negotiated since Truman's second term. While the number of treaties has remained relatively low, the number of executive agreements has dropped since its peak during the Carter and Reagan administrations. The George H. W. Bush and Clinton administrations wrote fewer executive agreements and the George W. Bush administration fewer still. In fact, the George W. Bush administration entered into fewer total agreements than any president since Franklin Roosevelt, which may reflect his tendency to take a more assertive, unilateral approach to world affairs.

Researchers have argued that presidents use executive agreements as political devices to circumvent the Senate, especially when it is controlled by the other party (Margolis, 1986; Martin, 2000). A 2008 work by Randall Smith shows that there are several types of executive agreements, only a few of which are original in nature. Most revise previous agreements or are authorized in treaties themselves. His research shows that executive agreements are not political devices, but they are convenient tools that accommodate the intricacies and details of the foreign policy environment. Tables 7-12 and 7-13 report the ratios between executive agreements and treaties. The data show no higher ratios when presidents faced an opposition Senate than when they enjoyed a Senate controlled by their own party. Executive agreements and treaties increased with Republican presidents McKinley and Theodore Roosevelt, both of whom benefited from Republican Senate majorities. The number of executive agreements did not consistently exceed the number of treaties until the time of Calvin Coolidge, a Republican president who worked with a strongly Republican Senate. In the aftermath of World War II and at the outset of the implementation of the Marshall Plan, executive agreements increased again with President Truman, whose party generally controlled the Senate.

Table 7-14 analyzes these issues further by classifying Senate action on all international agreements submitted for ratification in the postwar period. These statistics and the list of treaties killed by the Senate found in Table 7-15 demonstrate that since the beginning of the republic, the Senate has rejected just 24 treaties of the more than 10,000 offered. In the last fifty years, only 6 agreements have been rejected. When treaties are in danger of being rejected, presidents tend to withdraw them from consideration. The Senate may also leave an agreement pending at the end of a session, so that ratification is thereby delayed for a session or more.

The infrequency of presidential defeat does not imply that the treaty ratification process is moribund. Although executive agreements have replaced treaties as "the official instrument of foreign policy commitment" (Johnson, 1984, 12), the number of treaties, protocols, and conventions has also increased since the administration of Franklin Roosevelt (see Tables 7-12 and 7-13). Treaties and other agreements often involve important and controversial topics, which have included the creation of the North Atlantic Treaty Organization, strategic arms limitations, cooperation in the Middle East, and numerous trade and tariff understandings. These tend to be negotiated, at least informally, with the Senate before final negotiations take place with the signatories. This fact may account for the very low rejection rate. Table 7-16 lists the major arms control agreements that the presidency has prepared and the Senate has reviewed since the Eisenhower administration. Both institutions appear to respond in practical ways to an expanded policy environment: Incumbent presidents have not consistently maneuvered around Congress to avoid its constitutionally prescribed check on their diplomatic powers; neither has the Senate abdicated its consent role.

In sum, the number of executive agreements seems predicated more on the exigencies of U.S. involvement in foreign affairs than on presidents' attempts to circumvent the shared powers outlined in the Constitution. Executive agreements are convenient tools that can accommodate the policy complexity created by both routine and important foreign matters, regardless of who controls the Senate or the White House.

Conclusion

Presidents exercise their own presidential war-making power to order troops around the world. They act as the "sole organ of foreign relations" on behalf of the United States, issuing a vast array of international agreements. Presidents devote much of their personal time and energy to foreign affairs because they have such sweeping unilateral authority. They can direct the nation and its resources to a single international goal. Their advisers maneuver to give the best advice to the president on matters that may well shape history. At least at the outset, presidents typically command considerable public support for these efforts. Yet, presidents also face a dizzying, messy conglomeration of international problems, the values and interests that define acceptable solutions, and the many unintended consequences of the policies they choose. As much as presidents may have unilateral power to act, the reactions to this power are often cacophonous and complex. The very sweep of power presidents assert in military affairs has created a paradox for them. The broader the claim of presidential power, the more intractable the situations in which presidents find themselves. The broader the claim of presidential power, the more difficult internal White House politics becomes, the more recalcitrant Congress may become, the more likely public support erodes, and the less likely world leaders fall in line behind America's chosen course. Unfolding events, the perspectives of other world politicians, competing advisers, and ideological beliefs about enemies and friends shape presidents' foreign policy efforts and take away much of the independence that presidents have so vigilantly advanced.

Table 7-1 Declared Wars by the United States, 1787–2008

Year	*Name*	*Enemy*	*President requests*	*House action*		*Senate action*	
1812	War of 1812	Great Britain	June 1, 1812	June 4, 1812	Vote: 79–49	June 17, 1812	Vote: 19–13
1846	Mexican-American War	Mexico	May 11, 1846	May 11, 1846	Vote: 174–14	May 12, 1846	Vote: 40–2
1898	Spanish-American War	Spain	April 25, 1898	April 25, 1898	Voice vote	April 25, 1898	Voice vote
1917	World War I	Germany	April 12, 1917	April 6, 1917	Vote: 373–50	April 4, 1917	Vote: 82–6
1917	World War I	Austria-Hungary	Dec. 4, 1917	Dec. 7, 1917	Vote: 365–1	Dec. 7, 1917	Vote: 74–0
1941	World War II	Japan	Dec. 8, 1941	Dec. 8, 1941	Vote: 388–1	Dec. 8, 1941	Vote: 82–0
1941	World War II	Germany	Dec. 11, 1941	Dec. 11, 1941	Vote: 393–0	Dec. 11, 1941	Vote: 88–0
1941	World War II	Italy	Dec. 11, 1941	Dec. 11, 1941	Vote: 399–0	Dec. 11, 1941	Vote: 90–0
1942	World War II	Bulgaria	June 2, 1942	June. 3, 1942	Vote: 357–0	June 4, 1942	Vote: 73–0
1942	World War II	Hungary	June 2, 1942	June 3, 1942	Vote: 360–0	June 4, 1942	Vote: 73–0
1942	World War II	Rumania	June 2, 1942	June 3, 1942	Vote: 361–0	June 4, 1942	Vote: 73–0

Source: U.S. Library of Congress, Congressional Research Service, Report for Congress, "Declarations of War and Authorizations for the Use of Military Force: Historical Background and Legal Implications," Jan. 14, 2003, 4-6, www.ndu.edu/library/docs/crs/crs_rl31133_14jan03.pdf.

Table 7-2 Military Engagements Authorized by Congress, 1787–2007

President	*Country/ continent*	*Conflict*	*Date*	*Authorization*
Adams	France	French navy seizes American commercial ships	May 28, 1798	President is "authorized to instruct and direct" navy commanders to "seize, take, and bring into any port" offending French ships.
Adams	France	French navy seizes American commercial ships	July 9, 1798	President is "authorized to instruct the commanders to subdue, seize, and take any armed French vessel."
Jefferson	Tripoli	Tripoli pirates seize American vessels	Feb. 6, 1802	President is authorized to "subdue, seize, and make prize of all vessels, goods, and effects" used to attack U.S. vessels.
Madison	Algeria	Algerian navy seizes U.S. commercial vessels	March 3, 1815	President is authorized to "subdue, seize, and make prize of all vessels, goods, and effects" used to attack U.S. vessels.
Monroe	South America	Spanish colonies attack U.S. vessels	March 3, 1819	President is authorized to "subdue, seize, take, and send into any port" the vessels used to attack U.S. ships.
Monroe	Africa	U.S. Navy raids slave ships pursuant to act outlawing slave trade as piracy	May 15, 1820	March 3, 1819, language is applied to slave trade.
Buchanan	Paraguay	Paraguay attacks U.S. naval vessel	June 2, 1858	President is authorized to instruct U.S. Navy to seize Paraguayan vessels.
Eisenhower	Formosa	U.S. agrees to protect Formosa (Taiwan) from attack by mainland Communist China	Jan. 29, 1955	President "is authorized to employ the Armed Forces as he deems necessary for the specific purpose of securing and protecting Formosa."
Eisenhower	Lebanon	Insurgents in Lebanon threaten its stability	March 9, 1957	President is authorized to "use armed forces to assist any such nation or group of such nations requesting assistance against armed aggression from any country controlled by international communism."

(Table continues)

Table 7-2 *(Continued)*

President	*Country/ continent*	*Conflict*	*Date*	*Authorization*
L. Johnson	Vietnam	North Vietnamese naval units attack U.S. ships in Gulf of Tonkin	Aug. 10, 1964	"Congress approves and supports the determination of the President, as Commander in Chief, to take all necessary measures to repel any armed attack against the forces of the United States and to prevent further aggression."
Reagan	Lebanon	U.S. Marines are killed in multinational peacekeeping effort	Oct. 12, 1983	"The President is authorized for the purposes of the War Powers Resolution to continue participation by U.S. Armed Forces in the Multinational Force in Lebanon."
G.H.W. Bush	Iraq	Iraq invades Kuwait	Jan. 14, 1991	President is authorized to use "all available means after January 15, 1991, to uphold and implement all relevant Security Council resolutions and to restore international peace and security to the area."
G.W. Bush	Al Qaeda, Afghanistan	United States is attacked on Sept. 11, 2001	Sept. 18, 2001	"President is authorized to use all necessary and appropriate force against those nations, organizations, or persons he determines planned, authorized, committed or aided the terrorist attacks that occurred on September 11, 2001, or harbored such organizations or persons, in order to prevent any future acts of international terrorism against the United States."

G. W. Bush	Iraq	Iraq is believed to be hiding "weapons of mass destruction"	Oct. 16, 2002	"President is authorized to use the Armed Forces of the United States as he determines to be necessary and appropriate in order to— (1) defend the national security of the United States against the continuing threat posed by Iraq; and (2) enforce all relevant United Nations Security Council resolutions regarding Iraq."

Source: U.S. Congress, Library of Congress, Congressional Research Service, "Declarations of War and Authorizations for the Use of Military Force: Historical Background and Legal Implications," Jan. 14, 2003, www.ndu.edu/library/docs/crs/crs_rl31133_14jan03.pdf.

Table 7-3 Presidential Military Action without Congressional Authorization, Washington to G. W. Bush

President	*Year*	*Location*	*Action*
Washington	1788	Pennsylvania	Whiskey Rebellion: president orders militia, which he personally leads, to quell riots over a tax on liquor.
Jefferson	1806	Mexico	U.S. army platoon invades Spanish territory in Mexico.
Jefferson	1806–1810[a]	Mississippi Delta	U.S. gunboats routinely fire on French and Spanish privateers off the Mississippi Delta.
Madison	1810	West Florida (Spanish territory)	Governor of Louisiana occupies disputed territory on orders of president.
Madison	1812	East Florida (Spanish territory)	President authorizes temporary possession of Amelia Island, later disavowed by Madison.
Madison	1816	Spanish Florida	U.S. destroys fort known to harbor raiders into U.S. territory.
Madison	1816–1818[a]	Spanish Florida	First Seminole War: Gen. Andrew Jackson pursues Seminole Indians into northern Florida. Monroe authorizes Jackson to invade Florida and attack Spanish posts. Spain ceded Florida in 1819.
Monroe	1817	Spanish Florida	Under presidential orders, U.S. forces land on Amelia Island to expel smugglers.
Monroe	1818	Chile	USS *Ontario* rescues U.S. merchant ships captured by Spain.
Monroe	1818	Oregon	USS *Ontario* lands at Columbia River to take possession of Oregon territory.
Monroe	1822	Cuba	U.S. naval forces land on Cuba to attack pirates.
Monroe	1823	Cuba	U.S. naval forces land on Cuba to attack pirates.
Monroe	1824	Cuba	U.S. naval forces land on Cuba to attack pirates.
Monroe	1824	Puerto Rico (Spanish territory)	U.S. naval forces land on Puerto Rico to attack pirates.
J.Q. Adams	1825	Cuba	U.S. naval forces land on Cuba to attack pirates.
J.Q. Adams	1827	Greece	U.S. naval forces land on islands to hunt for pirates.

Table 7-3 *(Continued)*

President	*Year*	*Location*	*Action*
Jackson	1831–1832	Falkland Islands	USS *Lexington* seeks release of three American sealing vessels.
Jackson	1832	Sumatra	U.S. naval force attacks fort in retribution for earlier attack on U.S. ship.
Jackson	1833	Argentina	U.S. forces sent to protect U.S. interests during an insurrection.
Jackson	1835–1836	Peru	U.S. Marines protect U.S. interests during an insurrection.
Jackson	1836	Mexico	U.S. troops occupy disputed territory during the Texas war for independence to prevent Native American attacks.
Van Buren	1838–1839	Sumatra	U.S. naval forces land to punish locals for attacks on U.S. shipping.
Van Buren	1840	Fiji Islands	U.S. naval forces land to punish locals for attacks on U.S. shipping.
Tyler	1841	Drummond Island	U.S. naval forces land to avenge death of sailor murdered by locals.
Tyler	1843	China	U.S. naval forces land to protect Americans after clash with Chinese at Canton.
Tyler	1843	Africa	U.S. naval forces land to prevent piracy and slave trade and punish attacks on locals and U.S. seamen.
Tyler	1844	Mexico	President orders U.S. forces to protect Texas pending Senate approval of annexation, which was later rejected.
Taylor	1849	Smyrna	U.S. naval forces gain release of American held by Austrian officials.
Fillmore	1851	Turkey	U.S. naval forces in show of strength after massacre of foreigners, including Americans.
Fillmore	1851	Johanns Island (East Africa)	U.S. naval forces punish locals for unlawful imprisonment of Americans.
Fillmore	1852	Argentina	U.S. naval forces land to protect American interests during revolution.

(Table continues)

Table 7-3 *(Continued)*

President	*Year*	*Location*	*Action*
Fillmore	1853	Nicaragua	U.S. naval forces land to protect American interests during unrest.
Fillmore	1853	Japan	Commodore Perry's naval expedition shows U.S. force, leading to the "opening of Japan" with a letter from Fillmore.
Pierce	1854	China	U.S. ships protect American interests in Shanghai during Chinese civil unrest.
Pierce	1854	Nicaragua	U.S. naval forces bombard town to avenge insult to U.S. minister to Nicaragua.
Pierce	1855	China	U.S. ships protect American interests in Shanghai and Hong Kong.
Pierce	1855	Fiji Islands	U.S. naval force lands to seek reparations for actions against Americans.
Pierce	1856	Panama	U.S. naval forces land to protect American interests during civil unrest.
Pierce	1856	China	U.S. naval forces land to protect American interests in Canton during hostilities between Chinese and British.
Buchanan	1857	Nicaragua	U.S. naval forces block attempt of William Walker to take over country.
Buchanan	1858	Uruguay	U.S. naval forces land to protect American interests during a revolution in Montevideo.
Buchanan	1858	Fiji Islands	U.S. forces avenge killings of two U.S. citizens.
Buchanan	1858–1859	Turkey	Sec. of State requests naval force to avenge American deaths and "to remind the authorities of the power of the United States."
Buchanan	1859	Mexico	U.S. Army pursues bandit Cortina.
Buchanan	1859	China	U.S. naval forces land to protect American interests in Shanghai.
Buchanan	1860	Angola	U.S. naval forces land to protect Americans during civil unrest.
Buchanan	1860	Colombia	U.S. naval forces land to protect American interests during a revolution.
Lincoln	1861	U.S. southern ports	U.S. Navy establishes blockade of ports in Florida, Georgia, Louisiana, North Carolina, South Carolina, and Virginia at start of the Civil War.
Lincoln	1863	Japan	U.S. Navy ship retaliates against Japanese attack on U.S. vessel.

Table 7-3 *(Continued)*

President	*Year*	*Location*	*Action*
Lincoln	1864	Japan	U.S. naval forces protect U.S. minister to Japan.
Lincoln	1864	Japan	U.S. naval forces enforce treaties to open Japanese waters to foreign shipping.
Lincoln	1865	Panama	U.S. naval forces land to protect Americans during a revolution.
A. Johnson	1866	China	U.S. naval forces land to support American consul at Newchwang.
A. Johnson	1867	Nicaragua	U.S. Marines occupy Managua and Leon to protect American interests.
A. Johnson	1867	Formosa	U.S. naval forces land to punish locals for attacks on U.S. shipping.
A. Johnson	1868	Japan	U.S. naval forces land to protect American interests during civil war in Japan.
A. Johnson	1868	Uruguay	U.S. naval forces land to protect foreign residents during an insurrection in Montevideo.
A. Johnson	1868	Colombia	U.S. naval forces protect American interests at Aspinwall.
Grant	1870	Mexico	U.S. naval forces destroy pirate ship *Forward.*
Grant	1871	Korea	U.S. naval forces land to punish locals for attacks on U.S. shipping.
Grant	1873	Panama	U.S. naval forces land to protect American interests during hostilities between local groups and Panamanian government.
Grant	1873–1896[a]	Mexico	U.S. troops cross into Mexico to pursue cattle thieves.
Grant	1874	Hawaii	U.S. naval forces land to maintain order during coronation of new king.
Grant	1876	Mexico	U.S. naval forces land to police town of Matamoras temporarily without a government.
Arthur	1882	Egypt	U.S. naval forces land to protect American interests during warfare between British and Egyptians.
Arthur	1885	Panama	U.S. forces guard valuables in transit over Panama Railroad.

(Table continues)

Table 7-3 *(Continued)*

President	*Year*	*Location*	*Action*
Cleveland	1888	Korea	U.S. naval forces land to protect American residents in Seoul during political unrest.
Cleveland	1888	Samoa	U.S. naval forces land to protect American citizens during a civil war.
B. Harrison	1889	Hawaii	U.S. naval forces land to protect American interests during a revolution.
B. Harrison	1890	Argentina	U.S. naval forces land to protect American consulate at Buenos Aires.
B. Harrison	1891	Haiti	U.S. naval forces land to protect American lives on Navassa Island.
B. Harrison	1891	Bering Strait	U.S. naval forces stop seal poaching.
B. Harrison	1891	Chile	U.S. naval forces land to protect the American consulate during revolution in Valparaiso.
B. Harrison	1893	Hawaii	U.S. Marines land to protect American lives and promote provisional government. Action disavowed by U.S. government.
Cleveland	1894	Brazil	U.S. naval forces land to protect American shipping during a Brazilian civil war.
Cleveland	1894–1895	China	U.S. Marines land to protect American interests during Sino-Japanese War.
Cleveland	1894–1896	Korea	U.S. naval forces land to protect American consulate during Sino-Japanese War.
Cleveland	1895	Colombia	U.S. naval forces land to protect American interests during bandit attacks.
Cleveland	1896	Nicaragua	U.S. naval forces land to protect American interests during local unrest in Corinto.
McKinley	1898	Nicaragua	U.S. naval forces land to protect American interests during local unrest at San Juan del Sur.
McKinley	1898–1899	China	U.S. naval forces land to protect U.S. consulate in Peking and Tientsin during political unrest.
McKinley	1899	Nicaragua	U.S. naval forces land to protect American interests during insurrection against military government.

Table 7-3 *(Continued)*

President	*Year*	*Location*	*Action*
McKinley	1899	Samoa	U.S. naval forces land to protect American interests during political unrest.
McKinley	1899–1901[a]	Philippines	U.S. naval forces land to protect American interests after the war with Spain and take over island.
McKinley	1900	China	U.S. naval forces land to protect foreign lives during the Boxer Rebellion. A permanent U.S. legation was established in Peking.
T. Roosevelt	1901	Panama	U.S. naval forces land to protect American property on the isthmus and keep shipping open during a revolution.
T. Roosevelt	1902	Colombia	U.S. naval forces land to protect American lives at Bocas del Toro during a civil war.
T. Roosevelt	1902	Panama	U.S. places armed guards on all trains crossing the isthmus and stationed ships on both sides of Panama to prevent the landing of Colombian troops.
T. Roosevelt	1903	Honduras	U.S. naval forces land to protect the American consulate during a revolution.
T. Roosevelt	1903	Dominican Republic	U.S. Marines land to protect American interests in Santo Domingo during a revolution.
T. Roosevelt	1903	Syria	U.S. naval forces land to protect American consulate in Beirut.
T. Roosevelt	1903–1904	Abyssinia	U.S. Marines sent to protect U.S. consul general as he negotiates a treaty.
T. Roosevelt	1903–1914[a]	Panama	U.S. Marines sent to protect American interests and lives during revolution for independence from Colombia.
T. Roosevelt	1904	Dominican Republic	U.S. naval forces land to protect American interests during a revolution in Puerta Plata, Sousa, and Santo Domingo City.
T. Roosevelt	1904	Morocco	U.S. Marines land to protect consul general and force release of kidnapped American.
T. Roosevelt	1904	Panama	U.S. Marines protect American lives during a threatened insurrection.

(Table continues)

Table 7-3 *(Continued)*

President	*Year*	*Location*	*Action*
T. Roosevelt	1904–1905	Korea	U.S. Marines sent to protect American consulate in Seoul during Russo-Japanese War.
T. Roosevelt	1906–1909	Cuba	U.S. forces land to restore order and protect foreigners after a revolution.
T. Roosevelt	1907	Honduras	U.S. naval forces land to protect American interests during a war between Honduras and Nicaragua.
Taft	1910	Nicaragua	U.S. naval forces land to protect American interests at Bluefields.
Taft	1911	Honduras	U.S. naval forces land to protect American lives during a civil war.
Taft	1911	China	U.S. naval forces land in several locations to protect American lives and interests as the nationalist revolution approaches.
Taft	1912	Honduras	U.S. naval forces land to protect an American railroad from being seized by the Honduran government.
Taft	1912	Panama	U.S. troops supervise elections outside the Canal Zone.
Taft	1912	Cuba	U.S. troops protect American interests in Havana.
Taft	1912	China	U.S. naval forces land to protect American lives during a revolution.
Taft	1912–1925	Nicaragua	U.S. Marines land to protect American interests during an attempted revolution and remain to promote peace and stability through 1925.
Taft	1912–1941[a]	China	U.S. troops land to protect American interests, establish a guard at Peking and along the route to the sea.
Wilson	1913	Mexico	U.S. Marines land to evacuate American citizens from Yaqui Valley during civil strife.
Wilson	1914	Haiti	U.S. naval forces land to protect American lives during a revolution.
Wilson	1914	Dominican Republic	U.S. naval forces land to protect Santo Domingo City as a neutral zone.

Table 7-3 *(Continued)*

President	*Year*	*Location*	*Action*
Wilson	1914–1917	Mexico	Ongoing hostilities with Mexico including Gen. Pershing's expedition to northern Mexico.
Wilson	1915–1934[a]	Haiti	U.S. forces maintain order during political unrest.
Wilson	1916	China	U.S. forces land to quell a riot on American property in Nanking.
Wilson	1916–1924[a]	Dominican Republic	U.S. naval forces maintain order during period of unrest.
Wilson	1917	China	U.S. troops land to protect American lives at Chungking.
Wilson	1917–1922[a]	Cuba	U.S. forces land to protect American interests during an insurrection. Most forces leave by 1919, some remain until 1922.
Wilson	1918–1919	Mexico	U.S. troops enter Mexico in pursuit of bandit at least three times in 1918 and six times in 1919.
Wilson	1918–1920	Panama	U.S. forces keep order during unrest associated with elections.
Wilson	1918–1920	Soviet Russia	U.S. Marines land at Vladivostok to protect American consulate during fighting between Bolshevik troops and Czech Army.
Wilson	1919	Dalmatia	U.S. forces land to keep order between Italians and Serbs, at request of the Italian government.
Wilson	1919	Turkey	U.S. Marines land to protect U.S. consulate during the Greek occupation of Constantinople.
Wilson	1919	Honduras	U.S. Marines land to maintain order in a neutral zone during an attempted revolution.
Wilson	1920	China	U.S. Marines land for a few hours to protect American lives during a disturbance at Kiukiang.
Wilson	1920	Guatemala	U.S. forces land to protect American interests during a period of fighting between Unionists and the government.
Wilson	1920–1922[a]	Russia	U.S. Marines land to guard U.S. radio station at Vladivostok.
Harding	1921	Panama-Costa Rica	U.S. naval squadrons demonstrate on both sides of the isthmus to prevent war between the two countries.

(Table continues)

Table 7-3 *(Continued)*

President	*Year*	*Location*	*Action*
Harding	1922	Turkey	U.S. Marines land to protect American lives and interests against Turkish Nationals.
Harding	1922–1923	China	U.S. Marines land to protect American lives during period of unrest.
Coolidge	1924	Honduras	U.S. Marines land to protect American lives during election hostilities.
Coolidge	1925	China	U.S. Marines land to protect American lives in Shanghai during unrest.
Coolidge	1925	China	U.S. Marines land to protect American lives and interests in Shanghai during continued unrest.
Coolidge	1925	Honduras	U.S. forces protect foreigners at Ceiba during political unrest.
Coolidge	1925	Panama	600 U.S. troops land to protect American interests after rioting.
Coolidge	1926–1933[a]	Nicaragua	U.S. Marines land to protect American interests after a coup.
Coolidge	1926	China	U.S. Marines land to protect American interests after a Nationalist attack on Hankow.
Hoover	1927	China	Increase in American sailors and marines to protect consulate in Nanking and Shanghai during fighting between Nationalist forces and government.
Hoover	1932	China	U.S. forces land to protect American interests during Japanese occupation of Shanghai.
F. Roosevelt	1934	China	U.S. Marines land at Foochow to protect American consulate.
F. Roosevelt	1940	Newfoundland, Bermuda, St. Lucia, Bahamas, Jamaica, Antigua, Trinidad, British Guiana	U.S. troops guard "lend-lease" air and naval bases obtained from the British.
F. Roosevelt	1941	Greenland	U.S. troops protect Greenland from Germany.
F. Roosevelt	1941	Dutch Guiana	U.S. troops occupy country by agreement with the Netherlands to protect aluminum ore supply.
F. Roosevelt	1941	Iceland	U.S. takes over Iceland for strategic protection.

Table 7-3 *(Continued)*

President	*Year*	*Location*	*Action*
F. Roosevelt	1941	Germany	U.S. Navy patrols ship lanes to Europe, acts as convoys, and attack German submarines.
Truman	1945	China	50,000 U.S. Marines sent to North China to assist Chinese Nationalist authorities with the Japanese.
Truman	1946	Trieste	U.S. troops increased near the Italian-Yugoslav border.
Truman	1946	Bosporus Straits	Soviet threat to Turkish control.
Truman	1948	Palestine	U.S. Marines sent to Jerusalem to protect U.S. consul general.
Truman	1948–1949	China	U.S. Marines land sent to Nanking and Shanghai during communist takeover.
Truman	1950–1953	South Korea	U.S. troops fight the Korean War.
Truman	1950–1955	Formosa (Taiwan)	U.S. naval forces positioned to prevent communist attacks from mainland.
Eisenhower	1954–1955	China	U.S. naval forces land to evacuate Americans from Tachen Islands.
Eisenhower	1955–1960	Vietnam	U.S. military advisers help train the South Vietnamese army after the Geneva Convention partitions the country between north and south.
Eisenhower	1956	Egypt	U.S. Marines evacuate Americans during Suez crisis.
Eisenhower	1957	Indonesia	U.S. Marines wait to protect Americans during revolt
Eisenhower	1957	Taiwan	U.S. naval forces defend against communist shelling.
Eisenhower	1958	Indonesia	U.S. Marines and naval forces land to protect American citizens.
Eisenhower	1959–1960	Cuba	U.S. Marines land to protect American lives during Cuban crisis.
Kennedy	1961	Vietnam	U.S. military advisers increase to stabilize government and begin to train combat units.
Kennedy	1962	Cuba	U.S. Navy blockades Cuba during the missile crisis.
Kennedy	1962	Thailand	U.S. Marines land to protect country from communist threat.
Kennedy	1962–1975[a]	Laos	U.S. military support protects government against communist threat.
Kennedy	1963	Haiti	U.S. Marines position off the coast to ensure stability.

(Table continues)

Table 7-3 *(Continued)*

President	*Year*	*Location*	*Action*
L. Johnson	1964	Congo	U.S. provides airlift for Congolese troops during a rebellion.
L. Johnson	1965	Dominican Republic	U.S. troops land to protect American lives during a revolt.
L. Johnson	1967	Congo	U.S. transport planes provide logistical support for government during a revolt.
Nixon	1969–1970	Cambodia	U.S conducts secret bombing missions in Cambodia.
Nixon	1970	Cambodia	U.S. troops invade to clear out supply depots of North Vietnam.
Nixon	1974	Cyprus	U.S. naval forces land to evacuate Americans during clash between Turkish and Greek Cypriot forces.
Ford	1975	Vietnam	U.S. Marines and helicopters aid in the evacuation of Americans and others from Saigon as the North Vietnamese take over the city.
Ford	1975	Cambodia	U.S. forces aid the evacuation of Americans as government collapses.
Ford	1975	Cambodia	U.S. military forces retake the ship *Mayaguez* seized by Cambodia.
Ford	1976	Lebanon	U.S. Navy helicopters evacuate Americans and others during fighting between Lebanese factions.
Ford	1976	Korea	U.S. forces increase after two Americans killed.
Carter	1978	Zaire	U.S. military transport provide logistical support for Belgian and French rescue operation.
Carter	1980	Iran	U.S. transport planes and helicopters make an unsuccessful helicopter rescue attempt of U.S. embassy hostages.
Reagan	1981	El Salvador	U.S. military advisers sent to train government forces in counterinsurgency.
Reagan	1981	Libya	U.S. Navy planes shoot down Libyan jets.
Reagan	1983	Egypt	U.S. AWACS electronic surveillance plane arrives after Libyan plane bombs city in Sudan.
Reagan	1983	Honduras	U.S. military helicopters carry Honduran troops to Nicaraguan borders to repel Nicaraguan troops.

Table 7-3 *(Continued)*

President	*Year*	*Location*	*Action*
Reagan	1983	Chad	U.S. air support used to assist Chad against Libya.
Reagan	1983	Grenada	U.S. Marines land to protect American lives and respond to threats of instability.
Reagan	1984	Saudi Arabia	U.S. air support aids Saudi jets shooting down Iranian fighter planes.
Reagan	1985	Italy	U.S. Navy planes intercept hijacked Egyptian airliner.
Reagan	1986	Libya	U.S. forces attacked in the Gulf of Sidra by Libyan jets.
Reagan	1986	Libya	U.S. air and naval forces conduct bombing strikes on terrorist and military facilities in Libya.
Reagan	1987–1988	Persian Gulf	U.S. Navy escorts Kuwaiti oil tankers and are fired upon on several occasions.
Reagan	1988	Panama	1,000 U.S. troops sent to canal zone to protect American lives and interests and keep canal open during period of unrest.
G. H. W. Bush	1989	Libya	U.S. Navy jets shoot down Libyan fighters.
G. H. W. Bush	1989	Panama	U.S. troops added to existing forces after elections.
G. H. W. Bush	1989	Philippines	U.S. fighter planes assist government to block coup.
G. H. W. Bush	1989–1990	Panama	U.S. troops invade to protect American lives, bring Noriega to justice.
G. H. W. Bush	1990	Liberia	U.S. forces provide additional support for U.S. embassy and evacuate Americans during unrest.
G. H. W. Bush	1990	Saudi Arabia	U.S. forces increase after Iraq invades Kuwait.
G. H. W. Bush	1991	Iraq	U.S. forces go to northern Iraq to provide emergency aid to Kurdish rebels.
G. H. W. Bush	1991	Zaire	U.S. planes aid Belgian and French troops during rioting, also evacuate Americans.
G. H. W. Bush	1992	Sierra Leone	U.S. military planes evacuate Americans after government overthrown.

(Table continues)

Table 7-3 *(Continued)*

President	*Year*	*Location*	*Action*
G.H.W. Bush	1992	Kuwait	U.S. military exercises after Iraqi refusal to recognize new border.
G.H.W. Bush	1992	Somalia	U.S. forces arrive for humanitarian aid effort.
Clinton	1993	Iraq	U.S. pilots fire on targets in Iraq after antiaircraft fire directed at them.
Clinton	1993	Bosnia	U.S. forces conduct airdrop of relief supplies.
Clinton	1993	Bosnia	U.S. forces participate in NATO air action to enforce UN ban on unauthorized military flights over Bosnia.
Clinton	1993	Iraq	U.S. planes bomb antiaircraft sites.
Clinton	1993	Somalia	U.S. military effort protects humanitarian relief effort.
Clinton	1993	Iraq	U.S. naval forces launch missiles in retaliation for unsuccessful attempt to assassinate former president Bush.
Clinton	1993	Iraq	U.S. aircraft bomb antiaircraft site.
Clinton	1993–1994	Macedonia	U.S. soldiers deploy to help maintain stability.
Clinton	1993	Haiti	U.S. ships enforce UN embargo.
Clinton	1994	Bosnia	U.S. aircraft join UN peacekeeping mission.
Clinton	1994	Bosnia	U.S. aircraft patrolling the "no-fly" zone shoot down Serbian planes.
Clinton	1994	Rwanda	U.S. forces evacuate Americans and others during civil unrest.
Clinton	1994	Macedonia	U.S. forces increase to maintain stability.
Clinton	1994	Haiti	U.S. forces continue to enforce embargo.
Clinton	1994	Bosnia	U.S. aircraft attack Bosnian Serb heavy weapons.
Clinton	1994	Haiti	U.S. troops arrive to reinstate elected government.
Clinton	1994	Bosnia	U.S. aircraft attack Serb bases.
Clinton	1994	Somalia	U.S. forces assist the withdrawal of UN forces.
Clinton	1995	Bosnia	U.S. aircraft aid in NATO air strikes against Bosnian Serb army.
Clinton	1995	Bosnia	20,000 U.S. forces enforce peace agreement.
Clinton	1996	Liberia	U.S. military forces help evacuate Americans and others during unrest.

Table 7-3 *(Continued)*

President	*Year*	*Location*	*Action*
Clinton	1996	Central African Republic	U.S. forces help evacuate Americans and others during unrest.
Clinton	1996	Rwanda, Zaire	U.S. forces aid humanitarian efforts of UN.
Clinton	1997	Albania	U.S. forces help evacuate Americans and others during unrest and protect U.S. embassy.
Clinton	1997	Congo, Gabon	U.S. forces help evacuate Americans and others during unrest.
Clinton	1997	Sierra Leone	U.S. forces help evacuate Americans and others during unrest.
Clinton	1997	Cambodia	U.S. forces deploy to Thailand for possible evacuation efforts in Cambodia.
Clinton	1997	Guinea-Bissau	U.S. forces stand by for possible evacuation and protection efforts during a Guinea-Bissau army mutiny.
Clinton	1998–2007[a]	Bosnia	U.S. forces participate in NATO peace-keeping mission.
Clinton	1998	Kenya, Tanzania	U.S. forces enhance security after embassy bombings.
Clinton	1998	Albania	U.S. forces sent to enhance security at U.S. embassy.
Clinton	1998	Liberia	U.S. forces stand by for possible evacuations and to restore order during unrest.
Clinton	1998	Iraq	U.S. forces conduct bombing campaign against Iraqi industrial facilities deemed capable of producing weapons of mass destruction.
Clinton	1998–2001[a]	Iraq	U.S. forces conduct military operations against Iraqi air defense systems after Iraqi aircraft violate "no-fly" zones.
Clinton	1999	Yugoslavia-Kosovo	U.S. forces conduct air strikes against Yugoslavia in its campaign against ethnic Albanians in Kosovo.
Clinton	1999–2007[a]	Yugoslavia-Kosovo	Additional forces conduct air operations.
Clinton	1999–2001[a]	East Timor	U.S. forces sent as UN peace-keeping mission to restore order.
Clinton	2000	Sierra Leone	U.S. forces deployed to stand by to support evacuation efforts if necessary.

(Table continues)

Table 7-3 *(Continued)*

President	*Year*	*Location*	*Action*
Clinton	2000	Yemen	After attack on USS *Cole,* U.S. forces ensure better security for the ship.
G. W. Bush	2001–2008	Afghanistan	U.S. forces search for Taliban and al-Qaeda forces suspected of terrorism.
G. W. Bush	2002–2003	Philippines	U.S. forces aid Philippines' army in its antiterrorism capabilities and conduct other counter-terrorism operations.
G. W. Bush	2002	Cote d'Ivoire	U.S. military evacuate Americans and others during a rebellion.
G. W. Bush	2003	Pakistan	U.S. military engage in joint antiterrorism effort at Pakistan/ Afghanistan border.
G. W. Bush	2003	Liberia	U.S. forces enter territorial waters to support UN efforts to restore order.
G. W. Bush	2003	Georgia	U.S. combat forces deploy to aid country's counterterrorism capabilities.
G. W. Bush	2003–2006	Djibouti	U.S. combat forces deploy to aid country's counterterrorism capabilities.
G. W. Bush	2004	Haiti	U.S. combat forces aid U.S. embassy security and protect American citizens during a rebellion.
G. W. Bush	2004	Haiti	Additional forces arrive.
G. W. Bush	2004–2006	Kenya	U.S. combat forces deploy to aid country's counterterrorism capabilities.
G. W. Bush	2004–2006	Ethiopia	U.S. combat forces deploy to aid country's counterterrorism capabilities.
G. W. Bush	2004–2006	Yemen	U.S. combat forces deploy to aid country's counterterrorism capabilities.
G. W. Bush	2004–2006	Eritrea	U.S. combat forces deploy to aid country's counterterrorism capabilities.
G. W. Bush	2006	Lebanon	U.S. combat forces aid U.S. embassy security and protect American citizens during unrest.

Sources: U.S. Congress, Congressional Research Service, CRS Report for Congress, "Instances of Use of United States Armed Forces Abroad, 1798–2007," RL32170, Sept. 12, 2007, updated by the author.

Note: George W. Bush through 2007 only.

[a] Mission continues under next president(s).

Table 7-4 Summary of Instances of American Use of Force without Congressional Authorization, 1788–2007

President	*Instances of use of force*	*President*	*Instances of use of force*
Washington	1	B. Harrison	6
Adams	0	Cleveland	5
Jefferson	2	McKinley	6
Madison	4	T. Roosevelt	14
Monroe	7	Taft	9
J.Q. Adams	2	Wilson	18
Jackson	5	Harding	3
Van Buren	2	Coolidge	7
W. Harrison	0	Hoover	2
Tyler	4	F. Roosevelt	6
Polk	0	Truman	7
Taylor	1	Eisenhower	7
Fillmore	5	Kennedy	5
Pierce	6	L. Johnson	3
Buchanan	8	Nixon	3
Lincoln	5	Ford	5
A. Johnson	6	Carter	2
Grant	6	Reagan	12
Hayes	0	G.H.W. Bush	11
Garfield	0	Clinton	39
Arthur	2	G.W. Bush[a]	14
Cleveland	2	Total	252

Source: Table 7-3.

[a] Through 2007 only.

Table 7-5 Presidential Notifications under the War Powers Resolution, Ford to G. W. Bush, II

President	*Number of notifications*	*Number of troop commitments without notification*
Ford	4	3
Carter	1	1
Reagan, I	7	5
Reagan, II	8	4
G. H. W. Bush	6	4
Clinton, I	31	0
Clinton, II	30	3[a]
G. W. Bush, I	30	1[a]
G. W. Bush, II[b]	6	0
Total	123	21

Source: U.S. Congress, Congressional Research Service, CRS Report for Congress, "The War Powers Resolution: After Thirty Years" (RL32267), March 11, 2004; CRS Report for Congress, "War Powers Resolution: Presidential Compliance" (RL33532), June 12, 2007.

[a] At various times from 1998 to 2001, U.S. military operations were conducted to enforce "no-fly" zones in Iraq. These are counted here as single instances for each year but, in fact, reflect multiple missions.
[b] Through 2007 only.

Table 7-6 The Costs of War

War	*Years*	*Total Service Personnel*	*Battle Deaths*	*Other Deaths*	*Woundings*	*Expenditures (in billions of current dollars)*
War of 1812	3	286,730	2,260	—	4,505	$0.09
Mexican-American War	2	78,718	1,733	11,550	4,152	0.08
Civil War	4	2,213,363	140,414	224,097	281,881	1.00
Spanish-American War	1	306,760	385	2,061	1,662	0.27
World War I	4	4,734,991	53,402	63,114	204,002	33.00
World War II	4	16,112,566	291,557	113,842	671,846	360.00
Korean War	4	5,720,000	33,741	20,505	103,284	50.00
Vietnam War	10	3,403,000	47,424	42,785	153,303	111.00
Persian Gulf War	1	694,550	147	1,825	467	61.00
Iraq War[a]	6	218,500	3,175	726	28,870	607.00

Sources: Total service personnel and casualty data from U.S. Department of Defense, Statistical Information and Analysis Division, "DoD Military Personnel and Casualty Statistics" found at http://siadapp.dmdc.osd.mil/personnel/CASUALTY/castop.htm. Expenditure data from U.S. Department of Commerce, Bureau of the Census, *Statistical Abstract of the United States 1998,* "Estimates of Total Dollar Costs of American Wars"; U.S. Congress, Congressional Research Service, CRS Report for Congress, "The Cost of Iraq, Afghanistan, and other Global War on Terror Operations Since 9/11," RL33110, Nov. 9, 2007.

Note: "—" indicates not available.

[a] As of January 2008.

Table 7-7 War-Related Appropriations for Defense, Iraq and Afghanistan, 2002–2007 (in billions)

Year	*Appropriation*	*Cumulative Total*
2002	$ 31	$ 31
2003	76	107
2004	74	181
2005	100	281
2006	116	397
2007	165	562
2008	188	750

Source: U.S. Congress, Congressional Budget Office, "Analysis of the Growth in Funding for Operations in Iraq, Afghanistan, and Elsewhere in the War on Terrorism," Feb. 11, 2008, www.cbo.gov.

Figure 7-1 Public Attitudes toward the Korean, Vietnam, and Iraq Wars, 1950–2007

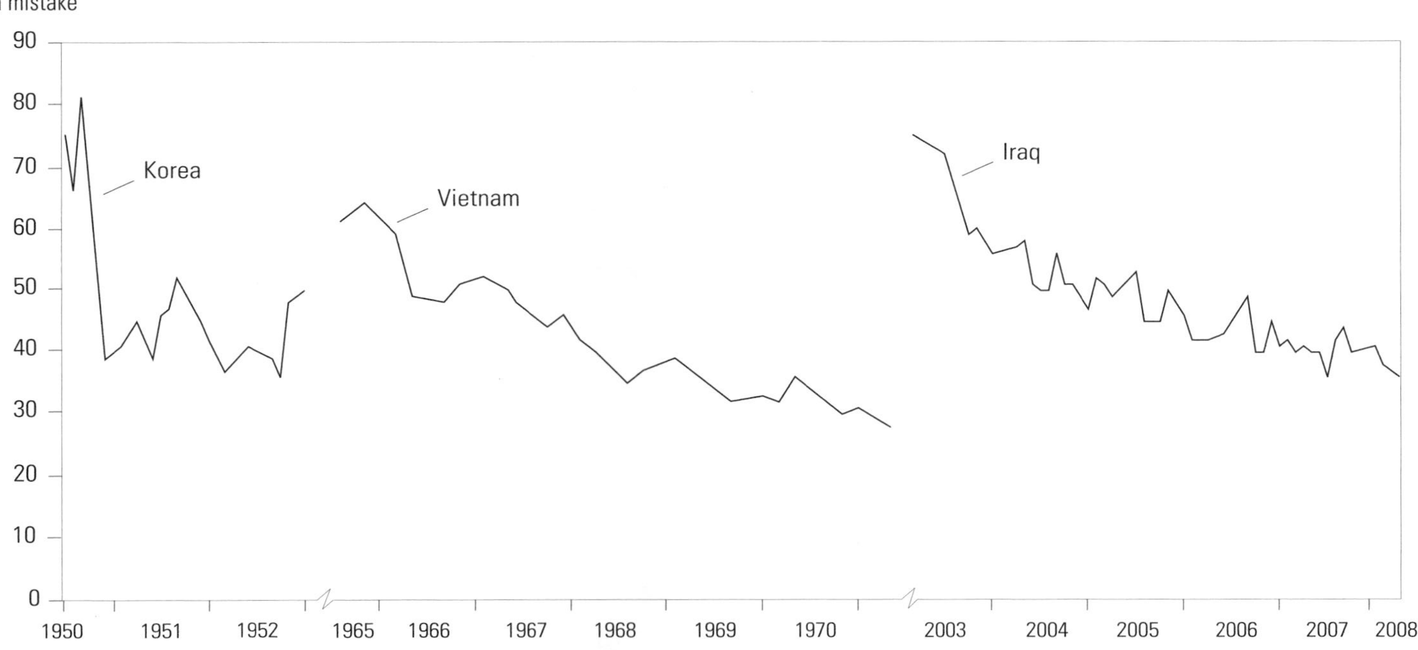

Sources: (Korea and Vietnam), John Mueller, *War Presidents and Public Opinion* (New York: John Wiley, 1973), 45–47, 54–55; (Iraq) Joseph Carroll, "The Iraq-Vietnam Comparison," Gallup Poll, www.gallup.com/poll/11998/IraqVietnam-Comparison.aspx.

Note: Entries are percent who said the war is not a mistake in answer to the question: "Do you think the United States made a mistake sending troops to [Korea/Vietnam/Iraq]?"

Table 7-8 Presidential Determinations (Foreign Assistance Funds), Kennedy to G. W. Bush, II

President/year	*Total*	*Funds for military support*	*Funds for nonmilitary support*
Kennedy			
1961	1	1	0
1962	1	0	1
1963	0	0	0
L. Johnson[a]			
1964	1	0	1
1965	0	0	0
1966	0	0	0
1967	3	3	0
1968	0	0	0
Nixon, I			
1969	1	1	0
1970	0	0	0
1971	0	0	0
1972	10	5	5
Nixon, II			
1973	11	10	1
1974	12	8	4
Ford			
1974	5	2	3
1975	17	10	7
1976	18	8	10
Carter			
1977	7	2	5
1978	15	7	8
1979	22	8	14
1980	21	8	13
Reagan, I			
1981	13	7	6
1982	11	5	6
1983	9	7	2
1984	10	7	3
Reagan, II			
1985	21	14	7
1986	19	7	12
1987	10	2	8
1988	26	5	21
G. H. W. Bush			
1989	20	10	10
1990	28	9	19
1991	30	10	20
1992	27	2	25

Table 7-8 *(Continued)*

President/year	*Total*	*Funds for military support*	*Funds for nonmilitary support*
Clinton, I			
1993	32	12	20
1994	44	15	29
1995	28	12	16
1996	55	16	39
Clinton, II			
1997	23	7	16
1998	19	0	19
1999	16	1	15
2000	9	3	6
G. W. Bush, I			
2001	16	0	16
2002	24	8	16
2003	21	7	14
2004	18	8	10
G. W. Bush, II[b]			
2005	9	0	9
2006	9	0	9
2007	13	3	10

Source: (1961–1997) *Code of Federal Regulations, Title 3,* Table 3, successive volumes; (1998–2006) www.access.gpo.gov; (2007) www.whitehouse.gov.

Note: Excludes transfers, waivers, and drawdowns.

[a] Includes full term from Nov. 1963 to Jan. 1969.
[b] Through 2007 only.

Table 7-9 Foreign Assistance Authorized by Presidential Waivers, Kennedy to G. W. Bush, II

President/fiscal year	*Number of waivers*	*Authorization (millions)*
Kennedy		
1962	10	$54.3
1963	12	85.7
L. Johnson[a]		
1964	12	128.2
1965	9	107.0
1966	8	114.6
1967	6	97.2
1968	4	11.7
Nixon, I		
1969	1	4.0
1970	5	62.9
1971	9	209.5
1972	8	198.6
Nixon, II		
1973	6	106.9
1974	11	194.6
Ford		
1975	2	77.6
1976	1	0.9
Carter		
1977	0	0.0
1978	0[b]	0.0
1979	2[b]	15.0
1980	2[b]	45.1
Reagan, I		
1981	5[b]	53.2
1982	2[b]	26.9
1983	1[b]	0.1
1984	2	—
Reagan, II		
1985	0	—
1986	1	—
1987	3	—
1988	2	—
G. H. W. Bush		
1989	1	—
1990	3	—
1991	4	—
1992	2	—

Table 7-9 *(Continued)*

President/fiscal year	*Number of waivers*	*Authorization (millions)*
Clinton, I		
1993	4	—
1994	2	—
1995	2	—
1996	3	—
Clinton, II		
1997	6	—
1998	6	—
1999	8	—
2000	9	20.0
G. W. Bush, I		
2001	8	55.0
2002	8	—
2003	21	—
2004	18	—
G. W. Bush, II[c]		
2005	11	—
2006	8	—
2007	8	1,694.1

Source: (1962–1984) U.S. General Accounting Office, *Use of Presidential Authority for Foreign Assistance* (Washington, D.C.: Government Printing Office, 1985); (1985–1997) *Code of Federal Regulations, Title 3;* (1998–2006) www.access.gpo.gov; (2007) www.whitehouse.gov.

Note: "—" indicates not available.

[a] Includes full term from Nov. 1963 to Jan. 1969.
[b] Minimum number of waivers for the year; others may not have been filed.
[c] Through 2007 only.

Table 7-10 Presidents' Foreign Assistance Fund Transfers, Kennedy to G. W. Bush, II

Date	*Region/country*	*Use*	*Authorized transfer (millions)*
Kennedy			
March 21, 1962	NATO	Administrative expenses	$ 2.0
March 22, 1962	Southeast Asia	Administrative expenses	3.0
June 5, 1962	Africa	Contingency funds	30.5
June 5, 1962	Africa	International organization funds	9.5
June 5, 1962	Africa	International organization funds	15.0
May 21, 1963	Central America	Alliance for Progress	10.0
L. Johnson			
March 21, 1964	Poland	Project Hope	1.6
May 19, 1964[a]	Not specified	Military assistance	50.0
June 26, 1964[a]	Southeast Asia/Congo/Turkey	Military assistance	25.0
June 26, 1964[a]	Southeast Asia/Congo/Turkey	Military assistance	15.0
June 29, 1964	Central America	Alliance for Progress	8.0
June 29, 1964	Central America	Alliance for Progress	6.0
June 22, 1965	Southeast Asia/Central America	Support assistance	18.0[b]
Jan. 18, 1966[a]	Vietnam	Support assistance	28.0
Jan. 18, 1966[a]	Vietnam	International organization funds	28.0
Feb. 10, 1966[a]	Vietnam	Support assistance	18.0
Feb. 10, 1966[a]	Vietnam	Support assistance	10.0
June 8, 1966	Vietnam	AID administrative expenses	1.4
Nov. 19, 1966	Vietnam	Administrative expenses	5.0
May 16, 1968	Vietnam	Administrative expenses	7.2
Nixon, I			
May 13, 1969	Vietnam	Administrative expenses	6.4
April 14, 1970	Vietnam	Administrative expenses	5.5
June 30, 1970	Cambodia	Military assistance	1.0
July 18, 1970	Not specified	Project Hope	0.5
Oct. 23, 1970[a]	Cambodia	Military assistance	50.0
Feb. 11, 1971	Cambodia	Military assistance	10.0
March 23, 1971	Vietnam	Administrative expenses	3.6
March 1, 1972	Vietnam	Administrative expenses	3.6
Nixon, II			
June 13, 1973	Vietnam	Administrative expenses	2.9
April 19, 1974[a]	Egypt	Security support assistance	8.0
May 16, 1974	Egypt	Security support assistance	0.7
June 30, 1974	Egypt	Security support assistance	20.0

Table 7-10 *(Continued)*

Date	*Region/country*	*Use*	*Authorized transfer (millions)*
Carter			
Sept. 13, 1979	Caribbean	Disaster relief	2.2
Jan. 24, 1980	Sinai	Air transport services	3.9
July 8, 1980	Not specified	AID expenses	7.0
Reagan, I			
Sept. 28, 1981	Lebanon	Peace-keeping operation account	9.0
Dec. 5, 1981	Chad	Airlift services	12.0
G.H.W. Bush			
June 21, 1990	Not specified	Anti-narcotics assistance	16.5
Clinton, I			
Sept. 28, 1993	Mexico	Economic support	0.4
Sept. 29, 1993	Liberia	Peacekeeping	—
Sept. 30, 1994	Haiti	Economic support	4.6
Sept. 30, 1994	Guatemala	Economic support	4.6
May 16, 1995	Liberia	Peacekeeping	3.0
Sept. 29, 1995	El Salvador	Economic support	2.8
Clinton, II			
Aug. 20, 1997	Agency for International Development	Operating expenses	17.5
Sept. 22, 1997	Africa	Peacekeeping	4.0
Sept. 29, 1998	South Korea	Non-proliferation, anti-terrorism	10.0
Sept. 29, 1998	South Korea	Economic support	5.0
Sept. 30, 1998	World Court	Proceedings on airline bombing case	8.0
Dec. 24, 1998	South Korea	Economic support	12.0
Sept. 22, 2000	South Korea	Economic support	29.4
G.W. Bush, I			
Sept. 22, 2001	South Korea	Energy development	29.4
Sept. 30, 2003	United Nations	Child survival and health	25.0
Dec. 5, 2003	Iraq	Relief and reconstruction	—
Sept. 30, 2004	General	Foreign assistance	25.0
G.W. Bush, II[c]			
Sept. 28, 2005	Libya	Chemical weapons destruction	—
Sept. 28, 2005	Libya	Defense articles and services	—
Sept. 29, 2005	G-8	Women's Justice and Empowerment Initiative	5.0
May 18, 2006	South Korea	War reserves stockpile	—
Aug. 28, 2006	Sudan	Defense articles and services	—

(Table continues)

Table 7-10 *(Continued)*

Date	*Region/country*	*Use*	*Authorized transfer (millions)*
G. W. Bush, II[c] (continued)			
May 2, 2007	Sudan	Defense articles and services	—
May 10, 2007	Liberia	Security	10.0
July 5, 2007	USAID	Antinarcotics assistance	1.8
July 10, 2007	Overseas Investment Corp.	Loan guarantees	5.0

Sources: (1962–1983) U.S. General Accounting Office, *Use of Presidential Authority for Foreign Assistance* (Washington, D.C.: Government Printing Office, 1985), appendix I; (1984–1997) successive volumes of *Code of Federal Regulations, Title 3,* Table 3; (1998–2006) www.access.gpo.gov; (2007) www.whitehouse.gov.

Note: "—" indicates not available.

[a] Transfers also demanded a waiver of the 10 percent limitation, which required that the president be allowed to move no more than 10 percent of the funds from one category to another.
[b] $13.8 million earmarked for Southeast Asia.
[c] Through 2007 only.

Table 7-11 Presidential Use of Drawdown Authority, Kennedy to G. W. Bush, II

Date	*Country*	*Purpose*	*Authorized drawdown (millions)*
Kennedy			
Jan. 3, 1963	India	Military assistance	$ 55.0
L. Johnson			
May 15, 1965	Vietnam	Military assistance	75.0
Oct. 21, 1965	Vietnam	Military assistance	300.0
Nixon			
Dec. 24, 1973	Cambodia	Military assistance	200.0
Ford			
May 13, 1974	Cambodia	Military assistance	50.0
Jan. 10, 1975	Cambodia	Military assistance	75.0
Carter			
July 1, 1980	Thailand	Military assistance	1.1
Dec. 9, 1980	Liberia	Military assistance to support coup	1.0
Reagan, I			
Jan. 16, 1981	El Salvador	Military assistance	5.0
March 5, 1981	El Salvador	Military assistance	20.0
Feb. 2, 1982	El Salvador	Military assistance	55.0
July 19, 1983	Chad	Military assistance	10.0
Aug. 5, 1983	Chad	Military assistance	15.0
Reagan, II			
Dec. 5, 1985	Israel	Military assistance (Iran arms)	15.0
Jan. 17, 1987	Iran	Military assistance	15.0
1986	Chad	Military assistance	10.0
1986	Honduras	Military assistance	20.0
1986	Philippines	Disaster relief	10.0
1987	Chad	Military assistance	25.0
1988	Afghanistan, Pakistan	United Nations support	0.2
G. H. W. Bush			
1989	Jamaica	Disaster relief	10.0
1989	Colombia	Counter-drug assistance	20.0
1990	Colombia	Counter-drug assistance	53.3
1990	Israel	Military assistance	74.0
Sept. 30, 1990	Philippines	Disaster relief	10.0
1991	Israel	Military assistance	43.0
Jan. 16, 1991	Turkey	Military assistance	32.0
April 6, 1991	Turkey	Humanitarian relief	25.0
April 19, 1991	Turkey	Humanitarian relief	50.0
May 26, 1991	Bangladesh	Disaster relief	20.0
1992	Senegal	Military assistance	10.0
Feb. 26, 1992	Mexico	Counter-drug assistance	26.0

(Table continues)

Table 7-11 *(Continued)*

Date	*Country*	*Purpose*	*Authorized drawdown (millions)*
G. H. W. Bush (continued)			
April 27, 1992	Israel	Military assistance	47.0
Sept. 24, 1992	Nagorno-Karabarkh	Military assistance	—
Sept. 30, 1992	Colombia	Counter-drug assistance	7.0
Sept. 30, 1992	Pakistan	Disaster relief	5.0
Clinton, I			
March 30, 1993	Israel	Military assistance	491.1
June 24, 1993	Ecuador	Disaster relief	2.0
1993	Somalia	UN peacekeeping	25.0
Sept. 30, 1993	Laos	Humanitarian assistance	—
Dec. 18, 1993	Egypt		—
March 16, 1994	Serbia, Montenegro	UN border, sanctions enforcement	5.6
1994	Egypt	Military assistance	13.5
March 30, 1994	Israel	Military assistance	161.9
March 30, 1994	Israel	Palestine police force	4.0
May 16, 1994	Former Yugoslavia	Military assistance	—
Aug. 8, 1994	Serbia, Montenegro	UN border, sanctions enforcement	—
Aug. 19, 1994	Rwanda	Disaster relief	75.0
1994	Haiti	Military assistance	50.0
Nov. 1, 1994	Israel		—
Nov. 15, 1994	Serbia, Montenegro	UN border, sanctions enforcement	—
March 16, 1995	Israel	Palestine police force	5.0
June 23, 1995	Haiti	Military assistance	7.0
Sept. 18, 1995	Serbia, Montenegro	UN border, sanctions enforcement	1.5
1995	Bosnia	Military assistance	12.0
1995	Bosnia	Military assistance	3.0
1995	Bosnia	Military assistance	17.0
Feb. 23, 1996	Jordan	Military assistance	100.0
March 7, 1996	Israel	Military assistance	22.0
1996	Bosnia	Military assistance	100.0
Aug. 24, 1996	Vietnam	Defense articles in exchange for locating POWs/MIAs	3.0
Sept. 4, 1996	Cambodia	Defense articles in exchange for locating POWs/MIAs	0.2
Sept. 12, 1996	Haiti	Military assistance	3.0
Sept. 30, 1996	Nigeria and others	Military assistance	10.0

Table 7-11 *(Continued)*

Date	*Country*	*Purpose*	*Authorized drawdown (millions)*
Clinton, I (continued)			
Sept. 30, 1996	Columbia, Venezeula, Peru, and others	Counter-drug assistance	75.0
Dec. 2, 1996	Mexico	Counter-drug assistance	37.0
Dec. 11, 1996	Iraq	Peace monitoring	4.0
Dec. 27, 1996	Iraq	Humanitarian assistance	10.0
Clinton, II			
Sept. 30, 1997	Columbia, Venezuela, Peru	Counter-drug assistance	20.0
March 13, 1998	Jordan	Military assistance	25.0
Sept. 20, 1998	Latin American states	Counter-drug assistance	75.0
Nov. 6, 1998	Honduras, Nicaragua, El Salvador, Guatemala	Disaster relief	30.0
Nov. 14, 1998	Honduras, Nicaragua, El Salvador, Guatemala	Disaster relief	45.0
March 25, 1999	Jordan	Military assistance	25.0
March 31, 1999	Kosovo	Peacekeeping	25.0
July 1, 1999	Tunisia	Military assistance	5.0
Sept. 21, 1999	East Timor	Military assistance	55.0
Sept. 21, 1999	Kosovo	War crimes tribunal	5.0
Sept. 30, 1999	Columbia, Peru, Ecuador, Panama	Counter-drug assistance	72.6
Oct. 29, 1999	Iraq	Training	5.0
Dec. 23, 1999	Venezuela	Disaster relief	20.0
Feb. 25, 2000	African states	Disaster relief	37.6
April 19. 2000	Sierra Leone	Military assistance	18.0
Sept. 22. 2000	Tunisia	Military assistance	—
G.W. Bush, I			
Aug. 18, 2001	Tunisia	Military assistance	5.0
Aug. 14, 2002	Tunisia	Military assistance	5.0
Dec. 7, 2002	Iraq	Military assistance	92.0
Feb. 13, 2003	Afghanistan	Military assistance	323.0
Feb. 13, 2003	Jordan	Military assistance	7.0
Dec. 16, 2003	Afghanistan	Military assistance	135.0
Oct. 22, 2004	Sudan	Peacekeeping	2.5

(Table continues)

Table 7-11 *(Continued)*

Date	*Country*	*Purpose*	*Authorized drawdown (millions)*
G. W. Bush, II[a]			
Jan. 4, 2005	Indonesia and others	Disaster relief (tsunami)	65.0
Jan. 27, 2005	Afghanistan	Military assistance	88.5
June 15, 2005	Afghanistan	Military assistance	161.5
July 12, 2005	Philippines	Antiterrorism assistance	10.0
July 15, 2005	Sudan	Peacekeeping	6.0
Dec. 30, 2005	Pakistan	Diaster relief	30.0
Feb. 7, 2006	Afghanistan	Military assistance	17.0
Sept. 29, 2006	Indonesia	Transport of peace-keeping forces to Lebanon	3.0

Sources: (1962–1983) U.S. General Accounting Office, *Use of Presidential Authority for Foreign Assistance* (Washington, D.C.: Government Printing Office, 1985), 8; (1984–1997) successive volumes of *Code of Federal Regulations,* Title 3, Table 3; (1998–2006) *Code* found at www.access.gpo.gov; (2007) www.whitehouse.gov. Additional entries with year only found at U.S. Department of Defense, Security Cooperation Agency, *Handbook for Foreign Assistance Act Drawdown of Defense Articles and Services,* Appendix 1, Dec. 15, 2000, www.fas.org/asmp/resources/govern/Drawdowns.pdf.

Note: "—" indicates not available.

[a] Through 2007 only.

Table 7-12 Treaties and Executive Agreements, Washington, I to Truman, I

President/year	*Senate majority party same as president's?*	*Total international agreements*	*Executive agreements*	*Treaties*[a]	*Ratio agreements: treaties*[b]
Washington, I					
1789	Yes	0	0	0	—
1790	Yes	0	0	0	—
1791	Yes	0	0	0	—
1792	Yes	0	0	0	—
Total	—	0	0	0	—
Yearly average	—	0.00	0.00	0.00	—
Washington, II					
1793	Yes	0	0	0	—
1794	Yes	1	0	1	—
1795	Yes	2	0	2	—
1796	Yes	2	0	2	—
Total	—	5	0	5	—
Yearly average	—	1.00	0.00	1.00	—
Adams					
1797	Yes	1	0	1	—
1798	Yes	1	0	1	—
1799	Yes	1	0	1	—
1800	Yes	1	0	1	—
Total	—	4	0	4	—
Yearly average	—	1.00	0.00	1.00	—
Jefferson, I					
1801	Yes	1	0	1	—
1802	Yes	1	0	1	—
1803	Yes	3	0	3	—
1804	Yes	0	0	0	—
Total	—	5	0	5	—
Yearly average	—	1.00	0.00	1.00	—
Jefferson, II					
1805	Yes	1	0	1	—
1806	Yes	0	0	0	—
1807	Yes	0	0	0	—
1808	Yes	0	0	0	—
Total	—	1	0	1	—
Yearly average	—	0.25	0.00	0.25	—
Madison, I					
1809	Yes	0	0	0	—
1810	Yes	0	0	0	—
1811	Yes	0	0	0	—
1812	Yes	0	0	0	—
Total	—	0	0	0	—
Yearly average	—	0.00	0.00	0.00	—

(Table continues)

Table 7-12 *(Continued)*

President/year	*Senate majority party same as president's?*	*Total international agreements*	*Executive agreements*	*Treaties*[a]	*Ratio agreements: treaties*[b]
Madison, II					
1813	Yes	0	0	0	—
1814	Yes	0	0	0	—
1815	Yes	1	0	1	—
1816	Yes	2	0	2	—
Total	—	3	0	3	—
Yearly average	—	0.75	0.00	0.75	—
Monroe, I					
1817	Yes	3	1	2	0.5
1818	Yes	0	0	0	—
1819	Yes	2	0	2	—
1820	Yes	0	0	0	—
Total	—	5	1	4	0.3
Yearly average	—	1.25	0.25	1.00	—
Monroe, II					
1821	Yes	0	0	0	—
1822	Yes	2	0	2	—
1823	Yes	1	0	1	—
1824	Yes	2	0	2	—
Total	—	5	0	5	—
Yearly average	—	1.00	0.00	1.00	—
J. Q. Adams					
1825	Yes	2	1	1	1.0
1826	Yes	3	1	2	0.5
1827	No	6	0	6	—
1828	No	3	0	3	—
Total	—	14	2	12	0.2
Yearly average	—	3.5	0.50	3.00	—
Jackson, I					
1829	Yes	1	0	1	—
1830	Yes	2	0	2	—
1831	Yes	2	0	2	—
1832	Yes	3	0	3	—
Total	—	8	0	8	—
Yearly average	—	2.00	0.00	2.00	—
Jackson, II					
1833	Yes	4	0	4	—
1834	Yes	0	0	0	—
1835	Yes	2	0	2	—
1836	Yes	2	0	2	—
Total	—	8	0	8	—
Yearly average	—	2.00	0.00	2.00	—

Table 7-12 *(Continued)*

President/year	*Senate majority party same as president's?*	*Total international agreements*	*Executive agreements*	*Treaties*[a]	*Ratio agreements: treaties*[b]
Van Buren					
1837	Yes	1	0	1	—
1838	Yes	4	0	4	—
1839	Yes	3	1	2	0.5
1840	Yes	3	1	2	0.5
Total	—	11	2	9	0.2
Yearly average	—	2.75	0.50	2.25	—
W. Harrison					
1841	Yes	1	0	1	—
Tyler					
1841	Yes	0	0	0	—
1842	Yes	2	0	2	—
1843	Yes	3	1	2	0.5
1844	Yes	6	0	6	—
Total	—	11	1	10	0.1
Yearly average	—	2.75	0.25	2.50	—
Polk					
1845	Yes	4	1	3	0.3
1846	Yes	6	2	4	0.5
1847	Yes	6	1	5	0.2
1848	Yes	5	1	4	0.3
Total	—	21	5	16	0.3
Yearly average	—	5.25	1.25	4.00	—
Taylor					
1849	No	5	3	2	1.5
1850	No	2	0	2	—
Total	—	7	3	4	0.8
Yearly average	—	3.5	1.5	2.00	—
Fillmore					
1850	No	3	1	2	0.5
1851	No	2	0	2	—
1852	No	8	3	5	0.6
Total	—	13	4	9	0.4
Yearly average	—	4.33	1.33	3.33	—
Pierce					
1853	Yes	10	5	5	1.0
1854	Yes	13	4	9	0.4
1855	Yes	4	3	1	3.0
1856	Yes	5	0	5	—
Total	—	32	12	20	0.6
Yearly average	—	8.00	3.00	5.00	—

(Table continues)

Table 7-12 *(Continued)*

President/year	*Senate majority party same as president's?*	*Total international agreements*	*Executive agreements*	*Treaties*[a]	*Ratio agreements: treaties*[b]
Buchanan					
1857	Yes	8	3	5	0.6
1858	Yes	10	1	9	0.1
1859	Yes	2	2	0	2.0
1860	Yes	4	2	2	1.0
Total	—	24	8	16	0.5
Yearly average	—	6.00	2.00	4.00	—
Lincoln, I					
1861	Yes	8	0	8	—
1862	Yes	7	1	6	0.2
1863	Yes	7	2	5	0.4
1864	Yes	3	0	3	—
Total	—	25	3	22	0.1
Yearly average	—	6.25	0.75	5.50	—
Lincoln, II					
1865	Yes	0	0	0	—
A. Johnson					
1865	Yes	0	0	0	—
1866	Yes	5	0	5	—
1867	Yes	7	0	7	—
1868	Yes	14	0	14	—
Total	—	26	0	26	—
Yearly average	—	6.50	0	6.50	—
Grant, I					
1869	Yes	3	1	2	0.5
1870	Yes	12	1	11	0.1
1871	Yes	5	0	5	—
1872	Yes	5	0	5	—
Total	—	25	2	23	0.1
Yearly average	—	6.25	.50	5.75	—
Grant, II					
1873	Yes	4	2	2	1.0
1874	Yes	9	5	4	1.3
1875	Yes	1	0	1	—
1876	Yes	4	2	2	1.0
Total	—	18	9	9	1.0
Yearly average	—	4.5	2.25	2.25	—
Hayes					
1877	Yes	2	1	1	1.0
1878	Yes	6	1	5	0.2

Table 7-12 *(Continued)*

President/year	Senate majority party same as president's?	Total international agreements	Executive agreements	Treaties[a]	Ratio agreements: treaties[b]
Hayes (continued)					
1879	No	2	1	1	1.0
1880	No	9	2	7	0.3
Total	—	19	5	14	0.4
Yearly average	—	4.75	1.25	3.50	—
Garfield					
1881	Yes	3	1	2	0.5
Arthur					
1881	Yes	2	0	2	—
1882	Yes	14	4	10	0.4
1883	Yes	6	4	2	2.0
1884	Yes	11	3	8	0.4
Total	—	33	11	22	0.5
Yearly average	—	8.25	2.75	5.50	—
Cleveland					
1885	No	7	5	2	2.5
1886	No	8	1	7	0.1
1887	No	7	3	4	0.8
1888	No	8	2	6	0.3
Total	—	30	11	19	0.6
Yearly average	—	7.50	2.75	4.75	—
B. Harrison					
1889	Yes	3	1	2	0.5
1890	Yes	4	2	2	1.0
1891	Yes	11	6	5	1.2
1892	Yes	9	2	7	0.3
Total	—	27	11	16	0.7
Yearly average	—	6.75	2.75	4.00	—
Cleveland					
1893	Yes	2	0	2	—
1894	Yes	5	2	3	0.7
1895	No	4	2	2	1.0
1896	No	6	2	4	0.5
Total	—	17	6	11	0.5
Yearly average	—	4.25	1.50	2.75	—
McKinley, I					
1897	Yes	5	2	3	0.7
1898	Yes	11	7	4	1.8
1899	Yes	18	9	9	1.0
1900	Yes	15	7	8	0.9
Total	—	49	25	24	1.0
Yearly average	—	12.25	6.25	6.00	—

(Table continues)

Table 7-12 *(Continued)*

President/year	*Senate majority party same as president's?*	*Total international agreements*	*Executive agreements*	*Treaties*[a]	*Ratio agreements: treaties*[b]
McKinley, II					
1901	Yes	4	2	2	1.0
T. Roosevelt, I					
1901	Yes	11	4	7	0.5
1902	Yes	20	9	11	0.8
1903	Yes	12	1	11	0.1
1904	Yes	20	7	13	0.5
Total	—	63	21	42	0.5
Yearly average	—	15.75	5.25	10.50	—
T. Roosevelt, II					
1905	Yes	17	10	7	1.4
1906	Yes	20	7	13	0.5
1907	Yes	25	15	10	1.5
1908	Yes	39	4	35	0.1
Total	—	101	36	65	0.6
Yearly average	—	25.25	9.00	16.25	—
Taft					
1909	Yes	11	7	4	1.8
1910	Yes	17	5	12	0.4
1911	Yes	10	2	8	0.3
1912	Yes	7	3	4	0.8
Total	—	45	17	28	0.6
Yearly average	—	11.25	4.25	7.00	—
Wilson, I					
1913	Yes	19	4	15	0.3
1914	Yes	30	7	23	0.3
1915	Yes	14	13	1	13.0
1916	Yes	9	7	2	3.5
Total	—	72	31	41	0.8
Yearly average	—	18	7.75	10.25	—
Wilson, II					
1917	Yes	5	4	1	4.0
1918	Yes	21	9	12	0.8
1919	No	18	7	11	0.6
1920	No	6	3	3	1.0
Total	—	50	23	27	0.9
Yearly average	—	12.50	5.75	6.75	—
Harding					
1921	Yes	27	14	13	1.1
1922	Yes	18	10	8	1.3
1923	Yes	14	7	7	1.0
Total	—	59	31	28	1.1
Yearly average	—	14.75	7.75	7.00	—

Table 7-12 *(Continued)*

President/year	*Senate majority party same as president's?*	*Total international agreements*	*Executive agreements*	*Treaties*[a]	*Ratio agreements: treaties*[b]
Coolidge, I					
1923	Yes	19	6	13	0.5
1924	Yes	46	18	28	0.6
Total	—	65	24	41	0.6
Yearly average	—	32.50	12.00	20.50	—
Coolidge, II					
1925	Yes	51	38	13	2.9
1926	Yes	28	21	7	3.0
1927	Yes	24	14	10	1.4
1928	Yes	64	23	41	0.6
Total	—	167	96	71	1.4
Yearly average	—	41.75	24.00	17.75	—
Hoover					
1929	Yes	47	26	21	1.2
1930	Yes	36	19	17	1.1
1931	Yes	29	22	7	3.1
1932	Yes	46	38	8	4.8
Total	—	158	105	53	2.0
Yearly average	—	39.50	26.25	13.25	—
F. Roosevelt, I					
1933	Yes	26	19	7	2.7
1934	Yes	37	21	16	1.3
1935	Yes	32	21	11	1.9
1936	Yes	51	26	25	1.0
Total	—	146	87	59	1.5
Yearly average	—	36.50	21.75	14.75	—
F. Roosevelt, II					
1937	Yes	36	23	13	1.8
1938	Yes	47	38	9	4.2
1939	Yes	40	30	10	3.0
1940	Yes	42	29	13	2.2
Total	—	165	120	45	2.7
Yearly average	—	41.25	30.00	11.25	—
F. Roosevelt, III					
1941	Yes	60	56	4	14.0
1942	Yes	134	130	4	32.5
1943	Yes	99	98	1	98.0
1944	Yes	89	83	6	13.8
Total	—	382	367	15	24.5
Yearly average	—	95.50	91.75	3.75	—

(Table continues)

Table 7-12 *(Continued)*

President/year	*Senate majority party same as president's?*	*Total international agreements*	*Executive agreements*	*Treaties*[a]	*Ratio agreements: treaties*[b]
F. Roosevelt, IV					
1945	Yes	35	35	0	35.0
Truman, I					
1945	Yes	90	85	5	17.0
1946	Yes	163	144	19	7.6
1947	No	192	174	18	9.7
1948	No	223	202	21	9.6
Total	—	668	605	63	9.6
Yearly average	—	167.00	151.25	15.75	—

Source: Adapted from Lawrence Margolis, *Executive Agreements and Presidential Power in Foreign Policy* (New York: Praeger, 1986).

[a] Treaties include protocols and conventions.
[b] The ratio is expressed as the number of executive agreements issued versus the number of treaties. In 1948, for example, 9.6 agreements were issued for every one treaty.

Table 7-13 Treaties and Executive Agreements, Truman, II to G. W. Bush, I

President/year	*Senate majority party same as president's?*	*Total international agreements*	*Executive agreements*	*Treaties*	*Ratio agreements: Treaties*
Truman, II					
1949	Yes	156	131	25	5.24
1950	Yes	176	154	22	7.00
1951	Yes	237	214	23	9.30
1952	Yes	329	305	24	12.71
Total	—	898	804	94	8.55
Average	—	224.50	201.00	23.50	—
Eisenhower, I					
1953	Yes	171	155	16	9.69
1954	Yes	223	204	19	10.74
1955	No	318	302	16	18.88
1956	No	259	236	23	10.26
Total	—	971	897	74	12.12
Average	—	242.75	224.25	18.50	—
Eisenhower, II					
1957	No	216	206	10	20.60
1958	No	224	206	18	11.44
1959	No	240	221	19	11.63
1960	No	294	284	10	28.40
Total	—	974	917	57	16.09
Average	—	243.50	229.25	14.25	—
Kennedy					
1961	Yes	252	237	15	15.80
1962	Yes	315	304	11	27.64
1963	Yes	215	202	13	15.54
Total	—	782	743	39	19.05
Average	—	260.67	247.67	13.00	—
L. Johnson					
1964	Yes	257	249	8	31.12
1965	Yes	217	200	17	11.76
1966	Yes	247	229	18	12.72
1967	Yes	230	211	19	11.11
1968	Yes	193	182	11	16.55
Total	—	1,144	1,071	73	14.67
Average	—	228.80	214.20	14.60	—
Nixon, I					
1969	No	169	152	17	8.94
1970	No	234	212	22	9.64
1971	No	244	217	27	8.04

(Table continues)

Table 7-13 *(Continued)*

President/year	*Senate majority party same as president's?*	*Total international agreements*	*Executive agreements*	*Treaties*	*Ratio agreements: Treaties*
Nixon, I (continued)					
1972	No	320	297	23	12.91
Total	—	967	878	89	9.87
Average	—	241.75	219.50	22.25	—
Nixon, II					
1973	No	250	226	24	9.42
1974	No	165	151	14	10.79
Total	—	415	377	38	9.92
Average	—	207.50	188.50	19.00	—
Ford					
1974	No	87	83	4	20.75
1975	No	251	232	19	12.21
1976	No	373	352	21	16.76
Total	—	711	667	44	15.16
Average	—	237.00	222.33	14.67	—
Carter					
1977	Yes	395	370	25	14.80
1978	Yes	422	402	20	20.10
1979	Yes	418	387	31	12.48
1980	Yes	354	319	35	9.11
Total	—	1,589	1,478	111	13.32
Average	—	397.25	369.50	27.75	—
Reagan, I					
1981	Yes	305	287	18	15.94
1982	Yes	339	322	17	18.94
1983	Yes	301	277	24	11.54
1984	Yes	338	322	16	20.12
Total	—	1,283	1,208	75	16.11
Average	—	320.75	302	18.75	—
Reagan, II					
1985	Yes	351	334	17	19.65
1986	Yes	313	293	20	14.65
1987	No	375	363	12	30.25
1988	No	355	336	19	17.68
Total	—	1,394	1,326	68	19.50
Average	—	348.50	331.50	17.00	—
G. H. W. Bush					
1989	No	286	273	13	21.00
1990	No	264	243	21	11.57
1991	No	214	199	15	13.27

Table 7-13 *(Continued)*

President/year	*Senate majority party same as president's?*	*Total international agreements*	*Executive agreements*	*Treaties*	*Ratio agreements: Treaties*
G.H.W. Bush (continued)					
1992	No	201	182	19	9.58
Total	—	965	897	68	13.19
Average	—	241.25	224.25	17.00	—
Clinton, I					
1993	Yes	127	113	14	8.07
1994	Yes	195	167	28	5.96
1995	No	184	162	22	7.36
1996	No	227	189	38	4.97
Total	—	733	631	102	6.19
Average	—	183.25	157.75	25.50	—
Clinton, II					
1997	No	226	194	32	6.06
1998	No	199	175	24	7.29
1999	No	160	138	22	6.27
2000	No	132	118	14	8.43
Total	—	717	625	92	6.79
Average	—	179.25	156.25	23.00	—
G.W. Bush, I					
2001	No	90	79	11	7.18
2002	No	127	120	7	17.14
2003	Yes	173	157	16	9.81
2004	Yes	153	148	5	29.60
Total	—	543	504	39	12.92
Average	—	135.75	126	9.75	—

Source: Randall Smith, "Capturing the Evasive President: Disaggregating Senate–Executive Interactions in Foreign Affairs," Ph.D. dissertation, University of Illinois at Chicago, 2008.

Figure 7-2 International Agreements, 1949–2004

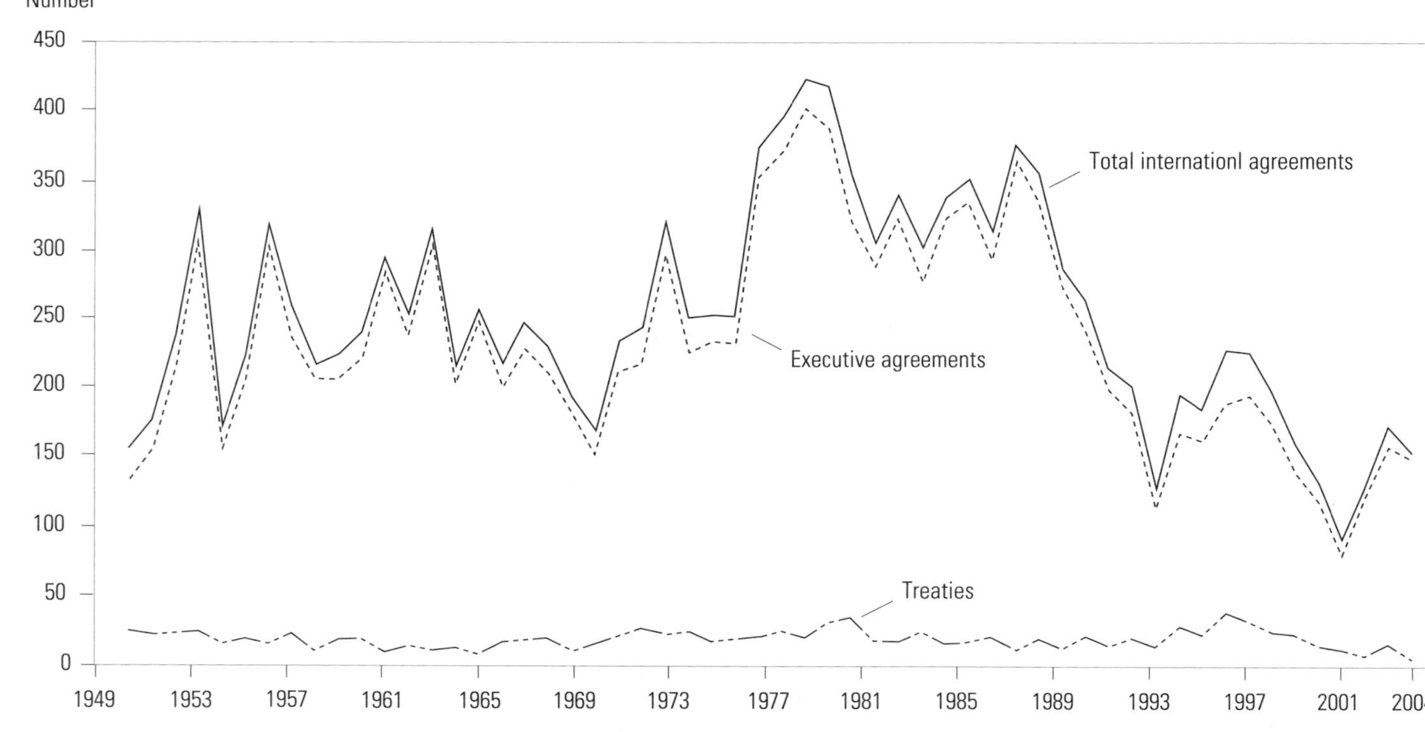

Source: Table 7-12.

Table 7-14 Senate Action on Treaties, Protocols, and Conventions, Truman, II to G.W. Bush, II

President/year	*Ratified*	*Pending*	*Withdrawn*	*Rejected*
Truman, II				
1949	9	19	7	0
1950	14	11	0	0
1951	15	39	1	0
1952	25	7	3	0
Total	63	76	11	0
Eisenhower, I				
1953	25	15	0	0
1954	6	24	1	0
1955	20	16	1	0
1956	12	14	0	0
Total	63	69	2	0
Eisenhower, II				
1957	12	15	1	0
1958	3	7	7	0
1959	8	15	0	0
1960	13	13	0	1
Total	36	50	8	1
Kennedy				
1961	9	18	0	0
1962	8	17	1	0
1963	8	27	0	0
Total	25	62	1	0
L. Johnson[a]				
1964	14	14	3	0
1965	6	17	0	0
1966	9	29	0	0
1967	25	17	2	0
1968	15	14	0	0
Total	69	91	5	0
Nixon				
1969	7	16	0	0
1970	10	18	1	0
1971	13	18	0	0
1972	18	23	0	0
1973	22	24	0	0
Total	70	99	1	0
Nixon/Ford				
1974	9	27	0	0
Ford				
1975	15	23	0	0
1976	14	24	0	0
Total	29	47	0	0

(Table continues)

Table 7-14 *(Continued)*

President/year	*Ratified*	*Pending*	*Withdrawn*	*Rejected*
Carter				
1977	5	34	0	0
1978	10	31	0	0
1979	16	45	0	0
1980	19	55	0	0
Total	50	165	0	0
Reagan, I				
1981	33	37	6	0
1982	7	9	0	0
1983	14	9	0	1
1984	20	40	0	0
Total	74	95	6	1
Reagan, II				
1985	6	45	0	0
1986	11	50	0	0
1987	3	60	0	0
1988	27	43	0	0
Total	47	198	0	0
G.H.W. Bush				
1989	9	50	0	0
1990	16	49	0	0
1991	16	50	0	2
1992	31	39	0	0
Total	72	188	0	2
Clinton, I				
1993	20	39	0	0
1994	8	13	0	0
1995	10	19	0	0
1996	28	10	0	0
Total	66	81	0	0
Clinton, II				
1997	15	21	0	0
1998	53	5	0	0
1999	13	7	0	1
2000	39	13	0	0
Total	120	46	0	1
G.W. Bush, I				
2001	3	1	0	0
2002	17	9	0	0
2003	11	8	0	0
2004	15	4	0	0
Total	46	22	0	0

Table 7-14 *(Continued)*

President/year	*Ratified*	*Pending*	*Withdrawn*	*Rejected*
G. W. Bush, II[b]				
2005	6	6	0	0
2006	14	4	0	0
2007	9	8	0	0
Total	29	18	0	0

Source: (1949-1996) U.S. Congress, *Executive Proceedings of the Senate* (Washington, D.C.: Government Printing Office, 1949–1993); (1997–2006) www.thomas.gov/home/treaties/treaties.html; (2007) www.senate.gov/pagelayout/legislative/d_three_sections_with_teasers/treaties.htm.

[a] Includes full term from Nov, 1963 to Jan. 1969.
[b] Through 2007 only.

Table 7-15 Treaties Killed by the Senate, 1789–2007

Date of vote	President	Country	Vote Yea	Vote Nay	Subject
March 9, 1825	J. Q. Adams	Colombia	0	40	Suppression of African slave trade
June 11, 1836	Jackson	Switzerland	14	23	Personal and property rights
June 8, 1844	Polk	Texas	16	35	Annexation
June 15, 1844	Polk	German Zollverein	26	18	Reciprocity
May 31, 1860	Buchanan	Mexico	18	27	Transit and commercial rights
June 27, 1860	Buchanan	Spain	26	17	Cuban Claims Commission
April 13, 1869	Grant	Great Britain	1	54	Arbitration of claims
June 1, 1870	Grant	Hawaii	20	19	Reciprocity
June 30, 1870	Grant	Dominican Republic	28	28	Annexation
Jan. 29, 1885	Cleveland	Nicaragua	32	23	Interoceanic canal
April 20, 1886	Cleveland	Mexico	32	26	Mining claims
Aug. 21, 1888	Cleveland	Great Britain	27	30	Fishing rights
Feb. 1, 1889	B. Harrison	Great Britain	15	38	Extradition
May 5, 1897	McKinley	Great Britain	43	26	Arbitration
March 19, 1920	Wilson	Multilateral	49	35	Treaty of Versailles
Jan. 18, 1927	Coolidge	Turkey	50	34	Commercial rights
March 14, 1934	F. Roosevelt	Canada	46	42	St. Lawrence Seaway
Jan. 29, 1935	F. Roosevelt	Multilateral	52	36	World Court
May 26, 1960	Eisenhower	Multilateral	49	30	Law of the Sea Convention
March 8, 1983	Reagan	Multilateral	50	42	Montreal Aviation Protocol
1990	G. H. W. Bush	Multilateral	—	—	Chemical weapons convention[a]
June 11, 1991	G. H. W. Bush	Multilateral	—	—	Annex II, international convention on load lines[b]
June 11, 1991	G. H. W. Bush	Multilateral	—	—	Amendments to Annex II, international convention on load lines[b]
Oct. 13, 1999	Clinton	Multilateral	48	51	Comprehensive Test Ban Treaty

Source: Congress A to Z (Washington, D.C.: Congressional Quarterly, 2nd ed., 1993), 395; U.S. Senate, *Treaties,* "Chapter 5: Rejected Treaties," www.senate.gov/artandhistory/history/common/briefing/Treaties.htm#5.

[a] Remains unratified although not formally rejected.

[b] Not formally rejected by a roll call vote, but instead returned to the president.

Table 7-16 Major Arms Control Agreements, Eisenhower to G. W. Bush

President	*Year signed*	*Agreement*	*Senate action*	*Provisions*	*Parties*
Eisenhower	1959	Antarctic Treaty	Ratified	Prohibits all military activity, including deployment of nuclear weapons, in Antarctica	Multilateral
Kennedy	1963	Partial Nuclear Test Ban Treaty	Ratified	Prohibits nuclear tests under water, in the atmosphere, and in outer space	Multilateral
L. Johnson	1967	Outer Space Treaty	Ratified	Prohibits all military activity, including deployment of nuclear weapons, in outer space	Multilateral
L. Johnson	1968	Nuclear Nonproliferation Treaty	Ratified	Prohibits acquisition of nuclear weapons by nations not already possessing them and establishes international safeguards to prevent the spread of nuclear weapons capability	Multilateral
Nixon	1971	Sea Bed Treaty	Ratified	Prohibits deployment of nuclear weapons on the ocean floor	Multilateral
Nixon	1972	SALT I ABM Treaty	Ratified	Limits size and number (two) of antiballistic missile systems in U.S. and Soviet Union. A 1974 executive agreement reduced number of sites permitted to one	U.S.-Soviet Union
Nixon	1972	SALT I Interim Offensive Arms Agreement	Executive agreement; no action	Established a five-year freeze on number of intercontinental ballistic missiles and submarine-launched ballistic missiles deployed by U.S. and Soviet Union	U.S.-Soviet Union
Nixon	1974	Threshold Nuclear Test Ban Treaty	Unratified	Prohibits underground nuclear test explosions greater than 150 kilotons	U.S.-Soviet Union
Ford	1976	Peaceful Nuclear Explosions Treaty	Unratified	Prohibits nuclear explosions greater than 150 kilotons for excavation and other peaceful purposes	U.S.-Soviet Union
Carter	1979	SALT II Offensive Arms Treaty	Unratified	Limits numbers and types of strategic nuclear weapons	U.S.-Soviet Union

(Table continues)

Table 7-16 *Continued)*

President	*Year signed*	*Agreement*	*Senate action*	*Provisions*	*Parties*
Reagan	1987	Intermediate Nuclear Forces Treaty	Ratified	Mandates the removal and destruction of all land-based nuclear missiles with ranges between 300 and 3,400 miles	U.S.-Soviet Union
G. H. W. Bush	1990	Conventional Forces in Europe Treaty	Ratified	Limits conventional weapons in Europe	Multilateral
G. H. W. Bush	1990	Chemical weapons convention	Unratified	Bans use, development, and stockpiling of chemical weapons	Multilateral
G. H. W. Bush	1991	Strategic Arms Reduction Treaty (START I)	Ratified	Limits numbers and types of strategic nuclear weapons	U.S.-Soviet Union
Clinton	1993	Strategic Arms Reduction Treaty, II (START II)	Ratified	Limits numbers and types of strategic nuclear weapons	U.S.-Russia
Clinton	1997	Strategic Arms Reduction Treaty (START III)	Proposed but not negotiated due to failure to implement START II	Proposed destruction of and further reductions in strategic nuclear warheads	U.S.-Russia
G. W. Bush[a]	2002	Strategic Offensive Reductions Treaty (SORT)	Signed, awaiting ratification by both countries	Proposed reduction of nuclear arsenals to 1,700–2,200 warheads	U.S.-Russia

Source: Guide to the Presidency, 4th ed. (Washington, D.C.: CQ Press, 2007), 771.

[a] Through 2007 only.

8

Presidential Policymaking

- **Executive Orders**
- **Presidential Tax and Appropriation Proposals**
- **Budget Surpluses and Deficits**

On September 24, 1957, President Dwight D. Eisenhower issued Executive Order No. 10730, directing the secretary of defense to order the Arkansas National Guard into the service of the United States. The Guard was to protect nine African-American teenagers who were attempting to attend Central High School in Little Rock but were being resisted by mobs of angry whites and the recalcitrant governor of the state, Orval Faubus. The Eisenhower administration acted to enforce a school desegregation order handed down by the U.S. District Court in Arkansas and, in so doing, carry out the requirements of U.S. law.

Lyndon B. Johnson, under authority of the Tariff Act of 1930, enacted Executive Order No. 11377 on October 23, 1967, authorizing the U.S. Tariff Commission to monitor the annual consumption of whisk brooms in America, noting the types, numbers, and uses made of them.

On August 21, 2002, George W. Bush issued Executive Order No. 13273, which gave the Coast Guard additional powers to protect the ports, harbors, and coastline facilities of the United States in light of the attacks on September 11, 2001. In taking the action, Bush's order asserted that "the security of the United States is endangered by reason of disturbances in the international relations of the United States that have existed since the terrorist attacks on the United States of September 11, 2001," adding that "such disturbances continue to endanger such relations. . . ."

This chapter examines presidential policymaking in two broad issue areas: domestic matters and fiscal economics. These policy areas reveal the four central features of presidents' policy efforts discussed in the previous chapter.

First, policy complexity defines the environment within which the modern presidency operates. This complexity is a reflection of the demands placed on the national government to do something about virtually everything. As a pivotal policy unit in the national government, the presidency makes a dizzying number of policies in all major domestic and economic issue areas and most minor ones. As a major policy initiative, George W. Bush's order on the Coast Guard to protect the U.S. shoreline was a reflection of the complexity that arose after the September 11 bombings. Yet Bush also signed numerous orders about less crucial matters, including the improvement of the coordination of youth soccer programs, the line of succession in the Office of Management and Budget, and adjustments for certain rates of pay for federal employees. The presidency acts on agriculture, health care, crime, drugs, the budget, business regulations, unemployment, banking, housing, safety, social security, welfare, nuclear power, natural resources, clean air, and civil rights. It sets policies on commemorative stamps, the length of government reports, and the shape of the national Christmas tree. Policy complexity is not only a feature of the environment but also an aspect of the presidency itself.

Second, as the examples reveal, presidents engage in independent policymaking. Eisenhower, Johnson, and George W. Bush acted unilaterally, without immediate congressional approval and without any coordinate decisions by Congress. These executive orders and other presidential efforts technically constitute execution of the law of the land. In these three instances, each president acted literally as chief executive. So that they may do so, Congress has granted presidents considerable discretion (and hence considerable autonomy) in the issuing of orders and other pronouncements. Although chief executives act under authority granted them in the U.S. Constitution and federal statutes, they are not bound by any specific instructions of Congress. Thus, in many instances presidents more genuinely create law rather than simply execute it. The presidency acts as a substitute legislative policymaker—identifying a problem, establishing a procedure or program to solve it, and allocating resources and personnel to put the program into operation.

Third, individual presidents may claim a personal role in independent policymaking. Eisenhower stood behind the Little Rock order. John F. Kennedy also issued executive orders on desegregation in Mississippi and Alabama and backed them with federal troops. The literature on presidential policymaking focuses heavily on the agendas and the successes of individual presidents; it looks upon policymaking as an incumbent-specific enterprise. And, certainly, differences in presidential policymaking can be significant. The differences between the economic plans of Franklin Roosevelt and George W. Bush are striking. Yet, these individual variations also reflect different partisan, ideological, and historical eras. These more systematic differences may be as telling as the differences among individual presidents.

Fourth, the presidency as an institution has an important, ongoing role in making presidential policy. Forced by the sheer number and varying types of decisions, spanning foreign, economic, and domestic policy spheres, presidents depend on the executive organization to get the job done. In many instances, they are only vaguely aware of the details of decisions that are made and ultimately go out under their signature. For example, Johnson signed, but undoubtedly did not ponder, the whisk broom order. The organization of the institutional presidency renders these decisions routine, making them less dependent on a specific individual. Thus, there is a distinction between individual presidents as policymakers and the presidency as a policymaking institution.

The chapter is organized in three parts. First, it considers the role of executive orders in independent presidential policymaking. Next, it examines the use of presidential signing statements as another mechanism of independence. Finally, it discusses presidents' efforts relating to taxes, spending, and budgets.

Executive Orders

Presidents engage in independent policymaking in domestic affairs through the use of executive orders. Like the executive agreements discussed in Chapter 7, executive orders do not require congressional approval. They are drafted in some instances in departments and agencies and sometimes in the Office of Management and Budget (OMB). In either case, OMB has developed a practice of "executive order clearance" in which all proposed orders are first screened by OMB to assure that they fit with the president's policy interests and existing law.

Executive orders since 1789 have been recorded, and those issued since 1949 have been classified by policy area and president. Table 8-1 shows the total number of known executive orders since Washington, who issued the first executive order on June 8, 1789, asking the heads of the original departments—state, war, Treasury, and the attorney general—to give "a clear account" of affairs connected with their departments (Lord, 1979, 1). As might be expected, early executive orders were infrequent; they began to see significant use only after the Civil War. During the nineteenth century, executive orders had two primary administrative purposes. The earliest was for external administration: the disposition of public lands, especially the withdrawal of land for Indian, military, naval, and lighthouse reservations. In the 1870s executive orders were used for internal administration. Numerous orders were issued concerning civil service rules, including the status of government employees, their work hours, salaries, pension requirements, and federal holidays. These two administrative forms are no longer the only types of executive orders, but they remain a significant proportion of the total number.

A relatively large increase in the number of executive orders appeared in Theodore Roosevelt's first term, and an even greater increase occurred in his second term. However, these orders continued to fit the nineteenth-century administrative mode; they did not advance major policy initiatives. The increase in executive orders during Roosevelt's administration did not represent an isolated flurry of presidential activity. Presidents who succeeded Roosevelt—including those who were activists, such as Woodrow Wilson, and those who were not, such as William H. Taft, Warren G. Harding, Coolidge, and Herbert Hoover—issued executive orders at roughly the same levels as Roosevelt. The new level of executive activity begun under Roosevelt became institutionalized for subsequent chief executives and reflected an expanded federal government.

Franklin Roosevelt extended the use of executive orders to include major policy initiatives, although the number of orders issued on administrative matters continued to be high and remained so until the early 1960s (see Ragsdale and Theis, 1997). Executive orders rose sharply between 1932 and 1933 (see Table 8-1). Roosevelt closed banks during the banking emergency of 1933, wrote rules under the authority of the National Industrial Recovery Act, and established the Civilian Conservation Corps. In addition, he issued orders for defense and national security. By executive order, Roosevelt established the Office of Price Administration and the Office of Economic Stabilization and mandated the internment of American citizens of Japanese ancestry living in the Pacific coastal states. The Supreme Court later declared unconstitutional the Japanese internment order, along with President Harry Truman's order to seize the steel industry.[1] However, the Court has usually upheld presidential executive orders, establishing them as having the same force in law as statutes.

Substantive policymaking through executive orders has also focused on civil liberties. Franklin Roosevelt established the Fair Employment Practices Commission in 1943 to prevent discrimination in hiring by government agencies and military suppliers. Truman ended segregation in the armed forces. As noted above, Eisenhower and Kennedy issued executive orders to enforce desegregation of schools in Arkansas, Mississippi, and Alabama. Lyndon Johnson created equal employment opportunity in federal hiring and in hiring by government contractors through a 1965 executive order. Indeed, the whole concept of affirmative action in federal employment stems from this order. The Reagan administration, which opposed affirmative action, proposed the issuance of an executive order that would have amounted to a "repeal" of Johnson's equal opportunity order (it never pursued this proposal, however). Bill Clinton set off a storm of controversy when he proposed an executive order to lift the ban on homosexuals in the military. Only after long negotiations with military commanders, Defense Department officials, and members of Congress did Clinton sign an order that was much less sweeping than the one he had originally intended.

An ongoing example of the use of the executive order as an independent policy device focuses on an order, first signed by Reagan and then continued by George H. W. Bush, that prohibited family planning clinics receiving federal funds from informing their clients about abortion options. The Supreme Court upheld this "gag rule" order in *Rust v. Sullivan* (1991). Congress tried several times to pass legislation to negate the order, but Bush vetoed one such attempt and threatened to veto others. Congress was unable to rally the two-thirds votes from both houses needed to override the veto. Within days of taking office, however, Clinton revoked the Reagan executive order and ended the gag rule. Then, on January 22, 2001, George W. Bush, during his first days in office, reinstated the Reagan order from two decades earlier. The order remained in effect throughout his administration.

Presidents have also used executive orders to create government units. Kennedy created the Peace Corps with an executive order and Congress later passed legislation formalizing its creation. Lyndon Johnson created the Office of Economic Opportunity out of which the "War on Poverty" was run. George W. Bush created the Homeland Security Administration by executive order, prior to the passage of legislation by Congress for the Department of Homeland Security.

Executive Orders and Policy Areas

In Table 8-2 executive orders are categorized by policy type. Apart from executive orders on federal government personnel and interagency and congressional requests, presidents use these orders in five principal policy areas: defense, foreign trade, economic management, natural resources, and social welfare/civil rights. Relatively few executive orders are issued in the areas of agriculture, federalism, and foreign aid. Agricultural executive orders deal principally with farming problems, which do not provide presidents with abundant advantages for building broad constituency support. When international agreements are made, agriculture figures much more prominently because it is an easy, economical, and broad-based avenue by which to aid nations and at the same time facilitate the distribution of American farm surpluses. By comparison, numerous executive orders have covered social welfare, economic management, and natural resource issues. Table 8-2 also reveals that executive orders extend beyond domestic affairs. They cover foreign trade, defense, and, to a much lesser extent, foreign aid. Oftentimes these orders establish guidelines for carrying out earlier international agreements.

Table 8-2 analyzes the policy emphases of executive orders by individual presidents and by party. Social welfare and civil rights issues were especially prominent under Carter. Kennedy, George H. W. Bush, and George W. Bush issued the most defense executive orders. Eisenhower issued the fewest executive orders on social welfare/civil rights matters. The economy received the most attention from Richard Nixon, Truman, and Reagan. Executive orders on natural resources have declined since Truman, whereas those on foreign trade increased markedly during the Carter and Reagan administrations. Democratic presidents are generally more likely to issue executive orders in the areas of resources and social welfare/civil rights than are Republican presidents. Although variations in policy emphasis between incumbents are evident, the policy complexity within which these variations occur is even more plain. The presidency is not free to ignore any policy area and must ultimately juggle the interrelationships and inconsistencies across the several types of issues.

Executive orders combine the interests of incumbents with programmatic priorities that attach to the institution of the presidency. The intricacies inherent in these orders are heightened by complexity across policy areas and diversity among groups. Presidents must rely on the Executive Office of the President and on departments and agencies to propose and draft executive orders. The occupant of the Oval Office is not personally issuing each executive order; instead, the institution turns this abundance of work into standard operating procedures, patterns, and expectations. The type and frequency of executive orders issued by any new president is thus predominantly a function of the institution of the presidency. Presidents influence the direction of executive policymaking, but only in incremental ways.

Signing Statements

Presidents have also expanded their independent policy role through the use of signing statements. These statements—sometimes as short as a paragraph, other times as long as several pages—are issued when presidents sign bills into law. They are recorded for presidents since Hoover in Table 8-3. Signing statements first began with President James Monroe. They were issued very sporadically until the 1950s, and were typically descriptive or congratulatory in nature. They typically announced what the new law was intended to achieve or congratulated members of Congress on its passage. But signing statements have also been used to make substantive administrative and constitutional claims. This began in 1830 when Andrew Jackson signed a bill that appropriated funds to build a road from Detroit to Chicago; Jackson sent Congress a message stating that he intended to stop building the road at the Michigan border. John Tyler expanded on Jackson's precedent by expressing constitutional misgivings on a reapportionment act. Congress rebuked Tyler, stating that a president had "only three options upon receiving a bill: a signature, a veto, or a pocket veto." To sign a bill and add extraneous matter in a separate document could be regarded "in no other light than a defacement of the public records and archives."[2] Other nineteenth-century presidents also issued signing statements, several explicitly claiming that sections of a law deprived the president of constitutional authority. Andrew Johnson signed a particular army appropriations bill, but protested that one of its sections "in certain cases virtually deprives the President of his constitutional functions as Commander in Chief of the Army."[3] The fight was not just about interpreting a bill's sweep as the law of the land, but also constituted a match-up between Congress and the president over presidential power and Congress's perceived encroachments of it.

Nevertheless, signing statements were few and far between until the 1950s. As shown in Table 8-3, Truman revived the signing statement and also issued several that questioned the constitutionality of key parts of the legislation he was signing into law. This continued until Gerald Ford, who increased the issuance of signing statements questioning the constitutionality of specific sections of bills being promulgated. These statements typically referenced sections of bills referred to as "legislative vetoes" or language that provided Congress final approval over regulations issued by the executive branch. The Supreme Court struck down the legislative veto in 1983 in *INS v. Chadha* (462 U.S. 919), but presidents since then have continued to look out for passages of legislation that might be construed as such vetoes in violation of the Court's decision. In addition, presidents continue to question bill language that asserts congressional infringement on presidents' power in diplomacy, as commander in chief, in making appointments, and in running the executive branch. As an example, President George W. Bush issued a signing statement on an appropriations act that asserted:

> The executive branch shall construe as advisory the provisions of the Act that purport to direct or burden the Executive's conduct of foreign relations, including the authority to recognize foreign states and negotiate international agreements on behalf of the United States, or limit the President's authority as Commander in Chief.[4]

Beginning in the Reagan administration, presidents have asserted their "right" to have signing statements serve as a part of the legislative history of a bill. This means that when a bill is subjected to litigation and interpretation by the courts, the executive's view of the legislation is a part of the record upon which the courts make their decisions. The courts have in fact taken note of several signing statements in their rulings since the Reagan years.[5]

Signing statements have caused considerable controversy during the George W. Bush administration. Unlike many of his predecessors who issued numerous signing statements for celebratory reasons, Bush chose to issue statements almost exclusively on constitutional grounds. As seen in Table 8-3, he issued fewer signing statements than his immediate predecessors Reagan, George H. W. Bush, and Clinton. But among the statements the younger Bush signed, virtually all of them raised questions about constitutionality of some part of the bill being signed into law.

This has opened a debate about the legitimacy of signing statements. At its core, the logic presidents invoke seems inherently flawed: they sign a bill, but say that they will not enforce some part of it because they believe it violates the Constitution or other federal laws. Seemingly, the correct course of action in this situation is to veto the bill rather than sign it. But presidents clearly see both political and constitutional advantages to picking and choosing the parts of a law they believe to be enforceable. Critics question whether presidents can have this "last word" on the constitutionality of certain portions of legislation they sign into law. Some constitutional law scholars maintain that, per Congress's remarks to John Tyler, presidents have only three options: veto, pocket veto, or sign the bill. They cannot sign *most* of a bill, but through a signing statement they can suggest that they will not enforce certain parts they find objectionable.

Determining the constitutionality of a law or parts of a law is, by this argument, a matter for the courts to decide. According to these experts, presidents thus fail to enforce the law—all of it—and thereby abrogate their own constitutional role as chief executive to "faithfully execute the laws." But the debate is far from resolved; meanwhile, George W. Bush firmly enlarged his independent policy role, maintaining that he has the ability to determine the constitutionality of individual passages within legislation. This permits the president to raise objections first, before the courts become involved. Since oftentimes the courts do not become involved, this leaves the president's views about constitutionality and presidential power as paramount. It is unlikely that future presidents will argue otherwise, recognizing that they gain political advantages by claiming such power.

The Economy

Presidents since Franklin Roosevelt have presented themselves as budding economists who will adapt fiscal policy to promote economic prosperity. They do so by three devices: (1) adjusting taxes, typically downward; (2) adjusting spending, typically upward; and (3) attempting to balance the budget.

Taxing Politics

Presidents since Truman have offered tax cuts as the primary instrument of economic management. Presidents typically propose the cuts as swift, short-term economic solutions that give taxpayers and businesses an immediate benefit. Tax cuts ultimately provide clear political advantages for the presidents and other politicians offering them, but they have ambiguous economic impact on the consumers and corporations receiving them. Table 8-4 summarizes presidents' tax proposals and congressional enactments from Truman to George W. Bush. As the table shows, presidents and Congress jockey over taxes, with presidents almost never getting what they have asked for. Presidents are faced with a Congress introducing its own initiatives without a prior proposal from the White House. For instance, Truman and Eisenhower reluctantly introduced tax cuts in 1948 and 1954 to stave off the larger cuts desired, and ultimately enacted, by Congress. The table also shows that every president since Truman has proposed at least one tax cut. In the span of just four decades, tax rates for the highest income bracket dropped from 91 percent in 1946 to 28 percent in 1986.

Tax cuts are the "easy" half of presidents' fiscal tax policy. How willing are presidents to adopt the "hard" part of fiscal policy—a tax increase? Table 8-4 shows that presidents have agreed to tax increases generally only in exchange for economic or other desired incentives. Lyndon Johnson resisted a tax increase until 1968 when, no longer running for reelection, he acquiesced to a Vietnam tax surcharge passed by Congress. Nixon sought the continuation of the surcharge in exchange for congressionally sponsored income tax reduction and repeal of investment tax credits in 1969. Two years later Nixon changed course, asking for a large income tax reduction and the return of the investment tax credit. During the post–oil embargo recession in 1974, Ford proposed a tax increase designed to pay for antirecessionary plans that included improved unemployment compensation and aid to the housing industry. Yet a tax cut for business also accompanied the increase. This increase was abandoned completely in 1975 in favor of a temporary tax cut to give the economy an immediate boost. Congress and President Reagan agreed on moderate increases in excise taxes in 1982 and 1984 in response to an ever-growing budget deficit. President George H. W. Bush agreed to assorted tax increases in 1990, but many of these were repealed in 1992. In the largest tax package in history, Clinton and Congress agreed to $56 billion in tax increases over five years in exchange for tax cuts of $152 billion. Despite a growing budget deficit, the George W. Bush administration continued to push for additional tax cuts well into its second term.

Spending Politics

Presidents also adopt programs designed to "spend" the economy back to health or to show the government's commitment to alleviating a particular problem. Table 8-5 records the differences between presidents' proposed spending totals and the amounts actually appropriated by Congress. Only Eisenhower, during his second term, met with much success in getting what he wanted. Congress has raised or lowered the requests of all other presidents since Truman. Table 8-5 reveals that presidents also advocate spending cuts. Cuts are typically offered as measures of immediate cost savings or as a matter of ideology—frugality is good. Much of the spending proposed by presidents and approved by Congress goes to mandatory programs that have become increasingly uncontrollable elements of the federal budget (54 percent of the total in 2007). The table also reveals an obvious partisan difference between Democratic and Republican presidents. Democratic presidents have typically asked for more nondefense spending than they actually get from Congress, while Republican presidents have requested more defense spending than they ultimately receive. The most vivid comparison is between Jimmy Carter and George W. Bush. Carter requested much less defense spending but much more nondefense spending than the Congress actually appropriated. Combining the two, Carter and Congress were actually more than $21.6 billion apart in their appropriations numbers. George W. Bush requested more defense spending and less nondefense spending than Congress approved, leading to an overall gap of $23 billion between his wishes and what Congress appropriated.

Budget Politics

Presidents' main economic policy instruments of taxing and spending ultimately depend on the budget and the budget process. The most that presidents can hope for is to modify the overall budget picture, but this is difficult to do because the budget is an amorphous document that never really exists in one place, nor is it passed at one time. The budget process is instead a confusing, fragmented, and decentralized process.

Because of looming budget deficits (Figure 8-1), budgeting increasingly went to the core of governing in the 1980s and 1990s. Table 8-6 indicates that, since 1947, the government has operated in surplus in only twelve years: 1947, 1948, 1949, 1951, 1956, 1957, 1960, 1969, 1998, 1999, 2000, and 2001. Structural deficits—the portion of the deficit that results from a basic imbalance in spending and revenues not due to recession—have been commonplace. Deficits during the 1960s were modest, averaging $5 billion from 1961 to 1967. A $25.2 billion deficit was amassed in 1968. This was followed by a surplus of $3.2 billion in 1969. A large jump in the deficit followed the first oil shock of 1974. The deficit increased tenfold from $6.1 billion in 1973 to $63.2 billion in 1975. It remained high throughout the Carter years after the oil shock of 1978. The average annual deficit from 1977 to 1980 was $58 billion. In 1981 the deficit almost doubled from the previous year (from $79 billion to $128 billion). In 1982 it nearly doubled again (from $128 billion to $208 billion). During the Clinton administration the deficit dropped for the first time since 1987—by $40 billion in fiscal 1993 and by more than $50 billion in fiscal 1994. In fiscal year 1998, the first surplus since 1969 occurred at $69.3 billion. This was followed by even larger surpluses in the next three years. The largest budget surplus ever—$236.2 billion—was recorded in fiscal year 2000. All this came to an abrupt end by fiscal 2002. The antiterrorism campaign, the war in Iraq, a slowed economy, and a growing number of baby boomers collecting Medicare benefits pushed the federal budget back into deficit. Indeed, deficits of $378 billion in 2003, $413 billion in 2004, and $318 billion in 2005 broke all previous records.

Finally, Table 8-7 examines the size of the federal government as a percentage of U.S. gross national product (GDP). These data bear directly on the ongoing debate regarding the appropriate size and purpose of government. One of President Reagan's chief objectives was to prove that the government was too large and to work to curtail it during his administration. Presidents George H. W. Bush and George W. Bush have echoed Reagan's claims. While Reagan's rhetoric may well have been successful, actual efforts to decrease federal spending have had little effect. As the table shows, the overall size of the federal government calculated as a percent of GDP has been fairly stable since 1968, averaging just under 21 percent. It was at its lowest in fiscal year 2001 at 18.5 percent and at its highest in fiscal year 1983 at 23.5 percent. Ironically, federal spending as a percentage of GDP actually grew during the Reagan years, in part because of the interest being paid on the rising budget deficits. While total federal spending was roughly 18–20 percent of GDP in the 1960s and 1970s, it rose to its highest levels in the 1980s and early 1990s. The percentage dipped below the 20 percent mark in the latter 1990s and from 2000 to 2002. Since then, the percentage has been at or above 20 percent. This pattern is examined graphically in Figure 8-2.

Conclusion

The prevailing model of presidential policymaking stresses the roles of key political actors, especially presidents. As a result, less attention is paid to the institutions within which these actors behave. This chapter focuses on the institution's impact on policymaking. The institutional presidency transcends individual presidents' specific actions. Although presidency watchers detail the idiosyncrasies of presidential officeholders, the contemporary institution is a much more complicated, although much more predictable, policymaker. It is elaborate, decentralized, and stable in its organization, with key ongoing units that have well-established practices and norms. The institution accommodates numerous policy areas that place different demands on presidents, create different incentives for them, and allow them different degrees of success. Institutional policymaking occurs at the point where the predictable institution encounters the complex and unpredictable policy environment. Only within the arena defined by the institution, policy areas, and target groups are the actions of individual presidents relevant.

Notes

1. Several tables in this chapter take Truman's second term as a convenient starting point. Truman's first term was marked by activities tied to the end of World War II and is therefore somewhat anomalous.
2. Material about Jackson and Tyler from U.S. Congress, Congressional Research Service, CRS Report for Congress "Presidential Signing Statements: Constitutional and Institutional Implications," RL33667, September 20, 2006, p. 2.
3. Memorandum for Bernard Nussbaum, Counsel to the President, "The Legal Significance of Presidential Signing Statements," Appendix, found at www.usdoj.gov/olc/sigining.htm.
4. Statement on Signing the Science, State, Justice, Commerce, and Related Agencies Appropriations Act, 2006, November 22nd, 2005, found at the American Presidency Project, www.presidency.ucsb.edu / signingstatements.php
5. U.S. Congress, Congressional Research Service, CRS Report for Congress "Presidential Signing Statements: Constitutional and Institutional Implications," RL33667, September 20, 2006, p. 4.

Table 8-1 Executive Orders of Presidents, Washington, I to G.W. Bush, II

President/year	*Numbered orders*[a]	*Unnumbered orders*[b]	*Total for term*	*Average number per year*
Washington, I				
1789	—	3		
1790	—	2		
1791	—	0		
1792	—	2	7	1.75
Washington, II				
1793	—	1		
1794	—	0		
1795	—	0		
1796	—	0	1	0.25
Adams				
1797	—	0		
1798	—	1		
1799	—	0		
1800	—	0	1	0.25
Jefferson, I				
1801	—	2		
1802	—	0		
1803	—	0		
1804	—	0	2	0.50
Jefferson, II				
1805	—	0		
1806	—	1		
1807	—	1		
1808	—	0	2	0.50
Madison, I				
1809	—	0		
1810	—	1		
1811	—	0		
1812	—	0	1	0.25
Madison, II				
1813	—	0		
1814	—	0		
1815	—	0		
1816	—	0	0	0.00
Monroe, I				
1817	—	0		
1818	—	0		
1819	—	0		
1820	—	1	1	0.25

(Table continues)

Table 8-1 *(Continued)*

President/year	*Numbered orders*[a]	*Unnumbered orders*[b]	*Total for term*	*Average number per year*
Monroe, II				
1821	—	0		
1822	—	0		
1823	—	0		
1824	—	0	0	0.00
J.Q. Adams				
1825	—	0		
1826	—	0		
1827	—	1		
1828	—	3	4	1.00
Jackson, I				
1829	—	1		
1830	—	2		
1831	—	1		
1832	—	1	5	1.25
Jackson, II				
1833	—	1		
1834	—	0		
1835	—	3		
1836	—	2	6	1.50
Van Buren				
1837	—	2		
1838	—	6		
1839	—	0		
1840	—	2	10	2.50
W. Harrison				
1841	—	0	0	0.00
Tyler				
1841	—	0		
1842	—	14		
1843	—	0		
1844	—	3	17	4.25
Polk				
1845	—	3		
1846	—	1		
1847	—	12		
1848	—	3	19	4.75
Taylor				
1849	—	3		
1850	—	1	4	2.66
Fillmore				
1850	—	1		

Table 8-1 *(Continued)*

President/year	*Numbered orders*[a]	*Unnumbered orders*[b]	*Total for term*	*Average number per year*
Fillmore (continued)				
1851	—	4		
1852	—	8	13	5.20
Pierce				
1853	—	6		
1854	—	15		
1855	—	11		
1856	—	3	35	8.75
Buchanan				
1857	—	2		
1858	—	3		
1859	—	8		
1860	—	2	15	3.75
Lincoln, I				
1861		3		
1862	1	6		
1863	1	14		
1864	0	20	45	11.25
Lincoln, II				
1865	0	3	3	9.09
A. Johnson				
1865	3	17		
1866	1	14		
1867	0	23		
1868	2	19	79	19.75
Grant, I				
1869	0	29		
1870	0	27		
1871	0	18		
1872	1	18	93	23.25
Grant, II				
1873	5	28		
1874	6	27		
1875	2	36		
1876	1	25	130	32.50
Hayes				
1877	0	24		
1878	0	12		
1879	0	29		
1880	0	27	92	23.00

(Table continues)

Table 8-1 *(Continued)*

President/year	*Numbered orders*[a]	*Unnumbered orders*[b]	*Total for term*	*Average number per year*
Garfield				
1881	0	9	9	[c]
Arthur				
1881	1	4		
1882	0	23		
1883	0	25		
1884	2	45	100	25.00
Cleveland				
1885	3	22		
1886	0	25		
1887	3	15		
1888	0	45	113	28.25
B. Harrison				
1889	0	29		
1890	1	38		
1891	1	35		
1892	2	29	135	33.75
Cleveland				
1893	3	26		
1894	15	22		
1895	29	17		
1896	12	18	142	35.50
McKinley, I				
1897	7	5		
1898	10	19		
1899	12	33		
1900	16	42	144	36.00
McKinley, II				
1901	6	28	34	[c]
T. Roosevelt, I				
1901	13	13		
1902	44	39		
1903	47	25		
1904	55	27	263	75.14
T. Roosevelt, II				
1905	164	9		
1906	165	2		
1907	188	5		
1908	330	6	869	217.00
Taft				
1909	79	15		
1910	129	38		

Table 8-1 *(Continued)*

President/year	*Numbered orders*[a]	*Unnumbered orders*[b]	*Total for term*	*Average number per year*
Taft (continued)				
1911	175	12		
1912	277	27	752	188.00
Wilson, I				
1913	135	13		
1914	243	6		
1915	188	12		
1916	252	10	859	214.75
Wilson, II				
1917	255	17		
1918	259	7		
1919	225	8		
1920	210	1	982	245.50
Harding				
1921	192	1		
1922	174	1		
1923	118	1	487	182.40
Coolidge, I				
1923	62	0		
1924	233	5	300	214.29
Coolidge, II				
1925	227	0		
1926	201	1		
1927	238	2		
1928	288	2	959	239.75
Hoover				
1929	183	0		
1930	268	0		
1931	247	0		
1932	273	0	971	242.75
F. Roosevelt, I				
1933	468	1		
1934	473	2		
1935	384	0		
1936	283	0	1,611	402.75
F. Roosevelt, II				
1937	249	0		
1938	249	0		
1939	287	0		
1940	274	8	1,067	266.75

(Table continues)

Table 8-1 *(Continued)*

President/year	*Numbered orders*[a]	*Unnumbered orders*[b]	*Total for term*	*Average number per year*
F. Roosevelt, III				
1941	365	—		
1942	288	—		
1943	122	—		
1944	121	—	896	224.00
F. Roosevelt, IV				
1945	8	—	8	[c]
Truman, I				
1945	139	—		
1946	148	—		
1947	103	—		
1948	113	—	503	125.75
Truman, II				
1949	65	—		
1950	105	—		
1951	118	—		
1952	115	—	403	100.75
Eisenhower, I				
1953	80	—		
1954	73	—		
1955	65	—		
1956	46	—	264	66.00
Eisenhower, II				
1957	52	—		
1958	50	—		
1959	60	—		
1960	56	—	218	54.50
Kennedy				
1961	70	—		
1962	89	—		
1963	55	—	214	71.33
L. Johnson[d]				
1963	7	—		
1964	56	—		
1965	74	—		
1966	57	—		
1967	66	—		
1968	65	—	325	65.00
Nixon, I				
1969	52	—		
1970	72	—		
1971	63	—		
1972	60	—	247	61.75

Table 8-1 *(Continued)*

President/year	*Numbered orders*[a]	*Unnumbered orders*[b]	*Total for term*	*Average number per year*
Nixon, II				
1973	59	—		
1974	40	—	99	59.28
Ford				
1974	29	—		
1975	67	—		
1976	73	—	169	72.22
Carter				
1977	83	—		
1978	78	—		
1979	77	—		
1980	99	—	320	80.00
Reagan, I				
1981	50	—		
1982	63	—		
1983	57	—		
1984	43	—	213	53.25
Reagan, II				
1985	43	—		
1986	37	—		
1987	43	—		
1988	45	—	168	42.00
G.H.W. Bush				
1989	31	—		
1990	43	—		
1991	46	—		
1992	40	—	160	40.00
Clinton, I				
1993	57	—		
1994	54	—		
1995	39	—		
1996	47	—	197	49.25
Clinton, II				
1997	38	—		
1998	38	—		
1999	35	—		
2000	41	—	152	38.00
G.W. Bush, I				
2001	66	—		
2002	31	—		
2003	41	—		
2004	45	—	183	45.75

(Table continues)

Table 8-1 *(Continued)*

President/year	*Numbered orders*[a]	*Unnumbered orders*[b]	*Total for term*	*Average number per year*
G.W. Bush, II[e]				
2005	26	—		
2006	27	—		
2007	26	—	79	32.67

Sources: (Unnumbered series, 1789–1941) Adapted from Clifford Lord, *List and Index of Presidential Executive Orders, Unnumbered Series, 1789–1941* (Wilmington, Del.: Michael Glazier, 1979); (numbered series, 1862–1935) adapted from Clifford Lord, ed., *Presidential Executive Orders, 1862–1935,* 2 vols. (New York: Hastings House, 1944); (numbered series, 1936–1997) compiled from successive volumes of *Code of Federal Regulations*; (1998–2007) successive volumes of *Code of Federal Regulations,* www.access.gpo.gov.

Note: Collation and numbering of executive orders did not begin until 1907. However, certain orders before that date were entered into the numbered series. Some unnumbered orders exist as late as 1941. In a project conducted by the Works Progress Administration in 1935 and 1936, the unnumbered orders were collected and analyzed from historical materials. This was the first and, in fact, only attempt to establish a list of unnumbered orders. Generally, such a list is difficult to compile because of a lack of agreement as to whether a document was an order, a proclamation, a land order, or some other executive communication. Those presented here are drawn from the 1935–1936 WPA project. For years in which a new term begins, orders signed prior to inauguration day (March 4 before 1937, Jan. 20 thereafter) are counted in the previous year.

[a] Numbered series begins in 1862; "—" in this column indicates no numbered orders.
[b] Unnumbered series ends in 1941; "—" in this column indicates no unnumbered orders.
[c] President did not complete full year.
[d] Includes full term from Nov. 1963 to Jan. 1969.
[e] Through 2007 only.

Table 8-2 Executive Orders, by Policy Type, Truman, II to G. W. Bush, II

President/ year	*Foreign trade/ diplomacy*	*Foreign aid*	*Defense*	*Social welfare/ civil rights*	*Government/ economic management*	*Natural resources/ environment*	*Agriculture*	*Ceremonial/ cultural*	*Federalism*	*Personnel, agency requests*	*Total*
Truman, II											
1949	10	0	3	1	15	14	0	2	0	20	
1950	9	0	23	6	27	15	1	5	0	19	
1951	10	0	32	11	18	17	0	3	0	27	
1952	13	0	21	6	11	27	0	6	0	31	
Total	42	0	79	24	71	73	1	16	0	97	403
%	10.4	0.0	19.6	6.0	17.6	18.1	0.2	4.0	0.0	24.1	
Eisenhower, I											
1953	9	3	25	3	13	6	3	6	0	12	
1954	3	1	9	5	15	11	2	3	0	24	
1955	7	1	26	3	3	9	2	1	0	13	
1956	1	0	19	2	5	5	1	2	0	11	
Total	20	5	79	13	36	31	8	12	0	60	264
%	7.5	1.9	29.9	4.9	13.6	11.7	3.0	4.5	0.0	22.7	
Eisenhower, II											
1957	6	1	9	3	10	6	2	2	0	13	
1958	5	0	13	3	6	11	0	1	0	11	
1959	5	0	11	1	9	12	3	6	1	12	
1960	4	0	10	0	17	5	2	3	1	14	
Total	20	1	43	7	42	34	7	12	2	50	218
%	9.2	0.1	19.7	3.2	19.3	15.6	3.2	5.5	0.1	22.9	

(Table continues)

Table 8-2 *(Continued)*

President/ year	*Foreign trade/ diplomacy*	*Foreign aid*	*Defense*	*Social welfare/ civil rights*	*Government/ economic management*	*Natural resources/ environment*	*Agriculture*	*Ceremonial/ cultural*	*Federalism*	*Personnel, agency requests*	*Total*
Kennedy											
1961	5	2	19	5	13	17	2	4	1	12	
1962	3	2	23	9	22	12	2	5	0	11	
1963	8	0	13	10	6	2	0	5	0	11	
Total	16	4	45	24	41	31	4	14	1	34	214
%	7.5	1.9	21.0	11.2	19.2	14.5	1.9	6.5	0.1	15.9	
L. Johnson[a]											
1963	1	0	1	1	1	0	0	0	0	3	
1964	7	0	10	7	10	7	1	3	1	10	
1965	13	2	6	10	4	8	2	4	0	25	
1966	12	1	7	6	8	5	1	4	0	13	
1967	5	1	10	6	10	12	2	0	0	20	
1968	10	0	8	11	8	5	0	2	1	20	
Total	48	4	42	41	41	37	6	13	2	91	325
%	14.7	1.2	13.3	12.9	12.6	11.4	1.8	4.0	0.1	28	
Nixon, I											
1969	3	0	5	10	5	5	1	4	1	18	
1970	7	0	11	7	13	9	1	4	0	20	
1971	5	0	7	5	12	6	2	6	2	18	
1972	7	0	4	5	9	9	0	5	1	20	
Total	22	0	27	27	39	29	4	19	4	76	247
%	8.9	0.0	10.9	10.9	15.8	11.7	1.6	7.7	1.6	30.8	
Nixon, II											
1973	2	0	3	3	9	15	1	4	0	22	

1974	6	0	4	5	5	6	0	0	1	13	
Total	8	0	7	8	14	21	1	4	1	35	99
%	8.0	0.0	7.1	8.0	14.1	21.2	0.1	4.0	0.1	35.6	
Ford											
1974	7	0	2	3	4	2	0	2	0	9	
1975	8	1	11	4	7	9	0	4	0	23	
1976	19	1	6	4	4	9	0	5	0	25	
Total	34	2	19	11	15	20	0	11	0	57	169
%	20.1	0.1	11.2	6.5	8.8	11.8	0.0	6.5	0.0	33.7	
Carter											
1977	7	0	5	12	3	9	0	4	0	26	
1978	12	0	4	18	11	6	0	1	0	26	
1979	18	3	5	8	7	15	1	5	0	15	
1980	37	1	6	13	4	15	1	2	0	20	
Total	74	4	20	51	25	45	2	12	0	87	320
%	23.1	1.3	6.3	15.9	7.8	14.1	0.1	3.8	0.0	27.2	
Reagan, I											
1981	15	0	3	3	6	7	0	4	1	11	
1982	18	1	4	9	11	3	0	2	1	14	
1983	16	0	4	8	13	5	1	0	1	9	
1984	12	0	5	1	11	0	0	1	0	13	
Total	61	1	16	21	41	15	1	7	3	47	213
%	28.6	0.1	7.5	9.9	19.2	7.0	0.1	3.3	0.1	22.0	
Reagan, II											
1985	11	3	8	3	7	4	0	0	0	7	
1986	8	1	5	2	12	1	1	2	0	5	
1987	7	0	3	7	13	3	0	1	0	9	
1988	9	1	8	1	14	4	0	1	0	7	
Total	35	5	24	13	46	12	1	4	0	28	168
%	20.8	2.9	14.3	7.7	27.4	7.1	5.9	2.4	0.0	16.7	

(Table continues)

Table 8-2 *(Continued)*

President/ year	*Foreign trade/ diplomacy*	*Foreign aid*	*Defense*	*Social welfare/ civil rights*	*Government/ economic management*	*Natural resources/ environment*	*Agriculture*	*Ceremonial/ cultural*	*Federalism*	*Personnel, agency requests*	*Total*
G. H. W. Bush											
1989	3	1	5	2	3	3	0	0	0	14	
1990	10	2	8	1	1	4	2	1	0	14	
1991	10	2	8	1	1	4	2	1	0	17	
1992	8	2	5	3	2	2	0	5	1	12	
Total	31	7	26	7	7	13	4	7	1	54	157
%	19.4	4.4	16.3	4.4	4.4	8.1	2.5	4.4	0.6	33.8	
Clinton, I											
1993	12	0	6	6	11	9	0	0	1	12	
1994	9	0	10	7	3	9	0	1	0	15	
1995	8	1	10	3	9	2	0	0	0	5	
1996	8	1	2	11	9	3	0	3	1	10	
Total	37	2	28	27	32	23	0	4	2	42	197
%	18.8	1.0	14.2	13.7	16.2	11.7	0.0	2.0	1.0	21.3	
Clinton, II											
1997	6	1	6	4	12	5	1	0	0	3	
1998	8	0	7	5	6	5	0	1	3	3	
1999	10	0	6	4	6	5	0	1	0	3	
2000	2	0	0	13	10	6	0	2	4	4	
Total	26	1	19	26	34	21	1	4	7	13	152
%	18.2	0.7	13.3	18.2	23.8	14.7	0.7	2.8	4.9	9.1	
G. W. Bush, I											
2001	10	0	5	12	12	8	0	0	2	17	

2002	2	0	6	12	1	2	1	0	0	7	
2003	10	0	6	5	3	4	0	3	1	9	
2004	7	0	6	11	4	9	0	1	1	6	
Total	29	0	23	40	20	23	1	4	4	39	183
%	15.8	0	12.6	21.9	10.9	12.6	0.5	2.2	2.2	21.4	
G. W. Bush, II[b]											
2005	4	0	6	4	4	0	0	1	0	7	
2006	6	0	3	7	6	2	0	0	0	3	
2007	5	0	8	2	7	6	0	1	0	1	
Total	15	0	17	13	17	8	0	2	0	11	83
%	8.2	0	9.3	7.1	9.3	4.4	0.0	1.1	0.0	6.0	
Total	586	36	514	353	521	436	41	145	27	821	3,412
%	15.6	1.1	15.3	10.3	15.2	12.8	1.2	4.3	0.7	23.5	
Republican presidents											
Total	275	21	281	160	277	206	27	82	15	457	1,801
%	15.3	1.2	15.6	8.9	15.4	11.4	1.5	4.6	0.8	25.4	
Democratic presidents											
Total	243	15	233	193	244	230	14	63	12	364	1,611
%	15.1	0.9	14.5	12.0	15.1	14.3	0.9	3.9	0.7	22.6	

Source: (1949–1997) Calculated by the author from successive volumes of *Code of Federal Regulations*; (1998–2007) *Code of Federal Regulations*, www.access.gpo.gov.

Note: Policy types were coded on the basis of title descriptions and, in some cases, the text of the orders.

[a] Includes full term from Nov. 1963 to Jan. 1969.
[b] Through 2007 only.

Table 8-3 Presidential Signing Statements, Hoover to G.W. Bush, II

President	*Signing statements*	*Constitutional questions raised*	*Constitutional questions as percentage of total*
Hoover			
1929	1	0	0.0
1930	2	0	0.0
1931	1	0	0.0
1932	12	0	0.0
Total	16	0	0.0
F. Roosevelt, I			
1933	5	0	0.0
1934	7	0	0.0
1935	6	0	0.0
1936	2	0	0.0
Total	20	0	0.0
F. Roosevelt, II			
1937	0	0	0.0
1938	1	0	0.0
1939	4	0	0.0
1940	4	0	0.0
Total	9	0	0.0
F. Roosevelt, III/IV			
1941	0	0	0.0
1942	2	0	0.0
1943	3	0	0.0
1944	8	0	0.0
1945	0	0	0.0
Total	13	0	0.0
Truman, I			
1945	6	0	0.0
1946	12	0	0.0
1947	11	0	0.0
1948	18	0	0.0
Total	47	0	0.0
Truman, II			
1949	19	0	0.0
1950	13	1	7.7
1951	16	1	6.3
1952	12	0	0.0
Total	60	2	3.3
Eisenhower, I			
1953	9	0	0.0
1954	35	0	0.0
1955	14	1	7.1
1956	31	2	6.5
Total	89	3	3.4

Table 8-3 *(Continued)*

President	*Signing statements*	*Constitutional questions raised*	*Constitutional questions as percentage of total*
Eisenhower, II			
1957	17	0	0.0
1958	20	2	10.0
1959	23	1	4.3
1960	7	1	14.3
Total	67	4	6.0
Kennedy			
1961	18	0	0.0
1962	17	0	0.0
1963	2	0	0.0
Total	37	0	0.0
L. Johnson			
1963	3	0	0.0
1964	11	1	9.1
1965	34	1	2.9
1966	55	1	1.8
1967	33	1	3.0
1968	39	0	0.0
Total	175	4	2.3
Nixon, I			
1969	10	0	0.0
1970	21	2	9.5
1971	17	0	0.0
1972	31	3	9.7
Total	79	5	6.3
Nixon, II			
1973	27	0	0.0
1974	11	1	9.1
Total	38	1	2.6
Ford			
1974	32	1	3.1
1975	28	2	7.1
1976	77	8	10.4
Total	137	11	8.0
Carter			
1977	32	6	18.8
1978	77	5	6.5
1979	26	1	3.8
1980	90	11	12.2
Total	225	23	10.2
Reagan, I			
1981	19	4	21.1
1982	28	1	3.6

(Table continues)

Table 8-3 *(Continued)*

President	*Signing statements*	*Constitutional questions raised*	*Constitutional questions as percentage of total*
Reagan, I (continued)			
1983	26	7	26.9
1984	48	11	22.9
Total	121	23	19.0
Reagan, II			
1985	19	3	15.8
1986	54	5	9.3
1987	23	7	30.4
1988	32	13	40.6
Total	128	28	21.9
G. H. W. Bush			
1989	43	9	20.9
1990	62	24	38.7
1991	36	14	38.9
1992	87	20	23.0
Total	228	67	29.4
Clinton, I			
1993	33	1	3.0
1994	38	10	26.3
1995	21	4	19.1
1996	73	7	9.6
Total	165	22	13.3
Clinton, II			
1997	36	7	19.4
1998	52	12	23.1
1999	42	13	31.0
2000	86	18	20.9
Total	216	50	23.1
G. W. Bush, I			
2001	24	7	29.2
2002	34	33	97.1
2003	27	27	100.0
2004	25	24	96.0
Total	110	91	82.7
G. W. Bush, II[a]			
2005	14	13	92.9
2006	23	18	78.3
2007	8	4	50.0
Total	45	35	77.8

Source: Coded by the author from the compilation of signing statements found at the American Presidency Project, www.presidency.ucsb.edu. Keywords "constitution" and "signing" were used in the search engine to create a database of signing statements with possible constitutional objections. From this population, individual signing statements were read to ascertain whether constitutional objections were in fact presented.

[a] Through 2007 only.

Table 8-4 Presidential Tax Proposals and Congressional Enactments, Truman to G. W. Bush, II (in billions of 1982 dollars)

	Presidential proposal		*Congressional enactment*		*Difference*	
President/year	First year[a]	Fully effective[b]	First year[a]	Fully effective[b]	First year[a]	Fully effective[b]
Truman						
1948	–3.2	—	–4.8	—	–1.6	—
1950	5.5	—	8.8	—	3.3	—
1951	10.0	—	5.7	—	–4.3	—
Eisenhower						
1954	–1.3	—	–1.4	—	0.1	—
L. Johnson						
1964	–6.3	–10.3	–7.7	–11.5	–1.4	–1.2
1968	7.4	—	10.9	—	3.5	—
Nixon						
1969	c	—	–2.5	—	–2.5	—
1971	–12.9	–9.3	–11.4	–10.0	1.5	–0.7
Ford						
1975	–16.0	—	–22.8	—	–6.8	—
1976	c	—	–15.7	–6.2	–15.7	–6.2
Carter						
1977	–13.8	–15.7	–17.7	–13.8	3.9	–1.9
1978	–24.5	–34.9	–18.7	–34.1	5.8	0.8
1980	c	—	3.6	—	3.6	—
Reagan						
1981	–56.6	–129.8	–37.7	–150.0	18.9	–20.2
1982	c	—	18.0	51.8	18.0	51.8
1984	c	—	10.6	22.5	10.6	22.5
1986	11.5	–11.5	11.5	–15.1	0.0	–3.6
1987	6.1	—	9.4	15.8	3.3	9.7
1988	c	—	0.4	—	0.4	—
G. H. W. Bush						
1989	5.3	—	5.6	5.1	0.3	–0.2
1990	8.9	20.4	15.6	26.6	6.7	6.2
Clinton, I						
1993	36.0	65.1	27.4	53.2	–8.6	–11.9
1996	c	—	2.0	20.0[d]	2.0	20.0
Clinton, II						
1997	–0.3	–135.0[d]	–9.5	–95.0[d]	–9.2	–40.0
1998	—	—	—	—	—	—
1999	—	–32.6	—	–792.0[e]	—	792.0

(Table continues)

Table 8-4 *(Continued)*

President/year	*Presidential proposal*		*Congressional enactment*		*Difference*	
	First year[a]	Fully effective[b]	First year[a]	Fully effective[b]	First year[a]	Fully effective[b]
G. W. Bush, I						
2001	—	–1,640.0[d]	—	–1,350.0[d]	—	290.0
2003	—	–725.7[d]	—	–333.0[d]	—	395.7
2004	—	–106.6[d]	—	–146.3[d]	—	–39.7
G. W. Bush, II						
2006	—	–58.8[f]	—	–70.0[f]	—	–11.2
2008	—	–145.0[g]	—	–150.0[g]	—	–5.0

Sources: (1948–1992) Lyn Ragsdale, *Presidential Politics* (Boston: Houghton Mifflin, 1993), 326; (1993–2008) *CQ Almanac,* successive years, http://library.cqpress.com.

Note: "—" indicates no proposal of that kind in that year. In 1992 two tax cut bills passed Congress, one cutting $77.5 billion over five years, the other cutting $27 billion over five years. Both were vetoed by G. H. W. Bush and override attempts failed. In 1995 Clinton proposed a seven-year, $105 billion tax cut package. Congress passed a $245 billion package, which Clinton vetoed. The 1997 package involved a gross tax cut of $152 billion offset by a gross tax increase of $56 billion.

[a] Expected revenue change first full year after law is passed.
[b] Expected revenue change first full year after law is fully effective, if different from first column.
[c] No presidential proposal.
[d] Over ten years.
[e] Republican Congress passed $792 billion cut over ten years that was vetoed by Clinton.
[f] Over five years.
[g] Over two years.

Table 8-5 Differences in Appropriations Proposed by President and Passed by Congress, Truman to G. W. Bush, II (in billions of 1982 dollars)

	Average annual difference[a]		
President/fiscal years	Defense	Nondefense	Total[b]
Truman (1947–1953)	17.5	–3.1	14.5
Eisenhower (1954–1957)	–4.6	–0.3	–5.3
Eisenhower (1958–1961)	–1.0	0.1	–1.0
Kennedy / L. Johnson (1962–1965)	–2.4	–7.4	–9.3
L. Johnson (1966–1969)	1.0	–10.4	–10.9
Nixon (1970–1973)	–16.0	2.5	–12.8
Nixon / Ford (1974–1977)	–9.2	25.4	15.8
Carter (1978–1981)	9.8	–32.3	–21.6
Reagan (1982–1985)	8.9	5.6	16.4
Reagan (1986–1989)	2.7	19.1	21.9
G. H. W. Bush (1990–1993)	–2.4	4.9	2.5
Clinton (1994–1997)	2.5	–24.3	–21.8
Clinton (1998–2001)	–17.1	20.3	3.2
G. W. Bush (2002–2005)	–10.5	10.4	0.1
G. W. Bush (2006–2007)	–30.8	7.8	–23.0
Average			
Republican administrations	–6.7	8.3	1.8
Democratic administrations	1.9	–9.5	–7.6
All years	4.6	10.7	10.6

Source: (FY1947–FY1997) Lyn Ragsdale, *Presidential Politics* (Boston: Houghton Mifflin, 1993), 329; (FY 1998–2007) *Congressional Quarterly Almanac,* successive years, http://library.cqpress.com/cqalmanac/toc.php?mode=cqalmanac-topic&level=2&values=Appropriations.

[a] Positive numbers indicate Congress authorized more than the president requested; negative numbers indicate the reverse.
[b] Includes defense, nondefense, and interest payments.

Figure 8-1 Budget Deficit or Surplus, Eisenhower to G. W. Bush

Billions of dollars

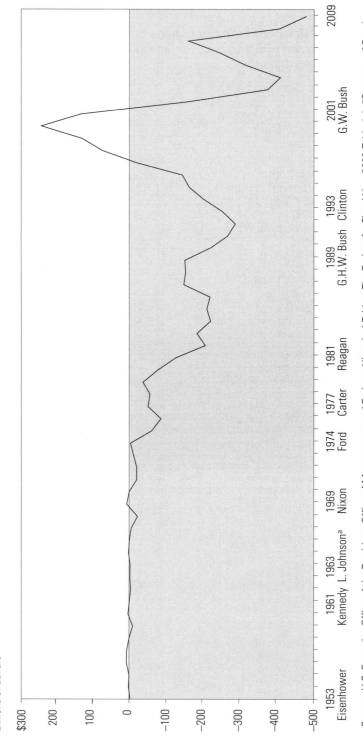

Source: U.S. Executive Office of the President, Office of Management and Budget, *Historical Tables: The Budget for Fiscal Year 2009,* Table 1.1, "Summary of Receipts, Outlays, and Surpluses or Deficits, 1789–2013."

[a] Includes full term from Nov.1963 to Jan. 1969.

Table 8-6 Federal Budget Receipts and Outlays, 1924–2008 (in billions of current dollars)

Year	*Receipts*	*Outlays*	*Surplus or deficit*
1924	3.9	2.9	1.0
1925	3.6	2.9	0.7
1926	3.8	2.9	0.9
1927	4.0	2.8	1.2
1928	3.9	3.0	0.9
1929	3.8	2.9	0.9
1930	4.0	3.1	0.9
1931	3.2	4.1	–1.0
1932	2.0	4.8	–2.7
1933	2.1	4.7	–2.6
1934	3.1	6.5	–3.3
1935	3.8	6.3	–2.4
1936	4.2	7.6	–3.5
1937	5.6	8.4	–2.8
1938	7.0	7.2	–0.1
1939	6.6	9.4	–2.9
1940	6.9	9.6	–2.7
1941	9.2	14.0	–4.8
1942	15.1	34.5	–19.4
1943	25.1	78.9	–53.8
1944	47.8	94.0	–46.1
1945	50.2	95.2	–45.0
1946	43.5	61.7	–18.2
1947	43.5	36.9	6.6
1948	45.4	36.5	8.9
1949	41.6	40.6	1.0
1950	40.9	43.1	–2.2
1951	53.4	45.8	7.6
1952	68.0	68.0	[a]
1953	71.5	76.8	–5.3
1954	69.7	70.9	–1.2
1955	65.5	68.5	–3.0
1956	74.5	70.5	4.1
1957	80.0	76.7	3.2
1958	79.6	82.6	–2.9
1959	79.2	92.1	–12.9
1960	92.5	92.2	0.3
1961	94.4	97.8	–3.4
1962	99.7	106.8	–7.1
1963	106.6	111.3	–4.8
1964	112.7	118.6	–5.9
1965	116.8	118.4	–1.6
1966	130.9	134.7	–3.8
1967	149.6	158.3	–8.7
1968	153.7	178.8	–25.2
1969	187.8	184.5	3.2
1970	193.7	196.6	–2.8
1971	187.1	210.2	–23.0
1972	207.3	230.7	–23.4

(Table continues)

Table 8-6 *(Continued)*

Year	*Receipts*	*Outlays*	*Surplus or deficit*
1973	230.8	245.7	–14.9
1974	263.2	269.4	–6.1
1975	279.2	332.3	–63.2
1976	298.1	371.8	–73.7
1976[b]	81.2	96.0	–14.7
1977	355.6	409.2	–53.6
1978	399.7	458.7	–59.0
1979	463.3	503.5	–40.2
1980	517.1	590.9	–78.9
1981	599.3	678.2	–127.9
1982	617.8	745.7	–207.8
1983	600.6	808.3	–185.3
1984	666.5	851.8	–222.2
1985	734.1	946.3	–212.3
1986	769.1	989.8	–220.7
1987	854.1	1,003.9	–149.8
1988	908.9	1,064.1	–155.2
1989	990.7	1,143.2	–152.5
1990	1,031.3	1,252.7	–221.4
1991	1,054.3	1,323.8	–269.5
1992	1,091.6	1,381.8	–290.1
1993	1,153.5	1,408.2	–254.7
1994	1,280.4	1,483.8	–203.4
1995	1,351.8	1,515.7	–163.9
1996	1,426.8	1,572.4	–145.6
1997	1,579.0	1,601.3	–21.9
1998	1,722.0	1,652.7	69.3
1999	1,627.6	1,702.0	125.6
2000	2,025.5	1,789.2	236.2
2001	1,991.4	1,863.2	128.2
2002	1,853.4	2,011.2	–157.8
2003	1,782.5	2,160.1	–377.6
2004	1,880.3	2,293.0	–412.7
2005	2,153.9	2,472.2	–318.3
2006	2,407.3	2,655.4	–248.1
2007	2,568.2	2,730.2	–162.0
2008[c]	2,521.1	2,931.2	–410.0

Sources: (1929–1970) U.S. Department of Commerce, *U.S. Historical Statistics: Colonial Times to 1970,* vol. 2 (Washington, D.C.: Government Printing Office, 1971), 1105; (1971–1984) U.S. Department of Commerce, *Statistical Abstract of the United States* (Washington, D.C.: Government Printing Office, 1986), 305; (1985–1986) U.S. Executive Office of the President, *The Budget of the United States* (Washington, D.C.: Government Printing Office, 1987); (1987–1996) U.S. Department of Commerce, *Statistical Abstract;* (1997–2008) *The Budget of the United States, Fiscal Year 2009,* Historical Tables, Table 1.1, "Summary of Receipts, Outlays and Surpluses or Deficits: 1789–2013."

[a] Less than $50 million.

[b] Transition quarter. In 1976 the beginning of the fiscal year was changed from July 1 to Oct. 1. A transition quarter (July 1–Sept. 30, 1976) was used. It belonged to neither fiscal 1976 nor fiscal 1977.

[c] Estimate.

Table 8-7 Outlays for Major Spending Categories as a Percentage of Gross Domestic Product, 1968–2007

Year	*Discretionary Spending*	*Mandatory spending* Programmatic spending	*Mandatory spending* Offsetting receipts	*Net interest*	*Total outlays*
1968	13.6	6.9	–1.2	1.3	20.5
1969	12.4	6.8	–1.2	1.4	19.3
1970	11.9	7.2	–1.1	1.4	19.3
1971	11.3	8.0	–1.3	1.4	19.5
1972	10.9	8.6	–1.2	1.3	19.6
1973	9.9	8.8	–1.4	1.3	18.7
1974	9.6	9.1	–1.5	1.5	18.7
1975	10.1	10.9	–1.2	1.5	21.3
1976	10.1	10.9	–1.1	1.5	21.4
1977	10.0	10.3	–1.1	1.5	20.7
1978	9.9	10.3	–1.0	1.0	20.7
1979	9.6	9.9	–1.0	1.7	20.1
1980	10.1	10.7	–1.1	1.9	21.7
1981	10.1	11.1	–1.2	2.2	22.2
1982	10.1	11.5	–1.1	2.6	23.1
1983	10.3	11.9	–1.3	2.6	23.5
1984	9.9	10.5	–1.2	2.9	22.1
1985	10.0	10.8	–1.1	3.1	22.8
1986	10.0	10.5	–1.0	3.1	22.5
1987	9.5	10.2	–1.1	3.0	21.6
1988	9.3	10.1	–1.1	3.0	21.2
1989	9.0	10.2	–1.2	3.1	21.2
1990	8.7	10.9	–1.0	3.2	21.8
1991	9.0	11.8	–1.8	3.3	22.3
1992	8.6	11.5	–1.1	3.2	22.1
1993	8.2	11.2	–1.1	3.0	21.4
1994	7.8	11.3	–1.0	2.9	21.0
1995	7.4	11.2	–1.1	3.2	20.7
1996	6.9	11.2	–0.9	3.1	20.3
1997	6.7	10.9	–1.1	3.0	19.6
1998	6.4	10.9	–0.9	2.8	19.2
1999	6.3	10.7	–.08	2.5	18.6
2000	6.3	10.6	–0.8	2.3	18.4
2001	6.5	10.9	–0.9	2.0	18.5
2002	7.1	11.5	–0.9	1.6	19.4
2003	7.6	11.9	–0.9	1.4	20.0
2004	7.8	11.7	–0.9	1.4	19.9
2005	7.9	11.8	–1.0	1.5	20.2
2006	7.8	11.9	–1.1	1.7	20.4
2007	7.6	11.9	–1.3	1.7	20.0
Average (1968–2007)	9.1	10.5	–1.1	2.2	20.6

Source: U.S. Congress, Congressional Budget Office, Historical Budget Data, Appendix F, Table F-6, p. 153, www.cbo.gov/budget/data/historical.pdf.

Figure 8-2 Federal Outlays by Category, 1950 to 2010, by Decade

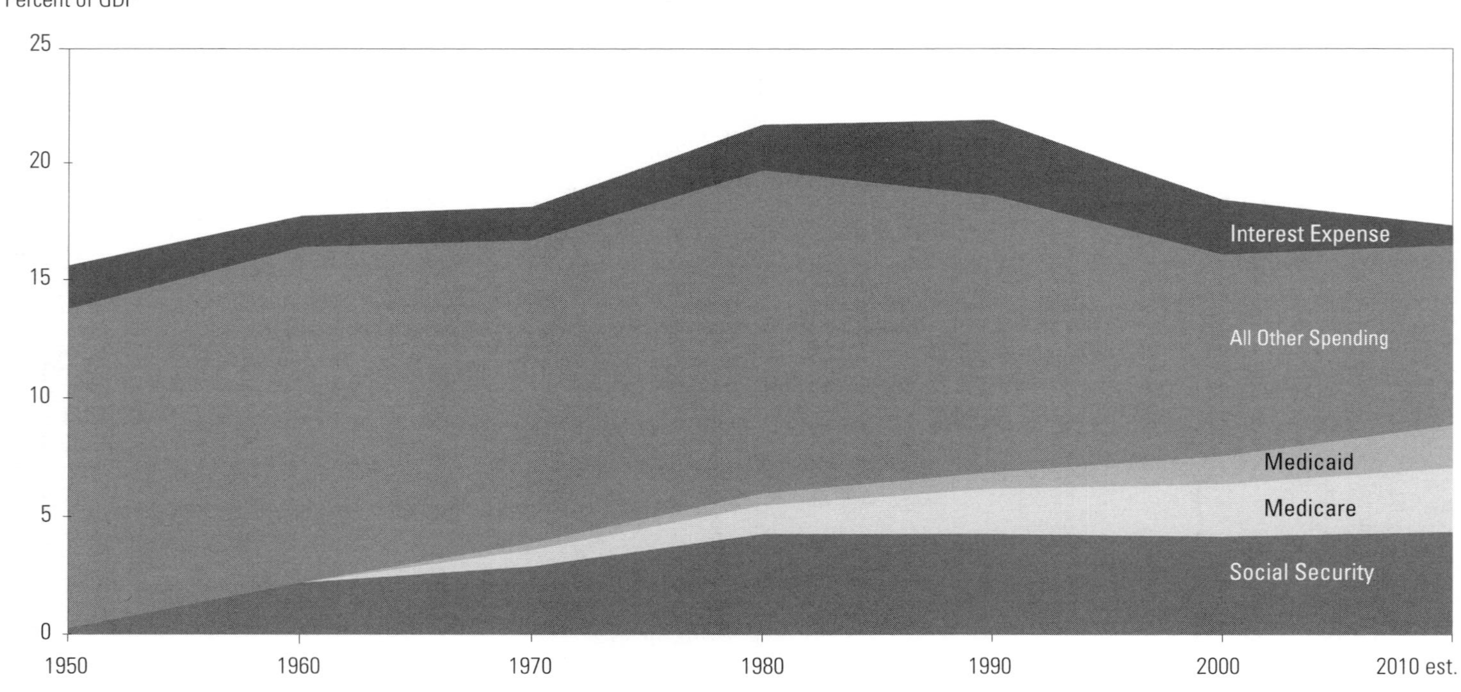

Source: U.S. Congress, Congressional Budget Office, "A 125-Year Picture of the Federal Government's Share of the Economy, 1950 to 2075," July 3, 2002, www.cbo.gov/ftpdoc.cfm?index=3521&type=0&sequence=0.

9
Congressional Relations

- **Political Parties of the Presidency and Congress**
- **Office of Legislative Affairs**
- **Legislative Clearance Process**
- **Presidential Requests to Congress**
- **Presidential Position Taking**
- **House and Senate Concurrence with Presidents' Positions**
- **Vetoes**
- **Presidential Policy Behavior**

In his eight years as president of the United States, George Washington publicly expressed an opinion on only five pieces of legislation. He recommended bills concerning the militia, the army, and a temporary commission to negotiate with the Indians, and he vetoed an apportionment bill on constitutional grounds and a bill on the military because it was poorly drafted. Washington's three recommendations were approved and his two vetoes went unchallenged. More than two hundred years later, George W. Bush, in his first year as president, took positions on 43 pieces of legislation and signed into law 383 bills passed by Congress. The nineteenth-century norm was to minimize presidential involvement in legislative politics; the twenty-first-century norm is to expect it. "The presentation of an annual program to Congress, the coordination of that program within the executive branch, the drafting of legislation, and the submission of special messages are now standard fare" (Wayne, 1982, 45).

In considering presidential involvement in legislative affairs, studies generally focus on presidents as individual policymakers rather than on the actions of the presidency as a policymaking institution. Presidents are depicted as "proximate policymakers" (Lindblom, 1968, 30n), as "policy actors," or as lone figures who try to impose a broad, national policy focus upon a parochial and wayward, if not annoying, congressional body. The image suggests that each president acts anew, asserting new legislative priorities, facing unique challenges presented by Congress, and adopting individual strategies to establish his priorities before the group.

This view belies the existence of institutional relations between the two branches of government. These institutional relations include organizational, behavioral, and structural elements of the presidency. Presidents rely on a well-developed organization in the Executive Office of the President to execute many of their legislative decisions. The Office of Management and Budget (OMB) monitors incoming requests for legislation, outgoing legislative proposals, and final bills from Congress. The Office of Legislative Affairs (formerly the Office of Congressional Relations) develops strategies to pass bills that the president promotes. While much of this appears to be undertaken by presidents single-handedly (indeed, the White House itself may wish to give this impression), these activities are ultimately carried out by dozens of people in the presidential organization.

The policy programs presidents initiate and the positions they take on legislation reflect institutional behavior. Presidents annually present policy proposals to Congress in their State of the Union messages. Each year, too, presidents submit the federal budget, as required by the Budget and Accounting Act of 1921. Although these actions are undertaken by individual executives, the expectations upon which they are based rest on institutional behavior. One of these expectations is that presidents handle the policy complexity of the political environment by proposing, or at least supporting, legislation to solve national problems in an array of issue areas. Harry S. Truman began a practice of using the State of the Union message to submit an annual legislative program to Congress. Although Dwight Eisenhower had no desire to follow Truman's lead, congressional Republicans criticized him for failing to submit a set of priorities, and Eisenhower relented. Truman's precedent became institutional behavior for future presidents.

Three structural features of the presidency influence its relations with Congress. These features are time, the political party system, and the U.S. Constitution. An institutional time line guides presidents' policy programs in Congress. The presidential cliché about "hitting the ground running" provides good advice. Time, calibrated by the next election, establishes a cycle of influence whereby the ability of presidents to succeed with Congress declines in proportion to the time they have spent in office.

The political party system is one of the primary institutional connections between Congress and the presidency. Table 9-1 documents the party composition of Congress since Washington. Party provides a basis of communication between the two institutions and helps to reconcile some of their differences, especially when the president's party holds a majority in one or both houses. But even during the years that the president's party does not have a majority in at least one house, party still serves to narrow the debate. Independent partisanship, the modern configuration of party first introduced in Chapter 2, plays a distinct role in the operation of the two institutions and their interrelationships. The concept pertains to politicians who seek election and reelection by devising independent campaign organizations, bases of support, and media strategies but still associate with a party label. This means that much of the support presidents get (or do not get) in Congress flows through the political parties, but the parties are made up of members who do not feel beholden to the president. This independent partisanship affects contemporary presidents' relations with Congress no matter who the president is, no matter what the issue is, and no matter what the president's policy position is.

The Constitution also establishes institutional relations between presidents and Congress. One of the president's most powerful mechanisms in his dealings with Congress is the veto—its use or the threat of its use. The efficacy of this mechanism is not accidental but stems from the constitutional requirement that two-thirds of both houses vote to override a veto. The veto offers a structural advantage for the presidency since getting two-thirds of all members of Congress to agree on a controversial action is a Herculean task, again no matter who the president, what the issue, or what the president's position. Thus, although presidents individually engage in certain activities, their efforts are neither new nor unique. Knowing who the president is may be less important than the ability to identify the organizational, behavioral, and structural types of institutional patterns that now exist.

Organizational Relations with Congress

Organizational units within the White House undertake two key congressional activities: (1) legislative liaison efforts that sell presidential proposals to Congress and (2) legislative management that supervises the flow of legislation, legislative requests, and budget proposals to and from the White House. As staff and resources have increased, the formal congressional liaison staff has expanded. Since the days of Washington, personnel in the executive branch have sporadically helped presidents communicate with Congress. Herbert Hoover tentatively formalized such assistance by relying on one staff member to supervise congressional liaison. Truman, who wanted help in pursuing annual legislative programs, introduced a staff with official legislative liaison responsibilities. Yet the two junior presidential assistants assigned the task were primarily messengers who did not speak for the president (Holtzman, 1970, 231–234). Not until Eisenhower was the Office of Congressional Relations established. It was renamed the Office of Legislative Affairs in 1981. Its size since 1981 is depicted in Table 9-2. The office has become a well-developed unit in the White House, with separate offices that handle the House and Senate. These units did not change, for instance, when Republican president George W. Bush took over from Democrat Bill Clinton.

The task of legislative management involves two processes that are handled within the OMB: legislative clearance and the handling of enrolled bills. The former was initiated in 1924, with the first Budget of the United States; the latter was begun in 1938. Figures 9-1 and 9-2 depict these two processes, respectively. A classic instance of the legislative clearance process at work, and its detachment from presidents' own involvement, took place on August 9, 1974, when Richard Nixon announced his resignation. A congressional staff member called a high-ranking White House official during the day to inquire as to whether a minor piece of legislation was "in accordance with the president's program" (reported by Heclo, 1981, 3). Neither a president nor a presidential program existed in those hours, but the institution of the presidency continued to operate. Likewise, the handling of enrolled bills (bills passed by the House and Senate that are awaiting a presidential signature) is very much an institutional process. Except in the case of particularly visible legislation or items the White House initiates, presidents are unlikely to keep tabs on legislation passed on Capitol Hill. The OMB steps in to determine whether the president should sign or veto a bill, presenting its own recommendations, which presidents typically adopt (Wayne, Cole, and Hyde, 1979).

The tasks of legislative liaison and management have become sufficiently elaborate that presidents exert less than full control over their processes or content. The use of proposals made by the executive bureaucracy that are channeled by the OMB, itself a large bureaucratic unit, and advocated by a good-sized liaison staff largely determines the extent of a president's involvement in the legislative process.

Institutional Behavior: Presidential Priorities and Congressional Concurrence

Contemporary presidents have fashioned two distinct types of institutional behavior by which to identify policy priorities. They both submit legislation related to their programs, and they take positions on bills introduced by members of Congress. Both establish the level of concurrence between the positions held by members and the positions held by presidents on the same legislation.

Presidential Programs

Since Truman, presidents have used State of the Union messages to capture congressional and national attention for their legislative programs.

The size and scope of these legislative programs are depicted in Table 9-3. The analysis indicates that presidents typically have made most of their policy requests in their first year in office. In later years, new requests generally decline and repeat requests increase. Ronald Reagan proved an exception: he made far fewer requests than other presidents and also had a fairly uniform number of requests each year during his two terms. As Table 9-4 indicates, the majority of policy requests during the first year of a president's tenure occur in the first six months. Indeed, except in Nixon's first term, the first-year requests occur most frequently between January and March.[1] George W. Bush made all his legislative requests in the first quarter of both his first and second terms.

These tables provide evidence that timing is a critical structural element of the presidency. Presidents face, in Paul Light's words, "a cycle of decreasing influence" (1991, 36). This cycle affects all presidents. They enter office with a complement of political capital: their popularity is at its highest point for the term, they can claim a mandate for policy initiatives based on their election victory, and their party often picks up seats in Congress during the presidential election. Yet, the political honeymoon soon ends: popularity declines, people forget about the election and turn their attention to governance, and the president's party loses congressional seats in the midterm elections. The gloomy circumstances of this cycle of decreasing influence mean that presidents must act early in their terms to secure major legislative victories in Congress.

Presidential Positions

Another way of evaluating presidential priorities is to observe the preferences that presidents reveal in the positions they take on congressional legislation. Position taking not only encompasses presidents' own initiatives and desires but also responds to congressional legislation in which presidents are not fully involved. Table 9-5 reports the total number of House roll call votes and the number of votes on which presidents have taken public positions from 1957 to 2007.

The most dramatic trend revealed in Table 9-5 is the sharp drop in position taking after Lyndon Johnson's tenure as president. Presidents beginning with Nixon have taken positions on roughly 16 percent of the total roll call legislation voted on by the House. An initial drop is not surprising; we would expect Johnson to take positions more frequently on legislation produced by the large Democratic congressional majority than would the Republican president Nixon. However, the drop persisted. Indeed, the decline has continued with Presidents Clinton and George W. Bush taking positions on only 12 percent of bills. Bush has actually taken positions on fewer bills than any president since Eisenhower, just 8 percent. The change may be partly explained by the dramatic increase in roll call votes, which nearly doubled in the early 1970s. But this shift cannot provide a full answer, since the number of roll call votes declined again beginning in 1981.

Another part of the explanation may be that presidents, wary of an increasingly independent-minded congressional membership, have come to actively support legislation only when it is of particular importance to them, in an attempt to minimize defeat. Presidents must build new legislative coalitions among independent partisans in Congress for each bill on which they take a position, bill after bill. Thus, limited position taking may be a form of institutional behavior that presidents of both parties have adopted to establish legislative priorities and ensure success.

Policy Complexity in the Political Environment

The political environment constrains the institutional behavior presidents undertake. One key aspect of this environment is policy complexity. Because of the scope of modern government, presidents take positions and Congress pursues legislation on a vast array of policy issues. This occurs regardless of whether the president and Congress are Democrat or Republican, liberal or conservative. Table 9-6 reports the number of bills on which presidents since Eisenhower have taken positions in seven policy categories—foreign trade, foreign aid, defense, social welfare, economic management, resources, and agriculture. Not surprisingly, presidents have taken greatest interest in policy areas that strongly define the core of government activity—social welfare and economic management. Since Eisenhower, all presidents have taken numerous positions in these two policy areas. This suggests the extent to which the political environment shapes presidents' legislative decisions and minimizes differences among them on policy issues.

Table 9-6 shows another equally clear pattern: all presidents since Eisenhower have taken fewer positions on agriculture than on any other policy area. Incentives to take stands on agriculture, especially for recent presidents who find the proportion of the population working on farms declining, are low. Instead, this type of policy better fits institutional behavior patterns found in Congress. The specialization and reciprocity that characterize Congress suggest that the positions taken by legislators representing agricultural regions will have greater importance than those taken by presidents.

Beyond these two strong general patterns, individual differences exist. Presidents Gerald Ford and Jimmy Carter gave sustained emphasis to energy policy, while President Reagan took more positions on defense than any other president under study. Overall, however, the similarities outweigh the differences. Considerable consistency exists in the presidential attention given these policy types—indeed, the consistency is such that it seems appropriate to refer to "presidential attention" generically rather than discuss the attention given by any individual president.

Congressional Concurrence with Presidents

Writers often comment on presidential success, or support, in Congress. Yet, this is not only a problematic concept to measure, but the notion of success itself is misleading. One might think of presidential success as how well the president does on legislative measures that actually originate in the White House. Many pieces of legislation on which the White House puts its stamp, however, have been developed for years in Congress, making it difficult to determine what in fact originates from the presidency. Another way of thinking about presidential success is to examine how well presidents do on major legislation dealt with by a given Congress. While this may adequately deal with the prominent issues that connect presidents and Congress, it does not encompass the smaller issues that also define presidential-congressional relations.

Thus, in considering presidents' relations with Congress, it is important to consider the range of issues on which the president takes a position. This includes the major pieces of legislation originating from the White House, those which come from Capitol Hill, and many less crucial bills that nonetheless constitute the work of Congress in any given term. This concept is most aptly termed congressional (or presidential) concurrence. It is measured here in two ways: vote concurrence and member concurrence. Vote concurrence is measured by the number of times a majority of members of Congress vote with the president's position on roll call votes. Member concurrence is the percentage of members who agree with the president's position on a roll call vote. Unlike the usual scholarly focus on success or support, the concurrence measures acknowledge that it is impossible to judge who influenced whom. Information is simply inadequate to ascertain the direction of influence. Members of both parties overwhelmingly support many roll call votes regardless of whether the president has a position.

Vote Concurrence. Figure 9-3 charts the vote concurrence rates for Congress since Eisenhower. Generally, presidents did best in the first year of their first elected term, regardless of their party or the majority parties of the two houses of Congress. This reflects the benefit of presidents hitting the ground running. President Johnson garnered the highest levels of vote concurrence: in 1965, a majority of Congress concurred with Johnson's position 93 percent of the time. President Reagan's seemingly magical legislative success during the 1981 Congress was not exceptional in comparison with the records of other presidents. Eisenhower, John F.

Kennedy, Johnson, and Clinton all exceeded Reagan's record; George W. Bush equaled it. Kennedy, Nixon, and Carter did slightly better in their second years, but differences between the first and second years were not substantial. Nor did divided government necessarily inhibit high degrees of vote concurrence. Eisenhower (1953) and Reagan (1981) faced divided government but had high concurrence rates. Yet Clinton's concurrence rate plummeted to the lowest of any president in 1995 after the Republicans gained control of Congress. A majority of Congress supported Clinton only 36 percent of the time in 1995 as compared with an 86 percent concurrence rate in 1994. Presidents clearly do less well in their second terms. Both Clinton and George W. Bush hit very low concurrence levels in 1999 (37.8 percent) and 2007 (38.3 percent), respectively.

Table 9-7 permits a more careful examination of the total vote concurrence rates for both houses. The data make clear that congressional vote concurrence has stayed fairly modest over the terms of the last nine presidents. These rates typically do not dip below the 50 percent mark. Still, Reagan in 1987 and 1988, George H. W. Bush in 1990 and 1992, Clinton in 1995 and 1999, and George W. Bush in 2007 all saw concurrence rates drop below 50 percent.

Table 9-7 also permits a separate analysis of House and Senate vote concurrence. It reveals that the House and Senate concurred with presidents since Eisenhower at fairly similar levels, with the exceptions of Reagan, Bush, and Clinton in his second term. In all three cases, the Senate was much more likely to concur with their positions than was the House, even when the Senate majority was of the opposite party. During the twelve years covered by their terms, only six of which saw Republican control of the Senate, the Senate was much more likely to concur with Reagan's or Bush's position than was the House. As an example, the Senate concurred with Clinton 71 percent of the time in 1997, while the House only agreed with him 39 percent of the time. One explanation for these exceptions may be that during the Reagan and Bush years conservative coalition victories were higher in the Senate than in the House, meaning that Republicans and Southern Democrats voted together more often in the Senate, presumably in ways that these two administrations supported (Ornstein et al., 1998, 203). For Clinton, the explanation is likely to be that the Senate, although in Republican hands during these years, was not overwhelmingly so, permitting the Clinton administration to forge victories with Democrats and key moderate Republicans.

Tables 9-7 and 9-8 suggest several generalizations about party as a structural link between the presidency and Congress. First, as one would expect, Democratic presidents were more successful in the Democratic House and Senate than Republican presidents (Table 9-7). George W. Bush saw the lowest concurrence rate from members of the opposing party of any president since Eisenhower; he posted a concurrence score among all

Democrats of 7 percent (among southern Democrats, 11 percent). The results, however, were not completely uniform. Although congressional vote concurrence with Carter was generally higher than for the Republican presidents, it was consistently lower than for Presidents Kennedy, Johnson, and Clinton. Table 9-8 reveals that strong party ties exist for southern Democrats, who are often considered more likely to agree with Republican presidents than Democratic chief executives. The table shows that although southern Democrats were somewhat more supportive of Ford and Reagan in his first term than were Democrats as a whole, this was not typical. Their support did not continue to be higher than all Democrats during Reagan's second term, nor for Nixon or Bush. Moreover, southern Democratic concurrence with Johnson, Carter, and Clinton rivaled that for Democrats as a whole. This, of course, occurred as the sheer number of southern Democrats dropped dramatically as more and more southern states elected Republicans to both houses.

Member Concurrence. Table 9-9 provides initial evidence about member concurrence. While vote concurrence determines whether a majority of congressional members supported the president's position on a roll call vote, member concurrence involves the actual percentage of members who concurred with the president's position on the roll call. This provides a more precise measure of agreement between individual members and the president. The high first-year pattern noted for vote concurrence is less clear for member concurrence. Especially for members of the out party, concurrence was typically not at its highest during the president's first year in office. Out-party members may have wished to assert their autonomy from the new president. For members of the in party, concurrence was fairly consistent across the president's term. Among the presidents studied, Ford obtained the highest level of member concurrence in 1974, largely due to very high out-party support in the aftermath of Watergate. Indeed, in that year concurrence from congressional Democrats exceeded that from congressional Republicans. Clinton received the lowest out-party concurrence in 1995 from the new Republican majority in the House—just under 23 percent concurrence. In general, member concurrence rates, like vote concurrence rates, stayed within a relatively narrow range—from 50 to 70 percent concurrence among all members. Reagan, in the latter part of his first term and throughout his second term, proved an exception, falling below the 50 percent mark. Clinton also fell below the 50 percent mark in his first term but not in his second.

The implication of this narrow range observed for both measures is that the institutions of the presidency and Congress shape individual presidents' success in Congress. Congressional decentralization, committee strength, and constituent policy interests place a ceiling on presidential support, whereas party loyalty, regularized liaison efforts, and strategic veto threats prevent this support from dropping too low. The congressional and executive institutions place constraints on and provide resources for actors within them, thereby narrowing the degree of difference and the variation in feasible behavior.

Tables 9-10 through 9-12 examine member concurrence by issue areas. The results indicate key policy similarities across presidents. Presidents consistently did well in matters of foreign trade and defense. From 1957 to 2004, the member concurrence rate was 62.4 percent on trade and 59.3 percent on defense. In addition, for 29 of the 47 years presented in Table 9-10, member concurrence with the president was highest in one of the three foreign policy areas (although the second highest category was one of the domestic policy areas roughly 40 percent of the time). This is most notable among members of the out party whose concurrence with the president was highest in one of the three foreign policy areas in 29 of the 47 years under study (Table 9-12). The ten presidents studied also obtained reasonably strong concurrence among all members on economic management issues (55.7 percent). Member concurrence in the other areas was more varied, especially by party. For instance, across his two terms, Bill Clinton received 82 percent concurrence from Democrats on social welfare issues but only 31 percent concurrence from Republicans. In 2001, George W. Bush received 97 percent concurrence from Democrats on defense but only 16 percent concurrence from them on energy, environment, and resource issues. In contrast, Republicans concurred with Bush 96 percent of the time on defense and 82 percent of the time on resource issues.

These results point to a mixing of issue content with institutional advantages and limitations. Presidents are constitutionally mandated to act in areas of diplomacy and defense. Statutes such as the Budget and Accounting Act of 1921 and the Full Employment Act of 1946 also give them an active role in economic policy. With these constitutional and statutory bases for action, presidents may commit greater resources to legislative efforts in these areas, and congressional members may be more willing to support presidential positions. In contrast, the remaining areas are characterized more by changing political stakes than by stable institutional attributes.

Structural Politics: Vetoes and Congressional Overrides

In his classic book, *Congressional Government*, Woodrow Wilson wrote that a president's "power of veto ... is, of course, beyond all comparison, his most formidable prerogative" (1973, 53). It is "the president's ultimate legislative weapon in that it gives him the weight of two-thirds of the members of each house of Congress" (Watson and Thomas, 1983, 257). It is also a "weapon" that is understood in notably structural terms within the institution. It is exercised infrequently and, by constitutional design, it is overridden rarely. Indeed, overuse of the veto power is sometimes identified as a sign of presidential weakness. Table 9-13 summarizes veto data since Washington. Presidents Ulysses Grant, Grover Cleveland, Theodore Roosevelt, Franklin Roosevelt, Truman, and Ford used the veto most often; Presidents Franklin Pierce, Andrew Johnson, Truman, and Ford saw their vetoes overridden most frequently. President George W. Bush vetoed no bills in his first term and only 8 in his second; this was the fewest number of vetoes for any president since Warren Harding. Table 9-13 also reveals that presidential expansion of legislative activity in the twentieth century has produced a concomitant increase in vetoes. Even when Cleveland is included, nineteenth-century presidents averaged some 32 vetoes during their terms (only 14 vetoes per term if Cleveland is excluded); twentieth-century presidents, beginning with Theodore Roosevelt, averaged 94 regular and pocket vetoes per term.

Table 9-14 examines vetoes by issue area. It shows a dramatic decline in the number of private bills vetoed after Eisenhower. Apparently presidents no longer saw such minor matters as worthy of presidential attention. Policy complexity can be observed in the other categories. The largest number of vetoes appears in the social welfare, economic management, and resources categories, the areas in which presidents take their greatest numbers of positions (see Table 9-6). Among the other areas, from 1946 to 2007 there was only one presidential veto of foreign aid legislation and only scattered vetoes in foreign trade. Defense policy vetoes occurred less frequently than vetoes in some of the domestic policy areas. Very few vetoes on agricultural matters are evident.

Congressional attempts at overriding presidential vetoes, along with the total number of vetoes, appear in Table 9-15. Congress has overridden presidents' regular vetoes just over 100 times in more than 200 years—a mere seven-tenths of 1 percent. Nearly 50 percent of these (46) have occurred since 1946. Despite the strong unilateral power the veto gives presidents, it is largely a negative institutional power. Presidents stop what they do not want, but they do not necessarily get what they want.

Presidents have long called for the ability to exercise a line-item veto, which would allow them to strike out specific projects from large appropriations bills. The rationale for the line-item was that presidents would eliminate waste and pork barrel expenditures that members of Congress were all too prone to approve. In tight budget times, the line-item veto was touted as a key money-saving device. Congress passed the Legislative Line-Item Veto Act of 1996, thereby giving presidents the ability to strike appropriation lines and targeted tax provisions from acts within twenty days of signing the full acts into law. So the line-item is quite distinct from the regular veto. With the regular veto the president refuses to sign into law the bill before him. With the line-item veto, the president signs the law, the law goes into effect, and then the president selectively vetoes specific projects within the newly enacted law. A federal judge declared the legislative line-item veto unconstitutional in February 1998 as "disrupting the balance of powers among the three branches of government." The Supreme Court then agreed to hear the case and it too declared the line-item veto unconstitutional on the same grounds in June 1998. There have been two attempts to reinstate the line-item veto in the Legislative Line-Item Veto Acts of 2006 and 2007, but neither bill passed.

Conclusion

The data in this chapter suggest three points about presidential relations with Congress. First, the presidency, not the officeholder, is the "policy actor" to watch. Many of the president's efforts are handled by a well-developed organization within the White House. Presidents must grapple with the presidential institution as it coordinates legislative proposals, legislative liaison work, and strategies to achieve legislative success. Presidents must engage in institutional behavior by advancing a presidential program even if they would prefer to minimize their role in the policymaking process. Structural constraints within the presidency, such as the cycle of declining influence and independent partisanship, influence the initiatives presidents propose, when they are proposed, and what degree of success they ultimately achieve.

Second, the impact of the institution is similar for presidents across various policy areas. The complexity of the policy environment affects different presidents in very similar ways. This institutional policymaking can be placed in clearer perspective by considering together the several types of policy behavior in which presidents engage. Figures 9-4 through 9-7 show presidents' legislative positions, vetoes, and, from data in Chapter 8, executive orders across all policy areas, and then separately for foreign, defense, and domestic policy since 1957. These figures provide a startling view of the many policy demands placed on the presidency and the many policy techniques available to presidents through both executive and legislative avenues. The complexity of policy types, the conflicts among techniques, and the diversity among targeted groups promote a reliance on institutional rather than personal decision making.

Finally, institutional relations between the presidency and Congress define the success of a president's performance on any single occasion. The organizational, behavioral, and structural elements of Congress establish these interinstitutional connections as much as do the same elements of the presidency. The organization of Congress is larger and more decentralized than the presidency, which itself is large and decentralized. The congressional organization places pressure on the presidency to be everywhere at once, creating greater distance between the presidential organization and the president (see Chapter 6). The slow pace of congressional activity means that presidents must be masters of timing in spotlighting their programs. Party and the Constitution structure both Congress and the presidency and make the two institutions interdependent, while at the same time creating great tension between them, given their frequently divergent time patterns and policy motivations. After all the political speeches are made and the congressional votes are counted, presidents are apparently not "chief legislators" who "guide Congress in much of its lawmaking activity" (Rossiter, 1960, 26), although the presidency is surely one of the two chief legislative institutions.

Note

1. A distinction should be noted here between the number of proposals submitted to Congress by the White House and the importance attached to any one proposal. The frequency with which proposals are submitted within a policy area provides one indication of the breadth of attention given the issue category by a president, but a single proposal may be viewed as a major priority by the chief executive. For example, although Lyndon Johnson did not submit numerous proposals on civil rights, a few central measures did show concerted attention to this policy area.

Table 9-1 Political Parties of Presidents and Congress, 1789–2008

				House					*Senate*					
				Majority		Opposition			Majority		Opposition			
Year	*President*	*President's party*	*Congress*	(N)	*Party*	(N)	*Party*	Other	(N)	*Party*	(N)	*Party*	Other	*Unified/divided government*
1789–1791	Washington	F	1st	38	F	26	OP	0	17	F	9	OP	0	UG
1791–1793		F	2nd	37	F	33	DR	0	16	F	13	DR	0	UG
1793–1795		F	3rd	57	DR	48	F	0	17	F	13	DR	0	DG-H
1795–1797		F	4th	54	F	52	DR	0	19	F	13	DR	0	UG
1797–1799	J. Adams	F	5th	58	F	48	DR	0	20	F	12	DR	0	UG
1799–1801		F	6th	64	F	42	DR	0	19	F	13	DR	0	UG
1801–1803	Jefferson	DR	7th	69	DR	36	F	0	18	DR	13	F	0	UG
1803–1805		DR	8th	102	DR	39	F	0	25	DR	9	F	0	UG
1805–1807		DR	9th	116	DR	25	F	0	27	DR	7	F	0	UG
1807–1809		DR	10th	118	DR	24	F	0	28	DR	6	F	0	UG
1809–1811	Madison	DR	11th	94	DR	48	F	0	28	DR	6	F	0	UG
1811–1813		DR	12th	108	DR	36	F	0	30	DR	6	F	0	UG
1813–1815		DR	13th	112	DR	68	F	0	27	DR	9	F	0	UG
1815–1817		DR	14th	117	DR	65	F	0	25	DR	11	F	0	UG
1817–1819	Monroe	DR	15th	141	DR	42	F	0	34	DR	10	F	0	UG
1819–1821		DR	16th	156	DR	27	F	0	35	DR	7	F	0	UG
1821–1823		DR	17th	158	DR	25	F	0	44	DR	4	F	0	UG
1823–1825		DR	18th	187	DR	26	F	0	44	DR	4	F	0	UG
1825–1827	J.Q. Adams	I	19th	105	IDR	97	JDR	0	26	IDR	20	JDR	0	DG
1827–1829		I	20th	119	JDR	94	IDR	0	28	JDR	20	IDR	0	DG
1829–1831	Jackson	D	21st	139	D	74	NR	0	26	D	22	NR	0	UG
1831–1833		D	22nd	141	D	58	NR	14	25	D	21	NR	2	UG
1833–1835		D	23rd	147	D	53	NR	60	20[a]	D	20[a]	NR	8	UG
1835–1837		D	24th	145	D	98	W	0	27	D	25	W	0	UG
1837–1839	Van Buren	D	25th	108	D	107	W	24	30	D	18	W	0	UG
1839–1841		D	26th	124	D	118	W	0	28	D	22	W	0	UG

1841–1843	W. Harrison/Tyler	W	27th	133	W	102	D	6	28	W	22	D	2	UG
1843–1845	Tyler	W	28th	142	D	79	W	1	28	W	25	D	1	DG-H
1845–1847	Polk	D	29th	143	D	77	W	6	31	D	25	W	0	UG
1847–1849		D	30th	115	W	108	D	4	36	D	21	W	1	DG-H
1849–1851	Taylor/Fillmore	W	31st	112	D	109	W	9	35	D	25	W	2	DG
1851–1853	Fillmore	W	32nd	140	D	88	W	5	35	D	24	W	3	DG
1853–1855	Pierce	D	33rd	159	D	71	W	4	38	D	22	W	2	UG
1855–1857		D	34th	108	R	83	D	43	40	D	15	R	5	DG-H
1857–1859	Buchanan	D	35th	118	D	92	R	26	36	D	20	R	8	UG
1859–1861		D	36th	114	R	92	D	31	36	D	26	R	4	DG-H
1861–1863	Lincoln	R	37th	105	R	43	D	30	31	R	10	D	8	UG
1863–1865		R	38th	102	R	75	D	9	36	R	9	D	5	UG
1865–1867	A. Johnson	R	39th	149	R	42	D	0	42	R	10	D	0	UG
1867–1869		R	40th	143	R	49	D	0	42	R	11	D	0	UG
1869–1871	Grant	R	41st	149	R	63	D	0	56	R	11	D	0	UG
1871–1873		R	42nd	134	R	104	D	5	52	R	17	D	5	UG
1873–1875		R	43rd	194	R	92	D	14	49	R	19	D	0	UG
1875–1877		R	44th	169	D	109	R	14	45	R	29	D	2	DG-H
1877–1879	Hayes	R	45th	153	D	140	R	0	39	R	36	D	1	DG-H
1879–1881		R	46th	149	D	130	R	14	42	D	33	R	1	DG
1881–1883	Garfield/Arthur	R	47th	147	R	135	D	11	39	R	37	D	1	UG
1883–1885	Arthur	R	48th	197	D	118	R	10	38	R	36	D	2	DG-H
1885–1887	Cleveland	D	49th	183	D	140	R	2	43	R	34	D	0	DG-S
1887–1889		D	50th	169	D	152	R	4	39	R	37	D	0	DG-S
1889–1891	B. Harrison	R	51st	166	R	159	D	0	39	R	37	D	0	UG
1891–1893		R	52nd	235	D	88	R	11	47	R	39	D	2	DG-H
1893–1895	Cleveland	D	53rd	218	D	127	R	7	44	D	38	R	3	UG
1895–1897		D	54th	244	R	105	D	40	43	R	39	D	6	DG
1897–1899	McKinley	R	55th	204	R	113	D	9	47	R	34	D	7	UG
1899–1901		R	56th	185	R	163	D	9	53	R	26	D	8	UG
1901–1903	McKinley/T. Roosevelt	R	57th	197	R	151	D	0	55	R	31	D	4	UG
1903–1905	T. Roosevelt	R	58th	208	R	178	D	0	57	R	33	D	0	UG
1905–1907		R	59th	250	R	136	D	0	57	R	33	D	0	UG
1907–1909		R	60th	222	R	164	D	0	61	R	31	D	0	UG

(Table continues)

Table 9-1 (*Continued*)

				House					*Senate*					
				Majority		Opposition			Majority		Opposition			
Year	*President*	*President's party*	*Congress*	(N)	*Party*	(N)	*Party*	Other	(N)	*Party*	(N)	*Party*	Other	*Unified/divided government*
1909–1911	Taft	R	61st	219	R	172	D	0	61	R	32	D	0	UG
1911–1913		R	62nd	228	D	161	R	1	51	R	41	D	0	DG-H
1913–1915	Wilson	D	63rd	291	D	127	R	17	51	D	44	R	1	UG
1915–1917		D	64th	230	D	196	R	9	56	D	40	R	0	UG
1917–1919		D	65th	216	D	210	R	6	53	D	42	R	0	UG
1919–1921		D	66th	240	R	190	D	3	49	R	47	D	0	DG
1921–1923	Harding	R	67th	301	R	131	D	1	59	R	37	D	0	UG
1923–1925	Coolidge	R	68th	225	R	205	D	5	51	R	43	D	2	UG
1925–1927		R	69th	247	R	183	D	4	56	R	39	D	1	UG
1927–1929		R	70th	237	R	195	D	3	49	R	46	D	1	UG
1929–1931	Hoover	R	71st	267	R	167	D	1	56	R	39	D	1	UG
1931–1933		R	72nd	220	D	214	R	1	48	R	47	D	1	DG-H
1933–1935	F. Roosevelt	D	73rd	310	D	117	R	5	60	D	35	R	1	UG
1935–1937		D	74th	319	D	103	R	10	69	D	23	R	2	UG
1937–1939		D	75th	331	D	89	R	13	76	D	16	R	4	UG
1939–1941		D	76th	261	D	164	R	4	69	D	23	R	4	UG
1941–1943		D	77th	268	D	162	R	5	66	D	28	R	2	UG
1943–1945		D	78th	218	D	208	R	4	58	D	37	R	1	UG
1945–1947	Truman	D	79th	242	D	190	R	2	56	D	38	R	1	UG
1947–1949		D	80th	245	R	188	D	1	51	R	45	D	0	DG
1949–1951		D	81st	263	D	171	R	1	54	D	42	R	0	UG
1951–1953		D	82nd	234	D	199	R	1	49	D	47	R	0	UG
1953–1955	Eisenhower	R	83rd	221	R	211	D	1	48	R	47	D	1	UG
1955–1957		R	84th	232	D	203	R	0	48	D	47	R	1	DG
1957–1959		R	85th	233	D	200	R	0	49	D	47	R	0	DG

1959–1961		R	86th	283	D	153	R	0	64	D	34	R	0	DG
1961–1963	Kennedy	D	87th	263	D	174	R	0	65	D	35	R	0	UG
1963–1965	Kennedy / L. Johnson	D	88th	258	D	177	R	0	67	D	33	R	0	UG
1965–1967	L. Johnson	D	89th	295	D	140	R	0	68	D	32	R	0	UG
1967–1969		D	90th	246	D	187	R	0	64	D	36	R	0	UG
1969–1971	Nixon	R	91st	245	D	189	R	0	57	D	43	R	0	DG
1971–1973		R	92nd	254	D	180	R	0	54	D	44	R	2	DG
1973–1975	Nixon / Ford	R	93rd	239	D	192	R	1	56	D	42	R	2	DG
1975–1977		R	94th	291	D	144	R	0	60	D	37	R	2	DG
1977–1979	Carter	D	95th	292	D	143	R	0	61	D	38	R	1	UG
1979–1981		D	96th	276	D	157	R	0	58	D	41	R	1	UG
1981–1983	Reagan	R	97th	243	D	192	R	0	53	R	46	D	1	DG-H
1983–1985		R	98th	269	D	165	R	0	54	R	46	D	0	DG-H
1985–1987		R	99th	252	D	182	R	0	53	R	47	D	0	DG-H
1987–1989		R	100th	259	D	176	R	0	55	D	45	R	0	DG
1989–1991	G. H. W. Bush	R	101st	260	D	175	R	0	55	D	45	R	0	DG
1991–1993		R	102nd	267	D	167	R	1	56	D	44	R	0	DG
1993–1995	Clinton	D	103rd	261	D	173	R	1	58	D	42	R	0	UG
1995–1997		D	104th	230	R	204	D	1	54	R	46	D	0	DG
1997–1999		D	105th	227	R	207	D	1	55	R	45	D	0	DG
1999–2001		D	106th	223	R	211	D	1	55	R	45	D	0	DG
2001–2003	G. W. Bush	R	107th	221	R	212	D	2	50	R	50	D	0	DG-S
2003–2005		R	108th	229	R	204	D	1	51	R	48	D	1	UG
2005–2007		R	109th	232	R	202	D	1	55	R	44	D	1	UG
2007–2008		R	110th	233	D	202	R	0	49	R	49	D	2	DG

Sources: (1789–1970) Adapted from U.S. Department of Commerce, *U.S. Historical Statistics: Colonial Times to 1970* (Washington, D.C.: Government Printing Office, 1971), 204–210; (1971–2008) U.S. Department of Commerce, *Statistical Abstract of the United States* (Washington, D.C.: Government Printing Office, various years).

Note: D—Democrats, DG—Divided Government, DG-H—Divided Government (House only), DG-S—Divided Government (Senate only), DR—Democratic-Republicans, IDR—Independent Democratic-Republicans, JDR—Jacksonian Democratic-Republicans, NR—National Republicans, OP—Opposition, R—Republicans, U—Unified Government, W—Whig.

[a] Eight members not affiliated with either main party gave their support, and thus a majority, to the Democrats.

Table 9-2 Size of the Office of Legislative Affairs, Reagan, I to G. W. Bush, II

President/year	*Size of staff*	*President/year*	*Size of staff*
Reagan, I		Clinton, II	
1981	39	1997	23
1982	39	1998	23
1983	34	1999	23
1984	28	2000	21
Reagan, II		G. W. Bush, I	
1985	24	2001	22
1986	25	2002	22
1987	22	2003	24
1988	27	2004	25
G. H. W. Bush		G. W. Bush, II	
1989	12	2005	25
1990	13	2006	25
1991	14	2007	26
1992	14	2008	26
Clinton, I			
1993	21		
1994	18		
1995	22		
1996	24		

Source: (1981–1998) Successive volumes of *Federal Staff Directory* (Mt. Vernon, Va.: Staff Directories, Ltd.) and *Carroll's Federal Directory* (Washington, D.C.: Carroll Publishing); (1999–2007) *Federal Staff Directory,* (Washington, D.C.: CQ Press), http://fsd.cqpress.com/scripts/index.cfm.

Note: Annual data not available prior to Reagan.

Figure 9-1 The Legislative Clearance Process

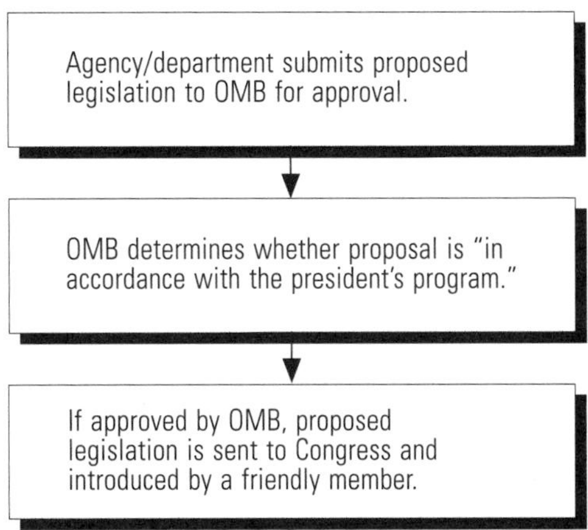

Figure 9-2 The Enrolled Bill Process

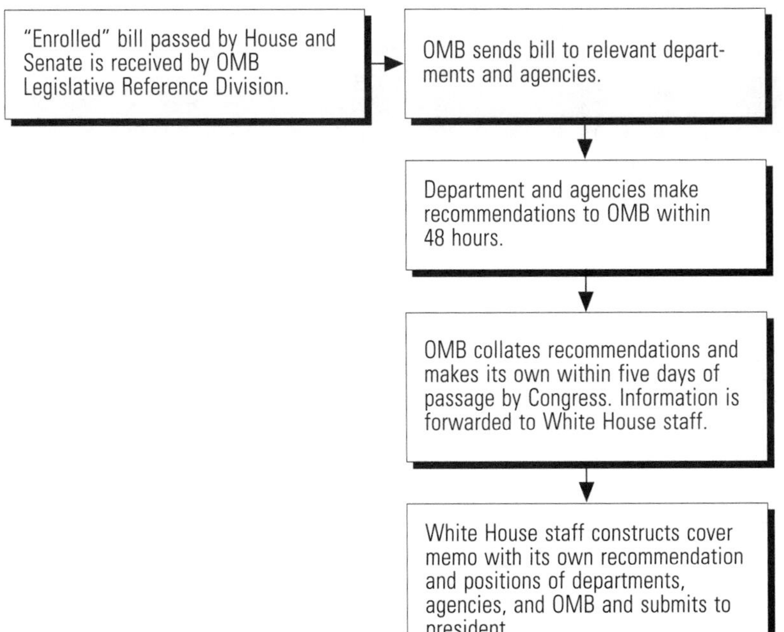

Table 9-3 Number of Presidential Requests of Congress in State of the Union Messages, Truman, I to G.W. Bush, II

President/year	*Total requests*	*Total domestic requests*[a]	*First-time requests*	*Domestic first-time requests*[a]	*Repeat requests*	*Domestic repeat requests*[a]
Truman, I						
1946	41	36	16	12	25	24
1947	23	20	21	18	2	2
1948	16	11	6	5	9	6
Truman, II						
1949	28	25	17	15	11	11
1950	20	19	9	9	11	10
1951	11	9	5	5	6	5
1952	19	18	7	6	12	12
Eisenhower, I						
1953	14	13	14	13	1	1
1954	39	30	35	26	4	4
1955	32	25	19	11	14	14
1956	42	37	23	19	19	18
Eisenhower, II						
1957	14	10	6	3	8	7
1958	4	1	4	1	0	0
1959	16	14	14	12	2	2
1960	6	5	1	1	5	4
Kennedy						
1961	25		25		0	
1962	24		16		8	
1963	18		6		12	
L. Johnson[b]						
1964	17		6		11	
1965	38		34		4	
1966	31		24		7	
1967	27		19		8	
1968	26		14		12	
Nixon, I						
1969	17		17		0	
1970	21		12		9	
1971	20		8		12	
1972	17		3		14	
Nixon, II	23		20		3	
1973	23		20		3	
1974	16		5		11	
Ford						
1975	13		10		3	
1976	13		6		7	

Table 9-3 *(Continued)*

President/year	*Total requests*	*Total domestic requests*[a]	*First-time requests*	*Domestic first-time requests*[a]	*Repeat requests*	*Domestic repeat requests*[a]
Carter						
1977	21		21		0	
1978	11		8		3	
1979	13		8		5	
1980	11		4		7	
Reagan, I						
1981	8		8		0	
1982	8		7		1	
1983	14		11		3	
1984	9		4		5	
Reagan, II						
1985	7		0		7	
1986	5		0		5	
1987	5		0		5	
1988	4		0		4	
G. H. W. Bush						
1989	34	33	33	33	0	0
1990	18	18	15	15	3	3
1991	20	17	12	9	8	8
1992	27	24	13	13	14	9
Clinton, I						
1993	30	28	30	28	0	0
1994	22	20	15	15	8	7
1995	25	22	17	10	9	6
1996	19	14	7	5	12	9
Clinton, II						
1997	20	19	18	17	2	2
1998	25	19	21	16	4	3
1999	27	24	20	18	7	6
2000	32	26	13	10	19	16
G. W. Bush, I						
2001	19	18	19	18	0	0
2002	16	15	15	14	1	1
2003	14	13	9	8	5	5
2004	15	14	11	10	4	4
G. W. Bush, II						
2005	20	19	9	8	11	11
2006	11	10	7	6	4	3
2007	10	6	6	3	4	3
2008	9	8	7	4	2	4

(Table continues)

Table 9-3 (*Continued*)

Sources: (Kennedy through Reagan, II) Updated by the author from Paul Light, *The Presidential Agenda,* rev. ed. (Baltimore: Johns Hopkins University Press, 1991), 42, 241. Reprinted by permission of the Johns Hopkins University Press.

Note: The tallies for Truman, Eisenhower, G. H. W. Bush, Clinton, and G. W. Bush were taken from State of the Union messages. Truman did not deliver a State of the Union address in 1945. Those for Kennedy through Reagan are from the legislative clearance records of the Office of Management and Budget and from State of the Union messages. The counts involve items that had cleared in accordance with the president's program and had been mentioned in at least one State of the Union message.

[a] Domestic requests refer to legislative proposals on agriculture, education, health, social welfare, the environment, the economy, and others. The difference between the first column and the second paired column is the number of foreign policy legislative proposals submitted to Congress. For example, Truman submitted five foreign policy proposals in 1946. Light does not distinguish between foreign and domestic policy proposals in his data for Kennedy through Reagan.

[b] Includes full term from Nov. 1963 to Jan. 1969.

Table 9-4 First-Year Requests for Legislation, Truman, II to G. W. Bush, II

President/year	*Jan.–March (%)*	*April–June (%)*	*July–Sept. (%)*	*Oct.–Dec. (%)*	*Total number of requests*
Truman, II					
1949	68	0	32	0	41
Eisenhower, I					
1953	52	41	7	0	27
Eisenhower, II					
1957	51	46	0	3	39
Kennedy					
1961	76	24	0	0	25
L. Johnson					
1965	94	6	0	0	34
Nixon, I					
1969	12	41	41	6	17
Nixon, II					
1973	40	30	15	15	20
Ford					
1974	—	—	28	72	18
Carter					
1977	33	57	10	0	21
Reagan, I					
1981	63	18	19	0	8
Reagan, II					
1985	31	61	0	0	7
G. H. W. Bush					
1989	79	0	21	0	34
Clinton, I					
1993	52	0	48	0	30
Clinton, II					
1997	100	0	0	0	20
G. W. Bush, I					
2001	100	0	0	0	19
G. W. Bush, II					
2005	100	0	0	0	20

Sources: (Truman, Eisenhower, Ford, Reagan, G. H. W. Bush, Clinton, G. W. Bush) Calculated by the author from all major addresses to the nation delivered during prime time, carried by the major networks and preempting regular programming; (Kennedy through Carter) OMB Legislative Reference Division clearance records in Paul Light, *The Presidential Agenda,* rev. ed. (Baltimore: Johns Hopkins University Press, 1991), 45; reprinted by permission of the Johns Hopkins University Press.

Table 9-5 Presidential Position Taken on House Roll Calls, Eisenhower, II to G. W. Bush, II

President/year	*Total roll calls*	*Positions*[a]	*Positions as percentage of roll calls*[b]
Eisenhower, II			
1957	100	54	54.0
1958	93	48	51.6
1959	87	53	60.9
1960	91	41	45.1
Kennedy			
1961	113	65	57.5
1962	124	60	48.4
1963	119	71	59.7
L. Johnson[c]			
1964	113	52	46.0
1965	201	112	55.7
1966	193	102	52.8
1967	245	126	51.4
1968	233	101	43.3
Nixon, I			
1969	177	47	26.6
1970	266	64	24.1
1971	320	61	19.1
1972	329	37	11.2
Nixon, II			
1973	541	125	23.1
1974	476	107	22.5
Ford			
1974	61	0	0.0
1975	612	89	14.5
1976	661	49	7.4
Carter			
1977	706	75	10.6
1978	834	115	13.8
1979	672	143	21.3
1980	604	114	18.9
Reagan, I			
1981	353	75	21.2
1982	459	75	16.3
1983	498	80	16.1
1984	408	111	27.2
Reagan, II			
1985	439	80	18.2
1986	451	90	20.0

Table 9-5 (*Continued*)

President/year	*Total roll calls*	*Positions*[a]	*Positions as percentage of roll calls*[b]
Reagan, II (continued)			
1987	488	99	20.3
1988	451	104	23.1
G. H. W. Bush			
1989	379[d]	86	22.7
1990	536[d]	108	20.1
1991	444[d]	111	25.0
1992	488[d]	105	21.5
Clinton, I			
1993	597	102	17.1
1994	464	78	16.8
1995	884	133	15.0
1996	454	79	17.4
Clinton, II			
1997	640	75	11.7
1998	547	82	15.0
1999	611	82	13.4
2000	603	69	11.4
G. W. Bush, I			
2001	512	43	8.4
2002	484	40	8.3
2003	677	55	8.1
2004	544	34	6.3
G. W. Bush, II[e]			
2005	671	45	6.7
2006	543	55	10.1
2007	1,186	117	9.9

Source: (1957–1996) Coded by the author from annual volumes of *Congressional Quarterly Almanac* (Washington, D.C.: Congressional Quarterly); (1997–2006) *Congressional Quarterly Almanac,* http://library.cqpress.com; (2007) Clea Benson, "CQ Vote Studies—Presidential Support: The Power of No," *CQ Weekly,* Jan. 14, 2008, 132, http://library.cqpress.com/cqweekly/weeklyreport110-000002654714 (accessed Feb. 17, 2008).

[a] Number of House roll calls on which president took a clear position.
[b] Total number of positions presidents have taken as a percentage of the total number of House roll calls.
[c] Includes full term from Nov. 1963 to Jan. 1969.
[d] Includes quorum calls.
[e] Through 2007 only.

Table 9-6 Presidential Position Taken in the House, by Issue Area, Eisenhower, II to G.W. Bush, II

President/year	*Foreign trade*	*Foreign aid*	*Defense*	*Social welfare*	*Economic management*	*Resources*	*Agriculture*	*Total*
Eisenhower, II								
1957	2	6	4	18	9	10	5	54
1958	5	4	9	13	7	8	2	48
1959	1	7	3	9	11	15	7	53
1960	3	7	1	15	6	5	4	41
Kennedy								
1961	5	10	5	12	18	9	6	65
1962	3	10	6	10	19	8	4	60
1963	3	9	8	14	23	9	5	71
L. Johnson[a]								
1964	4	9	5	14	9	10	1	52
1965	5	10	10	36	30	16	5	112
1966	7	13	4	24	36	18	0	102
1967	5	12	9	42	43	11	4	126
1968	5	10	7	29	26	18	4	99
Nixon, I								
1969	1	4	2	18	18	2	2	47
1970	1	5	2	21	20	13	2	64
1971	9	2	9	25	9	7	0	61
1972	3	3	7	8	11	5	0	37
Nixon, II								
1973	10	3	15	20	36	26	15	125
1974	2	11	15	23	35	21	0	107

Ford								
1974	0	0	0	0	0	0	0	0
1975	7	4	10	14	22	27	5	89
1976	3	1	5	11	10	19	0	49
Carter								
1977	4	9	11	10	15	25	1	75
1978	13	19	20	11	31	20	1	115
1979	32	21	14	31	17	28	0	143
1980	10	19	11	14	31	22	7	114
Reagan, I								
1981	4	1	15	4	21	15	15	75
1982	3	4	22	6	15	20	5	75
1983	5	6	27	20	8	9	5	80
1984	19	1	20	26	19	22	4	111
Reagan, II								
1985	6	13	19	4	14	12	12	80
1986	15	4	25	20	13	9	4	90
1987	12	4	27	13	18	25	0	99
1988	9	7	29	31	14	13	1	104
G. H. W. Bush								
1989	4	13	12	16	24	17	0	86
1990	13	6	12	32	24	16	5	108
1991	7	14	21	29	27	12	1	111
1992	13	3	13	27	29	20	0	105
Clinton, I								
1993	3	7	17	22	41	10	2	102
1994	7	0	15	19	26	11	0	78
1995	5	7	21	29	52	18	1	133
1996	10	5	8	17	26	13	0	79

(Table continues)

Table 9-6 *(Continued)*

President/year	*Foreign trade*	*Foreign aid*	*Defense*	*Social welfare*	*Economic management*	*Resources*	*Agriculture*	*Total*
Clinton, II								
1997	11	0	10	26	20	7	1	75
1998	13	1	0	30	31	6	1	82
1999	7	6	7	28	24	8	1	81
2000	12	0	2	23	23	9	0	69
G. W. Bush, I								
2001	6	0	1	17	12	6	1	43
2002	5	0	10	6	17	1	0	39
2003	6	2	6	22	14	5	0	55
2004	6	2	5	9	9	3	0	34
G. W. Bush, II[b]								
2005	8	1	7	13	13	4	0	46
2006	9	1	6	12	8	4	0	40
2007	4	1	23	30	42	14	3	117

Source: (1957–1996) Coded by the author from annual volumes of *Congressional Quarterly Almanac* (Washington, D.C.: Congressional Quarterly); (1997–2006) *Congressional Quarterly Almanac,* http://library.cqpress.com; (2007) Clea Benson, "CQ Vote Studies—Presidential Support: The Power of No," *CQ Weekly,* Jan. 14, 2008, p. 132, http://library.cqpress.com/cqweekly/weeklyreport110-000002654714 (accessed Feb. 17, 2008).

Note: Figures are the number of roll calls in which the president took a position in each issue area. Foreign trade—foreign trade, diplomacy, or immigration; foreign aid—various forms of assistance to other countries; defense—military, defense, veterans issues; social welfare—social welfare, civil rights, Indian affairs, and education; economic management—government and economic management, income tax issues, telecommunication, technology; resources—energy, natural resources, environment, and transportation; agriculture—agriculture and farm policy.

[a] Includes full term from Nov. 1963 to Jan. 1969.
[b] Through 2007 only.

Figure 9-3 Congressional Concurrence with Presidents, Eisenhower to G. W. Bush

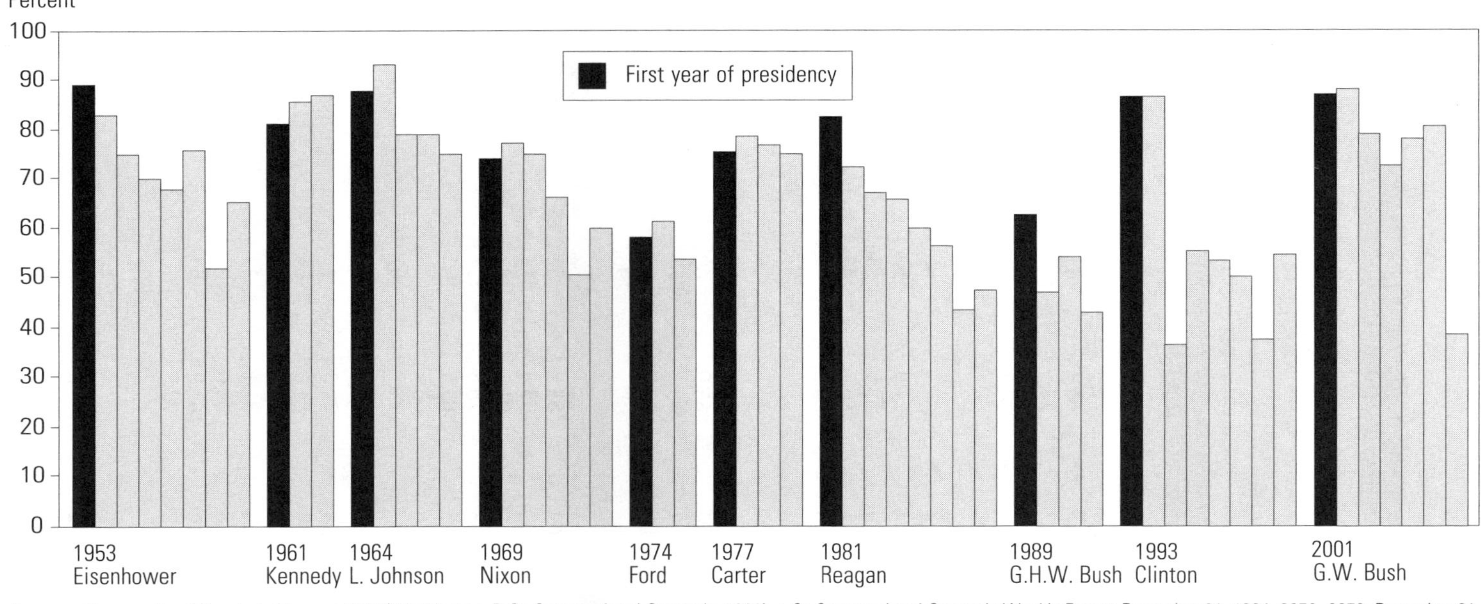

Sources: Congressional Quarterly Almanac 1993 (Washington, D.C.: Congressional Quarterly, 1993), 4-C; *Congressional Quarterly Weekly Report,* December 31, 1994, 3652–3653; December 21, 1996, 3427–3430.

Note: Concurrence is defined by the number of times a majority in Congress supported the president's position on legislation. Congressional Quarterly has tracked presidential positions since 1953. However, the decision rules and methods of recording positions were altered in 1957. Therefore, data from 1953 to 1956 may not be comparable with data after 1957.

Table 9-7 House and Senate Concurrence with Presidents, Eisenhower to G. W. Bush, II

President (political party)/year	*Total House and Senate concurrence*	*House*		*Senate*	
		Concurrence rate	Number of votes	Concurrence rate	Number of votes
Eisenhower, I (R)					
1953	89.2	91.2	34	87.8	49
1954	82.8	78.9	38	77.9	77
1955	75.3	63.4	41	84.6	52
1956	69.2	73.5	34	67.7	65
Average	79.1	76.8		79.5	
Total			147		243
Eisenhower, II (R)					
1957	68.4	58.3	60	78.9	57
1958	75.7	74.0	50	76.5	98
1959	52.9	55.6	54	50.4	121
1960	65.1	65.1	43	65.1	86
Average	65.5	63.2		67.7	
Total			207		362
Kennedy (D)					
1961	81.5	83.1	65	80.6	124
1962	85.4	85.0	60	85.6	125
1963	87.1	83.1	71	89.6	115
Average	84.7	83.7		85.3	
Total			196		364
L. Johnson (D)[a]					
1964	87.9	88.5	52	87.6	97
1965	93.1	93.8	112	92.6	162
1966	78.9	91.3	103	68.8	125
1967	78.8	75.6	127	81.2	165
1968	74.5	83.5	103	68.9	164
Average	82.6	86.5		79.8	
Total			497		713
Nixon (R)					
1969	74.8	72.3	47	76.4	72
1970	76.9	84.6	65	71.4	91
1971	74.8	82.5	57	69.5	82
1972	66.3	81.1	37	54.3	46
1973	50.6	48.0	125	52.4	185
1974	59.6	67.9	53	54.2	83
Average	67.2	72.7		63.0	
Total			384		559
Ford (R)					
1974	58.2	59.3	54	57.4	68
1975	61.0	50.6	89	71.0	93

Table 9-7 (*Continued*)

President (political party)/year	*Total House and Senate concurrence*	*House* Concurrence rate	*House* Number of votes	*Senate* Concurrence rate	*Senate* Number of votes
Ford (R) (continued)					
1976	53.8	43.1	51	64.2	53
Average	51.7	51.0		64.2	
Total			194		214
Carter (D)					
1977	75.4	74.7	79	76.1	88
1978	78.3	69.6	112	84.8	151
1979	76.8	71.7	145	81.4	161
1980	75.1	76.9	117	73.3	116
Average	76.4	73.2		78.9	
Total			453		516
Reagan, I (R)					
1981	82.4	72.4	76	88.3	128
1982	72.4	55.8	77	83.2	119
1983	67.1	47.6	82	85.9	85
1984	65.8	52.2	113	85.7	77
Average	71.9	57.0		85.8	
Total			348		409
Reagan, II (R)					
1985	59.9	45.0	80	71.6	102
1986	56.5	33.3	90	80.7	83
1987	43.5	33.3	99	56.4	78
1988	47.4	32.7	104	64.8	88
Average	51.8	36.1		68.4	
Total			373		351
G.H.W. Bush (R)					
1989	62.6	50.0	86	73.3	101
1990	46.8	32.4	108	63.4	93
1991	54.2	43.2	111	67.5	83
1992	43.0	37.1	105	53.3	60
Average	51.7	40.7		64.4	
Total			410		337
Clinton, I (D)					
1993	86.4	87.3	102	85.4	89
1994	86.4	87.2	78	85.5	62
1995	36.2	26.3	133	49.0	102
1996	55.1	53.2	79	57.6	59
Average	66.0	63.5		69.4	
Total			392		312

(*Table continues*)

Table 9-7 (*Continued*)

President (political party))/year	*Total House and Senate concurrence*	*House*		*Senate*	
		Concurrence rate	Number of votes	Concurrence rate	Number of votes
Clinton, II (D)					
1997	53.6	38.7	75	71.4	63
1998	50.6	36.6	82	66.7	72
1999	37.8	35.4	82	42.2	45
2000	55.0	49.3	69	65.0	40
Average	49.3	40.0		61.3	
Total			308		220
G. W. Bush, I (R)					
2001	87.0	83.7	43	88.3	77
2002	87.8	82.5	40	91.4	58
2003	78.7	87.3	55	74.8	119
2004	72.6	70.6	34	74.0	50
Average	81.5	81.0		82.1	
Total			172		304
G. W. Bush, II (R)[b]					
2005	78.0	78.3	46	77.8	45
2006	80.9	85.5	40	78.6	70
2007	38.3	15.4	117	66.0	97
Average	65.7	59.7		74.1	
Total			203		212

Source: Harold Stanley and Richard Niemi, *Vital Statistics on American Politics, 2007–2008* (Washington, D.C.: CQ Press, 2008), 264–265; (2007) Clea Benson, "CQ Vote Studies—Presidential Support: The Power of No," *CQ Weekly*, Jan. 14, 2008, p. 132, http://library.cqpress.com/cqweekly/weeklyreport110-000002654714 (accessed Feb. 17, 2008).

Note: R—Republican; D—Democrat. Percentages based on the number of congressional votes supporting the president divided by the total number of votes on which the president had taken a position.

[a] Includes full term from Nov. 1963 to Jan. 1969.
[b] Through 2007 only.

Table 9-8 House and Senate Concurrence with Presidents, by Party, Eisenhower, I to G.W. Bush, II (percent)

	House			*Senate*		
President/year	All Demo-crats	Southern Demo-crats	Repub-licans	All Demo-crats	Southern Demo-crats	Repub-licans
Eisenhower, I						
1953	55	N/A	80	55	N/A	78
1954	54	N/A	80	45	N/A	82
1955	58	N/A	67	65	N/A	85
1956	58	N/A	79	44	N/A	80
Eisenhower, II						
1957	54	N/A	60	60	N/A	80
1958	63	N/A	65	51	N/A	77
1959	44	N/A	76	44	N/A	80
1960	49	N/A	63	52	N/A	76
Kennedy						
1961	81	N/A	41	73	N/A	42
1962	83	71	47	76	63	48
1963	84	71	36	77	65	52
Johnson[a]						
1964	84	70	42	73	63	52
1965	83	65	46	75	60	55
1966	81	64	45	71	59	53
1967	80	65	51	73	69	63
1968	77	63	59	64	50	57
Nixon, I						
1969	56	55	65	55	56	74
1970	64	64	79	56	62	74
1971	53	69	79	48	59	76
1972	56	59	74	52	71	77
Nixon, II						
1973	39	49	67	42	55	70
1974	52	64	71	44	60	65
Ford						
1974	48	52	59	45	55	67
1975	40	48	67	53	67	76
1976	36	52	70	47	61	73
Carter						
1977	69	58	46	77	71	58
1978	67	54	40	74	61	47
1979	70	58	37	75	66	51
1980	71	63	44	71	69	50
Reagan, I						
1981	46	60	72	52	63	84
1982	43	55	70	46	57	77

(Table continues)

Table 9-8 *(Continued)*

	House			*Senate*		
President/year	All Democrats	Southern Democrats	Republicans	All Democrats	Southern Democrats	Republicans
1983	30	45	74	45	46	77
1984	37	47	64	45	58	81
Reagan, II						
1985	31	43	69	36	46	80
1986	26	37	69	39	56	90
1987	26	37	65	38	43	67
1988	28	34	61	51	58	73
G. H. W. Bush						
1989	38	49	72	56	66	84
1990	26	35	65	39	49	72
1991	35	43	74	42	53	84
1992	27	38	75	33	40	75
Clinton, I						
1993	77	78	39	87	82	29
1994	75	75	47	86	84	42
1995	79	73	22	84	80	29
1996	78	74	39	85	79	38
Clinton, II						
1997	73	68	31	87	83	61
1998	78	72	27	86	83	42
1999	75	70	24	86	84	35
2000	76	68	28	92	88	47
G. W. Bush, I						
2001	32	38	88	67	71	96
2002	33	40	85	73	81	95
2003	27	37	92	52	60	96
2004	31	42	83	63	70	93
G. W. Bush, II[b]						
2005	24	34	83	39	55	88
2006	32	46	88	54	64	89
2007	7	11	72	37	43	85

Source: Harold Stanley and Richard Niemi, *Vital Statistics on American Politics, 2007–2008* (Washington, D.C.: CQ Press, 2008), 266–267; Clea Benson, "CQ Vote Studies—Presidential Support: The Power of No," *CQ Weekly*, Jan. 14, 2008, p. 132, http://library.cqpress.com/cqweekly/weeklyreport110-000002654714 (accessed Feb. 17, 2008).

Note: N/A—not available. Concurrence indicates the percentage of roll calls on which members voted in agreement with the president. The percentages are calculated to eliminate the effects of absences as follows: support = (support)/(support + opposition).

[a] Includes full term from Nov. 1963 to Jan. 1969.
[b] Through 2007 only.

Table 9-9 Average Annual Roll Call Support for the President by Members of the House, Eisenhower, II to G.W. Bush, I

	All members		Out party		In party	
President/year	Number voting	Percent with president	Number voting	Percent with president	Number voting	Percent with president
Eisenhower, II						
1957	386	56.0	208	53.7	178	59.3
1958	375	64.4	199	63.1	175	65.6
1959	395	57.3	258	46.7	138	77.1
1960	392	53.3	251	47.5	141	63.6
Kennedy						
1961	391	65.2	157	40.8	235	81.4
1962	382	68.5	155	47.7	227	82.6
1963	379	65.2	157	36.5	220	85.4
L. Johnson[a]						
1964	383	67.4	161	43.2	222	84.8
1965	384	71.3	124	46.4	260	83.1
1966	343	69.8	114	46.3	228	81.6
1967	380	67.6	167	51.8	213	79.8
1968	363	69.9	161	60.0	202	77.9
Nixon, I						
1969	376	59.8	210	56.1	166	64.4
1970	359	71.4	201	66.1	158	78.3
1971	386	64.2	224	53.1	162	79.5
1972	366	64.0	215	56.4	153	74.5
Nixon, II						
1973	395	51.6	219	39.1	176	67.3
1974	381	55.8	214	48.8	166	64.8

(Table continues)

Table 9-9 (*Continued*)

	All members		*Out party*		*In party*	
President/year	Number voting	Percent with president	Number voting	Percent with president	Number voting	Percent with president
Ford						
1974	369	72.4	207	76.4	162	67.4
1975	406	50.2	270	40.8	136	69.0
1976	389	48.1	259	37.3	131	69.5
Carter						
1977	394	60.7	132	43.6	261	69.4
1978	384	58.9	130	39.7	254	68.7
1979	399	58.6	146	36.7	253	71.3
1980	387	60.5	143	44.4	244	70.1
Reagan, I						
1981	404	57.0	224	45.3	180	71.4
1982	393	55.4	218	43.8	175	69.9
1983	410	46.6	251	29.9	159	72.9
1984	402	47.7	246	37.2	156	64.3
Reagan, II						
1985	421	48.9	245	33.8	179	73.5
1986	397	42.5	211	29.7	169	68.7
1987	411	41.2	239	26.0	168	64.0
1988	400	42.0	233	27.0	165	62.0
G.H.W. Bush						
1989	413	52.0	244	42.1	169	70.9
1990	416	42.0	247	26.2	170	65.1
1991	395	50.6	241	37.3	152	71.5
1992	411	50.6	247	27.3	159	74.5

Clinton, I						
1993	423	63.5	171	40.2	236	84.2
1994	426	61.2	153	48.3	252	64.3
1995	415	48.0	218	22.7	196	76.6
1996	417	55.2	231	38.1	187	76.4
Clinton, II						
1997	423	38.7	225	31.0	197	73.0
1998	418	36.6	221	27.0	196	78.0
1999	417	35.4	214	24.0	200	75.0
2000	417	49.3	213	28.0	202	76.0
G. W. Bush, I						
2001	424	60.0	206	32.0	216	88.0
2002	421	59.0	202	33.0	215	85.0
2003	423	59.5	199	27.0	223	92.0
2004	434	57.0	196	31.0	218	83.0

Source: Each roll call individually coded by the author from annual volumes of *Congressional Quarterly Almanac* (Washington, D.C.: Congressional Quarterly).

Note: In party is the party of the president.

[a] Includes full term from Nov. 1963 to Jan. 1969.

Table 9-10 Support for the President on House Roll Calls, by Issue Area, Eisenhower, II to G.W. Bush, I (percent)

President/year	*Foreign trade*	*Foreign aid*	*Defense*	*Social welfare*	*Economic management*	*Resources*	*Agriculture*
Eisenhower, II							
1957	70.1	54.4	50.6	56.9	56.3	55.4	54.1
1958	70.1	60.0	80.6	63.2	62.8	51.4	50.3
1959	99.5	70.3	49.4	55.6	69.0	46.0	50.3
1960	56.1	58.3	46.3	55.6	34.8	55.2	72.5
Kennedy							
1961	84.2	71.6	85.1	70.1	55.6	51.9	60.1
1962	71.7	61.7	83.1	78.8	70.0	58.3	49.2
1963	69.6	54.5	71.3	74.9	62.7	65.6	55.0
L. Johnson[a]							
1964	74.3	64.5	49.4	65.3	63.0	84.6	51.0
1965	81.5	68.9	68.7	72.7	66.6	81.7	56.0
1966	75.5	69.9	53.1	69.4	67.1	77.1	—
1967	59.7	58.7	79.5	69.9	68.0	62.7	62.8
1968	68.6	70.0	77.2	72.5	61.7	75.4	72.5
Nixon, I							
1969	85.9	56.2	86.1	59.3	59.9	45.6	44.6
1970	76.3	64.8	68.2	58.1	82.8	80.5	56.0
1971	66.1	51.2	65.6	61.7	73.5	60.7	—
1972	80.1	65.2	68.0	55.9	61.7	66.2	—
Nixon, II							
1973	51.3	72.5	44.2	47.6	57.5	50.5	48.2
1974	55.3	49.4	48.6	54.9	57.7	67.0	—
Ford							
1975	69.9	61.8	52.7	30.5	49.0	52.5	57.2
1976	52.5	60.3	56.5	45.2	43.1	48.9	—

Carter							
1977	67.7	49.2	61.5	73.6	56.0	60.5	75.7
1978	55.0	52.8	54.9	58.5	64.3	62.8	64.1
1979	60.7	53.9	64.8	59.9	58.0	55.4	—
1980	72.8	50.8	55.4	66.2	59.9	59.3	72.7
Reagan, I							
1981	54.7	31.7	55.6	52.3	59.1	73.0	42.9
1982	67.7	61.6	65.8	47.6	41.1	56.1	46.6
1983	43.3	57.5	57.8	38.8	39.8	30.7	47.0
1984	56.5	50.6	55.5	38.7	47.4	41.2	62.5
Reagan, II							
1985	51.7	53.6	50.2	28.9	48.5	42.6	52.5
1986	37.4	40.3	49.5	40.9	47.3	41.8	—
1987	39.5	43.5	53.4	39.3	28.3	34.8	—
1988	39.4	68.0	53.3	32.4	27.3	31.2	95.5
G. H. W. Bush							
1989	58.4	55.2	51.5	48.9	58.5	39.6	—
1990	34.0	47.6	57.1	42.5	43.0	33.3	36.6
1991	52.1	43.2	58.6	48.5	48.5	43.3	93.6
1992	32.5	—	50.1	46.0	45.4	48.6	—
Clinton, I							
1993	68.6	62.2	55.3	73.0	62.5	56.5	—
1994	66.2	—	56.4	52.7	50.7	98.8	—
1995	50.0	48.0	40.6	53.0	50.4	45.3	51.2
1996	71.0	43.3	40.5	53.0	58.5	61.4	—
Clinton, II							
1997	36.2	51.3	40.8	53.3	52.4	48.1	22.1
1998	32.6	38.7	24.2	57.0	54.6	48.9	50.8
1999	44.6	45.2	56.9	51.6	48.4	50.4	41.3
2000	69.0	43.5	38.3	54.6	53.1	43.1	50.7

(Table continues)

Table 9-10 *(Continued)*

President/year	*Foreign trade*	*Foreign aid*	*Defense*	*Social welfare*	*Economic management*	*Resources*	*Agriculture*
G. W. Bush, I							
2001	57.1	N/A	96.2	59.9	65.4	49.6	38.5
2002	66.7	N/A	43.3	63.1	56.3	72.3	—
2003	52.5	66.0	58.8	64.5	59.4	57.9	—
2004	52.0	57.7	67.0	59.3	66.4	40.9	—

Source: Coded by the author from annual volumes of *Congressional Quarterly Almanac* (Washington, D.C.: Congressional Quarterly).

Note: Foreign trade—foreign trade, diplomacy, or immigration; foreign aid—various forms of assistance to other countries; defense—military, defense, veterans issues; social welfare—social welfare, civil rights, Indian affairs, and education; economic management—government and economic management, income tax issues; telecommunications, technology; resources—energy, natural resources, environment, and transportation; agriculture—agriculture and farm policy. In party is party of the president. "—" indicates that no votes were taken in that area. N/A—not available.

[a] Includes full term from Nov. 1963 to Jan. 1969.

Table 9-11 In-Party Support for the President on House Roll Calls, by Issue Area, Eisenhower, II to G. W. Bush, I (percent)

President/year	*Foreign trade*	*Foreign aid*	*Defense*	*Social welfare*	*Economic management*	*Resources*	*Agriculture*
Eisenhower, II							
1957	70.3	55.9	56.1	47.7	67.5	70.0	66.8
1958	59.1	59.2	93.1	58.1	62.9	52.4	82.4
1959	100.0	65.1	81.6	70.1	83.8	74.7	87.0
1960	63.0	63.2	63.0	60.3	50.8	79.2	92.4
Kennedy							
1961	93.5	81.2	87.1	86.9	78.8	71.9	77.7
1962	96.1	76.9	92.0	82.7	85.1	76.1	74.0
1963	88.9	80.7	85.9	84.3	87.0	86.2	85.6
L. Johnson[a]							
1964	89.4	82.8	66.2	85.1	84.3	94.3	84.8
1965	85.4	83.5	80.0	85.9	77.9	89.6	76.6
1966	84.0	80.8	66.2	81.2	81.7	84.9	—
1967	65.8	76.6	76.4	81.0	83.8	76.0	70.9
1968	80.0	78.1	93.2	78.2	68.4	85.2	79.4
Nixon, I							
1969	99.4	40.1	92.9	63.3	69.9	51.1	40.5
1970	71.0	63.4	92.8	73.1	88.4	79.8	50.8
1971	85.3	59.0	80.6	82.9	82.1	61.2	—
1972	77.2	58.8	91.4	68.9	76.4	63.6	—
Nixon, II							
1973	56.3	75.9	65.3	56.7	81.4	63.1	62.4
1974	78.3	52.1	60.1	59.4	68.1	74.6	—

(Table continues)

Table 9-11 *(Continued)*

President/year	*Foreign trade*	*Foreign aid*	*Defense*	*Social welfare*	*Economic management*	*Resources*	*Agriculture*
Ford							
1975	59.9	73.1	67.3	50.6	73.3	76.1	76.1
1976	67.4	86.7	81.2	65.1	59.9	73.5	—
Carter							
1977	67.1	58.5	71.7	85.5	59.9	71.1	92.4
1978	63.7	58.1	65.3	68.2	77.4	72.3	70.7
1979	78.4	68.6	69.0	73.0	68.7	65.9	—
1980	81.2	65.0	53.5	75.6	74.2	66.2	77.7
Reagan, I							
1981	66.4	21.9	68.7	76.7	92.0	76.2	43.8
1982	94.1	72.8	80.5	63.0	57.1	68.4	59.2
1983	71.3	51.3	87.7	69.3	64.1	65.8	62.5
1984	69.9	71.6	84.9	56.7	54.7	52.8	92.6
Reagan, II							
1985	70.8	85.5	75.5	27.3	62.8	54.7	70.0
1986	62.2	79.0	49.5	40.9	47.3	41.8	53.2
1987	48.8	79.9	80.9	78.3	48.3	45.8	—
1988	72.8	87.2	53.3	49.5	44.7	40.9	93.1
G.H.W. Bush							
1989	65.0	71.0	73.5	48.9	58.5	39.6	—
1990	45.3	90.0	85.8	68.0	69.9	50.7	41.1
1991	53.4	47.8	78.3	82.6	85.7	70.4	93.9
1992	59.9	54.6	84.0	71.2	85.3	73.2	—

Clinton, I							
1993	73.5	72.1	57.4	93.4	89.3	58.6	—
1994	65.2	—	71.8	75.9	66.2	98.4	—
1995	64.4	72.1	56.1	85.0	89.5	70.0	65.6
1996	67.9	55.3	63.7	81.7	85.0	72.3	76.4
Clinton, II							
1997	52.9	84.8	69.0	82.4	80.7	53.0	N/A
1998	41.9	64.6	24.9	84.2	81.8	81.5	57.2
1999	59.2	73.8	85.3	83.1	76.6	59.3	58.7
2000	60.3	73.9	66.3	74.2	80.4	73.2	82.6
G. W. Bush, I							
2001	77.0	N/A	95.7	88.5	97.6	82.3	47.7
2002	69.0	N/A	65.4	81.8	89.2	94.0	N/A
2003	78.6	90.6	83.8	96.1	94.1	91.5	N/A
2004	77.1	71.5	84.8	89.2	78.2	68.0	N/A

Source: Coded by the author from annual volumes of *Congressional Quarterly Almanac* (Washington, D.C.: Congressional Quarterly).

Note: Foreign trade—foreign trade, diplomacy, or immigration; foreign aid—various forms of assistance to other countries; defense—military, defense, veterans issues; social welfare—social welfare, civil rights, Indian affairs, and education; economic management—government and economic management, income tax issues; resources—energy, natural resources, environment, and transportation; agriculture—agriculture and farm policy. In party is party of the president. "—" indicates that no votes were taken in that area. N/A—not available.

[a] Includes full term from Nov. 1963 to Jan.1969.

Table 9-12 Out-Party Support for the President on House Roll Calls, by Issue Area, Eisenhower, II to G. W. Bush, I (percent)

President/year	*Foreign trade*	*Foreign aid*	*Defense*	*Social welfare*	*Economic management*	*Resources*	*Agriculture*
Eisenhower, II							
1957	70.2	53.3	46.3	65.2	46.7	44.4	43.1
1958	79.6	60.7	69.8	67.6	62.7	50.2	20.7
1959	99.2	73.2	31.8	47.6	61.1	30.5	29.9
1960	52.2	55.5	40.9	52.9	25.9	41.2	61.4
Kennedy							
1961	71.0	56.0	81.3	45.2	21.4	22.4	34.1
1962	37.2	39.4	69.6	73.1	47.5	31.9	12.4
1963	42.8	17.0	50.3	61.6	28.0	37.6	12.3
L. Johnson[a]							
1964	54.1	39.4	26.9	37.8	32.7	71.1	5.7
1965	73.6	38.1	45.1	44.4	43.3	64.6	11.8
1966	58.0	48.0	28.6	45.4	38	62.1	—
1967	52.4	35.2	83.3	55.5	47.6	46.1	52.2
1968	54.3	59.7	58.3	65.2	53.4	63.3	64.0
Nixon, I							
1969	75.0	69.1	80.5	56.0	52.2	41.2	47.9
1970	80.8	65.7	47.9	46.5	78.4	81.5	60.1
1971	52.2	45.6	54.4	46.5	67.2	60.5	—
1972	82.2	69.8	51.2	45.9	51.4	68.1	—
Nixon, II							
1973	47.6	69.9	27.2	40.1	38.5	40.4	36.8
1974	37.5	47.4	40.0	51.3	49.6	60.9	—

Ford							
1975	74.9	56.3	45.3	20.4	36.6	40.6	47.7
1976	44.7	46.8	43.9	35.3	34.4	36.6	—
Carter							
1977	69.6	31.2	41.4	50.4	48.6	39.2	43.4
1978	38.0	42.8	33.9	39.6	39.3	44.0	51.7
1979	30.4	28.4	57.6	37.2	39.2	37.4	—
1980	58.7	26.8	58.6	50.2	35.9	47.8	64.1
Reagan, I							
1981	45.4	39.6	45.2	32.6	32.7	70.3	42.0
1982	47.1	52.6	54.1	35.5	28.2	46.3	36.2
1983	25.3	61.5	38.8	19.3	24.7	8.82	36.9
1984	48.2	37.3	36.8	27.3	42.4	33.9	44.1
Reagan, II							
1985	37.9	28.0	31.6	30.1	37.4	33.7	39.6
1986	20.0	10.7	29.8	21.4	29.2	34.0	39.3
1987	33.0	18.0	34.0	12.2	18.3	27.0	—
1988	16.5	54.4	34.6	17.7	15.3	28.2	97.1
G. H. W. Bush							
1989	53.7	44.2	36.4	23.4	48.9	25.6	—
1990	26.2	18.6	36.8	25.0	25.6	21.3	33.4
1991	51.3	40.3	46.2	28.3	24.6	26.5	93.3
1992	13.1	67.6	28.7	30.2	21.3	33.1	—
Clinton, I							
1993	61.6	47.9	52.5	43.3	22.9	53.4	—
1994	68.3	—	39.8	23.3	27.8	99.4	—
1995	37.0	27.4	19.4	25.5	18.7	24.2	38.5
1996	73.6	33.5	21.3	29.4	38.0	52.3	—

(Table continues)

Table 9-12 *(Continued)*

President/year	*Foreign trade*	*Foreign aid*	*Defense*	*Social welfare*	*Economic management*	*Resources*	*Agriculture*
Clinton, II							
1997	18.2	13.7	13.7	39.5	39.7	37.6	—
1998	35	15.5	5.9	29.5	32.2	31.3	45.1
1999	30.8	17.9	30.5	21.8	25.2	41.7	24.8
2000	77.8	14.4	11.8	30.7	24.1	15.3	18.6
G. W. Bush, I							
2001	36.5	N/A	96.9	29.7	31.4	15.7	29.0
2002	64.7	N/A	20.6	43.5	21.7	49.8	—
2003	23.6	38.5	31.7	29.3	20.7	19.5	—
2004	24.8	42.8	47.5	25.9	53.1	10.3	—

Source: Each roll call individually coded by the author from annual volumes of *Congressional Quarterly Almanac* (Washington, D.C.: Congressional Quarterly).

Note: Foreign trade—foreign trade, diplomacy, or immigration; foreign aid—various forms of assistance to other countries; defense—military, defense, veterans issues; social welfare—social welfare, civil rights, Indian affairs, and education; economic management—government and economic management, income tax issues, telecommunications, technology; resources—energy, natural resources, environment, and transportation; agriculture—agriculture and farm policy. Out party is not the party of the president. "—" indicates that no votes were taken in that area. N/A—not available.

[a] Includes full term from Nov. 1963 to Jan. 1969.

Table 9-13 Presidential Vetoes, Washington to G.W. Bush

Years	*President*	*Total vetoes*	*Regular vetoes*	*Pocket vetoes*	*Vetoes overridden*	*Veto success rate*[a]
1789–1797	George Washington	2	2	0	0	100.0%
1797–1801	John Adams	0	0	0	0	—
1801–1809	Thomas Jefferson	0	0	0	0	—
1809–1817	James Madison	7	5	2	0	100.0
1817–1825	James Monroe	1	1	0	0	100.0
1825–1829	John Quincy Adams	0	0	0	0	—
1829–1837	Andrew Jackson	12	5	7	0	100.0
1837–1841	Martin Van Buren	1	0	1	0	—
1841–1841	William H. Harrison	0	0	0	0	—
1841–1845	John Tyler	10	6	4	1	83.3
1845–1849	James K. Polk	3	2	1	0	100.0
1849–1850	Zachary Taylor	0	0	0	0	—
1850–1853	Millard Fillmore	0	0	0	0	—
1853–1857	Franklin Pierce	9	9	0	5	44.4
1857–1861	James Buchanan	7	4	3	0	100.0
1861–1865	Abraham Lincoln	7	2	5	0	100.0
1865–1869	Andrew Johnson	29	21	8	15	28.6
1869–1877	Ulysses S. Grant	93	45	48	4	91.1
1877–1881	Rutherford B. Hayes	13	12	1	1	91.7
1881–1881	James A. Garfield	0	0	0	0	—
1881–1885	Chester A. Arthur	12	4	8	1	75.0
1885–1889	Grover Cleveland	414	304	110	2	99.3
1889–1893	Benjamin Harrison	44	19	25	1	94.7
1893–1897	Grover Cleveland	170	42	128	5	88.1
1897–1901	William McKinley	42	6	36	0	100.0
1901–1909	Theodore Roosevelt	82	42	40	1	97.6
1909–1913	William H. Taft	39	30	9	1	96.7
1913–1921	Woodrow Wilson	44	33	11	6	81.8
1921–1923	Warren G. Harding	6	5	1	0	100.0
1923–1929	Calvin Coolidge	50	20	30	4	80.0
1929–1933	Herbert Hoover	37	21	16	3	85.7
1933–1945	Franklin D. Roosevelt	635	372	263	9	97.6
1945–1953	Harry S Truman	250	180	70	12	93.3
1953–1961	Dwight D. Eisenhower	181	73	108	2	97.3
1961–1963	John F. Kennedy	21	12	9	0	100.0
1963–1969	Lyndon B. Johnson	30	16	14	0	100.0
1969–1974	Richard M. Nixon	43	26	17	7	73.1
1974–1977	Gerald R. Ford	66	48	18	12	75.0
1977–1981	Jimmy Carter	31	13	18	2	84.6
1981–1989	Ronald Reagan	78	39	39	9	77.8
1989–1993	George H.W. Bush	46	27	19[b]	1	96.3
1993–2001	Bill Clinton	37	36	1	2	94.4
2001–2008[c]	George W. Bush	8	7	1	1	71.4

Sources: Calculated by the author from *Presidential Vetoes, 1789–1976* (Washington, D.C.: Government Printing Office, 1978) and *Presidential Vetoes, 1977–1984* (Washington, D.C.: Government Printing Office, 1985); updated from successive volumes of *Congressional Quarterly Almanac* (Washington, D.C.: Congressional Quarterly) and www.senate.gov/reference/Legislation/Vetoes.

[a] Measured as percent of regular votes not overridden.
[b] Two pocket vetoes were not recognized by Congress, which passed subsequent legislation that did not encounter vetoes.
[c] As of Aug. 2008.

Table 9-14 Annual Number of Presidential Vetoes, by Issue Area, Truman, I to G. W. Bush, II

President/year	*Private*	*Foreign trade*	*Foreign aid*	*Defense*	*Social welfare*	*Economic management*	*Resources*	*Agriculture*	*Total*
Truman, I									
1946	36	0	0	3	2	4	4	0	49
1947	16	0	0	2	2	8	3	1	32
1948	29	0	0	1	3	5	5	0	43
Truman, II									
1949	22	0	0	2	1	2	5	0	32
1950	34	1	0	4	1	3	2	1	46
1951	10	0	0	4	0	1	0	0	15
1952	1	2	0	1	0	2	2	0	8
Eisenhower, I									
1953	8	0	0	0	0	1	1	0	10
1954	25	2	0	2	2	8	3	0	42
1955	4	0	0	1	0	4	2	0	11
1956	9	0	0	1	1	3	8	1	23
Eisenhower, II									
1957	8	0	0	1	0	2	1	0	12
1958	27	0	0	3	1	5	2	1	39
1959	9	0	0	0	3	2	4	2	20
1960	11	1	0	0	2	8	2	0	24
Kennedy									
1961	3	0	0	0	1	3	1	0	8
1962	8	1	0	0	0	2	1	0	12
1963	2	1	0	0	0	0	0	0	3

L. Johnson[a]									
1964	6	0	0	0	0	0	0	0	6
1965	4	0	0	1	1	0	1	0	7
1966	2	0	0	0	1	2	2	0	7
1967	1	1	0	0	1	0	0	0	3
1968	2	1	0	0	0	0	1	1	5
Nixon, I									
1969	0	0	0	0	0	0	0	0	0
1970	2	0	0	0	2	5	0	0	9
1971	0	0	0	0	2	2	1	0	5
1972	1	0	0	2	7	2	5	0	17
Nixon, II									
1973	0	0	0	2	2	4	2	0	10
1974	3	1	0	0	2	7	4	2	19
Ford									
1974	0	1	0	0	1	3	3	2	10
1975	0	2	0	1	3	4	4	2	16
1976	2	2	0	2	4	7	4	2	23
Carter									
1977	0	0	0	0	0	0	1	1	2
1978	1	2	0	3	0	7	4	0	17
1979	0	0	0	0	0	0	0	0	0
1980	2	0	0	1	1	4	4	0	12
Reagan, I									
1981	0	0	0	0	0	2	0	0	2
1982	1	0	0	0	0	7	3	0	11
1983	0	1	0	0	2	2	2	2	9
1984	4	0	0	0	2	6	5	0	17

(Table continues)

Table 9-14 (*Continued*)

President/year	*Private*	*Foreign trade*	*Foreign aid*	*Defense*	*Social welfare*	*Economic management*	*Resources*	*Agriculture*	*Total*
Reagan, II									
1985	0	1	0	0	2	1	1	1	6
1986	2	1	0	1	2	2	6	0	14
1987	0	0	0	0	0	1	2	0	3
1988	0	2	0	1	7	3	3	0	16
G. H. W. Bush									
1989	0	2	1	1	1	4	1	0	10
1990	1	2	0	1	4	2	1	0	11
1991	0	0	0	0	2	1	1	0	4
1992	0	2	0	0	6	7	5	1	21
Clinton, I									
1993	0	0	0	0	0	0	0	0	0
1994	0	0	0	0	0	0	0	0	0
1995	0	0	0	2	1	7	1	0	11
1996	0	1	0	0	2	2	1	0	6
Clinton, II[b]									
1997	0	0	0	1	1	1	0	0	3
1998	0	1	0	0	2	1	0	1	5
1999	0	1	0	0	1	3	0	0	5
2000	0	0	0	0	0	4	3	0	7
G. W. Bush, I									
2001	0	0	0	0	0	0	0	0	0
2002	0	0	0	0	0	0	0	0	0
2003	0	0	0	0	0	0	0	0	0
2004	0	0	0	0	0	0	0	0	0

G. W. Bush, II									
2005	0	0	0	0	0	0	0	0	0
2006	0	0	0	0	1	0	0	0	1
2007	0	0	0	2	4	0	1	0	7
Total	296	32	1	45	86	166	118	21	765

Source: Calculated by the author from *Presidential Vetoes, 1789–1976* (Washington, D.C.: Government Printing Office, 1978) and *Presidential Vetoes, 1977–1984* (Washington, D.C.: Government Printing Office, 1985); updated from successive volumes of *Congressional Quarterly Almanac* (Washington, D.C.: Congressional Quarterly) and http://www.senate.gov/reference/Legislation/Vetoes.

Note: Private—bills specifically providing relief for a named individual or individuals (all other categories include only public bills); foreign trade—foreign trade, diplomacy, or immigration; foreign aid—various forms of assistance to other countries; defense—military, defense, veterans issues; social welfare—social welfare, civil rights, Indian affairs, and education; economic management—government and economic management, income tax issues, telecommunications, technology; resources—energy, natural resources, environment, and transportation; agriculture—agriculture and farm policy.

[a] Includes full term from Nov. 1963 to Jan. 1969.
[b] Excludes line-item vetoes.

Table 9-15 Congressional Challenges to Presidential Vetoes, Truman, I to G. W. Bush, II

	Vetoes			*Veto challenges*		*Percentage overridden* [d]	
President/year	Total[a]	Pocket[b]	No challenge[c]	Sustained	Successful overrides	House	Senate
Truman, I							
1946	49	16	30	3	0	60.38	0.00
1947	32	19	10	2	1	73.25	67.20
1948	43	14	23	1	5	78.64	80.04
Truman, II							
1949	32	2	29	0	1	86.65	88.24
1950	46	6	35	3	2	88.53	70.44
1951	15	5	7	1	2	83.71	86.71
1952	8	4	3	0	1	71.28	68.67
Eisenhower, I							
1953	10	6	4	0	0	—	—
1954	42	25	17	0	0	—	—
1955	11	8	2	1	0	—	58.06
1956	23	14	8	1	0	48.91	—
Eisenhower, II							
1957	12	9	3	0	0	—	—
1958	39	24	14	1	0	52.88	77.53
1959	20	10	5	4	1	67.31	66.05
1960	24	12	9	2	1	72.44	65.38
Kennedy							
1961	8	2	6	0	0	—	—
1962	12	7	5	0	0	—	—
1963	3	2	1	0	0	—	—

L. Johnson[e]							
1964	6	2	4	0	0	—	—
1965	7	0	7	0	0	—	—
1966	7	4	3	0	0	—	—
1967	3	1	2	0	0	—	—
1968	5	5	0	0	0	—	—
Nixon, I							
1969	0	0	0	0	0	—	—
1970	9	3	0	4	2	62.51	71.35
1971	5	2	1	2	0	—	60.00
1972	17	13	1	1	2	78.27	88.28
Nixon, II							
1973	10	1	0	8	1	60.70	69.48
1974	19	2	8	5	4	80.19	84.27
Ford							
1974	10	9	1	0	0	—	—
1975	16	0	5	7	4	73.72	68.53
1976	23	7	6	6	4	73.42	65.57
Carter							
1977	2	0	2	0	0	—	—
1978	17	13	2	2	0	51.11	—
1979	0	0	0	0	0	—	—
1980	12	5	5	0	2	94.97	93.87
Reagan, I							
1981	2	1	1	0	0	—	—
1982	11	3	3	3	2	68.92	72.92
1983	9	3	5	0	1	70.38	100.00
1984	17	14	2	0	1	79.23	87.76

(Table continues)

Table 9-15 *(Continued)*

	Vetoes			*Veto challenges*		*Percentage overridden* [d]	
President/year	Total[a]	Pocket[b]	No challenge[c]	Sustained	Successful overrides	House	Senate
Reagan, II							
1985	6	0	5	0	1	92.22	92.71
1986	14	7	5	1	1	79.04	72.36
1987	3	0	1	0	2	88.35	76.50
1988	16	11	2	2	1	66.43	70.16
G. H. W. Bush							
1989	10	2	4	5	0	67.08	64.32
1990	11	5	0	6	0	66.44	65.00
1991	4	2	0	2	0	63.89	65.00
1992	21	10	2	8	1	68.32	65.37
Clinton, I							
1993	0	0	0	0	0	—	—
1994	0	0	0	0	0	—	—
1995	11	0	7	3	1	46.61	68.00
1996	6	0	3	3	0	48.70	41.00
Clinton, II							
1997	3	0	1	1	1	76.29	57.00
1998	5	0	5	0	0	—	—
1999	5	0	5	0	0	—	—
2000	7	1	4	3	0	36.67	35.35
G. W. Bush, I							
2001	0	0	0	0	0	—	—
2002	0	0	0	0	0	—	—

2003	0	0	0	0	0	—	—
2004	0	0	0	0	0	—	—
G. W. Bush, II[f]							
2005	0	0	0	0	0	—	—
2006	1	0	0	1	0	—	—
2007	7	1	1	4	1	16.67	16.67

Sources: Calculated by the author from *Presidential Vetoes, 1789–1976* (Washington, D.C.: Government Printing Office, 1978) and *Presidential Vetoes, 1977–1984* (Washington, D.C.: Government Printing Office, 1985); updated from successive volumes of *Congressional Quarterly Almanac* (Washington, D.C.: Congressional Quarterly) and www.senate.gov/reference/Legislation/Vetoes.

[a] Total number of vetoes of all types: public, private, pocket, and regular.
[b] There is no possibility of a congressional challenge for pocket vetoes in the legislative process, although there have been several unsuccessful court challenges.
[c] Number of bills not challenged among those that might have been challenged.
[d] Average percentage of the members of the House and Senate who vote to override on veto challenge motions; dashes indicate no challenges.
[e] Includes full term from Nov. 1963 to Jan. 1969.
[f] Through 2007 only.

Figure 9-4 Presidential Policy Behavior, Eisenhower, II to G.W. Bush, I

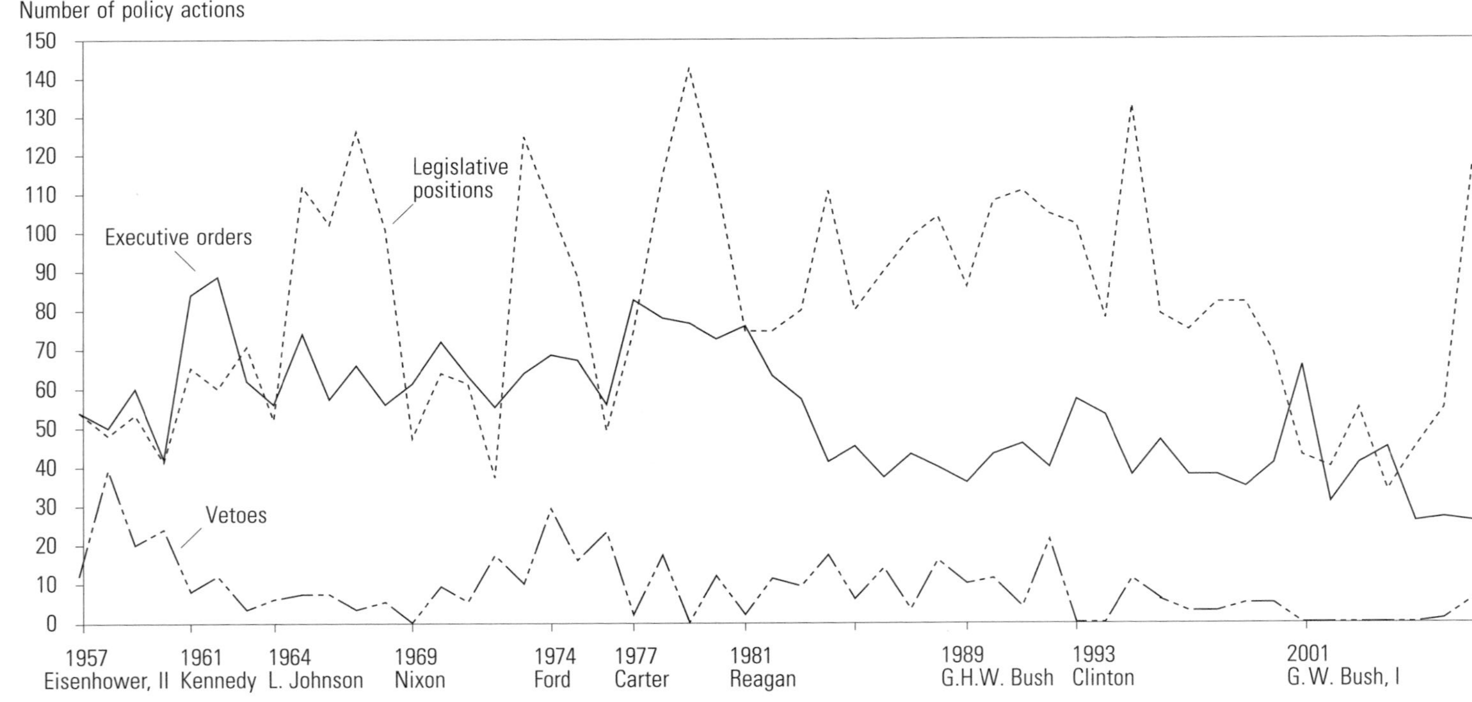

Source: Coded and calculated by the author.

Figure 9-5 Presidential Behavior on Foreign Policy, Eisenhower, II to G.W. Bush, I

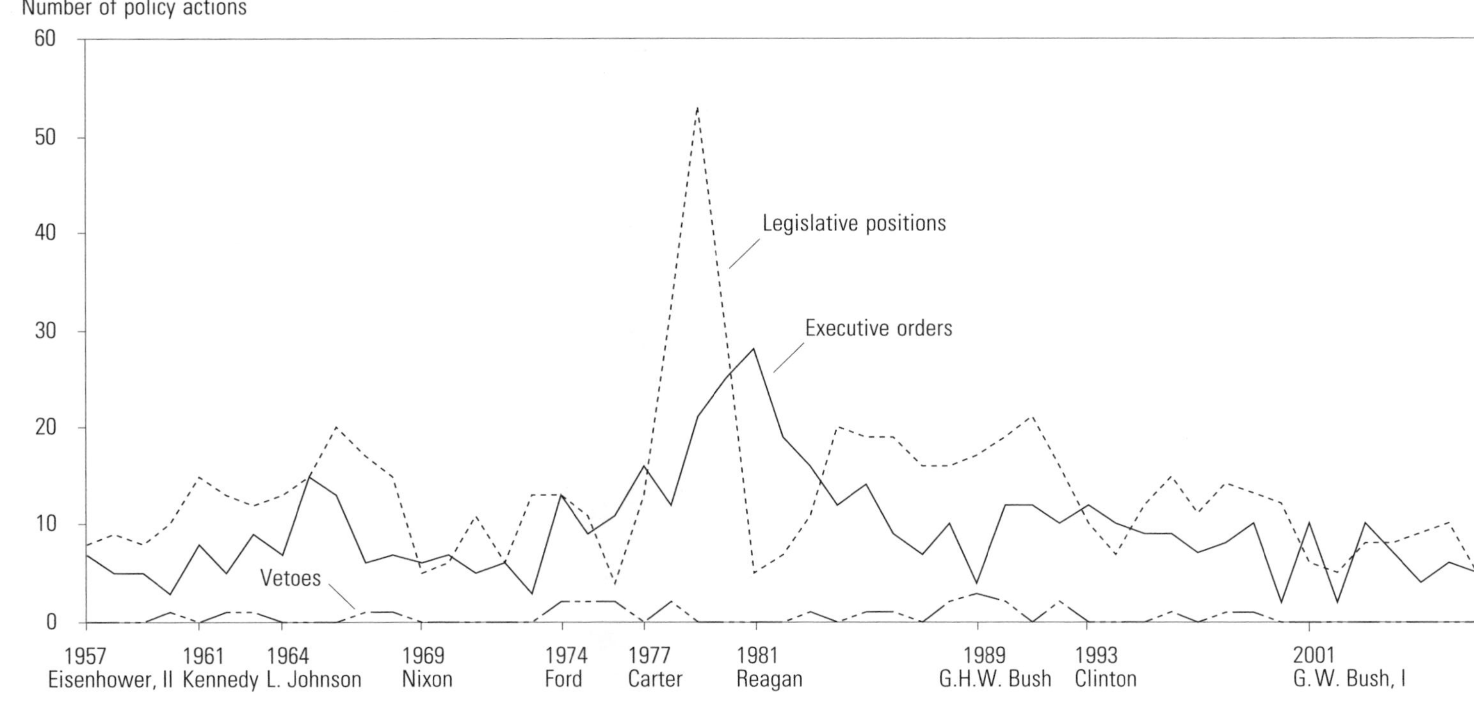

Source: Coded and calculated by the author.

Note: Foreign policy includes foreign trade and foreign aid.

Figure 9-6 Presidential Behavior on Defense Policy, Eisenhower, II to G.W. Bush, I

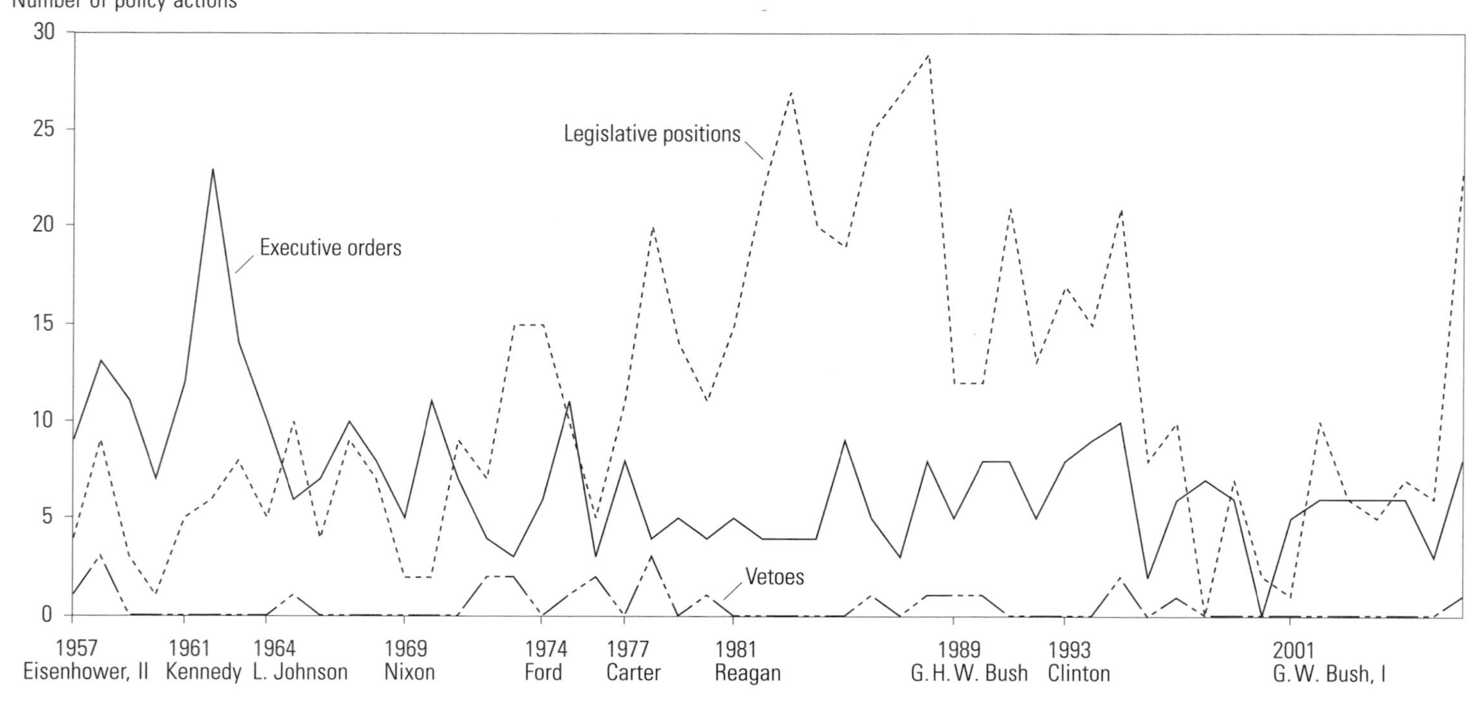

Source: Coded and calculated by the author.

Figure 9-7 Presidential Behavior on Domestic Policy, Eisenhower, II to G.W. Bush, I

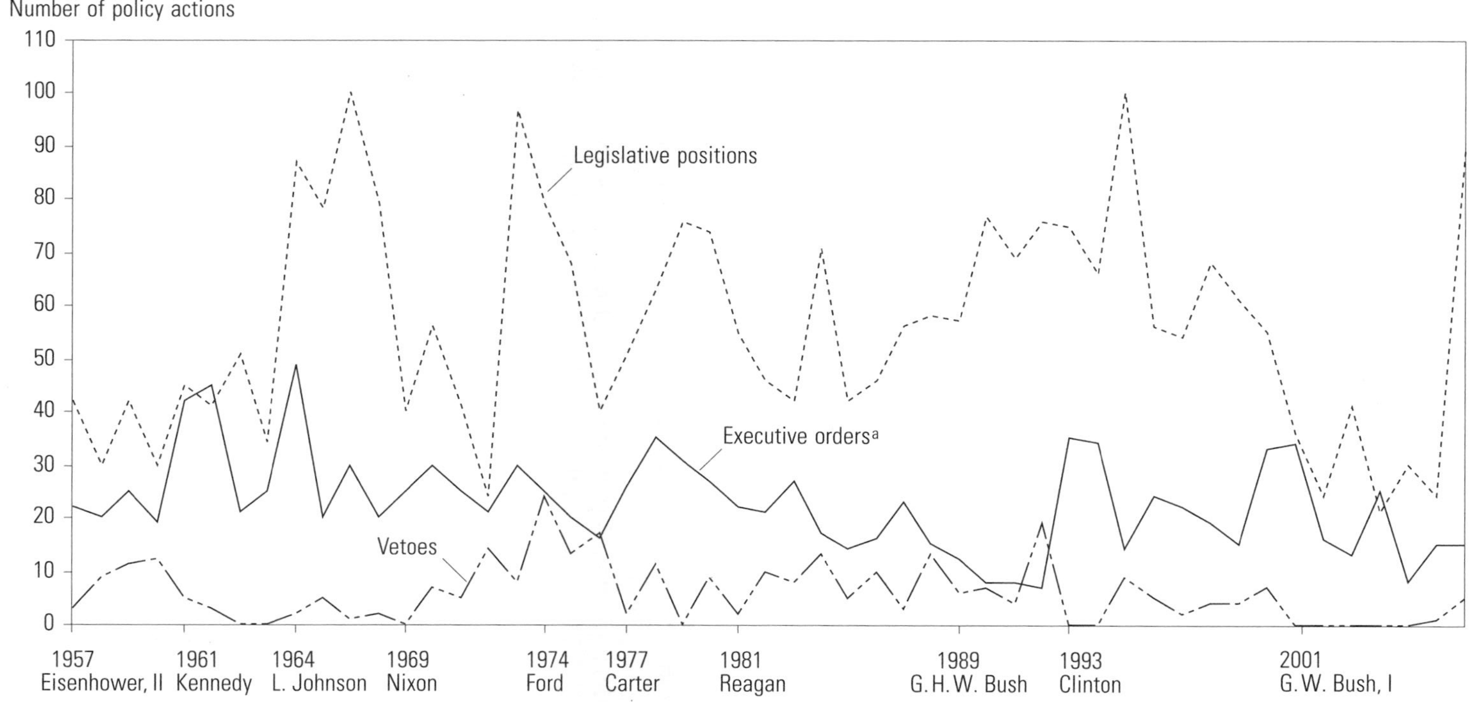

Source: Coded and calculated by the author.

[a] Excludes ceremonial, personnel, and federalism orders.

10

The Presidency and the Judiciary

- **Presidents' Nominations to the Supreme Court**
- **Court Nominees with Senate Problems**
- **Presidents' Nominations to Lower Courts**
- **Characteristics of Lower Court Appointees**
- **Success of the United States in the Supreme Court**
- **Supreme Court Rulings against the President**

Although presidential relations with the judiciary are more sporadic and less visible than those with Congress, they nonetheless rest on structural, organizational, and behavioral elements of the institutional presidency. The U.S. Constitution provides one key structural element of the presidential-judicial relationship: it specifies that presidents nominate and, with the advice and consent of the Senate, appoint judges to the federal courts, including the U.S. Supreme Court. The White House organization is heavily involved in screening potential nominees and running the confirmation process in the Senate. Senatorial courtesy—the practice of allowing senators to have control over lower court appointments—is a form of institutional behavior that links the presidency, the Senate, and the courts.

Data on presidential-judicial relations are more scarce than data documenting the connections between the presidency and Congress. This absence of data limits understanding of the presidential-judicial relationship. This chapter surveys four aspects of this relationship: Supreme Court nominations, lower court nominations, the degree of governmental success before the Supreme Court, and the Court's decisions as they relate to the presidency.

Supreme Court Nominations

High political drama typically accompanies a president's nominations to the Supreme Court. These decisions are commonly viewed as personal. The chief executive is depicted as heavily involved—culling a list of potential nominees, scrutinizing the credentials of the finalists, personally interviewing them, and announcing the selection with some fanfare. There is some truth to this portrayal. Presidents are often personally associated with their Court nominees. Franklin Roosevelt, Harry Truman, John F. Kennedy, and Lyndon Johnson had a personal relationship with nearly every Court nominee they submitted to the Senate. Richard Nixon, Ronald Reagan, George Bush, and Bill Clinton, all of whom were more concerned with the ideological credentials of their candidates, were less likely to know their nominees personally. George W. Bush pursued both directions. He knew Harriet Miers, his first Supreme Court nominee, quite well; she had worked for him both in Texas and at the White House. When her Supreme Court nomination appeared to be headed for failure due to strong criticisms of her lack of judicial experience, she withdrew. Bush then turned to a more ideological choice in Samuel A. Alito. Bush's choice of John G. Roberts as chief justice was similarly ideological in nature.

Presidents' nominations to the Court are more rooted in the presidential organization than this personal depiction suggests. Candidates face lengthy background checks, interviews, and analyses of their writings, carried out by the Justice Department, the Office of the White House Counsel, the White House personnel office, and the Office of the White House Chief of Staff. In addition, many of the nominations reflect internal conflict. Opposing camps within the presidential organization will champion one contender over another. For instance, after the defeat of Robert Bork's nomination to the Supreme Court, two camps in the Reagan administration battled over whether a moderate choice (Douglas Ginsburg) or a conservative one (Anthony Kennedy) should be next. Reagan ultimately decided to go with Ginsburg, whom he met for the first time only thirty minutes before announcing the nomination. Nine days later Ginsburg withdrew his nomination upon admitting that he had once smoked marijuana; Kennedy's nomination was then sent to the Senate and confirmed. There was also considerable jockeying between those officials in the Clinton administration who wanted Judge Stephen Breyer (the eventual nominee) to replace Associate Justice Harry Blackmun and those who supported Secretary of the Interior Bruce Babbitt. A similar contest between the Breyer and Babbitt camps had also preceded the appointment of Clinton's first nominee to the Court, Ruth Bader Ginsburg.

The clearest structural pattern discernible in Court nominations is that presidents overwhelmingly choose members of their own party as nominees to the Court. This is true regardless of the president, his party, the Court vacancy, or any other qualifications a prospective nominee may have. Although people often like to say that the Supreme Court is "above politics," it is in fact strongly tied to politics—at least through the party affiliations of presidents and justices. Evidence of this pattern is made clear in Table 10-1, which examines the number of appointments presidents since George Washington have made to the high court. Presidents have nominated someone of the other party to the Supreme Court only 14 times in 114 appointees.

Beyond party, presidents also consider other representational qualifications in making their Court nominations. This involves the extent to which a nominee can be identified with a significant portion of the American public. Region, religion, race, and gender have all been relevant attributes. Presidents, particularly in the nineteenth century, sought regional balance on the Court. Washington commented on his appointment of North Carolinian James Iredell to the Court in 1790 that no one from North Carolina had yet received a judicial appointment. Abraham Lincoln expressed dismay at having to fill two "southern seats," created at the start of the Civil War, with northerners. Franklin Roosevelt told Wiley Rutledge of Iowa upon his nomination that "we had a number of candidates for the Court who were highly qualified, but they didn't have geography—you have that" (Scigliano, 1971, 111).

A rise in religious, racial, and gender qualifications has accompanied the decline in regionalism. Observers refer to a "Catholic seat," a "Jewish seat," "a black seat," and, most recently, a "woman's seat." Since William McKinley's appointment of Joseph McKenna in 1898, there has been a Roman Catholic sitting on the bench almost continuously. Woodrow Wilson appointed the first Jew to the Court—Louis Brandeis. Brandeis's appointment in 1916 was followed by Benjamin Cardozo in 1932 (Hoover), Felix Frankfurter in 1938 (Roosevelt), Arthur Goldberg in 1963 (Kennedy), Abe Fortas in 1965 (Johnson), Ruth Bader Ginsburg in 1993, and Stephen Breyer in 1994 (both Clinton). George H. W. Bush continued to reserve a seat for an African American jurist when he nominated conservative Clarence Thomas to replace liberal civil rights advocate Justice Thurgood Marshall, who in 1967 became the first African American appointed to the Court. Reagan nominated the first woman, Sandra Day O'Connor, in 1981; Clinton appointed the second woman, Ginsburg, in 1993. When O'Connor retired in 2005, George W. Bush attempted to replace her with another woman, Harriet Miers, but, as noted above, Miers withdrew her nomination after intense objections that she lacked sufficient judicial experience.

Table 10-1 also reveals that there is little way of telling how many appointments a president will make. Only four presidents—William Henry Harrison, Zachary Taylor, Andrew Johnson, and Jimmy Carter—did not make any Supreme Court appointments. Among those, Carter was the only full-term president in history to be denied this opportunity. By contrast, William Howard Taft, also a one-term president, appointed six justices. Presidents average one appointment every twenty-two months.

Table 10-2 shows those Supreme Court nominees that encountered problems with Senate approval. Thirty nominees were rejected or withdrew their nominations for 20 seats on the Court; this amounts to roughly 17 percent of the total appointments made. (Four of those rejected were later confirmed.) Are there any patterns to these rejections? First, 22 of the 30 problems occurred in the nineteenth century, when the Senate had a history of asserting strong power over presidential appointments. It is also clear that when a president runs into a problem with one nominee, he may also encounter trouble with subsequent nominees for the same seat. For instance, John Tyler, who had great difficulty with Congress after he became president upon the death of William Henry Harrison, nominated five people to a vacancy on the Court, each of whom encountered problems. Tyler did not succeed until his sixth try. Nixon also failed in two successive nominations—Clement Haynsworth and G. Harrold Carswell—before succeeding in his appointment of Harry Blackmun. One strategy that presidents adopt when their nominations run into trouble is to withdraw them from the Senate calendar. This has occurred 10 of the 30 times a nomination has run into trouble.

Lower Court Nominations

Presidents have far less control over selecting lower court judges than they do in choosing nominees to the Supreme Court. In the 95 federal district courts, there are 645 judges. The 13 courts of appeals, or circuit courts, have a corps of 167 full-time judges. Table 10-3 records the number of nominations for lower court positions by presidents since Kennedy. With 50 or more judicial vacancies to fill in a year, presidents turn to the White House organization and the Justice Department to evaluate the candidates, make recommendations, and see that the eventual nominees are confirmed by the Senate. Of equal importance is the tradition of "senatorial courtesy," which influences the appointment of district court judges in particular. Based on an informal reciprocal arrangement among senators, this institutional behavior allows senators of the president's party from the state where the district court vacancy occurs to sponsor candidates they like and veto candidates they do not like. Other senators go along, knowing that they, too, will have an opportunity to recommend nominations at some point. Senatorial courtesy thus limits presidents' control over their own appointments to the federal district bench.

Consistent with the party pattern observed for the Supreme Court, Table 10-4 reveals the partisanship on the federal district courts, while Table 10-5 presents evidence of partisanship on the federal courts of appeal. The percentage of district court appointees of the president's party averaged 92 percent for all presidents from Grover Cleveland to George W. Bush. Each of these presidents exceeded 90 percent, with the exceptions of Taft, Ford, George H. W. Bush, Clinton, and George W. Bush. The last three presidents have made appointments from their own parties just below the 90 percent rate. Party was slightly less important in appointments to the circuit courts. Presidents since Cleveland have nominated members of their own party to the appeals bench 85 percent of the time.

Tables 10-6 and 10-7 examine some of the other characteristics of presidents' appointees to federal district courts and federal circuit courts, respectively. The backgrounds of the district court judges and appeals court judges have been very similar under the seven presidents from Lyndon Johnson to George W. Bush. Nominees to the courts are mostly white male lawyers. Only Presidents Carter and Clinton have been especially noteworthy in efforts to appoint African Americans, other ethnic minorities, or women to the federal bench. President Carter appointed 21 percent minorities to federal district courts and 21 percent minorities to federal circuit courts, while President Clinton appointed 27 percent minorities to federal district judgeships and 28 percent to circuit court positions. As shown in Table 10-8, from Lyndon Johnson to George W. Bush, nearly 90 percent of the judicial appointees were men. The characterization of a white male judiciary is made plain in the last column of the table: 77 percent of the appointments made by Presidents since Carter were white males. George W. Bush granted 85 percent of his nominations to white males.

Figure 10-1 shows how the judicial appointments of presidents since Franklin Roosevelt shaped the federal bench. Franklin Roosevelt, Dwight Eisenhower, and Reagan made more nominations relative to the total number of judgeships than did the other presidents studied. President Ford fared especially poorly in placing his stamp on the judiciary.

The Government and the Supreme Court

The presidency has some ability to influence what cases the Supreme Court hears and how it decides those cases through the Office of the Solicitor General in the Justice Department. The solicitor general is a presidential appointee who supervises the litigation of the executive branch. Put simply, the solicitor general is the lawyer for the executive branch. The Office of the Solicitor General can influence the Court's decisions in two ways. First, when the government is a party to a lawsuit, the solicitor general's office decides which of the cases lost by the government will be appealed to the Supreme Court and thus receive the considerable resources of the federal government. Although the Court controls its docket, it is much more likely to accept cases filed by the solicitor general than from others. In recent years, the federal government has been a party to about half the cases heard before the Court. As shown in Table 10-9, its success rate in these cases averaged 63 percent for the period from 1946 to 2004.

Second, the solicitor general's office participates in cases to which it is not directly a party. It files *amicus curiae* (friend of the court) briefs supporting or opposing the positions of other parties before the Court. As seen in Table 10-10, the solicitor general's office is very successful in advancing the position the Court ultimately upholds. Although the success rate has declined from highs during the Eisenhower, Kennedy, and Johnson years, it still remains quite strong.

In these two ways, the solicitor general's office has developed a fairly close working relationship with the Court. It clearly has more expertise and greater resources in dealing with the Court and its members than do other litigants. Although the solicitor general's office is independent of the presidency, presidents and presidential staff members nonetheless keep in close contact with it. On occasion, the White House has lobbied the solicitor general to take a particular case before the Court or handle a brief in a specific way. Thus, through the solicitor general's office, the presidency has an organizational avenue of influence to the Supreme Court.

The Supreme Court's Impact on the Presidency

While the presidency shapes the judiciary primarily through the appointments process, the courts also have the ability to shape the presidency. In a recent example, the Supreme Court handed down a decision in *Bush v. Gore* holding that Florida should stop its recount of ballots in the 2000 presidential election. Based on the reported vote, George W. Bush won Florida and thus had a majority of electoral college votes, even though Al Gore had won more popular votes nationally. In a wider context, the Supreme Court has throughout its history handed down various decisions that have done far more to expand presidential power than to restrict it. The Court has interpreted presidential power broadly in the areas of diplomacy, war, and domestic unrest. When the Court has stopped or chastised presidential action, it has often done so after an incident is over or a crisis has passed.

Table 10-11 examines the impact of the Court on the presidency. Although the Court generally upholds presidential actions, the table lists the number of times the Court has ruled against presidents from Washington to George W. Bush. It shows that in only 82 instances has the Court rebuffed presidents. The most recent instance was in 2006 when the Court rejected George W. Bush's establishment of military commissions by executive order to prosecute suspected terrorists. There have been other pivotal Supreme Court cases against U.S. presidents. In 1974 the Court handed down *U.S. v. Nixon* in which it unanimously held that Nixon must turn over the Watergate tapes. This was one of the key events that precipitated Nixon's resignation. In 1997 the Court decided that a sexual discrimination lawsuit filed by former Arkansas state employee Paula Jones could proceed against President Clinton while he was in office.

Conclusion

Although data on relations between the presidency and judiciary are sparse, those that are available reveal three patterns—two that arise from institutional elements of the presidency and a third that emerges from the political environment. First, just as party connects the presidency and Congress, so, too, does it connect the presidency and the judiciary. Party is a structural component of the presidency that provides an indicator of how closely a nominee's views will match those of a president. Although the stamp placed on the courts may look like that of an individual president, it is in fact the product of this much larger institutional partisanship. The data reveal no evidence of independent partisanship in presidents' judicial appointments. If this were so, an increase in the number of appointments of judges from the opposition party might be evident. Instead, the partisanship looks decidedly old-fashioned and one-sided. Since judges serve for good behavior, the presidents' appointments draw party lines in the federal judiciary that are long-standing.

Second, the recruitment environment within which the presidency operates strongly affects the types of nominations presidents make. Presidents rely on a readily available pool of candidates from the upper echelons of the law profession and law schools and from lower courts to fill open slots. Their appointments mirror the makeup of the legal profession in general and judgeships more specifically. Presidents do little to rock the legal boat in their appointments, so the white-men-preferred profile still predominates.

Finally, in its decisions the Supreme Court respects the presidency as a co-equal branch. This is a structural aspect of the presidency's relations with the judiciary implied in the Constitution. While presidents make individual appointments to the federal bench and the Court makes significant decisions for and against the actions of individual presidents, institutional dynamics nonetheless guide these incumbent-specific dealings.

Table 10-1 Presidents and Supreme Court Justices, Washington to G. W. Bush

President/seat number and justice	*Total appointees*	*Party*	*Home state*	*Years on Court*	*Age at nomination*	*Years of previous judicial experience*
Washington	11	Federalist				
1 John Jay		Federalist	New York	1789–1795	44	2
2 John Rutledge		Federalist	South Carolina	1789–1791	50	6
3 William Cushing		Federalist	Massachusetts	1789–1810[a]	57	29
4 James Wilson		Federalist	Pennsylvania	1789–1798[a]	47	0
5 John Blair, Jr.		Federalist	Virginia	1789–1796	57	11
6 James Iredell		Federalist	North Carolina	1790–1799[a]	38	0.5
2 Thomas Johnson		Federalist	Maryland	1791–1793	59	1.5
2 William Paterson		Federalist	New Jersey	1793–1806[a]	47	0
1 John Rutledge		Federalist	South Carolina	1795	55	6[b]
5 Samuel Chase		Federalist	Maryland	1796–1811[a]	55	8
1 Oliver Ellsworth		Federalist	Connecticut	1796–1800	51	5
J. Adams	3	Federalist				
4 Bushrod Washington		Federalist	Virginia	1798–1829[a]	36	0
6 Alfred Moore		Federalist	North Carolina	1799–1804	44	1
1 John Marshall		Federalist	Virginia	1801–1835[a]	45	3
Jefferson	3	Jeffersonian[c]				
6 William Johnson		Jeffersonian	South Carolina	1804–1834[a]	32	6
2 H. Brockholst Livingston		Jeffersonian	New York	1806–1823[a]	49	0
7 Thomas Todd		Jeffersonian	Kentucky	1807–1826[a]	42	6
Madison	2	Jeffersonian				
5 Gabriel Duvall		Jeffersonian	Maryland	1811–1835	58	6
3 Joseph Story		Jeffersonian	Massachusetts	1811–1845[a]	32	0
Monroe	1	Jeffersonian				
2 Smith Thompson		Jeffersonian	New York	1823–1843[a]	55	16
J.Q. Adams	1	Jeffersonian				
7 Robert Trimble		Jeffersonian	Kentucky	1826–1828[a]	49	11

(Table continues)

Table 10-1 *(Continued)*

President/seat number and justice	*Total appointees*	*Party*	*Home state*	*Years on Court*	*Age at nomination*	*Years of previous judicial experience*
Jackson	5	Democrat				
7 John McLean		Democrat	Ohio	1829–1861[a]	44	6
4 Henry Baldwin		Democrat	Pennsylvania	1830–1844[a]	50	0
6 James Wayne		Democrat	Georgia	1835–1867[a]	45	5
1 Roger B. Taney		Democrat	Maryland	1836–1864[a]	59	0
5 Philip P. Barbour		Democrat	Virginia	1836–1841[a]	52	8
Van Buren	3	Democrat				
8 John Catron		Democrat	Tennessee	1837–1865[a]	51	10
9 John McKinley		Democrat	Alabama	1837–1852[a]	57	0
5 Peter V. Daniel		Democrat	Virginia	1841–1860[a]	57	0
W. Harrison	0	Whig				
Tyler	1	Whig				
2 Samuel Nelson		Democrat	New York	1845–1872	52	22
Polk	2	Democrat				
3 Levi Woodbury		Democrat	New Hampshire	1845–1851[a]	55	6
4 Robert C. Grier		Democrat	Pennsylvania	1846–1870	52	13
Taylor	0	Whig				
Fillmore	1	Whig				
3 Benjamin R. Curtis		Whig	Massachusetts	1851–1857	41	0
Pierce	1	Democrat				
9 John A. Campbell		Democrat	Alabama	1853–1861	41	0
Buchanan	1	Democrat				
3 Nathan Clifford		Democrat	Maine	1858–1881[a]	54	0
Lincoln	5	Republican				
7 Noah H. Swayne		Republican	Ohio	1862–1881	57	0
5 Samuel F. Miller		Republican	Iowa	1862–1890[a]	46	0

9 David Davis		Republican	Illinois	1862–1877	47	14
10 Stephen J. Field		Democrat	California	1863–1897	46	6
1 Salmon P. Chase		Republican	Ohio	1864–1873	56	0
A. Johnson	0	Republican				
Grant	4	Republican				
4 William Strong		Republican	Pennsylvania	1870–1880	61	11
6 Joseph P. Bradley		Republican	New Jersey	1870–1892[a]	56	0
2 Ward Hunt		Republican	New York	1873–1882	62	8
1 Morrison R. Waite		Republican	Ohio	1874–1888[a]	57	0
Hayes	2	Republican				
9 John M. Harlan		Republican	Kentucky	1877–1911[a]	44	1
4 William B. Woods		Republican	Georgia	1880–1887[a]	56	12
Garfield	1	Republican				
7 Stanley Matthews		Republican	Ohio	1881–1889[a]	56	4
Arthur	2	Republican				
3 Horace Gray		Republican	Massachusetts	1881–1902	53	18
2 Samuel Blatchford		Republican	New York	1882–1893[a]	62	15
Cleveland (first term)	2	Democrat				
4 Lucius Q. C. Lamar		Democrat	Mississippi	1883–1893[a]	62	0
1 Melville W. Fuller		Democrat	Illinois	1888–1910[a]	55	0
B. Harrison	4	Republican				
7 David J. Brewer		Republican	Kansas	1889–1910[a]	52	19
5 Henry B. Brown		Republican	Michigan	1891–1906	54	16
6 George Shiras, Jr.		Republican	Pennsylvania	1892–1903	60	0
4 Howell E. Jackson		Democrat	Tennessee	1893–1895[a]	60	7
Cleveland (second term)	2	Democrat				
2 Edward D. White		Democrat	Louisiana	1894–1910[a]	48	1.5
4 Rufus W. Peckham		Democrat	New York	1895–1909[a]	57	9
McKinley	1	Republican				
8 Joseph McKenna		Republican	California	1898–1925	54	5

(Table continues)

Table 10-1 *(Continued)*

President/seat number and justice	*Total appointees*	*Party*	*Home state*	*Years on Court*	*Age at nomination*	*Years of previous judicial experience*
T. Roosevelt	3	Republican				
3 Oliver W. Holmes		Republican	Massachusetts	1902–1932	61	20
6 William R. Day		Republican	Ohio	1903–1922	53	7
5 William H. Moody		Republican	Massachusetts	1906–1910	52	0
Taft	6	Republican				
4 Horace H. Lurton		Democrat	Tennessee	1909–1914[a]	65	26
7 Charles E. Hughes		Republican	New York	1910–1916	48	0
1 Edward D. White		Democrat	Louisiana	1910–1921[a]	65	1.5[b]
2 Willis Van Devanter		Republican	Wyoming	1910–1937	51	8
5 Joseph R. Lamar		Democrat	Georgia	1910–1916[a]	53	2
9 Mahlon Pitney		Republican	New Jersey	1912–1922	54	11
Wilson	3	Democrat				
4 James C. McReynolds		Democrat	Tennessee	1914–1941	52	0
5 Louis D. Brandeis		Republican	Massachusetts	1916–1939	59	0
7 John H. Clarke		Democrat	Ohio	1916–1922	59	2
Harding	4	Republican				
1 William H. Taft		Republican	Ohio	1921–1930	63	13
7 George Sutherland		Republican	Utah	1922–1938	60	0
6 Pierce Butler		Democrat	Minnesota	1923–1939[a]	56	0
9 Edward T. Sanford		Republican	Tennessee	1923–1930[a]	57	14
Coolidge	1	Republican				
8 Harlan Fiske Stone		Republican	New York	1925–1941	52	0
Hoover	3	Republican				
1 Charles E. Hughes		Republican	New York	1930–1941	67	0
9 Owens J. Roberts		Republican	Pennsylvania	1930–1945	55	0
3 Benjamin N. Cardozo		Democrat	New York	1932–1938[a]	61	18

F. Roosevelt	9	Democrat				
2 Hugo L. Black		Democrat	Alabama	1937–1971[a]	51	1.5
7 Stanley F. Reed		Democrat	Kentucky	1938–1957	53	0
3 Felix Frankfurter		Independent	Massachusetts	1939–1962	56	0
5 William O. Douglas		Democrat	Connecticut	1939–1975	40	0
6 Frank Murphy		Democrat	Michigan	1940–1949[a]	49	7
4 James F. Byrnes		Democrat	South Carolina	1941–1942	62	0
1 Harlan Fiske Stone		Republican	New York	1941–1946[a]	68	0[b]
9 Robert H. Jackson		Democrat	New York	1941–1954[a]	49	0
4 Wiley B. Rutledge		Democrat	Iowa	1943–1949[a]	48	4
Truman	4	Democrat				
9 Harold H. Burton		Republican	Ohio	1945–1958	57	0
1 Fred M. Vinson		Democrat	Kentucky	1946–1953[a]	56	5
6 Tom C. Clark		Democrat	Texas	1949–1967	49	0
4 Sherman Minton		Democrat	Indiana	1949–1956	58	8
Eisenhower	5	Republican				
1 Earl Warren		Republican	California	1953–1969	62	0
8 John M. Harlan		Republican	New York	1955–1971	55	1
4 William J. Brennan		Democrat	New Jersey	1956–1990	50	7
7 Charles E. Whittaker		Republican	Missouri	1957–1962	56	3
9 Potter Stewart		Republican	Ohio	1958–1981	43	4
Kennedy	2	Democrat				
7 Byron R. White		Democrat	Colorado	1962–1993	44	0
3 Arthur J. Goldberg		Democrat	Illinois	1962–1965	54	0
L. Johnson	2	Democrat				
3 Abe Fortas		Democrat	Tennessee	1965–1969	55	0
6 Thurgood Marshall		Democrat	New York	1967–1991	59	4
Nixon	4	Republican				
1 Warren E. Burger		Republican	Minnesota	1969–1986	61	13
3 Harry A. Blackmun		Republican	Minnesota	1970–1994	61	11
2 Lewis F. Powell, Jr.		Democrat	Virginia	1971–1987	64	0
8 William H. Rehnquist		Republican	Arizona	1971–1986	47	0

(Table continues)

Table 10-1 *(Continued)*

President/seat number and justice	*Total appointees*	*Party*	*Home state*	*Years on Court*	*Age at nomination*	*Years of previous judicial experience*
Ford	1	Republican				
5 John Paul Stevens		Republican	Illinois	1976–	55	5
Carter	0	Democrat				
Reagan	4	Republican				
9 Sandra Day O'Connor		Republican	Arizona	1981–	51	6.5
1 William H. Rehnquist		Republican	Arizona	1986–	61	0[b]
8 Antonin Scalia		Republican	Illinois	1986–	50	4
2 Anthony Kennedy		Republican	California	1988–	51	12
G. H. W. Bush	2	Republican				
4 David H. Souter		Republican	New Hampshire	1990–	50	13
6 Clarence Thomas		Republican	Georgia	1991–	43	1
Clinton	2	Democrat				
2 Ruth Bader Ginsburg		Democrat	New York	1993–	60	13
3 Stephen G. Breyer		Democrat	Massachusetts	1994–	55	14
G. W. Bush	2	Republican				
1 John G. Roberts		Republican	New York	2005–	50	2
9 Samuel Alito		Republican	New Jersey	2006–	51	16

Source: Adapted from Harold Stanley and Richard Niemi, *Vital Statistics on American Politics, 2007–2008,* (Washington, D.C.: CQ Press, 2008), 281–286.

Note: Seat number 1 is always held by the chief justice of the United States.

[a] Died in office.
[b] Prior to appointment as associate justice.
[c] Jeffersonian Party also known as Democratic-Republican Party.

Table 10-2 Supreme Court Nominees with Senate Problems, Washington to G. W. Bush

President/year	*Nominee*	*Action*
Washington		
1793	William Paterson	Withdrawn[a]
1795	John Rutledge	Rejected[a]
Madison		
1811	Alexander Wolcott	Rejected
John Adams		
1828	John J. Crittenden	Postponed
Jackson		
1835	Roger B. Taney	Postponed[a]
Tyler		
1844	John G. Spencer	Rejected
1844	R. H. Walworth	Withdrawn
1844	Edward B. King	Withdrawn
1844	R. H. Walworth	Withdrawn
1845	John M. Read	Postponed
Polk		
1846	G. W. Woodward	Rejected
Fillmore		
1852	Edward A. Bradford	Postponed
1853	George E. Badger	Postponed
1853	William C. Micou	Postponed
Buchanan		
1861	Jeremiah S. Black	Rejected
A. Johnson		
1866	Henry Stanbery	Postponed
Grant		
1870	Ebenezer R. Hoar	Rejected
1874	George H. Williams	Withdrawn
1874	Caleb Cushing	Withdrawn
Hayes		
1881	Stanley Mattheys	Postponed
Cleveland		
1894	W. B. Hornblower	Rejected
1894	W. H. Peckham	Rejected[a]
Hoover		
1930	John J. Parker	Rejected
L. Johnson		
1968	Abe Fortas[b]	Withdrawn
1968	Homer Thornberry	Withdrawn

(Table continues)

Table 10-2 (*Continued*)

President/year	*Nominee*	*Action*
Nixon		
1969	Clement F. Haynsworth	Rejected
1970	G. Harrold Carswell	Rejected
Reagan		
1987	Robert H. Bork	Rejected
1987	Douglas H. Ginsburg	Withdrawn
G.W. Bush		
2005	Harriet Miers	Withdrawn

Source: Adapted from *Guide to the U.S. Supreme Court* (Washington, D.C.: Congressional Quarterly, 1979), 946–948; updated by the author.

[a] Later confirmed.
[b] Associate justice nominated for chief justice.

Table 10-3 Presidential Nominations to the Lower Courts, Kennedy to G. W. Bush, II

President/year	*Number of nominations*	*President/year*	*Number of nominations*
Kennedy		1984	37
1961	60	Total	144
1962	52	Reagan, II	
1963	15	1985	95
Total	127	1986	54
Johnson[a]		1987	52
1964	18	1988	46
1965	28	Total	247
1966	60	G. H. W. Bush	
1967	35	1989	17
1968	24	1990	61
Total	165	1991	63
Nixon, I		1992	67
1969	26	Total	208
1970	64	Clinton, I	
1971	61	1993	42
1972	25	1994	95
Total	176	1995	53
Nixon, II		1996	16
1973	22	Total	206
1974	17	Clinton, II	
Total	39	1997	79
Ford		1998	88
1974	17	1999	70
1975	17	2000	83
1976	30	Total	320
Total	64	G. W. Bush, I	
Carter		2001	73
1977	26	2002	102
1978	39	2003	115
1979	128	2004	30
1980	64	Total	320
Total	257	G. W. Bush, II[b]	
Reagan, I		2005	14
1981	40	2006	21
1982	37	2007	51
1983	30	Total	86

Sources: (1961–1996) Successive volumes of *Congressional Quarterly Almanac* (Washington, D.C.: Congressional Quarterly); (1997–2003) data from U.S. Congress, Congressional Research Service, CRS Report for Congress, "Judicial Nomination Statistics," www.senate.gov/reference/resources/pdf/RL31635.pdf.

Note: Includes only district and circuit court appointments.

[a] Includes full term from Nov. 1963 to Jan. 1969.
[b] Through 2007 only.

Table 10-4 Presidential Appointments to the U.S. District Courts, by Political Party, Cleveland to G. W. Bush

		Appointees				
President	*Party affiliation*	Member of same party	Member of other party or independent	Unknown party affiliation	Percentage from president's party	*Total*
Cleveland	Democrat	30	0	0	100.0	30
B. Harrison	Republican	18	1	0	94.7	19
McKinley	Republican	19	0	0	100.0	19
T. Roosevelt	Republican	55	0	0	100.0	55
Taft	Republican	26	6	0	81.2	32
Wilson	Democrat	54	1	0	98.2	55
Harding	Republican	37	1	0	97.4	38
Coolidge	Republican	49	2	0	96.1	51
Hoover	Republican	30	3	0	90.9	33
F. Roosevelt	Democrat	151	10	0	93.8	161
Truman	Democrat	105	10	0	91.3	115
Eisenhower	Republican	116	9	0	92.8	125
Kennedy	Democrat	93	10	0	90.3	103
L. Johnson	Democrat	115	7	0	94.3	122
Nixon	Republican	166	13	0	92.7	179
Ford	Republican	41	11	0	78.8	52
Carter	Democrat	187	15	0	92.6	202
Reagan	Republican	270	20	0	93.1	290
G. H. W. Bush	Republican	131	17	0	88.5	148
Clinton	Democrat	267	37	0	87.5	305
G. W. Bush[a]	Republican	172	31	0	84.7	203

Source: Adapted from Harold Stanley and Richard Niemi, *Vital Statistics on American Politics, 2007–2008* (Washington, D.C.: CQ Press, 2008), 293.

[a] Through 2007 only.

Table 10-5 Presidential Appointments to the U.S. Courts of Appeal, by Political Party, Cleveland to G. W. Bush

		Appointees				
President	*Party affiliation*	Member of same party	Member of other party or independent	Unknown party affiliation	Percentage from president's party	*Total*
Cleveland	Democrat	6	1	5	50.0	12
B. Harrison	Republican	8	2	2	66.7	12
McKinley	Republican	3	2	0	60.0	5
T. Roosevelt	Republican	14	3	3	70.0	20
Taft	Republican	11	2	0	84.6	13
Wilson	Democrat	19	1	0	95.0	20
Harding	Republican	6	0	0	100.0	6
Coolidge	Republican	15	2	0	88.2	17
Hoover	Republican	12	4	0	75.0	16
F. Roosevelt	Democrat	45	3	0	93.8	48
Truman	Democrat	23	3	0	88.5	26
Eisenhower	Republican	42	3	0	93.3	45
Kennedy	Democrat	20	1	0	95.2	21
L. Johnson	Democrat	38	2	0	95.0	40
Nixon	Republican	42	3	0	93.3	45
Ford	Republican	11	1	0	91.7	12
Carter	Democrat	46	10	0	82.1	56
Reagan	Republican	76	2	0	97.4	78
G. H. W. Bush	Republican	33	4	0	89.2	37
Clinton	Democrat	52	6	0	85.2	58
G. W. Bush[a]	Republican	45	4	0	91.8	49

Source: (Cleveland–G. H. W. Bush) Adapted from Lee Epstein, Jeffrey Segal, Harold Spaeth, and Thomas Walker, *The Supreme Court Compendium* (Washington, D.C.: CQ Press, 1994), 646; (Clinton, G. W. Bush) *Sourcebook of Criminal Justice Statistics Online,* www.albany.edu/sourcebook/pdf/t1822007.pdf.

[a] Through 2007 only.

Table 10-6 Characteristics of District Court Appointees, L. Johnson to G. W. Bush (percent)

Characteristics	*L. Johnson*	*Nixon*	*Ford*	*Carter*	*Reagan*	*G. H. W. Bush*	*Clinton*	*G. W. Bush*[a]
Race								
White	93.4	95.5	88.5	78.7	92.5	89.2	75.5	82.8
Black	4.1	3.4	5.8	13.9	2.0	6.8	17.1	5.9
Hispanic	2.5	1.1	1.9	6.9	4.9	4	5.8	10.8
Asian	0.0	0.0	3.9	0.5	0.7	0.0	1.3	0.5
Sex								
Male	98.4	99.4	98.1	85.6	91.6	80.4	71.7	80.3
Female	1.6	0.6	1.9	14.4	8.4	19.6	28.3	19.7
Religious background								
Protestant	58.2	73.2	73.1	60.4	61.1	64.2	N/A	N/A
Catholic	31.1	18.4	17.3	27.2	29.6	28.4	N/A	N/A
Jewish	10.7	8.4	9.6	12.4	9.1	7.4	N/A	N/A
Party								
Democratic	94.3	7.2	21.2	94.1	4.8	6.1	87.1	6.9
Republican	5.7	92.8	78.8	4.5	93.8	88.5	6.7	84.7
Independent	0.0	0.0	0.0	1.5	1.6	5.4	5.8	8.4
Law school education								
Public institution	40.2	41.9	44.2	50.5	35.4	44.6	44.4	48.8
Private (non-Ivy)	36.9	36.9	38.5	32.2	50.2	41.2	40.8	38.9
Ivy League	21.3	21.2	17.3	17.3	14.4	14.2	14.8	12.3
Experience								
Judicial	34.3	35.1	42.3	54.5	47.0	46.6	53.0	51.7
Prosecutorial	45.8	41.9	50.0	38.6	44.1	39.2	41.4	43.8
Neither	33.6	36.3	30.8	28.2	28.3	31.8	30.6	26.1

Occupation								
Politics/government	21.3	10.6	21.2	4.4	12.3	10.8	11.6	12.3
Judiciary	31.1	28.5	34.6	44.6	37.5	41.9	48.7	46.8
Law firm	44.3	58.2	44.3	47.7	49.3	45.3	26.0	37.4
Professor of law	3.3	2.8	0.0	3.0	2.1	0.7	2.4	1.5
Other	0.0	0.0	0.0	0.5	0.8	1.4	1.2	2.0
Total appointees	122	179	52	202	290	148	305	203.0

Sources: (Johnson–Bush) Adapted from Sheldon Goldman, "The Bush Imprint on the Judiciary," *Judicature* 74 (April–May 1991): 298; (Clinton, I) Sheldon Goldman, "Clinton's First Term Judiciary," *Judicature* 80 (May–June 1997): 261; (Clinton, II, G. W. Bush) adapted from *Sourcebook of Criminal Justice Statistics Online,* www.albany.edu/sourcebook/pdf/t1822007.pdf.

Note: N/A—not available.

[a] Through 2007 only.

Table 10-7 Characteristics of Circuit Court Appointees, L. Johnson to G. W. Bush (percent)

Characteristics	*L. Johnson*	*Nixon*	*Ford*	*Carter*	*Reagan*	*G. H. W. Bush*	*Clinton*	*G. W. Bush*[a]
Race								
White	95.0	97.8	100.0	78.6	96.8	89.2	73.8	79.4
Black	5.0	0.0	0.0	16.1	1.6	5.4	13.1	11.8
Hispanic	0.0	0.0	0.0	3.6	1.6	5.4	11.5	8.8
Asian	0.0	2.2	0.0	1.8	0.0	0.0	1.6	0
Sex								
Male	97.5	100.0	100.0	80.4	95.2	81.1	67.2	79.4
Female	2.5	0.0	0.0	19.6	4.8	18.9	32.8	20.6
Religious background								
Protestant	60.0	75.6	58.3	60.7	57.2	59.4	N/A	N/A
Catholic	25.0	15.6	33.3	23.7	29.4	24.3	N/A	N/A
Jewish	15.7	8.9	8.3	16.1	13.4	16.3	N/A	N/A
Party								
Democratic	95.0	6.7	8.3	89.3		2.7	85.2	5.9
Republican	5.0	93.3	91.7	5.4	97.8	89.2	6.6	91.2
Independent	0.0	0.0	0.0	5.4	2.1	8.1	2.9	2.9
Law school education								
Public institution	40.0	37.8	50.0	39.3	35.8	38.9	N/A	N/A
Private (non-Ivy)	32.5	26.7	25.0	19.6	37.5	33.3	N/A	N/A
Ivy League	27.5	35.6	25.0	41.1	26.8	27.8	N/A	N/A
Experience								
Judicial	65.0	57.8	75.0	53.6	62.1	62.2	59	61.8
Prosecutorial	47.5	46.7	25.0	32.1	26.6	29.7	37.7	35.3
Neither	20.0	17.8	25.0	37.5	33.1	32.4	29.5	23.5

Occupation								
Politics/government	10.0	4.4	8.3	5.4	5.9	10.8	6.6	20.3
Judiciary	57.5	53.3	75.0	46.4	56.2	59.5	52.5	47.1
Law firm	30.0	35.5	16.6	32.3	28.5	27.0	32.7	23.5
Professor of law	0.0	6.7	0.0	14.3	13.4	2.7	N/A	N/A
Other	0.0	0.0	0.0	1.8	1.1	0.0	8.2	8.8
Total appointees	40	45	12	56	78	37	61	34

Source: (Johnson–Bush) Adapted from Sheldon Goldman, "The Bush Imprint on the Judiciary," *Judicature* 74 (April–May 1991): 299; (Clinton) Sheldon Goldman, "Judicial Selection of Clinton," *Judicature* 78 (May–June 1995): 287; (Clinton, II, G.W. Bush) adapted from *Sourcebook of Criminal Justice Statistics Online*, www.albany.edu/sourcebook/pdf/t1822007.pdf.

Note: N/A—not available.

[a] 2001–2004 only.

Table 10-8 Women and Minorities Appointed to Judgeships, L. Johnson to G. W. Bush

	Women		*Black*		*Hispanic*		*White male*	
President	Number	Percentage of total	Number	Percentage of total	Number	Percentage of total	Number	Percentage of total
L. Johnson	3	1.9	7	4.3	3	1.9	N/A	N/A
Nixon	1	0.4	6	2.7	2	0.9	N/A	N/A
Ford	1	1.6	3	4.7	1	1.6	N/A	N/A
Carter	40	15.5	37	14.3	16	6.2	172	66.7
Reagan	28	7.6	7	1.9	15	4.1	318	86.4
G. H. W. Bush	36	19.4	12	6.5	8	4.3	134	72.4
Clinton	107	29.2	61	16.7	25	6.8	274	74.9
G. W. Bush[a]	51	20.2	18	7.1	25	9.9	131	84.7

Source: (Johnson–Bush) Adapted from *Congressional Quarterly Almanac* (Washington, D.C.: Congressional Quarterly, 1992), 324; (Clinton, II, G. W. Bush) adapted from *Sourcebook of Criminal Justice Statistics Online,* www.albany.edu/sourcebook/pdf/t1822007.pdf.

Note: Total reflects only appointments to U.S. District Court and U.S. Courts of Appeal. N/A = not available.

[a] Through 2007 only.

Figure 10-1 Total Number of Judicial Appointments, F. Roosevelt to G.W. Bush

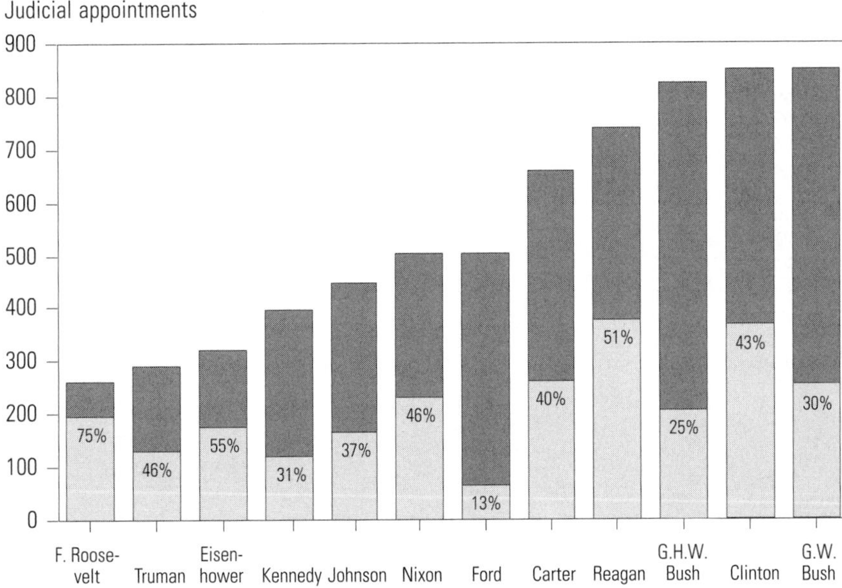

President	*Supreme Court*	*Court of Appeals*	*District Courts*	*Total*	*Total Judgeships*
F. Roosevelt (1933–1945)	9	52	136	197	262
Truman (1945–1953)	4	27	102	133	292
Eisenhower (1953–1961)	5	45	127	177	322
Kennedy (1961–1963)	2	20	102	124	395
L. Johnson (1963–1969)	2	41	125	168	449
Nixon (1969–1974)	4	45	182	231	504
Ford (1974–1977)	1	12	52	65	504
Carter (1977–1981)	0	56	206	262	657
Reagan (1981–1989)	3	83	292	378	740
G.H.W. Bush (1989–1993)	2	60	148	210	825
Clinton (1993–2000)	2	61	203	368	851
G.W. Bush (2001–2007)[a]	2	49	203	254	851

Source: *Congressional Quarterly Almanac* (Washington, D.C.: Congressional Quarterly, 1990), 517. Updated by the author.

Note: Light portion of the bar indicates percentage of judgeships appointed by a president; remainder of bar denotes judgeships appointed by previous presidents.

[a] Through 2007 only.

Table 10-9 Success Rate of the United States as a Party to a Case before the Supreme Court, Truman, I to G.W. Bush, I

President/year	*Total number of cases* [a]	*Percentage of cases won*
Truman, I		
1946	68	69.1
1947	51	66.7
1948	39	56.4
Truman, II		
1949	38	57.9
1950	51	64.7
1951	37	62.2
1952	43	58.1
Eisenhower, I		
1953	26	61.5
1954	34	61.8
1955	41	46.3
1956	59	44.1
Eisenhower, II		
1957	48	58.3
1958	35	62.9
1959	56	62.5
1960	51	68.6
Kennedy		
1961	36	44.4
1962	36	61.1
1963	37	56.8
L. Johnson[b]		
1964	24	79.2
1965	39	56.4
1966	30	60.0
1967	40	65.0
1968	31	61.3
Nixon, I		
1969	26	65.4
1970	40	70.0
1971	23	43.5
1972	40	72.5
Nixon, II		
1973	31	71.0
Ford		
1974	38	68.4
1975	33	84.8
1976	30	50.0
Carter		
1977	33	57.6

Table 10-9 *(Continued)*

President/year	*Total number of cases*[a]	*Percentage of cases won*
Carter (continued)		
1978	20	65.0
1979	38	65.8
1980	16	66.8
Reagan, I		
1981	18	72.2
1982	25	52.0
1983	30	83.3
1984	25	76.0
Reagan, II		
1985	25	88.0
1986	26	61.5
1987	24	66.7
1988	15	80.0
G. H. W. Bush		
1989	23	56.5
1990	14	64.3
1991	21	57.1
1992	30	60.0
Clinton, I		
1993	21	61.9
1994	14	46.7
1995	27	55.6
1996	17	70.6
Clinton, II		
1997	26	65.4
1998	11	45.5
1999	21	52.4
2000	12	50.0
G. W. Bush, I		
2001	14	87.5
2002	12	41.7
2003	13	69.2
2004	12	66.7
Total	1,794	62.7

Source: Lee Epstein, Jeffrey A. Segal, Harold J. Spaeth, and Thomas G. Walker, *The Supreme Court Compendium*, 4th ed. (Washington, D.C.: CQ Press, 2007), 692.

[a] Includes those cases where the *U.S. Reports* names the United States a party to the case, and criminal and habeas corpus cases where the *U.S. Reports* lists as the party the name of the official or office of the person who prosecutes or has custody of the accused or convicted person. If the United States is not the first named party in multiple party litigation, the case is not included.

[b] Includes full term from Nov. 1963 to Jan. 1969.

Table 10-10 Success Rate of the Solicitor General as an *Amicus Curiae* in Cases before the Supreme Court, Eisenhower to G. W. Bush

President	*Total number of cases*[a]	*Percentage of cases won*
Eisenhower	42	83.3
Kennedy	48	87.5
L. Johnson	41	82.9
Nixon	79	70.9
Ford	38	71.1
Carter	86	65.1
Reagan[b]	239	72.8
G. H. W. Bush[c]	110	78.2
Clinton[d]	163	59.3
G. W. Bush[e]	308	74.5

Source: Lee Epstein, Jeffrey A. Segal, Harold J. Spaeth, and Thomas G. Walker, *The Supreme Court Compendium,* 4th ed. (Washington, D.C.: CQ Press, 2007), 691. Updated by the author from the U.S. Department of Justice, Office of Solicitor General, "Amicus Briefs," www.usdoj.gov/osg/briefs/search.html. The position taken in individual briefs is compared against the ruling of the Court based on summaries found at http://caselaw.lp.findlaw.com/casesummary/index.html.

[a] Includes all cases where solicitor general filed an *amicus curiae* brief and the Court decided the case with an opinion on the merits.
[b] Includes 1980–1987 terms.
[c] Includes 1988–1991 terms.
[d] Includes 1992–1999 terms.
[e] Through 2007.

Table 10-11 Supreme Court Rulings against Presidents, Washington to G. W. Bush

President	*Number of decisions*
Washington	0
Adams	0
Jefferson	2
Madison	3
Monroe	1
J. Q. Adams	0
Jackson	0
Van Buren	0
W. Harrison	0
Tyler	1
Polk	0
Taylor	0
Fillmore	1
Pierce	0
Buchanan	0
Lincoln	5
A. Johnson	2
Grant	0
Hayes	1
Garfield	0
Arthur	2
Cleveland	1
B. Harrison	0
McKinley	0
T. Roosevelt	0
Taft	0
Wilson	2
Harding	2
Coolidge	3
Hoover	1
F. Roosevelt	8
Truman	3
Eisenhower	3
L. Johnson	2
Nixon	25
Ford	3
Carter	2
Reagan	0
G. H. W. Bush	0
Clinton	5
G. W. Bush[a]	4
Total	76

Source: Michael A. Genovese, *The Supreme Court, the Constitution and Presidential Power* (Lanham, Md.: University Press of America, 1980), 264. Used by permission. Updated by the author from the Court decisions found at www.supremecourtus.gov/opinions/opinions.html and http://supreme.lp.findlaw.com/supreme_court/decisions/index.html.

[a] Through 2007 only.

References

Aldrich, John. 1980. *Before the Convention.* Chicago: University of Chicago Press.

Alford, John, and David Brady. 1993. "Personal and Partisan Advantages in Congressional Elections." In *Congress Reconsidered,* 5th ed., ed. Lawrence Dodd and Bruce Oppenheimer. Washington, D.C.: CQ Press.

Aristotle. 1943. *Politics.* New York: Modern Library.

Basler, Roy P., ed. 1953. *The Collected Works of Abraham Lincoln,* 9 vols. New Brunswick, N.J.: Rutgers University Press.

Beck, Paul Allen. 1997. *Party Politics in America.* New York: Longman.

Bemis, S. F. 1956. *John Quincy Adams and the Union.* New York: Random House.

Berman, Larry. 1979. *The Office of Management and Budget and the Presidency.* Princeton: Princeton University Press.

Bond, Jon, and Richard Fleisher. 1992. *The President in the Legislative Arena.* Chicago: University of Chicago Press.

Brace, Paul, and Barbara Hinckley. 1992. *Follow the Leader.* New York: Free Press.

Brown, Roger. 1982. "Party and Bureaucracy: From Kennedy to Reagan." *Political Science Quarterly* 97 (Summer): 279–294.

Burke, John. 1992. *The Institutional Presidency.* Baltimore: Johns Hopkins University Press.

Cameron, Charles. 2000. *Veto Bargaining: Presidents and the Politics of Negative Power.* Cambridge: Cambridge University Press.

Chambers, William. 1963. *Political Parties in a New Nation: The American Experience, 1776–1809.* New York: Oxford University Press.

Cornwell, Elmer. 1965. *Presidential Leadership of Public Opinion.* Bloomington: Indiana University Press.

Corwin, Edward. 1957. *The President: Office and Powers.* New York: New York University Press.

Cronin, Thomas. 1987. "The Swelling of the Presidency." In *American Government: Reading and Cases*, 9th ed., ed. P. Woll. Boston: Little, Brown.

DeGrazia, Alfred. 1965. *Republic in Crisis: Congress against the Executive Force.* New York: Federal Legal Publications.

Dennis, Jack. 1988. "Political Independence in America, Part I: On Being an Independent Partisan Supporter." *British Journal of Political Science* 18 (Winter): 77–109.

DiClerico, Robert. 1985. *The American President*, 2d ed. Englewood Cliffs, N.J.: Prentice-Hall.

DiMaggio, Paul. 1991. "Constructing an Organizational Field as a Professional Project: U.S. Art Museums, 1920–1940." In *The New Institutionalism in Organizational Analysis*, ed. W. Powell and P. DiMaggio. Chicago: University of Chicago Press.

Edwards, George, III. 1989. *At the Margins: Presidential Leadership of Congress.* New Haven: Yale University Press.

Edwards, George, III. 2003. *On Deaf Ears: The Limits of the Bully Pulpit.* New Haven: Yale University Press.

Edwards, George, III, John Kessel, and Bert Rockman, eds. 1993. *Researching the Presidency.* Pittsburgh: University of Pittsburgh Press.

Eisenstadt, S. N. 1964. "Institutionalization and Change." *American Sociological Review* 29 (April): 235–247.

Epstein, Leon. 1986. *Political Parties in the American Mold.* Madison: University of Wisconsin Press.

Fenno, Richard. 1959. *The President's Cabinet.* New York: Vintage.

Ford, Paul. 1892–1899. *The Writings of Thomas Jefferson.* 8 vols. New York: Putnam.

Garand, James, and Donald Gross. 1984. "Changes in the Vote Margins for Congressional Candidates: A Specification of Historical Trends." *American Political Science Review* 78 (March): 17–30.

Grossman, Michael, and Martha Kumar. 1981. *Portraying the President.* Baltimore: Johns Hopkins University Press.

Hart, John. 1987. *The Presidential Branch.* New York: Pergamon.

Hart, Roderick. 1987. *The Sound of Leadership.* Chicago: University of Chicago Press.

Heclo, Hugh. 1981. "Introduction: The Presidential Illusion." In *The Illusion of Presidential Government*, ed. H. Heclo and L. Salamon. Boulder, Colo.: Westview Press.

Helmer, John. 1981. "The Presidential Office: Velvet Fist in an Iron Glove." In *The Illusion of Presidential Government*, ed. H. Heclo and L. Salamon. Boulder, Colo.: Westview Press.

Herring, Pendleton. 1940. *Presidential Leadership.* New York: Harcourt Brace.

Hess, Stephen. 1976. *Organizing the Presidency.* Washington, D.C.: Brookings Institution.

Holtzman, Abraham. 1970. *Legislative Liaison: Executive Leadership in Congress.* New York: Crowell and Readers Digest Press.

Howell, William. 2003. *Power without Persuasion: The Politics of Direct Presidential Action.* Princeton: Princeton University Press.

Howell, William. 2007. *While Dangers Gather: Congressional Checks on Presidential War Powers.* Princeton: Princeton University Press.

Hult, Karen, and Charles Walcott. 2004. *Empowering the White House: Governing under Nixon, Ford, and Carter.* Lawrence: University Press of Kansas.

Hunt, Galliard, ed. 1906. *The Writings of James Madison,* 9 vols. New York: G. P. Putnam's Sons.

Huntington, Samuel. 1965. "Political Development and Political Decay." *World Politics* 17 (April): 235–247.

Johnson, Loch. 1984. *The Making of International Agreements: Congress Confronts the Executive.* New York: New York University Press.

Kernell, Samuel. 1978. "Explaining Presidential Popularity." *American Political Science Review* 72 (June): 506–522.

Kernell, Samuel. 1984. "The Presidency and the People: The Modern Paradox." In *The Presidency and the Political System,* ed. M. Nelson. Washington, D.C.: CQ Press.

Ketcham, Ralph. 1984. *Presidents above Party: The First American Presidency, 1789–1829.* Chapel Hill: University of North Carolina Press.

King, Gary. 1993. "The Methodology of Presidential Research." In *Researching the Presidency,* ed. G. Edwards, J. Kessel, and B. Rockman. Pittsburgh: University of Pittsburgh Press.

King, Gary, Robert Keohane, and Sidney Verba. 1994. *Scientific Inference in Qualitative Research.* Princeton: Princeton University Press.

Kissinger, Henry. 1979. *The White House Years.* Boston: Little, Brown.

Koenig, Louis. 1964. *The Chief Executive.* New York: Harcourt, Brace, and World.

Krehbiel, Keith. 1987. "Why Are Congressional Committees Powerful?" *American Political Science Review* 81 (September): 929–935.

Kumar, Martha. 2007. *Managing the President's Message: The White House Communications Operation.* Baltimore: Johns Hopkins University Press.

Ladd, Everett C. 1981. "The Proper Role of Parties in Presidential Nominee Selection." *Commonsense* 4: 33–39.

La Follette, Robert. 1913. *La Follette's Autobiography.* Madison, Wis.: R. La Follette.

Light, Paul. 1991. *The President's Agenda: Domestic Policy Choice from Kennedy to Reagan,* rev. ed. Baltimore: Johns Hopkins University Press.

Lindblom, Charles. 1968. *The Policy-Making Process.* Englewood Cliffs, N.J.: Prentice-Hall.

Lorant, Stefan. 1951. *The Presidency: A Pictorial History of Presidential Elections from Washington to Truman.* New York: Macmillan.

Lord, Clifford, ed. 1979. *List and Index of Presidential Executive Orders, Unnumbered Series, 1789–1941.* Wilmington, Del.: Michael Glazier.

MacKenzie, G. Calvin. 1981. *The Politics of Presidential Appointments.* New York: Free Press.

Malek, Fred. 1978. *Washington's Hidden Tragedy.* New York: Free Press.

March, James, and Johan Olsen. 1984. "The New Institutionalism: Organizational Factors in Political Life." *American Political Science Review* 78 (September): 734–749.

Margolis, Lawrence. 1986. *Executive Agreements and Presidential Power in Foreign Policy.* New York: Praeger.

May, Ernst, and Philip Zelikow, eds. 1997. *The Kennedy Tapes inside the White House during the Cuban Missile Crisis.* Cambridge: Harvard University Press.

Mayer, Kenneth. 2002. *With the Stroke of a Pen: Executive Orders and Presidential Power.* Princeton: Princeton University Press.

Meyer, John, and Brian Rowan. 1991. "Institutionalized Organizations: Formal Structure as Myth and Ceremony." In *The New Institutionalism in Organizational Analysis,* ed. W. Powell and P. DiMaggio. Chicago: University of Chicago Press.

Moe, Terry. 1985. "The Politicized Presidency." In *The New Direction in American Politics,* ed. J. Chubb and P. Peterson. Washington, D.C.: Brookings Institution.

Moe, Terry. 1993. "Presidents, Institutions, and Theory." In *Researching the Presidency,* ed. G. Edwards, J. Kessel, and B. Rockman. Pittsburgh: University of Pittsburgh Press.

Mueller, John. 1970. "Presidential Popularity from Truman to Johnson." *American Political Science Review* 64 (March): 18–34.

Mueller, John. 1994. *Policy and Opinion in the Gulf War.* Chicago: University of Chicago Press.

Nathan, Richard. 1983. *The Administrative Presidency.* New York: Wiley.

Neustadt, Richard. 1960. *Presidential Power.* New York: Wiley.

Neustadt, Richard. 1975. "The Constraining of the President." In *Perspectives on the Presidency,* ed. A. Wildavsky. Boston: Little, Brown.

Norrander, Barbara. 1992. *Super Tuesday.* Lexington: University Press of Kentucky.

North, Douglass. 1990. *Institutions, Institutional Choice, and Economic Performance.* Cambridge: Cambridge University Press.

Ornstein, Norman, Thomas Mann, and Michael Malbin. 1998. *Vital Statistics on Congress 1997–1998.* Washington, D.C.: CQ Press.

Ostrom, Charles, and Brian Job. 1986. "The President's Use of Force." *American Political Science Review* 80 (June): 541–566.

Ostrom, Charles, and Dennis Simon. 1985. "Promise and Performance: A Dynamic Model of Presidential Popularity." *American Political Science Review* 79 (June): 334–358.

Pika, Joseph. 1988. "Management Style and The Organizational Matrix." *Administration and Society* 20 (May): 3–29.
Polsby, Nelson. 1968. "The Institutionalization of the U.S. House of Representatives." *American Political Science Review* 62 (March): 144–168.
Powell, Woodward, and Paul DiMaggio, eds. 1991. *The New Institutionalism in Organizational Analysis.* Chicago: University of Chicago Press.
The Public Papers of the Presidents: Hoover to Bush (1929–1993), American Presidency Project, www.presidency.ucsb.edu.
Ragsdale, Lyn. 1984. "The Politics of Presidential Speechmaking." *American Political Science Review* 78 (December): 971–984.
Ragsdale, Lyn. 1993. *Presidential Politics.* Boston: Houghton Mifflin.
Ragsdale, Lyn. 1997. "Studying the Presidency: Why Presidents Need Political Scientists." In *The Presidency and the Political System,* 5th ed., ed. Michael Nelson. Washington, D.C.: CQ Press.
Ragsdale, Lyn and John J. Theis, 1997. "The Institutionalization of the American Presidency, 1924–1992" *American Journal of Political Science* 41 (October): 121–139.
Richardson, J. D., ed. 1897. *Messages and Papers of the Presidents,* 11 vols. New York: Bureau of National Literature and Art.
Roosevelt, Theodore. 1913. *Theodore Roosevelt: An Autobiography.* New York: Macmillan.
Rossiter, Clinton. 1960. *The American Presidency.* New York: Mentor Books.
Rubin, Richard. 1981. *Press, Party, and Presidency.* New York: Norton.
Rudalevige, Andrew. 2002. *Managing the President's Program: Presidential Leadership and Legislative Policy Formulation.* Princeton: Princeton University Press.
Rudalevige, Andrew. 2006. *The New Imperial Presidency: Renewing Presidential Power after Watergate* Ann Arbor: University of Michigan Press.
Savage, Charlie. 2007. *Takeover: The Return of the Imperial Presidency and the Subversion of Democracy.* Boston: Little, Brown.
Schlesinger, Arthur, Jr., ed. 1973a. *The History of U.S. Political Parties.* 3 vols. New York: Chelsea House.
Schlesinger, Arthur, Jr. 1973b. *The Imperial Presidency.* Boston: Houghton Mifflin.
Schlozman, Kay, and John Tierney. 1986. *Organized Interests and American Democracy.* New York: HarperCollins.
Scigliano, Robert. 1971. *The Supreme Court and the Presidency.* New York: Free Press.
Selznick, Philip. 1957. *Leadership in Administration.* Evanston, Ill.: Row, Peterson.
Shepsle, Kenneth, and Barry Weingast. 1987. "The Institutional Foundations of Committee Power." *American Political Science Review* 81 (March): 85–104.

Sigelman, Lee, and Kathleen Knight. 1983. "Why Does Presidential Popularity Decline? A Test of the Expectation/Disillusion Theory." *Public Opinion Quarterly* 47 (Fall): 310–324.

Stanley, David, Dean Mann, and Jameson Diog. 1967. *Men Who Govern.* Washington, D.C.: Brookings Institution.

Stanley, Harold, and Richard Niemi. 2008. *Vital Statistics on American Politics, 2007–2008.* Washington, D.C.: CQ Press.

Stimson, James. 1976. "Public Support for American Presidents: A Cyclical Model." *Public Opinion Quarterly* 40 (Spring): 1–21.

Stuckey, Mary. 2004. *Defining Americans: The Presidency and National Identity.* Lawrence: University Press of Kansas.

Taft, William Howard. 1916. *The Presidency.* New York: Charles Scribner.

U.S. Congress, Library of Congress, Congressional Research Service. Jan. 14, 2003. "Declarations of War and Authorizations for the Use of Military Force: Historical Background and Legal Implications." Washington, D.C.: Government Printing Office.

U.S. Congress, Library of Congress, Congressional Research Service. Sept. 12, 2007. "Instances of Use of United States Armed Forces Abroad, 1798–2007." Washington, D.C.: Government Printing Office.

U.S. General Accounting Office. 1985. *Use of Special Presidential Authority for Foreign Assistance.* Washington, D.C.: Government Printing Office.

Watson, Richard, and Norman Thomas. 1983. *The Politics of the Presidency.* New York: Wiley.

Wayne, Stephen. 1978. *The Legislative Presidency.* New York: Harper and Row.

Wayne, Stephen. 1982. "Congressional Liaison in the Reagan White House: A Preliminary Assessment of the First Year." In *President and Congress,* ed. N. Ornstein. Washington, D.C.: American Enterprise Institute.

Wayne, Stephen, Richard Cole, and James Hyde. 1979. "Advising the President on Enrolled Legislation: Patterns of Executive Influence." *Political Science Quarterly* 94 (Summer): 303–317.

Weber, Max. 1947. *The Theory of Social and Economic Organization.* Glencoe, Ill.: Free Press.

West, William, and Joseph Cooper. 1985. "The Rise of Administrative Clearance." In *The Presidency and Public Policy Making,* ed. G. Edwards, S. Shull, and N. Thomas. Pittsburgh: University of Pittsburgh Press.

Wilson, Woodrow. 1973. *Congressional Government.* Cleveland: World Publishing.

Wood, B. Dan. 2007. *The Politics of Economic Leadership: The Causes and Consequences of Presidential Rhetoric.* Princeton: Princeton University Press.

Index

Years following presidents' names are terms of office.

E